ANCIENT POLYNESIAN SOCIETY

ANCIENT POLYNESIAN SOCIETY

Irving Goldman

THE UNIVERSITY OF CHICAGO PRESS
Chicago & London

International Standard Book Number: 0–226–30114–1
Library of Congress Catalog Card Number: 74–116028
The University of Chicago Press, Chicago 60637
The University of Chicago Press, Ltd., London

Published 1970
Printed in the United States of America

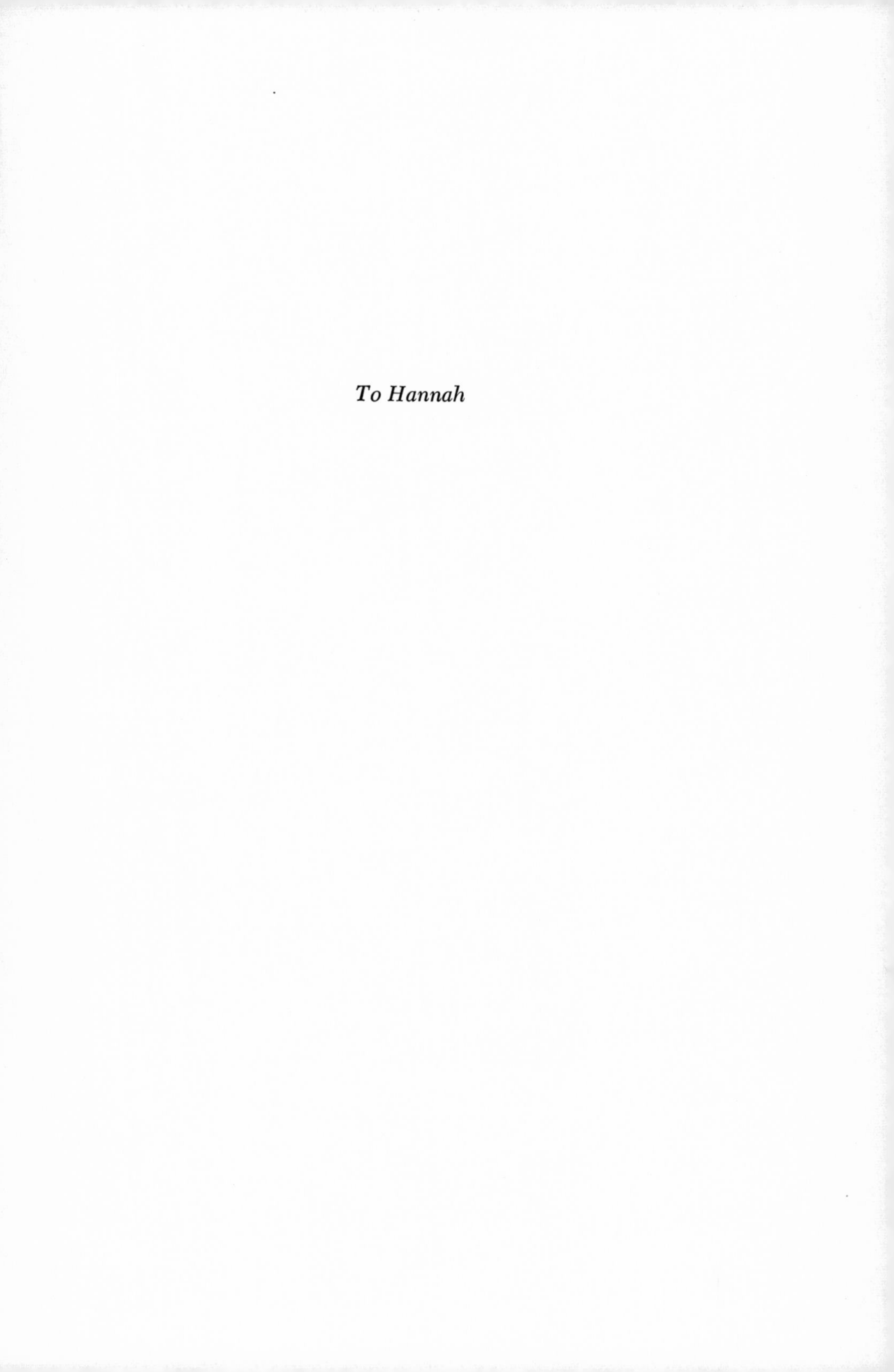

To Hannah

The noble of every age has done his best to invent a life which he, and he only, can live.

BALZAC

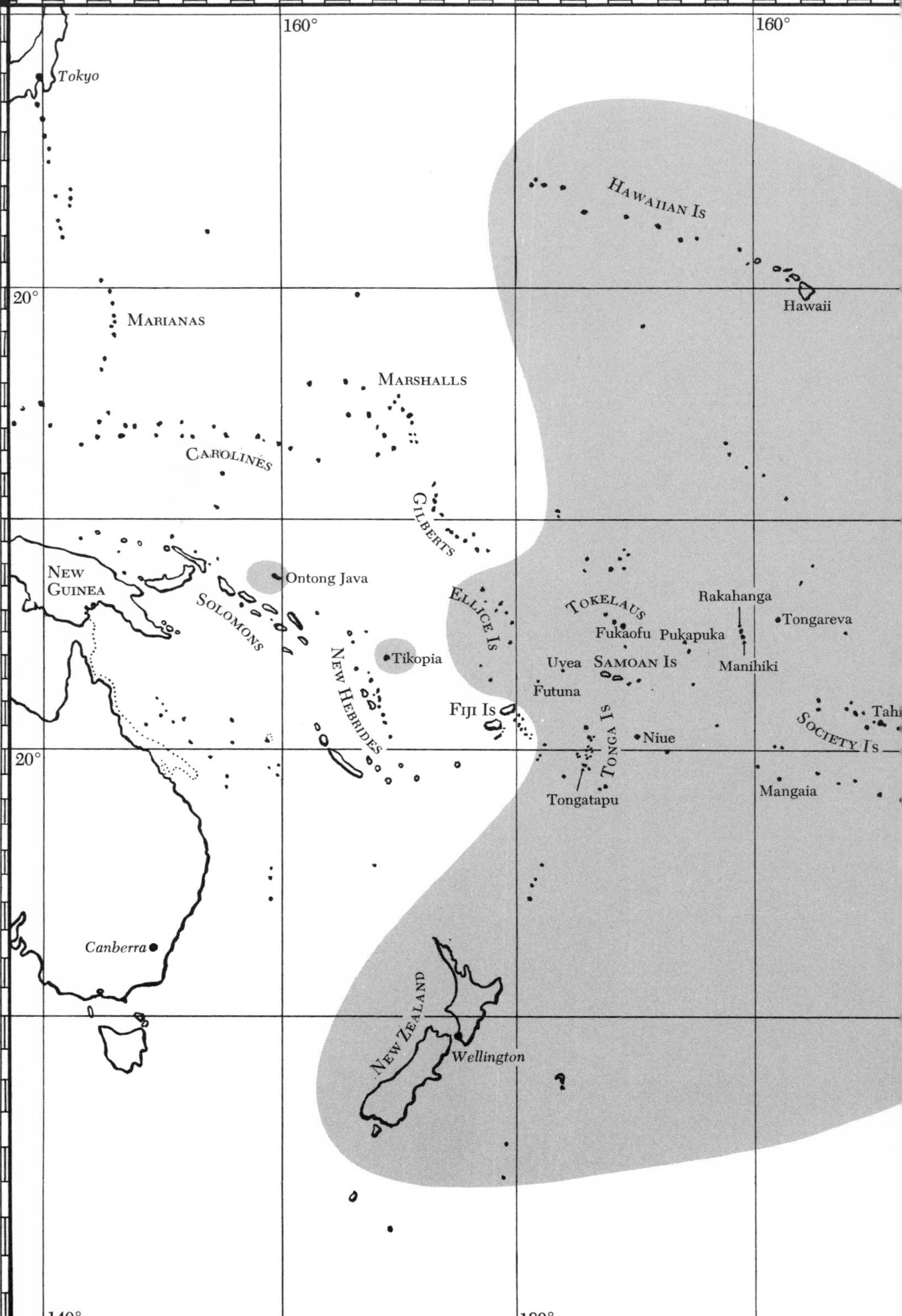

160°
160°
Tokyo
Hawaiian Is
20°
Marianas
Hawaii
Marshalls
Carolines
Gilberts
New Guinea
Ontong Java
Solomons
Ellice Is
Tokelaus
Rakahanga
Tongareva
Fukaofu
Pukapuka
Tikopia
New Hebrides
Uvea
Samoan Is
Manihiki
Futuna
Fiji Is
Tonga Is
Niue
Society Is
20°
Tongatapu
Mangaia
Canberra
New Zealand
Wellington
140°
180°

Preface

THE METHOD OF ANALYSIS EMPLOYED IN THIS BOOK IS NOT COMMON IN anthropology, although it is well enough known and its merits are generally recognized. (Boas, for example, was among the first to see the advantages of close study of limited geographic areas.) The subsequent rise of the culture area concept immediately called attention to the significance of variations within a single cultural tradition as a guide to historical reconstruction. When attention turned to the study of regularities of structure in society and culture, the method then offered—as Eggan aptly phrased it—the possibilities for "controlled comparisons." Its merit, of course, is that it reconciles the apparently divergent interests of the field in both the specifics of history and the generalities of sociology. It meets the requirements of the historian in acknowledging the relativism of context, and it responds at the same time to the scientific interest in general and formal propositions. For the truly zealous generalist, however, the approach may be too conservative. Its discoveries, such as they are, do not transcend culture, and their value therefore falls short of the ambitious hopes of social anthropology for a full-fledged "science of society." But even the most exuberant generalist may see the wisdom of retreating an intellectual step or two before leaping forward.

The study of variability does, in fact, illuminate structure and it does point to general propositions about society and culture. When culture areas that exhibit similar structures are eventually compared from the standpoint of our knowledge of their separate characteristics of variability, they may well yield deeper insights into general properties of systems and processes of development than are now available from more limited comparisons. From the standpoint of method, controlled comparisons drawing upon historical details have the rigorous advantage of being subject to immediate and sudden contradiction. Model constructors, by comparison, have the good fortune of a more sheltered life. Not altogether in the spirit of self-defense, I remind the reader that even though almost every general proposition I put forth is subject to immediate refutation or confirmation from readily available evidence (either in this book itself or in the published literature), our subject matter is not chemistry. I would be overstating my intentions grossly if I did not make clear that at bottom this is a work of interpretation. Its findings are to be regarded as hypotheses. I have used methodology to inform my judgments, and not to present Q.E.D. "laws."

Systematic comparisons such as I have attempted demand a great deal from the published literature. The sources must give comparable information on each point for each of the societies. There is no literature on any culture area that can fully sustain so systematic a comparative study—gaps are inevitable—and one must cut the cloth accordingly. Moreover, the literature on Polynesia is by current standards of analytic refinement rather unsophisticated. Much of the ethnographic work was carried out well after the aboriginal cultures had gone into decline. As for the eyewitnesses, they were all competent and wise men and women, but they were untrained and they often spent too little time in one place. We should not, however, exaggerate their biases, for almost all were products of the Enlightenment; they respected the "natives" and sought to understand them. But since the quality of description of each society naturally differs enormously, in every instance I inform the reader of my main sources and of their scholarly qualifications. By and large, however, the quality of the Polynesian literature is eminently respectable. There is enough of it from a variety of sources so that much of the most basic information can be evaluated. There are in fact rather few extraordinary discrepancies in the older literature, judging from their careful evaluation at the hands of the able ethnographers who came later.

The most problematic historical sources are the genealogical traditions. To the ancient Polynesians the traditions of chiefly lines were authentic history, often recorded by professional genealogists and transmitted by them with scrupulous regard for the rights of pedigree and family honor. One would not, however, accept the record of oral history without verification, no more than one would the unsupported evidence of a written document. Neither, for that matter, may one reject as ipso facto irrelevant or as grossly inaccurate a purported historical record that does not meet the standards of absolute verification. We work with what we have; and the traditions are objective data. At the very least they represent a Polynesian viewpoint on their own history, and in this important respect they reveal local historiography. They define Polynesian history as if it were true; how really "true" the traditions are we do not, of course, know. Raymond Firth —as skeptical as anyone—found Tikopian traditions to be reliable as far back as they could be judged by known historic events, and Robert Suggs—a leading archeological authority—found that genealogical traditions and archeological findings were often in substantial agreement. In appendix 1, for example, I have compared chronologies from the traditions, from archeology, and from linguistics; the degree of conformity is surprising. The dates from pedigrees, calculated at 25 years per chiefly presence, should not, of course, be taken as true chronology—but, on the other hand, who can say they should be disregarded? I cite them because they are part of the record and because they may well be at least as accurate as glotto-chronology, which in its present state offers little more than a systematic estimate. For that matter, my work does not rest upon dates, though it does welcome evidences of sequences in major features of social and political life. On statement of sequences, the traditions are relevant and possibly reliable, though one would hesitate to credit them with a faithful rendition of the distant past, since all historical viewpoints are in the final analysis likely to be contemporary. But they may by the same token have much to say about the next to recent past. I have considered them as invaluable in their description of specific historical changes that ushered in the present state of affairs.

An outsider such as myself who comes to work with the Polynesian literature has much to be thankful for in the standards of field research and publications of the Bernice P. Bishop Museum in Honolulu. The policy of the Museum has taken account of future interests in comparative study in its stress upon ethnography and in presenting Polynesian society from within a Polynesian perspective. The test of good ethnography is its serviceability for changing theoretical interests, and the Bishop Museum publications do not fail this test insofar as the present work is concerned. In any case, the works of Buck, Firth, Handy, and Mead stand as bright beacons illuminating the darker corners of all Polynesian cultures. Williamson's monumental compilations and historical observations are still invaluable even after others have covered the same ground; no one has evaluated the early sources as thoroughly as he has. Finally, there is Burrows' areawide surveys, in particular his "Breed and Border in Polynesia" which, as I now recall, was the paper that first drew my attention to the prospects of a Polynesian study.

This book does not pretend to cover all the pertinent works on Polynesia; this literature—as one can see at a glance from Taylor's truly monumental *A Pacific Bibliography*—is extensive. I had to conclude that one does not live long enough to read and absorb everything written on a subject so vast and complex, and I can only hope that my choices have been decent. Except for editorial revision (i.e., substantial rewriting), the manuscript was completed in 1966, so that with few exceptions my reading in the literature has not gone past that date. Without question the archeological picture, in particular, has changed since then. This, however, should not affect the analysis of the ethnographic data too much.

For aid in the preparation of this work I am gratefully indebted to Sarah Lawrence College for a faculty fellowship in 1953 that allowed me to get started; to the Class of 1966 for its generous grant (for the encouragement of faculty writing) that covered editorial and research expenses; and to Bollingen Foundation for a fellowship (1960–62) that financed research assistance and released time from teaching. Mrs. Joan Shepard Wilson was a most invaluable research assistant for several years, and Miss Beverly Emmons, Miss Arlene Mazak, and Miss Karen Heller assisted me for a shorter time.

Miss Mary Blackman helped to prepare the sketches for the chapter-opening maps. Except for that of New Zealand, which was freely adapted from general maps, all are based upon ethnographic sources: Tikopia from Firth (1936), the Hawaiian islands from Coulter (1931), and all the rest from the basic source works on specific Polynesian societies as published in the bulletins of the Bernice P. Bishop Museum, Honolulu; only details pertinent to the present work have been included. The engravings are details from those in Captain James Cook, *A Voyage to the Pacific Ocean* (London, 1784), provided by the photograph collection of the Rare Book Division of the New York Public Library.

I must express my special appreciation to Margaret Mead, who followed my thought on Polynesia over the years, encouraged me and counseled me, and was never sparing in her criticism. I wish also to thank Douglas Oliver and Alexander Lesser for their helpful comments on several chapters.

My ultimate acknowledgment is to Franz Boas who was my teacher and who inspired in me, as he did in all of his students, the deepest respect for the human beings whose thoughts and passions must animate whatever we write about them.

Introduction

Begun as an inquiry into the sociology of elementary aristocracies, this study of the ancient Polynesian societies turned finally into an account of their patterns of evolution. In retrospect the diversion of a sociological into an historical interest seems to have been both logical and inevitable and, without implying paradox, no diversion at all. All social systems are best understood as theme and variation. Aristocracy is no exception. Though its leading ideas are durable, they are not rigid. They bend before circumstances as much as they seek to bend circumstances to their own rules—but whether bending before or bending to, they insist on the rules. The rules always impose an order. Variations that ensue from accommodations and adaptations are thus neither random nor altogether circumstantial. They express the theme. Adaptation whether social or organic is specific. Each organic species exhibits its own characteristics of adaptation, and each social system has its own style of response and hence of development. Thus the description of aristocracy of a specific style demands an understanding of its themes and of the variations that express them and so make them comprehensible. The theme, let us say, is the most abstract statement possible about a system. Its variations endow the abstraction with historical reality. The abstract tends toward the timeless; the concrete is historical; neither is by itself comprehensible.

At bottom the aim of evolutionary theory is precisely that of delineating the continuity of patterns of change in specific structures. The linear interest, the concern with stages and direction of evolution, is part of the general aim, but hardly primary. Direction and sequences of stages represent at best selected strands from the multiple foliation of variations. If the characteristics of a structure are to be defined from their variations, then of course all variations must be taken into account. Yet one can hardly turn away from the urgent interests in the history of specific institutions. Retrospective history, like a proud genealogy, is selective, favoring the lines that have moved toward fruition and ignoring those that seemed to have accomplished little. In this study I have taken some account of the multiple foliations, but for the most part I have selected those strands, those patterned variations, that would seem most closely to elucidate the role of aristocracy in the development of civilization. Civilizations are, above all, political systems. Accordingly, I deal mainly with those variations in the theme of Polynesian aristocracy that help define the political evolution of the system. The political variations in turn define the precise character of Polynesian aristocracy.

Elementary Ideas of Aristocracy

From the standpoint of our age, aristocracy seems both special and archaic. Yet in the larger historical perspective, aristocracies have been the agents of the most powerful and significant cultural developments. All the early civilizations whose social systems are known to us were aristocracies, a circumstance that has sometimes been misinterpreted to imply that aristocracy—with its differentiation of statuses and ranks—has itself been a product of civilization (cf. Childe 1946, Hawkes and Wooley 1963). The reverse is more likely true: Civilizations are the product of developing aristocracy. Civilization as a special emergent is late in history, whereas the roots of aristocracy are ancient. Aristocratic principles have nourished some of the simplest societies, both those that have been remote in space from civilizations and those that have preceded them in time.

The elementary idea of aristocracy seems both simple and innocuous: the concept of the inherent superiority of a line of descent. Aristocracy enthrones a genealogical elite as possessor of the highest virtue and, thus, privileged to lead and to rule. In choosing its leaders mankind has never relied upon any single principle of personal virtue. It has placed its trust in the experience of age, and in the kinetic qualities of strength, valor, and skill; and along with these pragmatic virtues it has honored the idea of descent. The pragmatic virtues, efficacious as they are, have the defect of lack of continuity. They hardly encompass the life of one person, let alone readily connect one generation with its successor. These are technical difficulties that many societies have learned to overcome. From the moral perspective of kinship society, the main defect of pragmatic virtue is its ephemeralness: the fact of its being lodged in one being rather than in a line; the fact of its being associated only with the present rather than with the depth and weight of time. The pragmatic virtue is immediately the victim of the pragmatic test. The virtue of the ideal is that it can be taken for granted and given the benefit of the doubt. Aristocracy is at its core a specific concept of kinship. Kinship is a system of social order that asserts the superiority of that which is given over that which is acquired. In kinship the merit that resides in a line or in a categorical position—as, say, the mother's brother—is an additional dimension to the personal merits of an individual being. The merit of the line or categorical position resides in the principle of relationship and descent rather than in the person. The person is always subject to evaluation; the principle tends to be constant.

Thus in kinship society, leadership that descends from a line runs, so to speak, along the grain, coinciding with the constancy of reverences and respects that are owed to the genealogical order. Totemism in its social aspect, in its identification of a line with a revered nonhuman ancestor, or in its association of a line with an honorable emblem, expresses even more directly the elementary principles of aristocracy. Aristocracy draws upon totemic principles, but since the totemic principles are the more general, and are held to by the simplest and technically least sophisticated peoples, they are surely the older. Totemism honors a line of descent by endowing it with categorical identity and with associations of special significance. Totemism is commonly religious, in which case the associations take on a reverential and sacred aspect. Religious totemism is often lodged within an egalitarian setting that declares the emblems, the associations, and the identifications to be of equal value. But even societies that have the appearance of social egalitarianism may acknowledge the religious superiority of lineage or clan as a quality of its totemic character. Whether the totemic association is hierarchical or not, however, it is the notion of a distinctive quality added to the genealogical order that gives totemism its appeal. Aristocracy also holds to the concept of special virtue attached to a line of descent. But if aristocracy derives from the same principles that endow descent with inherent merit, it is, at the same time, a special development in that it adds to the concept of exclusiveness, which it shares with totemism, that of superiority.

Aristocratic leadership has then the advantage of being rooted in the deepest sources of sentiment—lineage and religion. We can distinguish between two styles of leadership, the utilitarian and the aristocratic. Utilitarian leadership being based on pragmatic evidences of value is, as I have said, discontinuous in its influence. In kinship society it achieves wide influence in time of crisis; under normal conditions it is reduced to a narrow influence. It must contend against the opposition of conflicting utilitarian interests. Aristocratic leadership draws its authority from religious sentiments which transcend the pragmatic tests of ordinary events, so that its influence has continuity unless challenged by some major crisis with which it cannot contend. Even then it has the advantage of religious authority. Moreover, aristocratic leadership is not individual but includes, in fact, a cadre of persons from the same or related pedigrees. A particular person may fail in leadership and the cadre will replace him.

Religious sentiments foster the formation of wider networks of kin and community than do utilitarian motives. Australian native communities that have no common economic interests, for example, join, nevertheless, in great ecumenical gatherings to carry out religious ceremonies. The *kula* networks of the Massim area in Melanesia link communities of diverse cultures in a ritual of exchanges of objects of pure sentiment. Ordinary trade may follow in the path of ritual exchange, but it is the ritual interest that maintains the links, not the utilitarian trade. Everywhere among kinship societies common ritual or religious interests draw people together far beyond their ordinary interests. In the simpler societies, at least, the utilitarian interests are ordinarily narrow and parochial; communities are essentially self-sufficient in the basic necessities of existence. Even in the early civilizations international trade began with luxury articles, not with objects of daily use. In our own historical tradition, Europe was Christian far beyond the boundaries of political authority.

Insofar, therefore, as aristocracy draws upon religious sentiment for its authority, it has the same characteristics as religion in extending itself. Aristocracies have the advantage in linking together lines of kin. A primitive community under aristocratic leadership is essentially a religious community, acknowledging in the religious sense the inherent superiority of a ruling line. Under these conditions, subordination in such a community is no more demeaning than is subordination before an ancestral figure, a god, or a spirit. Such subordination is accepted as part of the natural order. (Even in the European tradition it has always seemed possible for a nation to accept a foreigner as a ruler as long as he represented true principles of aristocracy.) In kinship societies, aristocracy makes it possible for distantly related kinsmen and for communities that are not related in kinship to cohere easily within a mixed religious and political-tribal organization. In this respect it has been a principal factor in social evolution, which has been generally defined as a process of enlargement and of coherent organization of the political community. Aristocracy, for the reasons I have cited, seems to have been the most suited to bringing this enlargement and organization about. Some clues as to how enlarged communities may have been formed under the leadership of aristocracies can be found in Polynesia, where the process of enlargement can be described in substantial detail.

The distinctions between utilitarian and aristocratic leadership are not quite as categorical as I may have presented them. Aristocracies also have their utilitarian and nonreligious aspects, while the effectiveness of utilitarian leadership must depend in considerable measure not only on the pragmatic test of the value of the end result but upon the idealistic admiration for efficacy itself. The transformations of aristocracy in Polynesia result in part from the interplay of both idealistic and utilitarian motives and interests within the aristocratic system itself and, of course, in the society at large.

A thorough historical study of aristocracy must draw upon much wider cultural sources than I have included here, but Polynesia seemed to have the special advantage of offering a range of aristocratic systems which, from the demographic point of view alone, includes small atoll populations of several thousand persons at one extreme, and great high-island populations numbering hundreds of thousands at the other. What the small atoll populations offer to theory are examples of pure structural forms of aristocracy in which senior lineages supply the chiefs and the genealogical elite, while the junior lines contain the commoners. On the large Society and Hawaiian archipelagoes, the same aristocratic structures embrace a more elaborate political and economic organization and therefore represent more developed forms. The elementary forms of aristocracy simply carry out the logic of primogeniture and of seniority of descent. The developed forms add on or proliferate administrative and religious offices and titles and generally expand the functions and powers of leadership. Polynesia thus offers a spectrum of aristocratic systems which at its upper end is comparable in form, if not altogether in dimension, with the complex aristocracies in such early civilizations as those of Middle America, the Andes, and Africa. In terms of magnitude, however, which is another criterion of evolutionary development, Polynesia even at its upper range in the Hawaiian Islands is a small-scale Early Civilization. The smallness of Polynesian societies is, from a scientific point of view, their most intriguing quality. The most elementary form of a complex structure is, after all, the most advantageous for study, for the elementary form is the basic model upon which the complex system has been constructed. While we have no assurances that the small Polynesian aristocracies and their social settings are, in fact, the elementary forms of more complex aristocracies and early civilizations elsewhere, we can hardly doubt that they are a class of elementary forms. We should eventually determine where they fit in the worldwide distribution of aristocracies and civilizations.

Social theories that assume that a stable order is inevitably established by the balance of internal forces look to external events for sources of variability. An internal order is indeed affected by direct foreign intrusions of persons, artifacts, and ideas, as well as by its more complex interplay with changing material conditions. Diffusion and ecological adaptation have been most commonly adduced in explanation of Polynesian cultural variability. Undeniably valid as such explanations are in general, they are only partial and incomplete insofar as they overlook the specifics of response of each social system and, above all, their internal characteristics of change. Social systems differ in responsiveness to external events and in their organization of internal equilibrium. Concepts of rank as social order and as social doctrine define the attitudes and the responsiveness to the physical environment and to the outside world, and they define the patterning of internal social relationships. The external response cannot be predicted from general theory, nor do the internal relationships conform to equilibrium hypotheses derived from views of a generalized social system. The concept of social equilibrium can only be taken as an explanation for continuity of pattern, not for the dubious assumption of a stationary order which only an external disturbance can dislodge from hypothetical immobility. Aristocracy in any case is no static social order. It is precisely its powerful internal movement that has given it its strategic role in social evolution. What this internal movement is and what it accomplishes is the main concern of this study.

The question of origins is not at issue here. I deal only with established aristocracy and not with its first emergence. Still, in theory the question of which forces brought a social system into being cannot be disassociated from questions of how the social system behaves. If genealogical rank and its associated doctrines and institutions had been an economic product, specifically—a response to "surplus" and to the complexities of social and economic management, let us say—then it would be reasonable to suppose the system would continue to respond to such conditions. There is, in fact, no direct evidence for an assumption that the system of genealogical rank is an adaptation to such specific economic conditions as level of production or to such specific social conditions as size of population. In Oceania, among Malayo-Polynesian speaking peoples, so small an atoll as Ifaluk supports a complex order of genealogical ranks among a population of only 500 persons who live mainly by fishing (Burrows and Spiro 1957). Ifaluk is not exceptional in this respect, so we must assume that aristocracy is in its basic forms not a product of social and economic magnitudes. Nevertheless, the character of a social order is not independent of the factors of scale or of multiplicity of relationships. Dependence, however, is mutual and interactive. But given the circumstance that elementary aristocracies coexist with social and economic systems of a wide range of magnitudes and complexities, the most significant question may be: How do societies living by aristocratic principles utilize the economy and other patterns of social relationships?

Polynesia as a Culture Area

Polynesia is a geographic designation for the easternmost group of Pacific islands, starting with the Samoan-Tongan archipelagoes as the western margin and extending eastward to Easter Island. The Hawaiian Islands form its northern point and New Zealand its southern. The area is roughly triangular and extends for some 4,500 miles in each of its three main directions. A number of islands west of the Samoa-Tongan divide, and well within Melanesian territory, are occupied by Polynesian-speaking peoples and are included therefore within the cultural domain of Polynesia. These are the islands of Tikopia, Ontong Java, Anuta, Duff, Rennell, Bellona, Sikaiana, Ndai, Taku, Kilimailu, Nissau, and Tanga. The Polynesian-speaking Ellice Islands border upon Micronesia; and Nukuoro and Kapingamarangi are Polynesian enclaves deep in Micronesian territory. There are no "foreign" enclaves within the Polynesian triangle. The history of these outlying Polynesian islands is still not known. Some consider them as examples of ancient Polynesian populations left behind in the general eastward movement (cf. Capell 1962), but as Elbert (1953) justly observes, Pacific populations have been moving westward as well, so that the history of each outlying island must be independently determined.

From the linguistic standpoint, Polynesia forms part of the distribution of Austronesian or Malayo-Polynesian–speaking peoples. This large linguistic super-family is considered to embrace over 500 languages (Grace 1959), some on the mainland of southeast Asia, but most occuping the islands. A very crude but commonly accepted subgrouping of the island language families is: Indonesian, Melanesian, Micronesian, and Polynesian (Capell 1962). The relationship among the major linguistic subdivisions of Austronesian is sufficiently close to imply a common history of no great antiquity, and suggests that Malayo-Polynesia may prove to have culture-historical significance as a super-culture area (cf. Schwartz 1963). The specific histories and patterns of cultural interrelationships within this great Oceanic area still remain to be determined. The entire region can certainly be seen as a cultural zone within which a common core of social features—systems of kinship, of status, of religion, of leadership—had evolved in multiple directions. A more comprehensive study in the evolution of aristocracy from some common cultural ground would include all of Malayo-Polynesia within its scope. But this is a task for the future that will be aided to the extent we understand processes of development in one of its parts. Within this great area Melanesia and Indonesia are undoubtedly the oldest, the first regions to be settled, and the most diversified with respect to language, culture, and physical type. Polynesia is the youngest of the subdivisions, evidently the last to be settled, and relatively homogeneous. Among the strictly aboriginal areas that have not been directly affected by later civilizations carried by Hinduism, Buddhism, and Islam, Polynesia was the site of the most fully evolved aristocracies among all Malayo-Polynesian–speaking peoples.

The historical unity of Polynesia is demonstrable on biological and linguistic grounds. Shapiro's assessment of the character of the Polynesian racial stock made a generation ago still stands (cf. Suggs 1960). Reviewing then all of the evidence, including his own studies, Shapiro wrote: "The Polynesian population possesses a fundamental unity in physical type which necessarily implies that the successive immigrants were derived from a common people (1943:7)." This common people was racially mixed before they entered Polynesia, and Shapiro assumes that the mixing took place in the original Asiatic homeland. The actual genetic composition of the Polynesian peoples has not been determined, and thus its history is necessarily conjectural.

Buck considers the Polynesians as primarily Caucasoid, with Indonesian (Malayan) and Melanesian (Oceanic Negro) mixture. Coon, on the other hand, defines them as basically Mongoloid, but as an "intermediate" form (1962:2, 369). The "intermediate" status of Polynesians is further implied by the frequencies of occurrence of the so-called shovel-shaped incisors, a distinctive Mongoloid trait. On this trait, Polynesian populations fall midway in frequency between Mongoloids and Europeans (Suzuki and Sakai 1964). In this respect they compare with Micronesians and Indonesians—also classed among Malayan peoples—and differ markedly from the Oceanic Negro Melanesian populations (Riesenfeld 1956).

Polynesian historical unity is more strongly established on linguistic grounds. Recent linguistic studies affirm earlier views on the relative uniformity of Polynesian languages (cf. Capell 1962, Elbert 1953, Grace 1964). Broadly speaking, the Polynesian languages fall into two related groupings, an eastern and a western, to which the outlying island languages are most closely related. Emory has summarized Polynesian linguistics as follows: "The fundamental unity within the Polynesian family of languages, marked by an even greater unity with the islands of West Polynesia and within those of Eastern Polynesia, means a common origin for the whole family and secondary common origins for the West and the East divisions (1963b:84)."

Race, language, and culture need not and often, in fact, do not coincide. Each finally develops its own history, as biological stocks split and separate, each new branch going its own way, mixing with others, changing its language and culture either moderately or drastically. The history of a race does not therefore stand for the history of a language or of a cultural tradition; and the histories of a language or of a culture do not by themselves account for the history of a particular people. These simple and indeed well-known characteristics of the historic process are sometimes overlooked as one follows the distribution of traits from a supposed homeland to their terminus in the Pacific. Nevertheless, in many instances race, language, and culture do coincide to establish an authentic ethnic coherence. Polynesia seems to be such an instance. The languages coincide approximately with specific regions, with a definable physical type, and with a particular set of cultural configurations. The degree of ethnic coherence that exists in Polynesia, however, defines only its recent history, that is, from the time of entry into the present habitat. But since this history encompasses some 2,500 years, it demarcates a substantial period of historical unity. Earlier historical theories explained diversity in Polynesia from diffusion—from supposed waves of immigrants, each bringing in new cultural traditions and new levels of complexity; all present evidence, whether from genetics, linguistics, or culture, including ethnology and archeology, converges towards the conclusion that the major Polynesian diversities have arisen from internal differentiation.

All human histories, needless to say, reflect both internal and external influences, and the task of the historian is to sort them out. In the Polynesian instance the external history concerns the places of origin, the courses of migration, the continuing contacts with cultures outside of Polynesia as well as the contacts and cultural exchanges within the area itself. The early history should give some image of the proto-culture, the basic social and cultural configurations that are subsequently added to and amended from the outside at the same time they are undergoing internal differentiation. The external history of Polynesia is as yet very little known. However, the new and very lively interest in Oceanic linguistics and archeology is certain before very long to supply the missing facts. As of now only the nature of internal differentiation can be described in satisfactory detail.

Since Polynesian is a branch of Malayo-Polynesian, the earliest history of its speakers must be considered as part of its broader history. Except for Heyerdahl (1952), the outstanding advocate of a theory of American Indian ancestry for Polynesians, Oceanic scholars derive the Polynesians along with all other Malayo-Polynesian peoples from mainland Asia. For reasons of geography, and from the distribution of languages, food crops, pottery, and adzes from early periods, the most reasonable source of the original homeland is believed to be southeast Asia and South China (Chang 1964). Evaluating present information on prehistoric pottery distributions on mainland Asia in the Pacific, Solheim (1964) suggests a connection between the western Malayo-Polynesian speakers (i.e., outside of Polynesia) and the Lungshan cultures of South China, a cultural tradition linked with North China and dated by Chang (1964) at about 2000 B.C. If authentic, this connection associates tangentially some branches of Malayo-Polynesians with emerging Chinese high cultures. Adze distributions, on the other hand, trace a movement from Indochina through the Philippines and then eastward out to Polynesia (Heine-Geldern 1945, Beyer 1948). Neither the pottery nor the adze distributions, however, have been dated objectively; and neither, needless to say, can actually identify the associated peoples or cultures. Beyer (1948:35), nevertheless, has put the age of Pacific island cultures as early Middle Neolithic (2250–1750 B.C.), while Solheim (1963:400), in close agreement, estimates from archeology and linquistics that "Malayo-Polynesians" left the mainland at about 2500 B.C. Linguistic evidence of the earliest Malayo-Polynesian movements is, if anything, even less certain than that of archeology. Grace, acknowledging the shortcomings of glotto-chronology, infers tentatively: "By about 1500 B.C., Austronesian languages were present on Taiwan, in all major parts of Melanesia, and probably in various parts of Indonesia and the Philippines (1964:304)." His estimate accords with what is still the earliest radiocarbon date of human occupancy of the outer Pacific islands: 1527 B.C. ± 200 from Saipan in the Marianas (Spoehr 1957). Thus the estimates of time and location are reasonable. The reader will understand, however, that artifacts do not identify either a language or a people. Even if the estimates of the age of the Austronesian languages are correct, we still do not know who their very early speakers were or where they lived. If Negroid peoples today speak Melanesian tongues closely related to Polynesian, then the complicating phenomenon of linguistic acculturation must be taken into account in all historical reconstructions.

The early history of the Polynesians themselves is even less certain. Again we have to consider separately the movements of a biological stock, a language, and a culture (represented for the earliest period only by adzes and pottery). In physical type Polynesians differ enough from all other branches of the Malayo-Polynesian–speaking family to stand as a group that had begun to differentiate itself early in its history. Shapiro, it will be recalled, believes the physical differentiation occurred on the mainland. The most recent linguistic studies suggest, however, that Polynesian had evolved from within Melanesia (Dyen 1965), specifically, according to Grace (1964:366), from one of the New Hebrides languages as early as 1000 B.C. The linguistic relationship between Polynesian and Melanesian establishes a specific historical connection between early Polynesian populations and those of southeastern Melanesia, but does not, of course, answer questions about the biological relations between Negroid Melanesians and lighter-skinned Polynesians.

The search for Polynesian ancestry cannot limit itself to tracing a single historical line. Even if, as now seems likely, the main line of Polynesians came from Melanesia, there is no reason to doubt that other lines came from other regions in Malayo-Polynesia. The nature of early Oceanic migrations presupposes a slow drift of populations carried by small canoes, many, as Sharp (1957) has convincingly argued, accidentally brought to an unanticipated landfall. In the course of over 2,500 years of developed open-sea navigation, all of Malayo-Polynesia has undoubtedly received people and their cultures from all parts of the Pacific basin, including its Asiatic and American shores. Consequently, Polynesian cultural traits show affinities with Melanesia, with Micronesia, and with Indonesia. Striking similarities in social structure exist between Polynesia and Malayo-Polynesian–speaking peoples on Taiwan (Chang 1957) and in what was formerly French Indochina (Le Bar 1964). Outside the range of the Malayo-Polynesian family, influences have been noted from the Americas (Heyerdahl 1952, Carter 1950), from Japan (Haring 1940), and from China (Heine-Geldern 1966, Ling 1957). If the Oceanic Negroid population should prove to be African, that would add to the diversity of the historical record.

Yet, even as we take account of the multiple strands of Polynesian history we cannot fail to be impressed by the coherence and unity of its social systems and cultural configurations. In part, this unity can be explained by the slow and gentle rate of diffusion. An occasional canoeload of visitors may leave its mark, but the impact is readily absorbed and enmeshed in the ongoing culture. There may be another and a more interesting explanation—the cultural character of Pacific Ocean voyagers. All such voyagers, whether accidental or deliberate must come from societies with a developed tradition of navigation, and canoebuilding. These as a rule are societies with developed chiefships, leadership, and craft specialization. In the Pacific basin they are mainly the rank- and status-oriented societies, many of them comparable aristocracies. Thus the main Polynesian contacts which we may assume to have been established and maintained for some 2,000 years were in all probability with compatible social systems.

The Melanesian relationships were, nevertheless, the most direct, by present knowledge. A radiocarbon date puts the occupation of New Caledonia, a likely embarkation point for the eastward move into Polynesia at 847 B.C. ± 400 (Gifford and Shutler 1956). A shared pottery tradition among ancient Samoans, Tongans, and New Caledonians confirms the Melanesian links and adds plausibility to conjectures that the New Hebrides and New Caledonia were early Polynesian homelands. By 124 B.C. the occupation of the Marquesas by what surely must have been a Polynesian population had begun (Shapiro and Suggs 1959). Occupancy dates for Samoa and Tonga, the more probable points of entry into western Polynesia, are somewhat later, but there is hardly reason to doubt that Polynesia begins to take shape as an ethnic entity shortly after the 847 B.C. date for New Caledonia.

Taking account of estimates from glotto-chronology and from positively dated archeological sites, we are able to give to Polynesian society an age of some 2,500 years. In this period Polynesian society advanced from "simple" Neolithic communities (Suggs 1961) that already had pottery and fully established horticulture to the great central administrations of Tonga, Tahiti, and Hawaii. We do not, of course, know the nature of the early social structures. Judging by historic distributions—no certain guide, to be sure—the earliest Polynesian communities may have already possessed the core traits of aristocracy, namely, primogeniture, seniority of descent, the ranking of descent lines, and religious leadership. The antiquity of these traits is suggested by their widespread distribution among all populations belonging to the Malayo-Polynesian family, whether on the mainland and its near islands or in the distant islands.

Even the aboriginal or "proto-Malay" Jukun of the east coast of Johore on the southern Malay Peninsula had ranked and titled statuses, and hereditary headmen who could also act as priest or "magician" with authority over local as well as a larger territorial community (Skeat and Blagden 1906). Systems of hereditary rank, with royal patrilineal lineages and sacred rulers were, of course, common among the more politically evolved Malayan communities and principalities of Malaysia (cf. Lebar, Hickey, Musgrave 1964). Chang (1957) has described "Polynesian" complexes among a "pocketed remnant of a proto-Polynesian population" on Taiwan, noting, in particular, lineages ranked by seniority into noble and commoner divisions. Parallel organizations are common in Indonesia, even among the more isolated and more "primitive" peoples of the Philippines, the Celebes, and Borneo. Among Bontocs and Ifugao of Luzon, for example, senior lines produce an hereditary aristocracy headed by a *kadangyang* who was at the center of ritual life. Micronesia, whose linguistic connections are with both Polynesia and Indonesia, has elaborately developed systems of hereditary rank everywhere, all based on common principles of primogeniture, seniority of descent, and ranked clans. Here, too, chiefs had sanctity and ritual authority. The system of hereditary ranks on Ponape is almost identical with that of Samoa and Tonga. Melanesian societies have generally developed along plutocratic lines, and allow for "social climbing" through possession and acquisition of wealth. Nevertheless, hereditary rank transmitted through primogeniture and seniority is widespread, running along the entire chain from the Admiralty Islands in the northwest through the Solomon Islands, the New Hebrides, and New Caledonia in the southeast. Fiji, the nearest of the Melanesian-speaking islands to Polynesia, falls culturally within the Polynesian orbit in this respect. In all Melanesian regions chiefs have the sanctity of *mana* or of special relations with ancestral ghosts.

This widespread distribution of primitive aristocracies among members of a common super-family, a distribution that reaches as far as Madagascar, conceivably represents secondary and later diffusions into the area from Asia and elsewhere or from developed aristocratic centers within Malayo-Polynesia. In that case we would still have to explain the ease of transmission of aristocratic institutions. Receptivity can be explained by congruence between existing and diffused institutions. If Malayo-Polynesians were receptive to aristocratic elaboration, they presumably had the elementary forms of aristocracy to start with. Upon such a base, evolutionary development is stimulated by internal and external and by combined internal-external conditions.

Western and Eastern Polynesia

The Polynesian languages fall into two major divisions: a western division including a proto-Tongan (along with Tongan, Futunan, Uvean, Niuean) and a proto-Samoan (along with Samoan and Tikopian); and an eastern division whose origins derive from a proto-Eastern (and Easter), a proto-Marquesan (Marquesan, Mangarevan), and a proto-Tahitian (Tahitian, Tuamotuan, Maori, Hawaiian) (Elbert 1953). This major linguistic division corresponds, on the whole, with a cultural subdivision of the Polynesian area (Burrows 1939) and defines for us its main lines of historical connections and divergences. Samoa and Tonga are identified as the two principal cultural centers of western Polynesia; the Marquesas and the Society islands as the corresponding centers of eastern Polynesia. The divergent character of the Easter Island language testifies to its early isolation. According to Grace (1964), who acknowledges the uncertainty of this glotto-chronological reconstruction, the separation between the eastern and western languages could have taken place between 40 B.C. and A.D. 580, that is, some time after the Polynesian "triangle" had been entered. The outlying islands seem to have separated at about the same time as the appearance of the east-west linguistic split (Elbert 1953). Taking 1800 as the terminal date for aboriginal society, it is clear that western Polynesia had at least 1,200 years of relatively independent development, and, in all probability, a good deal more, considering that the Marquesas which gave rise to eastern Polynesian languages had already been occupied by 124 B.C. Emory (1963), who has attempted to correlate linguistic and archeological evidence on the chronology of interior Polynesian dispersals, is convinced that Western Polynesian was the ancestral tongue of all Polynesia. By geography alone, it is reasonable to assume that Samoa and Tonga were settled earlier than the Marquesas, though the suggestion that western Polynesia (that is, Samoa and Tonga) is older than eastern Polynesia does not justify, in general, any assumption that a direct line of cultural development can now be traced from west to east in Polynesia. Some characteristics of social structure seem to have followed a course of progressive simplification from parts of Melanesia through western Polynesia and into eastern Polynesia, but on the whole each region has followed its own course of cultural diversification. The history of the western Polynesian islands has been strongly affected by contacts with Melanesia, while eastern Polynesia, by contrast, may have developed more independently.

ANCIENT POLYNESIAN SOCIETY

I

Principles of Status

ARISTOCRACY IS COMMONLY CONSIDERED A POLITICAL SYSTEM—AS "rule by the best," or by an hereditary elite. Aristocratic rule, however, is not to be interpreted narrowly as technical administration, but broadly as the imposition of a commanding and "natural" authority over the entire cultural domain. The Polynesian conception of chiefs as the sources of divine authority and power established them as the overseers of standards and of custom—as the *ariki,* the aristocracy. The standards of the ariki were the sources of merit, and governed basic relations of economy and government, and of kinship and religion. The Polynesian idea of a ruling elite is, at bottom, the expression of a cultural conviction about the whole social order, rather than a political invention. As we shall see, however, the idea soon becomes political, and aristocracy is eventually reduced from its broad and all-encompassing scope to a narrower, and more administrative realm. But even when aristocracy has become more strictly government, it still has the force of a broader cultural system. Even in its inevitable political demise, it remains as the exponent of a particular "style of life." Aristocracy, then, stands as a subculture within the larger culture.

What has given aristocracy its command has not been expediency, but a deep and elementary notion of distinctions in human worth. Specifically, aristocracy is a doctrine of social status. Its right to rule, and to assess standards, is a privilege of worth, one of many. Thus the way to an understanding of aristocracy is not through political theory, but through a theory of social status. When we assess aristocracy as a political system we are drawn to study consequences only and to overlook their sources. If aristocracy is indeed a system of social status, then the burden of analysis falls upon the effort to elucidate all principles of status, their combinations into patterns, their characteristics of variability, and their interaction with other social institutions such as economy, kinship, government, and religion.

Social anthropology has yet to develop a systematic theory of status systems. Recent students of social theory have slighted concepts of inequality and have preferred to define status very generally as, for example, "a relationship between individuals and groups with respect to a single class of objects or persons (Davenport 1959)." Or, when they do consider status more specifically as relationships scaled in value, they commonly treat them as side aspects of such more utilitarian systems as government, economy, and law.

Preliminary bases for a theory of status and of status systems have, however, been laid down by Linton and by Nadel. Linton offered the most generalized definition of status: "a position in a particular pattern" and "the minimum attitudes and behavior which [a person] must assume if he is to participate in the overt expression of the pattern (1936:113)"; and he contributed the now common distinction between "ascribed status" and "achieved status." A more restricted definition, and one more pertinent to questions of political evolution, has been offered by Nadel, who said, "By status I shall mean the rights and obligations of any individual relative both to those of others and to the scale of worthwhileness valid in the group (1953: 171)." The key term in Nadel's definition is clearly "the scale of worthwhileness," which declares status relationships to be hierarchical. It is in Nadel's sense that the term *status* is used in the present study. Following Linton, Nadel further noted: "Inasmuch as a group operates with ascribed status it is rigid and static; in the opposite case, it possesses mobility and implies competition (1953:171)."

In the tradition of Radcliffe-Brown, Nadel considered status, functionally, as a source of "internal order." But every system of social categorization is a source of "internal order." The real question is, how do different categorizations affect the organization and the development of the social order? By distinguishing rigid and static from mobile and competitive status, Nadel has implied that at least one type of status has a dynamic and, hence, an independent social role. We are asked to believe, however, that genealogical rank (ascribed status) establishes rigid and static social orders. Yet this cannot be so, since even the more primitive aristocracies are, or were, everywhere aggressive and expansive and, by no stretch of the imagination, rigid and static. Nadel evidently did not have history in mind, but rather a highly abstract sociological model of status within which a hypothetical single factor, hereditary rank, gave to the system an inevitable rigidity. The model as constructed is correct, but how real is it? It is altogether doubtful that a status system anywhere is formed around a single factor such as hereditary rank. Hereditary rank, as we shall see, is no single factor, but a compound of multiple genealogical criteria, while the complex that is genealogical rank is, in turn, linked with and dependent upon a variety of other status conditions which are not necessarily ascribed. An abstract model can readily distinguish ascribed from achieved status, but historical reality is ambiguous. When the heir apparent must meet standards of achievement to inherit the office, what do we call it? The point is, of course, that models are pure, while history, being concrete, is never pure. The model demands order of history; history for its part demands that the model reform itself by yielding some of its rigidity. In the specific case of genealogical rank, the model is needlessly rigid. Nevertheless,

Nadel's vision of status as a "scale of worthwhileness" implies no rigid concept at all, but points rather to a novel way of seeing all social relationships.

All social relationships—in particular, those of kinship, government, economy, and religion—can be usefully expressed in terms of a scale of worth. Role positions as, for example, chief, expert, warrior, priest, noble, commoner, male, female, elder, junior, and the like must inevitably be viewed from the point of view of relative worths. The principal advantage of defining relationships and roles in these terms is that we are able thereby to develop a "real" as against a teleological explanation of social systems. Teleological explanation seeks to identify the contributions of patterned relationships toward ultimate social ends. These ends, whether interpreted as social cohesion and continuity, or more generally as efficiency in carrying out social tasks, are not necessarily those of the participants. They are recognized for what they are by the observer. It is in the sense that the ends are believed to pertain not to persons but to social systems—which are theoretical constructs of the observer—that the explanation is not "real." To say that an explanation is not "real" is not to deny its value, but simply to classify it as one type of partial explanation. Social reality, on the other hand, is founded in the interests and intentions, whether conscious or unconscious, of people. Among the most characteristic personal interests are those of valuing, of defining the self in relation to others, and of reacting to the social valuations of others. The interests in valuing, in formulating hierarchical relations, in defining, asserting, defending, and in improvising upon the themes of personal and group identities are real and substantially explicit. Insofar as anyone can know anything precisely, chiefs, for example, have a precise understanding of their position, of the rules governing their position, of where they stand in the scale of worth, and of how they must behave in that scale. The same can be said, perhaps less precisely, about people in relation to kinsmen and in relation to all others in economy and in ritual.

Perhaps the interests of persons in valuing one another can also be included within the framework of teleological theory, but it is not necessary to seek to identify ultimate ends in order to deal systematically with the real interests of persons in status. Genealogical rank may, of course, be "explained" as a system that provides administrative efficiency, but even granted this is true, it does not follow that aristocratic systems evolved specifically to carry out general objectives of administrative efficiency. Administrative efficiency may well have been a by-product of systems of genealogical rank, along with powerful pressures for economic expansion. What we seek to understand, however, is not only the by-product, but also the actual characteristics of such systems, insofar as they can be elucidated. Granted that one aim of scientific enquiry is reductionist, another is clearly expansionist, the bringing out of the complex relations of a system. Reductionism elevates an explanation to the level of abstraction where it transcends history and culture. It is therefore a final step in ethnological explanation. But social anthropology knows so little about systems of social status—and little enough about such specific status systems as aristocracy—that the final step of reductionism is still irrelevant. Our present concern therefore is to understand a status system from the point of view of its participants and through its particular rules and principles.

A concept of status system is in itself sufficiently reductionist. What specifically is a status system? By status system I mean the principles that define worth and more specifically honor, that establish the scales of personal and group value, that relate position or role to privileges and obligations, that allocate respects, and that codify respect behavior. Since all social relationships involve, at some point, principles of honor and of worth, it would appear that "status system" is an all-inclusive concept. But for that matter, all systems that form part of a social structure are all-inclusive. When we speak of the "elements" of a social structure we may give the misleading impression of a total system made up of discrete parts that fit handily with each other, when, in actual fact, the notion of a social structure and of its component elements represents a theory as to how various principles of social categorization and of organization are interrelated. These principles may be shown within a theoretical structure of equilibrium, that is, in mutual interdependency and balance; they may be shown as linked in a coherent function of carrying out important social tasks. Or they may be shown as coming under the domination of one set of principles, in which case the structure is best described as having direction. In Polynesia, it is the status system—specifically, the principles of aristocracy—that gives direction to the social structure as a whole. Principles of status dominate all other principles of social organization. Here, then, in this part of the world, and in this type of social system, the variety of principles that in sum represent a social structure are seen to greatest advantage from the perspective of the special principles of social status.

All status systems are inherently dynamic because they all require some adjustment between their formal principles and shifting and flexible objective conditions. Status systems vary, however, in their ability to generate change. When age and skills are the main criteria of status, and prestige is their main privilege, a relatively "feeble" status system, with an equilibrium based on a repetitive cycle, is established. When, on the other hand, rank is joined to privileged land control as the centers of status, the system elaborates and expands, producing new variants. Status systems based upon hereditary rank, but granting only symbolic prerogatives, will develop more elaborate ritual forms; but if weak in such objective privileges as political power and command of wealth, they have little directive effect upon social structure as a whole. Polynesian status systems are all strongly dynamic. All are based upon complex patterns representing opposing concepts of ascription and of achievement, of sacred and secular, of formal and pragmatic. A status system like a kinship system or a total social structure is neither simple nor one-sided. It is inevitably a system of tensions demanding, as does life itself, the careful balancing of both opposing and disparate qualities. Seniority, for example, is in some balance with prowess. One quality is given, the other is achieved; one quality is precise, the other is ambiguous. Thus no position falls inevitably into place. The values of status are also, as they must be, of this nature, in part given, traditional, axiomatic, and thus objective; and in part created anew in each situation and so remeasured and reevaluated, and thus ultimately subjective. One can think of rudimentary status systems that are single-dimensioned in valuing achievement only. But fully developed status systems such as the Polynesian are most inadequately described as "ascriptive." Hereditary status is a principle incapable of leading a solitary existence.

The basic oppositions just mentioned provide one structural dimension to a status system; the counterpoint between position and prerogatives provides another. Position is real but formal as a single entity. It has potential but does not "realize" itself until it has been able to exercise the prerogatives that are appropriate to it. A prerogative is literally the right to be asked first and so have precedence in exercising a power. In its most general sense, then, a prerogative is a power. The counterpoint between position and prerogatives is that of form and action. Form and action are a dual combination; one presumes the other but does not obligate it. The chief is entitled to prerogatives, but must be able to exercise them; the commoner may seize the chiefly prerogatives, but must then be able to assume the royal forms. Moreover, a potential can be made kinetic by additional action. Thus a formal diagram of a status system must include a specification of appropriate actions to bring complementary conditions into their actual mutual relationships. Polynesia does not specify these actions precisely, demanding only general conformity with rules—once again, a balance of tensions between the formal and the improvised.

Polynesia does specify precise and formal criteria for ascribing status. Broadly speaking, rank is genealogical. Genealogy, however, is no single factor of hereditary status. Polynesia takes account of primogeniture, of senior descent lines, of sex line, of genealogical depth, and, in the overall, of genealogical distinction (that is, the history of the line). Each individual criterion of genealogical distinction establishes sharp divisions, but the combination of these four factors reopens ambiguity. Ambiguity is not to be taken as a "failing" in the system, but rather as an integral aspect of its inherent tensions.

The genealogical criteria determine basic ranks, which represent categorical social distinctions, in principle, but allow for ambiguities in particular cases. Another class of statuses starts from the ambiguous principle of achievement but allows itself to be drawn into the more categorical areas of rank. These are priests, craft experts, and warriors. Essentially specialists and particularists, in contrast to the ranks that are general and formal statuses, they form an ambiguous status division that may be either separate from or part of the basic rank organization. In principle, the highest ranks are also the priests, the experts, and the distinguished warriors; but in practice, which is an extension of principle, high rank specializes in political power and authority, leaving other specializations to others.

A status position stems fundamentally from an expectation of notable efficacy or the ability to control powers. In Polynesia, all powers are from the gods and, in principle, are transmitted genealogically, which is to say authentically along established lines. If Polynesia had rigidly recognized authenticity alone, or a single and exclusive rule of authenticity, power and rank would be solidly combined. But, in fact, powers are subdivided, and their transmission is granted a measure of uncertainty. While the gods conform to their own set principles, they retain the awesome power of deviation—as do men. While all powers come from the gods, some are direct and primary and others are indirect and secondary. In the course of events it is the indirect and secondary that may prevail. Power is the principal prerogative of status. It is a given, but it must also be taken, secured, and used. The form must be converted to action.

Mana

The central concept of power in Polynesia and in all of Oceania is *mana.* Durkheim, who sought for sources of religion among Australian aborigines, believed he had found it in mana, which he described as "indefinite powers, anonymous forces, more or less numerous in different societies, and sometimes even reduced to a unity, and whose impersonality is strictly comparable to that of the physical forces whose manifestations the sciences of nature study (1912:229)." Mana as a religious concept was first given currency by R. H. Codrington, a missionary and one of the great scholars of Melanesian ethnology. Writing in 1891, Codrington described mana from a first-hand knowledge of many Melanesian societies. Later field work has only verified his characterization, which still stands therefore as definitive:

> There is a belief in a force altogether distinct from physical power, which acts in all kinds of ways for good and evil, and which it is of the greatest advantage to possess or to control. This is *Mana.* The word is common I believe to the whole Pacific, and people have tried very hard to describe what it is in different regions. I think I know what our people mean by it, and that meaning seems to me to cover all that I hear about it elsewhere. It is a power or influence, not physical, and in a way supernatural; but it shews itself in physical force, or in any kind of power or excellence which a man possesses. This *Mana* is not fixed in anything, and can be conveyed in almost anything; but spirits, whether disembodied souls or supernatural beings, have it and can impart it; and it essentially belongs to personal beings to originate it, though it may act through the medium of water, or a stone, or a bone. All Melanesian religion consists, in fact, in getting this *Mana* for oneself, or getting it used for one's benefit—all religion, that is, as far as religious practices go, prayers and sacrifices (118, 119).

Closer to our interest in mana as an aspect of status is Codrington's observation that "all conspicuous success is a proof that a man has *mana;* his influence depends on the impression made on the people's mind that he has it; he becomes a chief by virtue of it. Hence a man's power, though political or social in its character, is his *mana* (1891: 120)."

Everywhere in Oceania, in Melanesia, Indonesia, Micronesia, and Polynesia mana is the primary condition of status. This does not mean that without mana there is no status, for there are other forms of prestige, worth, and personal effectiveness in Oceania that do not depend upon mana. Everywhere, however, the *ideal* of status depends upon mana, though the precise relationships between it and status vary in the area. In Polynesia, Indonesia, and Micronesia, mana, by and large, is regarded as an inherited quality. Those who are in the line of succession inherit mana and the right of office together. In Melanesia where the authority of chiefs is generally lesser, personal qualities are, as Codrington has informed us, a sign of mana, and the possession of mana entitles a man to office. These distinctions, it should be said at once, are not quite that sharp, for there is inheritance of mana and office in Melanesia, and acknowledgment of mana inherent in capability in Polynesia, Micronesia, and Indonesia. The differences I have described represent what appear to be the norms, the emphases.

In all of Malayo-Polynesia, ideal status, therefore, has a religious setting. Rulers, chiefs, and distinguished persons generally differ from the common people in the fundamental sense that they are believed to have been selected and endowed with a special quality of the highest worth. They form a true elite. On Sumatra in Indonesia, in almost all the Micronesian Islands, and almost everywhere in Polynesia, this elite is also sacred and separated from the common people in *tapu*, a term signifying a sanctity which demands reverential avoidance, hence it has taken on the more common meaning of "forbidden actions." In Polynesia the elite blessed with mana are also tapu. To speak of mana in Polynesia is always to imply tapu. Mana is, so to speak, the kinetic quality of religious force; tapu is its potential. The distinction between a category of a selected elite who are sacred and separate and those who are merely unusual is indeed an important one. The concept is worldwide, fundamentally distinguishing shamans, priests, elders, initiates from their nonsacred counterparts.

Status based on mana is almost obliged to be highly responsible, since mana is ordinarily a beneficent force in the service of the community. The point about the relationship of mana to status is that the concept, being so broad, is a highly variable one. Mana seems to have two modes of variation—one by gradation and another by polarity. Everywhere in Malayo-Polynesia, and Polynesia is no exception, mana is regarded as possessed in degrees, corresponding to specific manifestations and to specific achievements or to genealogical status. But whether acquired or inherited, mana gives to a status system a range of gradations as well as great flexibility. The concept of mana also includes the possibility of its lack. Thus in Polynesia mana is graded in quantity, but there are persons who have none. This definite quality of mana—a polarity between possession and nonpossession—allows for sharp and qualitative status distinction. There is in Polynesia still another polarity, and that is between the maximum mana distinguishing persons of highest sanctity from persons of lesser mana and lesser sanctity. The effect of this polarity is to create two avenues of status, one a fully ideal status moving along strictly sacred lines and strongly separated by mana, and the other a less ideal status and capable of moving along a variety of lines, but differentiated from that of the fully sacred. Within the sacred line itself there is the diversification that results from the unsharp distinction between chiefly sanctity and priestly sanctity. The distinction is not sharp because the Polynesian ariki always has some priestly function, and is sometimes the high priest as well. Despite this overlap of function, there seems to be a recognition among Polynesians that political and purely religious authority are separable. As we shall see, the bifurcation of authority along such lines is in fact common in Polynesia, as other students of the area have pointed out. The qualities of priestly mana follow the same gradations as the qualities of chiefly mana. Upper-rank priests match upper-rank chiefs, while the mana of lower-rank priests corresponds roughly with the mana of lower-nonpriestly ranks. Since priests always deal with powers, the situation of the lower-rank priests is necessarily a distinctive one. But this is a complex matter that is best dealt with in detail in its appropriate place. What we need to call particular attention to in the overlap of sanctity between chief and priest is that overlap or ambiguity is inevitably a source of rivalry and friction.

Considering the range of variability in the mana concept, and of all other related status variables, it is clear that this religious concept provides for flexibility in the establishment of status. The mana concept imposes no rigid rule, even though it does impose a general form upon a status system. Thus to stress the variability of mana is not to overlook its stabilizing effects. Mana sets limits, and it gives religious significance to the genealogical structure of status, endowing power and authority with special social responsibility and so counterbalancing purely self-assertive interests. Granted that purely self-assertive interests are held in check by the concept of mana, we cannot underestimate the significance of its loss or its lack for the person. To lose mana is to lose vitality and, therefore, from a Polynesian point of view, all genuine significance as a person. To lack mana is to lack significance—to exist in a lower sphere. Loss is worse than lack because it implies a betrayal of nature. Loss is always conspicuous; so is gain. In the final analysis, the person is constantly engaged in what can only be described as stupendous actions to defend his mana, his spiritual worth and hence the essence of his being. If born to a status that is low or lacking totally in mana, there is little to defend; on the other hand, there is much to gain, since the stakes defined as personal are the highest.

Tohunga

Tohunga represents a more specific concept of ability than mana, since it is a title of honor rather than a strictly religious quality. Tohunga has the connotation of expertness in specific activities. It does not necessarily include generalized chiefly qualities, but it does include religious skills, craft skills, and administrative skills. The overlap of the tohunga concept with that of mana is considerable, inasmuch as mana is itself so broadly conceived. Yet mana and tohunga seemingly start from opposite poles—mana as a sacred quality acquired in some unusual manner, and tohunga as the more secular aspect of skills that may be learned and mastered. Polynesian usage does not, however, polarize mana as sacred and tohunga as secular, but distinguishes between religious and secular forms of tohunga as well. Taking Polynesia as a whole, it is evident that the most varied interrelations are possible between a concept of mana and the concept of expertness underlying the tohunga title. When a priest is tohunga he is charged with sacredness to a high degree, but there are other crafts or skills also carrying the title in which sacredness is either minor or unimportant. The overlap between tohunga and mana brings out two features of Polynesian status systems: their emphasis upon capability, and the constancy of mana as a standard of worth. While the tohunga title has a parallel significance to that of mana, mana is the constant model. All evidence points to the chiefs, the ariki, as those who set the standards for the *tohunga* to follow. Like mana, tohunga is a graded quality that fits easily into a status system, constructed upon graded rank. Thus, while tohunga encompasses mastered skills, the title, nevertheless, is often inherited.

Like mana, tohunga is a special form of a more general status principle, the honoring of ability. The tohunga concept reaches lower down the status scale, singling out for titled distinction persons who would not qualify for a title by genealogical criteria alone, and so adds diversity to the status system. A concrete emphasis upon ability gives solidity to a status structure, bolstering symbolic concerns that by themselves might lack the vigor of constructive action; and, finally, by honoring ability, Polynesian societies placed themselves on the road of rapid cultural and technical development.

Toa

Toa meaning ironwood, the trademark of military hardness, is a title applied either to warriors generally or to those who have distinguished themselves in battle. Ideally, warriors came from the ranks of chiefs, but since nature does not necessarily bestow her very specific measures of personal quality by genealogical line, Polynesians—always realists in war—were often compelled to honor warriors regardless of rank. The prominence of war, the adulation of sheer power, not to mention the immediate political consequences of victory or defeat, almost inevitably elevated the warriors to a level where they could challenge the ariki. It was hard for Polynesians to overlook the implications of mana in military valor and success. Thus the ariki, who should hold all the virtues, faced the rivalry of priests and warriors when objective success was elusive. The outcome of these two distinct rivalries was, of course, profoundly different. Since priests were, in fact, high-born, as a rule, their ascendancy introduced only a minor modification in the organization of status. But when warriors who were not necessarily high-born were ascendant, their victory rocked the status system at its foundations. The potential conflict between toa and ariki was never simply one between brute force and formal honor, an opposition Polynesians would not allow. The conflict was made possible because strength was always idealized. The conflict could be visualized therefore as one of ideals.

Seniority

Principles of mana, tohunga, and toa provide solid bases for social inequality but do not by themselves institute a stable structure of status. What really organizes status differences in Polynesia into a strong system is the genealogical principle of seniority. Mana, tohunga, and toa are the variable principles of status representing the psychological or cultural aspects of the status system, while seniority, establishing, as it does, a stable and systematic organization, is a true structural principle.

All societies honoring first-born form some system of genealogical seniority. Polynesian systems are distinctive, however, for their inclusiveness, which is capable of assigning genealogical rank to all. Seniority of descent is derived from primogeniture, but is not identical with it since a title holder need not always be the actual first-born but only a descendant of a line of first-born. Primogeniture establishes an *ideal* of descent, whereas simple seniority, which gives some equivalence to all children of first-born, offers a line to fall back on when birth and personal qualities do not coincide. Thus, while genealogical rank by seniority seems inflexible in principle, the presence of a senior line gives to the system a definite margin of variability.

Order of birth has this mystical rationale: The first-born inherits most mana, the last-born least. This Polynesian view of primogeniture and of seniority is not at all unusual. Supernatural qualities such as mana can be transmitted either by chance, as is often the case in shamanism; they can be secured as an act of choice; or they can go automatically down a line of descent. In the latter case, seniority seems to have, judging by its widespread distribution in the world, the preference as a religiously logical mode. Seniority, therefore, is almost inevitably linked with the doctrine of sanctity of chiefs of other high-ranking strata.

Seniority in Polynesia carries some connotation of superiority at every genealogical level, ranging from statuses demanding the highest form of deference to those for whom a simple and almost casual offering of deference is sufficient. Polynesian social structures are literally built on the principle of seniority. Kin groups are traditionally organized around the relative seniority of descent lines. At the most elementary level of organization, the household, a distinction is drawn between the status and authority of senior and junior members. Polynesian kinship systems explicitly recognize this distinction by supplying terms for junior and senior siblings. The structural significance of seniority is in its provision for the orderly ranking of genealogical lines. Seniority also provides the appropriate fracture points at which new branches break out. It establishes the framework for the segmental organization of lineages, and for the orderly allocation of authority, responsibility, and privilege. Social structures based on ranked lineages are thus most effective organizations for the carrying out of sustained and disciplined effort.

Sanctity of the Male Line

Not all Polynesian societies unequivocally acknowledge the superiority, by virtue of sanctity, of the male line. Enough do, however, even in western Polynesia (an area of Melanesian relationships), so that there is little reason to doubt the importance of male line sanctity as one of the basic principles of status. The representation in New Zealand of the male line as the "erect penis" suggests perhaps virile potency as a source of reverence in this corner of Polynesia. The common native explanation of the preference for patriliny, which I designate as "pro-patriliny" to distinguish it from exclusive patriliny, is simply that men and the male line carry more mana than women and the female line. Why this should be so, we do not know. Matriliny and patriliny seem to be arbitrary choices, expressing in Malayo-Polynesia mystical rather than pragmatic values. In Polynesia, the honor of being descended from males must be weighed against the parallel honor of descent from lines of chiefs and from senior lines, generally; as against these modes of exclusive descent, the honor of the male line is always important but never paramount.

Supreme status, then, in Polynesia would be ideally defined as endowment with the greatest amount of mana by virtue of seniority of descent from a line of males and the demonstration of mana by skills and valor. The complexity of the system, of course, precludes the attainment of this ideal except in exceptional cases. Thus these five principles of status are inherently variable in their common relationship.

Seniority and the male line as basic genealogical principles of status allow for a variety of genealogical sources of status. These are the primary criteria that define a pedigree as distinctive. Derivative criteria are those of linearity and those of depth. Not all honored descent need be from a direct male line or from a direct line of seniority. Linearity of descent from a distinguished founder of a descent line and down a distinguished line of descendants becomes therefore a graded concept; the most direct line is the most honorable, the most circuitous the least. Genealogical depth is a related concept. The farther back the pedigree goes, the more honorable it is. All other conditions being equal, shallow genealogies are the least worthy. The metaphysics of genealogical linearity and depth are evidently related to the transmission characteristics of mana. Each generation by its own qualities affects in a sense the quantity of mana. Rich genealogies are additive, while poor genealogies subtract.

Prerogatives of Status

Rank has its privileges even in egalitarian-minded societies such as our own. Egalitarian-minded societies disdain, in principle, the very idea of preordained privilege. Aristocracies, however, live precisely by codified and preordained rights. Aristocratic rank rests upon a base of orderly precedence and formal definition of preordained rights—in the strict sense, prerogatives. The prerogatives are the exercise of rank and crucial to it. To deny rank its prerogatives is to challenge its authenticity and thus, in the end, to destroy it. Since the Polynesian concept of rank rests upon mana, a religious doctrine of efficacy, the vital prerogatives are concerned with powers: with power over person, over resources, and over the elements. But even the less vital prerogatives, those that set chiefs apart and denotate their precise standing, are not unrelated to powers; for alterations in orders of precedence and violations of sanctity or of the principle of separation of chiefs arise from changing estimations of chiefly power and from changing balances of powers among contending parties.

Thus, while prerogatives and rank are, in principle, fixed in an aristocracy, they are, in actuality, subject to the vicissitudes of political life. The political vicissitudes, it must be realized, are not somehow accidental and extraneous to the "system." They are part of the system; indeed, a central part. Efficacy demands measurement, and the measure of efficacy is in how it meets a challenge. The chief must be prepared to defend his prerogatives—to react swiftly and effectively against lese majesty—to give proof through his prerogatives that his mana is as it should be. Status and prerogatives are always in active interplay; indeed, this particular interplay is at the very heart of active variability in Polynesian status systems.

Prerogatives of status are ordinarily discussed under different subject headings: power over people is the conventional subject matter of political organization; power over resources falls between polity and economy; and, of course, power over the elements, or control of the supernatural, is the common subject matter of religion and magic. When we deal with these powers in conventional terms we may lose sight of their interrelationships with each other, and of the full range of influences that act upon them. From the point of view of status, these powers are linked within a common system and their exercise responds not only to the broad requirements of carrying out necessary social and cultural functions, but to the more specific requirements of carrying out the status interests of chiefs.

From a psychological point of view, it may well be true that the interest in power is basically personal. As an aspect of status, however, power is socialized, exercised in the interests of the community; at the same time, as a measure of efficacy and hence of worth it is inevitably personal. Ideally, personal and social interests coincide, and neither the arrogant nor the weak among the chiefs survive for long. The exercise of political power, nevertheless, is never constant, and in Polynesia the ways in which power is used varies from society to society with some regularity. To what causes are we to attribute variability? Political theory has paid most attention to the social side and has seen the growth in political power as a direct response to social "needs," to increasing complexity, and to growth in size of the community. C. N. Parkinson (1957), on the other hand, has aptly demonstrated the self-propelling features of a power system which creates the needs for itself to act upon. Polynesia demonstrates a dialectical relationship between power as personal and power as social. Since power is inescapably an aspect of status, it is the status system that directs its application.

As a matter of status, political office is a measure of capability and of the possession of mana. The practical exercise of the office in behalf of the community is a measure of responsible status. Since Polynesians judge status by concrete measures of capability, it is in the interests of a chief to seek to expand the size of his community. Thus it is not sufficient to say that the power of the chief gains in proportion to the size of the community; he hopes to enlarge his group to enhance the stature of his office.

Power over people in Polynesia is, then, both a prerogative of status and its measure. This dual role fosters the growth of power and its variability. The growth of power, nevertheless, is ordinarily held in check by many social and cultural conditions. In the most traditional Polynesian societies, of which Maori is perhaps the best example, the chief's power is restrained by the kinship unity of the genealogical network, by the doctrine of the lineage, by the system of land tenure, and by a limitation of his sacredness that allows him to move about freely and to work with his subjects. Maori society has from time to time called forth predatory and exploitative chiefs. On the whole, however, the Maori political system is one of balances.

The balance, though it is a delicate one and easily upset, is also readily restored. One chief may break with tradition, his successor will restore it. Such fleeting events are political vagaries, interesting as examples of delicate equilibrium but of no major consequence in political evolution. It is when particular circumstances provoke adaptive measures (such as shifts in rules of succession, the recognition of personal land tenure, the separation of sacred and secular powers, or rearrangements of territorial grouping) that variations assume evolutionary significance. Power over people is so vital for chiefly status that any threat to it is critical.

Political power rests upon economic efficacy, which is measured by the general aura of abundance within which a chief lives, by his ability to promote economic growth, and by his capacity as a donor. The first of these measures is largely symbolic, defining the physical setting of a chief. The second is a more active measure, testing both religious and secular capabilities. The third is the most specific measure, involving the chiefs in immediate and concrete relations with the community.

The ability to give is everywhere a mark of high status. As Mauss has said:

> To give is to show one's superiority, to show that one is something more and higher, that one is *magister*. To accept without returning or repaying more is to face subordination, to become a client and subservient, to become *minister* (1954:72).

In aristocracies the roles of giver and receiver depend upon rank, which governs the scope of giving and the patterns of reciprocity. The highest ranks are givers to the widest networks, the lowest ranks to the narrowest. Conversely, the principles of reciprocity cannot be allowed to disturb the hierarchy of honor; only equals may vie to repay more. True subordinates must measure carefully between the obligations of giving enough and not giving too much.

In Polynesia all exchanges at every social level from household to tribe follow patterns of social inequality set by the status system. These exchanges do not in fact abide by simple patterns of status hierarchy, though hierarchical principles, nevertheless, are never obscured. The details of hierarchical exchanges are left for later discussion. I wish at this point only to call attention to some general hierarchical principles. When chiefs and subjects exchange goods, the nature of the goods and the mode of exchange are clearly differentiated. Under some conditions, for example, the chief receives "first fruits." He is honored by receiving a product which carries the inherent honor of being a "first" and is, therefore, unique. When he reciprocates, it is an act of generosity and it is with generalized or more utilitarian examples of foodstuffs. When the chief pays for services, he is a giver of objects, and the people are givers of labor. Are objects and labor equivalent in honor? Presumably not, since no one pays the chief to do an equivalent service for him. If the principle that giving is honorific is sound, we must grant reciprocity of honor between chief and subject. The giver of first fruits to his chief also gains honor. He is giving freely and he is giving foodstuffs which have high status value. If, however, he were giving under stated coercion, or were giving labor rather than food, he would be losing honor. When the chief is a giver, he not only gains honor but, reciprocally, endows the recipient with honor. Generally speaking, therefore, reciprocal giving promotes reciprocal honoring. Reciprocal honoring need not and often cannot be symmetrical, since the grades of honor must be preserved.

If reciprocity involves mutual honoring, then a break in reciprocity must involve a corresponding break in the mutuality of honoring. Thus, one of the striking variations in Polynesian status systems results from the act of cutting off sections of population, such as slaves and commoners, from the chain of reciprocity. When this cut-off occurs, the social structure as a whole is profoundly affected, for it implies a fundamental cleavage. The question to answer is under what circumstances does the cut-off occur? The specific answers are more appropriate at the conclusion of this study, but in general it may be said that the break in reciprocity is made by the chief and represents, on his part, a final response to the variety of pressures upon him; and more broadly still the break reflects strains and conflicts with the organization of rank.

Finally, power over the elements refers to the priestly prerogatives of chiefs. Chiefs control religious powers directly through their personal mana or as agents of the gods. As agents of the gods, they have subordinate status and, accordingly, reduced religious responsibilities. Religious efficacy, nevertheless, remains a constant issue for chiefs. The issue of religious efficacy is most acute when the chief is also priest; it is least acute when religious and political office are divided. All three prerogatives of power—over person, over products, and over the divine sources of productivity—are in Polynesian thought unified under the single concept of efficacy as the measure of chiefly virtue. The context of efficacy, however, is never constant, and neither is the relationship among these power prerogatives.

Varieties of Status Systems

The variety of ways in which basic principles and prerogatives of status combine and modify one another gives rise to three basic variants in Polynesian status systems. In the first, which I call "Traditional," seniority is central. As the source of mana and sanctity, senior descent establishes rank and allocates authority and power in an orderly manner. The Traditional is essentially a religious system headed by a sacred chief and given stability by a religiously sanctioned gradation of worth. In the second system, which I call "Open," seniority has been modified to allow military and political effectiveness to govern status and political control. The Open system is more strongly military and political than religious, and stability in it must be maintained more directly by the exercise of secular powers. In the Open, status differences are no longer regularly graded but tend to be sharply defined. Finally, the third system, which I call "Stratified," is characterized by clearcut breaks in status that are far-reaching in their impact upon everyday life. In the Stratified system, status differences are economic and political. High ranks hold the rule and possess the land titles; the commoners are subjects and are landless. The Stratified represents a synthesis of Traditional and Open, combining respect and reverence for hereditary rank via seniority with necessary concessions to political and economic power. The system seems to have been an outcome of the intense status rivalry so characteristic of the Open societies. In effect, chiefs in the Stratified system had succeeded in consolidating their authority and had emerged therefore far stronger than chiefs in the Traditional and in the Open systems.

The distinctions marking these three types of status system are real and significant, as the study of specific examples will show. They are so far-reaching in their social and cultural effects that we are justified in referring to them as social systems. I speak therefore of Traditional, Open, and Stratified societies. Nevertheless, these three types of society are part of a single social order and cultural tradition. The differences among them are partly categorical, but mainly matters of degree. Stratified is the most clearly defined type because of the categorical distinction between landed and landless. The distinction between Traditional and Open, on the other hand, is one of gradation. By the single criterion of political power and authority, all Polynesian societies can be ranged along a hypothetical continuum from Traditional to Stratified. I have grouped the societies along this range as follows: *Traditional*—Maori, Manihiki-Rakahanga, Tongareva, Uvea, Futuna, Tokelau, Tikopia, Pukapuka, Ontong Java; *Open*—Mangaia, Easter, Marquesas, Samoa, Niue; *Stratified*—Mangareva, Society Islands, Hawaiian Islands, Tonga.

A description of Polynesian status systems is necessarily in political terms, if only because the central conception of status in Polynesia is that of power or capability. The concepts of mana, tohunga, and toa, the three pillars of Polynesian status, refer directly to power. The principle of seniority may be regarded as a logical form for the traditional allocation of power. This is not to say that seniority alone is not without status consequence, but only that seniority without power is incomplete.

If status and power are so closely identified in Polynesia, how are we to regard their relationship to one another? Are they completely parallel cultural and psychological motives? Is power an aspect of status, or is status one of the consequences of power? These are fundamental questions and they cannot be answered from within the limited terms of reference of a culture-area study. Each society handles the status-power relationship in its own way, either equating the two or subordinating one to the other. In Polynesian status systems, all three possible relationships exist: power and status are aligned as equal; status is dominant and power is subordinate; and power is dominant and status is subordinate. These Polynesian relationships between status and power are cultural, and they do not in themselves answer the psychological question of which of these, status or power, is more fundamental in human nature. Power is defined as control and is an objective condition, in the main, while status is defined as honor and is a subjective condition, in the main. This distinction, it must be emphasized, can only be sustained at a cultural level of analysis—not at a psychological level. We can distinguish readily enough between the deference paid a Polynesian chief in such ways as bowing, baring the breast, avoidances, symbolic offerings of first fruits, respect language, ritual precedences, and the like, and the claims the chief can make against crops, labor, and land. Deference is a clearly symbolic act and is owed to the status; in the Polynesian form, to the sanctity to the chief. We can also distinguish between prerogatives of dress, ornamentation, insignia, housing, diet, and prerogatives of tribute, ownership, leadership, and command. One set of prerogatives is what is automatically due to birth and to position; the other set is what birth and position can command providing there is also the power to do so. The distinction between what is owed to birth as a prerogative and what it can command as a prerogative is well illustrated by the Tahitian concept of *rahui,* the supernatural injunction against the use of crops without the permission of the chief. By birth and by his sacredness, the Tahitian chief has the prerogative of declaring a rahui. But the question in Tahiti is: does he have the power to enforce it? Psychologically, the deference a chief receives may be considered as a token of his power, but there is still the distinction between the token and the power itself.

The value of drawing distinctions between status and power is that the variable relations between these two linked psychological and cultural motives can be used to identify types of status systems and the directions in which they are developing. Along these lines we can say the following: In the Traditional societies, status is dominant and power is subordinate; in the Open societies, power is dominant and status is subordinate; in the Stratified societies, status and power are at an approximately even level but both are more consequential than in the Traditional societies. Taking Polynesian society as a whole, it is evident that the central issue is the steady growth in power. What is of real significance in Polynesian history is that power does not seem to develop either as an adaptation to complexity, nor in direct response to economic necessity. It seems rather to be an outgrowth of the rules of status. In Polynesia, at least, it is not too difficult to demonstrate that it is status that is primary and that power is political and a secondary development. The growth of political power as an aspect of status is, as we shall see, a consequence of status rivalry. Having stated that status is primary in Polynesia, we must, of course, observe that status itself is predicated upon mana, upon a concept of supernatural power.

The thesis that the growth of power in its economic, political, and religious forms can be laid to status rivalry has been presented thus far on essentially formal or logical grounds. The thesis corresponds to the logic of Polynesian status systems. Viewing status as a game in the manner of Huizinga (1958), and its principles or elements as its rules, we can say: This is the way the game is played and this is its probable outcome. Each challenge to power and status provokes a response that is potentially equal to or greater than the challenge. The thesis, of course, must be demonstrated empirically, but before we turn to the empirical evidence we may pause to consider the implications of the thesis. Its most striking implication would seem to be its apparent contradiction of the functional-structural theory on the nature of government. This theory regards government and its powers—as it does kinship, economic changes, or ritual—as devices for maintaining order. An early functionalist study of Polynesia (Hogbin 1938) presents a similar view, arguing that the power of chiefs is a function of economic productivity. According to this thesis, the more productive a society, the more goods there are to redistribute and the more power will be held by the chief. A more detailed version of this theory has been put forth by Sahlins (1959).

Taking a totally abstract view of culture—ignoring actual motives and the specific histories of cultures—it is, of course, possible to postulate a social model in which any aspect of culture can be shown to be adaptive, integrative, and contributing to equilibrium. In such a model, culture follows the analogy of a biological system in which all constituents contribute to a predictable outcome—adaptation, integration, equilibrium. Natural selection eliminates what is least useful until all adaptive and integrative components are stabilized. Still, in terms of a biological analogy, each cultural system has the task of compensating for periodic maladjustments and for adjusting itself to new conditions. Following this line of reasoning, we might explain the function of status as a stimulating mechanism. We might observe along with functionalist theories that status consciousness and status rivalry stimulate effort and promote skills, sorting out the efficient from the inefficient. The honor of status would simplify the task of efficiently organizing an administration. Power would then be explained as a supplement to status, bolstering respect for authority and smoothing over difficulties that sheer respect for status could not handle.

The difficulty with such an approach to status and power is that it is water-tight. It is a closed logical system immune to the data of history, psychology, or of cultural differentiation. A Polynesian chief may murder all potential rivals among his kin and precipitate a civil war at the end of which a triumphant chief establishes supreme authority over an enlarged political community. Seen from the perspective of the culture, the act of murder is an expression of personal ambition that is more or less consistent with the rules of the status system. It stirs up fears, suspicion, discord, and violence, turns kin against kin, interferes with every-day work, and imposes severe suffering on victor and vanquished alike. If we ignore these details, we cannot account fully for culture change, cultural adaptation, or cultural equilibrium. In brief, it is my contention that we cannot account for cultural evolution in Polynesia without full knowledge of the forms and circumstances of status rivalry.

Status Rivalry

Polynesian status systems are highly active. They are subject to self-generating conflict, dislocation, and readjustments. They evolve new customs and procedures. The focus of activity is status rivalry that draws into its maw members of the same kin community as well as outsiders. Rivalry is inherent although not inevitable in Polynesian status rules. From the standpoint of the status system, rivalry may be understood as a necessary response to ambiguity of rank. Ambiguity defies the ideal concept of genealogical rank, a concept of gradation, and so must be overcome. As chiefs see the situation, there is a question of who is most fit for leadership even by virtue of the variety of legitimate claims. From the standpoint of the person, then, ambiguity is intolerable and a challenge. Consequently, rivalry begins as confined to upper ranks. As long as it is confined to the upper ranks, rivalry need not be socially serious, but as rivalry moves down the social scale the outcome of status conflict becomes increasingly more significant.

The specific problem, then, is to analyze the nature of status rivalry, the specific conditions that give rise to it, the social consequences of rivalry, and the interaction or "feedback" between the consequences and the form of status rivalry. The problem is complex in proportion to the specificity of detail demanded of it. Complexity is reduced somewhat if we limit our analysis to that of the growth of power and to the effect of power upon the social system. Since status rivalry must abide more or less by traditional rules of behavior, the range of possibilities and of outcomes is relatively limited. This consideration, too, reduces the complexity of the analysis.

We may begin by considering the more elementary conditions of instability in systems of graded hereditary rank and proceed to the progressively more active and complex conditions of status rivalry. Under the most elementary conditions, rank follows seniority very closely, giving preference to males, so that the highest ranking chief is the senior male of a line of senior males. Generally the demands upon the chief are equal to his chiefly qualities. The chiefs live up to their obligations, contributing to the growth and well-being of the community. The community, for its part, acknowledges the sanctity of the chiefs and willingly grants them their prerogatives and privileges. In this condition (the Polynesian ideal), the chiefs are differentiated from the rest of the population by the status of sanctity, but they, together with all the ranks, are bound into an organic community that is modeled after the extended family or household. The chief is a paternal figure, responsible for the well-being of those below him. Those below acknowledge their acceptance of the chief by tokens of deference and respect.

This elementary condition approximates the ideals of the Traditional Polynesian societies. It remains relatively undisturbed if the expectations of well-being implied by endowing seniority with the honor of sanctity are fulfilled. The political community grows, it continues to be prosperous, and its honor vis-à-vis neighbors is upheld. The mana of the chief, who is the "father" of the community, is in the service of the entire community. If all benefit, then the Polynesians have reason to believe that the mana has been correctly allocated; from their religious point of view, the cosmic order and human affairs are in harmony.

Under such circumstances, internal disturbances need have minor consequences only. Population pressure is offset by fission and by the occupation of new territory and by more intensive and more efficient farming and fishing. The splitting-off of groups also reduces political and status pressures by allowing the ambitious to leave and start new communities elsewhere. Even when rivalry does arise, it is often dealt with decisively. A more competent chief replaces a less competent one and the system is, if anything, strengthened. Military attack can be beaten off and the campaign and the victory may also strengthen the system. The system can also tolerate economic setbacks and other natural disturbances, up to a point. Precisely what that point is, however, we do not know. (We do know that when a seismic wave struck some of the atolls a new political order was subsequently introduced.)

The Traditional system is at its best when the logic of seniority through males is most fully carried out. The advantage of a single line as against a double or alternate line of descent is the elimination of ambiguity as a potential source of conflict. In Polynesia, however, only Tikopia has consistent patriliny. Maori illustrates an interesting compromise. It allocates the highest rank to descendants of a senior line through males, and allows intermediate ranks to rest upon a compromise between seniority and patriliny. Since political rivalry in a hierarchical status structure tends to develop at the top, the Maori system affords good practical protection by giving to the high chief an unequivocal genealogical claim to the office. Generally speaking, those Polynesian societies that have a patrilineal bias have more stable status systems than those that freely follow primogeniture and seniority alone.

In practice, it is virtually impossible consistently to reconcile patriliny and seniority with requisite capability. If the senior male is incompetent, he is set aside in favor of a next of kin; chiefly descent lines approximate but do not ever coincide with the ideal. Consequently, depending upon the degree of deviation from the ideal of seniority of descent through males, a number of alternative genealogical claims to the chieftainship can be made. The elementary condition, therefore, is not without status rivalry. Status rivalry is contained, however, and is not allowed to spread. Tikopia and Maori are good examples of this state of affairs. When status rivalry gains momentum, the interaction between equilibrium and counter-equilibrium of the status system becomes considerably more complex. These more complex forms of status rivalry are best considered in their specific settings.

In the chapters that follow I describe the status systems of the eighteen Polynesian societies on which information is most complete. Since the status system has, I believe, the controlling influence over the evolution of Polynesian societies, it has been necessary to present each system in some detail so as not to obscure by generality the specifics of variability and of interaction between status system and the organization of kin groups. Status systems, as I have already indicated, are volatile, their organization at any moment in history being subject to the current conditions of status rivalry. To demonstrate the specific variations in the status system of each society and the role of status rivalry in bringing these variations about, I have placed each chapter within a relevant historical setting, drawing upon three sources of history: the archeological record, the genealogical traditions, and the published chronicles of European and American observers.

The chapters have been arranged partly to bring out a developmental sequence, but primarily to clarify continuities in the range of variations. Thus I have distinguished between eastern and western

Polynesia, treating each as a subculture area. Eastern Polynesia is the most distinctively "Polynesian" by contrast with western Polynesia, which in many respects has continuity with Melanesia. It has seemed more appropriate as a way of defining Polynesian aristocracy sharply to begin with the eastern societies, presenting them in an apparent developmental order. This developmental sequence is, of course, hypothetical and approximate. I certainly do not wish to imply that one can actually establish the precise rank order of eastern or western Polynesian societies. The question I have raised in this book is not of so specific a nature. I have asked rather whether variations in status system and related social structure have moved in some order of regularity from Traditional to Open and Stratified.

If I had thought it was possible to establish an actual historical sequence of development for each Polynesian society, I would have found it more reasonable to begin with the apparently older area of Polynesia—with western Polynesia and specifically with Samoa and Tonga, the probable gateways to Polynesia—and traced a movement to the Marquesas and then the complex diffusion of an early culture throughout eastern and western Polynesian society. Obviously, the history of diffusion of Polynesian culture has no direct bearing upon the attempt to reconstruct Polynesian social evolution. Societies are not ordinarily caught in arrested development, and Tonga, Samoa, and the Marquesas, the "old" Polynesian societies, were not, at the time of European discovery, representatives of archaic social systems but had undergone their own internal developments, influenced no doubt by persistent contacts with neighboring societies.

I have therefore arranged societies in a morphological order starting with the Maori—not as an example of *the* oldest form of Traditional Polynesian society but as a good example of a prototype form from the point of view of structure. Maori history, suggesting a branching from an early form of the Society Islands' social system, actually gives an historical foundation to the morphological view; Maori has some authenticity as an early social system.

When I present the eastern Polynesian atolls of Manihiki-Rakahanga and Tongareva after Maori, I do not imply a later development, but only mean to give examples of Maori structure as adapted to the smaller conditions of atolls. The order in which the three eastern Polynesian Open societies are presented should not be considered as a developmental sequence but as three variant forms of the Open condition. On the other hand, the three Stratified societies of eastern Polynesia do suggest an approximate evolutionary sequence.

For western Polynesia I have followed no evolutionary order. I have presented Samoa and then Tonga as the strongest expressions of the area and have discussed all other western Polynesian societies as variants of the Samoa-Tonga type. The evidence has dictated this order, since in western Polynesia there seems to be no sound reason to hypothecate an evolutionary sequence from the "simple" societies such as Tikopia, Pukapuka, Ontong Java to the more complex societies such as Samoa and Tonga. To bring out indications of developmental sequence in Samoa and Tonga, I have relied rather upon the internal evidence from archeology and the genealogical traditions.

Finally, each chapter sets forth its own historical inferences. The last chapter—on status and evolution—is an attempt to present a broad and general evolutionary perspective for Polynesia as a whole.

2

The Maori of New Zealand

THE MAORI TRIBES MAY BE CONSIDERED AS PROTOTYPES OF EASTERN Polynesian Traditional societies in a morphological if not in a strictly historical sense. They are classic examples of aristocratic organizations in which the basic principles of primogeniture, seniority of descent, graded rank, sanctity of chiefs, and the sanctity of the male line are well established but which show none of the specialized features—achieved chiefly position, sharp social stratification, and political centralism—of the Open and Stratified societies.

Unlike the Marquesas and the Society Islands, New Zealand was never a formative center of Polynesian culture; rather, like Easter Island, it was a relatively isolated outpost, remote from the active centers of cultural interchange. But if, as we have good reason to believe, the classic Maori were a migrant branch from the Society Islands, we have before us an interesting example of an offspring society that developed along different lines from that of its parent. If we accept Maori traditions on this subject, the separation must have occurred finally after A.D. 1350 and at a point in Society Islands' history when Tahiti was evolving a Stratified society. According to their traditions, the Maori were migrants who sought to escape from wars and excessive demands for tribute (Buck 1949:38). For a time after their arrival in New Zealand, the tribes continued to war against one another, later settling down to peaceable relations. In the Society Islands, such wars of conquest finally led to the formation of a territorial state.

If traditional Maori was indeed representative of Society Islands' society before it had become Stratified, it stands not only as a formal prototype but as an historical representative of the Polynesian Traditional, as well. We have, however, no truly satisfactory explanation for what seems to have been a case of "arrested" development in New Zealand. If Maori did not move in the same general direction as did the Tahitians, it may have failed to do so because of the historical accident of transfer out of a politically overheated atmosphere with its violent chiefly rivalries and stubborn wars for conquest. In a new land the continuities of old rivalries and antagonisms were easily broken and the evolutionary pattern interrupted. Perhaps the physical dimensions of the new land—with its almost limitless space, by Polynesian standards—allowed hostile and potentially hostile tribes to separate and find safety in distance. We cannot really claim that warfare and population density are closely associated in Polynesia. Nevertheless, the ultimate population density of 2.5 persons per square mile on North Island was extraordinarily low. While the fertile coastal plains and wide river valleys were, in fact, very heavily populated, the great interior forests, with their lakes and river valleys, were only sparsely settled and were attractive only to those refugees who felt pressed. General land pressure seems never to have been a serious issue in New Zealand, for, as Best had observed, the Maori had probably at no time fully used all their ready resources of fertile soils (1925:67).

Although the climate was colder than in the Society Islands, the New Zealand setting posed no formidable challenge. The familiar coconut, breadfruit, yam, and banana had to be abandoned as unsuitable, but the sweet potato (*kumara*), which the Maori had known in the old homeland, adapted readily to New Zealand soils and became the mainstay of the diet, supplemented by the familiar taro, along with fern root, fish, birds, waterfowl, and rat. Economic readjustment had no remarkable social consequences even for those Maori tribes such as the Tuhoe, for whom farming had become altogether secondary to fishing and gathering. If such an example is needed, Tuhoe may be cited in illustration of the adaptability of basic Polynesian social patterns to a variety of economic conditions. In general topography, New Zealand does not differ greatly from the large islands of the Society Islands archipelago. Like Tahiti, North Island, the center of Maori population, presents striking contrasts of terrain. The interior zone is high, rugged, volcanic, and heavily wooded. The coastal zones are open and gently rolling. The interior forests, lakes, and rivers were rather specialized habitats for Polynesians, but they were not deficient in foods. As on Tahiti, diversity of livelihood and of resources gave material substance to trade and other economic exchanges.

New Zealand geography placed no serious impediments in the path of cultural development. By Polynesian standards productivity was more than adequate to sustain the generous obligations of chiefly hospitality, to feed the thousands of persons who came together in great ceremonial feasts, to finance the construction of substantial and ornately carved meeting houses, and to support a cadre of priests and skilled artisans. Though the sweet potato in New Zealand could be harvested but once a year, the surplus was stored and was supplemented by other foodstuffs. If civilizations require economic abundance upon which to grow, New Zealand was a good provider; if not overall, then at least in selected areas like the Taranaki peninsula where the rich and powerful tribes lived. The material bases for conquest and for state formation were present; what was absent was the motive. Maori wars often verged on conquest, and chiefs understood the main principles of political domination. Why predatory and aggressive interests did not take hold in New Zealand is therefore an historical question that cannot be answered in general. The history of the New Zealand Maori has been neither peaceable nor benign, but it has been one of political restraint. As Buck has said:

> With the love of home territory strong, the desire to occupy other lands by conquest faded. The tribes continued to have their quarrels and feuds, but war parties returned home with plunder and captives after satisfying their desire for military glory (1949:381).

New Zealand had never developed the conspicuous ceremonial centers of the Society Islands homeland, in consonance perhaps, with its own less assertive political and religious style. The Maori *marae* (in New Zealand *marae* means "generosity") was the village clearing for group gatherings, while its *ahu*, or temple equivalent, was but a crude pile of stones hidden in the forest. On the other hand, what was lacking in massiveness was more than made up in elegance and sophistication. In turning from stone to wood, the Maori had in effect shifted the effort from centrally directed labor to the more intense skills and artistry of a few artisans. Scale was commensurate with village, and skills were directed to the domestic and personal. Maori clothing was the best in Polynesia. Meeting houses were substantial and richly carved. Stone carving was confined to small and delicate work in jade and nephrite. Agriculture often required the painstaking laying down of gravel beds and the construction of earthwork windbreaks to protect the potato crop from the severe climate. Such work required collective labor of a village, but was small-scale by comparison with the irrigation and terrace works of Tahiti and Hawaii.

The islands of New Zealand were first discovered by Tasman in 1642, whose presence, however, had no noticeable effect on Maori life. It was Cook's rediscovery in 1769 that began the cultural transformation. European occupation was swift and overwhelming, and by 1840 the Maori culture Cook had observed was gone. Yet no Polynesian people have been more voluminously and richly described by eyewitness observers or by diligent recorders of native traditions. The student of Maori must feel inadequate before the tremendous volume of published material. I have drawn mainly on the works of Elsdon Best, Peter Buck (who was also part Maori), and Raymond Firth. Like these authorities, I have been compelled to deal with a generalized concept of Maori. The study of variations among the scores of Maori tribes is a task for the New Zealand specialist.

The Archeological Record

Maori traditions claim a first settlement in New Zealand by Kupe ca. A.D. 950 (by genealogical reckoning), a second settlement by Toi ca. A.D. 1150, and then a great migration by a fleet (*heke*) ca. A.D. 1350. All migrants are traced to Hawaiiki, a now unidentifiable region presumably in the Society Islands. The traditions make the remarkably accurate claim that only the last migrants had brought agriculture with them.

The archeological evidence supports the chronological estimates from genealogies surprisingly well. Thus far, the earliest radiocarbon date for a New Zealand occupancy is ca. A.D. 1000 and the earliest circumstantial evidence for the presence of agriculture—storage pits for sweet potatoes—dates from the early fourteenth century (Golson 1961). It also supports the claim of at least two distinct settlements. Fairly extensive digging has suggested the presence of an "archaic" Maori who either had no agriculture at all or at best cultivated as a minor supplement to hunting the *moa,* the name given to several genera of large flightless birds which, by the seventeenth century, had finally become extinct. This archaic period is best known as Moa-Hunter, and while it cannot be dated exactly, since the moa disappeared at different times in different places, the dating from the traditions A.D. 950–1350 is an entirely reasonable demarcation of the period. The assemblage of artifacts from this archaic or moa-hunting period is definitely eastern Polynesian yet differs enough from later or Classic Maori (1350) to sustain the thesis of separate migrations. Apart from economy, the two periods differ in forms of implements and styles of art. Classic Maori shows a greater interest in personal ornamentations in its elaboration of jade and nephrite pendants than did the moa-hunters. There is no evidence for warfare among archaic Maori, but Classic Maori had brought in or developed in New Zealand weaponry, cannibalism, and fortified villages. Finally there is archeological evidence for the Society Islands' origin of Maori. Emory and Sinoto (1964) have found an artifact assemblage at a Society Islands' fishing village that resembles early or moa-hunting Maori dated from A.D. 1022 ± 70, or from about the time of the initial separation.

Genealogical Traditions

The bulk of Maori genealogical tradition stems from the later period of classic Maori, and gives an account of reasons for leaving Hawaiiki and of events in New Zealand up to the present. The Kupe tradition cites no political reasons for leaving, but the later traditions as narrated by Buck speak of political repression. The Aotea and Te Arawa canoes left as a result of quarrels over tributary payments to chiefs. According to Buck (1949:38), a Society Islands' chief argued that the tribute was not adequate, butchered his subordinate chief's son, and had him eaten. This led to reprisals and civil war, in the course of which the subordinate chiefs fled in a deliberate migration bringing with them the kumara (sweet potato).

Roberton (1957) has summarized the main events in New Zealand as revealed by the traditions of seven interrelated tribes. The consistencies among the genealogies of all seven argue well for the general historical validity of these traditions. The tribal traditions, of course, are not all alike. Yet even though they differ in details, they all illustrate expansion of tribal territory and influence through a combination of war and of intermarriage. While expansion strengthened the mana of a particular chiefly line, it did not establish great multitribal political chiefships. There is no evidence in the traditions, as narrated by Roberton, of any important changes in social system. Thus the traditions of the Tainui tribe, descended from a junior line, describe the first 100 years after settlement as peaceable; of expansion of chiefly influence by intermarriages with distinguished families from neighboring tribes. As the population grew, chiefs allocated lands to their sons and their descendants. Expansion of the tribe into new areas where they were compelled to fight with alien occupants was precipitated, Roberton insists, by family quarrels rather than by shortages of food which were, he notes, numerous. He adds: "Further expansion into Waikato was partly a result of disintegration of secondary family groups, but even more it was due to the ambition of men claiming a Hawaiiki father but brought up in an alien community where their standing was probably not recognized by the people of either the father or the mother (1958:53)." Some tribes were caught in internecine warfare and ground themselves down.

The general picture of political evolution is of gradual expansion of tribes, very likely accompanied by the strengthening of the power of tribal chiefs as war leaders. Yet, contrary to what happened in Tahiti, the zest for conquest evidently abated (Buck 1949:381), and land boundaries were stabilized. The earlier military interest in seizing new lands turned into the taking of captives and booty. But with the introduction of firearms by Europeans, a new wave of intertribal wars broke out, opening a fresh era of tribal military expansion. In this late epoch it would seem New Zealand history might have turned in the direction of the Stratified societies. But it did not. The predatory motive turned outward, not inward, and the tribal organization and its system of land tenure remained intact. In fact, when European colonists in the early nineteenth century began to acquire native lands by purchase, the Maori tribal chiefs banded together in a unity movement to oppose further land sales. This expression of the inalienability of tribal lands was the opposite of what happened in Hawaii, where chiefs took advantage of European law to acquire great private land-holdings for themselves.

The Status System

Polynesian status systems were organized—as already observed—around general principles expressing genealogical distinction, supernatural power, and sanctity, along with respect for outstanding competency in crafts, in warfare, in economic management, and in political leadership. The tribes differed in the precise ways in which they defined these principles and in the prominence they allowed them. Hence they differed in the manner of organization of general principles into a system. Maori, a prototype Traditional society, gave particular prominence to the principles of genealogy, supernatural power, and sanctity, but did not ignore factors of competency, which were considered, nevertheless, as dependent mainly upon genealogical rank and sanctity. The focus of the Maori status system was upon genealogical distinction and upon its attributes of religious authority. Genealogical distinction followed quite strictly upon principles of primogeniture, seniority of descent, male line descent, and genealogical depth.

Primogeniture

The first-born was distinguished in all families even though leadership itself, a prerogative of primogeniture, was restricted to males. The first-born male was the *matamua,* who was also honored with the title of ariki, unofficially among commoners and, of course, officially as the chiefly heir in highest ranking families. The female first-born carried the honorific distinction of being known as the *tapairu,* "first-born female," but was normally ineligible for office even when (as among some Maori tribes) she was also referred to as the *ariki tapairu,* and enjoyed the prestige of chiefly rank. The extraordinary respect paid first-born women in some Maori tribes—for example, among the Ngati Kahungunu (Buck 1949:344), where women were allowed to make public speeches, and among the Ngati Porou, where a female ariki was elevated to the paramount chiefship, a unique event in New Zealand—demonstrates the forcefulness of primogeniture. Even though the male and the male line were clearly superior in Maori doctrine, primogeniture pressed its own undeniable claims to high status, and in two tribes this principle emerged as the dominant one. If primogeniture could transcend the male principle in New

Zealand, it is not difficult to understand the appearance of bilateral primogeniture elsewhere in eastern Polynesia. Still, the intense respect for primogeniture was not absolute. The respect owed to seniority was permanent—the *tuakana* line (senior) was always the superior of the *teina* (junior)—but leadership could be lost in case of sheer incompetency. Nevertheless, the strong first-born son of a weak and set-aside ariki could, and generally did, reclaim the office.

Seniority of Descent

Insistence that the arikiship go down a line of first-born males or, in any case, down a line of first-born of either sex (Winiata 1956:26) established seniority of descent as a close to absolute principle of lineage organization. The status of families, of major lineages, and of all kindreds grouped around a chief was calculated by relationships of seniority. Whenever a genealogical relationship could be ascertained, the calculation that defined appropriate respect was that of relative seniority. The relative seniority of related chiefs defined the standing of their kinship following. Seen from the perspective of chiefs, the subdivisions, or segments, of the entire genealogical network were ranked in a fixed order of seniority. Senior lines descended from chiefly founders controlled the ariki titles; junior lines with no ariki titles were in permanent subordination. In broader perspective, the implications of seniority were more complex. Any senior male sibling was always tuakana and superior to all younger brothers, a relationship that moved down the generations, establishing all his descendants as superior to those of his junior (teina). Junior descendants of a tuakana were thus superior to senior descendants of their own teina lines. Except then for the rare senior descendants of the senior line of the entire network of kin, all men were subordinate in honor to some and superior to others. Women were only indirectly involved in these calculations. In short, the principle of seniority created a gross order of ranking based on chiefs and their descent lines, and highly varied and intricately differentiated ranks based on all relative birth orders. All but last-born males of last-born males could claim superiority over someone, even over persons of higher rank and station. However, it was gross seniority that opened the way to public rank and title. Interior seniority, as we may call the tuakana–teina distinctions, was a domestic affair, the source, in the main, of kinship respects.

The Male Line

As general doctrine, the Maori regarded males as tapu and women as *noa* (common), a distinction in conflict, at times, with reverence for primogeniture and seniority, and thus open to compromise. The first-born daughters of chiefs, for example, merited special respect, and in one known instance, qualified for office of ariki as senior descendant of a male line. On the other hand, a superior claim to seniority through a maternal line outweighed one of lesser significance through males. And if the wife held the higher rank it was to her husband's advantage to join her family, for the sake of the children (Winiata 1956:218). Since residence was also the source of land rights, it was the maternal side which then became the dominant center of both wealth and honor. Calculations of social advantage could lead through either sex, but the patrilineal claim, if honorable, was unquestionably the best, and no line was superior to that from uninterrupted links through first-born males. When the Maori designated such an extraordinary line as the *ure tu,* they were graphically depicting directness of descent in earthy imagery. We recognize as well the religious association of masculine mana with the specific fecundity and vigor that chiefly descent lines (the bone of the lineage) give to their dependents. As the "erect penis," it was signally appropriate for the distinguished line of chiefs to stand apart from all the others.

By associating women with childbirth—a passive sexual role—and with darkness and misfortune, the Maori inevitably stigmatized descent through females. Masculine–feminine was viewed religiously as complementary and antagonistic. The masculine represented the sky, light, and divine descent; the feminine, darkness, earth, the underworld. In myth they are in eternal conflict—in broadest terms that of life against death. Thus what is purely masculine, is life triumphant, so to speak; the feminine "mix" is a compromise.

Genealogical Depth

Maori history beginning only with the departure from legendary Hawaiiki is, of course, relatively recent. Genealogies, accordingly, lack the depth of those in Samoa, Tonga, the Marquesas, and the Society and Hawaiian Islands. The chiefly genealogies of the Tuhoe tribe, for example, as collected by Best (1924a:I, 344) included only 16 generations. All honorable genealogies had to connect with a founding ancestor, so that within the shallow limits of Maori history genealogical depth as a principle of status was indeed recognized.

Sanctity

Rank was unequivocally a religious condition defined by the two closely related concepts of mana and tapu. Mana was the religious condition that could be translated into specific qualities such as political authority, prestige, influence, psychic power (Firth 1929:244).

Tapu was the more general religious condition that has been defined as "sacred" and therefore commanding reverence. The precise relationship between mana and tapu as aspects of rank has never been made clear by the leading authorities on Maori, perhaps simply because neither concept had a precise meaning. Mana was a gift of the gods granted at birth in quantity proportional to rank, but depending, nevertheless, upon the proper carrying out of birth rites which secured the mana to the child. Mana therefore was definitely a variable quality in its inception. It was variable also in its development. Great deeds augumented mana and social disgrace diminished it. Persons possessing a high degree of mana could transmit it ritually, with fathers transmitting mana to their sons and teachers transmitting mana to their pupils. The volatility of mana is what made Maori so very "touchy" (Best 1924a).

Tapu expressed the sanctity of a person's *mauri,* or life force. In this respect it was a more general personal attribute than mana. Like mana, tapu was also a gift of the gods and a variable quality, the possession of which had to be zealously defended. Mana and tapu were brought into a very close relationship because their quantitative aspect was a function of rank. Since mana was sacred, it was spoken of as tapu. Chiefs who had most mana were most tapu. The traditional welcome for a chief was, "Welcome to power [mana], welcome to sanctity [tapu], welcome to dread [wehi] (Buck 1949:347)." Mana was demonstrated in the variety of capabilities of the chief or persons of quality. Tapu was demonstrated in the respects and avoidances demanded of those who associated with chiefs and persons of quality. Thus while mana and tapu were both god-given qualities of efficacy, in the broadest sense, and of the sanctity of efficacy that gave substance to the spirit or mauri of a person, they coexisted in a complementary manner, the mana standing for the person's responses, the tapu standing for the corresponding responses of respect toward the person. The relationship between mana and tapu is therefore best put in a hyphenated form, namely, mana–tapu. They rose in concert, and they fell in concert. If high mana provoked great respect in deference to high tapu, then any lack in respect or infringement of tapu was a threat to mana. However, while disrespect or violation of tapu inevitably threatened mana, loss of mana—as in cases of general inadequacy on the part of a first-born scion of a senior line—need not have diminished tapu as long as the chief and his kin were prepared to defend it. Mana then was the more specific religious quality of rank, and tapu the more general. An old man might no longer have the specific mana of forcefulness, but he would still possess the tapu appropriate to his rank and station. Moreover, the precise correspondence between mana and tapu was established only by the conditions of genealogical rank, so that the highest born had maximum mana and maximum tapu, but when mana increased markedly—as in the case of a warrior who had distinguished himself in a battle—the rise in tapu was not in proportion.

In summary, mana and tapu were supernatural qualities given at birth in proportion to rank and thereafter varying in accordance with the individual's fate, but mana possessed the highest variability, whereas tapu remained most closely associated with rank. Mana and tapu were both religious qualities, but the former expressed the broad range of personal qualities of competency, while the latter was expressed in the more specific range of ritual. Of particular importance to an understanding of status rivalry in New Zealand is the further characteristic of mana–tapu as testable qualities. Mana was definitely on the "firing line" at all times, tapu less so. Maori did not—as did the Tahitians, for example—provoke a challenging test of their tapu, but they did of their mana. What this distinction implies is that the sanctity of hereditary rank remained relatively secure in New Zealand.

As genealogically graded attributes, mana and tapu were associated with the majority of men. Only slaves were totally secular, lacking both mana and tapu. Since tapu was in fact the guardian of the mauri, or essential quality of the person, slaves were therefore spiritually defenseless and totally dependent upon their masters. In this important spiritual respect, then, slave status was categorically distinct from all others. Among Tongans, as we shall see, it was the commoners, a very large category of persons, who were considered lacking in spiritual quality. That women as secular creations of earth lacked both mana and tapu is a feature of Maori status that has already been considered. But first-born women of chiefly families were indeed sacred and subject to deference tapu. These ariki women formed a special category, since they alone among females were set apart.

Tohunga

Priest and crafts expert were in New Zealand, *tohunga,* sharing under this common and honorable title qualities of sacredness. It seems appropriate to translate tohunga in its Maori form as "priest," considering the craftsmen (tattooers, canoers, house carpenters) as the priests of their craft (they were, in fact, priests to the tutelary gods of their occupation). When an apprentice was drawn into a craft he was initiated through a religious ritual that brought him under the favor of the god. In a real sense, then, skilled labor was a ritual activity as was, in fact, the formal life of a chief. Only the master was the tohunga or priest; the apprentice was the neophyte who finally acquired the mana and the tapu.

All tohunga, whether craftsmen or true priests, were descendants of chiefly lines. In this way Maori remained true to their basic religious principle of attributing mana and tapu to genealogical distinction. Tohunga office therefore was hereditary and the tohunga apprentice was developed for his office in the same way that the ariki was developed for his. Tohunga were ranked, but in no precise manner. The priesthood proper, according to Best, was divided into ranks. He distinguishes "higher grade priests" who upheld the cult of Io, the Supreme Creator god; a second grade of priesthood concerned with rituals of war, agriculture, seafaring, fishing, woodcraft, and other industries; a third grade dealing with the ordinary concerns of people; and finally, a fourth grade of shamans (1924a:I, 244). The principle of ranking tohunga was similar to that of ranking leadership, going downward from the most general and esoteric to the most concrete and practical. In the religious sphere the bottom was a concept of evil. Esoteric knowledge was the exclusive prerogative of upper rank; sorcery the appropriate form of power for lower. The crafts themselves were not ranked, although wood carving as the favorite occupation of ariki was clearly highest. Whether the ranks of tohunga correspond with ranks of ariki and *rangatira* (junior chiefs) is not certain from the sources I have consulted. Logically they should correspond, and perhaps they did. The connection between high tohunga rank and the rank of the god he served demonstrates the logic of ranking. Curiously, highest and lowest orders of tohunga had in common the power to inspire fear and awe, the former the fear of the exalted (light, sky), and the latter the fear of evil (darkness and underworld). Finally, a mark of the importance of the *tohunga* in the status system of the Maori is the fact that the ariki who acquired specialized knowledge added thereby to their mana and so to their standing (Best 1924a:I, 345).

Toa

Chiefs were trained for war and were expected to show the qualities of toa. The title therefore was a chiefly prerogative. All men, commoners included, served as warriors and had the opportunity to show special skill and valor, but not to the disparagement of chiefs.

Wealth

Wealth was an attribute of rank in two major respects. First, and perhaps most important, chiefs were expected to move in an aura of material abundance and well-being. The ornately carved and fully provisioned storehouse and assembly house were prime marks of chiefly standing, as was the chief's possession of his descent group's traditional heirlooms—feather ornaments, shark's tooth ear pendants, carved *tikis,* cloaks, and mantles. A chief's standing was also judged by the number of slaves he held. A second and by no means minor aspect of wealth was the chief's reputation for hospitality and generosity.

We are indebted to Firth for a concise evaluation of the importance of wealth for the Maori chief. Remarking that the "honour of a Maori chief was bound up with his ability to entertain lavishly when necessary" and that through gifts and other forms of distribution the chief secured the allegiance and services of his followers, Firth adds the following important observation:

> His wealth was utilized for his own aggrandizement and influence, it is true, but in so doing it contributed greatly to the material benefit of his people. The analysis of the situation made it clear that this extensive command of wealth tended greatly to increase the authority of the chief of his tribe. In short, his economic position buttressed his social status (1929: 289).

A major aspect of wealth was land, but land itself did not enter strongly into status. While the Maori sought more crop lands, they did not measure rank directly by land holdings, even though chiefs did hold extensive personal tracts. Status honor was linked more directly with administrative rights than with possession as such. The chief was the guardian and the titular holder of tribal lands. Metaphorically, tribal lands were held to be extensions of parts of his body. In this way his honor was specifically bound up with the preservation of tribal land. Chiefs were often ambitious to extend tribal lands, whether by military or by pacific means, but they seemingly had no strong motive to accumulate personal holdings.

Political Hegemony

Logically, political hegemony was a function of genealogical rank. The highest-ranking chief ruled the most inclusive genealogical network; intermediate ranks ruled over intermediate networks; ranking family heads presided over households. In practice, hegemony and rank were only approximately related. An ariki, for example, had rank but might lack leadership. Lack of leadership, of hegemony, did not downgrade genealogical rank, but the new acquisition of leadership might, under some conditions, upgrade rank. Being designated to office as a replacement for an incompetent ariki was one way to gain rank. The upgrading of a descent group from a smaller to a more inclusive genealogical network was another. In the latter event, the chief and his kin gained in political rank even if not directly in genealogical rank. The growth of a political community was always an important factor in the honor of rank. The larger the tribe and its land area, the more prosperous its villages and the more formidable its fortifications, the greater was the prestige and influence of its chief. Growth being identified with power was honorable, and decline, accordingly, was degrading.

The Structure of Status

The distribution of Maori ranks may be visualized as forming a diamond. The bulk of the population occupies the bulging middle while only a small number of individuals fit into the upper and lower ends. Seniority grades all. Winiata (1956) has clarified for us the nature of the distribution. The ariki, as paramount chiefs, heads of the great lineages (*iwi*), and as sacred beings, formed a relatively closed and narrow elite, the pinnacle. Yet even this smallish group was further differentiated to extract the ultimate individual or individuals, the *tino ariki,* the possessors in full measure of all the chiefly qualities. In still another order of distinction, the *ariki matamua* was the traditional paramount, while the *upoko ariki* was one who had been designated chief because of other than purely genealogical attributes.

The masses were rangatira; in contemporary Maori thought, only a somewhat lesser aristocracy than ariki. Buck, and later Winiata, so describe them. But Winiata calls attention at the same time, to rangatira expansiveness as the inevitable outcome of grading without hard criteria. In the absence of a clear cut-off point, who would call himself a commoner? If rangatira includes all who can find some genealogical connection with an ariki no matter how distant, then it can hardly qualify as an aristocratic elite. A more apt translation would be "worthy" people, in the sense of the ancient Grecian freeman. The etymology of the term clearly sets them off from ariki. In Tregear's dictionary (1891) *ranga* and *tira* mean, respectively, "to arrange," "to set in order," "to set an army in motion," "to urge forward," "to raise up," and "a mast," "a company of travellers." The meaning is of one who directs, organizes, and guides. The Hawaiian form, *lanakila,* defined even more specifically as "a conqueror, a brave soldier" falls within the same category. As ariki has a religious connotation, rangatira is its secular complement; in this sense they are not mere grades of a common concept. The subchiefs were rangatira, but clearly not all rangatira held command. It is the intimation of efficacy and command—the substance of being a freeman—even without the actuality that endows the term with high honor. These connotations are so fundamental to Maori ideals as to form the essence of worth. To lack rangatira qualities is literally to be degraded.

Thus to translate the Maori term *tutua,* the lowest social rank, as "commoner" is, if not literally a distortion of the proper meaning, at least an inadequate rendering of the point of view. By all accounts tutua, which has been translated as "mean, low-born," refers to a degraded class. Rangatira who had disgraced themselves became tutua. The class included four kinds of debased persons: descendants of persons taken in war and then ransomed; descendants of prisoners who had not been ransomed; descendants of persons saved from death by the superior mana of a superior; and descendants of persons who did not protect their guests. Understandably, no self-respecting Maori could decently acknowledge tutua status. Certainly we have no serious reason to accept the common doctrine that tutua were simply the junior grades. Peter Buck, who saw ancient Maori society as falling into just two ranks, rangatira and tutua, by the abstraction of sheer seniority, confesses to his own perplexity when he says:

> It is somewhat difficult to understand the origin of the *tutua* class, since all members of the sub-tribe or tribe were descended from common chiefly ancestors and they were more or less related to the chiefly families of the period. . . . Therefore the most feasible explanation of the origin of the *tutua* class is that the descendants of junior families got farther and farther away from the prospects of exercising chieftainship over family groups and thus passed automatically out of the *rangatira* class (1949:338).

As a Maori himself, Buck sensed that the incapacity to rule or direct was in itself a form of degradation. But the most feasible explanation is not necessarily that of ultimate juniority.

Degradation is, of course, a relative concept; and the Maori concept was quite different from that of the Stratified societies. Tutua were low but not entirely without honor. Their lowness derived from a history of debasement and from their standing as a social category abruptly separated from chiefs. Ariki and rangatira were genealogically graded, but tutua were not. They formed a bin-like category of undifferentiated nonhonor. Nevertheless, they were not deprived of land rights—an ultimate of degradation—and they did not fall out of the traditional patterns of reciprocity with their chiefs. "The relationship of chiefs and commoners" Winiata remarks, "was one of filial and reciprocal respect involving specific rights and obligations (1956: 229)."

Tutua formed a genealogical grade, insofar as their status was the result of ancestral history. Maori also recognized degraded statuses that reflected specific personal circumstance. These were servants (*pononga*) and slaves (*taurekareka*). Servants were kinsmen who openly acknowledged weakness and accepted an inferior position in the household. Slaves were war captives. Both groups conceded loss of efficacy. Kinship, however, granted inalienable rights; slaves who had not even a claim to land were the very bottom. Where they were numerous, as in some tribes, they were an economic class, but only as outsiders. The interior constituency was socially graded, but not stratified.

Status Rivalry

Genealogical rank, as we have observed, was fixed so that upward status mobility was restricted mainly to the area of leadership. Even so, upward mobility was definitely limited. Downward mobility, on the other hand, affected all aspects of status, rank, leadership and prestige. When an ariki fell captive in war or in other ways violated the code of honor, he fell all the way. He moved downward by degree only insofar as he lacked competency. The moral requirements of honor were rigid. The same rules applied to the rangatira. The status "game," has two aims: one is defensive, that is, not to lose status honor, and the other aggressive, to gain status honor by excelling in the code, particularly in political leadership. Since either the loss of a defensive position or the assault upon a higher position resulted mainly from exceptional circumstances, status mobility, up or down, was limited. An ineffectual ariki was replaced by another of ariki rank, not by a rangatira. Since replacement was by an orderly procedure supervised by high-ranking kin and not by violence, political conflict and status rivalry were muted. The violence that could disturb Maori status strongly had to come from outside the genealogical network; it could hardly come from within.

To state that genealogical rank was fixed is to state the rule but not to assess all the possibilities of status mobility. Marriage also affected the ranking of the ensuing descent line. Since supreme rank was consistently defined by male primogeniture it stood as an absolute. But in bilateral descent all lower grades of rank found possibilities for manipulating the relative rank of ensuing descent lines. Marrying down, downgrades; marrying up, upgrades. This pattern of rank revision by marriage allows for a genealogical pruning by which lower grades are dropped from genealogical reckoning until the descent lines finally come to represent upper grades only. Such possibilities for genealogical manipulation through marriage explains why the lower grades accepted endogamy, while the upper grades, including the supreme ariki, preferred exogamy.

One other mode of altering rank was by upgrading a descent group to its next more inclusive level. When a "subtribe" became large enough to become a "tribe," its chief moved up in rank from rangatira to ariki. He remained subordinate in rank, however, to the ariki of tribes that had been formed earlier. Although his genealogical rank was unaffected by his political elevation, the possibility of moving politically from rangatira to ariki was bound, nevertheless, to foster all devices of political leadership that could hasten the growth of a descent group to a larger size.

Descent Group Organization

Maori descent group organization was segmentary, comprising four named hierarchical levels, the *waka*, the *iwi*, the *hapu*, and the *whanau*. To facilitate comparing the four named Maori "segments" with cognate descent groups elsewhere in Polynesia that are often not named, I shall identify them further as "segments" I, II, III, IV, respectively. The *waka* (canoe) was the most inclusive descent group. It represented all persons descended on both the maternal and paternal sides from the crew of a canoe that had arrived in New Zealand, according to Maori traditions, in the 1350 migration. The canoe crews were not necessarily kin, but often they were. If the canoe crews were not kin, the waka was technically a territorial grouping. But to call the waka a territorial grouping is to apply the concept too mechanically, inasmuch as the sentiment of linkage among members of a founding canoe was equivalent to that of kinship. The waka, nevertheless, had only a shadow structure, even when its founders were actual kin. This shadow structure held together by genealogical lines, by contiguity, and by claims to a common territory could become substantial in times of military crisis. The waka could unite all its iwi and hapu under its highest ariki, who then served as supreme military commander and as its political head. When the emergency subsided the supreme ariki lost his authority. The waka may be considered a latent political structure, with limited functions. I would consider the waka to be a loosely federated tribe, even though Maori specialists consider the iwi to be the tribe.

The difficulty is that "tribe" is still an unclear concept in social anthropology. The rule proposed by Fortes and Evans-Pritchard (1940) that the tribe is the largest grouping in which disputes can be settled by established procedures rather than by resort to war, does not suit the Maori case at all. For among the Maori it was common for the hapu to war with one another, and there is no basis whatsoever for considering the hapu as a "tribe." By all other conventional criteria, the waka was the "tribe." It occupied a coherent territory; it had a tradition of common ancestry; it commonly constituted a unified genealogical network. It shared common cultural traditions and it recognized an identity of interests. Finally, it had a chief. There seems, therefore, no reason not to define waka as tribe, other than an apparent reluctance to accord the Maori a "weak" tribal structure and to concede intratribal warfare as a regular feature of Maori life. If the waka (Segment I) is considered to be the "tribe," the iwi (Segment II) are to be considered as "subtribe."

In structure, the iwi was a replica of the waka. It represented, however, a narrower genealogical network, uniting all persons claiming descent through paternal or maternal lines from a founding ancestor, who was generally a member of the original immigrant canoe. Like the waka, the iwi was generally endogamous except for its ariki families, who married outside for status and political advantages. Endogamy helped overcome the dispersive capabilities of bilaterality and maintained the iwi as a compact territorial body. The iwi was under the jurisdiction of an ariki. Firth, having in mind the hapu as the principal Maori descent group, has minimized the significance of the iwi. He noted, for example:

> The economic functions of the tribe (*iwi*) were confined almost solely to participation in huge feasts and to an all-embracing over-right to the land within its borders; the latter was made manifest in the rallying of the *hapu* to defend the tribal land at any point invaded (1929:126).

The iwi, with weaker collective unity and fewer functions than the hapu, stood between the waka and the hapu. The hapu, by contrast, was a strongly collective entity. The iwi, on the other hand, was a structure held together in the main by the status interests of its ariki. From a political point of view, the iwi was a loose confederation of hapu, each alert to defend its own interests but reluctant to defend the interests of the others. It was the ariki who, to defend his own status interests, had to rally the constituent hapu to a common cause, as in the case of a military attack. An attack, after all, was an immediate threat to a particular hapu, but only a generalized threat to the iwi as a whole. Since sovereignty over iwi territory was vested specifically in the ariki, to whose body the land was symbolically attached, an invasion became an immediate affront to his honor. This he could not allow. Only the ariki could present a local issue in its broader terms. By defending his honor, he also defended the basic interests of the entire iwi. Nevertheless, he could only try to rally the hapu to his cause; he could not compel them to fight. Other than public opinion and an emergency convocation of hapu chiefs, the iwi had no agency other than the ariki to give it unity of action.

The economic unity of the iwi was also closely involved with chiefly honor. Most of the economic efforts of the ariki involved his own prestige directly and that of the iwi indirectly. The ariki had a claim to foodstuffs and other material forms of tribute from defeated tribes, and he had traditional rights to gifts and "first fruit" offerings from his own iwi. These offerings were more symbolic than substantial. They were given in deference to his rank and to his titular sovereignty over iwi territory. The ariki's wealth, as we have already observed, enhanced his status and his authority. He in turn distributed gifts, offered hospitality, and paid those who worked for him. The significance of the ariki's economic role for his own status was revealed most clearly in the rivalrous inter-iwi feasts, which, by Maori standards of food production, were on a grand scale. It is indeed proper to observe that these feasts "redistributed" foodstuffs over the entire territory of a waka. In the same way, the formal visiting of an ariki from hapu to hapu and from iwi to iwi promoted essential trade along with the customary exchange of gifts. The basic point remains that the economic activities of the iwi ariki were primarily in the interests of his status and of his effective sovereignty over the iwi; "redistribution" effects were secondary. That the ariki reciprocated each gift or offering demonstrates something more than a general principle of "reciprocity" as a "mechanism of equilibrium." It demonstrates as well a basic principle of status, which also demands "reciprocity." There is little value however, in discussing generalized reciprocity until we have a clearer understanding of particular forms of reciprocity. Thus, the story cited by Firth about the Maori chief who, having received only half a calabash of preserved birds, ordered the reluctant donor to be slain brings out the important point that reciprocity between dominant and subordinate follows its special rules of status (1929: 285). To give less to an ariki was called whakahawea—"to despise the recipient." When the ariki reciprocated a gift of preserved birds with a feast to the donors, he was displaying chiefly generosity. He was living up to his rank.

There is not enough detailed information to describe the full economic role of the iwi ariki, only enough to permit a general contrast between the hapu and iwi chiefs. The latter were largely sacred; the former, more fully secular and economic. Firth lists the following activities of the iwi ariki, all of which were ceremonial: imposing and lifting of tapu; carrying out ritual observances; fixing boundary marks; defining tribal territory; recital of curative magic; reception of visitors; recital of genealogies; giving and receiving presents; bestowing names on children; and the guardianship of tribal heirlooms and of the talismans of fisheries and forests (1929:93). These ariki functions demonstrate that the iwi was largely a ceremonial organization.

The iwi within a waka were subject to ranking on the basis of two principles: by the genealogical standing of their founder, and by the recency of their formation. The rank of the founder set up the primary rank order. Insofar as we know, the iwi founded by the chief of the canoe was highest and stood titularly therefore as the "dominant" iwi. All other iwi had a hypothetical graded rank. In the absence of strong hierarchical institutions such as a *fono,* however, or another formal order of precedence, their graded rank had no practical significance. On the other hand, those iwi that were founded late, by splitting from a parental iwi, had clearly subordinate rank and prestige as minor iwi. The "dominant" iwi had political significance because it provided the candidate for waka ariki. For the remainder, iwi rank had prestige but no other political value.

The hapu (Segment III) was unquestionably the principal Maori descent group. It was generally coextensive with the village (*kainga*) and had, therefore, the unity of common residence. Early writers, among them Best, referred to the hapu as a "clan." Buck uses "subtribe," and Winiata, has spoken of the hapu as "clan" or "subtribe." Firth, who has presented the most systematic analysis of Maori social life, accepted "clan" as convenient but later preferred "ramage," a term he had earlier introduced for a cognate descent group among the Tikopia. All writers have acknowledged the exceptional character of the hapu and there is some disagreement as to whether it is to be regarded as a descent group at all. The term "subtribe" stresses the political character of the hapu, while "clan," "lineage" and "ramage" have reference to a descent group. The question of the hapu as a descent group has been raised most sharply by Fortes, who said that the hapu is to be regarded as a "joint stock company in which the individual's right of 'membership' rests on the acquisition by purchase or otherwise of stock [rather] than that of a lineage or other type of descent group (1959:212)." In the Maori case, the title to "stock" comes from simple filiation.

Fortes' discussion of the hapu brings out two points of great importance: one is that the hapu really had a "political" character, meaning that it drew people together around their special interests; the other, that it stressed membership by filiation rather than by "perpetual descent," as do normal lineages. In these two observations, Fortes is quite right insofar as he is interpreting the theory of the hapu. But if Firth and Winiata are correct in their description of the hapu as largely endogamous, Fortes is arguing a hypothetical issue. If the bulk of hapu marriages were, indeed, endogamous, then the hapu had, in actuality, a rather minor political character, and the principle of lineal succession was actually a more important source of membership than filiation. What is most important to bear in mind about Polynesian social structures generally is their incompatibility with traditional classifications. We are compelled to deal not with an "either–or" problem, but with a situation imposed by flexible structures which may vary by degree more than by kind. Thus, while the Maori hapu did have the characteristics of political organization of a "stock company" formed by filiation, these characteristics were potential rather than actual. The political character shows up very strongly elsewhere in Polynesia. If we consider Polynesian social structures as a series expressing a consistent set of variations, then the Maori hapu belongs at the lineage and descent group end of the scale. This is not to say that the Maori hapu is either a conventional lineage or a conventional descent group. As applied to the hapu, the terms "lineage" and "descent group" have a statistical rather than a purely qualitative meaning. That is to say, for the bulk of its members the lineal ties back to a founding ancestor were more significant than the lateral ties to bilateral kin.

A hapu included some 200–300 persons and generally occupied a single village, called a *kainga.* Since hapu and village generally coincided, there may be some justification in regarding the terms hapu and kainga as equivalent. The question of equivalence of these terms is important, because while hapu had a limited distribution in Polynesia (confined to New Zealand), kainga with its derivative term kainanga was widespread. The hapu was directed by a chief with the title of rangatira. The rangatira organized and directed collective work on food plantations, in fishing, and in construction of public works, as well as all military operations. The hapu as a collective body owned a war canoe, a meeting house, large eel-weirs, and rat-runs. It had sovereignty over all the land surrounding the villages. In contrast to the iwi, whose functions were largely ceremonial, the hapu was largely a secular and economic organization. Iwi interests were recognized mainly through the prestige of the ariki, but the hapu was a strongly unified and essentially autonomous group in its own right.

The hapu included all kin through maternal or paternal lines who claimed descent from a founder going back some nine generations. This ancestor gave the hapu its name. The hapu did not regulate the marriage of its members. We need, however, to describe the composition of the hapu more specifically. Firth has recorded that ordinary persons married within the hapu, while persons of rank married outside, in order to advance their status interests. Since the male line carried highest status, the higher ranks in a hapu tended to form themselves around patrilineal descent lines whose maternal links were, however, with other hapu. In the case of the lower ranks, on the other hand, the maternal as well as the paternal lines were confined within the hapu. The upper ranks, as a rule, had the option of utilizing the whole of the genealogical network embracing the waka, while the lower ranks confining themselves to the more secular economic interests of the hapu utilized only a narrow segment of the entire genealogical network. In cases where lower ranks did marry outside of the hapu, actual residence of claimants—that is, of the children of such marriages—was required in order to maintain the genealogical connection. If residence was not taken up, the genealogical tie weakened and then lapsed. Winiata emphasizes endogamy in still another way: "Marriage was both endogamous and exogamous although the stress was on endogamy"; youths were advised, he continues, "Marry among yourselves so that when you quarrel, violence is between yourselves (1956:217). This was to avoid possibilities of interhapu strife.

Thus, the hapu appears to have been a complex type of descent group with a double composition: bilateral or endogamous in its lower ranks, preferentially patrilineal and patrilocal in its upper ranks. Since some Polynesian social structures—notably those of the Stratified societies—tended to split totally along lines of social and economic class, the genealogical diversification of the hapu suggests one of the ways in which the split may have developed.

Theoretically, at least, the hapu of any iwi were ranked by the genealogical standing of their chiefs. In this respect, hapu rank followed the same principles as iwi rank. Iwi rank, however, started from imprecise bases and so was never clearly defined. Hapu rank, on the other hand, started from more precise genealogical distinctions within the iwi and, therefore, could be more clear-cut. The hapu could, in principle, be ranked on a waka-wide basis, since each chief also had a genealogical rank within the waka. The literature on these questions, however, is uninformative. All that seems certain is the standing of the hapu of the senior line. Presided over by an ariki, it was the dominant hapu. Again, as in the case of the iwi, the practical issue of descent group rank depended upon the existence of institutional forms within which rank could be concretely displayed. In the absence of such institutions, hapu rank was more hypothetical than real.

The whanau (Segment IV) were the constituent households of the hapu. Representing three or four generations with a preference for patrilocal residence, the whanau developed as patrilineally extended families that were generally exogamous. Matrilocal residence prevailed only when the status of the wife was higher than that of her husband. A whanau was the most concrete land-holding unit, since hapu lands were allocated to particular households. Members of the whanau worked the land together and shared its produce. The whanau was directed by a household head called kaumatua; as a rule, he was the senior male. Women were often real whanau leaders. Theoretically, the whanau can also be ranked on a genealogical scale, but in practice the distinction seems to have been drawn only between the leading whanau of the hapu and all the others.

Status and Descent

The foregoing discussion of status system and of descent group organization has brought out the close interdependence between the two social concepts of status and of descent. We may now summarize this interrelationship in order to bring out some principles of interaction and to demonstrate more pointedly the principal thesis of this study, namely, that Polynesian kin group organization is in the service of social status.

The clearest and perhaps the basic relationship between status and descent is in the formation of the genealogical network that unites all segmental levels from waka down to whanau. The breadth of the genealogical network—that is, its lateral dimension—is, of course, a function of its depth—that is, of its lineal dimension. Segments, to be sure, can relate directly to parallel level segments by means of intermarriage and by the adoption of children, but the primary mode of relationship, of establishing lateral ties, is through a demonstration of common genealogical links through upper-level segments. Naturally, if the genealogical link goes only from whanau to hapu, for example, it covers only the whanau of the same hapu. If the link goes up to the iwi, it covers a wider range of whanau, and if it goes up to the waka, it covers all the whanau of a district. Since, as we have seen, genealogical depth is an aspect of status (rank, to be specific), we must conclude that the specific linkages both lateral and lineal are dependent on genealogical rank.

Segmental hierarchy, we have demonstrated, follows almost precisely the hierarchy of rank. The waka and the iwi depend upon ariki titles for their corporate character; the hapu, upon the hereditary rank of rangatira. In the case of the hapu, however, rank is not as crucial as it is for iwi or waka. Being a closely knit local group, the hapu inevitably creates its own leadership independent of genealogical rank, but the same cannot be said of iwi and waka, which are merely federations. Considering the weak corporate character of waka and iwi, along with the high degree of autonomy of the hapu, including willingness to war with one another, there seems hardly any other way of accounting for the presence of Segments I and II (waka and iwi) except by regarding them as honorific posts to accommodate the ariki titles. As for the hapu, we may visualize it as independent of genealogical rank only in theory. In actuality, the Maori hapu, through their rangatira, align themselves within the rank system as subordinate to the iwi. Thus the formal and orderly hierarchy of four segments, which is one of the striking characteristics of Maori social structure, must be attributed to the orderly hierarchy of genealogical rank.

The patrilineal bias in the Maori order of descent and in descent group affiliation is also a function of the status system. Patriliny and patrilocal residence have no discernible "adaptive"—that is, direct economic—functions. This conclusion is borne out by the fact that the lower ranks, including the lower rangatira, marry endogamously, while only the upper ranks of ariki and rangatira chiefs prefer patrilineal exogamy and patrilocal residence. Since land rights "cool" without actual residence, the preservation by the upper ranks of links in other iwi and hapu cannot have and, indeed, does not have, any other motive than the furthering of their genealogical rank. The higher the rank, the more patrilineal is the descent line.

The distinction between upper-rank pro-patriliny and lower-rank endogamy has the extraordinary effect, as we have already observed, of creating a composite descent group structure, a matter of particular consequence for the hapu. Upper-rank status requires strong genealogical ties to the important descent lines of the iwi and waka. To be sure, all persons "belong" to the common genealogical network, but the Maori distinguish between direct and indirect, between near and distant, and between patrilineal and ambilineal links to those descent lines. The purpose of upper-rank exogamous marriages is to establish links that are direct, near, and patrilineal. The lower ranks, lacking these possibilities, concern themselves largely with purely economic interests and these are seemingly best met by endogamy, which preserves the unity of whanau land-holdings. In their composite character, the iwi and the hapu resemble European monarchies whose upper ranks form an international genealogical network, while the lower ranks remain nationally endogamous. In Polynesia the distinction between the genealogical composition of the ariki and upper rangatira, on the one hand, and the lower rangatira and commoners, on the other, creates a potential cleavage point for the descent group. As we shall see, under the appropriate political conditions this cleavage becomes actual, as in Tonga, Mangareva, and Hawaii.

Upper-rank exogamy also creates the bases for the lateral ties between segments of the same level. Our information is not sufficiently detailed, however, to bring out the full social and economic value of such lateral ties for the Maori. What information we do have does not support an assumption that the lateral ties of the upper ranks provided any bases for more than ceremonial forms of intersegmental cooperation.

Finally, we may consider the relationship between status and descent group growth by budding and by branching. Conventional functional-structural accounts of these processes attributed them logically to population growth and the need to occupy new areas. There is no empirical reason to dispute this logical explanation. We are obliged, however, to consider all specific processes of budding and branching. Among those reported in the literature is the role of status. Buck (1949:338) has observed that one way to escape falling into the ranks of tutua was to move away and found a new line. Winiata implies the same:

> A younger son and his family together with his slaves may leave the subtribal (*hapu*) village to establish his household units in a neighboring part of the subtribal land. There would be constant communication with the subtribe and the old *marae*, especially at the beginning. However, in time, a new centre would be set up and a new village would be born. The processes of fission and of fusion would look after the growth of family groups till there is again another subtribe or tribe (1956:271).

By this process the younger son, having become the founder of a new line, upgraded his own rank. To form a new iwi, genealogical claim to an ancestor of note was required.

By providing genealogical sources for rank rather easily, the Maori were able to avoid the differentiation of descent groups into noble and commoner, such as occurred in other Polynesian societies. This development is, of course, in keeping with the structure of the status system, according to which the rangatira class is expansive and the tutua contractive.

The prosperity of a hapu, a function of leadership, was an important factor in its growth. Since the budding-off of family groups encountered no political impediments, growth was more than a matter of vegetative increase; it demanded a centripetal force as well. The centripetal force, it would seem, must be in the quality of leadership provided by the rangatira, who must hold a growing population in place and attract new adherents as well. In New Zealand, new adherents were generally of the genealogical network. They were subordinate kin such as servants (pononga) and in-laws with specific claims to hapu land. Taking into account the well-documented lower-rank endogamy of the hapu, one can only conclude that lower-rank persons must have come in as status subordinates attached to the households of upper-rank rangatira. Those who came in as in-laws with "rights" to hapu lands were bound, therefore, to be upper rank themselves. In New Zealand the addition of pononga to chiefly households did not add markedly to the political power of the chief, but it did add to his wealth and influence. The New Zealand political pattern restrained chiefly power, and so the addition of persons to the hapu added mainly to the relative influence of the hapu vis-à-vis other hapu. Perhaps the larger and more prosperous hapu gained a military advantage over the smaller and weaker hapu and were more likely, therefore, to attack them. Unfortunately, however, our information on the political and economic aspects of Maori wars is very incomplete. What is significant about the characterization of the hapu as a quasi-political organization is that this constitutes a pattern of organization that assumes vast importance in the Open and in the Stratified societies. In New Zealand itself the pattern was relatively undeveloped.

3

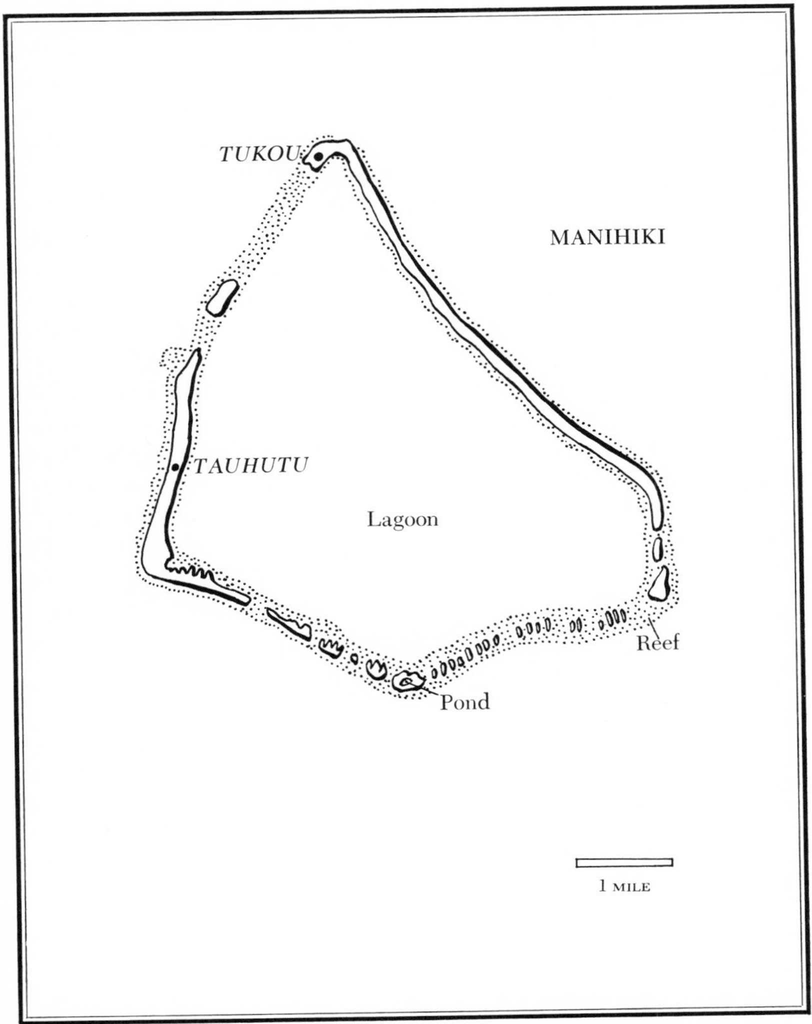

Manihiki-Rakahanga

THE TWIN ATOLLS OF MANIHIKI-RAKAHANGA IN THE COOK ISLANDS group were first settled by a single family that had come, the traditions say, from Rarotonga. The first residents occupied Rakahanga and then moved to cultivate Manihiki, some 25 miles away. As testimony to their sense of social unity, the population moved in a body first from one atoll and then to the other; it was not until 1852 that permanent residence was established on Manihiki, thus introducing the first physical separation of the people. The atolls are small, with a combined land area of only four square miles. In 1906 the population numbered 873, a figure close to what it had evidently been in the precontact period. These islets illustrate, therefore, the manner of development of the Polynesian social pattern upon a very small scale. By virtue of their more immediate history, they represent a direct variant of Rarotongan culture, which had gone on to evolve into an Open society (cf. chap. 5). In this respect the historical situation of the twin atolls is parallel to that of the Maori tribes. The parallel is more than superficial when we consider the very close linguistic affinities between Rakahangan and Maori. In a more general sense, then, both are common variants of an original Society Islands' system. The former developed in relative isolation on a monumental scale; the latter remained within the orbit of Cook Island cultural traditions. We recognize at once similarities with Mangaia, for example, and small as is the scale, the structure and style are unmistakably Polynesian and strongly cognate with New Zealand.

Peter Buck, the principal ethnographic authority on the atolls, spent only three weeks there in 1929. While his published report is of great value, it is understandably brief and general and, therefore, unsuitable for a detailed comparison with either Maori or Rarotonga. His account is of unusual interest, nevertheless, in that it illustrates processes of diversification of leadership and of kin groupings on a small scale and in a peaceable setting.

Genealogical Traditions

According to the traditions, the first settlers were headed by a man called Toa (warrior), a refugee who may have arrived sometime in the fourteenth century.[1] All four tribes on both atolls claimed descent from his line. Almost immediately the growing population formed itself into a dual grouping, one based on descent from an older

1. He may have come from Rarotonga in the Hervey Islands. According to the Rev. William Gill, the Rarotongans recognized Toa as a great warrior of the Ngati-Tinomana tribe (1856:II, 280).

brother who carried the ariki title and the other from a younger brother who was not an ariki. The senior line occupied the inner lagoon side of the island and the junior line the sea side. Both groups intermarried, the wives coming to live with their husband's family, although younger brothers, as Buck observed, would sometimes take up residence with their wives' relatives, a practice that would seem to associate matrilocality with lower status. High-ranking marriages, however, were endogamous as well. Thus, in the fifth generation the ariki married two wives, both from within his own division. The eldest son of the first wife inherited the ariki title and the eldest son of the second wife became the land distributor with a new title, *tuha whenua*. Each son then formed a new descent line which by the tenth generation had become distinct enough to be designated by specific names.

Buck, citing the genealogies, explains this first division in the ariki title as follows:

> The *ariki* of the 5th generation had two names, Huku-tahurou-rou-a-whara and Tapu-mahanga. He had two wives. By the first wife he had a son named Kaitapu and by the second wife a son named Huku-potiki. The title passed to Kaitapu who had the *pohatu* (the symbol of office), but the powerful family of the second wife brought such influence to bear that Huku-potiki was given the office of attending to the distribution of land among the families. The office was termed *tuha whenua* (land-distributor), and Huku-potiki received special grants of land to go with his office, Paerengi in Rakahanga and Haroi in Manihiki. Huku-potiki was also entitled to the *mata kairau,* a contribution of food from the people in recognition of his rank (1932b:45).

This first division of the ariki title into what was a senior and a junior line of descent occurred within the original senior line, among the lagoonside dwellers. In the eleventh generation a new division of the ariki title into two approximately equal ranking ariki titles and offices took place. This division, according to the traditions, was an accommodation to pressure from the original junior line, the seaside dwellers. Having intermarried consistently with the senior line, they had a strong genealogical claim to the title. To quote Buck again, "It must have required strong expression of divided opinion to bring about the change in social organization which occurred. The opposing factions were pacified by a compromise, for the native historians say that in the period of Temumatua and Tianawa-matua the authority (*pohatu*) was divided. The compromise was the creation of a dual *arikiship* (1932b:47)." One ariki was called the *Whainga-aitu* ("to follow the gods") and commanded the productivity of the land and the sea. The other ariki was called the *Whakaheo* ("to cause to surround with priestly influence") and was controller of the winds regulating the safety of canoes. At the same time the people also divided into four "tribes," two "tribes" supporting each title. The two old "tribes," it is said, supported the Whakaheo title and two newly created tribes—one in each division—came under the leadership of the Whainga-aitu.

We may pause to consider the significance of these successive divisions in authority. In both instances the point of view of the genealogies is that the division was caused by conflicting claims for the arikiship. What is striking in this connection about Manihiki-Rakahanga is that in neither case did the contenders go to war. For Polynesians confronted with a status dispute, they showed extraordinary restraint. Perhaps it was descent from a common ancestral line, as Buck believed, that favored the sentiment for compromise. Yet common descent did not keep the Maori hapu from fighting one another. There is no ready explanation. We are dealing perhaps with a matter of chance. In a conflict for office there are two possibilities: compromise or war. In similar circumstances most Polynesian societies chose war. Manihiki-Rakahanga was exceptional in choosing a peaceable compromise.

While status rivalry seems to explain the divisions of authority, we must also note such specific natural conditions as the growth in population and the filling up of the land area. Direct status rivalry provoked the first division in authority, and this, in turn, fostered a new social division, one following the senior ariki and the other the junior tuha whenua. The second division, on the other hand, was fostered by an already existing line of dual authority. The dual arikiship produced further social divisions.

One other point of interest in these divisions of authority is the light they shed upon the concept of ariki and upon the status values that underlay the office. In both instances economic functions followed the junior line, implying their lesser value. This we shall find to be a fairly consistent principle in the evolution of Polynesian status systems. The senior line chooses the less material functions when the choice is before it—almost invariably to its ultimate disadvantage. In the case of the tuha whenua division, the differentiation from the ariki was a strong one; the ariki retained the priestly prerogatives and the land administrator assumed all the secular prerogatives. In the second division, the distinction was seemingly minor, yet it too followed the model of economic versus noneconomic prerogatives. Among the Maori, as we have seen, the same principles governed the division of authority: the top-ranking ariki held the ritual functions and the lower ranking chiefs dealt directly with economic affairs.

Along these lines, the genealogies also indicate that when the four "tribes" were formed each was headed by an economic administrator, the whakamaru. The office of whakamaru absorbed the functions of the earlier tuha whenua. Buck notes: "The tuha whenua title that was instituted in the 6th generation became merged in one of the *whakamaru* titles that were evolved about the 11th generation (1932b:54)." The genealogies do not, however, reveal the descent lines of the whakamaru, and it is not known whether these offices went by descent, by election, or by appointment.

Finally, the genealogies reveal some interesting but puzzling features of chiefly descent. Buck claims that Manihiki-Rakahanga followed the principle of male-line seniority in chiefly succession. Yet the genealogies of the first eleven generations—that is, before the dual arikiship was formed—show no such clear-cut pattern of descent at all. In the genealogical samples offered by Buck, chiefly descent is in one case from a youngest daughter (1932b:26), and not uncommonly from junior lines. It was not until the period after the dual arikiship that succession finally fell into the traditional pattern. How are we to interpret this break in pattern? The most dismal explanation is that the early genealogies are simply defective and do not reveal the true conditions of descent. The fact is that the Manihiki-Rakahangans had no specialized priesthood, no trained genealogists as did the Maori. Buck, as well as the local Land Court that was investigating land claims, found witnesses to be confused and testimony contradictory on points of family-line descent for the first eleven generations. A more intriguing explanation is that the period of the single ariki was still a formative time when the immigrant descent lines that were not of ariki blood had not yet reconstituted the traditional principles of male seniority. There are a number of examples in Polynesia of plebeian lines reconstituting the traditional system in a new homeland, although they do not all follow a similar pattern of descent irregularity. Perhaps it takes time for official genealogists to iron out inconsistencies and to link up descent lines. The issue is left in doubt.

The Status System

Taking account only of conditions during the later period, that is of the dual *ariki*ship, the status system of Manihiki-Rakahanga appears as an almost classic example of the traditional type. Buck supplies no direct information on concepts of mana and tapu, but there seems little doubt that the priestly ariki were indeed sacred. There is no information either on the concept and function of tohunga, but this gap too is probably in the data alone. As for other functional principles of status, the parallels with Maori are fairly definite. Status was associated with economic well-being, and political hegemony was a prerogative of genealogical rank. It must be borne in mind, however, that the parallels are with the broad principles. The specific patterns, as one might expect, are distinctive.

In Manihiki-Rakahanga, the ariki seem to have had mainly a religious relationship to the land after the tuha whenua was set up. Unfortunately, we know nothing of the traditional claims of the ariki upon lands or upon food. We do know that the tuha whenua received special grants of land to go with his title and that he also became entitled to contributions of food from the people in recognition of his rank. Since these prerogatives went with the Land Distributor title, it is probable that the ariki had similar rights. We do not know whether the ariki or the Land Distributor had formal obligations to offer hospitality or to provide feasts or to distribute food in other ways. Insofar as we know, the redistributive functions of the tuha whenua, and later of the whakamaru, did not include food, but only land. Land redistribution, Buck maintains, was equitable and in accordance with the needs of individual families. The symbol of food abundance was not the full storehouse as in New Zealand, but the well-fed and fattened pubescent daughter of families of rank. As she approached puberty, the girl was secluded. We are told that "during the period of seclusion the best foods obtainable were contributed by the family and subtribe to make her well-nourished, for plumpness was one of the standards of beauty acquired and required by the upper classes (1932b:40)." What seems to differentiate the Manihiki-Rakahangan symbolism of abundance from that of the Maori is the scale of consumption. As against the extravagant feasts and displays of New Zealand, these little atolls devoted themselves to the more modest and more esthetic task of plumping up a few young girls each year.

The Structure of Status

What distinguishes Manihiki-Rakahanga most sharply from New Zealand is the apparent absence of derogatory status terms. There is no term cognate with the Maori tutua. The common people were referred to as *matakeinanga*, a term that also meant "tribe." Derogatory terms may have been overlooked. Yet there is no information either to suggest derogatory subordinate relationships. Since there were no wars, there were no war prisoners, no conquered peoples, and, in particular, no group of people who might have lost worth by unheroic conduct in war. The honorable titles were the traditional ones. The senior lines through males provided the ariki, and the close kin of the ariki formed a lower status group known as *hui rangatira,* from which the lower-ranking authorities were drawn. The entire body of hui rangatira of an ariki acted as a consultative body. For the rest, there were only administrative titles. Each ariki had an official called *moa* in one division and *papa* in the other who represented him before the whakamaru, the secular administrators of each of the four "tribes." These officials, however, were designated by the whakamaru. Although our information is not too clear, the whakamaru appear to have been relatively independent heads of "tribes." On matters of allocation of land they could not be overruled by the ariki.

In summary, there were three genealogical grades: ariki, rangatira, and untitled but not unworthy common people. The atolls had rich and poor families, but no class of landless. The only class division, therefore, was between titled and untitled. The status structure was, therefore, a simple one. We may attribute its relative simplicity mainly to the absence of war.

Status Rivalry

If the records of Manihiki-Rakahanga are reasonably correct on this point, we must conclude that status rivalry is not barred even when there is neither war nor warrior status. Legitimacy alone poses conflicting genealogical claims upon the title, while any dual organization provides a political basis for pressing conflicting claims. Male seniority does offer a direct and nonconflicting channel to the arikiship, but only in theory, for as is evident from Manihiki-Rakahangan history, the legitimacy of bilaterality gives flexibility to status descent and gives credence to conflicting genealogical claims. However, while legitimacy does provide an active channel for status rivalry, it seemingly has the means for controlling the consequences of status rivalry. Maori, which is our best documented example of a Traditional status system, demonstrated this most fully. Genealogical disputes serve to expand the segmental organization and to broaden the opportunities for rank. They do not transform the traditional system.

Descent Group Organization

The entire atoll population, descended as it was from a single biological family, formed a kindred. In its early stages the kindred were ruled by a single ariki, as we have observed. But even after the formation of the dual arikiship and the dual territorial division, the political unity of the kindred was not destroyed. The two ariki held complementary religious functions and led the entire group in common religious observances. Buck's information is not altogether clear, but his account of a chiefly council of hui rangatira, and his description of the offices of moa and papa as economic coordinators, suggests that the unity of kindred went beyond religious matters. In the periodic voyages from one atoll to the other, the entire population went as a body. We do not, however, know whether the moa and the papa and the chiefly council had any authority to organize collective plantings of taro or to regulate the periodic distributions of atoll lands. All we can reasonably conclude from information that is seemingly concrete is that the entire atoll population, the kindred, may be considered to be the "tribe" and to be cognate with the Maori waka. Since there is no native term for this political grouping, I shall refer to it as Segment I. For reasons of small population and compactness of territory, Segment I on the atolls had a greater degree of unity in religious and economic matters than the waka did in New Zealand. Segment I was naturally an endogamous group, but the early dual territorial grouping and the preference for patrilocal residence tended to form patrilineal kin groupings.

This dual grouping represented by seaside and by lagoonside populations has no native term and it is not adequately described. Yet it is clear that each formed a Segment II cognate with the Maori iwi. Segment II was organized around its own ariki, and, holding a compact territory, must surely have had common economic functions. We, know, for example, that the papa was an economic coordinator in one of these segments and the moa in the other. In Segment II the line of the ariki was clearly patrilineal, while that of lower ranks was preferentially but not absolutely patrilineal. Intermarriage between the two branches was common but not mandatory.

For Segment III we have the native term *matakeinanga,* which Buck has rendered as "tribe." There were four matakeinanga each headed by a secular authority the whakamaru. This was the segment with the most significant economic functions and of greatest kin unity, although this we must deduce from the described functions of the whakamaru. According to Buck, the whakamaru were the custodians of matakeinanga lands. They protected these lands against claims from other branches, settled land disputes, guarded crops against theft, and directed the planting of taro in communal beds as well as the planting of coconut trees. Finally, they had full responsibility and authority to redistribute common lands. Buck did not learn how the whakamaru were appointed, but he assumed that they were the senior males of the leading families in each group. In the light of its organization, the matakeinanga seems to be cognate with the Maori hapu. To use conventional terminology, we would designate it as a "lineage." Segment II would then be the subtribe.

The lineages bore what were apparently ancestral names, but these names did not link up with the genealogies that have been collected. There is, therefore, no way of knowing whether they were actually ranked, even though they were formed, according to the traditions, by a logic of rank. Because of the preference for patrilocal residence and the emphasis upon the male line, the matakeinanga must have resembled the Maori hapu in its composition of patrilineal upper-rank descent lines and its more heterogeneous lower-rank descent lines. Buck's observation that descent was matrilineal if the mother's line was more distinguished and wealthier bears out the theme of status descent. The identity and the territorial character of the lineages were maintained even after the entire population had consolidated residence in a single village on the islet of Kainga. A stone marker at the center of the village divided the lagoonside groups from the seaside groups, and other boundaries marked off the subdivision of each into two matakeinanga.

The four matakeinanga were subdivided into smaller groups called tukuwhare, a local term. Since *whare* means house, Buck has explained that this grouping conveyed the idea of kinsmen grouped into separate houses. There were a total of 25 tukuwhare, so they must have been quite small. Buck renders *tukuwhare* as "subtribe"; the native meaning of "house" seems preferable, however. Altogether, Segment IV, the tukuwhare, may be considered as parallel with the Maori whanau.

The genealogical records of the tukuwhare are incomplete but quite interesting. Buck collected them for the Whainga-aitu subtribes only. When the first Whainga-aitu ariki was established there were five sons of the then incumbent ariki. The eldest assumed the new ariki title and the others were made heads of tukuwhare in their own matakeinanga. The "house" of the eldest came to be known as the te-ware-ariki and henceforth carried the ariki title. The tukuwhare, therefore, were evidently ranked by genealogical traditions of seniority. Since only one matakeinanga of the subtribe held the ariki title, we must assume, although Buck does not say so, that the other subtribe was the lower-ranking one.

A sixth tukuwhare of the same matakeinanga traced its founding ancestor to the single ariki through a female descent line. Its founder, therefore, was not an ariki but a person of importance. It is said that this man had four sons. To the eldest he gave authority over his lands; to the second, authority over his group of people; to the third, the care of the family gods; and to the fourth, the position of herald. This item of information is interesting both as an illustration of a pattern of distribution of the patrimony that is parallel to the setting up of the tukuwhare, and as an illustration of a reversal of the order of status value we encountered in other repartitions of prerogatives. The suggestion here is that in a low-ranking house it is the economic functions that rank highest and the more ceremonial functions lowest.

Status and Descent

By and large, the relationship between the status system and the organization of descent groups was along the same lines as in New Zealand. The division between a senior and a junior line and the subsequent formation of new senior lines organized the total genealogical network into a succession of dual divisions. If the genealogical traditions are to be trusted, they document the important point that the formation of new descent group segments was spurred by status rivalry and by the requirement that each of the sons of a chief receive a title and an office. New descent lines grew around these offices and titles. One is struck by the fact that so small a population on so small an island formed itself into as many as 25 varied divisions (tukuwhare). The brief but significant genealogical records suggest that these were formed around titles and not around some peculiar ecological necessity. Atoll ecology, with its concentration of taro swamps and artificial pits, would seem to favor just as well the formation of large and less differentiated descent group segments. The fact that Manihiki-Rakahangans occupied a single village well into the Christian era would indicate that small group formation was not an adaptation to the location of resources. Even the early dual division between lagoonside and seaside dwellers cannot be accounted for by a theory of economic specialization. The division is supposed to have occurred early, so that each branch served as a nucleus around which the population grew. Further comparisons will in fact show that the division of territory in Polynesia followed strongly patterned traditions of segmentation rather than land contours or the distribution of resources.

There is not much specific information on the relationships between the descent group segments, but there seems little reason to doubt that the principal forms of economic cooperation, by which we mean specifically the collective planting of taro and the collective interatoll voyages, were regulated by the hierarchy of genealogical rank. On the other hand, marriage and bilateral kinships provided for small scale economic cooperation, that is, between individual households.

Finally, descent, as we have seen, followed the course of status linearity, preferring the male line but utilizing the female lines whenever the latter gave the advantage. In summary, Manihiki-Rakahanga possessed all the criteria of a status lineage.

4

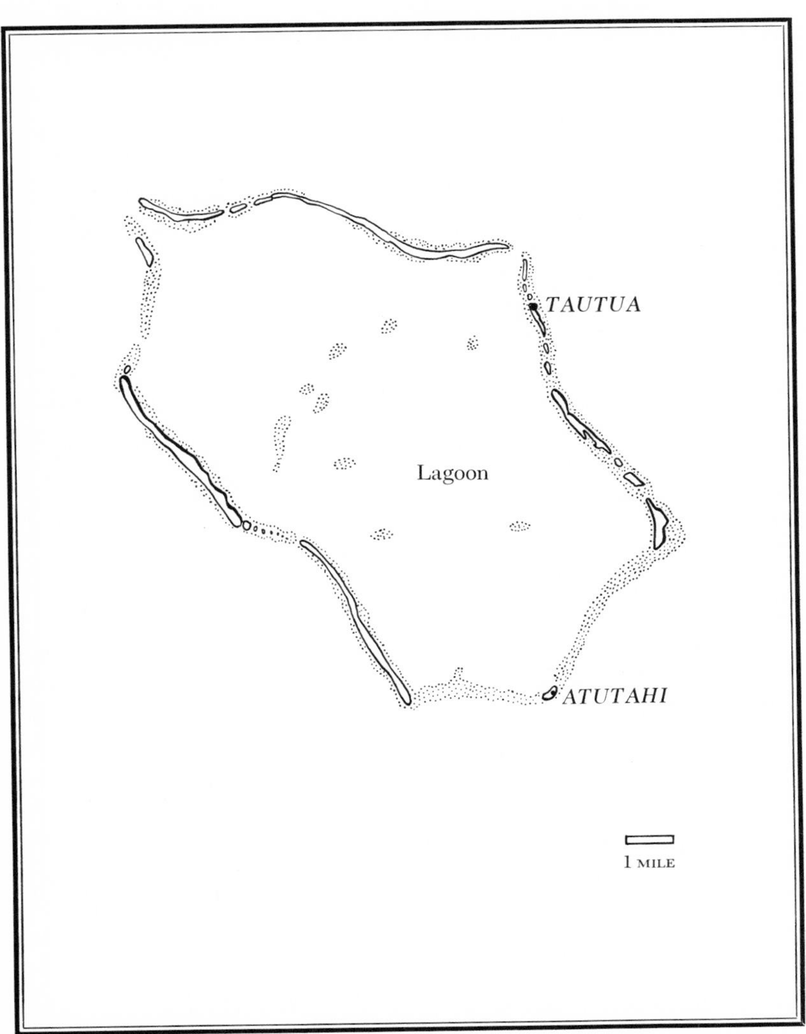

Tongareva

TONGAREVA IS AN ATOLL IN THE COOK ISLANDS WHOSE TRADITIONS link it with Manihiki-Rakahanga, with Rarotonga, and with Tahiti. The atoll consists of 15 islets with a total land area of six square miles. Native population has been estimated at 2,000, which would give a population density similar to that on Manihiki-Rakahanga. In 1864 Peruvian slavers reportedly took 1,000 persons away, so that in the 1906 census the population numbered only 420. The island was discovered by Lt. Watts of H.M.S. *Penrhyn* in 1788. It came under the London Missionary Society in 1854 and has been an administrative dependency of New Zealand since 1901.

For comparative purposes, Tongareva offers some variations on conditions in the neighboring atolls of Manihiki-Rakahanga. On this larger atoll wars were chronic and taro horticulture was lacking, the principal cultivations being the coconut tree and to a lesser extent the breadfruit. As a final point of contrast, settlement was by three distinct family lines. Tongareva offers then a test of the significance of several principal factors in the development of social structure: atoll ecology based on fishing and arbor-culture; descent from several ancestral lines; and a state of active warfare. Again, information based mainly on 17 days of field work by Buck (1932a) is very limited, but specific and significant on a number of key points.

Genealogical Traditions

The traditions indicate a rather shallow settlement period of some 18 generations, or of approximately 450 years. They mention three distinct ancestral lines, each headed by an ariki, that settled on different parts of the atoll and then intermarried to form a unified genealogical network. Buck speculates about an early period when families moved about the atoll freely, but the traditions themselves fix the population into closely held territorial divisions representing descent lines and their branches or segments. Despite the tripartite division of the ancestral lines, the tendency almost everywhere in the atolls was to form a dual division. If a large islet, it divided into a northern and southern division, and if a group of very small islets into two distinct groupings (Buck 1932a:69). On some of the very small islets, however, the groupings were more varied and fluid. The earliest groups were named after their chiefs, such as Ngati-Mahuta, but later each group took on a territorial name. There is no direct information to suggest that this change in designation was accompanied by a corresponding change in social organization. From the record of internecine warfare, we are led to surmise, however, that the use of territorial names reflected an acute state of local antagonisms. When a chief conquered a district it retained its territorial designation. Thus, while the genealogical network continued to provide a basis for atoll-wide kin unity, it seems to have been unable to overcome the powerful feelings for separateness. Buck has observed that earlier in Tongarevan history an ariki could combine two ariki titles: "With the later development of larger independent groups of people constantly at war with one another the combining of two *ariki* titles was untenable. The *ariki* had to live with one of the groups, and his claims over the other groups could not be enforced under the system that prevailed (1932a:48)."

Buck cites information from Mr. S. Savage, Registrar of the Court on Rarotonga, that at one period an ariki called Turua had declared himself at the head of the entire atoll and claimed the turtle tribute. Buck placed Turua in the eleventh generation and noted his descent from two ariki. He observes: "Later, in the period of Maiveriki, the turtle tribute was not exacted, and each chief or individual was entitled to keep what he caught. The power also passed more into the hands of the heads of the territorial groups (1932a:50)."

The traditions do not date the beginnings of atoll warfare, but by the time of Lamont (1853), who was the first European observer to describe Tongarevan life, wars had been devastating the atolls for generations. Not long before 1853 the people of Tautua were the most dreaded in the atoll. They had subjugated all territories on the east coast (their enemies later united and defeated them for good). No one, however, had been able to accomplish the military domination of the entire atoll.

Wars were fought for coconuts. We might attribute them to population pressure were it not for the fact that the Manihiki-Rakahangans had similar economic problems but resolved them collectively and peaceably. In fighting, moreover, the Tongarevans destroyed the coconut trees of their opponents. So while food scarcity may have been a cause of war, the effect of fighting was to destroy resources. Buck attributes war to sectionalism and to the ambition of chiefs.

What the genealogical traditions seem to reveal is first the consolidation of a traditional system, bringing the entire atoll under a single ariki, and then its breakdown, resulting in the division of this small atoll into a great number of independent territorial divisions headed by local chieftains and federating from time to time into unstable military alliances. The problem posed by this history is to account for the wars and for sectionalism, really aspects of the same problem. There is no ready answer. Settlement by three distinct descent lines may have been one factor, suggesting that genealogical unity through intermarriage alone was not always possible in Polynesia. Ecological conditions may be another factor. Arborculture, unlike taro cultivation on atolls, makes no demands on collective effort since trees are owned individually. In all likelihood, however, the failure to preserve the unity of the genealogical network was a political rather than an ecological condition. As we saw in Manihiki-Rakahanga, the proliferation into segments even of very small proportions is not necessarily governed by ecological conditions and is not necessarily restrained by a tradition of genealogical unity. In Manihiki-Rakahanga, the segments retained their linkages to the main stem, whereas in Tongareva they cast them off. The difference seems due to the evident adaptability of the ariki in Manihiki-Rakahanga and the apparent failure of Tongarevan ariki to provide for a hierarchical political organization. We cannot, however, go into direct causes. Of more immediate interest is the vulnerability of the traditional system to separatism and to war. This vulnerability, as we shall see, was not confined to the atolls.

The Status System

Buck's description of the status system portrays the traditional forms more strongly perhaps than they really were:

> Every district occupied by a number of families had its senior family which automatically supplied the district chief through primogeniture. When all the districts in an island or division of a large island combined for mutual protection or aggression one chief, by reason of the common descent from one ancestral family, was senior to all the others. His pedigree showed that his descent was from the senior family in each generation, and he was thus senior to all the other chiefs whose families had branched off from the main stem (*toro ahuro*). The other chiefs, who were descended from younger brothers who had moved off to other districts, were thus in the relative position of younger brothers. The junior chiefs were *hono tangata,* or the links which bound the smaller groups of families to the main stem and enabled the whole island or divisional group of people to act together under the senior chief of the largest group so formed (1932a:45).

In "two or more related territories," he continues,

> the senior family was known, and the senior chief of one of the linked territories was also, by descent, the senior chief of the combined territories. As the recognition of seniority prevailed, the status of the senior chief was increased not only by the

> number of collateral families in his own territory, but also by his position of seniority with regard to other territories. Seniority, through birth, had thus a wide-reaching influence. Absolute seniority within a group was expressed by the term *ariki* (1932a:45).

Finally, we are informed, the arikiship went in the male line, but the holder of the office had to have the capability.

Judging by information from Lamont (1867), who was shipwrecked on Tongareva in 1853, there were many ariki on the atoll. One was the head of the very small islet of Atutahi. We have no direct information on the relationship of the ariki to one another, but from the genealogical traditions, with their references to antagonisms, we may infer that the ariki title was assumed whenever a group achieved autonomy. When we speak, therefore, of the traditional status system on Tongareva, the reference is to a number of independent principalities. The literature does not give a full list of independent districts, but there seem to have been many as indicated by a map prepared by Buck. There were 24 maraes on the entire atoll, indicating an average of about 80 persons to a community. The jurisdiction of each ariki must thus have been over a very small population, for there was a tendency to divide the territory rather than the title. Lamont (cited by Buck 1932a:49), describes a conflict of hereditary claims to the office of ariki for which there was no direct heir. The community leaders resolved the dispute by dividing the territory (compare this with division of the office in Manihiki-Rakahanga), setting up two independent arikis, but avoiding war.

Subordinate chiefs were known as *tangata maro kura* ("men with red girdles"), a local term that refers to the Tahitian custom of girding high ariki with barkcloth bands covered with red feathers. Such girdles were not actually known in Tongareva, but the term gave honor to the title, and may have brought it closer to the status of the ariki. In genealogical terms (Buck 1932a:45), the lower-ranking chiefs were also *hono tangata* ("the link with the people"). It is not clear from Buck's account whether the term was also a title.

Since there were ceremonies investing a priest on the marae, but not an ariki, it is possible that the ariki in Tongareva had less sanctity than in other parts of eastern Polynesia. That he was a sacred figure would be indicated by his eating the turtle tribute on the marae. Moreover, it was the chief who was associated with the marae, and the marae was a monument to him (Buck 1932a:77). Drinking coconuts on the marae was also a mark of status and limited, therefore, presumably to chiefs. We do not know, however, whether the ariki had any priestly duties. Considering the apparent underdevelopment of ceremony, and the presence of a priestly group, the inference is that the ariki had only minor priestly functions, if any.

Buck refers to the priests (*taura*) as "another class within the community." They were the mediums, he says, of "certain lesser gods who were involved for assistance in cases of sickness, war, and economic and social troubles (1932a:50)." There were also seers (*karakia*), but these were individual experts, not a class.

There are no terms of low status, even though military conquest provides a natural setting for strongly demarcated status differences. The problem may simply be the lack of detailed information. Yet the stress on local autonomy, on the authority of the local community assemblies, would indicate that status differentiation was not very strong on Tongareva. Buck says as much:

> The power of chiefs and *ariki* was restricted and depended largely on the wealth of their food lands and the support they received from their people. The communities were comparatively small, and the resources of the atoll would not encourage the development of an elaborate ceremonial like that which was built up around similar positions in the larger and richer volcanic atolls (1932a:50).

Perhaps a more concrete indication of the limited powers of the ariki is the suggestion that the taboos on the harvesting of coconut crops (*masanga*) were imposed not by the ariki but by the community as a whole. Imposed to preserve a depleted food supply, the masanga was often an individual affair and affected only the trees of a family.

Tongareva thus presents a traditional status system with its two gradations of rank, ariki and tangata maro kura, corresponding to the rangatira in New Zealand. Status rivalry was active, but since it led only to the formation of new and autonomous sections or districts, it could not elaborate the status system. Neither the ariki nor the lower chiefs had specific economic prerogatives. The ariki were entitled to a symbolic offering of all turtles, which they ate ceremoniously on the *marae*. There were no formal feasts, and hospitality consisted largely of offering a guest a drinking coconut. The chiefs were neither land distributors nor redistributors of resources, since the economy was strictly a responsibility of the household head. Conquest did not add to the economic power of ariki; it added only to their scope of political hegemony, to their status. Military raids, on the other hand, were for coconuts, that is, for plunder, and not for conquest.

Tongareva recognized wealth distinctions and associated prestige with wealth, but since all owned coconut trees, only economic gradations and not economic classes were formed. The gradations, however, may have corresponded to genealogical rank, since as Buck observes, the senior descendant inherited the larger share of land (1932a:58). The ariki, therefore, were the wealthiest. Lamont, for example (cited by Buck 1932a:57), speaks of the daughter of a high chief as one of the richest heiresses, whereas her husband, a younger son, he notes, was poor.

Descent Group Organization

Buck's account of the kin groupings is incomplete and overly general in its depiction of a traditional order of seniority. A single ariki had succeeded in establishing authority by force over the entire atoll, and others also rose to command over smaller divisions by military or political means. Buck insists, nonetheless, that even when federations had formed for urgent defense the commander was still the senior ariki. He describes Tongareva as though it were small-scale Maori, but without segmental nomenclature.

The segmental order seemingly depended upon the actual state of political affairs at a given moment. Segment I was either a "conquest state" standing for the entire atoll, or it was a federation of related families forming a large division or district. All persons on the atoll were interrelated through intermarriage and formed, technically at least, a single kindred of blood relatives. From this point of view, Tongareva never became a territorial "state." The Tongarevan viewpoint, nevertheless, was separatist, and general kinship was considered as subordinate to the greater importance of ties to closer chiefly ancestors. The local concept was political, as demonstrated by active warfare; from the political standpoint, the unity of the atoll could only be accomplished by force in violation of basic principles of separatism.

The organization of smaller territorial divisions also reflected political, or—more accurately—military circumstances. Normally, local divisions represented kinsmen acknowledging descent from chiefly ancestors. We may speak of such a local group as a traditional Segment II in that it resembled the Maori iwi. It was headed by an ariki, the head of the senior line, who assumed authority in time of war. These local divisions either joined voluntarily into enlarged military coalitions or were consolidated by force into a single entity, in which case they were no longer bound by traditional seniority.

Segment III refers to what Buck has described as "village districts," aggregates of kinsmen under the jurisdiction of lower-ranking *hono tangata,* or secular chiefs. These, one gathers, were relatively stable kin groupings. Finally, the patrilocal extended household headed by a senior male stands for Segment IV. The households were the primary land and coconut tree holders. They were for most purposes economically self-sufficient and independent, reallocating their holdings from generation to generation in order of seniority, so that the eldest was also the wealthiest.

The economic focus upon household, upon the lowest level of segmentation, would seem to indicate that the development of a segmental order is unrelated to the distribution of goods. Tongareva illustrates two patterns of segmentation, one traditional, leading to the formation of the district organization, and another, more innovative, leading to enlargement by conquest. The powers of ariki have not been described either by Buck or by Lamont. There is no hint in the literature that either the traditional or the conquest chiefs had an economic role, even though scarcity of food was a major cause of war and therefore indirectly a factor in the growth of chiefly power. The power of the ariki—and the significance of the segments they headed—was essentially formal, a matter of status.

5

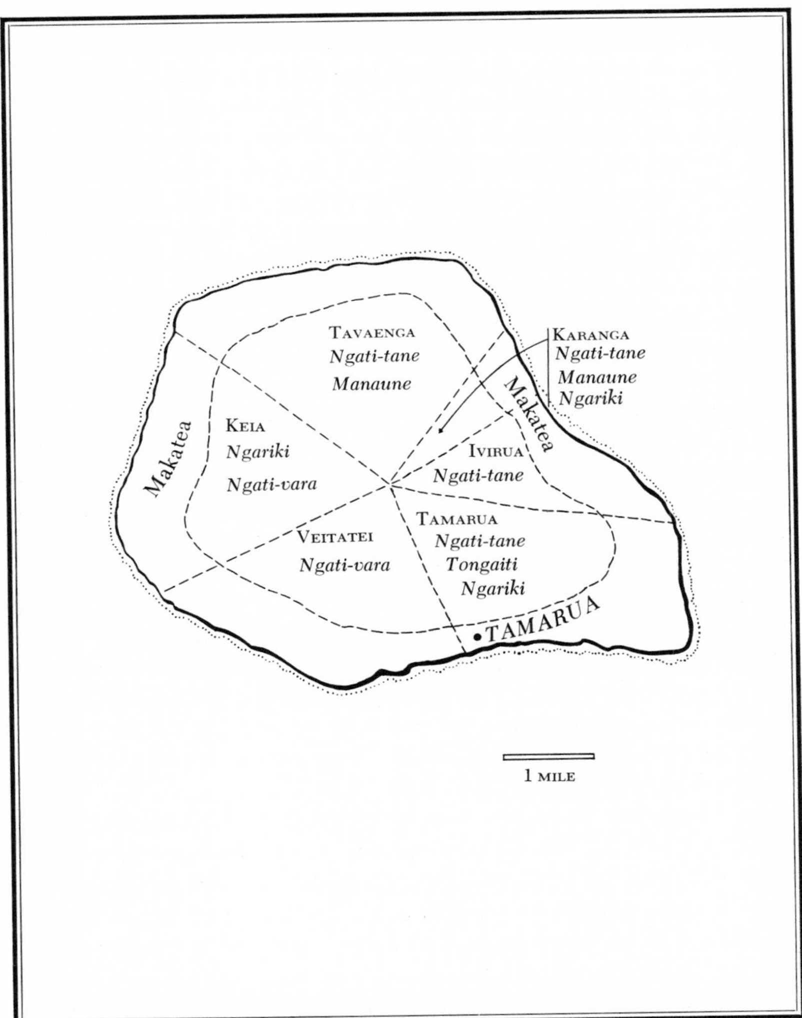

TAVAENGA
Ngati-tane
Manaune
KARANGA
Ngati-tane
Manaune
Ngariki
KEIA
Ngariki
Ngati-vara
Makatea
Makatea
IVIRUA
Ngati-tane
TAMARUA
Ngati-tane
Tongaiti
Ngariki
VEITATEI
Ngati-vara
TAMARUA
1 MILE

Mangaia

THE ISLANDS OF THE COOK ARCHIPELAGO REVEAL ALMOST THE FULL range of Polynesian social systems. And since almost all derive from the same sources in the Society Islands, they must surely express variations from a rather specific and common cultural base. We have already examined Manihiki-Rakahanga as a traditional atoll, and Tongareva as the Traditional society gaining social mobility. Pukapuka, to be discussed under western Polynesia (see chap. 17), is a special case of adaptation of eastern and western Polynesian traditions. Among the southern Cooks, which lie even closer to the Society group, Mangaia and its neighbor, Rarotonga, exemplify the fully developed Open society verging on economic stratification. By the evidence of their traditions—the only available historical information—Rarotonga was settled from Raiatea late in the twelfth century (Crocombe 1964), when the latter island was a citadel of Society Islands' traditionalism. Mangaia was then settled from Rarotonga three hundred years later (Buck 1934). Both Mangaia and Rarotonga, as their traditions reveal, became Open societies well after they had been settled. The transformation came somewhat earlier in Mangaia and was altogether more far-reaching than on Rarotonga. Both societies, however, seem to have undergone a parallel evolution, but with some important differences. On Rarotonga it was the traditional ariki who had seized the political power and reduced commoners to economic dependency (Beaglehole 1957, Crocombe 1964). On Mangaia it was commoners who had risen to the supreme political authority, reducing both ariki and the weak among the commoners to a state of dependency. On Rarotonga no ariki ever secured command of the entire island, but on Mangaia the outstanding warrior became, to use Buck's phrase, the "military dictator" over all the tribes (1934). Of the two, Mangaia was the most fully "open."

The Mangaian traditions were assembled in the late nineteenth century by Rev. W. W. Gill (1880, 1894), who had access to informants who still remembered the precontact period. In 1930 Peter Buck, then the temporary resident agent on the island, supplemented and evaluated Gill's writings. This is the sum and substance of our information on Mangaia. Cook, the discoverer, stopped over in 1777 but too briefly to add much to the historical record. The traditions are a vivid narrative of the wars and rivalries that finally brought the traditional order to a violent end.

A volcanic island with a diversified terrain, Mangaia must be considered among the more productive of the Polynesian habitats, even though much of its 27 square mile area was precipitous and stony. The central volcanic core, a common feature of the smaller high islands and ordinarily an agricultural wasteland, was on Mangaia rather low (554 ft.), and gently sloped (Marshall 1927). A system of terraces and water courses advancing far up the flanks added to the total crop yield as the population increased. Even the *makatea,* an elevated rim of broken coral rock that surrounded the interior, was finally brought under cultivation, but as very low-grade cropland. Between the makatea and the mountain slopes lay swamp flats (*puna*) ideal for taro, the major crop. And where the midsection of the island sloped markedly, it was built up into a series of descending terraces. The island was well-watered, and relatively free of hurricanes and drought, implying a stable food supply that was further assured by the presence of a substantial fishing lagoon.

However, as on most volcanic islands of Polynesia, it is not general productivity that is significant but the pattern of distribution of rich and poor farm lands. It is on this score that Mangaian geography proved to be problematic. The swamp flats were fiercely coveted and fought over, eventually becoming the prized possessions of the conquerors (Buck 1934). The weaker people were resettled up the slopes and on the makatea. We would be mistaken, however, if we dismissed the economic motive in Mangaian wars with the standard explanation of "population pressure." With a pre-European population of only 3,000 (Buck 1934), Mangaia had a relatively low density of settlement. The issue rather was power. Wealth was power. To humiliate an enemy one reduced him to poverty and thus to political impotence.

Genealogical Traditions

The traditions assert that the first settlers were ruled by three brothers, grandsons of the god Rongo, who all shared the royal title of *Nga-ariki* ("high chief"). Taking account of the brevity of the genealogical traditions, Buck has supposed that the first immigrants were plebeians from Rarotonga who had draped themselves with the mantle of aristocracy (1934:30). The ancestry of these first chiefs may be uncertain. It is clear though that they inaugurated a traditional order and that their credentials of aristocracy were never challenged. They did not, however, establish a unified rule. Rongo is said to have divided the authority among them, giving to the eldest the temporal authority, symbolized by the drum of peace; to the second, authority over food; and to the third, the priestly jurisdiction over prayers and ritual. Three lineages descended from these first founders, all three coming to be known as the royal lineages or Ngariki. Only the senior line assumed the authentic claim to the Ngariki designation; the other two carried the names of their founders. Thus

Mangaia offers a parallel to the fraternal divisions of chiefly authority that also took place in Manihiki-Rakahanga and Tongareva. On these atolls the order of values seemed to be different: the senior line received the religious authority and the junior line the secular. The difference, however, is more apparent than real, for the Mangaian temporal authority began as a priestly role and became secular only after a period of intertribal warfare had disturbed the traditional rules of chiefly succession.

The Mangaian peace was broken almost immediately by a series of fresh migrations from Rarotonga and other Cook Islands and from the Society groups. Wars for political control erupted and the tradition arose that military victory conveyed the temporal authority. The first invaders were the Tongaiti, not Tongan migrants as Gill and after him Williamson believed, but fellow Rarotongans (Buck 1934). The Tongaiti established themselves on Mangaia by sheer force and eventually became the commanding political power on the island. They were followed by the Ngati-tane, who were refugees from Tahiti, as Buck has reconstructed their history. The Ngati-tane were almost annihilated in war, but were reinforced by new arrivals and held on. A new Rarotongan invasion, followed in short order by military parties from the smaller Cook Islands of Atiu and Aitutaki, diversified the Mangaian descent lines still more, and added fresh fuel to a highly combustible political atmosphere. The Ngariki fought all new arrivals. The persistent enemy, however, proved to be the Tongaiti, and the carefully kept record of Mangaian wars and their victors and losers, chronicles the agonized rivalry of these two contenders for the supreme authority. Not until the final years, when Christianity had somewhat subdued the passions of political rivalry, did tribes heretofore relatively unknown join the select list of victors.

The history of Mangaia, Buck has said,

> illustrates the attempt of the Ngariki to keep the position of Temporal Lord of Mangaia within their own tribe, and their ultimate failure through the ambition of the warlike Tongaiti. Once precedent was broken down in this direction, the hope of establishing a hereditary *ariki* with temporal power over the whole island vanished. The principle that temporal power was the reward of war and not of hereditary descent led to frequent changes of secular government and offers a marked contrast to the social organization of Rarotonga where secular power remained in the hands of the *ariki* families and succession was hereditary (1934:54).

Gill compiled a list of 42 battles beginning with the first clash between Ngariki and Tongaiti and the final war that restored the

Ngariki dynasty, then already Christian (1880). Gill's list credits the Ngariki with eleven victories before the Tongaiti first won the temporal power. The Tongaiti victory was followed by the temporary superiority of another tribe, the Akatauira. Then the Tongaiti came back with a string of seven successive victories and chiefly successions. The Ngariki won the next eight battles. Thereafter the tide of battle and the secular crown shifted to several other tribes. The balance of power between the two great contenders was finally broken and political rivalry became more general. The wars between Ngariki and Tongaiti were amazingly bitter. The tribes sought nothing less than utter extermination of one another. They fought on the open battlefield. They struck with sudden and unsuspected raids; and they attacked each other, when all other means were unavailable, under the guise of friendship. Inexplicably, the Ngati-Tane were repeatedly victimized by the same ruse. Time and again they accepted an invitation to a "friendship" feast only to be slaughtered and roasted in the ovens that had been prepared for them in advance. The efforts to exterminate, nevertheless, fell short and the survivors from the safety of caves prepared a comeback. Since the victors often spent themselves in internal rivalries, revenge was not delayed for too long (Buck 1934, Gill 1880).

Throughout an unbroken history of terrible disorder, the Ngariki held almost to the very end all their traditional prerogatives of sanctity, preserving for the most part, the rule of seniority. Only the temporal authority, which had come to be defined as a military dictatorship, lost its traditional immunities. The title of Temporal Lord (*mangaia*) was at first also a priestly office with custody of the drum of peace. This religious title and office became dislodged from the senior lineage of the Ngariki almost from the very moment the Tongariki sounded the opening challenge. At one time each of the three Ngariki lineages held it. Whether the mangaia as a religious office was handed over amicably to the most capable leader or was seized by the strongest, the traditions do not say; but they do make clear that the mangaia had become a prize to be won well before the plebeian Tongaiti had wrested it from the royal lineages and converted it into a secular authority.

The fate of the ariki titles during this period of antagonism between royalist and nonroyalist forces seems to identify for us the actual issues of contention. The priestly functions, for example, were always immune from seizure; and priestly ariki lost their immunity as persons only after they had entered the political lists (Buck 1934:113). During the early periods of warfare the mangaia, too, seemed to be immune for, in at least one instance, the military victor awarded the title back to the Ngariki from whom he had wrested it. Presumably, the title then still held its priestly aura. Status rivalry thus was confined to the specific issues of political and economic controls and powers. The survival of the Ngariki despite their many defeats must be attributed to a generally accepted doctrine that rivalry for specifically political powers was, in fact, legitimate. The legitimacy of the rights of the lower ranks to hold the secular power was vouchsafed by the traditional doctrine that the jurisdiction of the highest-order chief was preeminently in ritual and that the specifically secular powers were a proper responsibility to be shared with lower ranks.

In summary, the Mangaian traditions define two periods in the island's history: an early period when the Ngariki, the traditional aristocracy, were in control and a later period when plebeian tribes held the military power. The first, or Ngariki period, resembles the Traditional society. The second, which for convenience we may call the Tongaiti period, is a classic example of an eastern Polynesian Open society.

The Status System

Except for the priestly office of Temporal Lord, with its divine authority to sound the drum of peace, the Mangaian principles of status are identical with those of the Maori, Manihiki-Rakahanga, and Tongareva. The history of the Temporal Lordship (mangaia) is not altogether clear. We do not know which privileges and authorities it controlled early in Mangaian history. In time of peace the military authority was undoubtedly formal and nominal. When the political character of the chiefship changed as a result of wars and conquests, gaining economic powers of land allocation and defying orderly rules of succession, the structure of the status system was drastically rearranged, though its formal elements remained intact. Mangaian history testifies to the durability of these elements and to the diversity of their combinations. The first-born was honored as *kiko mua* ("first flesh"). As Buck saw it, however, "Though seniority counted for much, junior lines could rise above their seniors in actual power within the tribe through the exercise of greater ability and leadership (1934:100)."

Primogeniture

There is no evidence that Mangaians ever abandoned this principle as the basis for office or title.

Seniority of Descent

In the period of Ngariki dominance, seniority of descent governed succession to all titles and offices. But in the Tongaiti period and thereafter, this principle no longer applied to the mangaia himself and had ceased to regulate succession to rangatira. Only the priestly offices held to it, illustrating the constant Polynesian association of seniority with sanctity.

Male Line

The Ngariki attached even more importance to the male line than did the Maori. Buck states at this point:

> The highest title (*ariki*) is vested in the *kiko mua* (first-born son of a first-born son) in each generation and cannot be held by a female. The fact that daughters may be born before a male child does not affect succession. A sister may be senior in birth to her *ariki* brother but, owing to the restriction of the relationship term of *tuakana* to the same sex her seniority is not recognized. When she marries, her children may be theoretically senior to those of her brother, but this is offset by the fact that they are *tama va'ine* (female line) and cannot supplant their cousins who are *tama tane* (male line). They have also passed out of the tribe and even their adoption cannot obviate their *tama va'ine* descent. This rule, however, has been broken on occasion (1934:109).

The stronger emphasis here on patrilineal descent suggests that the Cook Islands, and perhaps the Society Islands as well, were early centers of traditional honoring of the male line. Mangaia was able to preserve this tradition against almost inevitable erosion by introducing a novel rule—for Polynesia—of tribal exogamy. We cannot be sure, of course, that the defense of patriliny was their aim. Exogamy, nevertheless, does remove one major source of ambiguity about line of descent. Buck thought rather that the newly arrived tribes who followed the Ngariki onto the island had brought no wives with them and so were compelled to marry into the dominant Ngariki (1934: 92). Once the practice spread, it become an obligation. Whether or not the later arrivals had brought wives with them, we do not know. In any case, there is no precedent in Polynesia for an expedient solution to become a categorical rule. If the dominant Ngariki insisted upon exogamy, we must assume they did so to safeguard genealogical honor and their political dominance. Given the prominence of patriliny, exogamy would, in the first place, have been no threat to the genealogical quality of the ariki lines. Its specific advantage, however, would be its effect in linking up the family lines of newcomer tribes within a comprehensive kindred comparable to that of the Traditional societies. In this linkage, the Ngariki could retain their dominant status and hope for political stability. Exogamy would have had the further advantage of preserving the identity of the tribes by emphasizing their categorical distinctness. This aspect of exogamy may be interpreted as a compromise between opposing interests of tribal self-assertion, and the desire of chiefs for some peace and tranquility.

Genealogical Depth

The relative shallowness of Mangaian descent lines, including those of the royalist Ngariki, has been taken by Buck as a mark of their plebeian origins. Chiefly lines, he reasons, could have claimed genealogical connections with the ancestral homeland. By starting their chain of pedigree from the settlement period, the Ngariki conceded their newness and at the same time sought to conceal their commoner origins by attributing to themselves descent from the gods. By asserting a divine origin, they acknowledged adherence to the traditional principle of honoring a pedigree insofar as its roots went back to the first and pre-human origins. In traditional fashion, only the Ngariki claimed genealogical depth. The other tribes accepted their plebeian status in acknowledging the aristocracy of the Ngariki and did not claim godly descent. While the lower-ranking genealogies are not materially shorter, they are qualitatively different from those of the Ngariki. The most thoroughgoing differences in genealogical depth are among the chiefly descent lines. All the ariki titles go back to first origins, whereas the headships of the plebeian tribes held by military men represent only shallow descent lines. For the most part, these chiefly pedigrees have not been preserved. The title of Temporal Lord has genealogical depth, but the descent lines holding it do not. Genealogical depth appears then as a durable principle, dependent, however, upon the ariki title—in short, upon the preservation of aristocracy.

Linearity

Consistent patriliny along with seniority established the honor of linearity in Mangaia, but only for the highest-ranking lines among the Ngariki. All others faced the opposite prospect of assignment either to the mother's or to the father's side, depending upon which side was strongest and which side could make the strongest claim to a child.

Sanctity

All first-born (including females) and all "important" children, says Buck, received special ritual care. A high-ranking priest (*vaikea*) cut the navel cord and the child was dedicated to his tribal god. The knife was deposited on the marae, and the dedicated person was subject to being called upon as a human sacrifice if his tribe proved to be weak (1934:85). Soon after birth these children were raised upon the shoulders of relatives, a sign of fealty (1934:87). It is not clear, however, whether these examples of special treatment established sanctity or simply high prestige. Evidently the ordinary first-born were not subject to the usual avoidances that commonly denote actual sanctity. Definite sanctity may have been restricted to the High Priest, who was honored with the deference of avoidance only when confined to priestly duties. Even the Temporal Lord then approached him crawling on all fours (1934:116). But if the priest interfered in political affairs during war, he could be killed and eaten. The traditions record several cases, with the reminder that the gods could avenge the death of a priest. On two occasions women held the high priestly offices and were presumably honored as sacred. In one instance the woman was the sole survivor of a priestly line that had been virtually wiped out in war. The other instance carries no explanation. Sanctity, in sum, was genealogically derived, yet also situational.

Priesthood

There were two classes of priests, the holders of ariki rank who served the islandwide or national gods, and the local priests, the *pi'a atua,* or "receptacles" of the gods, who represented tribal deities. Both categories of priest had the power to intervene in political affairs. The Island High Priest as custodian of the drum of peace could launch himself against the rule of the Temporal Lord by refusing to sound the call for the laying down of arms. "The refusal of the high priest to conduct the ritual," Buck observes, "led to the venting of Rongo's anger upon the land. The slaying of people went on, the land was not legally redistributed and famine followed (1934:113)." Tribal priests, as oracles of the gods, had still wider scope for political intervention. They could raise up opposition against an incumbent chief and could declare the senior succession invalid. They were then drawn into active political struggle. When they had the power they assumed the chiefly offices. The Island High priests held the mangaia on several occasions, and tribal priests were often military chieftains. In self-defense, the secular authorities hoped to secure priests friendly to them. A powerful Temporal Lord installed his own candidate as Island High Priest. Victorious local chiefs promptly disposed of possible opposition by sacrificing enemy priests to Rongo. The Ngariki, who controlled the two high priesthoods and the national gods, had to contend with the very powerful priesthood of one of their own tribal gods, Motoro, for the Motoro priests enjoyed immunity against being killed within the Ngariki.

The overlapping of sacred and secular prerogatives, and the bitter conflicts it precipitated, violated utterly the traditional theory of orderly allocation of rights and jurisdictions. Yet, if our information is reliable, Mangaia never fully abandoned the traditional roles of priestly succession, of immunities, and responsibilities. The ariki offices were expected to move down the senior male line. The lower-ranking tribal priesthood, on the other hand, was inherited by males, but not in order of seniority. The genealogical link could not be broken; if there were no male heirs, a woman became the priest.

In the traditional Mangaian scheme, the priestly jurisdictions were well defined. The Island High Priest (*ariki-pa-uta*), the representative of Rongo, the national god, guarded the island against evil spirits coming from the east and was responsible for sacrifices to Rongo—who was a war god—after a military victory. The sacrifices placated Rongo and so preserved the peace. The priestly role was, in fact, politically neutral (Buck 1934:114), since war was the will of Rongo. The responsibilities of the second-ranking high priest, the *ariki-pa-tai,* the defender of the coasts, was still more circumscribed. But perhaps information on this priesthood is incomplete. The Ruler of Food (*te arikiite-ua-te-tapora kai*), the third-ranking high priest, had the specific jurisdiction over the fertility of land and trees, and could impose the *rahui* to conserve crops and fishing grounds. He was the administrator of the ritual economy, controlling the powers of production and the protocol of ceremonial distributions.

Tohunga

Priest and crafts experts were distinct positions. The former was *pi'a atua* and the latter held the title of *ta'unga.* While the ta'unga were treated with deference, and observed religious rites to give power to their tools, they were not a sacred group. They did not have their own marae nor their priests. The crafts were open to all, regardless of social status, but families guarded their trade secrets, passing them on from father to son. The ta'unga, however, lacked organization. Working as individuals, they could, in fact, pass on their craft skills to anyone, and they did, as Buck reports, "for a price (1934:131)." There is no reason to believe that ta'unga became wealthy or commanded special powers. They seem to have occupied a rather modest place in the social scheme, but with assured respect and an assured livelihood. A maker of ceremonial adzes, the most esteemed of the craftsmen, could buy immunity for himself and family after his tribe had been defeated and dispersed (1934:131).

Toa

In New Zealand, the toa were men of rank not lower than rangatira. In Mangaia, military ability alone counted, so that the outstanding war leaders soon overshadowed the traditional leadership (rangatira) of the tribes and achieved the supreme authority as Temporal Lord (Buck 1934:110). Well rewarded for their services with land grants, the warriors—regardless of official position—became local centers of wealth and of political power.

Wealth

We observe in Mangaia a rather marked shift in emphasis from the ritual to the pragmatic uses of wealth. The traditional esteem for abundance as a sign of divine grace, and generosity as demonstrations of rank, persisted mainly among the Ngariki, for whom property was the appropriate emblem of inherited rank. Against these essentially ritual uses of wealth, the rising warriors brought their own more urgent interests in property as the source of power. The source of wealth was land; since lands could be seized from the weak and redistributed among the strong, who came from all social ranks, the political uses of the economy were bound to surpass the ritual side in overall importance. We have, in fact, no specific information on the economic status of the Ngariki holders of rank, but we must assume from the character of the social system, which has been reasonably well described, that the traditional economy had been thoroughly disarranged, at least to the extent that commoners could equal, if not indeed surpass, the nobility in affluence. Noble and commoner had equal prerogatives in giving feasts and in distributing gifts of food, in the course of which they gained in honor.

The order of allotments of food at great tribal feasts, which were given by "powerful families" or the entire tribe, indicates some rearrangements in the traditional order, suggestive of a compromise between rank and status. The tribal priests received the first shares; the three ariki priests, the second shares; the Temporal Lord, the third shares and then, in order of political precedence, all the district and subdistrict chiefs. Those with neither title nor distinction ate from a common setting.

Political Hegemony

The issue of contention was power—power to award lands, to deprive of lands, to demand human sacrifices, to grant immunity from sacrifices, to attract adherents, to overcome enemies, to impose oneself as master, and to avoid becoming a victim. Power rather than rank gave jurisdiction, superseding finally some of the most zealously guarded prerogatives of the ariki priests. When the Temporal Lord had succeeded in imposing his own candidate as high priest, he assumed command of a centralized jurisdiction that embraced every territory and every secular function on the island. The rituals of installation of the Temporal Lord were surely intended to endow his authority with divine sanction, giving him some of the attributes if not the title of an ariki. But since even the true ariki had fallen, there was no safeguard for the Temporal Lord other than his ability to balance all the contentious forces that were subordinate to him. He could not sustain the balance for long, because even after the peace had been secured he was as dependent as ever upon all the local chiefs and warriors whose favor he had sought and whom he had raised up in power. Every jurisdiction contained a master-dependent relationship supported only partly by tradition and inevitably by the immediacies of power. When one such relationship was overturned, its repercussions threatened and often tore apart the entire political structure. Internal rivalry was but part of the threat to the central structure of power; the resurgence of the once vanquished enemies was another. What is remarkable about the Mangaian political organization is its consistent inability to transcend the temporal authority by any means other than force. So consistently was the hereditary succession avoided that we are moved to suspect the emergence here of a new and formal system of complementary power relationships: a genealogical succession for religious authorities and a military succession for secular authorities. Such a formal system achieves a conceptual coherence within a religious setting that raised up Rongo as the God of War and as the high god of the island, in contrast to traditional eastern Polynesia, where Rongo was the peaceable god of agriculture. The Temporal Lordship as a "military dictatorship" was a late development in Mangaia; it was also the logical development of an older religious idea.

The Structure of Status

Mangaian historical traditions have been particularly interesting in their portrayal of a series of transformations in the structure of status. In the Ngariki period, the status system was traditional and unitary. After the Tongaiti period, a dual system developed. How stable, we may now ask, is a dual system, even if it is founded, as the Mangaian seems to have been, upon the complementary functions of religion and politics? I have already suggested that power and tradition are not easily harmonized once they have been separated. Tradition without power loses its inner vigor; quite literally, its mana; power without tradition cannot assure its peaceable transference. The complements do not, in fact, support one another. Each lacks what the other has, compelling them to rivalry rather than to alliance. Over a short span of time there is no established outcome of such rivalry. In Mangaia the balance of forces shifted between power and tradition, depending on the tides of war. We have discerned, nevertheless, the erosion of tradition and the broadening and deepening of the pragmatic forces of political power. When we come therefore to describe the relationship of all the Mangaian statuses to each other, we must bear in mind a fluid rather than a stable and established historical setting.

Ideally, Ngariki traditionalism was founded upon the ranks of ariki, rangatira and matakainanga (the "people" or the commoners). The ariki, representing high-level segments and the senior lines, were responsible for ritual functions. The rangatira, representing lower-level segments and junior lines, dealt with practical affairs. The populace was genealogically related to the ariki and occupied a status of worth, unlike the Maori tutua. Since the rangatira were actually chiefs who headed a tribe, they were a small group, numerically contractive rather than expansive. The major social group was the matakainanga the truly expansive group. The traditional distribution of ranks followed the form of a triangle and not the diamond. When all the new tribes came under Ngariki jurisdiction, each tribe was headed by a rangatira, in harmony with the traditional structure of ranks. Thus the proportion of the ranks remained constant.

Under the Temporal Lord, an achieved office, a new status order developed that was strictly political and territorial. The entire island was divided into districts, each headed by a *pava,* and into subdistricts, headed by *kairanga-nuku,* who corresponded to the office of Land Distributor in Manihiki-Rakahanga and Tongareva. The Temporal Lord appointed the pava either from among the hereditary rangatira or from among distinguished warriors. The pava, in turn, appointed the subdistrict chiefs, who then had the specific responsibility for reallocating conquered lands among the victors and for dealing with all other land claims that might subsequently arise. A pava could also act as his own land distributor. In a fashion analagous to the Maori chief who named seized lands after parts of his body, the pava took direction of his lands in the name of his battle scars or wounds. When he delegated a land distributor (kairanga nuku), he chose him from among his own kin. In all significant respects the pava replaced the traditional rangatira as a political officer.

Those evicted from their lands formed a low class, stigmatized as the "fatherless people" (*ivi panga*). They were scattered among the victors as alien dependents who did the menial work; as tribute-paying subordinates who held lands on sufferance; or as desperate refugees awaiting a turn in fortune. Master-dependent relationships, though, were personal and flexible. Some dependents were eventually absorbed into the dominant tribe and thus were allowed to resettle on the less productive lands. The makatea became the exclusive territory of refugee bands under the inappropriate and undoubtedly ironic title of "ariki of the makatea (Buck 1934)."

Finally, there was a group of voluntary dependents—for whom there was no specific name—who accepted a menial and low status for the sake of relative safety.

The ivi panga resembled a "landless" class of the Stratified societies insofar as they were subject to eviction for failure to meet their obligations (Gill 1880:67). The distinction between the Mangaian forms of subordinate and low status land tenure and those of the Stratified societies are not profound, but they are historically interesting as a step in the gradual reduction of the commoner. The Mangaians reserved economic degradation for their military victims, yet even with these unfortunates the distinction they seemed most concerned to make was of quality of lands held rather than of quality of land tenure.

Descent Group Organization

In more recent times Mangaian society was organized territorially and did not have the traditional segmentary organization. There is some reason to believe, however, that a segmentary organization of the Maori type had once existed and had been replaced by the new political organization. For example, Mangaians were familiar with and used the traditional terms of segmentation such as *vaka, ivi kopu* and *'anau* · *Vaka,* along with *pare* and *e,* referred to "tribe," or the largest grouping based on a concept of common descent. *Ivi,* on the other hand, referred to a group sharing a common cause regardless of ancestry, as in *ivi panga. Kopu* was still another name for "tribe," while *'anau* retained its original meaning of "household." Polynesian segmentary terms are semantically general and cannot therefore be taken as conclusive evidence that other specific groupings had borne them. But since Rarotonga retained a segmentary organization, using some of these terms, it is hard to avoid the conclusion that Mangaia had also at one time done so. Certainly the social organization implied by the Ngariki chiefship is fully consistent with traditional segmentation. Ngariki as a tribe consisted of three genealogically linked and ranked lineages whose ariki were ritual heads. Ngariki as the vaka was Segment I. The component lineages headed by lower-ranking ariki would correspond to the traditional ivi as Segment II, while the subdivisions headed by junior branch rangatira resembled the Maori hapu. As in New Zealand, the vaka became a significant corporate entity in time of war. Since the Ngariki soon came under constant attack, their paramount chief gained in power as military leader and land distributor. In all four segments, including the household (IV), affiliation and descent were patrilineal and patrilocal.

The traditional social structure was fundamentally rearranged during the Tongaiti period. Of the ten tribes that then occupied the island, most were unrelated and several were perhaps ethnically differentiated. Under Ngariki leadership, a facsimile of the segmentary system had been organized within which the Ngariki as a tribe held the position that traditionally belonged to the senior lineage. All other tribes headed by chiefs no higher in the social scale than rangatira occupied the apparent status not of tribe in the traditional sense but of the equivalent of a hapu. This new system, which seems to have had the equivalence of an adoption, fell within the old mold, introducing within it, however, new conflicts and tensions. In time, of course, the pattern of intermarriages, accelerated under the influence of tribal exogamy, linked together the members of all the tribes into a semblance of a waka kindred. But the new kindreds, while offering persons new possibilities for affiliation, did not obscure the concept of tribe. Rather, two loyalties were created and persons had to choose, in time of war, between the conflicting pulls of family and tribe (cf. Buck 1934:106).

The facsimile of the traditional structure finally gave way during the Tongaiti period to a political and territorial system. Segment I was the central authority, headed by a military dictator, the new style Temporal Lord. Segment II represented the pie-shaped districts under the appointed pava. Segment III, a political subdivision in concept, could have been a kinship unit, since the subdistrict chief was usually a kinsman of the pava.

Primitive political systems inevitably retain a substantial part of a traditional kinship structure, no matter how far they carry centralization of authority. In Mangaia, too, the traditional structure was not supplanted; it was altered, over time. The traditions place the institution of the new territorial system at the time of Pangemiro, a Temporal Lord from the Manaune tribe who won the 41st battle shortly before the European era. By that time the long series of wars had already so dislocated the traditional order that the new system must have accomplished little more than put a formal seal upon existing conditions. Each war rearranged land-holdings and shifted about populations. It seems hardly likely that any traditional grouping could have remained intact.

The new territorial division, reaching from central peak in a wedge to the sea, followed a traditional concept of the land. But the number of districts, six, was symbolic. In the Tahitian manner, the island was visualized as a fish, as the "fish of Rongo" (Buck 1934:126). The fish lay with its head to the east and its tail to the west and was thought of as having been divided longitudinally into a right-hand and left-hand side and in three portions going from east to west, as head, body, and tail. There were thus two "head" divisions in the east, two "body" divisions in the center, and two "tail" divisions in the west.

It is not entirely clear whether the divisions were ranked or had equal honor. The fact that the left-hand divisions at the time of Pangemiro were said to "favor" the victor, and the right-hand divisions the vanquished, is reminiscent of the division of the land into two parties as occurred on other islands where an Open society had become established.

Each district was subdivided into as many as ten additional sections (*tapere*), which, as a rule, were also longitudinal strips from mountaintop to shore. The tapere populations were so small, averaging fewer than a dozen households each, that they were probably set up in response to the claims of warriors for honorific land tenure. The district and subdistrict organization met Mangaian standards for ecological equity in principle only, since the most powerful families monopolized the flat lands (Buck 1934:124). The subdistrict organization may have coincided generally with a hapu type of lineage, judging simply by the tendency of families to retain, if possible, their continuity of land rights. We do not, however, know how far the actual dislodging of families had gone. We know only that rights of conquest had indeed become established in Mangaian notions of tenure. Defeat may have compelled families to scramble for land, but in the poor zones of their original tribal territory. Victory, on the other hand, brought families into new territories. Thus, for a period of time, strong families were represented in different districts and certainly in different subdistricts. Kin and border, to employ Burrows' apt phrase, could not have coincided under these circumstances.

Households, in principle patrilineal and patrilocal, became more cosmopolitan in composition. Strong families gathered about them the weaker and poorer members of other families. Husbands joined the families of their wives. The strong adopted children from the families of the weak.

In the traditional system, the growth and branching of segments was largely vegetative, accelerated somewhat by the ambitions of junior lines to upgrade themselves. In the Mangaian Open system, growth—and decline—seems to have been rapid and regulated by centers of power. The strong gained adherents rapidly; the weak lost them. Size became a critical factor, since weakness invited attack. When lineages split they were apt to turn on one another and fight for the full authority. Social disorganization hit first at the weak and the lower ranks, who suffered the direct consequences of dispersal. The upper ranks, while not immune to disturbance, seemed to have been able to retain to the end some connections with the older genealogical order.

6

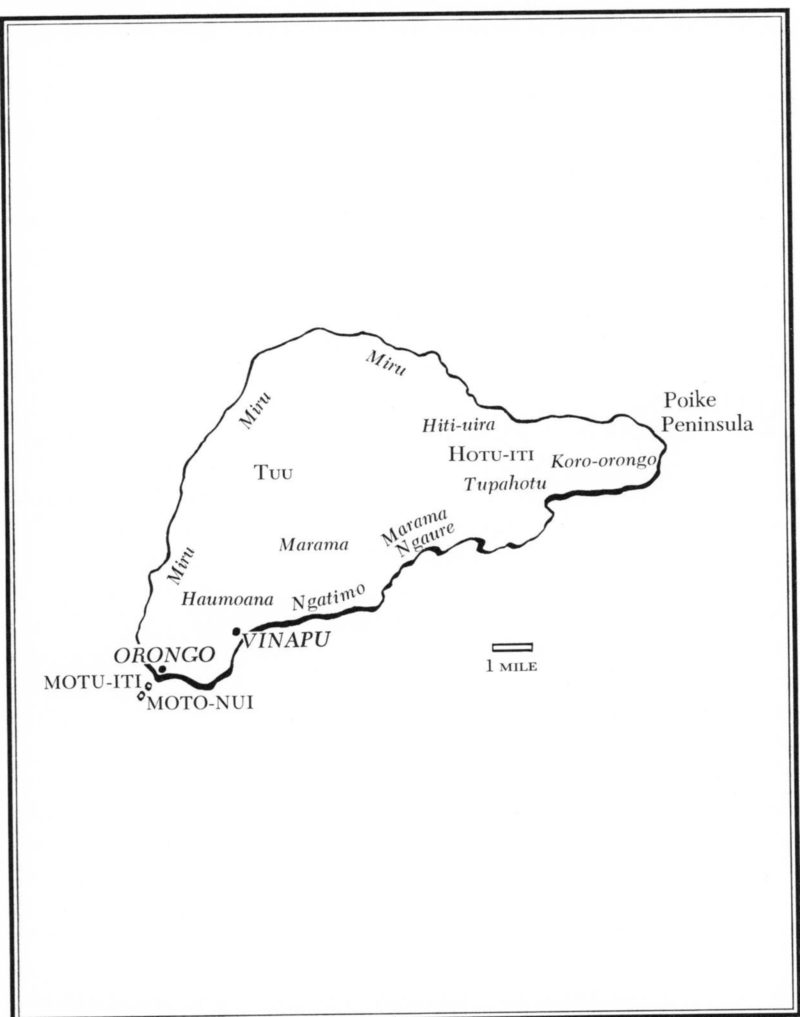

Easter Island

THE MOST ISOLATED AND AMONG THE MOST BARREN OF THE INhabited Polynesian islands, Easter was, nevertheless, the home of an impressively developed civilization. Its monumental stone statues and ceremonial centers and its esoteric script, evidently an "embryo writing" (Barthel 1958), stamp this remote Polynesian outpost as a "high culture," at least by technical standards. By social standards, it stands with the Open societies, which, like Mangaia and the Marquesas, had never evolved a central authority.

Easter has always given the impression of being the most mysterious and most alien of all Polynesian societies. All other Polynesian societies have been accepted, perhaps as strange, but hardly as inscrutable or as containing some coded message that when deciphered would suddenly bring into the open amazing historical secrets. If the "code" could ever have been deciphered, the opportunity has probably been lost for all time. The two great scientific expeditions of the eighteenth century—that of Cook and shortly thereafter that of the ill-fated La Pérouse—could have answered many questions about Easter Island culture that are now part of the island's mystery, but neither stayed long enough to record more than superficial observations. When a century later missionaries had settled in, the population had been reduced to the point where its continuity with past traditions had been all but lost.

Two of the more notable Easter Island mysteries are the scripts and the stone images. Both seem alien to Polynesia. The scripts incised on wooden tablets and used in religious ceremonies are the only example of "writing" in Polynesia. Some scholars have professed to see an historical connection between the Easter scripts and the use of knotted string in the Marquesas and in New Zealand, on the uncertain assumption that both were mnemonic. However, Barthel who submitted the scripts to cryptanalysis, found them to be both ideographic and pictographic and therefore not simply mnemonic. Von Koenigswald (1951) has sought to relate the scripts to patterns found on Sumatran silk embroidery, while Heine-Geldern (1938) has stressed similarities with prehistoric scripts of the Mohenjo-daro culture. Since Indonesia and Polynesia are in the same cultural orbit, the Sumatran connection is entirely plausible. What remains to be demonstrated, however, is the functional connection between the two scripts. The Indus Valley association is more problematic, for it is difficult to imagine how the Easter scripts, which seem to be relatively recent, can be connected with writings of the second millenium B.C. Others have called attention to resemblances between the Easter scripts and syllabary writings of the Cuna Indians of Panama.

But, as Metraux has asked, can we really compare modern syllabary writing developed under missionary guidance with a truly aboriginal script?

While the great stone images of Easter Island are more familiar as general examples of Polynesian megalithic arts, they are altogether distinctive in artistic style. Laval suggested that stylistically the Easter Island images resemble those of Mangareva; but a comparison of the small wooden effigies of Mangareva with the monumental stone work of Easter shows only a superficial relationship.

When we turn from such special features as scripts and statues to Easter Island culture as a whole, the strangeness and mystery quickly dissipate. The language is eastern Polynesian, closely related to Marquesan and Mangarevan, and the main social institutions and artifacts are also definitely Polynesian. Considering the isolation of the island and its relative antiquity, it is not difficult to imagine that some of the "alien" features are specialized developments and not necessarily foreign intrusions. But even if some traits were intrusive, it does not follow that they brought a wholly intrusive culture with them. Tobacco, after all, traveled about the world without taking with it the culture of the North American Indian. The fact of relative isolation is particularly important to our understanding of Easter Island society because it suggests that here we have what is perhaps the best example of relatively pristine internal development in all Polynesia.

For a volcanic island of some 60 square miles in area, Easter has a remarkably barren appearance. Several extinct volcanoes rise high above the landscape, but the terrain is rolling, rather than abrupt and diversified. Whatever trees had once grown on it are now gone and replaced by tall grasses. There are no streams, and much of the landscape is covered with an arid mantle of lava upon which cultivation is possible but unpromising. Skottsberg wrote about the "extremely poor flora" and the general aridity. "The great scarcity of water," he said, "makes the development of the culture astonishing (1920:I,6)." Nevertheless, substantial pockets of deep and fertile soils and good and reliable rainfall have sustained aboriginal populations estimated as high as 7,000. An ecological survey by the Norwegian Archaeological Expedition identified the fertile zones as Hangaroa, Metaveri, Vaihu, Rano Raraku, and Vaitea, areas concentrated mainly along the western coastal regions. In the east, the Poike peninsula is another fertile zone that, however, in aboriginal times was not fully cultivated. The subsistence problem was not crop yield, but availability of fresh water. Several crater lakes are great reservoirs of fresh water, but are so poorly located as to be, for all practical purposes, inaccessible. The islanders were compelled to rely rather on natural springs, or to construct reservoirs to impound rain water and sea walls to protect the reservoirs and springs. Even so, the water supply was always brackish. Sweet potato (*kumara*), the staple, grew very well in Easter Island soils, and this food supply was bolstered by good crops of yams, bananas, sugar cane, fern root and seaweed. The absence of a ringing reef, as in the Marquesas, reduced the importance of fishing, which was further impeded by the scarcity of wood for canoes. On the other hand, there was the native fowl, the ubiquitous Polynesian rat, and flocks of nesting seabirds. Food may not have been overly abundant, but the supply was reasonably reliable.

Like Mangaia, Easter Island is an example of an Open society in which warriors had succeeded in overcoming the authority of the traditional ariki. The warriors' supremacy had gone even further on Easter Island because here they had gained not only the political power, but had achieved an ascendant religious position as well. Nowhere else in Polynesia did commoners take upon themselves both the secular authority and prerogatives of mana and tapu which were not ordinarily theirs. This particular development, a carrying forward of the Marquesan tradition, lends special interest to Easter Island history. Unfortunately, Easter Island culture came to an abrupt end shortly after 1863. It was in that year that Peruvian slavers took some 1,000 persons off the island and the first missionaries arrived. In 1871 hundreds more left Easter Island for Tahiti and Mangareva. Early explorers, beginning with Roggeveen in 1722, and including Cook's party in 1774 and La Pérouse in 1746, did not record culture or traditions, but some of the early French missionaries did. When the Franco-Belgian scientific expedition arrived in 1934, the population had been reduced to 456. We are indebted, nevertheless, to Dr. Alfred Metraux, the ethnologist of that expedition, for a most thorough and judicious job of cultural salvage. We cannot answer many questions about details of Easter Island culture and of its development, but the general outlines are available. In 1955 the Norwegian Archaeological Expedition under Dr. Thor Heyerdahl began an extensive study of the stone monuments and other artifacts on the island. The results of that expedition provide an invaluable source of historical information to go along with the scattered native traditions. Thus, while we do not know as much about Easter Island social structure as we do about Mangaia, we have, on the other hand, some substantial archeological documentation of historical changes for which we have had to depend, thus far, upon the traditional records alone.

Genealogical Traditions

The traditions collected by several early students of Easter Island culture do not agree on details, but they all portray the same general picture of historical development. Metraux has evaluated and collected all the accounts and it is upon his version of the traditional history that we may rely. All accounts agree that an ariki called Hotu-matua, who came from Marae Renga, an unidentified island, was the founder of the social order. They explain his coming to the island as an escape after he had been defeated in a war of succession by his brother. Thus, the history of Easter Island begins in status rivalry. The traditions are not entirely clear on the important question whether Easter Islanders were all descended from a single body of related migrants or whether the population from the beginning consisted of several distinct parties. This question is important to our understanding of the profound antagonisms that soon divided the tribes. Mangaian social antagonisms could be laid to the natural conflicts between old settlers and newcomers. Was the same true on Easter Island, which resembled the Mangaian social system in so many important respects? The traditions can be interpreted to imply that this may have been the case, but they do not specifically assert it to be so. They refer, for example, to a party of six men who had preceded Hotu-matua on the island and do not identify them as kinsmen. They describe the Hotu-matua party as a large one that included another important ariki. The presence of two important ariki does, of course, suggest two distinct descent lines. Finally, the traditions describe how six "tribes" were formed after Hotu-matua had divided the land among his six sons. Since there were actually 10 to 12 tribes on the island, how are we to account for the extra tribes? Metraux has, for example, identified five tribes whose genealogical antecendents are not really known. There is reason to suppose therefore that the early settlers belonged to a number of separate lines. Yet, as Metraux has reasoned, the additional tribes may have later broken away from the original groups and lost the traces of their earlier connections. All Easter Island genealogies are exceedingly sketchy, and most tribes that consider themselves descended from Hotu-matua have no specific pedigrees to show their connections with one another. These specific family histories that might have told us whether Easter Island antagonisms were among blood kinsmen or among ethnic or genealogical aliens are lost to us. We are compelled therefore to fall back upon a more general historical consideration, namely, the point of view of the extant traditions. This at least is reasonably clear and leaves no doubt that the historical Easter Islanders thought of themselves as one stock and that when they fought it was one group of descendants of Hotu-matua against another group of his descendants. The wars, according to the traditional viewpoint, were internecine.

Those who believe that Easter Island had been settled by at least two different ethnic groups point to traditions of warfare between people known as Long-Ears and Short-Ears. The Long-Ears occupied the eastern part of the island, the Short-Ears the western side. In a great battle at the Poike ditch in the east, the Long-Ears, the eastern people, were, according to these traditions, virtually exterminated. The narrative of these warring groups is remarkably vague, and Metraux has concluded from an evaluation of all the relevant information that the war referred to was rather recent and that the tradition "presents no definite evidence of the existence of two different races on the island (1940:74)."

War is a recurrent theme in Easter Island traditions that dwell on the persistent rivalries between the eastern and western districts. According to the Hotu-matua tradition, the partition of the island may have represented at one time a royalist versus commoner division. The tradition states that Hotu-matua divided the lands among his six sons in order of seniority: He gave to his eldest, Tuu-maheke, the "royal lands," a stretch of the northern coast; to his second-born, Miru, a westward extension of the north coast; and, finally, to Hotu-iti, the sixth and youngest, the entire eastern side of the island. Each son founded a tribe. The western and royalist side came to be known as Tuu, and the Miru emerged finally as the one royal tribe. The entire eastern side of the island became known as Hotu-iti. On the strength of this, the principal tradition of social origins, the basic antagonisms were among related peoples and apparently between high and low ranks. The traditions, it must be noted, however, do not in fact describe the social issues in these major interisland rivalries. The genealogical references in several accounts of these wars place them in the eighteenth century (Metraux 1940:74).

On more recent periods the traditions and native recollections are more specific. Drawing upon these, Father Roussel, considered by Metraux to be the best source on aboriginal Easter Island culture, concluded that the power of the ariki was taken over by the warriors (*mata to'a*). Metraux quotes Roussel as follows:

> These kings who in the beginning were considered deities and had absolute power on the island, did not retain such authority for long, but only the prestige of supernatural power with certain personal privileges (1957:43). . . .

> In late times, although kings were still surrounded with respect by the natives who considered their persons to be sacred, their authority was nil and entirely disregarded. It had passed entirely into the hands of the *matatoa* who decided everything and carried on the war without beforehand consulting his majesty (1940:135).

In its last days, therefore, Easter Island had a dual status system almost identical with that in Mangaia. One aristocratic tribe, the Miru, retained rank and sanctity, while the chiefs of plebeian tribes held the actual power. But, as we shall see, the commoners' control of the strange cult of the Bird Man gave them sanctity as well. I shall reserve this discussion for a later point and will consider now the relationship of the archeological information to the oral traditions.

The Archeological Record

A radiocarbon date from what may have been a defensive ditch dug across the Poike Peninsula puts the occupancy of Easter Island at about A.D. 386 ± 100 (Heyerdahl 1961:394). This is a much earlier date than anyone had previously been prepared to believe, yet it is in fact consistent with estimates suggested by the list of 57 ariki compiled by Thomson in 1886. Allowing the usual 25 years for each generation gives a total of 1425 years, which, subtracted from 1860, places the first occupancy at A.D. 435, remarkably close to the radiocarbon date. The relationship, to be sure, may be fortuitous, yet the archeological dating checks with still another date from the traditions. A radiocarbon determination of 1680 for an apparent battleground site at Poike is almost identical with a possible date of ca. 1676 from the genealogical tradition for a major east-west war at this very site.

The Norwegian expedition did not establish a true stratigraphy, since it devoted itself almost exclusively to a study of selected monuments and surface collections of artifacts. But its study of the construction and reconstruction of the stone platforms, or ahu, does provide reasonable bases for delineating historic periods. Elsewhere in eastern Polynesia, *ahu* was the name given to the altar at one end of a ceremonial enclosure or *marae*. On Easter Island, *ahu* referred to the entire structure, which often included a central platform of massive stones and two long wings of stone, the whole structure enclosing a court. There were well over 200 ahu on Easter Island that varied greatly in size, in quality of construction, and in form as well as in function. As to function, some were altars, some were platforms upon which the statues were placed, and some were mainly burial sites.

Because of their great number, and the way in which they were distributed all along the coast where the population had been most dense, and in inland areas where it is known that native population had settled, there can be little doubt that the ahu were local ceremonial centers, constructed, that is, by local groups and maintained by them. The number of ahu, their location and their variations in size, adds important details to what is known about Easter Island social structure. Father Englert, who has made the most detailed compilation of ahu, observed three of unusual quality, one at Hangaroa on the west coast known as the ahu Tahiri, one at La Pérouse on the north coast and known as Hekii, and one on the east coast known as Tongariki. This last was the largest ahu on the island; it was 145 meters long and held 15 statues. Among these three exceptional ahu, one represented the western division and two the eastern. The location of the largest ahu among the plebeian tribes of the east underscores, as we shall see, the social upheavals that had rocked the island. Father Englert noted 12 other major ahu distributed among all "tribal" areas. Of the 15 outstanding ahu, six were located among the eastern tribes and nine among the western tribes. Since there were eight principal tribes, three in the east and five in the west, there seems to have been an approximately equal apportionment of great ahu by tribes. The apportionment could not be precise because tribes sometimes established a new ahu. All the remaining ahu were relatively small and probably belonged to tribal subdivisions. This was also the conclusion of the Norwegian expedition, which stated:

> It seems likely that each *ahu* belonged to an extended family or lineage. When a family line died out its *ahu* probably was abandoned and fell into disrepair. . . . eventually another family might rebuild an old *ahu* for its own use. In time of war an *ahu* might have been destroyed by another group and later rebuilt by the family that owned it. The rebuilding of *ahu* seems to have been the rule. (C. S. Smith in Heyerdahl 1961:183).

The fact that the ahu at a particular site underwent successive reconstructions and changes in form and function enabled the archeologists of the Heyerdahl expedition to delineate three historic periods in Easter Island; these are identified as: Early Period, 400–1100; Middle Period, 1100–1680; Late Period, 1680–1868.

The Early Period was notable for the quality of ahu construction. At Vinapu, one of the great ceremonial centers of this period, the ahu were then oriented toward the sun, implying that a solar cult may have been an early religious interest. Three ahu at Vinapu were dated by the expedition as belonging to the same period, yet one of these had been crudely constructed, while the others merited comparison in the quality of stone cutting and fitting with the monumental architecture of Andean civilizations. Evidently the three ahu, though side by side, were not part of a single complex, judging by differences in workmanship and by the fact that one of the three had been abandoned for a time and later reoccupied. There is no positive evidence that stone images were being made during this period. If they were, they were not emplaced on the ahu, which had clearly then a religious function unrelated to the use of statues.

In the Middle Period, the quality of ahu construction declined, while architectural and artistic interest shifted to the making and setting in place of the great images. The ahu had become essentially foundations upon which the statues were placed. The Expedition archeologists have described the new ahu of this period as "crude" and "structurally unsound." They lacked the symmetry of the older models and their solar orientation. The Orongo cult, whose construction center may have been in the Early Period, was fully developed at this time and was dedicated to Makemake, the patron deity of warriors. A new economic development was the expansion of cultivations up the slopes of the volcanoes with the aid of terraces.

The Late Period, which the Expedition dated with an apparent great battle at Poike between the Long-ears and the Short-ears, witnessed the decline of traditional Easter Island culture. During this period, which seems to have been one of great violence, the stone images were toppled and the ahu, reduced to mounds of rubble, became burial cairns. Abandonment of extensive quarries at Rano Raraku coincided, of course, with the end of megalithic stone carving. The Orongo center, however, persisted until the very end, according to native traditions which describe this period as one of chronic warfare.

While it would be naïve to assume that any particular artifact holds the key that will unlock the mystery of Easter Island history, there is no doubt that the stone images were a most important part of that history. Their production and emplacement defines the beginning of one era; their abandonment and overthrow, the beginning of another, the finale, so to speak.

There are some 600 images ranging in size from small 3-foot figures to one 70-foot giant that had never left the quarry. Only about 200 had been emplaced upon the ahu. The remainder had been set deep in the earth as independent figures. Most of the earth-emplaced figures—some 300—are in the eastern part of the island near the crater of Rano Raraku, the site of the most important quarry. Only minor differences in the rendering of features distinguish images of the same class, a reasonably definite sign that they were all of the same general period. All Easter Island images are legless, and all show the arms in the same manner along the sides of the body, the hands not quite meeting across the abdomen. Some had carving in front and back. All were made to wear "hats," which Metraux has shown to have been topknots. Among the images found at Tahiri, the average weight was found to be about 18 tons. The largest, the one never emplaced, weighed at least 130 tons. Easter Islanders also carved small stone figures in the same style and small wooden figurines representing emaciated men and elongated women. The wooden figures, probably ancestral images, are undoubtedly very recent, while all the stone work seems to be of the same general period.

Neither the meaning of the images nor the details of their construction or emplacement has as yet been fully explained. Native traditions reasonably attribute their manufacture to guilds of skilled carvers. There is reason to believe that the sculpting was brought close to completion at the quarry and that only such final touches as the carving of the eyes and the setting on of the topknot were carried out at the site of emplacement. Easter Islanders showed Heyerdahl how the great statues could have been stood up. In 18 days 12 men erected a quite large figure by building a mound of rubble beneath it until it could be pulled erect with ropes. What is more difficult to account for is how they were moved from the quarry to the site, sometimes a distance of ten kilometers. According to Heyerdahl's estimate it would have required up to 500 men to move one large image (1961:370). The native explanation, which is not without interest, is that the statues "walked" to their sites propelled by the mana of the ariki. It is certainly reasonable to assume that the figures were, in fact, measures of chiefly mana, and that they represented the chiefs. There is no evidence at all that they were deity figures. Cook, in fact, learned that some images carried the names of ariki, and La Pérouse took it to be fact that they portrayed chiefs. Metraux thought they were memorial figures for departed chiefs. But since images also stood on ahu which contained no burials, there can be no certainty they were associated with the dead. Metraux' information that Easter Islanders vied with one another in producing the largest images brings us back to the idea that whether they represented living or dead chiefs they were indeed specific symbols of the power of chiefs and of their lineages. Chiefs perhaps vied in terms of quantity as well, for while most ahu held an average of five images, some held many more. The ahu called Rikiriki on the southwest coast, for example, held 16, Tongariki and Akahanga in the east 15 and 13 respectively—but the great Vinapu held only 6.

We have no definite information on when the stone images were first made. Although Heyerdahl remains convinced that the Easter Islanders came from Peru or Bolivia, bringing with them developed arts of monumental stone architecture and carving, the specific archeological findings from his expedition do not support him on this. His earliest radiocarbon date from the Rano Raraku stone quarries is as recent as 1476, and his earliest dates for the emplacement of images on ahu are all after 1100, coinciding with his Middle Period. Whether stone images were carved at all during the Early Period is uncertain. Ferdon, the associate archeologist of the Expedition has summarized the evidence on statues as follows:

> The presence of statues during this Early Period is inferred on the basis of the finding of stone figures used in *ahu* constructions of the Middle Period. These are generally smaller and more naturalistic than the large, stylized figures of the Middle Period. . . . The round headed, kneeling statue at Rano Raraku is undoubtedly of this period. Its raised goatee style beard is similar to the Early Period plaza carving at Orongo as well as to certain pictographic heads from the same site. Since these latter appear to relate to the deity Makemake, it seems likely that this deity is connected with the Early Period. (Heyerdahl 1961:529).

The inference could not be stated more tentatively. Metraux impressed, as have been others, by the fresh appearance of the statues that had been carved in soft volcanic tufa, believed they were of recent origin. Their production, he observed, continued right through the middle of the nineteenth century.

The Cult of Orongo

At Orongo, a village on the southwestern tip of the island, the Easter Islanders had constructed their one great public ceremonial center. Orongo rests on a cliff overlooking the sea in the direction of the small islets Motu-iti and Motu-nui, the nesting grounds of thousands of sea birds, the sooty tern, in particular. In more recent times the center had been dedicated to the cult of the Bird Man which honored the sooty tern. In earlier times, as the Norwegian Expedition brought out, the cult center had concerned itself with quite different religious functions. The ruins of Orongo consist today of a long series of grouped stone houses with thick walls, corbeled roofs, and tunnel-like doorways facing the sea. At its narrow southern end a cluster of rooms radiate fan-like from a small natural court. The entire area is surrounded by large, natural boulders decorated in low relief or pictograph with representations of bird men and with an anthropomorphic face that probably depicts Makemake, the deity of the Bird Man cult.

The archeological study of the Orongo center proved to be most significant because it revealed evidence of a religious evolution, parallel in some degree to the social evolution suggested by the developments in ahu construction and function. Excavation brought to light a part of the ceremonial structure that dates to the Early Period and had become obscured during historic times. Since this structure seems to have had a solar equinox determination device, the archeologist who had conducted the study, E. Ferdon, considered it as historically related to the Vinapu ahu, which also showed a solar orientation. This part of the Orongo center was evidently abandoned between 1416 and 1420. The new ceremonial site that replaced it consisted of two centers of ritual activity. At one end of the site was a statue known as Hoa-haka-nana-ia, and at the other end were the representations of Bird Men and a plaza for the priests, or *rongorongo*.[1] This new area did not originally have stone buildings and was briefly abandoned between 1416 and 1540. After 1540 corbeled roof houses appeared. A later period of abandonment may have coincided with and, indeed, resulted from the aftermath of the historic Poike battle, an apparent turning point in Easter Island history in that it ended what must have been a prolonged and delicate balance of opposing military forces. Orongo was subsequently reoccupied and remained in use as a religious center until 1867 (Heyerdahl 1961:250). Native traditions claim that Orongo was simultaneously used for initiation rites and for the annual Bird Man festival, which had become the special cult of the warriors. The god of this cult was Makemake, the unique Easter Island divinity, creator of man and of the celestial bodies, and a bringer of the seabirds whose annual arrival was religously celebrated. Ferdon has inferred from the archeological evidence that Makemake must once have held the status of a more generalized deity and finally became the special patron of the so-called Bird Man cult and hence of its warrior clientele. I quote him on this point in part:

1. According to Routledge, the western half of the center was assigned to the rongo-rongo men of the western group of tribes on the island and the eastern half to those of the eastern tribes (cited by Metraux (1940:125). This division of the ceremonial center may reflect only the basic social division of the island, since there are no reports suggesting a dual division of religious functions by region.

> Whereas Makemake, as the creator and prime deity could not be reduced in status, a gradual increasing concern with the rites and powers associated with the bird cult demanded a modification. While the traditionally separate ceremonial centers of Makemake and the bird cult of presumably Haua were maintained, the old religious observances directly concerned with Makemake were reduced to groups of people assembling around the statue, Hoa-haka-nana-ia in the "house of the god," during the bird cult ceremony and the children's initiation rites. At the same time Makemake as the supreme deity became intimately linked with the beliefs and attendant ceremonial practices of the bird cult and, owing to his superior position, took over the lengendary function of having been the key figure in bringing the birds and the cult to Easter Island. With this merging and transference of ceremony and function, Makemake became completely associated with the bird cult and this cult's ritual became the prime concern of ceremonial observance (Heyerdahl 1961:253).

In the Bird Man cult, the victorious chiefs competed by proxy, so to speak, for the privilege of finding and bringing back the first egg of the sooty tern. The competition was for divine blessing and not a test of skills, so that it was not necessary for the chiefs to undertake a personal search; they sent their servants. The chief to whom this first egg was brought won the sacred title of Bird Man (*tangata manu*) and was for the entire year the incarnation of the god Makemake. As a god he was secluded, but presented by the entire island with offerings of food. Those who did not acknowledge the sanctity of the Bird Man were punished by the ruling party, who burned down their houses. Mrs. Routledge was told that the victorious party also showed its secular might by terrorizing and plundering all who could not resist them. As a result of such depredations and of the further roiling up of feelings during the sacred egg hunt, a fresh cycle of wars was initiated that ensured a new corps of contenders for the next season. The island ariki, the traditional sacred ruler, had no role in the Bird Man cult other than to signal the start of the egg hunt.

Historical Recapitulation

The Early Period appears only vaguely in the genealogical traditions and in the archeological record. Nevertheless, the specific information from both sources, meager as it is, does in fact suggest a Traditional society. Hotu-matua appears as a traditional ariki and the nature of the ahu, and in particular the quality of ahu construction, lend support to the supposition that this was a period when the religious authority of the ariki was most highly developed. The presence of a major ceremonial center at Vinapu and of scattered ahu over the entire island is also in keeping with the traditional segmentary organization of a senior ariki and lower level chiefs. The Segment I ariki probably had his center at Vinapu.

The archeology of the Middle Period depicts a more specific picture of a changing social order. The shift from a concept of ceremonial structure to one of images depicting persons does not by itself identify the specific nature of the changing order. What the shift in architectural focus does imply, however, is a break in the continuity of a particular style of authority. The unadorned ahu stand for a generalized religious authority, the images—if they are definitely not of gods—for a more personalized authority. The change in architectural interest from meticulous masonry work to a cruder construction suggests that the more personal authority lacked the stability of office of its predecessors. An apparent preoccupation with numbers of images rather than with quality of masonry is consistent with the assumption that military chiefs had begun to replace the exclusive authority of a religious ariki. The relationship may not be an absolute one, but as a rule quality is an expression of traditionalism, and mass production is the by-product of the political rivalries of the Open society. More specifically, quality architecture is an expression of highest rank, while mass defines best the interests of lower ranks. Thus Vinapu was evidently the focal point of the senior lines of the traditional ariki of the western part of the island. By contrast, the great ahu Tongariki at the eastern end of the island and the apparent stronghold of the lower-ranking lines had mass but poor masonry. This ahu, a major work of the Middle Period, and the largest on the island, held 15 images. The great variety in the number of images held by Middle Period ahu is consistent with Eastern Island traditions collected by Metraux and others to the effect that chiefs competed in placing the most images. Thus the number of images on an ahu would be generally proportional to the power of the chiefs and of their constituencies. By such standards of rivalry, Tongariki (the plebeian center with its 15 images) would seem to have surpassed aristocratic Vinapu (with only 6) as the major center of political power during the Middle Period. The extraordinary fact that a crude structure stood alongside the finest example of Easter Island masonry at Vinapu during the Early Period may perhaps be taken as evidence of lower-rank ascendance even during the most traditional period in the history of the island.

The Norwegian Expedition's reconstruction of the history of

Orongo lends additional support for the theory that the Middle Period had come to represent the Open society. This line of archeological evidence is especially persuasive because it points so definitely to a shift from a sun cult, or some other generalized cult, to a specific dedication to the Bird Man cult of the warriors. If the Middle Period instituted the Open society of warrior influence, then by all archeological and traditional sources the Late Period introduced nothing new. The overthrow of the images marks not a reconstruction but the inevitable chaos and violence of the militarized Open society. The Late Period was unquestionably, then, a period of social disintegration and of cultural decline.

Since each ahu evidently identified each of the principal political divisions on the island, we should be able to draw some further inferences about changing political conditions from ahu distributions. The total number of ahu has been put at 260. Of this number, 120 seem never to have held images and so belong to the Early Period; 80 definitely held images and are Middle Period or later; while 60 are in the form of burial cairns, and so very definitely Late Period. There may have been political consolidation over time. But considering the possibilities for overlapping in time and the decline in population that set in during the Late Period, there is no reason to assume that any drastic changes in the number of political segments had actually taken place.

If the Easter Island population never exceeded the most common estimate of 4,000 persons, then the average size of the political group appears to have been quite small. Assuming that the Early and Middle Periods averaged 100 ahu, the average political segment would have numbered 40 people. This figure, while feasible, is low and implies a much larger earlier population, perhaps the 7,000 estimated by Routledge from a calculation of the carrying capacity of Easter Island soils. Whether population was 4,000 or 7,000, the general conclusion remains the same: the political unit represented by an ahu was undoubtedly Segment III. The major ahu, such as Vinapu and Tongariki, would have represented, therefore, Segments I or II, more likely the latter. Orongo most likely was, considering its island-wide significance, a Segment I center. The persistence of Segment III as an ahu-building and therefore corporate body bears out the traditional genealogical records on Easter Island political separatism, a major characteristic of the Open society.

If the relative proportion of the social and political segments remained essentially unchanged, there is ample evidence pointing to very important changes in other areas of social and economic life.

The traditions describe a community of specialized artists and craftsmen who occupied the site of the main stone quarries of Rano Raraku. Such specialist communities—possibly guilds—were in Polynesia a distinctive characteristic of Open and Stratified societies. They do not appear in any of the Traditional societies. Thus the simultaneous appearance in Easter Island of "guilds" or communities of specialized carvers fits all expectations of a developing Open society.

The transportation of the great statues from the quarries over considerable distances, then, and their emplacement raises questions of technical and political means. The Norwegian Archaelogical Expedition estimated that an average statue required as many as 500 men to move and set it in place. Certainly no Segment III could erect an image on its ahu unassisted. Neither, for that matter, could a Segment II, which was some ten times the size of Segment III and numbered no more than 700 men, women, and children.

There are two ways by which the labor force capable of moving and installing the statues could have been assembled. One, is under the direction of a Segment I or II ariki. In the large Stratified societies such as Tonga, Tahiti, and Hawaii, central authorities did assemble labor for great public works and monuments. There is no reason to believe, however, that a central authority ever undertook the construction of local monuments. Since all but the few major ahu were local, they must be assumed to have been constructed under local auspices. Everywhere else in Polynesia local maraes were always the product of local labor. Polynesia offers examples of islandwide cooperation in economic activities of mutual benefit—in the construction, that is, of taro beds, fish ponds, and irrigation ditches—but none for the construction of local ceremonial centers. Easter Island could hardly have been the exception to this rule, in view of the evidently rivalrous nature of the image ahus.

Thus we must turn to an alternative explanation for the construction of image ahu; that is, the use of force or captive labor. In the Middle Period, wars were common. We know from Late Period accounts that the conquered peoples (*kio*) were drawn into the tribe and put to hard labor. Presumably this system prevailed during the Middle Period also. In any event, it would have provided the appropriate labor supply. It would also account for rivalry in image placing, and would give substance to the Easter Island belief that the statues were moved to their site by the mana of the chief. Specifically, we may assume that the chief of a victorious military coalition allotted kio among his allies to post a monument, probably a victory memorial. Each statue would therefore be a sign of military victory and in that very specific sense it could be said to have moved to the site by the mana of the chief. Whatever information we have about the image ahu is consistent with this theory of their military nature. They were erected in the spirit of status rivalry and they were toppled when the local chiefs were defeated in war or otherwise lost their mana.

We have not yet accounted for the 300 large image statues located near Rano Raraku and emplaced in the earth rather than on the ahus. Two opposing theories have been offered. Günther (Metraux 1957: 161) considered them as very late, coming after it was no longer feasible or fashionable to place them on ahu. Lavachery (1935), the distinguished French archeologist, thought rather they were experimental productions that preceded the ahu period. There is really no precedent for such extensive experimentation with megalithic carving. It would seem more likely that the earth-emplaced statues, which differed only slightly from those on ahu, served a similar purpose, that is, as memorials to distinguished persons. If the ahu images honored lineage heads, then may we not infer that the giant figures set along the slopes of Rano Raraku in the commoner area of the island were in honor of other persons of merit who had not, however, won actual leadership? Such persons would be craftsmen, priests, and warriors. The great number of statues in this category is consistent with the general impression of great status mobility during the Middle and Late Periods.

The history of the Orongo cult center implies in parallel fashion the concept of symbolic rivalry as an exact parallel to actual political rivalry. In the Orongo cult of the Bird Man, the warrior chiefs acquired the sanctity of impersonating the creator deity; in the cult of image ahu, they evidently acquired another form of sanctity in terms of the mana of military victory that was memorialized in the sacred precincts of an ahu. Through both cults the local chieftains had assimilated the ariki standards of sacred status. By the Late Period, however, the burden of war had begun to reduce the sanctity of the local chiefs. Yet, while their mana, in the form of images, was "overthrown," they still had the privileges of sanctity offered by Orongo. But only one chief impersonated Makemake at one time. In this respect, therefore, the Open society had succeeded in shaping itself to the more centralized standards of the traditional ariki. As a Bird Man, however, the dominant warrior was not quite the image of a political authority. Religious centralism clearly did not imply political centralism, judging only by the short duration of periods of peace.

The Status System

Easter Island, like Mangaia, had a dual status system: one, traditional, organized around sacred ariki and their descent lines; the other, highly mobile and representing warrior chiefs and their separate descent lines. The relationship of these two systems was both complementary and antagonistic, depending upon the point in time from which they are being considered. At some point in history, perhaps early in the Middle Period, the ariki were the central religious authority, while the warrior chiefs, the *matatoa,* had become the secular rulers. This complementary division of authority seems never to have stabilized itself, however. Once the division was formed, the authority of the ariki was assailed by the matatoa and progressively constricted to its purely religious functions. At the same time, the matatoa added powerful religious prerogatives comparable to those held by the ariki. Thus in a formal as well as in a very real sense the antagonism between ariki and matatoa had finally shifted the balance of powers. The ariki who had at one time held the general authority, retained to the very end their sanctity and the prestige of genealogical rank; the matatoa, who had begun with a secular authority and had gained sanctity, remained, nevertheless, in a lower status category outside the realm of authentic pedigree.

Primogeniture

Our information on chiefly succession is general and not drawn from detailed genealogical lists. The general traditions, however, affirm primogeniture and imply senior descent lines for the Miru, the one tribe that remained to the very end the source of Easter Island aristocracy. Since all other tribes were headed by warrior chiefs whose position depended upon military victory, consistent primogeniture and seniority of descent lines was evidently limited to the Miru. According to the Hotu-matua traditions, the Miru were actually descendants of the second-born son of the founder. But this seems to have been a singular historical event rather than a significant breach of the principle, which remained in force among the Miru until well into the nineteenth century. The Hotu-matua tradition carries the only reference to ranked descent lines. If all the main tribes were indeed once genealogically ranked, they finally lost their connections to the main descent line. The break in pedigree may have resulted from wars that elsewhere in Polynesia disrupted traditional affiliations. Or, as is even more likely, the serious depopulation of the island simply erased all accurate genealogical information once and for all, leaving all other tribes in the lowly status of total genealogical separation from the traditional rulers.

Male Line

All chiefly descent among the Miru was from father to first-born son, implying a consistent patrilineal pattern among the single aristocratic tribe. In a variation of the Marquesan custom, the son succeeded his father upon his marriage. But marriage came late, so that the Easter Island ruler had a longer tenure than his Marquesan counterpart. Descent and affiliation were patrilineal generally, but among the remaining tribes the mother's side could enlist a man's loyalty in time of war (Routledge 1919:226). And, as Routledge was informed, when a man had sons by more than one wife, each claimed his corpse after death for the ahu of the mother's side; finally, however, the corpse returned to the rightful place with the male line. The patrilineal preference may account for the belief reported by Metraux (1940:124) that women of the Miru were once forbidden to marry commoners of other tribes. On the other hand, the daughter of Ngaara, one of the last of the Miru ariki, did marry into a commoner tribe. This marriage coming in the Late Period, however, may have represented a lapse of the patrilineal tradition. "It is certain," Metraux remarked, "that the king [Miru] had to marry in his own tribe, though not in his own lineage. Other men of the Miru could marry into any descent line (1940:124)."

Genealogical Depth

The lapse of genealogical records for all but the Miru may, as I have suggested, be reasonably attributed to population decline. Yet such a lapse is consistent with Late Period social organization, when all but this one tribe were plebeian. If the Miru retained a list of more than 30 generations of hereditary ariki in the face of one social catastrophe after another, there is good reason to credit Easter Island aristocracy with the traditional attachment to genealogical depth. Thomson's list of Easter Island ariki offers 57 generations, but is disputed by Metraux as inaccurate. Nevertheless, a 57-generation pedigree calculated at an average of 25 years is so close to the radiocarbon date of earliest occupancy as to invite belief in it. All other tribes had some claim to genealogical depth, but only through the general tradition of common descent from the founding ariki.

Sanctity

Two forms of personal sanctity had evolved on Easter Island, a traditional and permanent sanctity of the *ariki mau* and of his Miru tribesmen, and a special and temporary sanctity of the Bird Man. Both forms were equivalent, insofar as they involved increased powers over nature and associated their holders with divinity. In religious essence they differed fundamentally: the ariki mau was the possessor of mana transmitted down the genealogical line from Tangaroa and Rongo, the ancestral gods; the Bird Man had the lesser sanctity as impersonator of the god Makemake. The traditional mana was part of the "chain of being," the source of highest honor. The special powers of the Bird Man, while impressive during the period of their tenure, suffered from the limitation of having been bestowed only upon a person and not upon a descent line. Aristocracies value the genealogical prerogatives more than they do the personal. In this most discriminating manner, aristocrat and commoner were in part equated but never really made equivalent. The duality of the status system was partially bridged but never overcome.

As lineal descendant of the great gods, the ariki mau was as sacred as any Polynesian ariki. His great personal sanctity persisted well into the European period, when well-intentioned missionaries sought to cut the hair of the last and very youthful spiritual ruler and offended and frightened the child. Ordinarily, no one dared touch any part of the ariki mau's body. His head was particularly sacred and his hair was never cut. To violate the ruler's tapu was to risk supernaturally caused death. The royal tapu extended to all his possessions. No one was allowed to see either the ariki mau or his son as they ate or slept, and none but other ariki could enter the royal hut. The contagiousness of the royal sanctity confined the ariki's activities to fishing and to making fish line and nets. Metraux has, in fact, suggested that a legend describing an ancient ruler as being carried in a litter may refer to the fear that the royal presence would contaminate the ground on which he stepped (1940:131). Such an extreme tapu was definitely applied only in the case of the highest Tahitian rulers.

The ariki mau controlled the growth of crops and the abundance of edible marine life directly through his mana. In a chant collected by Metraux, the ruler is described as responsible in a fully god-like manner for the favorable presence and growth of everything of value, including foods, "the stars, the sky, the heat, the sun, the moon—worms, earwigs, beetles—the chiefs, the chiefesses (1940:134)." He dealt with drought by sending his son or another lower-ranking *ariki* to perform rain-making rites. He inaugurated all new houses and all new canoes. He supervised the priestly reading of the tablets and judged the quality of tattooing. Finally, he initiated the harvest of all crops and received first fruits. Routledge was told that all Miru tribesmen shared in the royal sanctity. Because all had the power to make hens lay eggs, they were known as "fowlheads." They were even more potent after death and their skulls incised with fish designs were transmitted as family heirlooms (Routledge 1919:240). It is not clear, however, whether all or only priestly Miru skulls were incised and venerated. In all likelihood it was the latter, since a lower category of ariki, the *papa-ariki,* and a specialist caste of rongorongo or chanters were, along with the ariki mau, the priests of the Miru and, accordingly, of the island as a whole.

The sanctity of the Miru was special in its association with increase powers. According to Metraux it would appear that able persons had general sanctity. The heads of all children were sacred and subject to the touching tapu until they were married. When children were tattooed on the legs at the age of eight or ten, a maternal uncle gave them gifts of fowl called "fowls for the legs" which became tapu for ordinary eating within the family and were reserved for ritual distributions among kinsmen. Any ritual association with fowl was a mark of sanctity. Thus when children were submitted to seclusion rites at ages 13–15, they became known as Bird Children (Metraux 1940: 105). If our information on general sanctity is authentic (understandably a somewhat doubtful assumption because of its vagueness), it points to the most widespread generalized personal sanctity in all Polynesia, an all-inclusive sanctity that applied to all men, women, and children. The prominence of vulva motifs at Orongo adds to the impression that women were included among sacred persons.

Tohunga

Craftsmen and experts—in recent times called *maori* but currently *tohunga*—were accorded the highest respects (Metraux 1940:177). The stone carvers, who had been organized in a "guild" in which membership went from father to son, had a prestige comparable to that of royalty. Under the category of maori, Easter Islanders also included genealogists, wood cutters, and fishermen. Whether these crafts were actually ranked is not known, but there seems little doubt that the image carvers and the genealogists, or *tangata rongorongo,* were the most esteemed. According to one reputable source (Thomson 1891:514), the rongorongo, who controlled knowledge of genealogies and of the tablet scripts, were all members of distinguished families, either royalty, district chiefs, or sons of chiefs and priests and leaders of sacred lore. Metraux, however, states that other sources describe rongorongo as very numerous, and thus not necessarily of the nobility (1940:137).

Priests were not in the same category with other specialists. They were *ivi-atua,* or kinsmen of the gods and, according to Metraux, held a rank just below that of ariki. Easter Island traditions commonly identify the priests performing the most important ceremonies as papa-ariki, that is, as members of the family of the ariki mau. The high priests then would definitely be of the royal lineages. Metraux, noting that missionary reports do not mention ivi-atua, infers that they had lost their power and position long before 1864, the date of the first mission (1940:136). Conceivably, the ivi-atua, if of royalty, might have been eclipsed by the Orongo cult of Makemake, no longer under active royal patronage. Regrettably, however, early accounts of this cult, which persisted well into the nineteenth century, do not conclusively identify the class of priests who officiated at Orongo. Routledge describes *"ivi-atua"* as seers, but offers no specific comment on their rank or prestige; however, she identifies one *"ivi-atua"* as a "poor relation" of an incumbent Bird Man, and thus hardly a person of consequence (1919:264).

Toa

Matatoa, or distinguished warriors, were set apart from ordinary warriors (*paoa*—"club") as the war leaders whose presence on the field of battle assured victory. Metraux considered them as being virtually professional warriors who did no other work (1940:138). By all accounts the matatoa were also the heads of tribes and, if only temporarily as a result of a major victory, rulers of the entire island. Roussel noted that the matatoa had won the privilege of receiving the tuna offering formerly reserved for the ariki mau (cited by Metraux 1940:138). As the Bird Men, they acquired for the period of their incumbency a social status parallel and in many respects equivalent to that of the ariki mau, including rights to first fruits. An achieved status, the office was open to all contenders.

Wealth

The main privileges of status were political and religious powers. Wealth, nevertheless, conferred its own prestige when it was properly distributed. Men who financed feasts won the honorific appelation of *tangata honi,* or "great generous man." Warriors quarrelled at public feasts demanding large contributions from their followers, on the one hand, and the privilege of receiving the largest share, on the other (Metraux 1940:343). There were at least three major types of property distributions (foodstuffs, particularly fowl): the *paina,* a memorial feast for a deceased relative; the *koro,* an honoring feast for living relatives, namely, father, mother, father-in-law, mother-in-law; and the *areauti,* a display-of-wealth feast. The paina, financed by a group of close kin, assembled a great many guests; the koro involved a more limited distribution of several hundred fowl among close kin; the *areauti* was given to the public. As in New Zealand, the food at all these feasts was displayed on conical towers (Metraux 1940:343).

The paina feast and ritual is particularly interesting because of what it reveals about the function of the ahu, at least in later Easter Island history. The ceremony of honoring was held at the ahu under the direction of a priest (ivi-atua), and called for a placing on the altar of a great human image made of rods and reeds covered with barkcloth. The host, usually the son of the deceased, entered the hollow image carrying a chicken in his hand and then spoke to the assemblage through the mouth of the image (Metraux 1940:345). The parallel between paina images and stone images placed permanently on the ahu suggests a common religious significance. The antiquity of the paina image ceremony is not known, but it definitely continued long after the stone images had been overthrown. Conceivably this ceremony carried forward in a new form the older ritual of emplacing stone images.

Information on wealth and its role in status is sketchy. Such as it is, it suggests that on Easter Island the main role of economic redistribution or recirculation lay not with the ariki mau, but with heads of commoner groups. When the ariki mau received the tuna catch that was his ritual tithe, he distributed it only among the "important old men" (Metraux 1940:132). Warrior chiefs, by contrast, gave to great public gatherings. Thus it was the warriors, the commoners who had achieved high military status or who had acquired wealth, who held the honorific role as centers of economic redistribution. On the basis of scanty information, the traditional aura of abundance normally associated with Polynesian chiefs was set out only in the quality of his residence site and not in material abundance. But if the ariki mau did not present himself as a symbol of wealth, confined as he was to a rather narrow religious role, his royal kinsmen among the Miru did have a prominent role in traditional distributions. There is no reason to believe, however, that their economic role was a commanding one.

Political Hegemony

The nature of the political authority of the traditional ariki mau has never been clearly defined. Thomson said that the king was undisturbed by the results of wars and had the authority to remove or put to death any district chief and then to name a successor (1891:472). But this view of the royal power is flatly contradicted by the very able Roussel, who said that the royal authority had become "nil" (cf. quote in Metraux 1940:134). From our knowledge of traditional authority in Polynesia, the ariki mau was probably never a powerful secular ruler, but he may have been the titular holder of lands and the central figure in ritual and property distribution. These functions, along with the authority to prevent or declare wars, may have been stripped from him. The political evolution of Easter Island is perhaps best described not as a transfer of powers from ariki to warrior but rather as a growth in political power resulting from the emergence of the matatoa as an independent force. There is certainly no suggestion from any source that the ariki mau ever presided over conquered populations. Roussel, however, obtained detailed accounts of the treatment of kio, defined by Metraux as "serfs" (1940:139). The conquered peoples either remained on their own lands and paid tribute to their overlords, or were kept in caves as a slave population and put to work on the lands of their masters. When they were released after some time, they were still subject to demands for tribute. Rather than produce for a conqueror, they planted only a portion of what they needed for their own sustenance. Roussel may have overstated the plight of the kio, but—as Metraux has observed—the Easter Island traditions describe their misery just as graphically.

These accounts of treatment of conquered peoples, together with the information from the Makemake cult, presents a portrait of predatory political powers during the Easter Island Middle and Late periods. Routledge has told how the followers of the Bird Man of the year terrorized those who were reluctant to pay their tribute, and Metraux narrates a legend with a similar theme. A party of men claiming to be Makemake went about the island and demanded from the terrified people food, chickens, wooden images, and other goods. The deception was finally uncovered, but most of the imposters escaped. There seems little reason to doubt that political overlordship had become largely predatory and had lost whatever constructive and organizing functions it had once had, even if we were to judge such a conclusion from the solitary evidence of the near total overthrow in war of all the ahu images.

The Structure of Status

Graded rank may have existed in the Early Period in the time of Hotu-matua. But if ranks were graded at all in later times, the practice was almost certainly confined to the Miru. Yet all we really know about the Miru is that the ariki-mau was the senior head, probably of the senior lineage, and that all other Miru lineage heads were papa-ariki, or nobility. All other people on the island were *huramana,* or commoners. The demarcation between ariki and huramana may once have been a matter of gradation, but it finally became categorical. These were the two genealogical ranks. Easter Island lacked the transitional rank of rangatira. This position, which in Traditional societies was ordinarily held by segment heads below the rank of ariki, was on Easter held by rankless matatoa. From the point of view of the ariki, status consisted only of traditional ranks. The ariki had the highest priestly privileges. From the point of view of the matatoa, however, status appeared in the harsher light of political dominance and subordination of master and of mastered. Among the masters, status was graded by accomplishments, by military achievement, and by reputation for economic capability. The kio do not quite comprise a landless class because their captivity was only temporary. Traditional land rights were never abrogated and so no economic stratification developed.

From the point of view of traditional rank, the distribution of status was pyramidal in form. High rank was narrowly restricted and the great bulk of the population were commoners. From the point of view of achieved statuses, however, no stable order was ever formed. All depended on the fortunes of war, and, in the special case of the Bird Man, on divine grace.

Status Rivalry

The versions of Easter Island history that have been so sketchily pieced together imply a pattern of very active status rivalry outside the realm of genealogical rank. The achieved statuses, so to speak, commanded the political arena and fought one another for power and influence, seeking to emulate the ariki but never to overcome them. The effect upon the social system of this circumscribed status rivalry was essentially the same as it was in Mangaia, namely, the establishment of a dual status system within which the role of the ariki became specialized and restricted. As in Mangaia, the initial impetus for status rivalry came from the dual division of tribes within the framework of the traditional order.

Descent Group Organization

For an account of early descent group organization, we have only the uncertain evidence of the Hotu-matua legend to go by. For all its ambiguities, this tradition does imply an initial segmentary order. We have of course, no absolute assurance that the six districts dividing the island in historic times had their origin in the original six lineages descended from Hotu-matua. Except for a few, including the royal Miru, who do connect genealogically with the great founder, all other pedigrees have been lost. In the historic period the Miru alone had aristocratic standing, and all others were plebeian. Thus, between the implied early social order, indicative of the Traditional society, and the later organization into districts, whose descent lines were evidently discontinuous, there is a gap to be accounted for. The genealogical situation of the Miru and the history of internecine wars suggests a progressive reorganization of the traditional lineages, or *mata*. This is the conclusion to which Metraux, an especially cautious historian, finally came. Discussing the history of the mata (which he had translated as "tribe"), he writes:

> At one time every tribe had its own territory, which was known by the name of the group. Later the tribes became more scattered and isolated members or entire households of one tribe lived within the limits of another district; in some regions along the coast representatives of more than three groups were mixed. The old territorial divisions thus came to be mere districts where the main part of the *mata,* perhaps the senior line, was settled and had little to do with the actual distribution of the tribes (1940:20).

Metraux' interpretation of events brings Easter Island history within the Mangaian pattern. Descent lines are dispersed by war and other conditions, and their cores become the centers of a territorial organization. In Mangaia, differentiation took its start from conflict and cleavage between autochthonous and immigrant groups; in Easter Island, the basic antagonisms were interior. The results, though, were similar, even to the genealogical isolation of a royal lineage.

Segmentation

The entire island was a social unit that corresponded quite closely to the Maori waka, even to the point of ambiguity as to its kin unity. The Maori waka, it will be recalled, were either of the same kin or held to a tradition of common kinship. Such a tradition of kin unity existed on Easter Island as well, along with the opposing tradition of a strong division between eastern and western tribes. The supreme ariki, the ariki mau on Easter Island, had a fluctuating position. At one time, it seems, he was actually a powerful ruler, while in more recent times he had begun to resemble more the chief of the Maori waka in having the honor of supreme seniority and the rather limited prerogatives of regulating ritual. At times, too, the entire island was ruled by a matatoa, in which case it must have resembled Mangaia under its Temporal Lord. The entire island as a social entity may be considered as Segment I. There is no native term for this grouping (just as there was no definite native term for the island as a whole).

The most striking feature of Segment I was its unstable political character. Mangaia had already established a principle of full political and religious unity, but Easter Island was committed only to the principle of religious unity, political ties remaining tenuous. The political tradition was separatist. It is surely significant, therefore, that victorious warrior chiefs established their preeminence through religion—that is, through the Bird Man cult—the mode of the ariki, rather than through sheer political power. Since, under all circumstances, the entire island acknowledged some genealogical unity as well as a common ariki, common culture, and a common religion, we must regard Segment I as the tribe.

Segment II consisted of the ten or so mata that Metraux has translated as "tribe." But in this instance Metraux has been following the standard of Polynesianists who have tended to identify as "tribe" that social grouping with the strongest marks of unity. Mrs. Routledge, bearing in mind the unity of the island under the ariki mau, identified the mata as "clans"—that is, as tribal subdivisions; "clan," however, has too specific a meaning to be appropriate for the Easter Island Segment II. The mata had no constant social composition. According to the theory of the genealogical traditions, the mata were major lineages that had branched off from the original ariki mau. The Miru, although descendants of the second-born, became the royal lineage; all the other lineages became plebeian or huramana. As Metraux, whom I have already cited on this point, has observed, wars broke up the genealogical unity of each mata, scattering their members among those who were the strongest. Therefore, each mata must have consisted of a core of kin who had a long historical continuity with the original lineage, and a group of other people who could not actually establish genealogical links with the core group. One cannot say they were not kin at all, since theoretically all on the island were "kin." The important point is that each mata consisted of persons who were markedly different in their status as members.

The internal composition of the Miru was evidently very different from that of the other mata. The Miru were basically a traditional status lineage, with its preference for patrilineal descent and in its allocation of rank, title, and office along the lines of seniority. Members of other mata were evidently incorporated among the Miru as kio and probably as lesser forms of subordinates. The Miru had their senior lineage which gave to the mata, as a whole, its ariki mau and junior lineages, each of which was headed by an ariki papa. The plebeian mata, insofar as we know, maintained no genealogies and had no regular forms of genealogical rank. Each was headed by a warrior chief who had assumed command because of his military successes rather than by genealogical succession.

At the level of Segment II, Easter Island presents a divided social structure, one mata conforming approximately to the traditional type, the others having a distinctive structure. This division in social structure was one of the striking developments in Polynesian social evolution and we shall see more examples of it in the Stratified societies. The term *mata* is significant in this connection because it had a broad connotation in eastern Polynesia. It was generally combined with the word *kainga,* or *kainanga,* to mean simply "the people," or "district," and in some instances "commoner." The Maori term *ivi* ("bone"), which has the more specific connotation of lineage, was used in Easter Island to refer to descendants of a common ancestor. This distinction between ivi and mata in itself suggests the changes that have taken place in Segment II. Metraux has identified the ivi as "lineages" or subdivisions of the mata.

The mata were originally the principal land-holding groups, but, as Metraux has brought out, they had eventually become fragments of a territorial organization. The political and economic function of the mata, therefore, was to serve as the traditional nucleus of the newly emerged territorial organization. Even the Miru, the most traditional of the mata, were widely scattered among other mata. Other mata, such as the Ngatimo, had a clearly defined area of their own, but this area had the disadvantage of poor fishing. Still another group of mata did not even have a claim to a traditional area. These were the eastern mata.

The mata were not graded in rank as were the Maori ivi, except for the presence of the one high-ranking Miru. They differed in status, though, depending upon their wealth and their military successes. A number of mata may have been branches of larger mata, but we have no details on how these branches developed nor on how they maintained links with one another.

Segment III consisted of subdivisions of the mata which Metraux has called "lineages." He has also translated ivi as "lineage," but his information is not clear as to whether the specific groups he has identified as "lineages" were actually referred to by the Easter Islanders as ivi. It may be that we have no native term for Segment III. Again, it was the Miru who had a traditional organization that included thirteen descent lines ("lineages"), ranked apparently according to seniority of descent. One of these, the Honga, was the senior line and always produced the ariki mau. Ideally, each subdivision of a mata had its own territory and probably, as most authorities believe, each had its own ahu. While there is some information on the subdivisions of the Miru, there is none at all on those of the other mata. We must assume, however, that all or most of the mata were subdivided to account for the distribution of the many small ahu.

Segment IV refers to the households for which Metraux has given the term *ivi,* again in its connotation of an extended family. There is no information on its early form. The existence of large canoe-shaped houses of rush built over a stone foundation does suggest that the household was an extended family. Judging by the strength of paternal authority at the time of first contact, the houses were probably patrilineal and largely patrilocal. The extended family was the unit that worked the cultivated plots in common.

7

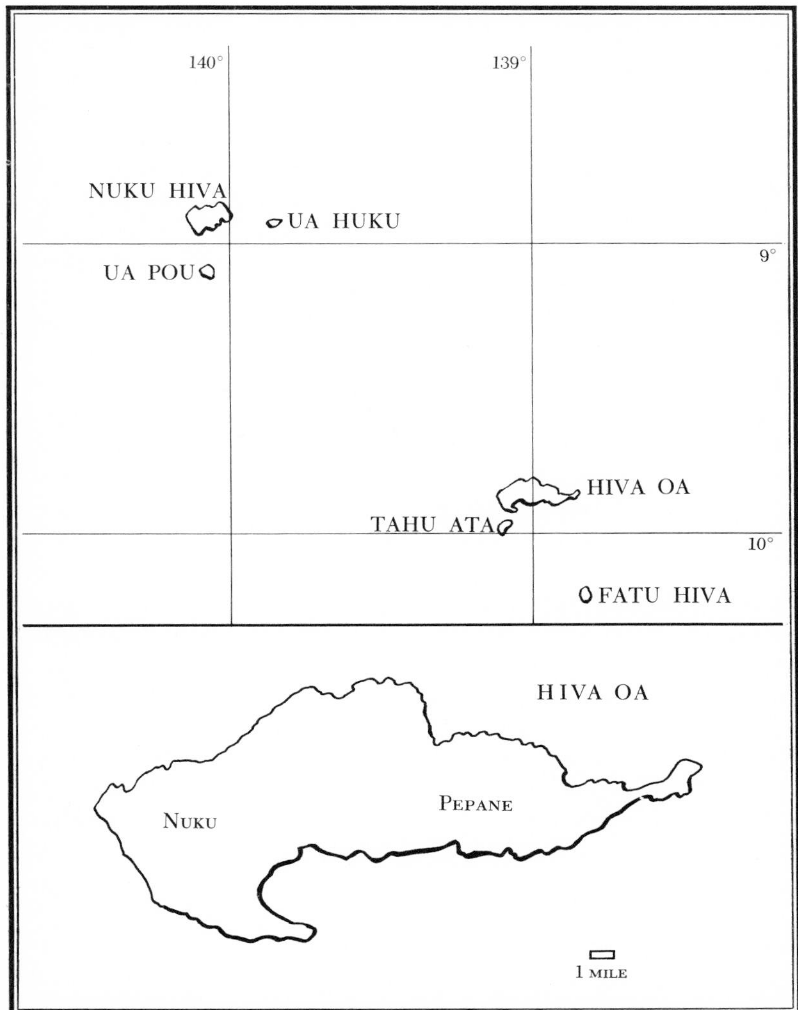

The Marquesas

PERHAPS THE FIRST OF THE EASTERN POLYNESIAN ISLANDS TO HAVE been settled, the Marquesas are also the most fully evolved example of an Open society. Mangaia and Easter Island in the process of becoming "open" had split the chiefly authority, giving to the ariki command over religion, and to the ascendant warriors jurisdiction over lands and people. The religious-secular division was most complete in Mangaia and less so in Easter, where warrior chiefs had succeeded in acquiring a special religious role through the Bird Man cult. In the Marquesas, however, all chiefly authority, whether descending from an illustrious ancestral line or achieved by force or political skill, was of the same character in combining religious and secular roles. Thus, if Mangaia and Easter represent two phases of "dual" status, the Marquesas differ in having evolved an open status system that was unitary. Marquesan chiefs did not lack sanctity; the distinction between sacred and secular chiefs was simply not made. If Mangaia stands as an example of emergent dualism, and Easter is an example of dualism in process of being overcome, we may then consider the Marquesas as an example of synthesis, of equalization of genealogical and achieved status. From a structural point of view, such a synthesis seems to be in accord with the eastern Polynesian systems of status and their patterns of status rivalry. Whether such a synthesis had in fact taken place in the Marquesas is a more doubtful matter, yet there is some specific historical evidence pointing to general parallels with Mangaia and Easter and suggesting that the unitary status system of the Marquesas may indeed have evolved from a dual system. In this respect the Marquesas may be said to represent the Open society in its most mature form. The Marquesas also brought forth ephemeral forms of Stratified society, but for the most part Marquesan chiefs fought one another to a bloody stalemate.

The ten Marquesan islands (of which only six were regularly inhabited), with their combined land area of some 500 square miles, are among the largest in Polynesia, and their pre-European populations —variously estimated at between 50,000 to 100,000—established them as one of the major centers of Polynesian civilization. The two main islands, Nuku Hiva and Hiva Oa, average over 100 square miles each, and even the smaller islands range in area from 20 to 40 square miles. These islands, though, were not among the attractive habitats in the Pacific, at least from the single standpoint of subsistence. Melville's Taipi valley on Nuku Hiva was very fertile, as were other valleys, but the total aspect of the Marquesas moved Linton to say: "From the point of view of the primitive settler the Marquesas could hardly be considered desirable country (1923:265)." In arriving at such a gloomy estimation, Linton undoubtedly had in mind the rugged topography, the densely wooded, razor-backed mountains that carved each island into pockets of near isolated valleys, the unreliable rainfall, the scorching droughts, the cramped beaches and coastal plains, and, finally, the absence of a circling reef, this compelling the Marquesans to do their fishing in the treacherous open sea.

Breadfruit was the main crop, and was generally abundant, since it yielded four harvests a year and could be grown even on mountain slopes. The fermented breadfruit mash (*poipoi*) stored well in leaf-lined pits and provided a reserve when drought reduced the crop. Along with breadfruit, the Marquesans grew taro, for which they had prepared stone-walled terraces, and coconuts, bananas, and sugar cane. To compensate for an uncertain supply of fish, they had pigs and fowl, which had been brought to the islands by the first settlers. The economic picture of the Marquesas was thus not so much one of austerity as it was of uncertainty, and of extremes of uneven distribution of natural resources, of good crop years and famines, of fertile valleys and near-desert, of rich and strong, and of poor and weak tribes. In the particular Marquesan setting, inequality encouraged wars of conquest, but geography favored the weaker defenders, placing truly formidable obstacles in the way of the aggressors and their hopes for political unification.

The Marquesas were early one of the major centers of stone work in Polynesia, but not for monumental architecture. The local talent turned toward the cruder and smaller constructions, to the erection of walls, house and ceremonial platforms, and terrace facings. Stone was cut and fitted, but not with the refinement that distinguished the monuments of Tonga, Hawaii, or Easter Island. Marquesan walls combined cut with untrimmed boulders to create durable but crude structures. Marquesan artistic talent ignored architecture and favored image-carving in stone and wood and the ornamentation of the body and of useful implements and utensils. Stone image-carving executed in deep relief approached monumental proportions (some of the large deity images were about 8 feet in height) and was undoubtedly the work of experts. Wood carving and tattooing were very highly developed.

The islands fall into a northern and a southern grouping whose populations differed from one another only in minor physical and cultural respects. Handy, taking account of these differences, has seen them as local variations upon a basically common stock and culture (1923:22). Linton, on the other hand, came to believe that two different migrant groups had brought to the islands two distinctive traditions. An eastern Polynesian population of the Maori type, he reasoned, settled in Hiva Oa, Tahu Atu, and Fatu Hiva of the southern group, and an older western Polynesian people had established itself much earlier on the northern islands of Nuku Hiva, Ua Pou, and Ua Haka (1923:265).

That Marquesan culture combines features of both eastern and western Polynesia is a fact beyond dispute. The Marquesan language, for example, is closest to Tikopian, a derivative of Samoan-Tongan, while other traits, as Linton has shown, indicate a close relationship with Maori. For that matter, all Polynesian societies combine both cultural traditions. Are we always to explain this constant combination by the standard assumption of two streams of migration meeting on one island? Suggs' archeological studies on Nuku Hiva suggest rather that the Marquesas were settled from Melanesia and western Polynesia as early as 150 B.C. and then underwent an internal evolution without any marked disturbance from foreign sources. The evidence from continuity in the forms of artifacts certainly does not support theories of dual migrations, although, as Suggs has observed, it does not exclude the probability of sporadic contacts with other parts of Polynesia that might have modified specific cultural details. Thus the very close parallels between Marquesan and Maori cultures that Linton had brought out may be attributed partly to diffusions from eastern Polynesia and in the main to parallel developments. The great importance of Suggs' findings for Polynesian culture history is precisely its support for the theory that the eastern Polynesian cultural tradition was in large part a development upon an archaic Melanesian-western Polynesian base. In terms of this theory, Marquesan culture is not an example of fusion of two traditions, but an example rather of transition from one to the other. If Marquesan culture is transitional, its "open" status system cannot be considered to be a direct transformation of, let us say, the Maori Traditional, but rather as an example of a variant of a more general traditional form.

Our knowledge of traditional Marquesan culture is based largely upon the field work of Handy, who was the ethnologist of the Bayard Dominick Expedition in 1920–21. By that time, however, there was little left to observe of aboriginal Marquesan life. With annexation by France in 1842, native culture entered its final days, and by 1920 disease and despair had reduced the population to a mere 1,800 miserable souls. Handy's field work became merely a matter of salvaging information from the memories of the older inhabitants. Among those who saw native life in its prime and wrote about it, there is, of course, Herman Melville, whose unforgettable account of life in Taipi valley of Nuku Hiva in 1842. A more systematic description of Marquesan society comes from the astute pen of Father Mathias Gracia (1943), a clear-headed French missionary who came to the Marquesas in 1858. An earlier and informative narrative is the journal of Captain David Porter of the U.S. Navy, who took gratuitous part in native wars in 1813, and tried unsuccessfully to annex the islands to the United States. Briefer glimpses of the islands go back to Mendaña, the discoverer in 1595 and, among others, to Captain James Cook in 1772. On the whole, therefore, Marquesan culture is moderately well known. Our knowledge of its history has been deeply extended by the archeological work of Robert C. Suggs of the American Museum of Natural History in 1956–57, and, as in the case of Easter Island, we can attempt to reconstruct phases of Marquesan history both from the genealogical traditions and from the archeological record.

Genealogical Traditions

The people regarded themselves as descended from a common deified ancestor called Atea who is said to have come from Tonga. The longest genealogical record cited by Handy places the arrival of Atea some 90 generations back or, by conventional reckoning of 25 years per generation, to about 300 B.C. Shorter genealogies based entirely on chiefly names that are still extant go back to A.D. 950 or 1100. For obvious reasons, long genealogies are unreliable. Yet the long genealogy, which Handy understandably mistrusted, is not far from the dates yielded by radiocarbon analysis, and it accords with specific material evidence of the western Polynesian provenience of the earliest Marquesans.

Like those of Easter Island, the extant traditions are chronicles of war, and of the movements of displaced peoples from valley to valley and from island to island. One tradition cited by Handy (1923:25) has a precise parallel with those of Easter Island in its account of the formation on each of the major islands of a western and eastern political division. Here, as on Easter Island, the western division went to a senior brother and the eastern to his junior. These divisions became bitter enemies and fought many wars against one another. In the seventeenth century, by the genealogical records, a great war was fought on Hiva Oa, the largest island of the southern group, between the Nuku, or western division, and the Pepane, or eastern division, in which the easterners were wiped out. On Ua Pou a chief of the eastern division of the island defeated a western coalition in 1860 and assumed authority over the entire island (Handy 1923:30). This solitary example of political centralism came rather late in Marquesan history to be consequential. It informs us that political unification was, in fact, a chiefly goal. These regional coalitions, however, rarely held together. When free of an external threat, the tribes fought among themselves as did the Maori hapu of the same iwi. Apart from the chronicle of regional conflict, the genealogical traditions add little to our knowledge of early Marquesan history. For that record we draw upon the archeological studies of Suggs.

The Archeological Record

Suggs has divided Marquesan history into five main periods: Settlement (150 B.C.–A.D. 100); Developmental (100–1100); Expansion (1100–1400); Classic (1400–1700); and Historic, from 1790 to final collapse under European rule in the late nineteenth century.

Settlement Period (150 B.C.–A.D. 100)

The earliest settlement was found on Nuku Hiva, the largest of the islands, and one of the northern group, but Suggs believes that all the main islands were settled at about the same time. This first site had a population of fifty or so, which may have represented a single canoe load, judging by the known carrying capacity of Marquesan canoes. The people lived in canoe-shaped thatch houses—reminiscent of Easter Island—and were well supplied with livestock, pigs, and dogs. Their main crops then were roots, taro, and yams, but they also cultivated coconuts and breadfruit. They had pottery and they wore a shell disc headdress similar to the *kapkap* of Santa Cruz in the New Hebrides. The settlement had within it an ahu, an oblong enclosure of small stones only a few inches high, within which stood a pair of columnar basalt uprights around which the dead were buried. The burials revealed evidence of cannibalism. Male skulls were preserved, indicating to Suggs an "ancestral cult," although it is possible that the skulls might have been of high-born chiefs whose heads were known to be sacred in later times. Suggs deduced, however, from the absence of grave furniture "a lack of pronounced status differences (1960: 113)." Finally, the prevalence of small local ahus suggested private rather than public ceremonialism.

Developmental Period (100–1100)

The basic settlement pattern remained unchanged, but the houses were now placed on stone pavements called *pae pae*. While status differences at this time were not marked, Suggs observed that "the increased sizes of some of the house structures later in this period suggest that a gradual increase in prestige or rank may have prevailed at this time (1961:182)." During this period the ahu, which Suggs believes to have been the model for the ceremonial structure in Easter Island, was replaced by temples in the form of houses. Breadfruit was becoming more important, and the population was still concentrated in the valleys and along the favorable east coasts of the islands.

Expansion Period (1100–1400)

This was a period of active internecine warfare, referred to in the traditions and demonstrated conclusively by the appearance of substantial fortifications. Since the population had now begun to move into the interior, occupying the more hidden valleys, there is reason to assume with Suggs that "population pressure" had now forced the Marquesans to fight for land. It is also possible that in the Marquesas, as in New Zealand, wars dispersed the population, compelling the weak and the defeated to seek asylum in remote and sheltered valleys. The Expansion Period also saw the appearance and elaboration of great ceremonial centers which were the physical symbols of tribal prestige. Suggs sees these centers, or *tohua,* as the "beginning of the intergroup rivalry that was so marked in the Historic Period and as evidence of the "beginning of a rise in the prestige of the priesthood (1961:83)." Possibly also associated with a growing interest in status is the appearance at this time of stone images representing distinguished persons.

Classic Period (1400–1790)

The population reached its highest peak during this period. Nevertheless, the general community pattern did not change, for the Marquesas never did establish large communities, not even after the population had begun to exceed 100,000. The people began to leave coastal areas where they were subject to sea raids and established themselves in the interior valleys and where possible along the mountain slopes. Suggs found evidence of extensive agricultural terracing for taro fields, something that earlier archeological surveys had overlooked. Breadfruit had now become the mainstay of the diet and was stored as a fermented mash, in slab-lined or else in leaf-lined underground storage pits. The dog had begun to disappear, but pigs were still numerous and an important part of the diet.

It is the architecture that brings out the salient traits of the social structure. The Classic Period was notable for megalithic construction. Nuku Hiva was the main center of great stone constructions for all the Marquesan Islands, but Hiva Oa had important stone works as well. House terraces of large stones were now prominent, the tohua had become larger and more elaborate. Monumental stone carving comparable in general form, although not in specific style, to that of Easter Island, appeared all over the islands. Suggs has made the interesting observation that the use of cut slabs of volcanic tufa in personal dwellings had become "an index of personal prestige (1961: 185)." House structures differed in size and in the monumentality of their stone foundations. The houses, Suggs believes, expressed individual rivalry, while the tohua that had begun to appear in clusters in each subtribal district expressed the status differences between tribes.

The specifically religious *me'ae* also became larger and more abundant. Some were small and belonged to a family; large ones were tribal. Suggs has credited status rivalry among priests, who were generally the younger brothers of the chiefs, for the sudden increase in construction of ceremonial centers.

Characterizing the Classic Period generally as one of acute status rivalry ("The Classic Period archeological remains . . . demonstrate an increase in prestige rivalry; one might say that the importance of achievement in status might be traced back at least to that time [1961: 186]"), Suggs has suggested that this may have been the historic period that corresponded to my definition of the Open society. I quote Suggs on this point:

> The condition of acute prestige rivalry that manifests itself in the archeological record of this period may actually have caused a change in the basis for attainment of chieftainship. Goldman has suggested that a traditional status system was the basis for Polynesian social organization, and that this may have changed to a system in which status could be achieved. Achievement appears to have been quite possible during the Historic Period, if one examines the record of extremely intricate palace politics involving the Taiohae tribe, its chiefs and those of Ha'apa in their attempt to establish one rule for both valleys (1961:186).

Handy's distinction between the northern and southern Marquesan islands is corroborated by Suggs' archeological work, which also established the prominence of monumental stone architecture in the northern islands and the greater development of figure carving in stone, in wood, and in bone among the southern islands.

The Marquesan images were known as *tiki,* and represented deified tribal ancestors, according to Handy (1923:276). They were chiefs as well as priests who had become famous and after death became titular spirits or gods. These images were generally placed on the ceremonial platforms.

Historic Period (1790 to Late Nineteenth Century)

The historic period brought status rivalry to a head, as Suggs has remarked. It is noteworthy mainly for the rapid decline of native culture under European influence. The Europeans brought smallpox, leprosy, tuberculosis, venereal disease, and firearms. But the Marquesans, with the assistance of nature, did much on their own. While normally breadfruit grew abundantly, periodic and severe droughts brought dreadful famines that took a heavy toll of life. The Marquesan mode of warfare, as late as the Historic Period, was to ring the breadfruit trees of their enemy, destroying them for good. Captain Porter, who made his own contribution to the Marquesan mortality rate, was an eyewitness to the destruction of breadfruit trees.

Historical Recapitulation

Archeology and traditions are in general agreement on a number of important points: on the period of earliest settlement, on the probable derivation of the population from a common ancestral source, and on the transformation of the social system under the pressure of internecine warfare. There is no definite information on the important question of whether the entire Marquesan population was part of a single waka or of many. If population had increased during the early period at 2 percent a year, doubling in a century, a single canoe load of fifty people would have reached the limit of 100,000 by the end of the Developmental Period, or just before the period of active warfare would have begun to check further increases. Thus an assumption of descent from a single canoe is plausible, even if entirely uncertain.

Despite the appearance of physical differences between the inhabitants of the northern and southern islands, the archeological evidence suggests rather a single culture that had developed local variations. The significance of these cultural distinctions is, however, by no means clear. Linton's interpretation of the fusion between tohua and me'ae on Nuku Hiva suggests that this island, in particular, and the northern group of islands, in general, had become the center of a developed Traditional society with strong and sacred chiefs. Evidence that a Traditional climax had been achieved on Nuku Hiva is rather strong, for this island was also the focus of monumentality in stone works that would seem to be the product of strongly organized chieftainship. Following the analogy of Easter Island, where the stone images were evidently associated with more independent groups, it might be reasonable to speculate that the southern Marquesan islands, with their emphasis on carving—requiring less group effort—represented a parallel social system of relative decentralization. In Easter Island, however, the phase of image construction came after the period of monumentality in ceremonial centers and was identified as a development of an Open society. There is no evidence, however, that the southern islands and their specialization in carving represented either a later phase or an Open society in the Marquesas. The Easter Island images were definite marks of status. In the Marquesas it was the size and monumentality of pae pae and of tohua that conveyed the status of the group. Thus we may consider the southern islands as a divergent branch of development and the northern islands as the mainstream. Viewed this way, the entire development on Nuku Hiva up through the end of the Expansion Period represents a "maturation" of the Traditional society. The Classic Period is its culmination as well as the beginning of the establishment of the Open society. That the Historic Period marked the culmination of the Open society phase seems reasonably certain, since for this period we have eyewitness accounts as well as the recollections of native informants to document the characteristics in detail.

The archeological record cannot very well explain the origins of status rivalry or the causes of internecine war. Suggs believes that population pressure "intensified to an extreme the rivalry apparently present in most Polynesian societies (1961:186)." The fact that status rivalry intensified at about the same time the population had reached its peak of 100,000 or more would seem to bear him out. The difficulty with this explanation, though, is the vagueness of the meaning of "population pressure." If population pressure refers to the absolute relationship between nutrition and resources, then what is intensified is not status rivalry but sheer competition for food. There is no substantial evidence, however, that the Marquesans fought for food. Destroying the breadfruit trees of an enemy is not the act of a hungry aggressor. Father Gracia, the best of early sources on Marquesan life and a witness to their wars, never mentioned hunger as a cause. He thought the need for captives as human sacrifices to the gods was the main cause of war. Perhaps this is the biased view of a missionary, but he has stated further:

> La jalousie de quelques peuplades contre une autre qui est plus riche; l'ambition d'un chef qui veut, pour agrandir sa ré'putation ou son district, y ajouter ceux de ses voisins; la vengeance d'une insulte faite, même à un simple particulier, dans une tribu étrangere; la violacion d'un tapu, comise par des alliés, et qu'il faut venger (1843:90).

Marquesan warfare, then was, in the main, a form of status rivalry, its most direct form, but not a competition for food in the direct sense. The intensification of status rivalry is an important process in social evolution, but it is a process of great complexity. Population pressure is unquestionably a factor in building up the momentum of status rivalry. But it is only one factor.

The Status System

The basic elements of the Marquesan status system are of the Maori type, and hence eastern Polynesian. The divergence from Maori is solely in pattern of organization arising from specific emphases on different issues. Thus even if we have no assurance that the Marquesan Open was an actual historical development from a specifically Maori Traditional there is good reason to regard the Marquesan system as a structural variant of a type similar to that of Maori.

Primogeniture

All first-born males (*matahiapo* or *hamua*) also received the title *haka-iki,* and were heads of households. This title identified, in general, all chiefs, whether heads of minor groups or of tribal confederations, and its widespread use has been considered by many observers as one of the marks of Marquesan democracy. The first-born sons of chiefs had, of course, the advantages for status and for political prospects of distinguished family and of pedigree. Nevertheless, since all haka-iki could rise by their own efforts to high office, the sheer fact of primogeniture tended to blur the significance of seniority of descent. Elsewhere in Polynesia, primogeniture either became subordinate to seniority—so that in minor families being first-born had only limited significance for status—or, as in Samoa, disappeared altogether from the status system. But in the Marquesas, primogeniture was the more strongly accented principle. All first-born, whether male or female, were eligible for political office, but only the male acquired the full sanctity that raised him above the ordinary.

Seniority of Descent

The partition of Hiva Oa into a dual political division (one reckoning descent from an elder brother and the other from his junior) conveys the general idea of senior and junior descent lines. We have no evidence, however, that chiefly descent lines were, in fact, systematically arranged by seniority. We observe in the Marquesas the general idea of seniority but, for reasons stated, senior lines could not actually develop.

Male Line

Basically the Marquesan male had the same prerogatives of sanctity and of rule as his Maori brother. In the Marquesas, however, the higher status of the first-born male did not necessarily produce a male line of honorable descent. Nor was the male–female duality as strongly developed as in New Zealand, even though the principle of duality was recognized. While the son was the proper heir and had the highest sanctity, a woman could become chief and if she was the first-born daughter of a chief, she assumed sacredness just as she did in New Zealand. The elementary conditions for the formation of an honorable male line were therefore present, but as in the parallel condition of the relation between primogeniture and seniority, it was the patterns of status as a whole that governed the formation of a descent line. In the Marquesas, the equivalent of the Maori male line did not appear because of the prominence given to achieved status and the wide diffusion of the haka-iki title. If sanctity was a necessary condition of chiefship, it was a prerogative of both birth and of accomplishment. Since achievement also compensated for pedigree, a condition of generalized genealogical distinction inevitably became more significant than linearity. Perhaps it is reasonable to claim that the special conditions of Marquesan bilaterality, as expressed in the differentiation of terms for maternal uncle and paternal aunt, and the special respects granted these relatives, were potent factors in the blocking out of pro-patriliny. The case for this consideration is weakened, though, by the example of Tonga, where a very strong male line developed under rather similar conditions of bilaterality.

Sanctity

In the traditional Polynesian manner, the Marquesans attributed some sanctity to all males and regarded ordinary women as common. But they also venerated the head of any person, male or female, giving in this respect some equity in sacredness to women. First-born males were sacred to a higher degree. Not only were their heads sacred, but they were treated from birth with special ritual care. They were the *tama tapu,* or sacred children, entitled to ritual respects including the chiefly prerogative of first fruits. Whatever came into contact with the body of a first-born son had to be deposited by his mother in a sacred place. In adult life, however, contact was not injurious to personal tapu. The sanctity of the head continued to be respected. Chiefs, male or female, were somewhat more tapu than first-born males, but not, as Handy has remarked, in any distinctive way (1923:52). The chief shared the same general sanctity of other first-born males, although infringement of chiefly sanctity was a more serious offense and was punished by sorcery (Handy 1923:52). Nor, according to Handy, were there any special rites for chiefs or for their families. If the rites for the first-born of chiefs were more elaborate, it was not because of greater sanctity but because of greater wealth. The person of the chief did not lack religious significance. As living head of his tribal group, he embodied its procreative powers. The mention of his genitalia in fishing rites suggests a wider extension of his mana. The skills of tribal priests also had efficacy in fishing rites.

We have no difficulty in recognizing the traditional features of chiefly tapu in the Marquesas. We recognize, at the same time, a Marquesan preference for diffusing sanctity rather widely through the population and for minimizing the social and ritual separation of chiefs from their public. The sanctification of all heads is a remarkable example, for Polynesia, of democratization of tapu. In their relations with the public, chiefs were notably informal; they were also free to marry commoners (and when they preferred chiefly marriages the reasons were those of political expediency rather than of caste). The offspring of marriages between chiefs and commoners were legitimate and entitled to all prerogatives of royal birth. Nowhere in the Marquesas was the concept of chiefly sanctity so fully developed as it was in the Society Islands or in Hawaii. Ua Pou and Nuku Hiva were the major centers of chiefly sanctity in the Marquesas. Here the house, the coconut trees, and all personal possessions of the chief were sacred and to be avoided. Elsewhere in the islands the principle of sanctity was recognized, but no great attention was paid to it (Handy 1922:51). Even where the sanctity of the chief was very strongly respected, it was still secondary to the sanctity of the *tau'a* or the inspirational priests who need not have been of chiefly stock. In relative terms, then, the chiefs as sacred personages did not stand out too strongly. The ritual expression of chiefly sanctity depended on wealth, which was often also available to lower-level chiefs. In any case, his sanctity was subordinate to that of priests who need not have been of chiefly stock at all. Finally, chiefly sanctity was a source of respect and, as I have explained, of certain general supernatural powers, rather than of specific powers, which were the special prerogatives of the priests. Handy's statement that in more recent times priests had begun to come more frequently from chiefly families, emphasizes, of course, the persistent Polynesian view that chiefly and priestly powers are inherently of the same nature. When the powers are differentiated the chiefs move to occupy the priestly prerogatives and the priests utilize their sanctity to gain chiefly prerogatives.

Tohunga

Nowhere in Polynesia were the skills of craftsmanship more highly honored than in the Marquesas, even though the crafts themselves were not as formally organized as were the "guilds" of Samoa and Hawaii. The Marquesan labor organization approximated the guild system in some respects. Those who constructed stone platforms for houses, the house builders, the canoe builders, and the fishermen worked under the direction of a master craftsman, or *tuhuna,* and constituted during their period of labor a consecrated group. Since organized labor was regarded as a sacred activity, and was accompanied by ritual feasting, religious observances and avoidance of contamination from women, the workman himself and the directors, in particular, gained the status of sanctity. They had enormous prestige and good prospects for becoming wealthy and thus politically powerful. Handy quite properly considers the tuhuna to have been a social class. The term was applied to any outstanding demonstration of skill, but it was also used as a formal title designating the skilled professional and the director of labor. The master director was *tuhuna nui,* or "great tuhuna," a man who gathered about him apprentices and pupils. In the office of tuhuna nui lay the potentiality for a guild system that never developed because of the mobility of labor. The apprentice or pupil was free to choose his own associations, just as a commoner could choose the chief under whom he preferred to live. Thus the important skills were open to all males who were, at the same time, free to advance themselves according to their personal circumstances. Many tuhuna were unaffiliated professionals such as bards (the most esteemed of all), tattooers, and artistic workers in ornamentation, string figures, and drum making. The outstanding tuhuna were the men associated with chiefs as advisors on military and political affairs and as directors of formal public rituals. These tuhuna, somewhat like the Tongan *matapule* were deeply involved in tribal administration, the focus of status. Others, even on the political fringes, could advance themselves in influence through whatever affluence and respect their skills brought them.

Priests

Two orders of priest were categorically distinguished—the learned experts of ritual who were *tuhuna o'ono* or masters of prayer, and *tau'a,* the holy men who were the inspired voices of the gods. The tuhuna were literally religious craftsmen; they knew the chants and the conduct of ritual, and they taught novices for a fee. As priests they were sacred. Their professional stock, though, was knowledge, the letter-perfect recitation of the chant, for which they were often tested in public competitions. The tuhuna who was bested was said to have lost his mana and had to be deposed. Some claimed he was put to death for his shame (Handy 1923:229).

The inspired mystics were the more feared and the more honored. They were thought of as gods (*atua*), that is, as the physical presence of gods, and were treated with utmost prudence. When a tau'a died, no one dared touch his body, and it was allowed to decompose where it lay. As divine voices, these priests presided over the major rituals and were responsible for the care of the dead. They were generally men of the chief's close family and were allied with him as the sacred arm of the administration. The convenience of such a governing partnership had to be weighed, however, against the impressive merits of choice. The gods named their own spokesmen, choosing unexpectedly, from any family or rank—a woman, if they so desired. The signs of choice were sudden convulsive fits and new and extraordinary capabilities, such as not having to eat for a long time and not to be desired as food by sharks. Having been thus set apart, the tau'a was the equivalent of a chief.

Toa

The political importance of warfare notwithstanding, the professional warrior, capable as he was, did not rise above the sheer technical limits of his craft to join the exhilarating power contests, as did his comrades-in-arms in other Open societies. The Marquesas demanded a wider range of talents of its chiefs, among these the ability to win people by affable means. There is no compelling reason why the Marquesan warrior could not have broadened his own range of talents or innovated political standards more in keeping with the martial mode and so have advanced himself. For whatever reasons, the toa remained a professional, a priest of war in the service of the more generally talented chief. Chiefs declared war, negotiated the peace, raised and provisioned the army, and with the advice of other consultants set the strategy of combat. The toa, it seems, were not even combat leaders since Marquesan battle tactics always resolved themselves into the multiplicities and particularities of personal combat. The mission of the toa was to inspire his own side by a demonstration of skill and fearlessness and to chill the élan of the enemy by his awesome appearance and demeanor. In battle all warriors were sacred agents of Tu, the war god. The professionals, however, stood apart as the sacred core of the army. They had their own insignia of necklaces and bark cloth and distinctive tattooing. In peace they resembled a praetorian guard, occupying the Marquesan counterpart of a barracks within the chief's establishment.

Wealth

In the sense that leadership grew out of a widening of personal influence and of extended alliances for which foodstuffs and other goods were necessary, it can be said that the control of land was the ultimate political reality. Power growing around the control of scarce means was rooted in the economy. Many had the genealogical requirements for chiefship, but only those who had the means would take and hold the office. The senior male who headed his household or extended family was given at once the economic advantage as custodian of lands. His purpose, if he was politically ambitious, was to expand it and move up. As a tribal haka-iki, he was keeper of the famine reserve to which one of the four annual breadfruit crops was allocated. From this reserve he drew the costs of official expenditures, namely, the payment of artisans, priests, and warriors, and of hospitality and public ritual. The very substantial costs of marital exchanges in behalf of his children, which was a main source of his political influence, he had to draw from his own lands and from his more immediate kin. Wealth manifested mana and divine approval. Politically, it was the material magnet that held the loyalty of one's own tribe and could detach the unstable elements from weaker chiefs. Depending upon the particulars of geography, the wealth of a tribe, nominally at least the possession of its chief, could be increased either by war alone or by pacific means, by conquest or its threat. Thus the control of lands, an urgent obligation at all times, was inescapably at the center of political rivalry. For the lower ranks, requiring abundance for general status and influence, the well-being of the tribe and the capabilities of its chief were for obvious reasons equally essential. All the ambitious families, the energy centers of the tribe, were thereby bound in mutual economic interests.

Political Hegemony

The ultimate test of political power was the ability of a chief to attract and hold followers. All chiefly prerogatives and all chiefly talents had significance only insofar as they helped meet this test. If the chief could not build a following—if he could not control his kinsmen and allies—he had nothing to show for his title. He was either a political chief or, to all intents and purposes, none at all. The pragmatic test of leadership applied at every level of command—from the family head who took advantage of an attractive wife to enlarge his polyandrous household to the great divisional chief whose political talents covered the spectrum. The Marquesan concept of chiefs as political officers contrasts with the traditional idea by substituting quantitative for qualitative criteria. In principle, and as implied by the wide use of the haka-iki title, the small chief is a proportion of the large chief. His status can be measured by increments of jurisdiction.

Power was incremental. What were the actual capabilities of chiefs? We have only general information. All sources agree in describing the chief as a patriarch, as paternal defender of his kin tribe, but as more awesome and more potent in vital affairs with each increment of jurisdiction. The divisional chief—heading a coalition of tribes—was no religious supernumerary. Gracia seeks to distinguish between war and peacetime uses of authority, and between local and distant jurisdictions. Every chief, he says, had the right to defend his privileges and his honor, by capital punishment, if need be. In peace and within his own tribe this power was rarely used (1843:104). We must assume variability with respect to power over life as over property. As to the latter, we have information about chiefs who overstepped the lines of paternal custodianship to more personal despotism.

The single political standard is one of the special characteristics of Marquesan governance, and may be seen as an apt reflection of the concept of haka-iki, literally a "made chief." The authority may follow primogenitural succession, but is not allowed to fall into an assigned and preordained place. The authority must be devised, improvised, and imposed so as to fulfill the complementary requirement of being made. Yet the first born-son of a chief, the exemplar of genealogical succession, brought about at once, from the moment of his birth, the demotion of his father. The newborn assumed the title and the father became his regent. In this epiphany of the potency of primogeniture there would seem to be an utter contradiction of the achievement ethic. The first-born secures his place with his first outcry, and without lifting a hand or planning an alliance. Instant succession may be understood, of course, as practical politics, as insuring the continuity of administration. Viewed structurally, however, the administration appears as split. The infant now holds the honors, and little else; the father retains de facto jurisdiction as he defers symbolically to the higher status of his son. Such a division is true Polynesian, and reminds us of western Polynesian patterns in which honor and power are allocated between female and male lines respectively. The Marquesan pattern differs in choosing a self-liquidating polarity, that between incipience and maturity. The common intent would seem to be the obligation to liberate administration from the extreme restraints of honor. Thus the haka-iki concept is, in fact, preserved. The wielder of power from the time of the birth of his son to his own death is not fully the authentic ruler.

The Structure of Status

The status system can only be described broadly and imprecisely since information is incomplete. Two features, perhaps the decisive ones, seem reasonably clear, though, and help depict the basic structure. One is the commitment to genealogical rank through the single and poorly focused element of primogeniture; the other is the parallel insistence upon political efficacy as the agent of definition. The result is a flexible structure that, adhering to traditional guide lines, concludes with no fixed forms. Handy has described the system as follows:

> Social position tended to become hereditary, but there was nothing to prevent any man or woman in the tribe from rising to the highest positions, those of chief and of inspirational priest. There are examples of the attainment of such positions by those who had no hereditary claim to them. The factors determining social position were the function of a person in relationship to tribal activity dependent upon ability and personality; wealth, dependent partly on inheritance but chiefly on success in making favorable social alliances; energy and business ability; and lastly, personality, intelligence and skill (1923:37).

The combination of genealogy and efficacy is Polynesian. The variables are in the weightings. From Handy's summation, well-supported by all the data, the Marquesan system differs from the Traditional. In the latter system, grade set the jurisdiction and its perquisites; in the former, the reverse was always a possibility. The successful man acquired rank and sanctity regardless of how he had begun. Thus Williamson concluded from a review of the literature that the most powerful Marquesan chiefs were as sacred as any in Polynesia (1924: II, 397), a tribute as much to their achievement as to their generalized pedigree.

Aristocracies must focus and intensify the qualities of leadership until they reside most fully and potently in a very few. In the Traditional societies, this was accomplished largely by genealogical means. In the Marquesas, primogeniture as a sole genealogical factor tended to diffuse leadership so that political rivalry had to accomplish, in democratic fashion, the ultimate selection of the ruling elites.

The Marquesan system thus appears as an elementary form of aristocracy. Its nomenclature of ranks connects it at once with the traditional Polynesian order, either as an archaic version of it or as a severely reduced model. The historical evidence can be read either way. In the light of well-documented status rivalry, the latter interpretation seems the more probable. As we observed earlier, the apparent social distinctions between the northern and the southern group of islands suggests the appearance of both Traditional and Open societies. What appears to have been a Marquesan Traditional in the northern islands must be understood as a variant of a generalized Traditional order. But it was evidently distinct from the more flexible forms—the subject of the present discussion—that had established themselves on Hiva Oa, Tahu Atu, and Fatu Hiva.

On Ua Pou, according to Handy, the chiefs had once formed a "restricted class." In one valley of this island those known as the chiefly tribes, the *poi tiketike* ("high people"), lived on the eastern side of a stream; the commoners, on its western side. This arrangement resembles that of Mangaia and Easter Island. The so-called high people formed two distinct but intermarrying divisions, one the *papa haka iki,* or high chiefs, the other the *haka te pe'iu,* which may be translated as "the female chiefs" (1923:37). Handy's fragmentary information is tantalizing, for it suggests, in this respect, a common western Polynesian dual structure.

The northern islands recognized three ranks, *haka-iki, anatia* (rangatira), and *mata-ei-nana.* The first were the chiefs of great families; the second, their close kin; and the last their most distant kin, the commoners. There is no evidence the order had been formed by seniority; more general genealogical determinants could have accomplished the same. The anatia were described to Handy (1923:57) as "landed proprietors" who had received special land allotments from their chief in proportion to their importance in the tribe. Normally these land grants remained within the families, but chiefs could revoke title for cause. A feudal pattern is implied. The commoners were not a "landless" class. Their mobility, nevertheless, suggests a mode of land tenure somewhat less certain than that in the Traditional societies. The attachment to the soil, and perhaps economic autonomy, has lessened in the course of shifting from one chief to another.

The rank order was simplest on the southern islands where anatia was not a commonly recognized category, and where mata-ei-nana meant simply "the people," rather than "commoner." Here there were only chiefs and their constituencies, an essentially political model of organization. We detect a tendency towards individualization of statuses away from class or formal rank. The category of chief was genealogically expansive, even if finally politically restrictive. Relatively few were deprived of honor, leading Handy to declare flatly, the Marquesans had "no conception of a low class (1923:39)." If they had no degraded class, they were not unmindful of reduced statuses—but as products of circumstance. Libertine youth (*ka'oi*), the more informal counterparts of the Tahitian *arioi* (even to their religious role as a closed society of entertainers), were included among the lower grades as living outside the usual channels of political or religious powers.

Even more reduced were the secondary husbands (*pekio*) of polyandrous households, who were compelled to assume the menial duties of cooking and water carrying. Marquesan polyandry has been explained as an adaptation to an anomalous sex ratio (2.5 men to one woman). In its own fashion it offered the joys of domesticity to the surplus males and exacted the price of being only second and subordinate. There was, to be sure, the hope of succeeding to first place. In the most elevated households the secondary husbands were in a true sense members of the court, so to speak, and enjoyed the honor of their high association.

The true menials were all the weak and rootless people, the frightened and the displaced, the victims of war and of disturbed relations with chiefs. They were known contemptuously as common water (*vai noa*). They attached themselves to chiefs as servants with no landed status, for when they chose to be on their own again they had only fishing to fall back on. The lowest status would have been that of war captive, if they had been allowed to live long enough to perfect their own degradation.

Status Rivalry

The Marquesan is readily visualized as the prototype of Open society. It insists upon few givens, and leaves the field wide open for attainment. A comparison with Mangaia, which illustrates a traditional Rarotongan order tenaciously resisting and remorselessly being undermined, is instructive. Mangaian rivalry predicated upon the absolutes of sudden elevations and reductions was understandably bitter and treacherous. The Marquesans who did not appreciate live captives were not cast in the image of the gentle warrior. They were as implacable as any in war. The direction in which they were moving, however, seems to have been away from the absolutes and toward the gradations of compromise. The portrait of the Marquesan chief that all sources have drawn is of the political animal planning his advancement step by step. We are speaking now of the southern group, the most politically developed, and where statuses had become most fully generalized. Mangaia, too, had begun to submit to the gradations of political compromise. The resistance, though, may be measured by the extent of fracture of the status structure. The dual status system preserves the core of traditional categorization. The Marquesan, drawing upon broader standards of worth, responded by reducing categories and softening boundaries.

Gradation of status is, of course, a fundamental characteristic of the Traditional society. The Marquesan innovation was to reverse the order. Traditional gradation is genealogical, a given; the gradation of the Marquesan Open is in what has been made. The former starts as a product of the divine order of descent; the latter evolves as a product of human agency. Traditional gradation is postulated upon an organic fixity; Marquesan gradation, upon the kinetics of status rivalry.

Descent Group Organization

Whether all of the Marquesas formed a single genealogical network around one line of immigrants—a single waka, so to speak—or consisted of many originally distinct lines of relatives we do not really know. Since the archipelago never came under a single native administration, the question is not too important. For that matter, we do not even know what was the genealogical composition of one island such as Nuku Hiva. We can assume merely that all the inhabitants of an island were related, on the grounds that there were no restrictions against intermarriage, that descent was fully bilateral, that populations moved a great deal, that the islands were occupied for over 2,000 years and that genealogies of chief families had extraordinary depth. From the Marquesan point of view, the significant kin were those who came under a single jurisdiction. Those of the same tribe were close kin; those of allied or enemy tribes on the island were distant kin. It is difficult to evaluate the respective pulls of kinship and of political allegiance in the Marquesas, since segments of the same tribe fought against one another. Kinship relationships did not prevent the Maori hapu from fighting one another either, but in the Maori case the commoners of the hapu were endogamous, so that their connections with relatives in other hapu would have become, in the course of time, more a matter of tradition than of true sentiment. In the Marquesas there was a similar tradition of endogamy for the commoner, but people deserted one chief for another in the same valley. Thus when one subdivision of a tribe fought against another, it was as in Mangaia, kin against kin. The point of attraction in group formation was in the Marquesas largely political, but not exclusively so, for the link between the chief and his people was one of kinship.

Chiefs and commoners on the Marquesas used widespread kinship ties for their respective political interests. The chiefs used kinship to sanction their political relations with the people under their jurisdiction, and they used kinship to widen their alliances. The commoners used the wider kinship relations to gain sanctuary under the jurisdiction of another chief. What is noteworthy is that the uses by the commoners of their wider kinship ties in order to move to another jurisdiction depended not upon the specific relationship with a kinsman in another location but upon the relationship to its chief. This chiefly role suggests that in the fusion between the kinship and the political relationships in the Marquesas, the latter were emerging as the dominant forces of attraction.

In the Marquesas the kin group that formed a community—occupying a territory under the jurisdiction of a chief—was a true kindred including both maternal and paternal relatives. Descent was consistently bilateral and residence depended entirely upon which side had the best land. If a woman was the first-born and inherited the most land, her husband or husbands would come to live with her. A chief, on the other hand, resided generally on his paternal lands and brought his wife to his community. His residence tended to be patrilocal. The residence of subordinate husbands, however, was always matrilocal, so that in the Marquesas we again see some distinction between patrilocal residence and higher status and matrilocal residence and lower status. Since they preferred the male to succeed to the chiefship—only a preference and not a mandatory rule—there was also some tendency for the traditional patrilineal emphasis to assert itself. The chiefs, as I have said, married outside the tribe for political advantage, while the commoners, having less political advantage to gain, settled for the convenience of marrying within the tribe. In short, the conditions for establishing an affiliation to a community within the tribal area were completely flexible. Residence was a matter of choice and since everyone could claim a genealogical relationship with almost everyone else in the tribe, the wide choice of community affiliation did not violate the tradition that a community was a body of kin. Thus a person was either born into the kin grouping he lived with, joined a kin group of his choice, or arranged an adoption to a kin group if the genealogical links were too frail or had been forgotten. For all those engaged in advancing themselves, affiliation was entirely by status. On this matter Linton has said:

> Since the Marquesans traced descent through the parent of highest standing in each generation, there was always some point in the line of descent at which one of the ancestors was higher than a contemporary ancestor of some other individual. Genealogies could thus be used to justify actual social relations. The various households went up and down in social prestige and in position, and household heads selected which of the possible relationship terms they would use on the basis of which was superior or inferior. Because of the in-breeding it was always possible for a person actually on top to find a line of descent that was higher at some point than any other line. (1939: 150).

Segmentation

Information on Marquesan social structure is far from complete. With the population having suffered so sharp a decline immediately after European contact, it is not at all unlikely that the large group organizations, the tribal and multitribal units, would have changed. Granted these possibilities for error in reconstructing the aboriginal segmentary organization, there seems every reason to believe that in the Marquesas the formation of branches did not go by the principles of seniority as it did in the Traditional societies. This we can assert with some confidence for the Historic Period, since no observer has reported that the heads of tribal subdivisions were junior members of the senior line. The evidence rather goes the other way, asserting that powerful men established themselves as centers of population in control of a territory. Being part of the kindred, they were broadly related to the paramount chief, but they were not necessarily of his junior line. Moreover, heads of groups that were growing in power could challenge and usurp the office of the tribal chief. Linton has explained that one way in which a chief could counter the challenge of an upstart rival was to adopt the latter's son as his own heir (1939: 157). Adoption did not sever ties with the natal group; rather it brought both family groups into the same network. It therefore gave the politically ascending line a more legitimate claim to the chiefship. If, on the other hand, the ruling chief were overcome politically, the orderly rule of seniority would be upset in still another way. The evidence of status mobility is so very positive that it would be difficult to imagine under what circumstances the traditional order of branching by seniority would have been sustained. From the archeological record, this rearrangement of line could have been well under way during the Classic Period.

A further indication that the traditional forms of segmentation did not prevail in the Marquesas is the total absence of a segmental nomenclature. This absence of terms cannot be taken as positive evidence of the absence of the segments, but it is an item of information that cannot be ignored either. Any group occupying a territory and acknowledging a chief—haka-iki—was a *huaka* (waka). The term had a very general meaning and covered as it did in New Zealand, a very large band of people. Handy defined it as follows: "*Hua'a* (huaka) meant specifically blood and foster relatives, though extended in general application to all the members of the tribe, and even of related tribes. The same name meant also troupe or band (1923:67)." An adequate evaluation of the significance of a single descriptive term to describe all groups requires a full comparative study, which is reserved for a later chapter. At this point, however, it is appropriate to note the apparent relationship between the wholesale usage of "haka-iki' as a term for chiefs, subchiefs, and household heads, and the wholesale use of "huaka" for all levels of organization. The simplification of nomenclature does not portray by any means the full political realities of Marquesan life, but it does bring out the widespread equalization of status among people of honor. Even the household was a smaller version of the tribe. According to Handy (1923:61), as many as five or six families lived in a single establishment. The more affluent the family, the larger was the household and the more closely did it resemble a small tribe.

A segmental structure did exist, although not apparently upon any uniform basis of internal relationships. In the northern group of islands, in Nuku Hiva and Ua Pou, for example, the dual division between east and west represented by tradition a distinction between the senior and the junior branches of a common line. Such a division was a traditional one and as in other Open societies of eastern Polynesia each had the characteristics of a Segment I. This large segment, like the Maori waka, had no formal organization but was a federation of independent groups, tribes, that could be joined in a common military alliance on the traditional grounds of common ancestry. There is no reason to believe that the chief who brought the tribes into this grand division was necessarily, or even commonly, the scion of the senior line. Thus Handy has reported that in 1860 a chief on Ua Pou got together an alliance of east coast tribes, defeated the west coast tribes, and became chief over the entire island. Because of the instability of office, it is likely that the powerful chief of the moment was the head of the federation.

Segment II was headed by the paramount chief or papa haka-iki. This grouping seems to have corresponded to the district organization on Mangaia and on Easter Island. Williamson, for example, has called attention to the interesting fact that islands or portions of an island were generally divided into multiples of three or six. Taipi-vai on Nuku Hiva, for example, was divided, according to Captain Porter, into twelve sections, which were further subdivided into four groups of three each. A large grouping known as the Happah consisted of six sections, as were the Taeeh, also on Nuku Hiva. Ua Pou, which came under the jurisdiction of a single chief had six districts. Williamson concluded "that a system of districts subdivided into connected subdistricts prevailed and that there were head chiefs of the former having jurisdiction over chiefs of the latter (1924:I,323)."

The structure of the division, or Segment II, is not fully known, but it seems to have been variable, consisting in some valleys of branches of a single family line and in others of a grouping of allies each under a chief. Nor are the bases of group action clear. Segment II, like the Maori iwi, was not a zone of peace, for its component "tribes" fought against one another. It was, however, a zone of trade, and of exchanges of foodstuffs and goods through the medium of feasts and district ceremonies organized by the head chief and by local chiefs. The visits of the head chief, as among the Maori, also provoked exchanges of goods. In corporate respect, then, if not in genealogical structure, the district or Segment II was analogous to the Maori iwi. Its chief had special sanctity and headed the major ceremonial center (at which human sacrifices could be offered).

There is, unfortunately, no consistent nomenclature in the literature on the Marquesas, so that in compilations of "tribes" a district that is headed by a chief is included along with its subdivisions. Karl von den Steinen, an authoritative ethnographer, compiled a list of 113 "tribes" or "clans" (1925:28). On Nuku Hiva he listed 48 tribes located in 11 regions. This list included Taipi, which had the standing of a district according to Captain Porter, since it included 12 tribes, as well as groups that were smaller divisions of the Taipi. Captain Porter's list of "tribes" is perhaps the most useful since it was compiled early by a military man who became quickly involved in tribal warfare (1815). Porter distinguished between what was evidently a district (Segment II) and the tribe. For example, he indicated that the Happahs (hapaa), who occupied the valley of NW

Comptrollers Bay, consisted of six tribes, whom he named. Since he fought against the Happahs, his information may well be professional. He also names the chiefs of five of these six tribes. He estimated that the Happahs had 3,000 warriors, the Typees 3,500. This gives some indication of the size of Segment II.

Segment III is what most writers, including Porter, have listed as the "tribe." Linton has estimated the size of the aboriginal tribe at about 1,000 persons, a figure that is approximately in line with Porter's information that what he called a "great" tribe consisted of as many as six tribes. Each tribe was headed by a chief who held the title to the land. In this respect he had authority and power. In terms of corporate character, Segment III was the strongest social unit in Marquesan society, corresponding in this respect to the Maori hapu. The tribe had a strong collective organization parallel to that of the Maori hapu. Lands were allocated by the chief, who received services, first fruits, and other offerings. Handy has said that the breadfruit harvests were collectively organized by the chief. In good seasons there were four harvests. The first and smaller harvest belonged to the chief, but of this, part was stored as a tribal reserve in case of famine and the rest supported the large establishment of the chief and was the source of his hospitality and generosity. The chief also organized fishing expeditions and the distributions of fish. Through the great variety of feasts that accompanied all ceremonies, almost all the food of the tribe was consumed collectively. The second and ensuing harvests were for the individual households. Each tribe had its own tohua and me'ae for its local ceremonies.

Segment IV consisted of households which included as many as five or six nuclear families. Since households aimed at expanding themselves to the point where they would have the standing of tribes —with a titled chief and above all with the political influence of the tribe in its federation or district—their size must have varied considerably. The household head was not necessarily the senior male any more than the head of the tribe was the senior of a senior line. With combinations of polyandry, polygyny, and no fixed rules of residence at marriage, each household was an assembled group of kin rather than an arbitrarily formed kin group. The discontent of British anthropologists with naming Polynesian kin groupings as "descent groups" is fully justified in the case of the Marquesan groups, all of which may be considered as enlarged households. The household was the day-to-day producing unit; each owned its own breadfruit trees and stored its own supplies.

8

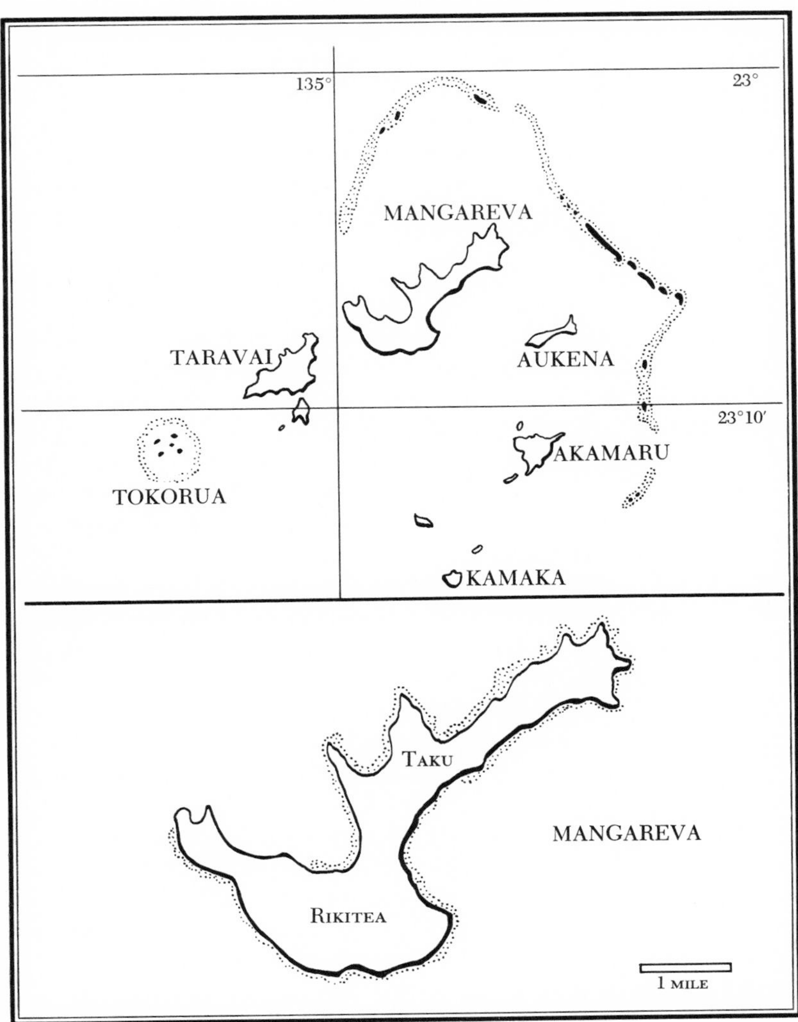
135°
23°
MANGAREVA
TARAVAI
AUKENA
23°10′
AKAMARU
TOKORUA
KAMAKA
TAKU
MANGAREVA
RIKITEA
1 MILE

Mangareva

MANGAREVA WAS SETTLED SOMETIME BEFORE A.D. 1100 (GREEN 1961), in all probability from the Marquesas, with which it has the closest cultural affinities (Buck 1938:512). Mangarevan society may therefore be regarded as the Marquesan system brought to fruition, but in a more meager and harsher physical setting. Poverty simplified but did not arrest the course of Mangarevan history; on the contrary, it added urgency to all political conflicts. Whereas in the Marquesas warring chiefs never quite realized their full political ambitions, in Mangareva they did. They secured a tight and dominant tenure over scarce crop lands and they established a firm central authority. Mangareva became a small version of the Stratified society.

The appearance of a Stratified society on these small and isolated islands that resemble atolls refutes at once the conventional thesis that political evolution can be explained from conditions of economic surplus. If Mangareva illustrates any economic thesis at all, it is rather the opposite—the stimulus of economic scarcity. The four islands comprising the archipelago have a combined area of no more than six square miles, the size of Tongareva atoll. Mangareva, the main island, measures only four square miles, most of it rocky and barely cultivable. The islands have no permanent streams, no secure water supply other than a few springs, rain runoff, and seepage. The small areas of fertile soil lie in scattered patches along coastal flatlands and within the short mountain valleys. Terracing and skilled impounding of water seepage extended the area of cultivation to its reasonable limits, and still did not provide lands for all.

Breadfruit yielding four crops a year with normal rainfall was the staple crop. The fermented mash was stored in pits though not, as might have been reasonably expected, as a famine reserve, but for ceremonial occasions. Taro, and to a lesser extent sweet potato, yam, arrowroot, banana, plantain, and coconut, were supplementary crops. In the end it was the sea, the "garden of the poor" that proved most dependable. On balance there was rarely enough food. Hunger drove people to steal growing crops, and from the breadfruit pits. Under extreme duress they resorted to fresh meat cannibalism and to robbing graves of their newly buried corpses. Hunger has been described as a common cause of war. Yet, having evicted an enemy from his land, they celebrated possession by shaking down the growing breadfruit and coconuts, and by cutting down young trees. War ravaged the thinly drawn economy even as it cut into the population. Caillot, a knowledgeable authority, estimated the Mangarevan population at an incredible 6,000–8,000 (1914:233). But even Buck's more modest calculation of "several thousand" implies a high density.

The mountainous terrain divided the island into natural districts, but of unequal economic value. The most important physical division was between the lagoon side, with access to the important fishing grounds, and the seaward side. The unequal distribution of resources embittered all traditional rivalries, for eviction from fertile areas often meant starvation.

Our knowledge of Mangarevan society, which is quite detailed in many respects, comes mainly from Father Laval, who was resident missionary from 1834 to 1871. Buck spent several months on the island in 1934 and was able to supplement Laval's information. Laval captured Mangarevan culture in its prime, having arrived shortly after Beechy's pioneer visit in 1825. I have drawn mainly upon Buck, whose study incorporates that of Laval. Archeological investigations have just begun, but since detailed results are not yet available, we must rely upon the genealogical traditions for a reconstruction of Mangarevan history. In evaluating the credibility of these traditions, we note the rather close correspondence between the radiocarbon date of 1100 with the genealogical date for first settlement of 1250.

Genealogical Traditions

"The history of Mangareva," Buck has written, "consists of the struggle between different families and districts in their attempts to gain power or avenge defeats (1938a:36)." The traditions begin with a narrative of rivalries and wars. Although Mangareva, like Mangaia, had apparently been settled by different groups of immigrants, some from Rarotonga, the conflict between old and new settler, while present, had not become a major issue. The main contention was between senior and junior lines of the same lineage and between commoners and nobility.

Mangarevan history begins with Tururei, the first ariki, whose reign, going back 26 generations from 1900, has been dated by Buck at 1250. "Warriors who refused to accept him" prevented Tururei's son from succeeding him. Two generations after this event a new ruler and a recent arrival was overthrown as a tyrant and a younger son of his, who would ordinarily have represented the junior line, assumed the rule. This was the illustrious Anua-motua, the legendary founder of the basic social order, the first ariki to unify the islands. This first unification is described as peaceable. In Marquesan fashion, Anua-motua's daughters married into the families of local chiefs, bringing them within the paternal lineage; and Anua-motua won the allegiance of a pivotal warrior chief who drew others with him. Apart from the advantages of daughters and a large family, Anua-motua held open the material attraction of large tracts of some of the most fertile lands. After his death, all his lands were formally divided among ten descendants, who became the founders of the ruling chiefly lines of their land districts. This first land division was given supernatural sanction: the allocation was made not by the living Anua-motua, but, as the traditions say, by his corpse as it lay in state on the marae. His daughters inherited land equally with sons. It was, in fact, a daughter who conveyed the senior line. She married a commoner who was a fisherman. Thus when her son succeeded to the paramount chiefship, he lacked traditional claims to authority. Thereafter the authority of the senior line atrophied further and the districts turned against one another.

The history of this early period just after the death of Anua-motua is punctuated by violent events that stirred up deep animosities and full-scale wars. An example of irascibility is the account of an exchange between farmer and fisherman conducted in the form of a "potlatch." The commoner fisherman offered more fish than his noble partner could pay for in breadfruit. The loser, shamed, killed him out of pique. The traditions also tell of uncles who killed their nephews who rose too high. "Jealousy of power was the cause of the killings," the traditions explain (Buck 1938a:33). In the course of district wars, two major confederations were formed, Taku and Rikitea, that then fought one another repeatedly for the supreme authority.

De jure, but not de facto seniority for the chiefly succession lasted for some ten generations after Anua-motua. The principle of seniority was then formally abandoned in favor of a new doctrine that gave the chiefship to the child born on the royal marae, regardless of genealogy. Whichever party could seize the marae by force acquired the succession legitimately; it then had only to be able to hold it.

It is reasonable to suppose that the mounting scale of warfare that followed was directly related to the new policy. Rikitea finally won and reunified the islands by force. Anua-motua had been a traditional, a priestly ariki. The new chief, Apeiti, was a military man. He became, says Buck, "the first real king of Mangareva (1938a:58)." The traditions of Apeiti's momentous victory pay great attention to the exploits of warriors and to their important role in the outcome of the wars. They describe local antagonisms and the instability of land holdings. Land tenure was, of course, inevitably jeopardized by war. In the post-Apeiti period, lands had also to be defended against kinsmen. To control the violence of land quarrels the successor to Apeiti instituted wrestling for lands. He is quoted as having said to his quarreling sons: "I will have no shedding of blood. Wrestle with your hands and the land shall go to the victor (1938a:163)."

The state of internal order depended on the nature of the central authority. When the paramount chief was just, the land was at peace. When he neglected the proper food distributions, the people rose against him. Of the ariki Makorotau the traditions say:

> No fighting arose in his days. The high lands were given peacefully into the hands of the people. There was no begging for food, hence no fighting. Though some commoners were seeking to obtain power, they had no followers (Buck 1938:69).

But the ariki who followed Makorotau took much and returned little. He was overthrown in a civil war. A commoner then did get a following and seized the paramount command, but only for a short time. The ariki forces rallied and regained the power in a bitterly vengeful war of extermination.

Two brothers shared in the restoration of aristocratic rule, one described as mild and the other as "savage in every way (Buck 1938a: 79)." The mild brother, it is said, held the greater power, but could not pacify the opposition. Both were then compelled to abdicate in favor of their sons. The younger son of one demanded and was given a third share in the rule. The triple authority, however, only added a fresh source of discord, and a new and more violent civil war erupted. Te Mahuru, one of the three rulers, captured 20 young men of royal birth, had them cooked alive and distributed their flesh in a feast clearly intended to both inflame and humiliate his enemies. Again lands changed hands rapidly. The chronicle of this period sounds a new and despairing note in its references to suicide. Suicide had become common among women driven to frenzies of rage by insult and domestic quarrel. They hurled themselves from the cliffs of Mt. Duff which, as Buck observed, "became the regular suicide cliff in Mangareva (1938a:86)."

A single authority finally took power just before the period of European occupation and restored a traditional senior line. The new ruler, Te Mateoa, was conciliatory, demanding only occasional human sacrifices. In the post-European period one final insurrectionary effort was planned by a high priest who had hoped the missionaries would side with him. They did not and he became again a loyal supporter of traditional authority.

Historical Recapitulation

The opening stages of Mangarevan history reveal a traditional society already well along the road toward a new social order. Warriors interfered with the succession and the paramount chief had come to power as a descendant of the junior line. The initial land distribution may have followed traditional principles, but it prepared the way for a district organization that was more political than familial in composition. On Mangareva, as on Easter, Marquesas, and Mangaia, the decisive political event was the formation of an antagonistic dualism that followed so closely upon the heels of the formal land division that we must regard the two developments as related.

The tradition of formal land allotments within a setting of dissension among kinsmen may be interpreted as a legendary justification for the autonomy of land-holding groups that claimed, nevertheless, a common descent. The tradition seeks to reconcile the differing interests in both separatism and unity. The ability of traditional authority to reassert itself would seem to demonstrate that a concept of legitimacy had never been abandoned despite antagonism. Even when antagonistic dual divisions arose and disrupted seriously the gradations of rank, they did not break the ultimate bonds of respect for seniority. The traditions incidentally, do not speak of the superior mana of chiefs unless the chief was at the same time an inspirational priest. Thus the personal status of the Mangarevan chiefs as portrayed in the traditions was similar to that of the Marquesan chiefs, who could be warriors or priests or political leaders.

The dual rule and then the triple rule were also in a formal sense variations of traditional principles and were encountered in Mangaia and in Manihiki-Rakahanga. But in those societies the divisions followed a functional allocation of authority, dividing religious and economic functions. In Mangareva there was seemingly no functional division at all. The brothers simply divided the lands. The dual rule was a dual division of territory along new lines. It led promptly, as we know, to a new and more bitter round of civil wars.

One can point to events that seemed to have special significance, but one cannot point to clear stages of transformation. We see rather all of Mangarevan history as a record of political unrest and of acute rivalries for power. In the course of these struggles the principles of traditional status were never really overcome or abandoned. They were stretched, and even reshaped to meet the actualities of political life. The senior line was periodically overcome, but it could always reassert itself. The resiliency of the senior line cannot be attributed entirely to respect for the principle of seniority but, judging by the traditions, to its political resourcefulness—the ability to line up support and allocate lands—and its military successes. The change in land tenure, on the other hand, was fundamental, placing the traditional seniority system in a new and distinctive context.

The Status System

Mangareva, like Tonga, illustrates the capabilities of a traditional status system for evolving a powerful centralism and thereby intensifying traditional distinctions between aristocrat and commoner. The Mangarevan nobility, able finally to surmount challenges to their natural authority, emerged stronger than ever. At the same time, warriors also won a place for themselves by opening a distinct realm as a middle class between aristocrat and commoner. Insofar as achieved status was locked within a category of its own, the Mangarevan status system, unlike that of the Marquesan, was dual.

Primogeniture

As in the Marquesas, all first-born, regardless of sex or social standing of family, were granted avoidance respects and were addressed by titles that set forth the special esteem in which they were held. In the most general sense they were the *tama'ere'ere,* those "treated with greatest love (Buck 1938a:119)." All carried the honorific *te-ma,* a name prefix that distinguished them from the more common *teiti.* Thus even after a commoner had become chief, his appelative *teiti* labeled him permanently as a junior. The rule could shift; honor remained constant. More in the traditional than in the Marquesan manner, the Mangarevans also divided male from female first-born. To the male, the *tama a o mua* ("the son who will rule first"), went the actual authority; to the female if she were the first, the respects and honor of being *kura-riki,* "the precious chief." It was in several respects therefore that honor and power had divided in Mangareva.

Seniority of Descent

Mangareva was not so revolutionary as the Marquesas in generalizing primogeniture to the point of erasing the senior lines. On this issue Mangarevans were conservatively traditional. Perhaps it was Rarotongan influence that shored up the senior lines. However, unless we assume even more formidable pressure capable of transforming an established system, we must be prepared to accept the possibility that Mangareva had retained an earlier phase of Marquesan society. Having separated from the Marquesas sometime between A.D. 900–1000, the Mangarevans would have represented the period just prior to the major eruption of status rivalry and when religious monuments were under development; in short, a period suggestive of the Traditional society. If traditionalism then had included senior lines, the Rarotongan migrations in later centuries would have helped sustain an established system.

Under attack, the traditional structure of seniority gave way, not only insofar as traditional unities of line and rule were concerned, but more fundamentally in respect to the unities of senior and junior branches. Buck recognized this important change in Mangarevan society. "In most Polynesian societies," he writes,

> the recognition of relatives sprung from junior branches as *teina* was useful as adding strength to the extended family. In Mangareva, however, is an instance in which the ruler Ohokehu objected to being addressed as a *tuakana* by a fisherman relative. He felt that he was the keel of the rule and stood out alone, so he killed his junior relative (*teina*) for his familiarity (1938a:139).

The incident reveals a strain in kinship loyalties at a critical point. We recognize it as falling within a developing pattern of intrafamilial antagonisms. Conceivably antagonism had gone so far as to break the actual genealogical connections between senior and junior branches, thus carrying out fully the logic of a functional division between landed and landless. Surface evidence suggests that a genealogical break had indeed occurred. "Genealogical records" Buck reminds us, "were as important in Mangareva as in other parts of Polynesia (1938a:15)," yet except for the ruling families none of the chiefly lines had bothered to transmit their pedigrees in the usual manner and none accepted the offer of missionaries to record precious pedigrees in writing. But the Mangarevans have explained this apathy as a desire to break with the pagan past (Buck 1938a:15)—a credible, but not entirely convincing explanation, considering that the ruling line was as zealously Christian as the rest.

Male Line

The fundamental right of the senior male to authority within the family and lineage was asserted in the distinction between *atariki* ("in the image of the chief"), held by the first-born son regardless of how many sisters had been born before him, and *tama'ine* (first-born daughter). The first-born daughter of the paramount chief assumed the honorific *tepeiru*, but, to quote Buck, "she could never be called *tuakana* to her brother and could never succeed to the rule in Mangarevan society (1938a:138)." Thus the political division between male and female was categorical in the traditional manner. While the right to rule was masculine and effective authority depended upon control of lands, women were not entirely outside the political realm. The traditions, for example, reveal that Anua-motua had given substantial land grants to some of his daughters from whom major lineages had subsequently descended (Buck 1938a:156). Moreover, within a pattern of royal polygyny, only the senior wife bore the true heir. Both examples point to a concept of complementary relationships which gave to royal wives and mothers deciding roles but denied them authentic authority. In this respect, too, Mangareva was closer to traditional eastern Polynesia pro-patriliny than the Marquesas. Women do, in fact, appear in the royal lists. According to Buck's explanation they are there not as rulers but as links to authentic ruling lines (1938a:157). Mothers became politically decisive when their sons—brothers to each other—fought for the supreme authority. Then the legitimate heir, the son of the senior wife, drew upon the male line for his support, while his opponents had to depend upon the kin of their mothers. The female lines were thus a politically creative force.

Genealogical Depth

The upper aristocracy alone retained its genealogical connections with first founders. For whatever reason, the lesser chiefs allowed their pedigrees to lapse; the traditional doctrine that honor is equated with depth of pedigree held.

Sanctity

The Mangarevan concept seems to have been in transition from a focus on the inherent to the bestowed. While the potential of sanctity lodged in line and order of birth, the powers could not be authentic without proper ritual on the marae. Under ordinary circumstances validation was automatic and followed the religious cycle in which human agency completed what the divine order had already set in motion. Political rivalry, however, could reverse the order so that control of the marae alone could endow the political authority with sanctity. Control alone was evidently not decisive in overriding the priorities of birth. It was important enough, however, to have become a political issue. For while forced access to sanctity was not admirable, it was allowable.

The idea that sanctity could be "made" is conveyed in the term for high chief, which is shared with the Marquesas. Mangareva, nevertheless, was the more aristocratic and more deeply committed to widening the gulf between *'akariki* and all others. Royal sanctity was expressed in the usual tapus of person, house, and belongings. These tapus were extended to the pregnant royal wife and to all places where the royal child was being reared. Royal infants were hidden away as though to emphasize their exclusive cycle of emergence and growth. Separation is traditional. Mangareva sought also to demonstrate the dread of the sacred, allowing the chief to spear to death any who violated his tapus. Dread of royal sanctity is the theme of this chant:

> Sacredness ascends to the peak of Mangareva
> The sacredness of the high chief Rikitea
> The heart throbs with awe.
> Sacredness surmounts the peak of Aorere
> The sacredness of the high chief Hopokai
> The heart flutters with dread.
> Sacredness envelopes the peak of Taravai
> The sacredness of the high chief Tuata-eriki
> The heart beats with fear.
> Sacredness enshrouds the peak of Mukotaka
> The sacredness of the high chief of Tupou-eriki
> The heart contracts with dread (Buck 1938a:152).

Royal sanctity seems to have been expressed as abstractly awesome. The high chief was a god-equivalent. In one chant he is the "god of the underworld." As an exalted being he is removed from utility. In the Marquesan tradition, applied sanctity, to coin a phrase, was the province of priests, who could be commoners. The Marquesas, however, had set their chiefs forth as political beings. Mangareva in its exaltation of the chiefly concept distinguished between source and management. The ruler was equivalent to a sacred source. He was not an agent of the gods, he was their earth-residing counterpart. They were the sources of crop, of health, and of safety, while he stood on earth as representative of the majesty of power. Priests with their own form of sanctity were in the direct line of transmission of the gods. The ruler had power directly within himself—it is in this sense that he was a source. The priests were possessed by the gods; their sanctity and power was thus fully secondary and derivative. The derivative powers dealt with crops and health; the source power dealt with great issues of human life and death.

Wealth

It is reasonable to assume that objective scarcity gave to food its special significance as symbol of honor, for how else does one account for the distinction between cultivated crops as *kaikai akariki*, "food of the chiefs," and wild plants called "food of the hungry"? The distinction is metaphoric, for commoners did, of course, eat breadfruit and taro. Nevertheless, the metaphor had a bite, for the commoners ate crop food as a royal benefice; deprivation was degradation. Food was the substance of wealth as honor and as power. The high privileges were to fatten and to distribute. The greatest joy in the words of traditional chants was to be an owner of land.

> If he becomes an owner of land
> His people will jump with joy
> The annual breadfruit will come
> The fermented food will follow
> The foods of a king
> To him, the owner of land (Buck 1938a:199–200).

Mangareva more than any other Polynesian society delineated economic honor in diet and in the enjoyment of food. The great antithesis was between crop and wild plant. Crop and fish entered into a more complementary balance. The traditions derive the present population from fishermen, acknowledging that even chiefs once fished. Later, high honor shifted to land and commoners alone became professional fishermen. Since fish were exchanged for crop, the fishermen were only partially reduced. While they were under obligation to trade, they could dare to withhold their fish. The chief who could not compel the fisherman to trade with him had lost his power. The fisherman as a commoner had thus the honor of leverage: he could extract crop and he could weaken the sources of power. This aspect of command stands as a counterpoise to agrarian authority. Its power, however, was circumscribed by the inability of fishermen ever to command a following. If a fisherman could upset a rule by demonstrating its inner weaknesses, he could not establish one. Only land could draw followers as dependent workers, renters, or leaseholders and as recipients of ceremonial distributions.

Corpulence was a religious concept as a sign of divine bounty and as evidence of personal power. The Mangarevans carried out with exuberance the common Polynesian preference for body mass in a chief. Chiefs sent their first-born sons and daughters to secluded fattening centers where they were force-fed from infancy on. At adolescence, barely able to support their own weight, they made a ceremonial appearance—and to be judged. As extravagant manifestations of economic fecundity, the "stoutest were the most esteemed and feared in the islands (Buck 1938a:118)."

Tohunga

Buck gives *ta'hunga* as one of the terms for master craftsman, but not the one in common use. Mangarevans had parted from the Marquesan and Society Islands' tradition by designating both crafts and religious experts as *taura,* the common term for priest. It is not unusual for Polynesians to link priests and craftsmen, but ordinarily they do so under the tohunga concept. The concept of tohunga is so varied we cannot point to a clear distinction between the two modes of combination of specialized abilities. Taura in Mangareva has the particular connotation of powers bestowed by the gods. Ultimately, anyone of whatever social rank could be chosen for a sacred calling. The taura need not be confined to a particular descent line.

Strictly speaking, only the carpenters, the "priests of wood," were material specialists; all other taura were either priests or specialized practitioners within the ceremonial order. The carpenters themselves were part of the ritual establishment, confining themselves to major works. They built the great double canoes, the houses of chiefs and all ceremonial structures, including god images. They were in the service of high gods and so received deference owed to general priests. Other taura were tattooers, undertakers, spirit catchers, healers, sorcerers, dancers, and chanters. Each specialty was granted the honor that was proportional to the standing of its patron deity. Highest honor, though, moved toward the more general functions. The highest priests, usually of the royal line (but not the high chief himself), were in charge of crops. The specialists were inevitably plebeian.

As priests the commoners moved within the atmosphere of high rank. They had sanctity, mana, and often land, the source of formal social position. Thus they were able to enter a new realm in more than the religious sense. In principle, the distinction between high priest and specialist was categorical: the first was born to the position; the second was raised to it. Under some circumstances, however, the plebeian could become a high priest—breaking a barrier in the religious realm—even if he could never become a noble. If the god could be made to remain long enough in an ordinary priest to boost his power and mana, his status would change from ordinary to high priest. The ability of a priest to move into a higher orbit offers a parallel to the de facto ennoblement of commoners who could force their way on to the chief's marae.

Political Hegemony

Mangareva may have preserved more fully than the Marquesas the traditional order of genealogical rank. Nevertheless, de facto power had here too threatened to become the true source of sovereignty. In its later years the great social distinction had come to be that between *pakaora* and *iga;* that is, between victor and vanquished, a distinction comparable to that between the parties of the strong and of the weak in Samoa. There, however, the issue was more symbolic than real. In Mangareva, mastery had harsher consequences. The victors seized lands, thus bringing their victims to close to total reduction in status. Pedigree, though, was irreducible and was always a potential source for recovery.

From the standpoint of actual powers, warfare was the pivot for total reversals in social position. Aristocrats wagered all for what was often only a small quantitative gain. Yet if the stake was absolute control, the small increment represented, nevertheless, the difference between the relative and the total. Thus high chiefs dealt in the absolutes of power: win all, lose all; lower landed ranks risked all for relative gains; but the landless had the most favorable stakes of wagering nothing (but their lives, as did everyone else) for a major reversal of status. As victors they acquired lands and, on a small scale, the status of masters. They became small centers of power.

The traditional source of power, pedigree, was never cut off. It was a constant that could be activated or put to rest depending upon its state of material resources. We are now simply restating the basic Polynesian formulation of power. Mangareva seemed to have been exploring the various capabilities of this formulation. Power was at its height when it fused pedigree, sanctity, and military efficacy. Then the high chief was godlike. He could have people killed for real or fancied slights; he could select a victim at random to avenge a death or to assuage a personal grief. He could also intervene to spare a life. In demonstrating these formidable powers, he also accepted the risks of excess. Public opinion could turn against him and he would be deposed. One suspects that excess was not just an idiosyncrasy of temperament, but a feature of the concept itself. Excess and risk were surely at the heart of the incredible Mangarevan wars.

Sheer physical power was most effective at the middle ranges of status. Buck does not recognize the Mangarevan *ragatira* as a significant social class. As in Tahiti, it had become an economically defined status. The Mangarevan ragatira were originally a genealogical rank that was "later . . . extended to include landed proprietors who rose from plebian stock . . . (Buck 1938a:147)." The point of significance is precisely the capability of economic power to open up a genealogical rank. Pakaora, by comparison, set forth a general concept of power.

The Structure of Status

The pakaora–iga category standing outside genealogical rank sets off achieved as against traditional status and exemplifies the dual character of the system. Duality is the conservative response to stress within the status system. It preserves the traditional order while yielding to the imperatives of power. But it is clear that the ability of a traditional rank order to sustain itself by means of a counterpart system is a demonstration not of weakness but of strength. In the Marquesas, the merging of opposing principles of status virtually eliminated the old order. In Mangareva, even more than in Mangaia, traditionalism met its challenges by intensifying the power of the traditional chiefs and by deepening distinctions between royalty and commoners. Even if genealogy had retained an orderly gradation of ranks, the more categorical distinctions in quality of land tenure would have provoked clear-cut stratification. It is the intentions that are conservative; the effects of economic stratification are not. Stratification preserves traditional ranking at the cost of the social structure as a whole. As for the rank order, it is its formal structure alone that is retained. And while the personae stay put within the structure even as they swing wildly between the extremes of victor or victim, the gist of what they are has been radically transformed.

Genealogical Rank

Mangareva has improvised new terms for rank indicative of structural modifications. *'Akariki* (the cognate form of Marquesas *hakaiki*) had become highly restricted, applicable only to high chiefs. It had become a title of office rather than a general rank in the traditional sense. For aristocrats, generally, a new term, *togo'-iti,* also with the meaning of "chief," has been introduced. Innovations in lower rank terms are common in Polynesia. Aristocrats are generally more conservative and tenacious of old titles, particularly of those as traditional and ancient as *ariki.* Thus we may regard the distinction between 'akariki and togo'iti as somewhat more than nominal. The Mangarevan dictionary (Tregear 1899) defines *'akariki* as "king, lord, high chief." It renders *togo'iti* similarly, adding, however, "the title of a person of dignity or a landowner when addressed by his inferiors, tenants, etc." The distinction might seem to be, then, between a generalized and more specifically economic status. In the term *ataeiki,* which Tregear mentions as the synonym of *'akariki,* the reference is still more general and in particular, nonmanagerial. It means, "to do nothing, and to dress richly in a luxurious way." Etymology thus conforms rather closely to sociology in this instance, adding support to historical evidences of shift in emphasis from pedigree to land. The social distinctions between 'akariki and togo'iti hinge upon command and upon acquired sanctity. In principle, the 'akariki should represent the senior line; in fact, he was often the head of the most powerful line. The very close kin of the paramount chief could also be called 'akariki; their ordinary designation though was *momomomo,* an untranslated term that served to set them apart from togo'iti.

Following the traditional system, ragatira should be recognized as a rank (despite Buck's omission), as a newly evolved conglomerate that included, on the one hand, the junior range of nobility and, on the other, newly elevated commoners who had acquired land of a size to support servants. Ragatira was the highest formal status open to commoners by virtue of economic standing and of honorific association.

'Urumanu is an innovative term for commoner, meaning, generally, "the poor, the herd" (Tregear 1899) and hence somewhat derogatory as compared with Marquesas *mata-ei-nana.*[1] Tregear suggests an etymology that defines the category even more specifically as "lowly." He considers the term to be compounded of *uru,* which means the southwest wind, the hair on the body, feathers, and, in another direction, to repair. The related term *urunui* means feeble and sluggish. *Manu* has another set of meanings, referring to sore mouth, nausea, as well as to bird, or beast. The full meaning may be unclear, but the implications of softness and of weakness are quite unmistakable.

In this instance, too, etymology fits sociology. The 'urumanu, who were the great majority of the population, are not to be regarded merely as junior descendants of noble lines. They are a true class of social and economic subordinates. The quality of their land tenure may be crudely described as "landless." They were, of course, for the most part, cultivators settled on lands they could bequeath to their own heirs. Tenure, however, was regulated by togo-'iti, or by pakaora (and fundamentally by the 'akariki), who also set conditions of occupancy which allowed them to evict for various causes, among them failure to pay rent, neglecting to weed, or personally offending the landowner. Land was so scarce that 'urumanu competed for this kind of tenancy. They would spread scandalous tales about tenants to bring about their eviction.

Genealogical commoners were economically diverse. The wealthiest gained a notch in rank; the iga escaped the stigma of being mere tenants. Some were but land laborers, who had no cultivations to transmit. These were *kio,* a term meaning "to extinguish," an implication of status reduction that speaks for itself. Those who had no association with the land at all were at the very bottom. They were

1. But see *Huramana* in Easter Island.

kiore, or "rats," who were often compelled to rob graves for food. Fishermen, also commoners and also landless, escaped reduction because of the special relationship of autonomy and reciprocity vis à vis the nobility.

In summary, Mangareva exhibits some of the main processes of conversion (incomplete to be sure) of ranks into economic classes. The upper ranks as centers of political and economic power had become restricted: only one family was 'akariki; only some ten families were great landholders and togo'iti. The contraction of aristocracy was accompanied by an expansion of the middle represented by ragatira and commoner-swelled pakaora. In terms of the principles of the status system, 'urumanu would remain relatively stable.

Status Rivalry

Mangareva reveals the familiar cycle of rivalries that starts among kin, divides them, and finally turns them to seek one another's subjugation or destruction. It is out of desperation at conditions into which they have driven themselves that the chiefs and their allies are compelled to abandon revered traditions and submit themselves to the uncertainties of open combat. They may not have welcomed the consequences, but the choice of endowing risk with honor was surely voluntary. What is distinctive about the Mangarevan cycle of rivalries is little more than its intensity.

Intensity of rivalry and the polarization of statuses suggests at least one of the conditions by which traditional land tenures are changed. In similar social settings in the Marquesas, in Mangaia, and in Easter Island economic subjugation had become both symbol and utilitarian prerequisite of the new master–subject relationship. Polarization postulates victimization; denigration of quality of land tenure is for farmers as harsh a definition of victim as can be stated. Polynesia offers at least four examples of economic stratification based upon conditions of land tenure. In three of these, commoners had become landless under quite different ecological circumstances. Thus objective scarcity may not be the critical factor. More basic is the concept of polarization, an inevitable by-product of rivalry. This question, though, is best left to the final chapters.

Descent Group Organization

Although Mangareva was settled originally by several unrelated families, there is reason to suppose an eventual linking-up of most families through intermarriages. But the supposition of kinship unity is hypothetical and does not represent, in any case, the Mangarevan conception of kinship. The organic links that really counted were those that bound people firmly to important chiefs (Buck 1938a:139). From the example of the chief who had killed his brash but well-meaning plebeian kinsman for unwanted intimacy, we detect a novel and dangerous mode of familial fragmentation. The political tie generally had begun to replace that of kinship.

To describe its members as organic descendants of a common line, most tribal names carry the prefix *ati* before the name of the founding ancestor. The system of naming must refer to a more traditional period, since the tribes were not in fact composed of kin. The actual genealogical composition of a tribe is not really known. What is known is its general makeup: All important tribes incorporated dependent and defeated peoples from other groups (Buck 1938a:140). A few tribes used only the definite article *te*, which carries no connotation of descent. Given the circumstances of war and of defeat, the difference between *ati* and *te* is not one of actual but of traditional composition.

Mangarevan traditions imply traditional segmentation—as in the Anua-motua narrative. In the more recent historical period, there is very little suggestion of the traditional segmental order. Perhaps the change was more apparent than real, resulting from nothing more than a technical factor, namely, loss of interest in pedigree. Yet the general question is relevant. Can a segmentary order survive the physical dislocations and the ideological disorientation of prolonged antagonism? At best, Polynesian segmentation has a political quality. In Mangareva, history and the simplification of nomenclature suggests a Marquesan type of development. There were but two categories of kin grouping, the *u* ("people") as most inclusive, and the *ina'o* ("family, tribe") as its subdivision. Only the latter category specifically implied kinship.

Segment I, the u, was a political entity. It encompassed each of the two great divisions of Mangareva, Taku, and Rikitea, and the entire island whenever the authority had become central. Buck, always having in mind the traditional Polynesian organization, visualized its political leader ('akariki) as the senior descendant of the senior ina'o. Originally, this may have been the case. But when Buck is speaking of specific Mangarevan history he sees the social structure in a different light. Describing the paramount chiefship he says:

> Certain chiefs with strong family groups extended their influence over other weaker family groups who allied themselves with the stronger group to avoid trouble and to consolidate their own position. The chief who extended his influence be-

> came a *'akariki,* and this extended authority was termed *ao* (rule). . . . Maintenance of the rule of a *'akariki* depended on the strength of his own tribe and the support he received from alliances with other tribes (1938a:157).

The great power of the 'akariki, especially when he had won his office, gave to the u the attributes of a political state—in miniature. The u was then a focus of ritual life centered in the marae of the chief; and it was the economic center insofar as the 'akariki redistributed land holdings after a military victory.

The relationship of ina'o to the entire political community may have been genealogical at one time. The known connections were rather religious and expedient. The political concept was more feudal than familial. The paramount chief ruled his u according to political realities. Some of its tribes represented autonomous federations of allies; others were bound together hierarchically as master–dependent. In sum, the relationship of ina'o to its 'akariki depended upon its own standing among fellow tribes. Regardless of political ties, all accepted a more equal membership in the religious community of the u. The local chiefs passed along first fruits and a portion of their breadfruit yield for public distribution at harvest festivals. The connections of the 'akariki were with the tribal chiefs and not directly with the people.

Segment II is ina'o, and like the Marquesan hua'a it most often represented a patrilineal core of original descendants around whom adhered a mixed population of kinsmen and others. Buck believes the ina'o was originally ruled by its senior line. As he says, "the rule [of seniority] was broken occasionally through the ambition and personality of juniors. The question as to whether or not departure from the pattern became established depended on their being able to hold by force of arms the position they had usurped (1938a:157)."

Buck calls attention to the difference between ina'o and ivi. The latter, he says, "stresses the genealogical relationship of the family"; the former "implies the large families expanding into a tribe." The distinction is one of degree. The absorption of the weak and the subjugated allowed ina'o to grow politically: "People in stress sought the protection of the chief who had land and power (Buck 1938:143)." Outside the genealogical lines of togo'iti, it was the politically determined land connections that replaced kinship ties. Political fortune was the active variable in the ina'o, regulating its size, its rate of growth, its internal composition, its internal hierarchical structure and its standing within the divisional coalitions.

The mixed political-genealogical character of ina'o is illustrated best by its territorial relations. Most tribes were contained within a defined territory where a variable combination of rights established the status of particular families. Only two actual families were represented in different tribes, an indication not of the family character of the tribe, but rather of the incapacity or indifference—it is hard to say which—of the families to segment. Of the two that could sustain branching across the political barriers, one was the *Ati-kura,* an aristocratic family of very high standing.

The tribal chief was *'akao,* a term with the connotation of having acquired power (*aka*—to make; *ao*—to have authority over [Tregear 1899]). His assembly place (*to'ua*) was also an administrative and ritual center, parallel to that of the 'akariki. Economy was a tribal concern only at critical points of redistribution. The organization of production was not a tribal, but a local concern.

Subdivisions of tribes were large extended families which could be known as *ivi* when the actual blood lines were being considered, or as *vao* or *pa'a* when the issue was territorial. Vao has the specific meaning of uninhabited land, while pa'a refers in a similar vein to a bay. The territorial significance of both terms is best understood as a contrast to *kaiga,* which refers to the cultivated lands of a household. In Mangareva, kaiga had no reference to a social group. Vao and pa'a thus identify a population from the more strictly territorial standpoint. The vao (or pa'a) is then Segment III. Its composition and social character also depends upon its political status; that is, upon the standing of its head. It would hardly be possible under existing conditions for a vao to cohere without a strong chief at its head.

Segment IV was the household of three or more lineal generations occupying one or more dwellings and possessing kaiga. With residence commonly patrilocal (unless the wife were of higher status), the family too tended to exist as a patrilineal core which could add to itself servants and other dependents. Ultimately, the social composition of the ina'o was the sum of the political statuses of its individual families and households. The strong cohered; the weak dispersed.

9

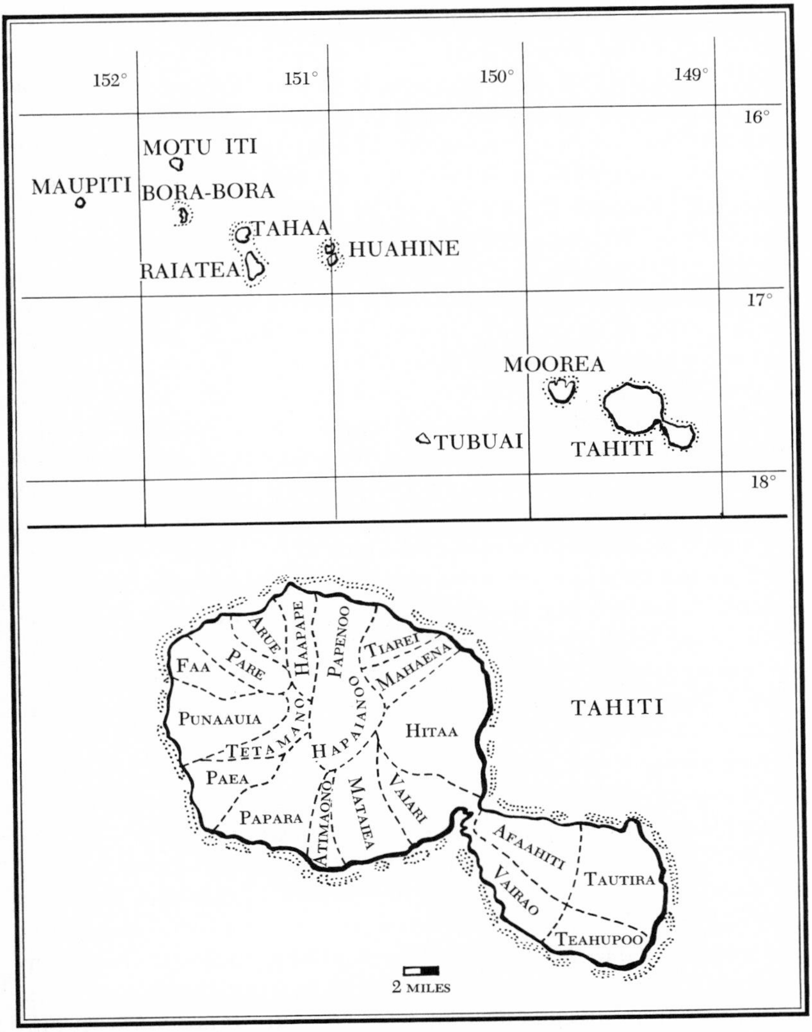

The Society Islands

LIKE THE MARQUESAS, THE SOCIETY ISLANDS STAND AS PRIMARY AND formative cultural centers of eastern Polynesia. The Marquesas would appear to be the older and perhaps the parent culture, but if they are, the separation would have occurred as early as A.D. 500 by one calculation (Elbert 1953), or 100 B.C. by another (Emory 1963). Even if at the more probable later date, the separation would have taken place during the early part of the Marquesan Developmental Period, when cultural differentiation had not fully asserted itself. Since Marquesan and Tahitian (Society) are the two principal divergent language groups of eastern Polynesia (Green 1966), we must assume that both cultural traditions subsequently developed in relative independence of each other. Mangareva, for example, had to be considered as a specific elaboration of the early part of the expansionist period of Marquesan history. Society Islands culture and its achievement of stratification and political centralism was more fully an indigenous product. Thus the parallels between Mangareva and the Society Islands suggest the operation of similar historical processes of internal growth, rather than effects of continuous contacts. The antiquity of Society Islands culture it should be said at once has been assumed from linguistic and general historical inferences and not from direct archeological knowledge. Specific radiocarbon dates do not antedate A.D. 1100 (Sinoto 1964), but resemblances between a Tahitian burial site (undated) and what has been designated as the New Zealand Moa-hunter period (ca. A.D. 950) suggest that the Society Islands may have been settled somewhat earlier, as Emory (1963) and others believe, and thus are more likely to have in fact been a center of secondary diffusion.

Even before it had reached its apogee as a European kingdom, the social system of the Society Islands, with its focus in Tahiti, had evolved beyond the Mangarevan, at least in complexity and in magnitude. The basic principles of stratification and of centralism were the same, but the greater size of the Society Islands and their economic vitality obviously provided opportunities for social elaboration that were denied to the more impoverished Mangarevans. The Society archipelagoes are among the largest in Polynesia and held a pre-European population estimated as high as 200,000, compared with only several thousand on atoll-sized Mangareva. The most impressive material manifestations of magnitude were the maraes, which, on Tahiti, had reached their highest development in all of Polynesia, and the systems of terraces and irrigation comparable to those of Hawaii. In terms of political development, the Tahitian "state" was closer to the Mangarevan than to the Hawaiian in its aboriginal condition. When the Tahitian kingdom was established it was more fully a European creation than its Hawaiian counterpart. Hawaii, as we shall see, had already begun to move in new directions. Tahiti and the Society Islands generally, on the other hand, had developed along more traditional lines.

The fourteen islands of the Society group fall into two geographic divisions. The Windwards, lying eastward, include Tahiti, Moorea, Meetia, and Tetuaroa; the Leewards, lying westward, include Raiatea, Huahine, Tahaa, Borabora, Maupiti, and several small atolls. The Tuamotu atolls are geographically distinct but came under Tahitian political and cultural influences in the eighteenth century. All the islands shared a common culture and were interwoven into a single genealogical system. Two divergent traditions, however, had developed among them. Raiatea had risen to eminence as the citadel of aristocracy and Tahiti, known also as Tahiti *manahune*, "plebeian Tahiti," had become the center of military and political power and eventually the seat of the central authority. The rise of Tahiti and the political eclipse of Raiatea defines rather closely the pattern of social evolution on these islands.

The Societies are among the most fertile and productive of all Polynesian islands. Tahiti was shipping surplus foods—breadfruit, coconut, fowl, and pigs—to all neighboring islands and as far away as the Tuamotus long before the European period (Maude 1959).

All the Society Islands had the reputation among early mariners as bountiful where supplies could be replenished. While the cone-shaped volcanic islands such as Tahiti were virtually uninhabitable at their center, they were well-watered, and all possessed extremely fertile coastal plains which were able to sustain almost the entire population. Tahiti's coasts were densely packed, with as many as 1,000 persons per mile (Adams 1947). The Tahitians added space by moving up into the higher interior valleys, terracing and irrigating as far as the precipitous terrain would allow.

This picture of productivity is, of course, general. As almost everywhere in Polynesia, local conditions varied widely, depending on the direction of the trade winds. East-west valleys are generally hot and dry; those facing north-south, cool and moist. On Tahiti, towering peaks interfered with rainfall so that even adjacent regions had very different climates. All the Society high islands are rugged and ecologically diverse, with rich and poor zones, and hence with rich and poor, and strong and weak tribes. But if regions were deficient in crops, they were almost certain to have fish in plenty; the islands are surrounded by reefs that enclose fishing lagoons. The Tahitians also constructed artificial fish ponds; they fished the rivers and the lakes. Agriculture was diversified. The major crops were breadfruit, banana, plantain, taro, yam, sweet potato, and sugar cane. Hogs were very abundant, and fowl and dog completed the inventory of animal food.

The Society Islands reached their political climax and their precipitous cultural decline almost at the same time. When Europeans began to arrive in numbers in the late eighteenth century, the island chiefs were already at war with one another for political domination. Whether any had then the exalted ambition to rule over all the far-flung Society Islands we cannot be sure; but chiefs had already brought neighboring islands within their political scope. In any case, Pomare I was not slow to seize upon the opportunities for unification given him so gladly by his European friends. He and his successor, Pomare II, created a European style rule that presided over the dissolution of native life and custom. In 1797, only nine years after the ill-fated Captain Bligh and his bully crew had joined in the civil wars, the population of Tahiti, which Cook had put at 100,000, had fallen to 16,000. By 1815, when all resistance to the central Tahitian command had ended, the count stood at 10,000.

Quiros, in 1606, was the first to sight the Society Islands. The honor of the first European visit, however, goes to Wallis, who spent five weeks on Tahiti in 1767. Bougainville arrived in 1768 and Cook in the following year. The European influence did not make itself felt until 1788 when the Bounty dropped anchor and began to trade guns for pork, and Bligh had thrown his weight behind Tu (later Pomare I), then still a local chieftain. When the London Missionary Society established itself on Tahiti in 1797, many chiefs, who had already witnessed the ineffectiveness of their familiar gods in protecting them, were easily drawn into the new and more potent faith.

Native institutions and traditions were erased before they could be fully investigated, but the historical record is by no means bare. The Reverend Ellis of the London Mission, and Judge Orsmond described with scrupulous care the native life as they saw it and as they heard it from Tahitian narrators from the combined period from 1817 to 1856. Ellis' very rich and early account is first-hand. De Bovis, particularly apt on political life, recorded native events and recollections between 1845 and 1891. In 1891 Henry Adams transcribed the memoirs of an old chiefess of the leading Tahitian line. The *arii* Taimai had the vivid recollection of the past that is the gift of the set-aside aristocrat. In 1923 Handy salvaged the last remaining crumbs from local memory. Finally, Douglas Oliver has now compiled and evaluated virtually the entire corpus of Tahitian records (not yet published).

Genealogical Traditions

The genealogical record consists of lists of chiefly lines from the main islands that extend back for 42 generations, or to ca. A.D. 900. These lists are not, however, consistently associated with particular events that make up the traditional lore of the islands. The traditions cannot be consecutively dated, but are useful as indications of broad and general patterns of development. They suggest, for example, that traditional aristocracy had reached its highest development on Raiatea and then spread outward, reaching Tahiti and other Windward islands. In the course of its development and movement outward, the Raiatean aristocracy became converted from what seems to have been a religiously oriented to a more politically oriented system. At the same time, the small military chiefdoms of Tahiti had grown in size and had assumed a more aristocratic character. Finally, speaking now very broadly, the mature form of Tahitian Stratified society may be explained as a fusion of the two. Handy has indeed presented a similar idea in his view that the Raiatean aristocracy had conquered "plebeian" Tahiti, imposing over a common population an arii rule. Conquest and superimposition imply a more violent and drastic meeting of the two cultures than the actual historical evidence would suggest. We see rather a fusion between two closely related social systems that had, however, evolved at different rates.

Tahitian traditions describe Raiatea as the great center of traditional aristocracy (Henry 1928:119). Raiatea was divided from earliest times into districts that were subordinate in rank to Opoa, which held the island-wide marae of Taputapu-atea, which eventually became the religious hub of all the Society Islands in a religious confederation that Mühlmann (1938) has compared with the amphyctyony of the Greeks. Originally, the traditions say (Henry 1928:120), Taputapu-atea was the national marae of Raiatea and represented only its eight districts and their chiefs. Then, as a result of intermarriages between Raiateans and families on other islands, the genealogical connections with the central marae spread outward. We can only assume that if Taputapu-atea at Opoa became an "international" religious center, then—in a manner comparable to that of the Great Fono of Samoa—it had come to represent the highest rank within an extensive genealogical empire. In time the Opoa center became more militant. Enemy skulls were brought to it, and branches of the central marae, bearing the same name of Taputapu-atea, were established on Tahiti and elsewhere in the Windwards. The outward spread of this marae was carried by intermarriages, since it was customary for members of the same pedigree to give religious sanction to the connection by building a new marae around foundation stones taken from the older. Thus each new marae was as much a literal branch of the old as was the newly formed family connection. As Tahitian families intermarried with Raiatea, they built branches of Taputapu-atea on their own island. We must assume, therefore, that Opoa retained its religious and social influences over the new Tahitian branches, but without political authority. The Tahitian traditions speak of violent opposition to the burden of so many new marae. "Crushed will be Tahiti before the marae," says the historical chant. The building of the new maraes evidently was accompanied by an outbreak of wars, because they were embellished with human skulls in honor of Oro the god of war. Since Opoa had already become an Oro or war cult center, the spread of its influence presumably carried the militant doctrine with it. We must, however, suspect a political set of causes for war, because the marae in eastern Polynesia was inevitably a center of local authority; and the building of new maraes in densely populated coastal zones must be taken to imply some form of political expansion.

The great Opoa religious confederation finally broke apart as a result of quarrels some time in the fourteenth century, by genealogical dating (Henry 1928:127), and only the religious associations between Raiatea and Tahiti were retained. In time even the religious connection had become a symbol of the genealogical relationships, rather than a branch of a cult. In any case, the more specific history of Tahiti describes an autonomous island made up of several independent districts.

The most numerous grouping from which a central authority finally arose was a section of the island occupied by what the arii Taimai has called a "clan." This clan, known as Teva, was divided into eight districts—a common pattern of subdivision in the Society Islands—one of which, in Raiatean style, was recognized as the senior and thus the dominant line. The first recorded senior branch of the "clan" was the Vaiari. We do not know the nature of Vaiari authority. It must have had political prerogatives, however, because when sometime in 1400 the Vaiari were "overthrown" by a junior branch, the Papara district, the result, as Taimai narrates the event, was to separate politics and the prestige of pedigree. Taimai, herself of Papara, comments,

> But while Papara took the political headship, it could not take the social superiority, for as long as society should last the

> Marae of Farepua [Vaiari] must remain the older and superior over all the Maraes of Papara (Adams 1947:18).

What may have been a parallel decline in the traditional aristocracy took place on Huahine, whose royal line was connected matrilineally with the royal line of Raiatea. The traditions say that the first Huahine dynasty was overthrown by a warrior chief, a distant member of its royal line. He then founded a new dynasty that ruled into historic times (Henry 1928). On Tahiti, on the other hand, the trend of history went in the opposite direction before it turned again. Most ancient Tahiti, the traditions record, was once physically part of Raiatea and then broke away. The statement may be a metaphor for political detachment or, more likely, for social contrast, since Tahiti was then supposed to be without royalty and without gods. In the words of the traditional chant: "There was no royal family upon Tahiti of the warriors as it came away; the warriors who owned it and their clans took charge of the land as it broke loose; for this cause it was named Tahiti-*manahune* (Henry 1928:439)."

Papara's political supremacy did not go unchallenged. The next major event took place in 1650, when a civil war had loosened the political grip of Papara. The effect of this minor upheaval was to disturb the balance of forces on the island. For when Bougainville came to Tahiti in 1768 he found that the Tevas under Papara were confronted by a coalition of two newly formed groups of districts which had heretofore not disputed their position on the island. Immediately after Bougainville's departure, Papara was attacked and defeated. Taking part in the attack was one of the district chiefs of the Teva who was related to the Papara line. Political power on the island passed from Papara to the coalition. The *maro ura,* a red-feather girdle and the symbol of highest rank, was then transferred from the marae at Papara to the marae of Attahara, one of the conquering districts. With this event the traditional order was seriously dislocated. The aftermath was a new round of civil wars in which former allies turned upon each other. Taimai has explained the civil wars of Tahiti as a typically violent reaction against excessive concentration of powers. If the English had not intervened in behalf of Pomare, she believes, he could never have become ruler. As a descendant of an inferior chiefly line, he lacked the traditional credentials, and he would not have been tolerated by local chiefs jealous of their autonomy and of their ancestral prerogatives. Yet in the end Pomare, who had been relatively low in the scale, took all the power and the glory—the rights to genealogical superiority. Taimai, who must be regarded as the authentic chronicler of these events from the inside, says it was "English guns" that brought Pomare to his eminent position. But she does not see him as a foreign puppet. On the contrary, as she observes from the distance of a lost past, Pomare had a clear vision of his road. As she explained to Henry Adams:

> Pomare could gain his object in no other way than by destroying one after another the whole of the old chiefly class. . . . He was a consummate politician, for the art of politics was the life of the chiefly class, and every chief knew by instinct and by close personal contact the character and thought of every other chief on the island. Pomare knew that what he was trying to do could be done only by wholesale destruction, and that, in order to do it, he must depend on outsiders; white men, or Raiateans or savages from the Paumotos (1947:138).

In the light of Taimai's evaluation of Pomare, the ultimate unification of the Society Islands must be recognized as the result of adding external means to the native intent. Without English arms and missionary effort, Pomare might have been defeated and the balance of unstable powers restored. The intent of conquest and even the concept of unification was, however, Tahitian.

The Archeological Record

Recent archeological investigations have not yet added much to the traditional records. To the extent to which these can be verified at all, there is only the surface examination of maraes to go upon. The study of maraes has verified some cultural distinctions between the provinces of Raiatea and Tahiti and suggests at the same time a process of gradual enlargement and a special pattern of distribution of aristocratic and commoner populations. In the Leeward islands the stone tradition was "megalithic," employing large trimmed slabs of limestone to build small and rather simple maraes. In the Windwards, centered on Tahiti, the marae structures were monumental and architectually sophisticated but were built of small stones that were expertly and painstakingly dressed and shaped. Emory (1933:6) has judged the Tahitian type of marae as later on the grounds of stylistic development, thus adding weight to the tradition on this point. The Tahitian maraes, true to the more intense political rivalry on that island, were the largest in the Societies, but the maraes of the Raiatean area also grew progressively. On Tahiti, Emory distinguished between the smaller and simpler inland maraes, which were little more than paved rectangular courts surrounded by a low wall (as in the Hawaiian Islands), and the coastal marae structures, which combined a court with a truncated pyramid. The great marae in Papara—which was being built when Wallis arrived—had an 11-step pyramid 50 feet high, and an attached court that measured 367 by 267 feet. Tahiti also had a third type of stone monument, the ahu, a one-step platform faced with cut stone. The ahu appeared everywhere on the island. In the light of the widespread distribution of simple rectangular courts and single-step platforms in eastern Polynesia, Emory's surmise that the coastal marae was the most recent form that combined the two is entirely reasonable. The coastal maraes could only have been built by chiefs who commanded large populations. Tahitian traditions describe an early settlement pattern which oriented rank in space by giving to the upper ranks the use of the jutting capes, to the lower gentry the indented bays, and to the commoners the inland zones. The actual distribution of types of marae only approximately fits this pattern. The large and more complex coastal maraes demarcated the territory of the senior lineages, and the smaller and simpler inland maraes marked the local centers of their subordinate branches. By the evidence of genealogy, the large coastal maraes were built late; probably, Emory believes, after 1600. They may have been replacements for simpler maraes that stood just behind them. If this interpretation is correct, it documents in stone the evidence from traditions that larger and more powerful chiefships had replaced a smaller political system. The construction of larger maraes on Tahiti than on Raiatea attests to growing power of the former, for the size of marae was the constant Polynesian index of political standing.

Historical Recapitulation

Neither traditions nor archeology are substantial enough to delineate more than sketchily the currents and tides of Society Islands' history. Therefore it would be misleading to say that archeology confirms the traditions. Still, both lines of historical evidence do run parallel and thus support certain very broad conclusions; namely, that what seems to have been a traditional aristocracy had become subordinate to more aggressive political forces; Tahiti underwent a later development and surpassed Raiatea. There may be some social clues in the styles of stone work, but can we really say that the cutting and use of very large stones is more aristocratic than the use of small stones? Size is a more intangible matter, and the significance of the complex Papara marae dwarfing the renowned traditional center of Opoa is unmistakable. In summary: archeology and traditions define an Early Period with a religious and traditional focus in Raiatea from which an inter-island ecumenical community depended; a Middle Period when the religious focus weakened and a more fully military and political emphasis developed in Tahiti; and, finally, a Late Period, coinciding with the coming of Europeans when active warfare for conquest laid the foundation for a state. The Early Period fits in general the picture of the Traditional Society; the Middle Period is Open; and the Late Period which is historical Tahiti is, of course, Stratified.

The Status System

Social conditions in the Society Islands were undoubtedly diverse even into the Late (or historic) Period. It is the Tahitian system that became dominant and it is in fact the only one known in appreciable detail. The Tahitian status system was complex. It resembled in some respects the dual system of Mangareva in its recognition of distinctive categories of genealogical rank and of achieved statuses, but allowed for a mixed status that combined rank and achievement and offered a greater variety of opportunities for commoners. Nevertheless, respect for genealogical rank never wavered.

Primogeniture

All first-born were honored, regardless of sex or station. In principle, and by preference, only the first-born male, who alone bore the title of *matahiapo,* could assume leadership. Yet the political prominence of women in later Tahitian history can only mean that order of birth finally outweighed the preference for the male. As in the Marquesas the matahiapo became the family "head" immediately upon his birth, superseding his father in rank but not immediately in authority. Investiture was necessarily postponed until after adolescence. The Tahitian view on primogeniture was the most extreme in Polynesia, for it insisted that no one could stand before the first-born. Among high-ranking or arii families where the issue of succession to command was of great consequence, the first-born son of a first-born female was also named matahiapo, and so recognized as a potential heir.

Seniority of Descent

The fidelity with which all chiefly lines, including that of Pomare, adhered to primogeniture as the rule for chiefly succession must demonstrate, if only indirectly, the consistent Tahitian regard for the senior line. As Taimai explained, the authority could leave seniority, but the rank-order of prestige could not deviate. In the end, as the

Pomare history reveals, the principle of seniority could be breached but never flouted. The Pomare dynasty having been established, it validated its claim both to power and to prestige by demonstrating its genealogical connections to the senior chiefly lines of Raiatea and Huahine. An example of a disputed succession, cited by Taimai (Adams 1947:33) asserts, however, a special Tahitian version of seniority: the first-born had the undisputed claim to the chiefship, but the younger sons were not ranked, and each had an equal claim. Genealogical rank, accordingly, was governed by seniority, but was not graded by it. Taimai, for example, speaks of senior and junior branches as two categories of rank. Gradations, as she illustrates them, arise from the general pattern of genealogical distinction and not from degree of closeness to a senior line of chiefs. In short, the extraordinary degree of deference for primogeniture (a further variation of the Marquesan pattern) reduced and generalized all other birth orders and endowed seniority with an absolute quality. The implications of this system of ranking for social stratification are self-evident. Gradation by order of birth unifies an ethnic community; the Tahitian system categorizes it. Beyond the realm of first-born of first-born, there was a closely related order of near descendants of chiefly lines. Beyond this select group lay a new and distinct order of status. Arii were heads of districts which were either the senior line or the junior branch. The districts were not ranked. The Society Islands' aristocracy were drawn into a comprehensive hierarchy that granted each arii general honors and prerogatives that were recognized everywhere, in addition to those he held exclusively in his own territory. There is no evidence that even this comprehensive hierarchy recognized gradations of seniority.

Male Line

The early generations of the Pomare line followed the male line exclusively. On the Tahitian branch, for example, no female is even listed among royal offspring until the 29th generation, or fewer than 100 years before Pomare's own accession to a chiefship. The mother of Pomare was the first female chieftain in this genealogy. As the senior of four children (two male, two female), she succeeded to the chiefship. At this very late date in Tahitian history, then, the rights of primogeniture overrode those of the male line (Henry 1928:247–49). On Raiatea the first female chieftain was not installed until 1881. A 14-generation genealogy from Borabora leads to the same conclusion, namely, that the male line was politically supreme until very late in Tahitian history. Whatever the earlier position of women had been, they had truly risen to extraordinary prominence. The arii Taimai, with understandable pride in her sex, spoke of the "tremendous" importance of women. Her examples show women as masterful and militant actors on the political stage, quite capable of pushing their men back into the wings. Early European chroniclers thought they had detected in Tahiti evidences of an ancient matriarchy, insofar as the mother was more influential for the child's rank than his father, when the marriage had not been among equals.

There is no doubt therefore that in the new Tahiti women had scored a major political triumph. The change in the status of women has its counterpart in the reduction of the status of the male line. Status descent became bilateral among chiefly families. Outside the chiefly lines, the traditional Polynesian doctrine that regarded men as sacred and women as profane still prevailed, according to Ellis, a most reliable eyewitness (1831:I, 129). Birth rituals, he noticed, were held for males but not for girls except among the highest ranking families (1831:I, 259). The great disproportion of men to women (4–1), which can only be explained by a high rate of female infanticide, must surely reflect upon the lower status of women, at least among the general public.

Genealogical Depth

A deep genealogy back to a "first beginning" was essential for the validation of rights to land and rights to rule. The Pomare genealogy is a case in point. It goes as far back as it can on Tahiti and then picks up branches on other islands, including the Raiatean, for maximum depth. In land disputes, the antiquity of the pedigree decided the issue (Davies 1851:iv). The genealogical connection evidently involved somewhat more than the recitation of lines of descent; it was founded in the very solid notion of the continuity of the family marae, the religious center of the prerogatives of a lineage. When a new branch was founded elsewhere, the new marae was built around stones taken from the old, and so rights in the old marae were transferred to the new. Genealogical depth implied, therefore, more than continuity; it also implied the multiplication and generalizing of rights. The lower ranks had not only fewer but also more restricted rights.

Sanctity

The image of a ruler astride the shoulders of a retainer who carries him about so that the royal feet should not taboo the ground has doubtless created in the European mind the most bewildering impression compounded of the awesome and the absurd. Pomare no doubt added to this bewilderment when he told Cook mock-boastfully how superior he was to the King of England, who merely rode a horse while he, Pomare, rode a person. In setting Cook down, Pomare reveals the same wry Tahitian humor that also enlivens the Tamai commentary. But, of course, he also identifies for us the meaning of the royal sanctity in Tahiti. The tapu is the sanctity of separation that places the ruler in a category from which all others must be excluded. Through separation he is elevated; his elevation demands a corresponding degradation; and that is the visible role of his bearer.

It is difficult to say where in Polynesia the royal sanctity was most dramatically displayed in its dual aspects of separation and of elevation–degradation. Tahiti, Hawaii, and Tonga made the same claims for their high chiefs but portrayed the theme of sanctity somewhat differently. I deal with the general questions of aristocratic sanctity in Chapter 23. The concern here is with the Tahitian pattern which is as extreme as any Polynesian statement on the theme of royal sanctity. Yet awesome as the display of royal dignity may have been, the ruler could just as suddenly be degraded and reduced to the common level. When chiefs had become "despotic and detested," Henry writes, the priests and the council of chiefs denounced him, saying: " 'Go and eat the leg of pork seared with dung! Thy royalty is taken from thee, thou art put down to tread the sand, to walk like common men' (1928: 196)." Thus, while the royal sanctity was carried in Tahiti to unusual heights, it and the man were separable. What is extraordinary about the Tahitian concept of loss is that it was not as in New Zealand the penalty for weakness, but for excess. To penalize excess is to introduce a political concept of social equilibrium. The Tahitians accepted and may have admired the symbolic display of excess, but they demanded respect for the actual balance of powers.

Symbolic excess was displayed in tapu of contact and association. These tapus have been summarized by Rev. Ellis:

> Everything in the least degree connected with the king or queen—the cloth they wore, the house in which they dwelt, the canoes in which they voyaged, the men by whom they were borne when they journeyed by land, became sacred—and even the sounds in the language, composing their names, could no longer be appropriated to ordinary significations. Hence the original names of most of the objects with which they were familiar, have from time to time undergone considerable alterations. The ground on which they accidentally trod, became sacred; and the dwelling under which they might enter, must for

> ever after be vacated by its proprietors, and could be appropriated only to the use of these sacred personages. No individual was allowed to touch the body of the king or queen; and everyone who should stand over them, or pass the hand over their heads, would be liable to pay for the sacrilegious act with the forfeiture of his life. It was on account of this supposed sacredness of person that they could never enter any dwellings, excepting those that were specially dedicated to their use, and prohibited all others; nor might they tread on the ground in any part of the island but their own hereditary districts (1853:III, 101–2).

The aspect of awe that certifies to the power of royal sanctity was brought out through human sacrifices. Sacrifices are to honor gods; when they accompany the main transitions in the life of royalty they endow them with attributes of divinity as well. In Tahiti human sacrifices were offered during various stages in the growth of the royal heir; again at the inauguration of a new marae, and at the preparation of the red-feather girdle, the principal symbol of royalty; and finally, to signal military victory, the expression of royal power, and at military defeat as a way of offsetting the apparent decline in royal power.

The sources of sanctity were divine and were carried only by the genealogical line through primogeniture and seniority. Sanctity could be lost; it could not be acquired. The highest chiefs were descendants of the high gods and were entitled to wear the feather girdle, the costume of the gods (Henry 1928:229). They carried the mana of the people. The chief, in the words of Handy, was "*mai iho,* which means umbilicus, path, core, the first fruit, the medium through whom flowed fertility to the land, prosperity to the people in peace time, and power in war (1928:46)."

The imagery of royalty was of the sky. The high chief's houses were the clouds of heaven; his canoe was the rainbow; his voice, thunder; the torches in his dwelling, lightning. When he travelled he "flew" like a bird (Ellis 1853:II, 359–60).

Sanctity was not restricted to royalty. High chiefs took their sanctity from the high gods, from Oro, for example. Lower ranks took theirs from lesser ancestral deities. Whoever had rights to a marae had a claim to sanctity which was transmitted to the first-born. Presumably the manahune, who had no independent land rights and thus no maraes, would have lacked sanctity. There is, however, no specific information on this point. But if the father in every family was its priest, as Ellis claims, then some sacred character would extend to all families. Sanctity was graded by the status of the marae, each marae standing as a sacred precinct representing a portion of the total territory. Outside of the marae, sanctity was necessarily of a different order; it was entirely particular and unconnected. As Ellis has remarked about the lower ranks: "The raatiras or inferior chiefs imitating the example of their superiors endeavored to secure renown for their children by performing corresponding ceremonies at their family *maraes,* but no attention was paid to it, except by the members of the relatives and dependents (1853:I, 259)."

If sanctity as measured by its specific associations with gods and their shrines was presumably graded, what about mana? There is no specific information. If Tahitian religious theory was consistent on this issue, mana would be graded in proportion to the standing of the gods.

Wealth

Taimai, who has so much to say about the privileges and the concerns of the great chiefs, does not speak of their wealth. She relates, rather, that

> every *Arii* or chief, great or small, had four properties belonging to his rank. None but those who have been mentioned could wear the Maro-ura red feather girdle and only head chiefs could order human sacrifices; but all equally possessed a Moua, or mount, an Outu, or point; a Tahua, or gathering-place, and a *Marae,* or temple (Adams 1947:14).

She does not speak of their great land holdings, of the tributes that were paid to them, of their considerable stores of food, or of the bales of tapa cloth they owned. The Society Islands chiefs lived in the traditional aura of abundance. They had the conventional obligations of generosity and hospitality; they used wealth to secure allies, dependents, and retainers; they were the supporters of the artisans, of genealogists, and of priests. Poverty would have diminished the chief's retinue and constricted his circle of influence. It certainly would have spoken ill of his mana and of his divine connections. We need not assume that the arii Taimai, who had been married to an Englishman (Salmon), had forgotten what wealth means to royalty. She was insisting, it is obvious, on the essentials of royal dignity. These were the apparel of the gods, the rights to life of the gods, the sanctuaries of the gods, and the distinguishing features of the land, its vista points and its close connection with the sea.

Wealth was a secondary interest because it did not categorically distinguish the highest-ranking from the lower-ranking chiefs. All chiefs demanded foods, cloth, and canoes from their dependents; and if the high chief received more, he gave away more. A good ruler, Ellis has remarked, was one who distributed among his chiefs whatever he received and never refused anything for which they asked (1853:I, 128). The economic issue was, of course, power. The obligation to give acknowledged fealty: largesse defined noblesse, and the ability to impose a *rahui* on the produce of the land was the ultimate test of internal authority. Its interest, in any event, was to accumulate for ritual use.

Land was the prime wealth. It is to be understood in its dual significance as patrimony and as source of authority and power. As patrimony it represented the honor of the family; and since honor was associated with traditional holdings, the matter of size was pertinent but not crucial. The paramount chief was often a smaller landholder than those who ranked beneath him. As a political resource, the issue of land was more complex. The highest ranks were in fact least dependent on direct tenure for assuring themselves of support and produce. By consecrating all local maraes within their jurisdiction, they acquired a ritual form of tenure which sanctioned their requests for support. And as beneficiaries of gifts and tributes, they had the means to reward aid and allegiance. The lower ranks depended directly upon their own holdings. The pressure for acquiring new lands came from the middle ranks.

Land boundaries were closely guarded against thieves, whose patron deity was Hiro, son of Oro, the god of war. Even so, thieves when caught were killed on the spot. The crime of theft and the fear of it are strange for a land so bountiful and so rich in hospitality and generosity. We can only imagine that theft was not economic but an act of internal warfare, an assault upon the honor of the land. In this respect theft would have been little different from interdistrict warfare, which must also be seen less as economic than as an assault upon honor. When Taimai discussed war with Henry Adams she spoke only of avenging affronts, not of the economic advantages of conquest.

Tohunga

In the Marquesan tradition, *tahu'a* included craftsmen and priests, defining their common quality as skilled makers or, to use Henry's translation, "authors." Tahiti also distinguished between inspirational priests (*etua*), who were simply the submissive and untitled spokesman of particular gods, and the learned and ritually directed priests, who were the tahu'a. In general, and certainly in the case of tahu'a priests, craft's status and social rank were closely aligned. The highest priest was either the high chief, himself descended from the god and the "owner" of the marae, or his younger brother, who then acted as "agent" of the chief. Since priestly ritual was conducted on the marae, the rank of the priest had to be equal to the social standing of the marae. The social standing of other tahu'a is less clear. Inspirational priests who could acquire great influence through prophecy were self-made men, and women, and could presumably come from the lower ranks. Perhaps sorcerers and counter-sorcerers, who also worked outside the established order of skills and had prospects of great power and influence, were another group that transcended rank. Wilson (1799:333) observed only that commoners made cloth, built houses, and assisted in laborous work. Apart then from the somewhat unorthodox and non-tahu'a priestly vocations, there is no strong reason to assume that in Tahiti the skilled crafts provided the manahune with special opportunities for rising in status.

The tahu'a vocations never reached the degree of organization of western Polynesian "guilds." Each branch of skill had its patron deity as did the guilds, but no formal leadership except perhaps in the priestly and scholarly fields. In those branches a formal system of schooling with private and public examinations undoubtedly gave order and control to the profession, establishing standards of competency. All tahu'a were highly respected and were evidently handsomely rewarded for their services. The ranks of tahu'a included in addition to priests and teachers, curers who were skilled in bone setting, marae builders, house builders, canoemakers, experts on fishing seasons, tattooers, and embalmers. Judging by the school curricula listed by Henry (1928:154), the range of intellectual skills embraced history, heraldry, geography, navigation, astronomy, astrology, mythology, time, numbers, seasons, and genealogies.

Toa

"War," said Ellis, was "the most important end in life (1853:I, 295)." War advanced the standing of all who were successful in it. Nevertheless, the outstanding warrior (*aito*) respected as he was, and ample as were his rewards, did not have quite the commanding position in Tahiti as he had in other militant Polynesian societies. The warrior was overshadowed by priests, themselves seized with political ambition and interest in power. Priests more than warriors won praise for military victory. All Polynesians acknowledged divine intervention in war, the Tahitians more directly. Thus all others held subordinate positions in battle, even the chief unless he appeared on the battle ground in his role as priest. Priests made the war arrangements and accompanied the troops. Inspirational priests known as *rauti* spurred the troops, exhorting them to fight, sometimes dying of oratorical overexertion. The aito, ordinarily lower-ranking chiefs, represented only the secular and at that the less important branch of the army. All other professionals had their own marae; the warriors did not. Their reward was, nevertheless, consequential, but in the secular realm. They were awarded lands and advanced in the lesser ranks of chiefs and gentry. A commoner could distinguish himself in war if he could overcome his lack of a command. According to Ellis he did. The title of aito, Ellis reports, "was not, like the chieftainship and other prevailing distinctions, confined to any class but open to all; and many from the lower ranks have risen as warriors, to a high station in the community (1853:I, 396)."

Political Hegemony

The formal division between authority and power, on the one hand, and genealogical honor, on the other, seems to have been brought about rather late in Tahitian history. The division that occurred when Papara overcame Vaiari reveals first that the prestige of genealogical rank was absolute, and second that while the split between rank and power was feasible, it was not tenable. Rank without power was diminished. If a chief could not enforce a rahui, or retain command of the chiefly paraphernalia associated with his marae, he was left with only the shadow of his substance. Power without rank was incomplete. It had all the material substance but not the authentic stamp of genealogical justification. The history of the Pomare family demonstrates once and for all how much the supreme command depended on the unity or upon the unification of rank and power. Late Tahitian society had no specific or titular role for the arii who had been pushed into the background. It did not provide an acceptable division between a sacred and secular authority. Consequently, rank and power could not remain permanently and comfortably split. When the separation had taken place, the advantage thereafter lay with power. The Pomares, for example, readily acquired the genealogical justification after they had secured the political power. It had become possible, as Wilson (1799) observed, to seize the ritual prerogatives of a royal marae as the new ceremonial center of a district. So striking a violation of royal rights was not, it must be said, gladly accepted; but accepted in fact it was. Permanent as were the credentials of pedigree, the marae had to be protected. In this manner Tahiti and Mangareva were alike.

We do not, unfortunately, have specific information on the nature of chiefly power during early periods. In the Late Period, powers were allocated among the chiefly grades more or less according to the traditional manner. The paramount chief controlled mainly the religious authority; the subchiefs, the more utilitarian. Rights to demand human sacrifices, a religious power with political implications, were reserved to the paramount chiefs, as was also, apparently, the right to declare lese majesty a capital offense. These chiefly rights to take human life asserted the awesomeness of chiefly sanctity, which—according to the traditions—gained in intensity over time. The history of Opoa and of the Taputapu-atea marae emphasizes the development and then the spread to other islands of a war cult, explaining how the number of human sacrifices increased as internal troubles grew more acute. The political implications of human sacrifices are brought out by Henry, who in explaining how sacrificial victims were chosen mainly from among war captives added the observation that they also included "those middle classes who had made themselves obnoxious to the men in power (1928:197)." The victims, it is important to note, were delivered by their subchiefs, who were obliged to obey the royal edict or suffer loss of their lands and property (Henry 1928:197). Since the land-holdings of subchiefs were ordinarily immune from seizure except at enemy hands, this extension of the divine chiefly prerogative must be recognized as a vital encroachment upon traditional autonomy. A further invasion of local autonomy was the right of the paramount chief's bodyguard to seek out and execute those who had offended the chief's sanctity. Such offenses, including refusal to offer first fruits, defying a rahui, and holding back on tributary offerings, were as political as they were religious.

The political power of high chief was ordinarily restrained by the combined resistance of local leaders, who have been compared by Ellis to "feudal barons" (1853:III, 210). They accepted a superior and acknowledged, when compelled to, the weight of superior force, but their authority, Ellis says, was more far-reaching in its powers over persons and property than that of the paramount chief over his political realm. Lacking an independent military force, a high chief could extend his political hegemony by fitting together a coalition and then trying to hold it. Only Pomare with "English guns" had found the key to stable overlordship.

The Structure of Status

A Tahitian chant describes the formation of social classes as follows: "The high royal family of the 'ura girdle . . . were descended of the gods from darkness." They were "begat" from Ti'i and Hina.

The "common people, the plebeians of the world" were "conjured into being" by the gods. The gentry were "begat" from intermarriages between royalty and commoners." The nobility, or lesser arii were "begat" from intermarriages between royalty and gentry (Henry 1928: 402–3). Thus commoners with the stigma of not having a line of descent stand alone as an absolute category. The highest arii stand alone as god-descended, and the two intermediate classes form still a third category, with merits of descent line and of connection with arii, but with the indelible blemish of mixture.

The highest rank were the *arii rahi* or *arii nui,* the sacred or great arii. The second rank were the *arii rii,* the small chiefs; the third were the *raatira;* the fourth, the *manahune.* The theory of class brought out in this chant differs from that of traditional Polynesia by ignoring gradations of seniority and by distinguishing rather by criteria of descent–non descent, endogamy–mixture, and near–distant (with respect to arii rahi). In traditional theory all classes are organically linked by grade to a common descent line. This concept of common descent—except for manahune—is in fact still adhered to, but indirectly. In traditional theory, common lines gradually separate as a result of endogamous marriages. In Tahitian theory, discrete lines are brought together by exogamous marriages. Once the full range of classes was formed, however, Tahitians also expected endogamy to preserve the established categories. Infanticide was the alternative to endogamy. Infanticide, as Ellis learned, even enhanced the status of the partners of a mésalliance, but at the obvious risk of extinction of the line. The Tahitian alignment of rank appears altogether traditional, but the ranks are like beads on a string rather than segments of the string itself.

An aphorism cited by Handy from a manuscript by Marau describes the Tahitian sentiment about rank (1930a:42): "The types of men are three. Take a breadfruit. When it is cooked take off the skin—that is for the people [*taata*]. The meat, that is eaten by the *arii.* The core is given to the *manahune.*"

Genealogical Rank

The rank of arii rahi was contractive, since it was more likely to lose membership by dilution and by extinction in war than to gain by natural increase. The rank was small in principle and was limited to the senior chiefly line in a district, generally a ranking district, or the commanding district of a confederation. Taimai, who dismisses the arii rii as "too numerous to mention," remarks there were in the Society Islands "only about a dozen important and old *marae* (Adams

1947:15), that is, seats of arii rahi. The title was held by the incumbent, and his close kin were apparently (information on this point is not clear) also considered as of this grade. The arii rahi were themselves ranked, the highest order wearing the red-feather emblem, the lower order that of the yellow-feather. The basis for the distinction seems to have been not simple seniority but the more general criterion of genealogical distinction. The Opoa traditions and the Pomare history imply strongly that all arii rahi were closely intermarried and hence part of a single kindred.

Arii rii were a relatively large group, expansive in times of peace and decimated in war. Our knowledge of who they were is rather vague, however. Early writers speak of great chiefs and of smaller chiefs without specifying rank. Small chiefs could certainly have included raatira as well. Walpole, for example, puts the number of major chiefs on Tahiti at 10 and the lesser chiefs at about 200 (1849: II, 85), but we cannot be too sure that this represented the actual proportion of arii rahi to arii rii. As for genealogical standing, the previously cited tradition of "miscegenation" states a viewpoint and not an established sociological fact. It seems most improbable for arii rii to have been composed only of fallen aristocrats who had not wed wisely. They must inevitably have included, as indeed Marau insists they did, the junior branches of arii rahi. Most likely, then, the rank included both, the mismarriages standing as the true links with non-noble gentry. Henry describes the arii rii as the "nobility of the land" with "no right to the imperial insignia" living "in the same way as the arii nui, but on a smaller scale (1928:229)." The smaller chiefs headed the less important districts, either small and autonomous or politically and/or socially subordinate to arii nui. In major districts, Marau says they were the *iatoai,* or military corps, of the arii nui, and held jurisdiction as subdistrict heads (Handy 1930a:42).

Raatira, an expansive rank, were plebeian heads of ordinary subdistricts under arii rii. Although connected with arii by legend, they were in fact a categorical social class (as Pomare II evidently believed, for in his formal ordering of the native class system he combined all arii into a single assemblage of nobility, leaving the raatira outside as, following European usage, a landed gentry). Ellis refined the category, distinguishing an "aristocracy" of raatira whose landholdings exceeded 100 acres, and a petty gentry who held smaller plots of from 20 to 100 acres. His distinction is useful because it separates those landholding subchiefs who had held from the beginnings ancestral lands and had added new grants received as awards from arii from the very small gentry (possibly including raised up manahune) whose dependency was directly upon raatira subchiefs (1853:III, 97). Thus the raatira rank was graded in a series of what may be properly called feudal dependencies in which land title was granted for tribute and military assistance. All authorities have spoken of the "independence" of raatira, pointing to their economic autonomy and the stability of their land title. Handy, for example, claims that raatira were not stripped of their land title even after all else had been destroyed in war (1930a:43), and that arii might banish a landholder but could not interfere with the inheritance of land. Handy may have overstated raatira independence, for there is certainly a good deal of information on land seizures and reallotment of enemy lands in war (cf. Henry 1928), and such authorities as Waldegrave (1933), Moerenhout (1837), Ellis (1853), and de Bovis (1855) all speak of expropriation of enemy lands. All, however, saw the raatira as a "middle class" acting as the familiar social balance, the checkrein upon chiefly powers.

That manahune were the low order is definite; it is their status as an economic class that is difficult to define with desirable clarity. Henry says only: "They served as retainers and workers for the upper classes, but also enjoyed their own hereditary possessions (1928:230)." De Bovis also describes them as living on the lands of arii and raatira, as enjoying the usufruct of their labor, as rarely dispossessed and as transmitting their particular rights to their heirs (1855:390). These observations could be understood as implying gradation rather than categorical separation of manahune from raatira. On this matter, Ellis, the earlier observer, may have been closer to the aboriginal condition. The extraordinary population decline that immediately followed European occupancy made it possible for anyone to take up a tract of land. Originally there were two classes of manahune, Ellis explains: servants of chiefs, and, I quote, "all who were destitute of any land, and ignorant of the rude arts of carpentering, building, etc., which were respected among them, and such as were reduced to a state of dependence upon those in higher stations (1853:III, 96)." They were not only landless, but unskilled, and so lacking in two main credentials of honor.

The meaning of landless in Polynesian law has already been discussed in terms of concepts of honor. Tahitian land titles resemble in principle the Mangarevan, and manahune of Tahiti is like 'urumanu of Mangareva. Both groups of commoners lived on lands of which the authentic or honorable titles belonged to arii and to raatira who had the maraes and genealogies to certify them. The place of the commoner on the land was utilitarian. His residential tenure was secure because there was no need ordinarily to dispossess him. That he could leave the land of one raatira to settle as dependent upon the land of another demonstrates, to be sure, his freedom as a person, but also his lack of connection with a primary source of status and honor. Ellis compares manahune, I think aptly, despite the trans-cultural reference, to English cottagers of his period.

Arii, raatira, manahune formed the three great Tahitian "estates," separate in category yet linked by the organic imagery of the lesser order of intermarriage, to be sure, but linked nevertheless. War captives (*titi*) and servants (*teuteu*) formed a special group of low-grade statuses, either as tragic victims or as self-made subordinates. It is unlikely that servants were anything but manahune; prisoners became at least by technical definition, manahune, for, to quote Ellis:

> Individuals captured in actual combat, or who fled to the chief for protection when disarmed or disabled in the field, were considered the slaves of the captor or chief by whom they were protected. The women, children and others who remained in the districts of the vanquished, were also regarded as belonging to them, and the lands they occupied, together with their fields and plantations were distributed among the victors (1853:III, 95).

As suddenly reduced people, the titi were also known as *taata ino,* or mean and low people, equal in ignobility to the Mangarevan kiore.

Achieved Statuses

Status mobility was confined to a narrow range, far more so than in Mangareva. Arii held the principal priestly and military posts; raatira served as subordinate war leaders under arii, as orators and as teachers, and controlled most of the skilled crafts. Commoners could advance in dignity with skill, and in grade for military distinction, and for service in the *arioi* dancing society.

The Arioi Society

In the arioi society, in essence an agricultural fertility cult elaborating the familiar theme of sexual licentiousness, we see revealed at the same time the complement of Tahitian principles of genealogical rank. The Tahitian arioi are undoubtedly cognate with the Marquesan ka'oi and have in common the function of honoring youthful sexuality and of relating human sexuality with plant fertility. In Tahiti the cult assumed special significance as a counterpart status system. It provided a rank order outside the traditional order within which persons advanced in honor but mainly within an enclosed and specialized orbit which in many respects depicted the thesis of genealogical rank in inverse fashion.

Henry defines the arioi as "comedians," which they were in their public capacity as entertainers. As entertainers who toured the country during harvest periods, they were revered and treated royally. At times, communities reduced themselves to utter want as they lavished feasts and gifts upon the itinerant troupes.

A metaphoric royalty—like actors in royal roles—the arioi were also representatives of the paramount chief, who was their patron with authority to name the ranking and commanding orders of the society. Arioi and paramount chief also shared a common divine patron, Oro, the national god. Oro was the first arioi, and the society was founded on earth by Tamatoa, the legendary warrior chief of Raiatea, who arranged to have the arioi brought to earth as a reincarnation of the national god. The arioi, like royalty, were an endogamous society. They were uniquely organized into male and female sections, each with its own chief; but again, like royalty, they formed eight grades, presumably parallel to the ancient Raiatean organization of eight ranked districts. Members advanced up the grades by talent and seniority, finally reaching eligibility for appointment to the top grade. The top grade was categorically distinguished from the rest in an obvious parallel with the organization of genealogical ranks. The top rank alone wore a replica of the *maro 'ura*, a mulberry girdle sprayed with red and yellow pigments; and only the top rank was allowed to transmit its titles and honors down a descent line. All other ranks were held to obligatory infanticide and so denied the honor of descent. While the highest rank of arioi held the honor of descent, in effect from Oro, the descent line was metaphoric rather than real, first because the arioi chief was actually appointed by the paramount chief—from among title holders—and, second, because the society membership as a whole was selected for grace, beauty, and dance talents rather than by ancestry. All ranks, including commoners, are said to have been drawn into the arioi. The society held the greatest social advantages for lower ranks; when manahune retired from the society, as they were always free to do, they were given royal grants of land and became gentry (*raatira*). After death, all arioi who had remained active were assured of a heavenly paradise, another royal prerogative. However, unlike arii rahi and high priests, the most sought-after prizes of war, the arioi had immunity from molestation.

From the point of view of the lower ranks, the arioi society opened new roads to honor. It elevated commoners, holding out to them the most glittering prospects of sacred descent and, more realistically, of more modest advancements. Perhaps we may see in this society of honored entertainers an outlet for restless ambitions otherwise constrained by a society that had increased the powers of chiefs and widened the gulf between high- and low-born. But if the arioi society was a new avenue to honor, it did not lead to the destination of the arii. The two roads were parallel and their separation was complete. There is actually no compelling reason to assume so specific a social function for this society. It can as readily be seen as an extension or further elaboration of the concept of chiefly rank—an extension that enhanced chiefly rank by the complex counterpoints of inversion and parallelism of symbolic forms of status.

Status Rivalry

If rank was secure, position was not. Realistically, then, rivalries were for power, and war, as almost everywhere else in Polynesia, was the testing ground of chiefs. Military might rearranged the hierarchical order of districts and of their chiefs; it broke down chiefly autonomies and forged new alliances and allegiances. It lifted up commoner and raatira, for whom position was in any case more significant than rank. The utilitarian interest in war is unmistakeable. Lands were seized and redistributed and tributes and services were secured. Wealth, as we have repeatedly observed, fed position. Yet if a proper emphasis is to be placed on Tahitian warfare, it must rest just as heavily upon the symbolism of power, upon the religious aim. Mature warfare worthy of a great state serves mainly economic and political ends and uses religion only as a justification and support. By this standard, the Tahitian state was still immature. The hot desire to crush and to annihilate an enemy seems to have been as strong, perhaps even stronger than the cooler calculation of how to subdue and to incorporate. African states, for example, had mastered the political arts of incorporation, finding an honorable place within the new administration for those who knew how to yield gracefully to superiority, but in Tahiti, as Henry has brought out, submission gained an enemy no benefits at all. The highest-ranking prisoners were decapitated and cut into as many portions as there were districts in the conqueror's domain. The paramount chief then received the head and the district heads the body portions (Henry 1928:315), incorporating thereby the spiritual substance of the enemy. At the same time, they laid waste the land, tore down the marae, killed the priests, and carried off the sacred treasures. War devastated the upper leadership, but without leaving room at the top. Raatira did not move up into vacated arii ranks; they advanced within grade and in influence, like an army which, losing its officer corps, must turn to its noncommissioned ranks. The fierceness of the attack upon the arii and the relative immunity of raatira reveals the complexity of viewpoint—in part the rage against a rival sanctity, and in part the astute calculation of chiefs, mentioned by Taimai, that the key to success depended precisely upon annihilation of their only true rivals.

A remarkable Tahitian chant cited by Henry (1938:307) states the meaning of warfare. I quote a section of it, including Miss Henry's parenthetical additions:

> War is growth (extension) to the land
> Establishment of rock strata (great men)
> Spreading out of land (population)
> Take the spade (war weapons)
> Dig the holes (drill the lines)
> War is fertile soil
> Soil that will produce seeds (extension)
> Soil that will be verdant (power)
> Soil spread out
> Soil for leaning slabs (increase of priests)
> Soil for pavings (for marae)
> Soil that shifts (changes rulers)
> Soil inaugurated
> Land was inaugurated in Hawaii (Raiatea).

The balance of forces in Tahitian society was carefully contrived to sustain stability. The sharp separation of ranks did not rule out antagonism, but it ruled out supplanting. Lower arii and raatira could bring down the most sacred chief. To do so, however, they risked their own status in civil war. In any case, they had to act in concert or not at all. The very real interdependence between arii nui and subchiefs safeguarded at the same time, the chiefly title from the likely opposition of a junior line. Tahitian history testifies to the effectiveness of this system of balances. The system was stable but not static. While the pattern of status relationships varied little, the constant tensions within the system would seem to have, in fact, strengthened the role of chiefly sanctity. Or, to see the process of development as a strategy of power, principles of separation and of religious terror and awe became the reliable—as reliable as any political strategy can be—techniques of reestablishing balances on a new level. The tradition of the steady increase in the terror of human sacrifices speaks to this point. We have also seen evidence of limits placed upon excessive growth in sanctity. Religious separation clearly carries with it the hazard of loss of connection with temporal affairs. But the most direct counterpoint to the increasing chiefly religious powers was the parallel power of priests. When a priest was possessed by a god, none could oppose him, it has been said (Henry 1928). He could ask for anything, even the wife of a paramount chief—and get it. Insofar as he was in a different social and spiritual realm, he could not usurp the power. The possessed priest was rather a reminder of the limits of religious power. Perhaps the most acute reminder of limits was the capability of a sorcerer, conceivably a commoner, and a major power at the lower end of the social scale, who, while not able to attack the office of chief, could endanger his person (Henry 1928:208).

Descent Group Organization

Many key details on Society Islands descent group organization are missing, and so we must, like the archeologist, reconstruct the system from the known facts and by interpolation. The most ancient social systems are naturally the most faintly delineated. Nevertheless, we do not go too far afield when we see in the Raiatean traditions intimations of the traditional order: the genealogical ranking of chiefs; a segmentary order of genealogically connected and hierarchically arranged districts; a ritual authority vested in the dominant district; and an expanding order of Segment I chiefs by way of intermarriages. The persistence in parts of Tahiti of a very similar organization up into the historic period adds credibility to this reconstruction. Tahitian history is altogether more definite, and points even more clearly to an early Traditional system of branching lineages and its eventual transformation into a political-territorial organization. At the point of European contact, both systems coexisted on Tahiti and were already actively being altered.

The Tevas, described by the arii Taimai as a "clan," were, as their traditions claim, represented by four districts whose arii recognized one (Vaiari) as its senior line. Papara, as we have learned, later assumed political ascendancy, altering the order of ranking but not apparently the genealogical segmentation and the close kinship connections among the principal chiefly lines. Subsequently the Teva extended their influence over sections of the small peninsula of Taiarapu, incorporating within a federation four of its districts. The original four were then known as Teva *iuta,* or "inner Teva," and the new group as the "outer" Teva. The latter may have been related to the inner group through ancient connections, but they were nevertheless regarded as political additions and not as organic branches.

They were, moreover, military and political rivals, even though within what had become the fashionable Society Islands' constellation of eight districts. On the main part of the island, two major districts, Attaharu and Faa, joined the Teva in military alliance. The remaining districts were independent and ruled mainly by small chiefs. By the historic period, all social and political relations on Tahiti had become acutely unstable. As Taimai reminds us, when all eight Teva districts accepted Papara as "political head," the dominant chief of the Taiarapu districts was "sometimes politically the stronger (Adams 1947:8)." The organization of districts on Taiarapu, she says, "were much changed by war, and the names have not kept their old meaning (Adams 1947:17)." Districts formed new federations or were conquered and absorbed.

Thus prior to the 1815 establishment of the Tahitian state, the question of how to define the maximal unit of organization depends upon specific histories. If we take Teva and its four inner districts, we have an apparent equivalent to the Maori waka. And, in fact, this "clan district," to follow Henry's terminology, was called *va'a mata'-einana* (1928:70). When we add the outer Teva, this grouping then resembles the Mangarevan u, whose political unity also depended upon the chief's capability of holding together a potentially unstable coalition. We cannot regard this coalition as a "conquest state," if only because the outer Teva had not, insofar as is known, been subjugated. Small conquest states, however, did exist on the small peninsula. The subdivisions of Tautira, for example, were called "Land-eating-small wood," which, as Henry explains, meant "they were tributary to a conquering power ruling over them, a condition to which they were subjected after conquest by the chiefs of the south when they erected a wall of heads. Upon these sub-divisions were placed chiefs and *marae*s from the south, according to the custom of conquerors (1928:87.)" The precise nature of political authority within a conquest state or within the Teva confederation has unfortunately never been described. We know, however, that it included rights to tribute and labor, and authority to redistribute conquered lands among allies and friends. It had then acquired a substantial secular character alongside its traditional religious character.

Within a confederation, Segment II, also called va'a mata'-einana, was a district headed by either a high chief or an ordinary arii. When districts were autonomous, their subdivisions were always an arii rii jurisdiction. Insofar as raatira, probably, and manahune, certainly, were not connected with chiefly genealogies, these subdivisions also stand as territorial–political rather than as kinship organizations.

They were, nevertheless, organic branches through their arii lines of the larger organizations. If in Segment I the religious authority outweighed the secular, in Segment II the balance was shifted to the secular in the sense that the lower-ranking chiefs were the principal war leaders.

Segment III had evidently become a political subdivision under the arii, administered by warrior chiefs with whom there was no organic connection other than the sanctification of the land title. The social composition of the populace allied to a chief of raatira rank was a composite of land-owning kinsmen of dependents to whom he had given land, of unrelated manahune, and, in some instances, of war captives. This segment, known by the general term, mata'einana, had its marae and its own ceremonies. It was, however, the focus of the economy, and the raatira were the true administrators of the land.

Finally, Segment IV, for which we have no nomenclature, was the household of fluctuating composition. The senior male was household head, descent was bilateral; residence after marriage followed no fixed rules. Whoever held title to property assigned it to chosen heirs just before his death. Tahiti had no villages. Manahune lived on the landholdings of raatira, and the residence of each arii formed a local capital of kinsmen and dependents.

10

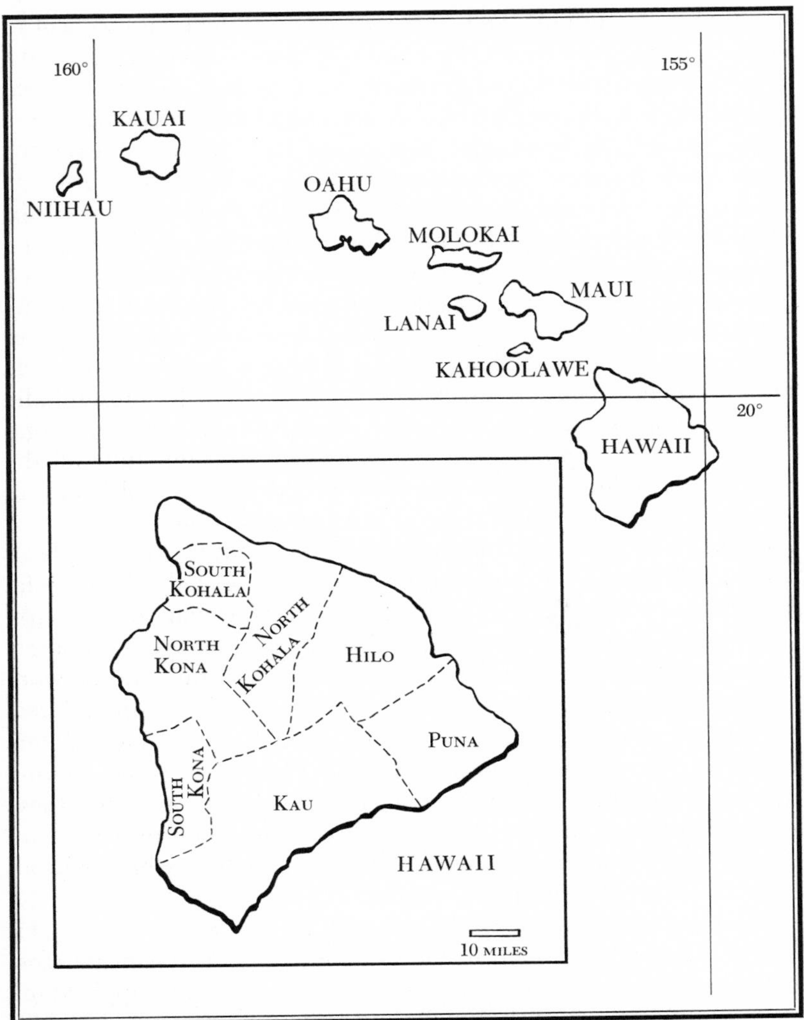

The Hawaiian Islands

POLYNESIAN SOCIAL EVOLUTION REACHED ITS GREATEST DEVELOPment in the Hawaiian Islands, where all changes in direction or further elaborations of traditional forms under way elsewhere finally came to fruition. The climax marked by the establishment of a central authority over all the islands of the archipelago came late. In 1778, when Cook entered the scene, the Kingdom had not yet been established, but the course had been set and all the major chiefs were racing toward the same goal. Europeans have been given far too much credit for their part in bringing about a new social order in Hawaii; they were only the midwives. Without them the new births might have been delayed, but probably not for too long. Even before the newcomers could intervene, Hawaiian chiefs had already seized command of all the large islands and were reaching out for more. Centralization of authority was no special Hawaiian accomplishment —Tongans, Mangaians, Mangarevans, Tahitians had done as much. The Hawaiian chiefs had finally succeeded in replacing substantially the traditional lineages with a tightly controlled administrative organization. All other Stratified societies had brought out fully all the political capabilities of the Traditional order. Hawaii had begun to introduce a new order and to move in a new direction.

If the Hawaiian Kingdom is to be considered as an example of "early civilization" or "high culture," it must be judged by social rather than by material standards. Materially, Hawaiian society ranks below small Easter Island which had produced a script and impressive megalithic arts. Hawaii had developed no writing and its work in stone was mediocre. The Hawaiian *heiau* was inferior in architecture and in quality of masonry to the best of the ceremonial centers of Easter, Marquesas, Tonga, and Tahiti. Hawaiian wood carving and house building lacked the refinement and virtuosity that these arts had acquired in New Zealand. There is no more primitive implement anywhere than the Hawaiian digging stick, which did not even have the efficient Maori footrest.

Hawaiian technical culture was, in fact, by no means inconsequential. If it failed to develop in the esthetic directions taken by most civilizations, it was remarkably effective in pragmatic application. Hawaiian chiefs turned their skills and their administrative capabilities to the quick and efficient organization of labor. The hallmark of Hawaiian public works is the standard of doing the most with the least effort. When stone was employed in temple building or in agricultural terraces, little effort was made to shape or dress it. The heiaus were crude and unimposing structures that created, nevertheless, the ample facilities for public worship. The agrarian works, however, were extensive and carefully executed. To promote wet taro cultivation, the Hawaiians irrigated and terraced low lands, protecting the crops from salt with great stone seawalls. They pushed terracing far up the mountain slopes, facing them where necessary with natural stone and linking them with well-engineered irrigation ditches. The outstanding example of ditch construction is in the Waimea valley of Kauai, where a deep ditch was lined with cut stone blocks fitted closely together with joints (Bennett 1931:105–6). It seems characteristic of the old Hawaiian culture that even on very traditional Kauai the best stone work went into a utilitarian construction. Generally speaking, the Hawaiian terrace-irrigation works are not comparable with those built by the politically primitive Ifugao and Bontoc on Luzon in the Philippines. But then the Hawaiian construction may have begun later. Other major constructions included fishponds built up in shallow waters where fish were husbanded and fed poi, baked taro, and other foods. There is no doubt as to the cultural stature of Hawaii. Yet there is always the puzzling judgment of L. H. Morgan, who could so misunderstand the Hawaiian culture as to rank it with the Australian aborigines.

The Hawaiian chain includes eight fully inhabited islands, of which Hawaii, with a land area of over 4,000 square miles, was the largest and most heavily populated. Maui, Oahu, Kauai, and Molokai were the remaining major islands of the group. Lanai, Niihau, and Kahoolawe were minor settlements. The main islands are among the most mountainous and rugged in Polynesia: only 16 percent of their land area, it has been calculated, is cultivable (Freeman 1951:328). The remainder is either too steep or too dry. What regions were available for farming were well-watered and fertile and able to sustain dense populations. The calculation of population density for the islands can hardly be exact in the absence of firm figures for either total population or for local distributions, but the Cook Expedition estimates (1779), ranging between 300,000 to 400,000, may have been accurate, since by 1853, when the first actual census was taken, there were still over 70,000 Hawaiians left, a remarkable survival rate by comparison with the fate of other Polynesian populations. Local population distributions have been plotted from this census (Coulter 1931). Even if we accept the high figure of 400,000, gross density is very low (approx. 65 persons per square mile). In the areas of cultivation, however, it approaches 400 persons per square mile—among the highest in the islands. Average densities, of course, obscure the range of variations, a factor of great importance in social systems as competitive as the Hawaiian. Not only were the productive zones of unequal value, but not all islands or island regions were cultivated with equal care. Irrigation, for example, was more extensively carried out on Hawaii and Kauai than on Oahu (McAllister 1933). As for population distributions, on Hawaii the Waipeo valley was very heavily populated and still produced taro surpluses which were sent in trade to Kawahaeo on the opposite side of the island (Coulter 1933). The valley of Kalalau on Kauai was the most intensively cultivated in all the islands (Handy 1940:60). On Oahu, the Wainiha valley had a very dense population. The pattern of population distribution was spotty on all islands. People were scattered in patches of heavy and light concentrations often separated by almost unpopulated areas. The great populations were coastal (cf. Coulter's maps, 1931). On the good lands food was plentiful. Taro was the major crop almost everywhere, yet the average consumption of *poi* from the secondary breadfruit cultivations averaged five pounds a day (Coulter 1933:7). Other supplementary foods included coconut, yam, sweet potato, sugar cane, arrowroot, and wild fern root. Fish were the common protein, but for ritual events the Hawaiians feasted heavily on pig and dog. In general, then, the islands were well favored to develop the economic capacity for social complexity. But the history of tribal expansions suggests that unequal distribution of resources and of populations was a more significant factor in political evolution than general prosperity.

The origins of the Hawaiian people and of their initial culture are not fully known, but there is no doubt of the close relationship between Hawaii and Tahiti, judging by strong similarities in language (Elbert 1953) and in ancient artifacts (Emory 1963). It had been generally assumed that the Hawaiians came originally from the Society Islands (Emory 1963) and then maintained some continuity of contact with their original homeland. Unfortunately for this theory, the dates of occupations—based, to be sure, on preliminary archeological surveys only—show the Hawaiian Islands to have been inhabited long before the Society Islands were. The earliest occupation date for Hawaii is A.D. 124 (Emory, Bonk, Sinoto, 1959); for the Societies, as late as 1100 (Sinoto 1963). Thus Emory (1963) has proposed a new theory, namely, that the Hawaiian Islands were settled initially from the Marquesas and were invaded sometime in the twelfth century by Tahitians. I shall return to these historical questions later. At this point it is sufficient to say that whether the initial settlement was from the Marquesas or from the Society Islands, the linguistic similarities alone compel us to view the Hawaiian culture as a variant of later stages of the Tahitian.

When Cook arrived he found, as he had in the Society Islands, a state of war, of intense political rivalry. Four of the great chiefdoms were at one another's throats, while each chief was, at the same time, trying to defend himself against internal opposition. Each of the populated islands had already been brought under a single authority, but neither was yet strong enough to conquer its opponents. Chief Kalaniopu, for example, had extended his jurisdiction from Hawaii to a district on neighboring Maui. The Maui chief, while holding to what remained of his island, had extended his rule to three neighboring islands. On Oahu a single political authority had already been established, but on Kauai, which had brought the island of Niihau into its political sphere, a chiefess who had just seized the power was maneuvering to retain it. Finally, Maui and Oahu were locked in struggle for control of Molokai.

Cook tragically lost his life in Hawaii before he could leave his own mark on events, but Europeans and Americans who arrived in short order understood the Hawaiian political scene only too well. They intervened promptly with advice and arms, and helped Kamehameha I overcome all opposition and to establish for the first time a central authority over all the islands. In 1782 the man who became Hawaii's first ruler was still a minor chief. By 1810 he had become the king. In 1819 his son and successor had launched the Hawaiian cultural revolution that broke with the traditional religious order. Thereafter Hawaiian history moved quickly into a European orbit. While much that happened after 1819 continued to follow older Hawaiian political patterns, the divergencies grew increasingly more radical. Up until 1819 Hawaiian political and cultural evolution simply carried out the momentum of the pre-European period. An all-Hawaiian authority was an innovation only in the sense that chiefs had found the concrete means to accomplish old ambitions. At its inception, at least, the rule of Kamehameha I was but an enlargement of the islandwide political authority. It would be false to conclude that the European role was negligible in this phase of Hawaiian political evolution, but we should not exaggerate its importance. Hawaiian chiefs took immediate advantage of the new post-European order to enrich themselves at the expense of commoners. They took legal title to lands and they engaged in the profitable sandal trade, to the serious detriment of food production. The European commercial tradition is evident. Yet Maori chiefs in similar circumstances fought against land expropriation. Hawaiian history points to a remarkable degree of convergence between the interests of chiefs and the European powers: Both saw virtue in power and in the growth of the state.

The traditional Hawaiian culture vanished before it could be properly recorded. Information on pre-European traditions and institutions is, nevertheless, abundant. Missionaries, journalists, and other early visitors recorded voluminously and encouraged Hawaiians to set down their recollections in their own language. The texts of Malo, Kepelino, and Kamakau are major archival sources. Handy and Pukui's study of social organization is modern and authoritative. The old Hawaiian system of land tenure has been described with special care because questions of land title and land distributions became an immediate concern of Hawaiian-European administrations, starting with the first Hawaiian constitution of 1840.

Genealogical Traditions

Hawaiian genealogical traditions were assembled by Judge Abraham Fornander during the 1870's, or two generations after Christianity had become the state religion, and so their authenticity may have been impaired. Sequences may have become rearranged and European viewpoints intruded. Fornander was not unaware that genealogical relationships had been rearranged by ambitious chiefly families, but the question of the European viewpoint poses a more difficult problem. For example, one of the early traditions dealing with the very first chief is a tale of brothers conspiring to get rid of a hated younger brother. The tale has all the earmarks of a "Joseph" tale, from which it may well have been derived. On the other hand, the theme of "sibling rivilary" is so common in the Hawaiian chiefly traditions that it is just as credible to assume that the Joseph tale found ready access to the minds of the genealogist and that the theme of the Biblical tale and the Hawaiian native themes merged. There are, of course, similar problems in evaluating the historical authenticity of all Polynesian traditions, but Hawaii poses a special problem because of the continuity of a Hawaiian ruling class and a Hawaiian literati well into the Christian period. That is to say, the native historians and genealogists had not only become Christian but had acquired a political role in which their view of history had political significance and was in any case of more than antiquarian interest. But the problem of bias is not unusual in history. It does not invalidate the traditions; it only reminds us to view them with necessary reserve and caution.

The fullest genealogical record is quite naturally that of the Kamehameha family, and covers 99 generations. The native historians have divided these traditions into five epochs. The first, of 16 generations, deals with events leading up to the arrival from "Tahiti" to Hawaii. The second epoch consists of eight generations, and the third of only four generations. The first three epochs were considered as generally peaceful and uneventful. Beginning with the fourth epoch, a period of 57 generations, and concluding with the fifth, of 14 generations leading to Kamehameha, the traditions describe wars and important social changes. Fornander, calculating a generation at 30 years, put the beginning of the fourth epoch at A.D. 1100. It may well have been several hundred years later, since many of the *ali'i* did not have a very long reign. This Epoch IV initiating a time of unrest has been called by Fornander the "Migratory Period" on the assumption that it was foreign invasions that had upset the earlier calm. The evidence for foreign invasions is not actually in the traditions—which describe only internal dissensions—but is a shrewd deduction made by Fornander, who believed that invading chiefs had conquered an indigenous folk and had reduced them to the status of commoners. Epoch IV, essentially the beginning of the Late Period in Hawaiian history, is presented in fairly rich detail.

The first recorded political disorder of Epoch IV concerns the removal of a chief from office by a high priest, who then installed a new chief. Subsequently, although not in response to this event, a "congregation of chiefs" (*aha ali'i*) was established on the island of Maui to authenticate the genealogical record and to preserve chiefly rank even after position and power had been lost. Those whose pedigrees came from the aha ali'i might be taken as prisoners of war and they might be offered as sacrifices, but they could not be enslaved or denied the deference due their rank. This important development marks a sharp break with the Traditional status system in which the degradation of military defeat and capture destroyed the mana of the chief and, hence, his rank. We may see in this immunization of rank an intensification of the genealogical principle and still another example of separation of rank and political power. Fornander has explained the aha ali'i "as a necessity of the existing condition of things during the 'migratory period,' as a protection of the native aristocracy against foreign pretenders and as a broader line of demarcation between the nobility and the commonality (1880:II, 30)."

It was during Epoch IV that the office of paramount chief over an entire island first came into being, and with it the new chiefly title *ka-moi,* or "supreme chief." Previously, chiefs of the island districts were politically independent and were known merely as *alii nui.* Fornander has described this change as follows:

> At this time commenced the development of the idea of a sovereign lord or king *ka-moi* over each of the principal islands of the group. Previously, it appears each chief was entirely independent of every other chief, and his authority was coextensive

> with his possessions. When the legends referring to that time speak of an *alii nui* of Kauai or an *alii nui* of Hawaii it simply means that he was the most powerful chief on that island for the time being, and that by inheritance, conquest or marriage had obtained a larger territory than any other chief there. But after this period the word *moi* appears in the legends and *moles* [chants] indicating that the chief who bore that title was by some constitutional or prescriptive right, acknowledged as the suzerain lord of his island, the *primus inter pares* of the other chiefs of said island, to whom the latter owed a nominal, at least, if not a real allegiance and fealty. Nor were the territorial possessions and power of the acknowledged *moi* always the source of this dignity, for the legends relate several instances where the wealth in lands and retainers of a moi were inferior to some of the other chiefs who, nevertheless, owed him allegiance and followed his banner (1880:II, 64).

The traditions of this epoch also describe the rise of priestly power, the first, but not the only example of which was the removal from office of a high chief. Perhaps another sign of priestly power was the change in the form of the heiau. At this time (Epoch IV), a four-walled ceremonial center replaced the open court that contained a truncated pyramid. In the older form the people could see the ceremonies. After the walls, which were about five feet high, were built, only the presiding chiefs and priests and other privileged persons were admitted to the enclosure; all others remained on the outside. The new heiaus. Fornander believes, came at a time when the great departmental deities, Kane, Ku, and Lono had replaced in importance the local ancestral gods. Fornander saw in the traditions of this period a new religious mood:

> To the influence of this period may be attributed the increased stringency of tabus and probably the introduction, or at least the more general application of human sacrifice. In support of this surmise I may state that in all the legends or allusions referring to the period previous to this migratory epoch I have found no indications of the practice of human sacrifices, though they may have existed; but subsequent to this period the inhuman practice became progressively increasing, until in the latter days of paganism hardly any public affair was transacted without the preamble of one or more human victims (1880:II, 16).

Fornander has characterized the fourth epoch generally as one in which the power of chiefs became more prominent and in which status distinctions hardened, enhancing the privileges of the nobility at the expense of the *makaainana*. The published traditions do not actually speak of any change in the condition of the commoners; this must be deduced from references to chiefly prerogatives. What they document in detail is the record of chiefly expansion and of chiefly rivalries, both internal and external. Since this was a period of wars and of civil unrest in which the orderly bases of genealogical rank and rule were frequently upset, it illustrates the Open Society phase of Polynesian social evolution. As chiefly lines finally consolidated their authority, establishing, above all, their rights to the reallocation of lands, this phase moved progressively, although not at a fixed time, into the Stratified Society; essentially the same processes of development are described for each of the main islands.

On Hawaii, the traditions attribute the beginning of the paramount chieftainship to Kalanuihua (1270), who succeeded in conquering Maui and Molokai and invaded Oahu, which, at the time, was divided into several independent territories. He was finally defeated and taken captive on Kauai but allowed to return to Hawaii where he resumed as *moi*. Fornander notes that during this period the priestly power was not yet very strong, for Kalanuihua had a legendary reputation for killing priests who crossed him.

Subsequently, in the time of Liloa (A.D. 1420), a high priest is reported by the traditions as receiving a grant of land in the Kona district of Hawaii which remained secure through all the vicissitudes of war and rebellion until the time of Kamehameha I. This land grant may indicate a gain in priestly influence. At the time of Liloa, the authority was divided, the lands going to the first-born son and the religious authority to the younger son. Subsequently, it was the younger son, Umi, who seized the full authority and became one of the most famous of paramount chiefs on Hawaii. As the traditions narrate the events, it was the priests in concert with lesser chiefs who conspired with Umi, as their champion, to overthrow the moi, who had a reputation for treating the priests disrespectfully and for capricious cruelty generally. When people were praised in his presence he arranged to have them killed (Fornander 1916–17:IV, 204).

The reign of Umi, dated by Fornander at 1450, is described in some detail by the traditions. From these accounts the social system at the time had reached its final or classic form. Thus Umi is said to have divided the lands of Hawaii into six great districts: Kau, Puna, Hilo, Hamakua, Kohala, and Kona, each of which he allocated to a friendly chief. This division of the lands may not have been the very first to follow a political rather than traditional principle of allocating lands among a group of siblings or other close kin, but it is the earliest specific reference of the kind in the traditions. The traditions dealing with Umi, it should be said, are not entirely consistent, for his authority over all of Hawaii is attributed, on the one hand, to his succession by force to the chiefdom and, on the other, to specific conquests over each of the districts. Since Umi was Hawaii's great legendary ruler, it is likely that the traditions have generalized his administration, attributing to it general rather than specific historical features. The traditions, for example, credit Umi with establishing all the standard features of paramount rule and with setting up the basic divisions of function.

The tradition says:

> Umi-a-Liloa set the laborers in order and separated those who held positions in the government. He separated the chiefs, the priesthood, the astrologers and the skillful in the land. He separated the cultivators and the fishermen, and the canoe hewers. He set apart the warriors, the spear-warders, and every department with proficiency, and every laborer in their respective lines of work. So with the governors, district superintendents, division overseers and section wardens; they were all set in order (Fornander 1916–17:IV, 228).

The use of cut stone in heiaus is dated from Umi.

The traditions portray Umi as a defender of the people against the nobles and retainers of his own court. He is said to have moved his residence from Waipio, where paramount chiefs usually lived, to the rich Kona district so that he could protect its people. There, the traditions say, he received tribute from chiefs and landowners.

The reign of Umi is held up as an interval of order and consolidation. The post-Umi period, after he was succeeded by his eldest son, was a return to "internal war, rivalry and confusion," to quote Fornander. The succession was soon contested by a younger son, who seized the rule and then put down a revolt of district chiefs. It seems certainly to have been a period of opportunity for lower-ranking chiefly families. Thus the traditions refer to Iwikauwikaua, a low-ranking alii who, with no land rights of his own, succeeded, nevertheless, by an advantageous marriage in having his daughter succeed as moi of Hawaii through his wife's side. During her reign one of the families on Hawaii had become so powerful as to be, to all intents and purposes, independent of the paramount chieftainship (Fornander 1880: II, 128). Between paramount chief and the district or lesser chiefs there seems to have been a relentless struggle for political advantage, a competition that was matched only by the rivalries between brothers for the same office. Speaking of this post-Umi period, Fornander has said:

> It was no uncommon event in those days for a chief to disembarrass himself of an obnoxious and powerful vassal against whom open force or other violence would be inadvisable, by the process of praying to death, "*anaana*" or by secret poisoning, "*akua hanai*"; and as late as thirty years ago, the belief was common that if a person died suddenly in the prime of life without any known cause of death, he had either been prayed to death or poisoned by secret enemies (1880:II, 142).

A common source of civil unrest was dissatisfaction with land distributions at the start of each new reign. When an heir was dissatisfied with his allotment he began a rebellion. The traditions document several such rebellions, some of which had very substantial political repercussions.

On Maui the unsettled period fell between 1180 and 1330, by Fornander's calculations. After the reign of Kauilahea (1330), the island was unified under a single moi and a stable administration continued in effect until the time of Kamehameha I.

The traditional history of Oahu develops in detail with Moikeha (1090), an alii nui. Through marriage he acquired a high chiefship on Kauai as well, and subsequently established its ruling line. The successor to Moikeha, his eldest son, is described in the traditions as having begun the system of having the farmers work a particular number of days in each month for the landowner. The sons of Moikeha on Kauai are described as having been overthrown by a revolt, the lands which had been descending in the family being seized by the victorious chief, who then installed a legitimate heir to the chiefship and took for himself the office of land administrator (*kona kuhina*). This may have been, therefore, an early example, if not the first of land reallocation as a prize of power (Fornander 1916–17:IV, 152). The period of stability on Oahu set in with Mailikukahi (1360). He came at the end of a disorderly interval and was appointed to the supreme chiefship by the local chiefs. He is said to have established the first permanent land boundaries. He built heiaus and honored the priests and he bolstered the bases of genealogical rank by instituting compulsory chiefly education for all first-born male children. The importance of the senior male at this stage of Hawaiian history is to be considered against the fact that during the fifth epoch women chiefs became quite prominent. Prior to Liloa—the end of the fourth epoch—no female chiefs are listed in the official genealogies.

On Kauai, a branch line of Oahu, the period of instability began in 1180 with Lamamaikahiki. Kauai had the prestige in the Hawaiian Islands equal to that of Raiatea in the Society Islands. Its chiefly lines had the highest rank and were sought after in marriage by chiefs in all the islands. But at some time unspecified in the genealogies its prestige began to decline. Still, Kauai had the distinction of never having been conquered—until 1824 when it ceded authority to Kamehameha I in order to forestall an invasion.

The Archeological Record

It is the earliest period of Hawaiian history that is in doubt. The date of a fishing station that was occupied as early as A.D. 124 sets the approximate age of the Hawaiian civilization but does not define for us its early style. Emory, who sees an historical relationship between early Hawaiian and Marquesan fishhooks, supposes that the first phase of Hawaiian society was a continuation of the Marquesan. A second phase was introduced ca. 1200 from Tahiti also, Emory reasons from fishhook comparisons. An analysis of over 4,000 fishhooks taken from 33 different excavations indicates, however, that the two phases were probably not discontinuous but merged smoothly. Over the entire course of their history covering at least 1,000 years, the series of fishhooks show only "small, gradual change (Emory, Bonk, Sinoto 1959:41)." In view of the late known dates for the Society Islands, a Marquesan derivation of early Hawaiian society seems reasonable. Nevertheless, Suggs, the unquestioned authority on Marquesan archeology, sees no substantial evidence for such a connection. (personal communication, June 14, 1963). Emory's belief that Tahitian influence "*overwhelmed* [italics mine] the Hawaiian Islands" in the twelfth century is out of proportion with specific evidence of continuity of development, whether we consider fishhooks or megalithic remains. If the Tahitian influence did come later—a reasonable supposition from glottochronology which dates the separation of Tahitian and Hawaiian at ca. A.D. 1000 (Elbert 1953)—that influence was more likely "in phase" with the course of developments in Hawaii.

The value of Hawaiian stone monuments as guides to historical sequences is considerably diminished by the fact that after 1820 many were systematically destroyed. Conceivably those that survived do not represent the full series of types that may have existed. The Hawaiian monuments are called heiaus and resemble the Tahitian ahus. On the outlying Necker and Nihoa islands, the most remote Hawaiian outposts, the heiaus are definitely of the early Tahitian type (Emory 1928). On the main islands, all the known heiaus are variants, or rather further developments, of this basic form. The Hawaiian heiaus seem never to have attained the grandeur of the Tahitian stepped pyramids. They remained essentially rectangular areas paved with uncut stone and surrounded often with a low stone wall. Each heiau also enclosed smaller structures of stone or timber, either as altars or as supporting buildings. While there is no consistent pattern in this respect, it is a fact that the largest Hawaiian heiau is of the walled type, in support of the tradition that walls were a later innovation. In no case are the surviving heiaus remarkable examples of construction. Bennett, who studied Kauai, noted that neither angles nor dimensions were very carefully calculated. Often the Hawaiians merely followed the slope of the terrain, rather than terrace to create a level (1931).

Bennett has identified five types of heiau (1931): the large sacrificial temples constructed by great chiefs and dedicated to Ku, god of war and used as chiefly burial places; agricultural shrines to bring rain; fishing shrines built along the shores; small family structures for private prayer and worship; and a miscellaneous group of small courts used by lesser chiefs and priests.

The sacrificial heiaus reveal most about earlier political conditions. These were rebuilt each time a new chief took office. The temple architects sought to incorporate all features of old heiaus that were believed to have brought success to their chiefs. Thus no two heiaus were alike. Perhaps it is for this reason of experimentation that heiau styles did not move forward in a continuous direction. Size of heiau, nevertheless, remained a constant index of chiefly grandeur. The largest heiau was on Oahu, the center of political power. This was a great terraced structure that reached a total length of 467 feet on both its levels and had surrounding walls ten feet in height (Thrum 1908). On Kauai, the center of traditional authority, the heiaus were smaller. But perhaps even more interesting, they were all of the same approximate size, leading Bennett to the reasonable conclusion that on this island the chiefly power was evenly divided (1931:35).

Historical Recapitulation

Archeology has not yet decisively established whether Hawaiian evolution was mainly internal or a product of foreign intrusion. But evidence of continuity in all available measures of change leads only to the conclusion that Tahitian influences most likely introduced a new stimulus but not a new direction. The traditional record is also one of continuity of development in which changes come about as a result of the rivalries of chiefs. The traditions identify one of the causes of unrest as dissatisfaction of chiefs with land allotments. Are we to interpret this observation as the familiar land pressure explanation for war? The extent of social turmoil on Hawaii, the largest island, and the relative quiet of Kauai, the smaller, reminds us that land pressure is more than a simple expression of population density. The social and political implications of density are always functions of the social system. In the Hawaiian Islands the land interest of chiefs, as the traditions amply indicate, were identified directly with their social ambitions, a consideration related, but only indirectly, to the issue of subsistence.

The traditions describe a sequence of cultural stages that accord readily with the hypothesis that a fully evolved Stratified society had gone from a Traditional and then through an Open phase. With only the most minor modifications, we may rearrange Fornander's five epochs into three main historical periods as follows:

An Early Period (A.D. 124–1100—Epochs I, II, III) when Hawaiian society was most traditional. Seniority ruled succession to title, authority and land holdings; chiefs were sacred and held religious prerogatives; the male line was preeminent; the power of chiefs was largely formal and ritual; and social distinctions between chiefs and commoners had not yet reached their full prominence.

A Middle Period (A.D. 1100–1450—Epoch IV) when Hawaiian society entered a phase transitional to full stratification. During this period chiefs redistributed lands among their allies; paramount chiefs (moi) took control of island-wide administrations; a formal council, the aha ali'i, was established to safeguard the rights and privileges of the nobility; the prerogatives of genealogical rank became more formal and less political and economic; the political authority of chiefs became more commanding; priests acquired new influence; the separation of chiefs and commoners gained momentum; new special roles and statuses were established; political rivalry grew more heated and the chiefly authority shifted from one family line to another.

A Late Period (1450–1820—Epoch V) when the Stratified society was fully established and the consolidation of political authority was completed. The period begins with the practice of redistributing lands with each new administration. The social upheavals that resulted from the dislodging of landholders, and the dissatisfaction of chiefs with the lands given to them, touched off a sequence of wars that did not stop until forcibly ended by the Kamehameha conquest.

The Status System

Hawaii eliminated the raatira rank, thus at least nominally widening the categorical gap, already manifest in Tahiti, between royalty and commoner. In principle, alii and makaainana—the one sacred, the other secular—were constituted as distinct realms. The former held the titles, the honorable forms of land tenure, and most prerogatives of authority; the latter held positions of worth as tillers of the soil, but were also the menials and persons without distinction. The system was dual even though some ali'i could slip down into the mire of commoner society and some makaainana could rise to ali'i. The gap was, in fact, more nominal than real. Where raatira in Tahiti had held a "middle" role, the Hawaiian ali'i had moved in to occupy comparable positions. Ali'i had become the expansive rank, spreading so wide as almost to lose distinction. In response, the ali'i were formed into eleven grades whose upper reaches separated themselves even more distantly from the rest. As the top ali'i ranks entered a new stratosphere of sanctity and distance, an obverse low rank was separated from makaainana as a true pariah caste. That the small pariah *kauwa* caste was structurally related to the formation of a super-rank of ali'i in terms of a principle of complementary opposition is suggested by its dual role as pariah and beyond even the pale of commonness as *akua* (gods) with a special relationship to chiefs. The Hawaiian status system was energetic and effervescent, moving simultaneously in two opposite directions: toward a consolidation and intensification of traditional principles in which sanctity was emphasized, and toward the opening up of new and essentially utilitarian channels.

Primogeniture

All first-born, male or female, were ritually honored; and even though men were preferred as actual chiefs and as family heads, the rule of primogeniture finally outweighed the sex consideration. The degree of devotion to primogeniture is reminiscent of the Marquesas, but the Hawaiian pattern of differentiating ranks foreclosed the possibility of spreading the honors too widely. As in the Marquesas, the first-born was known either as *makahiapo* (or *hiapo*), or as *mua*. The former was the term of special honor, a true title of status, derived, as Handy explains, from the banyan tree from which bark loin cloths were made for aristocrats (1958:47). Mua, on the other hand, a term referring, for example, to the forward end of a canoe, was the more general term, referring to all first-born, including those of commoner families. Special ritual honors naturally distinguished *ali'i* from commoner. The first-born was seen as "opening the way" for all other offspring of a family, and whatever blessings he received fell upon them as well. Thus he (or she) was the natural ritual center for his generation. Ritual interests were strongest among ali'i for whom the concept of a progenitive line was most important. Thus it was only among ali'i and related priestly families that the genitalia of the hiapo received ritual attention. The preeminence of the first-born must be considered against the very special affection bestowed upon the youngest child, who was playfully called *haku,* or family head. The youngest did not, however, stand simply as the pole of affection as against the pole of respect represented by the senior scion. In instances cited by Fornander (1890) it was indeed the youngest who succeeded to the paramount chiefship. In the complexity of factors entering into categorization of rank, as I shall explain below, primogeniture had ceased to be an absolute.

Seniority of Descent

In traditional fashion, Hawaiian kinship consistently delineated senior-junior relationships so that each family was conscious of those lines to which it was senior and those to which it owed respect as junior. In the district of Ka'u on Hawaii, a last stronghold of traditional kinship in the islands, the senior male of the senior line normally assumed the headship of his commoner kindred. Among ali'i however, seniority had become embedded in a distinctive pattern of rank distinctions governed largely by marriage. The form of marriage which modified the otherwise absolute character of seniority had become most important among the highest ranks of chiefs for whom finer discriminations had become imperative. Brother-sister marriage produced offspring of the highest rank; marriages between children sired with her by each of the two husbands of a chiefess, and then marriages between classificatory siblings produced offspring of second and of third rank respectively. Seniority was not negligible, but it was not, in these instances, the sole determining factor in rank. Senior lines, rather, had introduced additional criteria to allow for finer gradations. Kamehameha I, for example—his titles a product of senior lines—claimed an increment of rank because he had been sired by two fathers, both illustrious chiefs. In effect, it would appear that his seniority had been multiplied. The Hawaiian genealogists recognized their task as exceedingly complex—as it would be, considering the variety of factors they had to deal with.

Male Line

Early Hawaiian genealogies favored the male line; and even after the tide had begun to turn during the Middle Period men were still preferred as high chiefs, a condition that favored patrilineal succession. Nevertheless, bilateralism and with it the social and ritual equality of women had become overwhelmingly powerful forces. We have reason to assume that when Liholiho finally broke the *kapus* that had separated men and women in some ritual respects, his action was no mere response to Christian or to general political influences, but was indeed the culmination of an irresistible movement toward sexual equality. At the beginning of the nineteenth century Hawaiian culture presented the incongruous-seeming spectacle of extraordinary taboos that prevented husband and wife from eating together or freely sharing domiciles, while at the same time women had become powerful political personalities, and in the highest ranking families had achieved god-like sanctity. The separation of the sexes reflected, of course, the familiar Polynesian dictum of sacred male and profane female. This most conservative of all Polynesian religious notions the Hawaiians had also modified. While observing and even intensifying the forms of separation, the Hawaiians had modified the content by attributing to women descent from their own pantheon—a Polynesian version of the doctrine of equal but separate.

Both Fornander and Malo believed that the inheritance of rank—the real issue in linearity—had become pro-matrilineal. The examples do not bear them out. The impression of matriliny is understandable, however, in a setting of expanding bilaterality. The historical question is whether bilaterality was, in fact, developing or expanding or whether it was perhaps "old" Hawaiian? Hawaiian bilaterality resembles the Marquesan. In the Marquesan case we did not know whether bilaterality was original or late. Since the Hawaiian Islands had probably been settled first from the Marquesas, it would not be difficult to assume on general historical grounds an old bilateral tradition. (Again, to avoid misunderstanding, I remind the reader that the references to bilaterality in this discussion are not to kinship categories but only to patterns of transmission of title and rank.) However, specific historical evidence from Hawaii points to the characteristic Polynesian pro-patriliny as the older tradition. Thus, the kindred organization of Ka'u, an example of Hawaiian conservatism, follows the traditional practice of giving headship to the senior male of the senior male line (Handy and Pukui 1958:47). Even more impressive evidence is from the chiefly genealogies, all of which show that up until the beginning of the twelfth century (Middle Period) only males succeeded their fathers in office. Thereafter, as we observed in the Society Islands, women came to be named chiefs and men inherited office from their mothers. The shift was from patriliny to bilaterality. The Hawaiian history in this respect adds weight to what is only a conjecture of an earlier condition of pro-patriliny in the presumed Marquesas homeland.

To seemingly confuse the issue of apparent straight-line evolution from patriliny to bilaterality, there is the matrilocality of Ka'u (Handy and Pukui 1958). Residence and descent are, however, only loosely related conditions. The matrilocality of Ka'u, essentially a plebeian area, follows the rules of status residence (see chap. 20), according to which upper rank pro-patrilocality is matched by lower rank pro-matrilocality. In Hawaii, status bilaterality had, in fact, upset the sheer patrilocality of the upper ranks. Thus the pronounced matrilocality of low-rank families in Ka'u may be represented as response to a pattern of status differentiation—as an adjustment that preserved the contrast between upper and lower ranks.

Genealogical Depth

Depth was vital to honor. The Kamehameha pedigree reached back 99 generations to the gods; lower-ranking descent lines were founded by human ancestors. Depth was one of the conditions of genealogical thickness and rootedness. More specifically, it gave authenticity to the claim to general rule, for ultimately the entire Hawaiian population—the highest ranks by specific pedigree—claimed common descent from Wakea and Papa, the sky god and the earth goddess.

Sanctity

Sanctity (*kapu*) was a minutely graded quality inherent in pedigree, but only as a potentiality, and then made operative by means of proper observances. The gradations were most discriminating at the upper levels of rank in the normal Polynesian manner. The concept of sanctity as existing in a dual state, differentiating what is only potential and what is actually kinetic, is also standard in Polynesia. The Hawaiians only varied the pattern, creating to all intents and purposes a more conservative version. By identifying sanctity with the willingness to observe it, the Hawaiians evidently sought to spare it the harsh tests of political efficacy. The institution of the *aha ali'i* is a case in point. With the sanctity of rank immune to a greater degree than ever from the consequences of political rivalry, the Hawaiian aristocracy was free to develop the minutiae of ritual observances. Thus the political radicalism of Hawaii as expressed in the abandonment of the segmentary organization was matched by an increasing conservatism as expressed by an exaggerated ritual formalism in the assertion of rank.

Kapu in Hawaiian has a double meaning, denoting that which is prohibited and that which is a special privilege of sanctity (Pukui and Elbert 1965). The first meaning refers to the general pattern of avoidances, essentially common to all Polynesia. The second is specific, referring to the particular prerogatives of demanding obeisance and of freedom from obeisance. The *kapu moe* was the specific prerogative of highest rank. It demanded full prostration from subordinates below a prescribed rank in the presence of the Source or of any intimate object belonging to him. Lesser kapu prerogatives (*kapu wohi*) demanded that subordinates kneel before the source when he was eating, and that they appear before him clean and properly attired. Ranks close to the source held specific exemptions from the kapu moe. In the main, kapu wohi established the separation of ranks by the usual imposition of physical distances. A lower-ranking shadow could not fall upon the source or his house or his intimate belongings. Boundaries of the chiefly residence could not be trangressed; the garments of chiefs could not be handled; and no lower rank could appear in a superior canoe to that in which the source was presently seated. A chief's bathing stone was sacrosanct. The prerogatives of kapu moe and of kapu wohi were inherited as distinct units, for the kapu moe, even though it was clearly transcendent, did not specifically subsume the kapu wohi. Thus John Papa Ii notes that Liholiho (Kamehameha II) was the "most kapu" of all chiefs because he had inherited kapu prerogatives from both sides, the kapu moe from his mother and the kapu wohi from his father (1959:51). Whoever inherited the wohi did not have to submit to the kapu moe.

Violation of the moe or wohi subjected the offender to the death penalty, also an inherited prerogative of sanctity, known as *kanawai*, the common Hawaiian term for "edict, law" (Elbert and Pukui 1957). That is to say, the right to impose the death penalty, either by burning or by strangling, or by other means, was, in practice, subsumed under the prerogative of kapu, but was in principle also specified as a unit privilege. Kanawai were not necessarily in defense of kapu, as, for example, the special hereditary right to pluck out the eye of a man who had committed no offense (Kamakau 1964:14). Royal and chiefly lines accumulated unit prerogatives which they then passed down the pedigree. According to Papa Ii, inheritance was not automatic. He tells of a chiefess who gave her moe to one child and reserved the wohi for others (1959:52). Women inherited the awesome privileges of sanctity equally with men, despite the general kapu that declared women even of the highest rank as profane with respect to eating. The eating kapu (to which I shall turn shortly) defined the general pattern of ritual relations between men and women; the kapu moe and kapu wohi defined the more specific relations between persons of different ranks regardless of sex. It is not difficult to understand the restraints generally placed upon the sanctity of women who are not otherwise removed from the domestic sphere, for the logic of separation and of ritual contamination would place a barrier between mother and child. Yet in Hawaii some women of ali'i descent had so much sanctity of rank they dared not rear children for fear their powers would either cripple the new-born infant or kill it. Such women gave their children away to relatives for rearing (Handy and Pukui 1958:195–96).

The Hawaiians leave no doubt as to what they regarded as the ultimate source of kapu. Sanctity was not a generalized quality of lineage. It was specifically a quality of the gods and, in graded proportion, of their human descendants. Deference was thus to the gods and to the divine-descended. The offspring of high rank sibling marriages acquired the highest kapu because they were in fact gods. Like the gods they were said to be fire, heat, raging blazes. In the hierarchy of sanctity, gods and their human descendants were included within a single order. The gods held the first rank, their human descendants the ensuing ranks. To leave no doubt as to the unity of this order, the Hawaiians equated the offspring of the sibling (incestuous) marriages with the gods. The gods were the specific sources of sanctity; they were the specific sources of mana, which they transmitted in response to prayer, but in acordance with the protocol of rank. Mana corresponded in grade to kapu. The gods with highest-rank kapu had the highest-potency mana. Yet just as chiefly kapu could be matched as equivalent to that of the gods, so could the mana of chiefs be in effect countered against that of the gods.

Kamakau tells, for example, that chiefs had the power (mana) to spare the life of one who had perhaps inadvertently trespassed upon chiefly kapu. If the specific kapu of a god were violated, the death penalty was normally obligatory, since this was an offense outside the realm of sanctity of a chief. Nevertheless, Kamakau points out, "If a *kapu* of the chief and that of a god were combined, the man could be absolved through the *kapu* of the chief, and if the breaking of the god's *kapu* carried a death penalty he could be saved (1964:12)." He does not explain how the kapus are combined. The point, however, is that chiefs and gods met in the same realms of sanctity and of power. The chiefs were divine manifestations of the gods, to cite Kamakau. Since they were gods, though of lower degree, their relationship even to the great deities—Kane, Lono, Ku, Kanaloa—carried the inevitable ambiguity posed by distinctions in grade but not in kind. The power of the chief had become equivalent to the power of a god and could be conceived therefore as capable of counteracting it.

Chiefly powers then were truly godlike. We need to consider, however, the domain in which these powers ruled, since power in Hawaii had become specialized. The terrifying powers over life were in the service of special religious interests, and particularly in defense of specified kapus. In principle, sanctity and political qualifications coincided. Yet the association was not inevitable. Sanctity and rule, in fact, separated in the course of Hawaiian history. Kamakau has described this important development so aptly, I quote the relevant passage at length:

> The pedigrees (ku'auhau) of the chiefs in the line of succession (mo'o ku'auhau) from ancient times down to those of Kamehameha I are not the same. As their descendants spread out, the ranks ('ano) of the chiefs lessened. Sometimes the hereditary chief lost his land, and the kingdom was taken by force and snatched away by a warrior, and the name of "chief" was given to him because of his prowess. He then attached himself to the chiefly genealogies, even though his father may have been of no great rank (noa noa), and his mother a chiefess. Therefore, the chiefs were not of like ranks, and the islands came under the rule of different chiefs who were not all of high chiefly status (kulana)—not from generations of chiefs. One might be an ali'i kapu, a "sacred" chief of highest rank, another an ali'i noa noa, a chief of no particular rank, or an ali'i ho'opilipili, a chief who had "grafted" himself into a chiefly genealogy (1964:4).

The *aha ali'i,* the code in defence of aristocratic sanctity, gave official sanction to the separation of religious and political powers. We should not, however, confuse this Hawaiian separation of powers with that of Mangaia, which it resembles in principle. The Hawaiian concern was for the inviolable unity of pedigree and sanctity, and not with the relegation of the *ali'i kapu* to a specialized religious realm. Kamehameha and his son Liholiho were both kapu chiefs, emphasizing the Hawaiian preference for associating political hegemony with the highest degree of sanctity. Considered exclusively from a political standpoint the recurrent separations of power and sanctity are possibly to be understood as respect for efficacy, that is, realpolitik. From a religious point of view, however, the question to be answered is how vital was chiefly sanctity to the well-being of the political community. If, for example, productivity is seen as dependent upon chiefly mana and tapu, then a secular chief is a handicap unless supported, as in Mangaia, by a priestly aristocracy. Hawaii had a priestly aristocracy of high priests (*kahuna nui*) who were members of the royal line, in some respects more sacred than the ali'i, and with direct access to the gods. A sacred paramount chief was not therefore vital. The Hawaiian view, however, was that religious powers were quantitative and so the preference for a kapu ali'i was a matter of wanting the utmost of sanctity. The essential religious figures were the high priests, who represented directly all the gods including Kane the Creator. When priests opposed high chiefs, the consequences were not as drastic as when chiefs acted against the high priests. In the first instance, civil disturbances ensued; in the second, the gods smote the land with drought and famine. The violation of chiefly kapu was satisfied simply by direct retaliation upon the offender; the violation of priestly kapu endangered the land. Thus, in this particular respect, the chief's orbit of sacred power was narrow, that of the high priests wide. Since narrow orbits are lower in status, the sanctity of the kapu chief must be considered to be lower than that of the priests.

In his special role as a high worshiper of Lono, the god of agriculture, and in his ritual supremacy in the *makahiki,* or harvest festival, the paramount chief did indeed control one wide orbit—representing national prosperity. But he was certainly not the key to national well-being. Hawaiian religion had become extraordinarily diversified and specialized, and no one sector of authority held the controlling religious power. Each held a limited jurisdiction revolving about its special interests. According to Malo, the chiefs' special interests were to increase their lands. ("Land was the main thing which the kings and chiefs sought to gain by their prayers and worship . . . [1951:157].) The general public, on the other hand, prayed to Kane for all the general benefits of health, prosperity, and the well-being of chiefs. Each craft, of course, as indeed elsewhere in Polynesia, sought the aid of craft gods in behalf of their labors. Women had their own deities. In short, each rank, each occupation, and each sex had its own gods.

Whoever made an offering to a god received mana. Mana was thus not simply or directly an attribute of pedigree, but a benefice of the gods granted to whom they would favor. Many people, not only the high chiefs or priests, could acquire the mana of the gods, and so be feared. Many had the power to "pray to death in broad daylight, a mana so powerful that it caused solid rocks to melt (Kamakau 1964: 36)." If such godly mana—represented by the idea of a raging fire—was not the exclusive prerogative of rank—and if it was, moreover, exceedingly specialized—then, of course, there would be no religious difficulty in separating the efficacy of rule from the potential efficacy vested in pedigree alone. The most sacred chief could occupy his role as god and enjoy the privileges of personal sanctity even if he did not hold the temporal authority.

The apparent contradiction between the increasing political role of women and their deification among highest ranks, on the one hand, and the extreme separation of the sexes, on the other, is perhaps also to be explained by the principle of specialization of sanctity. The familiar Polynesian doctrine of men as sacred and women as profane was modified in Hawaii. Men and women were separated because they came under the jurisdiction of different classes of gods. Men, Handy and Pukui explain, ate in the presence of their family gods, and that is why women could not join them (1958:9). A more specific explanation must be that men were in the presence of male gods to whom they had been dedicated in early childhood. Thus women were also tabooed from eating pork, fowl, turtle, several kinds of fish, coconuts, and any other food offered in sacrifice to the great male gods (Ellis 1853:IV, 397). Insofar as they came under the jurisdiction of their own class of deities, among them Pele, the goddess of fire and volcanoes, women had access to mana and came under their own order of sanctity. The female order was, however, subordinate. Men and women ate in separate houses, but it was the male house that was taboo. Eating was exclusively a male sacrament. In this specific but most prominent order, women lacked sanctity. The highest ranking women, who had their own realm of extraordinary sanctity, could reverse the rule and be served by men who entered their eating houses. But such men held, in fact, the low status of spiritual eunuchs.

Wealth

In the well-endowed Hawaiian Islands, many could be wealthy; the "aura of abundance," while desirable, could not, however, differentiate ranks. Hawaii recognized the nobility of a chief living in poverty yet displaying pride of ancestry in his regal demeanor. As in Tahiti, the power to demand property and to govern it counted for more than direct possession. The land title held by the moi was, of course, a political authority. His personal land-holdings representing his particular pedigree put him on an equivalent plane with other aristocratic land holders. The political title set him apart. As an estate-holder, the paramount chief was conceivably less wealthy than his subordinates. In periodic redistributions of conquered lands, chiefs were eager for a personal share, but also mindful of the political advantages of bestowing the largest allotment upon an ally. The political consideration gave higher status than possession per se. Ordinary people enjoyed the high prestige of abundance which allowed them to retain servants, to acquire quality goods such as houses, canoes, and mats, and to expend in sacrifices. They held, so to speak, the lower status of the consumer, as against the higher status of the manager and mover of wealth.

Hawaii, however, did not emphasize either conspicuous consumption or invidious display. Thrift, Malo has said, was one of the major virtues (1951:74). There are no references in the literature on Hawaii to the "potlatch" type of rivalrous exchange. The size of the ground plan of a house accorded with rank and status, but elevation was rivalrous. The Hawaiian judgment, however, declared adjacent houses to be good if they were alike and of the same height. Then, it was said, they would not be in opposition to one another (Fornander 1880:VI, 76). The conspicuous chiefly display was also nonrivalrous and noneconomic: the insignia of chiefs, the red and yellow plumage worked into splendid helmets and capes, were symbols of divinity; and while the feathers were the most valuable, and desired offerings given to chiefs, they did not comprise economic wealth since they were nonnegotiable.

The great aura of abundance was represented in the tribute collected during the makahiki, the harvest festival. This tribute included the main food stuffs—pigs, dogs, fowl, poi—and durables—tapa cloth, dress tapas, malos, shoulder capes, pearls, ivory, iron adzes, and the red and yellow feathers. The quantity contributed was a measure of the chief's standing. If he judged the tribute insufficient, he had the district plundered (Kamakau 1964:20). According to Kamakau, only the precious objects were delivered to the chief. The foodstuffs and lesser objects were distributed at once to the crowd that followed the religious procession around the island. Kamakau may have had only small makahiki collections in mind. Kepelino mentions 20,000 calabashes of poi and 40,000 pigs collected in an island tour (Beckwith 1932:188–89). For such quantities the distributions were systematic, following the order of hierarchy. But Malo says: "No share of this property, however, was given to the people (1951:188)." The "people" were omitted, we may assume, because all giving was in the name of chiefs. The makahiki itself was a collective display of chiefly wealth within which the general principle that rank corresponds with wealth was expressed as a ritual statement.

To sense the crosscurrents of the varieties of chiefly interests in wealth, we must take notice of how chiefs began to manage the economy shortly after the European era began. The chiefs took immediate advantage of legal land titles to acquire new personal holdings; and they turned their attention from subsistence agriculture to the more enriching sandalwood trade. Low-status tenure became true landless tenure; crop productivity declined and people hungered. The preoccupation of chiefs with self-enrichment should not be credited solely to the new European morality. The older Hawaiian tradition, according to Malo, recognized the self-interest of lower-ranking chiefs and counted upon the moi to hold his political subordinates in check. The great prestige of European morality naturally offset that of the ruler. Malo sought to render a fair verdict when he called attention to differences in the moral character of chiefs. "Some," he said, "were given to robbery, spoilation, murder, extortion, ravishing. . . . The amount of property which the chiefs obtained from the people was very great. Some of it was given in the shape of taxes, some was the fruit of robbery and extortion (1951:85)."

Tohunga

The rule was diversification. Kahuna, a title for both professional priests and craftsmen, implied in both fields a ritual office. The crafts kahuna was its religious leader. The common craftsman was known only by his specific occupation: "one who makes adzes," or, if an acknowledged expert, as a "skilled person" (*malalaioa*). Warriors were *koa*, and each administrative officer was known by the specific title of his function. Crafts and technical administrative skills were not formally ranked as, for example, in Tonga. But this is not to say that all were regarded as equivalent.

Priestly kahuna were ranked (but really by pedigree, since the offices of high priest fell to aristocratic families), and held rank and prestige parallel to that of the ali'i. The priests of Ku, the war god, held, according to Malo, the first rank, the priests of Lono the second (1951:210).

Commoners entered into the lower orders of priestly kahuna and shared the honor of the exalted title. Dealing with minor gods, with lineage deities, and with domestic interests, they were a distinctly lower order of priest in the same broad category with high priests, but in function separate. Sorcerers (*anaana*), who prayed people to death, were kahuna of the lowest degree. In the upper ranks, the kahuna title was hereditary. Among commoners it was granted after an apprenticeship. All kahuna status was of high honor because the title implied the power to accomplish with utmost efficacy. By contrast, kahu represented the passive function of the caretaker. And though the kahu had honor rub off on him by his associations with high-rank persons, he did nothing but look after. (Modern Hawaiians call the owner of a cat its kahu.)

Administrative function, apart from ali'i and chief priest, no matter how important, did not constitute a generic category. Each was distinct and known by a descriptive term. Most secular specialists were persons of rank attached to the high chief's establishment as individual dependents and not, as in Tonga, as an administrative corps (*matapule*). The chief's household included guardians, foster parents, wet nurses, all kahu, a keeper of the household goods, a chief executioner, night guards, a chief steward, a treasurer, a reader of signs, an orator, a guardian of the royal genitals, a pipe lighter, and massagers. The administration consisted of a chief counselor, a chief priest, a war leader, a council of military strategists, common warriors, historians, and readers of omens (Kepelino in Beckwith 1932: 124 ff.).

The most important secular office in the administration was the *kalai-moku,* the island administrator. We recognize in the kalai-moku the familiar eastern Polynesian division between sacred ariki and secular land administrator. According to the tradition, the kalai-moku was in earlier days a junior member of the chiefly lineage. In the late period just before European contact, the office had begun to go to commoners and had become a technical post. As such it was immune to political upheaval; the experience of a skilled kalai-moku served all chiefs. As long as they were commoners they could not aspire to command.

The kalai-moku was responsible to the paramount chief for the collection of tribute and for the proper management of farms, irrigation works, fish ponds, and fishing. He supervised a corps of *konohiki,* or local overseers, who were lower ali'i by rank and subordinate officials by office. Since district chiefs were also land administrators by right of rank, the Hawaiian administration was divided between the traditional sources of rule and the technical. The latter was inevitably the stronger insofar as the district chiefs' tenure over land had become increasingly more dependent upon the victorious moi. In the reign of Kamehameha I, the konohiki had already achieved the ascendancy.

There is not enough information to allow us to assess accurately the relative importance of the craft specialties as against the service and administrative forms of specialization. Judging simply by degree of diversification of titles, the crafts were relatively few. The Hawaiian interests were turned more toward the care and management of people, toward entertainment and the bodily arts. Among the lowest but nonetheless most popular group of specialists were professional athletes and gladiators.

Toa

Distinguished military service benefited all social classes. As we have observed, the outcome of war—victory or defeat—had no major bearing on rank. But it was the source of power and authority, and ultimately great warrior chiefs who had married wisely into ranking families did raise the pedigree of their descendants. In the army, command positions were reserved for ali'i, the troops were commoners. Malo says the kalai-moku was the chief military planner and strategist, suggesting thereby that war, like land administration, had come under professional aegis. Perhaps that was the trend. But as Ellis has observed the military ranks were not professionals (1853:IV, 48). All went back after battle to other roles and occupations. We do not, however, know the nature of the military councilors, whether they were permanent appointments or were assembled for an emergency. But the fact that a military council was provided to aid in planning military strategy, that land and naval forces were taught to proceed in specified formations, and that the troops were given training in marksmanship testifies to the development of a professional point of view.

Political Hegemony

The moi-ship established finally the new Hawaiian principle of leadership, gave authority to military power, and left rank with only the certainty of deference. The appearance of an islandwide head chief did not actually augment the traditional powers of chiefs. Rather, it conveyed what had always been august powers into new and more utilitarian channels. As we have seen, the chief's kapu had endowed him with the prerogatives of demanding extreme deference, of offering human sacrifices, of exacting the death penalty for the violation of kapu. These were awesome powers over persons and they asserted the dreadfulness of a human divinity. Political overlordship carried out the same theme of dread. The Hawaiian "spoils system," the complete reorganization of land holdings with the induction of newly victorious moi, made it quite clear that land tenure was no longer the organic product of pedigree, but an artificial management established by the chief. From a Polynesian point of view, the abrupt allocation of lands normally moving naturally down the generations was nothing short of a revolutionary demonstration of personal power.

If the moi were not in fact divine, his powers from military efficacy gave him the appearance of a god.

Cruelty and the arbitrary exercise of power was evidently a requisite of chiefly office at any level of authority. Dread was the sign of divinity. I quote Malo:

> The conditions of the common people was that of subjection to the chief, compelled to do their heavy tasks, burdened and oppressed, some even to death. The life of the people was one of patient endurance, of yielding to the chiefs to produce their favor. . . .
>
> If the people were slack in doing the chief's work they were expelled from their lands, or even put to death. For such reasons as this and because of the oppressive exactions made upon them, the people held the chiefs in great dread and looked upon them as gods.
>
> Only a small portion of the kings and chiefs ruled with kindness; the large majority simply lorded it over the people (1951: 87).

If dread was the authentically divine or the facsimile of the divine aspect of Hawaiian rule, benignity was its other side. The moi intervened between the people and the harshness of their chiefs. When dread was unrelieved by considerateness, the people revolted.

Political power has its intensive and its extensive dimensions. Dread, the power over life and property is the intensive dimension. In respect to this dimension, the sacred ali'i as a god was undoubtedly supreme. But strictly as a sacred being, his power for all its formidableness had a narrow dominion, limited essentially to his personal being and to the zone of his personal possessions. He was, so to speak, a very hot center within a very small zone. The political ali'i, a more fully secular being, was less incandescent, he had less formidable powers. But his domain was extensive. The highest ranking kapu ali'i held what were to all intents and purposes fixed and absolute powers. The condition of *akua* could not be augmented or transcended. Extensiveness, however, was a relative quality, eminently expansible. Putting the distinction in metaphoric terms for the moment, we may say that the two kinds of ali'i equated, vis-à-vis each other, spiritual incandescence with political scope. Since it was the moi alone who could command human sacrifice (a power comparable to that of supremely kapu ali'i), we may assume that a political zone of the size of an island was the equivalent to the intensive dimension of a human akua.

The Structure of Status

Like the Tahitians, the Hawaiians visualized their state, their status system, as a coherent entity. Tahiti set forth the image of a ship with its rigging. The Hawaiian image was as traditional and organic as that held by the Maori. The state was the moi and its parts were his limbs. The moi was the head; the subchiefs, his shoulders and chest; the priests, his right hand; the kalai moku his left hand; the warriors, his right foot; and the farmers, his left foot. Lesser figures were his fingers and toes (Malo 1951). The image evokes the familiar Polynesian doctrines about the sanctity of the head, and the powers of shoulders and chest and the more common ideas of the superiority of the right side to the left side.

As between ali'i and commoners, the Hawaiian doctrine was the same as the Tahitian. All had a common origin and shared, therefore, an original organic link. The separation occured later. I have not found in the Hawaiian literature any traditional account of the separation. Fornander attributes the separation to a gradual political process of increasing chiefly prerogatives and the "systematic setting down if not debasement of the commoners (1880:II, 63). Malo, reasoning along similar lines, assumed the gradual separation occurred as commoners for unknown reasons lost their genealogical connections. With the loss of genealogical connection, though, the separation was complete.

The status system was dual but with a tendency of moderate proportions to reconstitute the older organic unity. The extraordinary expansiveness of ali'i is an example of the counter-trend. Hawaii had no named "middle" rank. Nevertheless, we may consider the great range of low-ranking ali'i, some of such low repute they were barely distinguishable from commoners, as a functional "middle class" within the formal framework of a basic two-class system. The perseverance of a two-class system speaks for Hawaiian conservatism, for its adherence to the genealogical sources of worth. Mangareva, a more radical example of the Stratified society had evolved a true middle class, that is, a class founded upon a new principle, that of landholding. In some few instances Hawaiian commoners received land grants and titles of ali'i, but this was exceptional. Genealogy remained the foremost consideration and status differentiation followed the lines set by pedigree. Pedigree served to differentiate gradations of sanctity and to define conditions of land tenure.

Traditionally, of course, rank authenticated land title, and to a limited degree, and with respect only to stable estates that had never been seized in war, the traditional system continued in force through the Late Period. The new system, the so-called "spoils system" of reallocation, ended once and for all authentic and traditional titles and replaced them with relationships of dependency upon a single titleholder. Since each subchief owed his land-holdings to a political decision, his relationship in principle to his superior was equivalent to that of the commoner to him. The differences in form of tenure between ali'i and commoner, therefore, are defined only crudely by the categories, landed–landless. In aristocratic societies, highest honor accrues to inherited prerogatives. In terms of this absolute principle, maximum honor in Hawaii had left the economic realm. For all political lands tenure was no longer authentic. A secondary principle of honor, however, remained, and that was the honor of relative dependencies. The moi headed this order of rank; the commoners were at the bottom. The honor of dependency is a distinct form of land tenure that carries with it the rights and obligations that are precisely recognized in terms of the rank of the donor and, in a hierarchical order of transmission, by the rank of all recipients. Since these rights and obligations are substantially those of ownership in Traditional societies (minus the authenticity of descent title), they grant the status at least of de facto ownership. Taking a legalistic view (as if there were in fact a Hawaiian code defining all the variant relations to land), one can assert that commoners, too, held de facto titles. Theirs, then, would be the title of least honor. In the final analysis, tenure of land in systems of primitive aristocracy can only be defined in terms of kinds and grades of honor.

Social stratification, drawing upon such absolute qualities as pedigree and sanctity, was categorical, allowing us to identify ali'i and maka'ainana as distinct classes. Economic differentiation, however, was graded, and economic stratification may thus be represented in terms of a two-class system only if we bear in mind commoners as the bottom of a continuum denoting degrees of honor.

Genealogical Rank

The eleven grades of ali'i were authentically recorded in *A Book of the Lineage of Chiefs for the Information of Liliuokalani* (Beckwith 1932:195–98). They are, in order:

1. *Niaupio:* The offspring of a marriage between brother and sister of the highest rank. The marriage was a "loop" that turned a genealogy back on itself and so achieved the highest sanctity. The niaupio were gods (akua) on the principle, it may be assumed, of the ultimate concentration of mana and kapu which reached a divine density. Such a marriage was literally a "hot" union in the sense of utmost intensity of merger. That is why the offspring in whom the merger was expressed were said to be a "fire," a "raging blaze." All other forms of marriage were a dilution of mana and sanctity. The niaupio transcended sex dif-

ferences and politics and exceeded, needless to say, parental rank. The kapu of niaupio was so severe it must have effectively interfered with all ordinary chiefly duties, among them the round of the island during the makahiki festival. The niaupio chiefs moved only at night so as not to interfere with the life of the country.

2. *Pio* represented the same transcendent rank, as they were the offspring of the next generation of brother-sister marriages, the children of uterine niaupio siblings.
3. *Naha* were the offspring of niaupio parents who were not uterine siblings. The naha chiefs formed a second rank, since they represented a diluted marriage. Their sanctity was nevertheless very close to that of the pio.
4. *Wohi* represented a significant drop in grade. The naha chief could dare the sanctity of the pio because of proximity, but if the wohi chief transgressed their kapu, he was burned alive. Wohi were offspring of niaupio, pio, or naha father and of a mother from the junior branch of a high chiefly line. These were the most common grade of high-ranking chiefs. Kamehameha I was of this grade.
5. *Lo* were a reserve corps of chiefs who had the status of sanctity of the aforementioned grades but lived in isolation in the mountains. They were referred to as the *po'e lo ali'i* "people from whom to obtain a chief."
6. *Papa* were the offspring of niaupio, pio, or naha mother and of a lower-ranking father. They were, then, a grade below their mother and had more sanctity than their father.
7. *Lokea* were offspring of niaupio, pio, or naha father and of a mother who was of a chiefly family that belonged to a younger branch of their father's family.
8. *La'au ali'i* were the offspring of the secondary matings within high ranking families. They were also known as "second pedigree chiefs."
9. *Kaukau ali'i* were the offspring of second pedigree chiefs of the high chiefly families.
10. *Ali'i noanoa* were the commoner children of aristocrat and commoner. The term *noa noa* stated, of course, the absence of sanctity and hence of rank.
11. *Ali'i maka'ainana* were those of chiefly lineage living incognito like commoners, not as chiefly reservists but as refugees, and therefore reduced in status.

The eleven grades form no more than three basic subdivisions, which are comparable to aristocratic ranks elsewhere in Polynesia, namely, a supreme and god-like rank, a high and political rank, and finally a second-grade rank equivalent to raatira in Tahiti. Only the supreme ranks were absolute and transcendent, transcending sex differences, political authority, and seniority. All other ranks were by contrast ambiguous and dependent upon a multitude of genealogical conditions. Reservists formed a different order. They were products of political instability, the party temporarily not in power. The first category of rank was contractive, all others were expansive in order of descent.

Commoners

The designation of commoner as *maka'ainana,* translated as "dwellers on the land," is an attribution of worthiness. Nominally the Hawaiians followed the more egalitarian Marquesan point of view (Ua Pou and Nuku Hiva), rather than the more polarized class doctrine of the Tahitians. Menehune were indeed known in Hawaii but only as a mythical "little" people. Assuming the Marquesas were the earliest source of Hawaiian culture, *maka'ainana* would be an old term that was retained despite the introduction of a new and more segregationist point of view from Tahiti. One cannot build too much history upon terms, yet retention in the face of a new concept must be recognized as a particularly significant event. What this seems to signify in Hawaii is a modification of the Tahitian order of status polarization that places the hard contrast between kapu ali'i and kauwa, rather than between chief and commoner.

The nominalistic recognition of worth comes not only from the honorific of "dwellers on the land," but from the synonym for commoner, *hu,* a term referring to the swelling and expanding of poi (Malo 1951:87). The *maka'ainana* were thus the growing bulk of the population. Honor, of course, does not move along a single dimension. The commoners had worth by function—that is, as farmers—but were reduced by lack of genealogical distinction and the quality of their land tenure. Malo, perhaps already from a Christian point of view, saw the common people as fallen, so to speak, from grace. They had been ali'i, he believes, and having carelessly given themselves up "in pursuit of their own gratification and pleasure" had lost interest in preserving their status (1951:87). Whether or not Malo's observations are sound history, he has identified the concern with genealogical form as the critical distinction between the social classes.

The estimation of commoner as of any other grade of worth evidently took into account a variety of conditions, some positive, some negative. The negative conditions were all from the defects of pedigree. That they were not a subjugated class stands as a positive condition, but rather reduced in significance since the ali'i had already detached the issue of rank from political fortune. As a dweller on the land, the commoner was subject to eviction, but so were the ali'i. Commoners have been described as "tenants at will" (Hobbs 1931: 28), free to leave the service of one chief or land supervisor for another. Mobility is freedom, but in the aristocratic tradition of rootedness, not necessarily honor. From the point of view of honor, it may not have mattered too much whether the commoner was evicted or left because of grievances. In either case he lacked traditional rights. His truly traditional and, therefore, honorable rights were to a substantial part of his own produce and to other produce of the land, firewood, thatch, timber, fish (Hobbs 1931). As the ultimate producer, the commoner was in a technical sense a donor, a source of benefice—an honorable position. This honor could not be totally denied him in the Hawaiian code, but it could be reduced, and reduced in significance it was by the fact that much of what he gave was on demand—what his superiors gave was a gift—and was given only to his lowest-ranking superior. Those above the rank of commoner who gave gifts came within the etiquette of reciprocity. The commoner was not entirely excluded from reciprocity. He was at the disadvantage in that what he gave was specified; what he may have received ultimately from his immediate superior was not.

Kauwa

This pariah group illustrates as an absolute negative the Hawaiian concept of status honor. We do not know the history of kauwa. They are described as slaves and as descendants of slaves. The term slave as applied to kauwa must be taken strictly in the euphemistic sense denoting a people totally without connections and hence without value. They had once been absolutely degraded, we can be sure, but they were not war captives. They were considered rather as "corpses." And it is this view of them that explains their utter worthlessness. The living dead were the absolute antithesis of the "raging blazes" who were the god-like ali'i. They were the metaphoric inert to the metaphorically incandescent; they completed by their presence a structure of status in which each grade had its appropriate counterpart. The kauwa were the reverse image of the pio. They were few in number; contact with them defiled all and therefore they were totally separated. They held their own lands. If a commoner trespassed, he had become "dirty" and was executed as a defiled being (Beckwith

1932:144). Their land and its produce was a separate domain, as though it were not of this world. So were their houses and they as persons. They covered their heads and dared not look at others. They were most polluting to commoners, setting up a status distance at the lower end of the scale equivalent to that between sacred chief and commoner. On the other hand, they had a close and paradoxically a "high" position in relation to chiefs, to whom they were a class of god. There is no specific information on the kind of gods they were. Their designation as "corpses" and by a variety of terms for decay can only mean they were the dark and underworld gods. Thus the conceptual antithesis between pio and kauwa stood, in fact, for the familiar Polynesian religious opposition between the light and the dark, the sky and the *po*.

Achieved Status

Certainly from the Middle Period on, rank and position were matched more by merit, by accomplishment in war and administration, than by the fixed standards of pedigree. Kamehameha I had appointed a commoner as governor of an island and the Kalai-moku had also come to be chosen from the common ranks. The barriers between chiefs and commoners were never fully breached, but a salient had been opened in the pragmatic sphere of politics. The system of rewards for services continued to favor the ali'i as the preferred corps of administrators, but the order of rank and the hierarchy of position were no longer in line. An important distinction was drawn between rule, organized by new political standards, and honorific office in the chiefly establishment, where the traditional order of ranks was feasible. The aristocracy, needless to say, was not on the verge of dissolution. It was necessity alone and not a democratic doctrine that had disrupted the traditional correspondence between rank and office. Hawaiian chiefs always sought to restore the old aristocratic forms. They schooled themselves to meet the tests of fitness when they already held hereditary rank, and they sought the legitimacy of rank when they had secured their political position.

Status Rivalry

Since rank was more or less above the strife, the issue was power. Rivals could not strip one another of their pedigree and the fixed honors that went with it, but they could deprive rank of administrative powers. Polynesian status rivalry constantly nourished the implacable aim of degrading the opponent. Hawaii modified and refined this aim to avoid total degradation, resorting instead to still another tradition, that of splitting the content of a title. In principle the stripping of political power from rank was an act similar to the separation of chiefly and priestly ariki offices. We must assume that any splitting of powers is reductive, even though it carries with it the compensation of immunizing the religious powers against further loss. In principle, the Hawaiian pattern of rivalry was parallel to that of Mangaia.

Status of chiefs consisted, then, of two orders of gradation—one fixed, the other movable. Both orders, however, were part of a more comprehensive and single system of chiefly rank. Thus, between the fixed and the movable aspects of hierarchy there was a constant instability—from the point of view of chiefs, the prospect of great expectations—itself a factor perpetuating rivalry. The goal of paramount chief through conquest is also made comprehensible through this pattern of matching fixed against movable gradations. As I have suggested earlier, the moi, by becoming first in movable rank, achieved some equivalence in status to that of pio in fixed rank. The presence of one order of rank stimulated activity in its parallel order.

Considering now the range of political possibilities open to expansive systems, we must ask what kind of policy dictated the decision to unseat all losers. Tahiti, for example, settled realistically for tributary relations. The Hawaiian system was inherently unsettling. It created total losers and dissatisfied winners among chiefs who resented their share in redistributed lands. Hawaii, it should be said, had no unique policy of political reconstitution. It had, however, developed an underlying Polynesian policy to its fullest degree. We recognize in this policy the absolutist doctrine of aristocracy. The full implications of the structure are to be carried out. As the pio chief is the head of an absolute organic order derived from the gods, the political chief becomes the head of an absolute "made" order in which the total political economy is of his creation.

Descent Group Organization

The organization of kin groups in the Hawaiian Islands had diverged so strongly from the traditional Polynesian type that at first glance Hawaii seems altogether unrelated in this respect to Polynesia generally. It should be said at once that we do not really know the actual composition of the territorial groupings. We know only their political composition and it is from the political standpoint only that the Hawaiian descent group organization can be discussed. The political standpoint, however, has been our constant reference point anyway, so the basis for comparison is still sound. Moreover, a study of the "backward" region of Ka'u on Hawaii, a region where the older family system had persisted almost into the modern era, offers at least a glimpse into the actual relationships between kinship and rule.

By the time of European contact, the territorial organization of Hawaii had become altogether political, and a sociological concept of descent group organization no longer applied to it, even in the broadest possible sense. The island of Hawaii, for example, had been divided into six pie-shaped divisions running from the mountain crests in the interior to the sea. These divisions had no reference at all to traditional tribal or kin groupings. They were strictly political. The large divisions were repeatedly subdivided into fixed numbers of subordinate divisions or political segments, each of which had an appointed chief immediately responsible to the superior directly above him. When the central government was changed the entire chain of command changed with it. Ruler and ruled were related neither by genealogical fact nor by sentiment. Commoners and chiefs were by the conditions of genealogical rank distinct and unrelated. In the political organization of the territories, there was no requirement that the chiefs and their subordinate chiefs be related. Chiefs, in fact, held lands and commands in different and in scattered regions. I have found no evidence in the literature on Hawaii that paramount chiefs followed the political principles of indirect rule.

Kinship considerations may have been removed from the specific and hierarchical organization of the main island divisions, but they were not irrelevant to Hawaiian political life generally. The cadre of chiefs, for example, was formed along a number of genealogical lines. There is every reason to believe that with the chiefly interests in negotiating politically expedient marriages being as strong as they were, all the chiefly descent lines on a single island were interrelated. The Kamehameha family had branches on several islands. The chiefs, therefore, constituted a great status lineage in which ancestral lines were pruned, weeded, and evaluated to establish the strongest possible genealogical chain. It is inaccurate to call the chiefly descent lines "bilateral," because the chiefly interest was not in giving equal value to claims upon maternal and paternal lines, but to search out with minimum impediment the most advantageous lines for genealogical rank. The chiefly descent lines were not "corporate." Their value lay mainly in the claim they gave to genealogical distinction or to rights of succession to chiefly office.

As everywhere else in Polynesia where chiefs intermarried widely, the chiefly lines were dispersed over the islands. This was certainly the case in New Zealand. Among the Maori, however, the commoners, endogamous within the *hapu,* formed a compact community. In Hawaii the commoners were also dispersed; not as widely as were the chiefs, but judging by conditions in Ka'u, at least within a major district. Among the commoners, kinship ties were utilitarian in the ordinary and non-honorific ways of gift exchange and barter. In Ka'u, the last stronghold of traditional Hawaiian family organization, the dispersed community of commoners had, nevertheless, a geographic center in a particular locality called an *'aina.* (Handy and Pukui 1958:2), and was cognate in this respect to the more common Polynesian system. Elsewhere the kindred of commoners may have been even more widely dispersed. There is, however, no information, and we are obliged to use Handy and Pukui's account of Ka'u for an understanding of family life. Ka'u in any case represented nothing more "backward" than the pre-Kamehameha period.

Family Life on Ka'u

The commoner kindred were referred to as an *'ohana,* or "family." Handy and Pukui point out that the term comes from *oha,* "to sprout," and means therefore, the offshoots of a family stock. The 'ohana included all persons related through maternal and paternal lines. The entire stock of kin, including the ancestors was known as a *kupuna,* the term for grandparents, but also for ancestors. *Kupu* means "to grow," so that kupuna has the sense of a stock from which the 'ohana was descended. A major subdivision of an island or of a large island district consisted of many 'ohana (Handy and Pukui 1958:5). Since the 'ohana was the most extensive network of kin, it is fair to conclude that the kupuna or ancestral stock had little genealogical depth. That the 'ohana did not have great depth among commoners is clear from the fact that only chiefs had a genealogical interest. Handy and Pukui however, speak of senior lines among the 'ohana from which its leadership came. They offer, however, no genealogies and do not distinguish between family lines of chiefs and commoners. Their discussion as a result is unfortunately vague. In some instances they speak of 'ohana as though it were a corporate body, having common activities and interests, and in other connections, in terms of the simple meaning of the term as "relative" or "kinsman." Thus when they say:

> Between households within the *'ohana* there was constant sharing and exchange of foods and of utilitarian articles and also of services, not in barter but as voluntary (though decidely obligatory) giving (1958:5),

they are speaking of a corporate body. But when they say about the connection between social status and genealogy, "the *'ohana* of a particular lineage depended on an elder who was known as the Mea-pa'a-kiauhau (1958:196)," (the genealogist) they are speaking simply of relatives, since chiefs and commoners did not share a common genealogy. Handy and Pukui do not claim that they did, but they leave the issue undecided, even though they cite the common information that genealogy was the special preoccupation of the ali'i (1958:195).

With reference to the 'ohana as a corporate body, Handy and Pukui speak of its senior line as providing the leadership of the entire kindred. The head was called *haku,* a term meaning leader or director in the strictly secular sense, without reference either to sanctity or to genealogical distinction, and altogether distinct, therefore, from ali'i. They describe him as the "elder male of the senior branch of the whole *'ohana* (1958:6)," and list his functions as dividing catches of fish, presiding over family councils, and supervising the entertaining of guests and of visiting ali'i. He was in charge of all communal work of the 'ohana (1958:7). The dispersal of the members of the 'ohana provided for a movement of coastal products inland and of inland products to the coasts, but from household to household and on a small scale. Within this common grouping, the economic exchanges were not redistributive, but were conducted on simple reciprocity. The haku was not a "redistributor," but rather an arbiter of an equitable distribution of a catch of fish among those who had taken part.

As a dispersed body of kin with limited tenure rights to land, the 'ohana was a "weak" corporate group at best. It was in no way comparable to the Maori hapu. If it can be compared at all, it would be closer to the iwi, whose membership had a sense of kinship and the occasional opportunities to exchange products in an uncomplicated way. The 'ohana, however, had no name, and, lacking a particular territory or any other means of demarcating itself, could have been a rather vague grouping only. Yet the levy demanded by the ali'i during the makahiki festival fell upon the 'ohana rather than upon individuals (Handy and Pukui 1958:6). Since the makahiki levy fell upon territorial divisions from the point of view of the paramount chief, it seems reasonable to conclude that it was the political territorial division that demarcated the 'ohana as a corporate body, limited as these corporate functions were. The 'ohana must be considered, therefore, in a double sense: as an amorphous group of all persons who regarded themselves as bilaterally related and who used their kinship claims to expect mutual aid, and as a more compact group within a political division that had the opportunity for more active forms of mutual aid and which came under the administration of a lay leader who was its representative before the ali'i. Inasmuch as commoners had de facto tenure on the land, the 'ohana with its haku had a degree of autonomy. In the organization of the 'ohana, Hawaiian society retained a semblance of kin group organization. The 'ohana, however, was not related to a segmentary organization, for segmentation —by which is meant an organization of subordinate and dependent units—applied in Hawaii only to the political structure. The 'ohana were not related to one another as groups; only individuals were related to one another. If the 'ohana did indeed have a senior line, as Handy and Pukui claim it did, seniority did not produce dependent branches. In a technical sense, the individual households' *hauhole* ("dwellings") might be considered as segments of the 'ohana, but an organization of related households does not constitute a segmentary organization. There is no specific suggestion that the households were ranked, other than the statement of the superiority of status of the household of the haku.

The concept of territory, *'aina,* had ceased to be a vital aspect of the 'ohana. At one time in Hawaiian history, Handy and Pukui believe, the 'ohana was a local group occupying a particular section of territory that later came to be known by the political designation of *ili*—the smallest territorial subdivision. They say: "It is to be inferred that the *ili* with its inland and seaward expanses was essentially and probably originally the province of a single 'ohana (1958:5)." By intermarriage the group would ramify outward, retaining, however, its feeling about the original domicile and in some cases leaving behind a core of kin, as happened to one 'ohana in Ka'u.

The household was known simply as *hale* ("house"), and consisted of kinfolk as well as of unrelated dependents known as *'ohua,* a term meaning passengers on a ship. The head of the house was called *po'o* ("summit," head of any kind of organization) and was not necessarily its senior member (Handy and Pukui 1958:5). We must assume, therefore, that he was head by virtue of his leadership and accomplishments. Well-to-do households were the larger ones since they attracted dependent outsiders as well as held more kin together. Among commoners, residence was matrilocal, since each family head regarded a son-in-law—who, of course, was or at least could be considered as an outsider—as a very desirable addition to the family. The literature on Hawaii offers no "functional" explanation of matrilocal residence. Actually the conditions of livelihood were served equally—from a functional standpoint—by residence with the husband's or with the wife's family. But residence everywhere in eastern Polynesia has been regulated by social status. Where the male line automatically conferred higher social standing, residence was patrilocal; where the male line was less important, postmarital residence was ambilocal, that is, dependent entirely upon considerations of advantage. Since the male line was preferred as a line of status descent in most of eastern Polynesia (and perhaps originally everywhere in eastern Polynesia), it was common for the lower ranks to be matrilocal. With few exceptions, after all, leadership was a masculine prerogative. This political condition in itself is no determinant of postmarital residence, for a man can still be the head of a matrilocal household; the point of matrilocality is that it readily establishes a category of dependent males, a status most sharply revealed in the polyandrous households of the Marquesas. In the Hawaiian household, the male was considered as the "feeder of the parents-in-law," a dependent status since he was adding to the strength and prosperity of the household headed by another male. Matrilocality seems to have been the common form of residence for the commoners, nor was it unusual among chiefly families. Among chiefly families, however, it was always the younger sons, judging by the traditions, who went off to live with the family of the wife. In every instance the traditions drive home the point, however, that the hero overcomes the disability of matrilocal residence. He marries the daughter of a chief and receives her "kingdom," or he becomes powerful and returns home to seize his rightful or his preferred patrimony (cf. Fornander 1916–17: IV, 236 ff.; 66–68; 112 ff.; 178 ff.). Fornander, it should be noted in this connection, believed that Hawaiian rank went along the female side, but the genealogical evidence is entirely against him.

The households were widely scattered, according to Handy and Pukui, because of the rugged terrain, but more probably because they had no strong collective basis for unity of residence. The obligation of the commoner households was to the primary economic interests of the chiefs. Thus the commoners lived on the cultivations over which the chiefs had the decisive jurisdiction.

The basic organization in Hawaii, including the district of Ka'o, was political and not kinship. This organization had a segmentary structure of dependent administrative groupings that seems to have lacked, however, the qualities of autonomous corporate character that are commonly identified as "segmentary social structures." The reference to the administrative organization as "segmentary" is to be taken in the historical sense as indicating homology of form with the true segmentary structures of Traditional eastern Polynesia. There is, however, no specific historical evidence pointing to the actual transformation of a segmentary kin-based social structure into a system of dependent administrative units. The relationship must be advanced on logical grounds.

Prior to unification of the islands, the largest administrative unit was the *moku,* which meant either an island or a politically autonomous division of the island. In either case, the moku was headed by a paramount chief. The character of the moku depended upon the qualities of the paramount chief. When the paramount chief was politically strong, the moku was the focus of religion, of decisions about land tenure, of the accumulation of goods for redistribution, and for the allocation of political offices. It was then no mere ceremonial center but the effective corporate body. The moku is parallel to Segment I of the segmentary societies.

Segment II, according to Malo was a district called *apana* ("pieces") or *moku-o-loko* ("interior divisions"). There were six districts on Hawaii and six on Oahu, implying that these were arbitrary divisions. In the recent past of each island, the territory corresponding to a district had been the site of an independent chiefdom. After conquest, however, the defeated paramount chief was removed and was replaced by an appointed high chief. The apana, however, were evidently not the formerly autonomous territories of other tribes but were new territorial configurations arranged after an island had been unified. The names given to districts, for example, were geographically descriptive and not, as on Tahiti, the names of tribal ancestors. Thus the district of Puna on Hawaii means "spring of water," Kona, the leeward side, Hilo, a variety of grass, and so on.

Segment III was a subdivision of an apana and was called either a *kalana* or *okana* (Malo 1951:37). These were sometimes further subdivided into a *poko,* which seems to mean "smaller thing."

The basic subdivision of the apana or kalana was, however, the *ahu pua'a* (Segment IV), literally "pig heap of stones," in reference to its boundary markers of a pile of stones surmounted by the image of a pig. The *ahu pua'a* was then Segment IV. The ahu was actually the altar corresponding to the marae in other eastern Polynesian islands upon which rested the legal title to the land. The altar, as described by Alexander who was superintendent of Government Surveys in the Kingdom of Hawaii (1891), was erected at the point where the boundary of the land was intersected by the main road that ran around each island. Upon this altar was deposited the annual makahiki tax.

The typical ahu pua'a was, by Alexander's account, a narrow strip extending from the mountain tops to the sea, giving to its chief a share of the variety of products of a region. Each ahu pua'a had, therefore, an ecological integrity and took into account the natural conformation of the land and the distribution of its products. On Maui, however, the ahu pua'a were extremely unequal in size and value, their formation having evidently followed some principle of political advantage. Some of these subdivisions monopolized an entire mountain as well as the deep sea fisheries, leaving to the smaller ahu pua'a fishing grounds where the water was only five feet deep. Maui, of course, had remained relatively free of central administration, so that its subdivisions conformed more to the traditional political organization, within which chiefs held relative autonomy.

The ahu pua'a were generally but not necessarily divided into *ilis* ("strips"), which formed a Segment V. Each ili had its own name and a carefully defined boundary. Alexander reports two kinds of ili, one simply an administrative subdivision of an ahu pua'a. The other, called *ili kupono,* or *ku,* or a "truly meritorious ili," was the province of an independent family that did not pay taxes and was immune to administrative shifts of tenure. The relationships of these two kinds of ili to their larger divisions of ahu pua'a were strikingly variable, reflecting no doubt the unequal rate of political development on a single island. On Hawaii, for example, the ahu pua'a of Waimea included within its territory independent ili kupono that covered 90 percent of its area (Alexander 1890:106). Some independent ilis lay as enclaves outside of any ahu pua'a. On Oahu some ili were discontinuous sections of land known as leles ("jumps"), presumably as adjustments to political necessity.

Finally, the ili were minutely subdivided into patches of cultivation, each also with its distinctive name. Patches cultivated exclusively for the chief were known as *koele* or *hakuone,* which had the connotation of something reserved for the chief. The other strips were called *moo.* These ili subdivisions allocated to households formed Segment VI.

We have only fragmentary knowledge of the social and political composition of these land or territorial subdivisions. By all indications they did not follow entirely regular principles, but corresponded rather to specific historical circumstances.

The social composition of Segment I as a conquest state incorporating populations of distinctive kin groups is reasonably clear to us. On Segments II and III there is no real information. We know only the general principles upon which they were formed. Those high-ranking ali'i who were allies of the victorious moi retained their traditional holdings and must have shared in the redistribution of holdings of the defeated. In that event, Segment II was a replica of Segment I. The same principles probably applied to Segment III; that is, it, too, was a smaller scale model of I. The ahu pua'a, on the other hand, seems to have been a somewhat different kind of entity, for being a taxpayer it was under the jurisdiction of lower-ranking chiefs who owed allegiance to the ali'i nui rank.

The ili differed still more, for except for those that were politically independent, they were held by commoners and were administered by overseers, *konohiki,* appointed by the chiefs. The ili subdivisions belonged to households.

In Hawaii no terms of segmentation were found to be cognate with the segmentary nomenclature of eastern Polynesia. If the Hawaiian Islands had been settled very late, it would have been possible to reason that the traditional terms had never arrived. But if A.D. 124 is the true early settlement date, then we may well conclude that these terms had been lost in the course of changes in the social system. The term *iwi,* for example, is in the Hawaiian vocabulary as "bone" and has the general connotation of a close blood tie, but it has no reference to a social group.

The one common term is *maka'ainana,* with the meaning of a group related broadly by kinship elsewhere in eastern Polynesia, and with the meaning in Hawaii of "those belonging to the land." On Hawaii this term had taken on the exclusive connotation of a status, standing for the common people, as distinct from the chiefs. This shift in usage illustrates what seems to have been the general process in Hawaii of submerging terms with kin group references in favor of political terms.

Status and Descent Group Organization

The allocation of chiefly office as a reward for political services and without reference to the genealogical relationship of the appointed chief to his constituency was a more solidly established principle in Hawaii than anywhere else in Polynesia. The ranks of chiefs constituting a general corps of potential administration, as in a European monarchy, were fully detached from their genealogical network, except for purposes of establishing their own rank. It was undoubtedly this thorough cleavage between chiefs and the people working the land that disrupted and transformed so completely a segmentary organization originally rooted in kin and based on orderly subdivisions of the genealogical network. The modes of branching of the

Polynesian descent groups were, as we have seen, always governed in the main by the interests and the activities of the chiefs. Such an arrangement could sustain the sentiments of mutual aid of kin groups but not their systematic organization and growth. It could sustain the traditional networks of chiefly lines but not the organic links of chiefs with their constituencies.

II

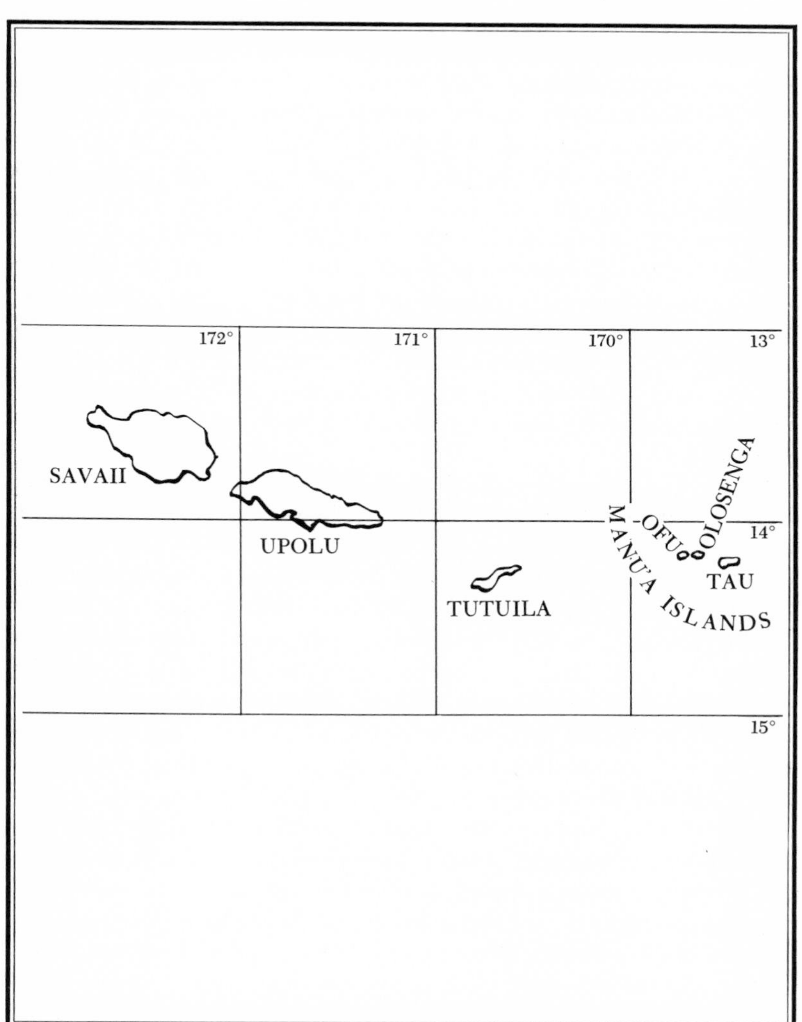

The Samoan Islands

HISTORIC SAMOA AS IT BECAME KNOWN FROM THE LATE EIGHteenth century onwards cannot, of course, be regarded as the ancestral Polynesian culture. Very early Polynesian features may have been preserved there, as indeed they were elsewhere in the islands, but these islands have also lived through some 2,000 years of history, have received fresh cultural impulses from Melanesia, from Micronesia, and from eastern Polynesia, and have gone through their own internal evolution.

If we do not find in Samoa what early Polynesian culture was like, we do, however, find there what is no less important, namely, an example of a new line of social and cultural diversification. Eastern and western Polynesia could not conceivably have developed in total isolation from each other. Still, the degree of linguistic differentiation between them can only mean their separation was genuine, if incomplete. Thus general similarities in organization, and certainly in patterns of historical development, are more likely to have resulted from independent parallel developments than from direct cultural influences.

In its basic principles all of western Polynesia has run the same historical course as have the islands of the east. The Samoan Islands appear as types of Open society; Tonga equates with Tahiti and Hawaii as a Stratified society. This difference between Samoa and Tonga is parallel to the sets of variations we have already observed in eastern Polynesia. However, there is this difference: Tonga is close to eastern Polynesia patterns; Samoa, more distant. But when we distinguish Eastern and Western Samoa as notably differing examples of Open society, the problematic character of the apparent eastern–western Polynesian divergences disappears. The triad of societies, which, after all, have always been historically close, represents rather a gradient of cultural variations along which the small islands of Eastern Samoa, namely, Manu'a, occupy one end, Tonga the other, and Western Samoa, in particular Upolu and Savaii, the middle. In view of continuity of variations, Tonga no longer looms as an eastern Polynesian intrusion. In this region of Polynesia the character of aristocracy and the course of its development shifts easily between eastern and western Polynesian patterns. This, however, is as it should be, since the gap between eastern and western Polynesia is only a matter of divergence and not of separate ancestry.

The Samoan archipelago embraces four main groups of islands. The two very large islands of Savaii and Upolu of some 700 and 400 square miles in area, respectively, dominate the western division; Tutuila (54 square miles) and the trio of tiny islands that make up the Manu'a group form the eastern group. The Manu'a islands and the three large islands have had rather different histories and have accordingly developed in different directions. The entire archipelago was, nevertheless, a single culture and shared a common aristocracy. A few great families were represented on all the islands, among which the Tui Manu'a, a sacred chief, was held to be the highest ranking notable in all Samoa. Before the year 1200, all of Samoa must have been substantially of the same cultural complexion. Aristocratic families created a ritual unity for all the islands, within which villages and small districts preserved traditional political and economic autonomy. Then Tongans invaded and occupied the three large islands of Savaii, Upolu, and Tutuila, holding their control for perhaps as long as 400 years until they were forcibly expelled. Experience with politically aggressive Tonga, including, of course, the wars of independence, naturally brought about the social ascendancy of war leaders. After the Tongans, the Samoans fought their own wars. The old traditional ranks did survive the new wars in the manner of eastern Polynesian Open societies; the new war leaders, however, began to resemble the Mangaian Temporal Lord.

Perhaps because they were so small, the Manu'an islands escaped the Tongan wars and developed along more pacific lines. Rivalry for social position was no less active but more delicate, relying upon persuasions of wealth and eloquence. The patterns of Open society that emerged on the three large islands is already familiar. It is the more subtle Manu'an version of "openness" that merits close attention.

For their size, population, and abundance of food, the Samoan islands were undistinguished in the production of those large works by which we customarily measure a civilization. The Samoans used stones in such simple constructions as house platforms and to face low earthen mounds upon which they erected important (but thatch) buildings. They did not cut or face stone and they did not develop any of the monumental arts for which nearby Tonga had become notable. Samoa had the facilities of terrain for terrace and irrigation works, but relied rather upon the more rudimentary techniques of slash-burn horticulture. Samoan technical skills, which were of a high order, turned rather to smaller works which could be produced by individuals or by small groups. The social importance of personal skills is conveyed by the growth of highly prestigious "guilds."

The islands as a group are unquestionably among the most benign and productive of all the Polynesian habitats. The large islands in particular, rugged and mountainous as they are, are outstanding in Polynesia for the fertility of their soils and the general ease they allowed their occupants to enjoy. The islands are heavily forested and well-watered, although, like all Pacific islands, they are subject to drought and to violent winds. Upolu, though not the largest, is the most favored of the group; it has the most extensive areas of fertile soils and is ringed with the longest reefs and lagoons. Much of Savaii, on the other hand, is lava-covered, but then this island is so much larger. The best soils were in the coastal areas on all the islands, and that is where the population tended to concentrate. The interior valleys and the mountain slopes, though heavily wooded, were also cultivable, and cultivated they were.

The Reverend John B. Stair, who lived among the Samoans between 1838 and 1845, when the native culture was still vigorous, remarked:

> This rich soil is so easily cultivated that the small amount of labor usually bestowed upon it, simply scratching the surface, in fact, is quickly rewarded by a large supply of excellent vegetables, such as yams, taro, sweet potatoes, and also banana plantains, and other valuable fruits (1897:53).

Reverend Turner, who lived in Samoa during the same period, corroberates Stair, noting that "after meeting fully, however, all home wants, large quantities of yams, taro and bananas, with pigs and poultry, were still to spare, and were sold to ships which called for water and supplies (1884:171)." Mead has said: "Economic conditions in Manu'a must be understood against a background of economic plenty. . . . In Samoa there is no winter, no lean season, no period when scrimping and saving are necessary (1930:65)." Coulter, a geographer, reported the same after a detailed study of the smaller islands that now comprise American Samoa (1941). On these as on the large islands, land was never scarce. On American Samoa only one-third the arable land was under cultivation, allowing for a proper rotation of crops. Everywhere terrains were diversified. Highland, lowland, forests, dry soils, and swamps suited different crops and growing conditions. The large island of Upolu was heavily grown to breadfruit, which was so abundant that reserve supplies could be stored as poi for years. Taro giving up to three crops a year grew well on all islands in cleared forest beds and in swamp areas that were drained and built up as damp beds. The cultivations were scattered and often distant from the villages, which clustered on the beaches. The aim of food production, as Coulter observed, was to exceed subsistence. Much of what was raised was given away in feasts that accented the social position of chiefs and family heads.

Abundance nourished the status system, and in that sense was critical for Samoan social stability. Yet the prominence of wars on the richer large islands, and the peaceableness of the Manu'an group, would seem to dispose of any simple relationship between economy and social conflict, or, for that matter, between economy and form of government.

Samoa came to European attention as late as 1722, when Roggeveen sighted the eastern group of islands. It was 43 years later before Bougainville hove into view of Tutuila and Upolu, and several years after that when the unfortunate La Pérouse completed his survey of all the islands. The European period does not begin, however, until 1830, the year the London Missionary Society established itself on Upolu. Samoan culture, however, proved more durable than most.

The unremitting vigor of Samoan cultural life in the presence of Europeans cannot be laid to European indifference to Samoan affairs. On the contrary, the great powers, Great Britain, the United States, and Germany, entered actively into Samoan political life. They intervened in local wars, introduced new systems of government, tried to arrange settlements of internal disputes, and, on their own account, established naval bases and trading stations. The powers came close to open warfare among themselves over their Samoan policies. Samoan life could hardly have remained unaffected, yet it continued to go its own way. When Mead came to the Manu'an Islands in 1925, she found a culture that had not lost much of its traditional vigor. The large islands of Western Samoa were vigorously alive in the late nineteenth century when English missionaries and German ethnographers turned their attention to it. Our understanding of Samoan life and custom is thus reasonably complete.

In Samoa, too, the European period opened at a near cataclysmic moment in native affairs. A chief of Upolu, the famous Malietoa Vaiinupo, had just established his hegemony by conquest over all the islands in a manner reminiscent of events in Tahiti and Hawaii. The parallel with eastern Polynesia was more apparent than real, however, for the Malietoa laid no claim to real power. The wars were violent, and the issues were deeply felt, but they were not the issues of economic control, of seizure of lands and territory; they were issues of rank and title, of dominance or subordination as an affair of honor. From the Samoan point of view, such issues could never be resolved. Even after Malietoa Vaiinupo became a Christian and was recognized by Europe as "King," the old disputes between who was up and who was down continued. Malietoa was succeeded at his death by a half-brother who was still a pagan and, of course, a new war for domination followed. As late as 1881 the European powers—still seeking a Samoan peace formula—arranged a wholly conventional compromise that divided authority between the rival parties. This, too, failed, for at stake was not the pragmatic issue of stabilizing authority so that social life could run a smooth course, but to the Samoans the more spiritual question of who was to wear the mantle of natural superiority.

Genealogical Traditions

The recorded Samoan traditions are not as detailed nor as chronologically coherent as those of Tonga. Especially vague and fragmentary are those dealing with the founding period. They do not, however, lack historical interest. At very least they reveal Samoan historical conceptions. These claim descent of illustrious founding lines from Tangaroa, the western Polynesian high god, and the autochthonous origins of all Samoans. The beginnings of social life are placed in the small islands of Manu'a, and the Tui Manu'a, their most illustrious title, is given the distinction of first descent from the high god. Williamson (1924) has painstakingly pieced together fragments of traditions and of genealogical lists to show that Tui Manu'a stood as founder and head of all the great lineage of Samoan chiefs. If his demonstration is not altogether convincing, the fact remains that Samoans regard their illustrious families as interconnected from the earliest days.

Men are declared to be the products of rivalry, as the following origin tradition states (Turner 1884:6):

> Fire and water married, and from them sprang the earth, rocks, trees, and everything.
>
> The cuttle-fish fought with the fire and was beaten. The fish fought with the rocks, and the rocks conquered. The large stones fought with the small ones; the small conquered. The small stones fought with the grass, and the grass conquered. The grass fought with the trees; the grass was beaten and the trees conquered. The trees fought with the creepers; the trees were beaten and the creepers conquered. The creepers rotted, swarmed with maggots, and from maggots they grew to be men.

This striking concept of a descending spiral of successive overcomings expresses the Samoan conviction, fully carried out in social life, that each position of authority engenders a lower-ranking opponent who can then rise. In the early traditions the younger tricks the older into losing his titles and rank to him. In a similar fashion, a son tricks his father. Sibling rivalry is implicit, and a father warns his sons immediately not to war on each other (cf. Williamson 1924:I, 53, 54). The point is made that division of function and rivalry are integral. The Tui Manu'a position is set up with either a high priest or a *tulafale* (talking chief) counterpart. Though complementary statuses, they are shown to be antagonistic.

The theme of small overcoming the big is expressed in the social superiority of Manu'a over all the great islands. In the same way, great Upolu comes under the jurisdiction of very small Manono. In the first transmission of ranks, it is the minor titles that are handed down first; the major titles come last. If the traditions simply render the contemporary social doctrines of seemingly endless possibilities for advancement, they also declare mobility to be part of the natural order. The natural order was established at once when the islands were partitioned among sons of a founder and the titles were handed down.

A new era bringing changes in traditional powers and authority starts with what the genealogical records call the Tongan occupation. The dating of this period is, to say the least, uncertain. Krämer's narratives and pedigree lists (1902), which are the most ample, put the event at ca. 1200. Von Bülow dates the expulsion at ca. 1600 (cited by Williamson, 1924:I 69). The Tongans arrived after the social influence of the Tui Manu'a had declined on Upolu. The traditions ignore the details of the Tongan occupation and understandably dwell on the wars of expulsion which are associated mainly with the history of Upolu. There a local chief who had distinguished himself received the newly coined title of *malietoa* ("brave warrior") and founded a new dynasty that with ups and downs entered the modern period as one of the most powerful families of Samoa.

The pre-Tongan period was "traditional" in the sense that a fully hereditary and divinely based title, Tui Manu'a, held the highest rank over all Samoa, while political and economic authority was local, lodged in essentially autonomous districts and villages. Thereafter titles became the active prizes of war. Upolu, for example, became a new battleground for the paramount authority. It suddenly produced a new title, the tafa'ifa, an apparent parallel to Tui Manu'a, which gave authority over all of Samoa except for the Manu'an group. The tafa'ifa was a conquest title that went to the possessor of the four leading titles of Upolu. The title was not continuous, since control of its four constituents was always uncertain. These were acquired by inheritance, by forcible seizure, and by political agreement—usually as a reward for vital military aid. In the event of conquest, title and sovereignty went together; in political agreements, only the title was given. Thus the tafa'ifa as a new title was evidently a compound of the traditional concern with the honorific and a new and more aggressive concern with power. (The malietoa as an independent title was entirely one of power.) A further indication of its compound nature was the provision that the official grant of the title had to be made by the *alataua*—the great and semi-divine orator chiefs of neutral districts. In appearance, then, the great title was freely granted by men responsible for the preservation of traditions and genealogies. Since it was a woman who was named first tafa'ifa of Samoa on the strength of her actual genealogical claims to all four titles, it is fair to assume the original emphasis was upon the honorific. Only subsequently did the element of aggressive power become the more prominent component. When Europeans first arrived they found the large Samoan islands ablaze with sectional warfare. The prize was tafa'ifa. In the early nineteenth century Tamafainga, a distinguished chief of the Malietoa lineage, forcibly declared himself ruler of all Samoa. He was assassinated almost immediately, but was avenged by a Malietoa kinsman, Vaiinupo, who then seized the four component titles and the Tafa'ifa. Embracing Christianity, Vaiinupo was recognized by Europe as King. Malietoa Vaiinupo ushers in the Modern Period.

The archeological record thus far tends to substantiate the traditions of a Tongan invasion. A Samoan village of the seventeenth century had, for example, the Tongan features of mounds. Very early Samoan sites, on the other hand, indicate cultural independence from Tonga (Suggs 1960). Finally, the antiquity of Samoan culture is suggested by a radiocarbon date of A.D. 9 (Shutler 1961). On the transformation of Samoan Society from Traditional to Open, only the traditions bear witness.

The Status System

The Tongan experience may account for the main divergences between status systems of Western Samoa and of Manu'a. This experience was the historical event, the energy factor, so to speak, that broke an older traditional pattern and split the head (Manu'a) from its body. An awareness of an all-Samoan unity thereafter weakened but did not disappear and so another pattern, a variant of the old, could reestablish itself. Manu'a severed from the body evolved in isolation. The head, as was its traditional role, continued to develop along the lines of status formalism. Having lost its body, it had lost much of its efficacy, its mana, so that much of the older religious awesomeness once associated with Tangaroa-descended Tui Manu'a drained away. In Polynesian aristocratic thought, religious power to be most effective had to be strongly focused and concentrated in a person or descent line. Mana had most force when it was intense. Dilution of mana was in one sense an affront against a chief and his sanctity. In a more far-reaching sense it was a disturbance of the natural religious order, which could not survive dilution. Samoa, having lost much of its religious focus, responded by placing all reliance upon the democratic principle of decentralization. Instead of one source, there were countless sources of divine power.

The large islands, to continue with the organismic analogy—which is, after all, of Polynesian making—found themselves headless and were confronted with a parallel problem of reassembling some form of customary centralized structure. As lower-order segments of what was once a larger system, their approach was, figuratively speaking, more somatic, and, encouraged no doubt by the Tongan experience, relied upon physical forcefulness to establish a political equivalent of the mana of a Tui Manu'a. The tafa'ifa of Western Samoa in his combined roles of form and power must be considered the new version of the now distant and cut-off Tui Manu'a.

Once separated, neither the headless body nor the bodiless head could restore the older organic order. Each was left with a novel incompleteness and a distinctive character. Each in its own mode had to create what I have called before a "made order." Samoa represents more clearly than any other Polynesian society the special combination of organic and "made" features that gives to a status system a dual character. The Samoan status systems were not, however, dual in the Mangaian style. They were rather bipolar. That is to say, whether one considers the authenticity of a single status or the table of organization of statuses, some combination of organic (genealogical) or "made" (political or military) will be involved. Dual systems separate organic and "made"; bipolar systems combine them almost in the way an electrical circuit is formed. Since mana is conceived as a flowing force, the analogy to a circuit is a relevant one. The flexibility, the openness, of both Samoan status systems is therefore of a distinctive nature for Polynesia.

Primogeniture

Primogeniture had all but vanished in Samoa along with the concept of senior lines. A few features remained to lend credence to the assumption, concurred in, for example, by Mead, that respect for the first had once been more significant. In Manu'a the first birth was most important. It sent the mother back to her own village, the male line source, for the parturition, providing she was of high rank, and it called for more extravagant exchanges between the infant's two families. The honor though, Mead points out, fell upon the mother rather than upon the child (1930:90). As elsewhere in Polynesia, the first-born was called *ulumatua,* a titular honor only, for he received no special privileges. Western Samoa honored the first-born only slightly more. He inherited his father's low-ranking title as household head, but not the higher ranks, which were in the jurisdiction of the fono. All other privileges were conferred and not inherited.

These slight examples do not demonstrate the degeneration of seniority, only its limitations. More positive evidence of earlier conditions come from the traditions. In these the first-born does inherit the major ranks and is then challenged by a junior sibling. The complex character of Samoan views on this subject is exposed in the Upoluan traditions. Pili, the divine founder, divided the island at his death, giving to his eldest son, Tua, one large land division and authority over agriculture. He gave the orator's staff, a secondary rank, to Tuamasanga, the second-born, and the very small island of Manono to the youngest. At this point the special Samoan point of view appears. The head of Manono is given jurisdiction over all of Upolu—the lower overcomes the higher. In the end it is the implausibility of the idea that Samoa alone, or virtually alone, in Malayo-Polynesia would lack the special respects for the senior, that compels us to assume a transformation.

Male Line

Samoa and Western Polynesia generally had established complementary parity between male and female lines of descent. In principle the male line transmitted the highest ranks and the chiefship. As the local group whose members were firmly bound together by the attraction of common residence, the male line (*tama tane*) held effective authority. It fostered a compact and well-defined lineage within what was actually a more comprehensive kindred and within which the female lines (*tama fafine*) held their own exclusive titles. But as the tama fafine were dispersed over many villages, their titles carried honor and rather less effective authority. Within the kindred (*aiga*), the male line was executive, the female held the veto. The tama tane possessed the progenitive honor of perpetuating direct descent; the tama fafine held the opposing honor of the power to curse its complement with the blight of barrenness. The father's sister, a link-pin between both sides of the kindred, was honored and feared as the holder of the curse. Obversely, the mother's brother, the male link, was honored as a ritual benefactor. (For details see chap. 21.)

These formal divisions between the male and female lines cannot be defined as bilateral, for they are not even-handed. Bilaterality did, however, develop in Samoa as part of a more general and all-encompassing easing of the rules for acquiring status honor. The role of pedigree was very strongly affected. Eventually, specifically male titles went to women. Women became headmen (*matai*), chiefs (ali'i) and family priests. The position of honored virgin (*taupou*), traditionally the privilege of sister's daughter, was allowed to go to a chief's own daughter. If women did not play more of a political role in later Samoan life, it was because they were uninterested. The doors had opened.

Genealogical Depth

Length of pedigree was the sole remaining categorical element of genealogy that Samoa had retained. The highest chiefs recorded genealogies back to their divine foundations. Lower ranks had shorter records. Antiquity, though, was shared by many families and so was only one of many factors to be considered by electors to title.

Sanctity

In the rank of Tui Manu'a we recognize at once the familiar eastern Polynesian concepts of divine and sacred chiefship. The Tui Manu'a was as revered as were the Tahitian and Hawaiian sacred chiefs. Moreover, the patterns of sanctity were alike in their separation of potential from kinetic. Through excess, the Tahitian chief lost sanctity, while the hidden country chief of Hawaii had the potential which he was required to activate. The Samoan version of this pattern was more formal. The Tui Manu'a was born with the genealogical potential. His sanctity did not, however, become manifest until after he had been anointed and invested with the symbols of office. In Samoa, it has been observed, sanctity was a property not of the person but of the title (Mead 1930). This democratic doctrine did not, however, apply to Tui Manu'a, whose claim to the title was specifically genealogical. To complete the circuit, figuratively speaking, the electors had to ratify a decision already made by the gods. This was the bipolar system: the gods declared, men ratified or vetoed. The children born to Tui Manu'a before ratification were ordinary; those coming after became the *alo tupu sa,* "children of the sacred king" (Mead 1930:184).

The Tui Manu'a rated the prostration tapu of the Hawaiian pio chiefs. His glance withered the fruit on the trees. His person, his food, and all his intimate belongings, and all places associated with his were sacred and dangerous. Even inadvertent contact could be deadly. As in Hawaii, the inadvertent offender could be absolved and decontaminated by the sacred chief. The rituals of the Tui Manu'a office declared his uniqueness and separation from all others. He was a figure of sudden transformation, ordinary and mingling freely with others one day, godlike and unique the next. This quality of electric change would seem to shift the religious viewpoint from Tangaroa to the electors. This seems precisely what the Manu'ans had in mind. As one said: "The people of old had Tagaloa and the village, and the village was the greater of the two."

To continue with the Hawaiian comparison, the Tui Manu'a was to other sacred chiefs as the pio were to the wohi. He was in a class alone. Stair names 18 sacred chiefs (*ali'i pa'ia*) of all Samoa, among which 12 were in a very high category and six in a lesser order. Their tapu was limited to the realm of food. They ate apart, and none dared touch their discarded food for fear of a supernatural death. In other realms they were accorded the respects of distance, but as etiquette and not as response to dangerous sanctity. Much of the wide area of tapu of Polynesia had in Samoa been converted to the lesser currency of etiquette.

The Samoan term *sa* may be correctly translated as "sacred." Yet it is applied, as Mead observes, to any statement of what is forbidden, regardless of whether the restraint is owed to association with divinity, has been imposed by the secular authority of the village council, or is simply a requirement of good manners. Like that of sanctity of persons, the concept of sa is graded, shading imperceptibly from the sacred to the secular realms.

The gradations of sa are all variations on the management of respects through separations and distance. Acts that would be sacrilegious before the Tui Manu'a are reduced to discourtesy before lesser chiefs. All persons are normally owed similar respects. Decorum, Stair tells us, was so elaborate, possibilities for offense were numerous. To throw food over a person, to walk in front of company, to stand before a person who was seated was insulting. Insults of this sort were common causes of war (1897:124).

The gradations in sanctity from reverences to respects represent the Samoan interest in diluting of honors. Samoa, having diluted the quality of its high chiefship, proceeded to carry out a widespread and democratic dilution of the sources of access to sacred powers. Each family head was also priest; each person at birth acquired his own tutelary spirit: each village had its own god. Everyone who could afford to be tattooed became momentarily a sacred being. Sanctity was then ritually removed, leaving behind only the honor of having had the body ornamented. While the Tui Manu'a and other chiefs retained their sanctity, of which in fact the lesser ones could be stripped for good cause, that sanctity was—even more so than in Hawaii—the ornament of rank rather than the source of productive powers.

Tohunga

The essence of the Polynesian patron-craftsmen relationship emerges with special clarity in Samoa. Here the relationship is definitely that of mutual honoring. It is a ritual connection as far removed from the utilitarian interest as is, ideally, that between priest and parishioner. We may no more speak of a craftsman hired for a fee than we may speak of Samoan bride price as the purchase of a woman. Both are instances of honorific exchanges between the essential parties. In the crafts relationship, the patron initiates the exchanges, giving one kind of goods and performing certain ritual acts to honor the workers; the *tufuga* reciprocate, delivering products and performing services that elevate the patron. The manner of labor and the pattern of social intercourse between patron and tufuga asserts their basic equivalency. Samoa distinguishes between craftsman and priest (*taula*), giving to each a special role and special honor. Of the two, the higher crafts have the greater honor. The crafts status in Samoa is, however, one of several coordinate and overlapping categories of honor. The crafts category standing outside the traditional system of genealogical ranks and the "made" system of titular ranks is modeled, nevertheless, precisely upon these two systems.

The Samoan crafts have been compared to European "guilds," which they do resemble in their plan of organization. Like the guilds, the principal Samoan crafts have corporate continuity, a firm internal organization of rules and regulations and, of course, the hierarchy of masters and apprentices. Each craft unit carries a name and a trademark by which all of its products can be readily identified. It is mainly in the character of the exchanges—as against payment for services—that the two systems differ. European exchanges were pecuniary, the Samoan, ritual. Before turning to the form of Samoan craft organization, we need to take note of the diversity of specialized skills that were recognized.

Stair (1897:142) lists the following: house builder, canoe maker, small canoe maker, wooden bowl maker, paddle maker, fish-bait preparer, sail maker, drum maker, preparer of turmeric, preparer of lamp-black, club maker, spear maker, maker of split bamboo fishing pots, barber, tattooer, maker of tattooing instruments, fishhook maker, maker of fishing nets, maker of stone hatchets, maker of nets, weaver of garment mats, weaver of house mats, siapo maker, arrowroot maker, basket weaver, ornamental screen maker, and plaiter of sennit.

Skill was a minor issue in such meticulous specialization. To quote Mead:

> There was no genuine dependence of the bulk of the community upon a few experts, except probably the tattooers who disappeared so long ago. The simple matter of lending a relative one's slightly superior skill is cloaked beneath a smothering amount of ceremony. The *tufuga* only held the position of dictator to his employer by virtue of this ceremonial round (1930: 69).

Since specialization of this degree of refinement was not a utilitarian response to technical complexity, it must be recognized as still another mode of formal categorization of statuses. In totemic systems, kin groups are classified, as a rule, by the "given" categories of nature. In the Samoan crafts, the order of classification is by that which is "made." The crafts take their place in the total structure of status as a "made" category, but with features of the "given," so that by Samoan standards of proper structure they have completeness. The Samoan crafts lack the systematic ranking of the Tongan system. Their major intent rather is to emphasize the honor of the special and the unique. The general, of course, is always common. In the Samoan crafts, the one who is a commoner by ordinary genealogical standards becomes special and highly honored. He holds the title of tufuga, and the special insignia of his craft.

The Samoan crafts have a broader system of ranking than the Tongan. Of all the aforementioned crafts, three stand apart as major; the rest are minor. The three are house carpenter, canoe builder, and tattooer. What these three have in common that distinguishes them from the rest is highest skill, longest apprenticeship, and costliest product. Their exchanges have magnitude. Whoever cannot finally afford to complete the payments, let us say, on a canoe, has failed to uphold his honor. Carpenters hold the highest rank among the three, tattooers the lowest; the minor crafts are not ranked at all. The three major products are, in the current vernacular, the main "status symbols" of the Samoans. Tattooing confers temporary sanctity; houses and canoes are also embellishments of person and of family. So the craftsman creating sources of honor is granted commensurate honor. That commoners are, nevertheless, admitted to such distinguished professions is but another example of the Samoan system of extending the blessings of aristocracy to the many.

The system of crafts was basically the same in Western Samoa and in Manu'a. In pre-European days the Western crafts were more formally organized, and were more fully a replica in miniature of the larger society. Members of the same craft unit are normally kinsmen who live in the same village and constitute themselves as a patrilineal lineage; they call themselves an aiga to emphasize their family character. Each has its own matai, who is also its chief master craftsman, and its priests. In Western Samoa each craft family has its own fono and its own stock of craft titles. The carpenters, for example, form a distinct genealogical entity, tracing descent through males from that great chief and carpenter, Malama. Like the traditional status lineage of eastern Polynesia, all carpenter craft units or societies are branches of a common descent line and are ranked in order of genealogical closeness to the direct line from the founder. Thus craft society and individual tufuga hold genealogical rank of a specialized type. In the Samoan system, however, the tufuga title, as any title, must finally be granted by a council which takes account of both pedigree and skill or, broadly speaking, achievement.

Priests

Priests, although categorically separated from tufuga, were, by general Polynesian standards for the profession, in effect reduced; by contrast the three top crafts were elevated. By Samoan standards, priests and artisans were leveled to approximately equivalent standing. We may judge reduction in standing by the objective criterion of scope. For Samoan priests, the scope had become narrow and local. Samoan religion was concerned mainly with family gods, incarnated in various animal and plant forms and with the active ghosts of the dead (Mead, 1930:163). All came within the jurisdiction of the family matai who doubled as priest and was then known as *o taula aitu-o-ainga*. Village gods were on a somewhat higher level and were served either by local chiefs or by a hereditary local priesthood. The national god, Tangaloa, had no priesthood. While gods of Heaven and the numerous war gods transcended strictly local interests, their priests (*tupai*), though credited with great powers, were, nevertheless, only slightly above the parish level. The worship by the very high chiefs of the great gods, the atua, who were above family and were not materially incarnated, involved a still higher order of priest—who could be the chief himself—but no formal office of high priest. The tulafale ("orator chiefs"), the executive officers of chiefs, were also priests. Again, their title relegates the priestly function to secondary importance. The priesthood, in short, was not clearly defined. A hereditary priesthood with important functions did exist, but unlike the tufuga had no preemptive role. As Stair has said: "Although there were in Samoa as elsewhere in Polynesia, various classes of priests, the head of a social group, great or small was its natural priest (1897:4).

References in Samoan traditions to earlier sun worship and to human sacrifice suggest that Samoan religious life may have undergone a long-range reduction in scope, reaching its low point with the decline in the stature of the Tui Manu'a. Hints of an ancient sun cult, possibly related to intimations of sun worship in early Easter Island history, raise intriguing conjectural possibilities, but are not substantial enough to attest to a decline of a central priesthood via democratic decentralization. The fact that the Tongan priesthood was of the same character, but in the opposite social setting of political centralism, implies rather that western Polynesia may have long had—and perhaps from the beginning—a somewhat different religious and priestly tradition from eastern Polynesia.

Ceremonial Setting

Even today when utilitarian pressures have undermined ritual in all parts of the world, both Samoas, the American and the independent state of Western Samoa, are still the despair of the western world. Protocol expertise and oratory, enjoyed as ends in themselves or as embellishments of the larger drama of honor, rank among the most esteemed of the Samoan skills. The ceremonial setting—the gesture, the word, the placement of persons, the order of precedence, the sipping of the kava cup—the respect for the minutiae of decorum is for the Samoans a statement of the very essence of social life. At least since the Tongan period, form has not been the solitary foundation of status in Samoa. It has been, let us say, one of its sturdy pillars. In Manu'a more than in Western Samoa, it was the central post. To grasp the prominence of form in holding up the Samoan status structure, we have only to consider how here it was the tulafale, the orator chief, the dean of eloquence and the master of protocol, who could use these ornamental arts as the point of departure for greater powers. In eastern Polynesia it was more often the administrator of lands who moved forward and surpassed the ariki. In Samoa it was he who knew where everyone belonged and all the signs, insignia, and other formal prerogatives that belonged to everyone.

Toa

Manu'a having finally eschewed war, had no place for warriors or for war priests. This was not so in Western Samoa, where war had increasingly become the main source of power and of honor. In this militant region, war gods and their priests had risen to prominence. Warriors, however, did not attain professional status. They were, of course, honored and rewarded. They and chiefs were the exclusive possessors of the special underworld of Pulotu, an important honor. They lacked the specific title that distinguished the great fighting men of eastern Polynesia. In Samoa the military skills were simply aspects of being a chief, of being a mature male. In place of the specialized warrior, Samoa in its own collective fashion had elevated villages to be vanguard units. One village in each large district jealously guarded this privilege and accepted the heaviest casualties. All ranks fought; the local chiefs of a district acted as a war council to the district paramount upon whom the military command necessarily fell.

Wealth

In the agrarian society, land is the natural source of all wealth; in agrarian aristocracies it is, in addition, the source of all honor. Thus the bitter conflicts in the eastern Polynesian Open and Stratified societies over the control of lands, the struggles to seize lands, to dispossess rivals and so humiliate and degrade them, seemed but the inevitable and direct expression of uncompromising rivalry. In Samoa, land was no less the ultimate source of wealth, and status rivalry, diverse as were its forms, demanded the currency of goods, as it did everywhere in Polynesia. Yet the economic point of view was decidedly different. The focus was not on the source, but on derivatives. As in the Traditional societies, land was securely embedded in the family. Persons could be expelled from the village by chief or fono; the land remained a family possession. Wealth, then, was measured in movable goods, in mats, tapa cloth, grass skirts, coconut oil, dyestuffs, canoes, weapons, ornaments, houses and food stuffs—crop, live pig, and fowl. The measurement was not of accumulation, of display, but of movement. All who valued rank and title engaged in exchanges, giving, as a rule, mats and tapa known as *toga* for foods known as *oloa.* Toga had high value as the gift of chiefs; oloa low value as the return gift of lower ranks. But in at least some situations everyone was a giver of one and a receiver of the other. No commodity remained accumulated at any one locus of status or power for long. The economy as a whole was set to be in fluid balance. Any individual, of course, was at any moment either ahead or behind in the balance of exchanges. However, since property moved from one group to another, from one person to another on so many different occasions—marriages, births, deaths, consecrations of houses, of ranks, launching of canoes, entertaining visitors, soliciting the labor of tufuga and the good will of chiefs and titled men—imbalances either of glut or of embarrassing shortages were almost inevitably temporary. The poor had a record of consistently meager participation in exchanges. On the other hand, it was not unusual for a great chief to impoverish himself to meet his very heavy ritual obligations.

Land in Samoa was abundant; it was there to be annexed from the uncultivated wilderness. It stood outside the active channels of status rivalry. That constant aspect of honor, tenure, was secured to all. The wealth that entered into the play of status was not inconsequential, demanding heavily of personal and family efforts. Neither was it crucial for everyday subsistence needs. Thus in its economic aspect, status rivalry was a low-risk affair. Persons and their families advanced their claims to honor or fell behind. No one rose to such heights he could no longer be overtaken; no one was so reduced he could not rise again. No one suffered the total degradation of utter economic destitution. Samoans recognized distinctions between rich and poor without regarding them as pertinent (Mead 1930:65).

Political Hegemony

Manu'a may be said to have been the center of intricate patterns of personal and collective powers; Western Samoa, of direct and crude distinctions between strong and weak. Still, to describe the differences between the two in this manner is to call attention to divergences at their widest, thus oversimplifying the actual situation in Western Samoa. In their local and internal arrangements both were almost alike. The point of difference was simply the Western Samoan concept of an external enemy, a concept lacking in Manu'a. This concept of direct antagonism, of opposition between strong and weak was, nevertheless, given a collective rather than the individual setting of eastern Polynesia. The antagonistic parties were districts, that is to say, kin groups. Chiefs, of course, had the semblance of hegemony as heads of group, but—to quote Robert Louis Stevenson's cool appraisal of what they could really accomplish—"The President of a college debating society was a far more formidable officer (1892:8)." All power resided in the fono; all decisions called for negotiation and compromise. Each decision, each expression of power, had to, as in any deliberative body, shift even if imperceptibly the balance of forces. Only at the time of war itself could a chief as respected leader stand out as a personal figure of power. Then he might have been able to award enemy lands to a warrior ally. But "in the ordinary affairs of life," Ella said of the chief in 1892, his powers and prerogatives "are little more than nominal (1892:631)." Ella, an authoritative source, saw Samoan rule as "almost democratic" adding "for the most part each man acts according to his own will (1892:631)." He defined the duties of a chief as "administering municipal laws, settling disputes, punishing transgressors, appointing feasts and general tabus, and in leading in wars (1892:631)." The description is, of course, still too general to depict adequately an attribute that is by its nature intensely concrete. What is clear though from Ella, and indeed from all other witnesses of early Samoan life, is the Samoan image of a chief as one among many, and never as the omnipotent and awe inspiring figure of other Open Society chiefs. It was Stair who said of Samoa: "The difficulty is not in finding a chief but in recognizing him."

Power in its cruel and awesome aspect had its proper place in dealings with the external (non-kin) community or, as very much the same thing, in punishing seriously criminal behavior. In the latter event, the fono either condemned the entire family to banishment and loss of property, or to face the destruction of its household goods and the ringing of its breadfruit trees. For lesser offenses, the culprit was ordered to injure himself violently in the presence of his judges, or to submit ignominously to being trussed like a pig and exposed to the broiling heat of the sun. For such offenses as murder or adultery, the offender submitted to the *ifonga*, a ritual self-humiliation, along with the payment of indemnity. The humiliation was to sit inertly before the aggrieved. Stair, who has described the ifonga, adds the important observation that subject peoples also submitted to the ifonga (1897: 101), thus bringing out a common concept governing internal and external expressions of anger. Offense considered a humiliation had to be rectified by a corresponding humiliation plus an indemnity, so that the equilibrium of honor was restored. While antagonistic relations with the external community could also be moderated in this manner, the interest was rather to maintain a stable dominance. Western Samoa, recognizing the permanence of two parties—the strong (*malo*) and the weak (*toilalo*)—joined in the common aristocratic contempt for the weak. In one respect, external antagonism was provoked by a quarrel, and so resembled a criminal and humiliating offense. In another, as brought out by Turner, the antagonism was "a desire on the part of one, two, or more of the districts to be considered stronger and of more importance than the rest (1884:189)."

In normal dealings with the segmentary internal organization, the issue is power in all its political complexity: in power as prestige, as influence, as the right to receive deference, to exert leverage, to regulate affairs, to be an executive and legislator, to be active—never inert.

Such powers are held by chiefs in collaboration with others, by fonos, by headmen, by artisans, by all the honored kinsmen, and, in short, by any restless and ambitious spirit who has the talent for the game.

The Structure of Status

The main structural principles of Samoan status may now be summarized. They represent, it should be said first, the same elements found everywhere else in Polynesia, including some recognition of primogeniture, seniority, descent lines, and patrilineal succession. The new structure, however, offers the greatest possible flexibility by invariably coupling a categorical with an optional principle of status. Thus the categorical is modified and the optional encounters limits. All status systems have, in fact, the same structure, which is as fundamental as organic life where fixed and flexible, as nature and nurture are inextricably linked. What gives the Samoan status structure its distinction is the systematic and formal manner in which this inevitable principle is formulated. The systematic formulation is itself a positive principle of form that leaves the actors a script, and the privilege of improvising within the stated themes. The script, moreover, is more than ample enough to incorporate new roles without in any way risking the anarchy and chaos of radical departure from both the constants of hierarchy and the careful observance of reciprocal respects. No one is fully separated from the rest; each is ultimately dependent for his honor, if not upon all, upon many. Samoa had come close to broadening the concept of aristocracy to include the common man.

Genealogical Rank

Samoa accomplished its mission of extending aristocratic honors by broadening the great avenues of genealogical rank, those of ali'i, of tufuga, of priest, and of family headship. In theory a restricted rank, the title of ali'i had become as common and about as meaningful as "colonel" in Kentucky. All descendants of chiefs, without regard to sex line or to seniority, could claim that distinguished and traditional title. To the early missionaries it seemed as though everyone were ali'i. The tufuga as honored craftsmen carried a second order of titles that were considerably more exclusive because limited severely to those who had survived a long apprenticeship. Even so, there was some special honor to be gained from almost any technical accomplishment. Priests had become as numerous as family heads. However, the most open and, in the end, the most significant road to aristocratic distinction was created by elevating the name of every extended family to the exalted stature of a title. The Samoan term for title is *a'o;* the name of the family was its a'o. Large families had through their intermarriages acquired several a'o and were represented in their fono by a number of title holders. The honoring of a family through its name is, needless to say, standard in Polynesia, where the lineage as *ngati* or *ati* carries the name of its founder as a proud title. Samoans, drawing upon this venerable and undoubtedly very ancient tradition which elsewhere was but an extension of the arikiship, gave it new stature. In their own fashion they made it separate, coordinate, overlapping, and, finally, antagonistic to the arikiship.

In principle, arikiship and family a'o are alike. Both are concepts of genealogical rank honoring the title holder and the family line. They start, however, from different directions in the social organization. Ali'i starts from the concept of a pinnacle and spreads down the social scale. All ali'i are presumably descendants of three great founding ali'i families. The family a'o, as organized into a hierarchy, acquires its standing in diverse ways, moving down from a pinnacle and moving up from the grass roots. The title of ali'i is generic, traditional, and associated in its higher levels with sanctity. The family a'o is particular; it resides in the family and emphasizes its specific and local character. It represents a newer system; it is secular, administrative, and, therefore, at the center of social life. In the dialectics of Samoan history, the ali'i fades and is overcome by the newer and initially lower. In eastern Polynesia coordinate systems of status diverged, the traditional moving into sanctity, the newer into political power. The two Samoan coordinates of status, rank (ali'i) and title (family name), move in no such decided directions. If anything, they tend to converge toward a common state within which sanctity is reduced to etiquette and administration is elevated to ritual. The system of rank is traditionally built around generic titles; the system of titles has in its convergence developed its own generic titles. Tulafale, for example, is a generic title representing the families. Thus, when ali'i and tulafale are administratively paired together, the two systems of status are joined and made operationally coordinate. In both systems the order of hierarchy is historical ("made"), rather than organic.

Ali'i

As in Hawaii, the great extensiveness of ali'i is corrected by further categorization. The lower or ordinary ali'i may be common as water; the ali'i pai'a form a sacred and endogamous elite. They are still further subdivided into an *afio* class and a somewhat lower *susu* class. The secular ali'i have also an elite grade within the afio class (Stair 1897:65). The genealogical authorization for such categorizations is not entirely clear. It depended, presumably, upon directness of descent and upon the wishes of the last incumbent. The designations of afio and susu have honorific significance only; they refer to forms of address and order of ritual precedence. Traditionally, the highest ranking ali'i in an area comprising many villages held the special generic title of *tui* ("lord").

If we consider ali'i as genealogical rank pure and simple, then we must conclude that Samoa had reduced it, as all information insists, to insignificance. Samoan concepts of honor are not, however, purist or monistic. Ali'i rank could, and generally did, acquire title and, thereby, administrative efficacy. The title, requiring collective assent, came at the expense of aristocratic autonomy. But the advantages were incalculable. All the great chiefs of Upolu, for example, had reached their powerful positions by just such a combination of rank and title. Rank was not per se political; it had great political advantages.

When the chief of high rank also held title, he presided over a court similar to that of Hawaiian chiefs. This court included official counsellors, the *atamai-o-ali'i,* stewards (*o le fa 'atama*), jesters (*o le salelelisi*), and personal attendants (*songa*) who were barbers, cup-bearers, trumpeters, and special messengers. A retinue of young men (*taule alea*) worked on his plantations, prepared food for the household, and bore arms for him.

To be efficacious, chiefs were bound to the collectivity of the fono. In still another kind of linkage, a council or blood brotherhood of chiefs, they declared their aristocratic autonomy. The details of *uso ali'i,* the brotherhood of chiefs, are dim. Grattan describes it only as a "flexible" and informal conclave of related chiefs who accepted one of their own as *sa'o,* or superior. He looked after their interests and they owed him allegiance and service (1948:20). The uso ali'i reminds one of the Hawaiian aha ali'i, still another example of aristocratic inner circle. The Samoan uso ali'i also guarded pedigrees, submitting its own candidates and their credentials to the official electors. The pure aristocracy, those who held authentic old titles from their ancestors in the strictly traditional manner, were distinguished as the *faletai*—as "real" chiefs, so to speak. Yet, while Samoa acknowledged the very idea of aristocratic purity, it could not and would not abandon its trend toward flexibility. Grattan, an experienced and hardened administrator, was amazed to hear that, in fact, even those who were not chiefs were admitted to the inner circles.

Tui Manu'a

At least in recent times the Tui Manu'a was chosen by the tulafale of the islet of Tau and not by his own family, which had no voice in the election (Mead 1930:178). He was thus the elected sacred chief, rather than one bestowed. The forms of the traditional sacred chief were retained, but on the issue of critical importance for aristocracy, the continuity of a descent line, the break with tradition was close to complete. The son of a Tui Manu'a was least likely to succeed him. In recent times the political position of Tui Manu'a has been in steady decline. At the time of Mead's study (1925), he held honorary office as high chief of all Manu'a, receiving tribute of fish and breadfruit from all, though not all acknowledged his ascendancy in the same way. Mead notes, for example, that one Manu'an village, Faleasao, had a high chief of its own. Tui Manu'a is the nearest Samoan approximation to a high chief of the traditional eastern Polynesian type. The line, god-descended by tradition, had finally retained only the abstraction of continuity and had lost the concreteness of genealogical descent.

O Le Tupu (The Grown)

Tui is an old title modernized. *Tupu* is the new political title representing modern conditions. Like tui, tupu is also an example of variability of the genealogical concept. Ordinarily the tupu, as ascendent chief over an entire island, begins as ali'i, the sole acknowledged genealogical rank. He demonstrates political efficacy by acquiring all pertinent titles of his jurisdiction, by intermarriage and, of course, by force. Tupu is unquestionably a conquest title. Yet in bringing out its "made" character, we need not lose sight of the constant genealogical substratum. The tupu, like the Hawaiian moi, had broken with the traditions defining categorical succession, but not with the central core of aristocratic rule. In the same way, the tafa'ifa, the supreme tupu, had to hold the five most important traditional tui titles to accredit properly his jurisdiction. The tafa'ifa was established by an Upolu family that already bore one of the highest family titles in Samoa. (Williamson 1924:II, 32).

Manaia

The heir apparent of the chief (except in the realm of Tui Manu'a), the *manaia* is usually of the family, as a rule the son. He has the hereditary right and is formally appointed by the tulafale. The manaia then acquires the practical position as head of the *aumaga,* the council of untitled young men; he leads his age group in the everyday labors of the village, cooking for the headman, cultivating taro, building roads, and taking care of visitors. For its practical efforts the manaia with his aumaga was "the strength of the village (Mead 1930:14)."

With respect to the structure of status, the manaia acquires a distinctive position. He is no junior chief, but in one important sense, as head of a group which represents sheer utility, he stands in opposition to the incumbent, who as ali'i represents form. In another sense he is parallel to the ali'i, who has a tulafale counterpart to his own position as counterpart to an untitled body of men, which has, of course, a higher standing collectively than a single untitled individual. In the community of Tui Manu'a, the manaia was not of the royal line. A more fully honorific position, more akin to that of Tui Manu'a, was held by a young man of his lineage and known as the *silia*. In other words, the lower level of chiefship sets up stronger contrasts than the highest level.

Taupou

In the villages the rather pragmatic role of manaia is contrasted with the far more ceremonious role of the honored virgin. The taupou has been described as the "female ornament of the chief's rank, combining the honor of princess and queen (Mead 1930:14)." In a role that is in one respect parallel to that of manaia, she presides over the assembly of untitled women, the *aulama*. The corps of untitled women does not concern itself quite so much with being useful to the village. It tends the mulberry plantings, but its main task is to look after the taupou. They are her court. As a sacred girl, a daughter of the ali'i or of his sister, she is second in rank in the village. The chief himself names her, so that she moves strictly in the solitary orbit of rank. She is addressed in the special courtesy language reserved for chiefs.

The roles of manaia and taupou demonstrate the two poles of the chief's office, its responsibility for form most appropriately portrayed through a virgin girl (the quintessence of the female side), and its regard for the practical and the efficacious represented by an energetic young man. Both are declared to be royal when mats, the gift of chiefs, are presented in their behalf to the tulafale at the ceremony of their appointment.

Tulafale

Both Stair and Williamson have recognized in the tulafale the eastern Polynesian rangatira. The comparison is apt, even though the actual historical connection between the two is at best circumstantial. Both, nevertheless, are lower-order chiefs representing the practical administrative side of rule. In New Zealand, rangatira are the junior lines of chiefs, whereas tulafale can only be, in the absence of senior lines, general kin of Samoan chiefs. The nature of the genealogical connections are hardly crucial to the historical question, since the relationship between rangatira and ariki is in eastern Polynesia most variable. The broad similarities do suggest a common cultural base.

The Samoan pattern is, of course, distinctive. Alii and tulafale are not related as ranks; they are, as we have already observed, paired as complements. Mead makes this relationship quite clear, by showing the structural parallel between tama tane and tama fafine and alii and tulafale, one as executive, the other as holder of the veto (1930:27). In high-ranking families, she observes, the tulafale have in fact taken over—vis-à-vis the ali'i—the female line prerogatives. In this respect, tulafale represent the elevation of kinship function to a political level. We encounter a parallel situation in Tonga. Mead's structural observation leads to an understanding of ali'i–tulafale as a representative Samoan "bipolar" relationship. The relationship between chief and orator chief connects the two orders of status, rank, and title, binding them into the essential mutual dependence between form and function.

The designation "orator" chief illustrates an important aspect of this dependency. In Samoa, speech had evolved a special code to separate the chiefly from all other realms. Speech has great meaning in content, of course, and in manner of presentation. The speech made by tulafale opens every important occasion and is given an appropriate setting. One village (Fitiuta) had created an ordeal of silence (*alofi sa*) during which the assembly sat mute and immobile for several hours until tulafale broke the spell and began his oration. In the past, it is said, the hapless individual who could not contain his restlessness was put to death. As for content, each official oration announced the order of rank within the fono, paying tribute to the established hierarchy. Eloquence and rhetoric, the embellishment of rank, comes as a reciprocal tribute from executive tulafale to ali'i, on the one hand, and all matais on the other. All matters relating to the chief's personal or intimate affairs had to be described euphemistically, that is to say, honorifically, in their presence. *Ava,* for example, is the common term for wife. The wife of Tui Manu'a is *masiofi,* of a chief, *faletua,* of a talking chief, *tausi,* and as a matter of courtesy to others, *toalua* (Mead 1930:114, 115). The speaker to the chief acknowledges distance; the chief does his part in defending boundaries by allowing his tulafale to speak for him. By acting as the bridge over the gulf dividing chief-nonchief, the tulafale is by standards of rank lower, for the simple reason that the Polynesian concept of a status bridge is that of gradient. As speaker, tulafale is executor, but evidently in the sense in which the priest is executor of the will of the god. Tulafale is not priest: he is to ali'i, as priest is to god. Like a priest, he carries out the concept of chiefship.

Tulafale, nevertheless, is not in the chiefly realm. He is in the area of titles where he represents families and local interests. He manages the formalities of protocol as the honorific side of his prerogatives, and bestows or withdraws powers as its utilitarian side. No wonder all Europeans observing an ali'i as apparent figurehead, and tulafale as the doer, came to the same conclusion as to where the real power lay. One observer (Schultz 1911) claims chiefs were originally the dominating power and tulafale were their servants, then the balance of power shifted. Stair, a most reliable scholar, also saw these two figures of power in constant rivalry, with one in command in one locality, the other in command in another. There is no specific evidence of rivalry. Yet the specific authority of tulafale to empower a chief, to bestow titles, to depose a chief, and submit him to the humiliation of exile clearly creates a rivalrous situation. Candidates for a title and hence for a voice in council (fono) decisions gave presents of mats to the tulafale. In the Euro-American political context, presents are "bribes," corrupting the judgment of the electors and giving unfair advantage to the wealthy. From this point of view, tulafale truly command a strategic post in the power structure. If, however, the internal issues in Samoan village life are not consequential powers but rituals of influence, then it becomes more meaningful to see tulafale as ritual executors of both sides, for the chiefs and for the families whose interest they speak for when they elect or when they depose. The presentation of mats to tulafale is aboveboard, and so is part of the traditional pattern of ritual exchanges. Ali'i assert their own honor by giving mats for food to tulafale. When candidates give mats, they are honored with the same chiefly prerogative.

Rivalry for status is no less real in Samoa than elsewhere in Polynesia. Rivalry is not a defect in what seems to be a stable structure of complementary relationships. It is rather, again as everywhere in Polynesia, integral with the structure. Rivalry imposes on each side the constant test of efficacy. In the Samoan system, the tulafale, as critical links between high and low and between hereditary and achieved statuses, were the best-placed arbiters of personal and family ambitions.

Matai

The system of titles links up with genealogical rank, and has its own table of organization, identified by the generic title, *matai. Matai* means "holder of a title." He is thereby any representative of a family.

He may be ali'i or ordinary household head. Whatever his grade, he holds the honor and dignity of a title bearer, which gives him a voice in the council, the privilege of kava, and the insignia of the fly flap. His specific grade and influence is regulated by history, by a complex and not fully predictable combination of such factors as the traditional rank of his family title, the size of his family, his wealth and personality, and his segmentary level. The common title of matai ranges, then, over the entire spectrum of Samoan rank. The title divides the population categorically into two divisions, the true stratification of Samoan society. As ali'i stands for the formal, the matais are the practical administrators of family affairs, the supervisors of lands and production, and in the fono the voices of the entire village. Precisely because the matai is concerned with practical affairs, with the bread and butter issues of his family, he has an independent jurisdiction. He may be outranked in formal orders of precedence—that is, in sheer honor—but as family head he cannot be bossed. His responsibility is to his own family. On practical matters, the untitled have the final voice on how they are to be administered. Since they name and also depose their own matai, they are truly the ultimate granters of honor. In a large family with branches which hold together, the *matai sili,* or chief matai, has a nominal jurisdiction.

Commoners

Samoa does not lack distinctions between high and low worth. We have considered such absolute status categories as chief–nonchief, titled–untitled, rich–poor, master–subject, specialist–nonspecialist, priest–non-priest. It is the variety of categories, their overlap, and their intricate subdivision of the entire range of honorable roles and activities within which a person in one way or another or at some point or other gains honorable recognition that gives to Samoan society its extraordinary openness. It is possible for Samoans to fall permanently into the bottom bin of sheer nondistinction. At some point the ali'i title does become meaningless; all families have a limited number of titles. Not every family carries the specialist's license. The poor families living in the backwoods lack the goods to make a good show on required ceremonial occasions. Undistinguished and poorly regarded persons there are. What is lacking is a broad encompassing concept of generalized low status as counterpart to generalized high status. The Samoan concept, in the classic spirit of the Open society, is that all can make the grade. If a family is willing to accept the economic challenge, it can split its titles, allowing several to share them. The cost of the feast validating a title is high; but then land is not scarce. Thus, as Grattan has said, "progress from untitled to titled rank is the normal aspiration sooner or later of most adult males (1948:14)." The undistinguished are generally the young. Yet what can "undistinguished" mean when in the final analysis the entire aiga, titled and untitled alike, has a decisive voice in bestowing honors?

Status Rivalry

Rivalry is to status as low is to high: one affirms the other. A position cannot be asserted as worthy unless, as the saying goes, it is worth fighting for. Status systems therefore differ only in their methods of rivalry. Eastern Polynesian rivalry was direct. The lower toppled the higher, replaced them, or pushed them into more specialized positions. These familiar direct actions are not alien to Samoa; they follow the traditional script. Samoan rivalry, however, had evolved and perfected still another version. It reared up counterpart systems. Direct rivalry is openly antagonistic; the counterpart acknowledges the durability, the authenticity, and the uniqueness of the original (ali'i). It rivals by emulating. Emulation includes recognition, of course, of the quality of uniqueness. As a consequence, the status system gains in complexity. Like a jungle growth it luxuriates and reduces contrasts. The focus of status is no longer confined to a center; it disperses itself. Dispersal increases opportunities inhibiting, at the same time, the excesses of antagonisms. While ambition is given latitude the ambitious are restrained by their dependence upon the consensus of councils. Wealth, Mead has observed is "dynamic," since it is convertible to titles. Again, the obligatory pattern of complementary exchange of foods against durables opposes accumulation—lower status giving what is abundant and higher status giving what is scarce—and thus reduces the leverage of wealth. Wealth serves most the interests of the titular system. If title-holders could ever have acquired great wealth and thus a dependent following, their power would surely have heavily overwhelmed the prestige of ali'i. At no point, however, does any person or group break out. All rivalry is restrained. If Samoa had once had a more traditional status system, as Tonga most certainly did, its transformation must surely have occurred slowly.

Descent Group Organization

In general terms, aiga bears a relationship to fono parallel to that between rank and title. Aiga, as an indefinitely extended bilineal family, is the traditional and organic organization. It forms branches, establishing a hierarchically segmental order, and sustains its unity through specific genealogical records. One half of the aiga, its localized and executive branches, resembles the traditional pro-patrilineal lineage and is, in fact, the common line for transmission of ali'i rank and the executive office of matai. The entire aiga, in its extensions of male and female lines, connects with near and distantly related branches from common ancestors, and by criteria of genealogical proximity authenticates rank.

The fono, in its present composition as an organization of family representatives who have created for themselves both the right to sit and a grade in their own rank order, is—like the titular system—a "made" order, but only to a degree. Like the relationship between rank and title, the differences are not polar. The similarities, rather, are out of phase. The organization of the fono runs approximately parallel to that of the families. It, too, has a segmental order, ranging from the Great Fono embracing all of Samoa to the small local fono of villages, and each fono has its independent and self-perpetuating administration. Since the fono is composed of families whose qualities and characteristics it must reflect, it must parallel the aiga organization. But just as title is a more flexible modification of rank, so fono introduces new ranges of possibilities for families. Each family exists in two dimensions: as aiga, with its male and female branches, and managing its own affairs, and as a member of a fono, which gives it specific recognition as an honorable entity. As autonomous, the aiga is concerned mainly with utilitarian interests such as management of land; as member of a fono, it is concerned vis-à-vis others with its grade, with its honor. In a village, all representatives in a fono may be and probably are kinsmen. But while the concept of aiga emphasizes unity of common kinship, the parallel concept of fono must emphasize distinctness. The very idea of a seat in the fono with a backrest at a house post emphasizes particularity. Again we see the appositeness of the fono relationship: fono is to aiga as title is to rank. The fono allows kinsmen to reclassify themselves, to particularize themselves more finely. The Samoan descent group organization includes, therefore, aiga and fono, the latter as an extension of the former.

The Samoan concept of what is its most comprehensive social entity is shadowy and uncertain, drawing upon the archaic tradition of a founding Tui Manu'a lineage. This tradition, nevertheless, implies a sense of an all-Samoan unity. It is a "clan" idea of common origin without genealogical specificity. Presumably this vast genealogical concept of a Segment I has been in recession. Its echoes, however, remain in the ceremonial outcry, "Tui Manu'a thou art my Lord," uttered everywhere in Samoa by the warrior who has taken a head in battle, by mourners at a high chief's funeral, by the court jester of

Opolu at the installation of the tupu, and understandably on Manu'a at all important court occasions (Mead 1930:191–92). The sense of oneness under a god-descended founder is thoroughly traditional, and not entirely void of social significance. It was the basis for the subsequent political unification of Western Samoa and for the parallel concept of an all-Samoan Great Fono.

Too little is known about the Great Fono for us to place it with certainty within a comprehensive Samoan social order. Mead describes it as if it were a conceptualization of the highest order of titles represented throughout the archipelago. It has not assembled, at least in historic times, and may for all we know never have had an actual existence. But it is almost certainly the conceptual counterpart of fono to aiga at the most inclusive social level; or, from the specific point of view of status, the counterpart of title to the concept of highest rank.

Segment I is thus Tui Manu'a and Great Fono. Both are noncorporate, serving mainly as pinnacles for traditions of family honor.

The relationship of the conquest state formed by Savaii, Upolu, and Manono to Segment I is obviously unsettled. The first aim of a state is to establish sovereignty over the entire area incorporated within its traditions. In abstract sociological terms, a corporate Segment I supplants a shadow Segment I. The Samoan "state" was never completed. Within its own territory, however, it had supplanted an older and had become a new Segment I. By all accounts, the Samoan state was still politically undeveloped. The tafa'ifa, or supreme tupu, had reached his paramountcy by force, but the actual authority still rested with lower-order local officials.

In the manner of authenticating the tafa'ifa title and office, we still see the persistent Samoan insistence upon linking two avenues of status and authority. To be acknowledged as paramount, the tafa'ifa had to have at least the appearance of election by the major constituent fonos of the islands.

When we say the Samoan state was undeveloped, we refer, of course, in the main, to the power and authority of the tupu or of the supreme tupu. His powers have been insistently described as "nominal." More accurately it was his official authority that was so uninspiring to Europeans. His powers depended on his personal character. Some conquest chiefs are described as arrogant and oppressive, their followers even more so. Such rulers provoked revolt. Oppression of the toilalo was part of the ritual of humiliation and was not necessarily constant policy. When the tupu made his first royal visit—in the manner of the Hawaiian moi—to all the districts which owed him homage, his followers and attendants who came much behind him damaged the plantings and seized whatever they could carry off (see Stair 1897:81). This was obviously a demonstration of the proper uses of conquest power. On the other hand, the demonstration of the newly established subordinate districts called for reciprocal exchanges of food for mats. The tupu received large quantities of food from the districts, assuming then the heavy burden of repaying with mats. This pattern of complementary exchanges, in essence a ritual defining honorable relations between upper and lower ranks, is about all that can be declared as "economic" in the authority of the tupu. The offerings, Stair reminds us, were really sacred. All food given to the tupu was called *o le taro pa'ia,* "the sacred taro" (1897:82).

The difference between traditional Segment I and its conquest state counterpart is visible but not glaring. The new element is that of force. Rearrangement of the status relations among districts had already been carried out under the title system. Conquest gave to the fono of the dominant district custody of the leading titles in the entire domain. The tupu, after all, was as much a subject of his fono as was any matai. The titles which gave him his scepter and orb were in the repository of his district fono. Since titles normally moved up from lower to higher fonos, force of conquest or of voluntary submission was but one of their several conveyances. The Samoan "conquest state" does not materially alter the structure of Segment I. It remains quasi-kinship (clan model) and ritual.

Segment II is the district, a major subdivision of an island. In pre-European Samoa, there were 10 such subdivisions of equivalent and unranked standing for which there is no generic term. But since the district was headed by a chief who held the traditional title of tui (to which the district name was added), it was undoubtedly an ancient and basic subdivision. Even under tupu or tafa'ifa, the districts remained fully autonomous, subject only to honorific exchanges. The tui, a god-descended chief, is, at least in principle, the ranking head of the ranking family. He represents traditional rank and stands as a founder. The genealogies of all families within a district do not necessarily interconnect, but the concept of common origin and of related descent is, to be sure, quite strong, again on the model of the clan, in the absence of specific information on consanguinity. The aiga of the entire district are represented, though in no regular manner of election or delegation, in its fono, the most comprehensive fono which does, in fact, meet. Having a fono which deliberates on war and peace, on the marriage of its tui, on the reception of distinguished visitors, and finally on ratification of hereditary authority, the district is indeed a corporate and representative body. It is in a limited way the governing body for affairs of the great extended families whose matais are its deliberative officers. The district is a territorial concept. It does not "own" land; it encompasses a territory, the boundaries of which are precisely defined and guarded by "boundary villages," which are first to sound the alarm of encroachment, and it has as its "capital" the village of its tui. Since the tui is more of a religious than an administrative figure, his capital has never been an economic center. He was never entitled to tribute other than exceptional first fruit or gift offerings. His economic relations with subordinates are in terms of the ritual of honorific exchange.

Segment III is what Williamson has called a "village district," a grouping of related villages, and closer, therefore, to a consanguineal concept. However, to identify or to seek to identify the village district as a body of kin is to ignore the Samoan point of view, which chooses to distinguish between aiga and fono—that is between kinship and title. Even if kinship were indeed the actual substratum of relationship in Segment III, we would still need to acknowledge the Samoan distinctions between self-governing aiga, the effective kin, and generalized kinship.

In manner of organization, Segment III resembles II. The differences are largely quantitative: generalized ties are more frequent, the territory is smaller, the chief is of lower rank, and the involvement of the fono in domestic and economic affairs is greater. The ali'i of the village district has only minor authority. The fono, however, acts as a court with authority to punish severely, imposing fines, even the death penalty, and ordering the destruction of property. Villages represented in the fono are often closely related, some linked as branches of each other. Meeting at the village of its elected chief, the fono of the village district recognizes one of its villages as ascendant, and as its capital center. Representation is, of course, dual, including, on the one hand, each village as a social and economic entity concerned with the practical issues of administration, and, on the other, each representative matai as the holder of a title and conscious of the appropriate order of precedence. Since precedence implies influence, quality of title and voice in practical affairs are inevitably related. The practical affairs are the deliberations on punishment. The preoccupation is with affairs of honor, namely, adultery with chief's wife, insult, and theft. Theft in an economy of subsistence collectivism is nothing less than the insult of internal aggression.

The village (Segment IV) repeats the structure of the village district. Except in war time, no village is actually under the jurisdiction of a higher body. Only persons and particular families come under the wrath of the village district; but the village as represented by its own fono has no peacetime master. It deals with other villages bilaterally and not through a higher fono. It has its own standards of residence and may refuse to admit a high-ranking chief from another village. Each village, except for those deficient in titles, has all the organs and positions of honor and authority available to higher organizations. It is a complete and essentially self-sufficient organism. It has its own god, its priests, its ali'i, its tulafale, its matai, its fono, its taupou, its manaia, and its own code of ceremonial precedence. When a village is represented in a higher fono, it gains in honor and loses nothing in sovereignty. Since warfare does bring villages under higher authority, Western Samoa had a more dependent segmental structure than Manu'a.

Samoan villages are large, averaging in Western Samoa some 300–500, and including from 10 to 20 titled heads of families as representative matais in the fono. If the village district comprises related families, the village is almost inevitably an aggregate of kin. Nevertheless, kinship is not the principle of its organization. Again, it is the title, whose precise function is to segregate generalized kin, that gives the village fono the appearance of a political council rather than that of a family conclave. The Samoan conception of social structure is of consciously asserted autonomy. The nature of linkage through a series of councils does not overcome autonomy. On the contrary, the ritual life of the fono, which is its most compelling interest, proclaims in every action that its constituents are integral and autonomous.

In the village fono, however, where the scale is small and where the social title of the village invites collective action, the point of separation between autonomy and coordination cannot be precisely located. This fono has a truly sweeping jurisdiction: it undertakes to build a chief's house, and a village guest house; to organize fishing expeditions; to build and maintain municipal fish traps; to organize the collective food supply for all village ceremonies by regulating consumption and then gathering in the supplies; to ration foods in an emergency. It has judicial authority, and it is the judge of who shall exercise the prerogatives of rank and title. Sweeping as this jurisdiction seems, its principal concern is, nevertheless, with the status of its constituents, and rather less with its subsistence. Bread-and-butter issues still remain the private concern of the individual family.

Aiga

Since it is represented in the village fono by virtue of the titles it holds in trust, the aiga might be considered an ultimate constituent of each village and thus a Segment V. Aiga, however, is more than household. With its two branches of local male line and dispersed female lines, it extends past the boundary of village. When it is the powerful and high-ranking family of a great chief, its membership and its branches have in effect a national distribution. Such large aiga are branched to a degree in a manner resembling traditional status lineage segmentation. No Samoan observer has suggested, however, that aiga segmentation has been systematically carried out, even among the greatest families, where conditions for branching are most suitable. As for unimportant families, they inevitably remain small and local.

Aiga and fono share jurisdiction over land. Aiga is the primary holder of tenure; it is the primary producer and primary consumer. Its matai holds the administrative authority for assigning cultivations and supervising joint labors. The tama tane, the resident branch, has what Mead has called the active rights of administration; the tama fafine has the perpetual right to claim membership in the local group or, most generally, rights of cultivation. Aiga membership thus gives persons economic rights beyond the village. There is no conflict between such two-sided claims on land. Land is not scarce and a matai can only welcome more people. At the same time, the assignment of administrative rights moves clearly within its local channels down the male line.

Following the pattern of fono is to aiga as tama fafine is to tama tane, the fono has its own claims over aiga lands and produce. As I have said before, the fono exacts what is due to its honor, whether this is a matter of levying assessments for ceremonial events, destroying crops and trees punitively, or banishing offenders. It has, however, no rights of administration over aiga lands.

Status and Descent Group

The almost complete disappearance in Samoa of a consistently ramified descent group organization must be attributed specifically to the rise of the fono. Mead has said as much:

> The present structure of Manu'a society suggests very vividly the way in which the political unit, the *fono,* had usurped, borrowed, readapted, or paralyzed the functions of the different members of the descent groups and of the descent groups themselves. This gradual accretion of power has followed two main lines: the ever-increasing control exercised by the *fono* over the choice and behavior of *matais,* and the arrogation by the village organization of the role of the descent group of the highest chief (1930:26).

Mead sets off politics (fono) against kinship (aiga) and, correspondingly, local group (village) against descent groups. The fono though is more heraldic than political: it is concerned more with honor than with administration. When the fono represents locality, it is again the administration of honor. We may conclude, therefore, that the Samoan descent group organization was transformed as everywhere else in Polynesia, namely, by alterations in the system of status.

The fono is, after all, the family system reclassified by more flexible means than the traditional categories of seniority, primogeniture, and male line descent allow. The titles upon which the fono organization rests are status subdivisions of families, replacing traditional and named branches of senior and junior lines. In their privilege of electing their own membership, the fono act as elite academies. In the main they choose from among their most prestigious constituencies, anyway. Still, having a choice and being influenced by several kinds of considerations, they eventually create a new, their own kind of ranking, not radically different from the old, but different. Once the academies have taken clear control of the most important of all Samoan duties, the certification of status, the aiga are reduced. They hold only one pole of status, in itself incomplete, and can concern themselves more directly with their primordial bread-and-butter business. To the extent to which descent groups become utilitarian, they cease to grow. In aristocracy, growth is an affair of honor.

12

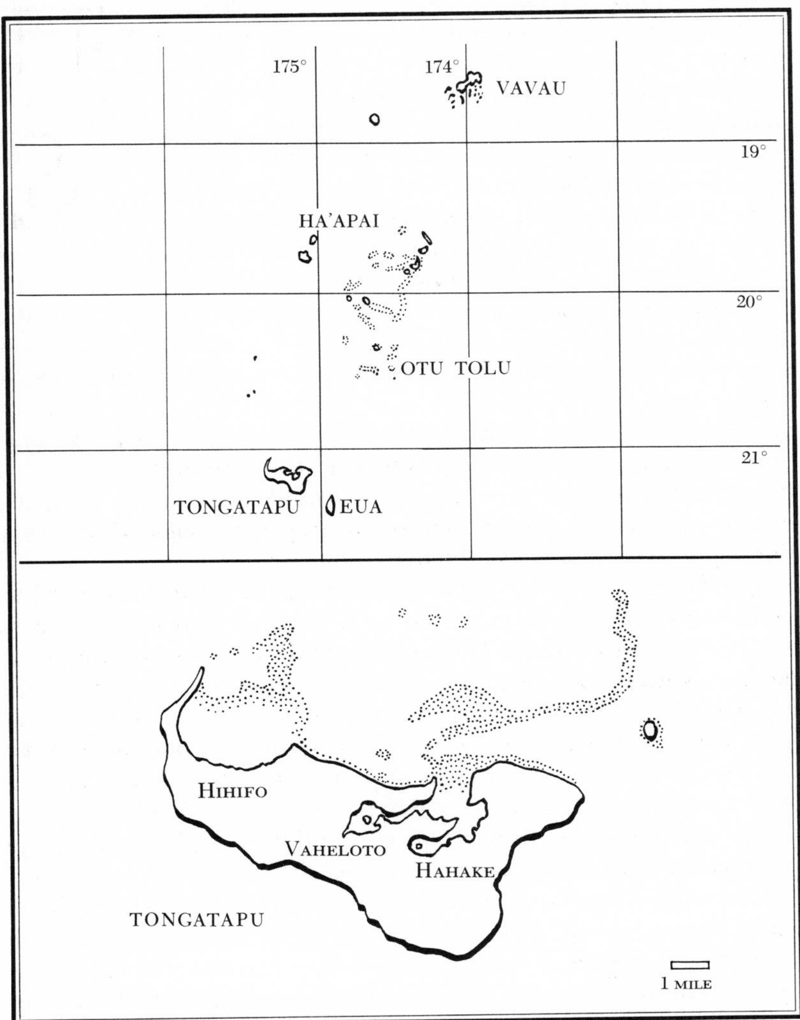
175°
174°
VAVAU
19°
HA'APAI
20°
OTU TOLU
21°
TONGATAPU
EUA
HIHIFO
VAHELOTO
HAHAKE
TONGATAPU
1 MILE

Tonga

TONGA IS THE STRATIFIED FORM OF THE WESTERN POLYNESIAN status system, having carried forward a political evolution that in Western Samoa, for example, was still incomplete. Variations between Tonga and Samoa do not, however, move in a single direction; they diverge as much as they run parallel. The main parallels are with Western Samoa; the divergences, with Manu'a. Where Manu'a, in particular, had elaborated dual and bipolar patterns of status, casting off seniority, and single line pro-patriliny, Tonga retained seniority, orderly genealogical rank, and branched pro-patrilineal lineages. Only in its later periods did this traditional Polynesian system begin to change. In parallel with Samoa, Tonga had evolved its own and more fully political version of dual and bipolar social structures.

Tongan and Samoan social systems are unquestionably cognate. Their divergences are no doubt due to the normal "drift" of physical separation. Linguistically, for example, Samoan and Tongan are much further apart than Tongan-Uvean or Samoan-Tikopian or, speaking of eastern Polynesia, Tahitian, Hawaiian (cf. Elbert 1953). Separation accounts only for general divergence. The specific differences are in political direction—in the degree of centralization and in the quality of power and of authority. The nature of power seems to have been the major variable in social differentiation.

Specific and close relations between Samoa and Tonga, referred to in the traditions of both, are dated by archeology back to at least A.D. 100 (Golson 1961). Early Tongan pottery points to even earlier connections with New Caledonia. The long-continued association with Fiji, the closest Melanesian-speaking society, is also early. Like Samoa, Tonga was involved in two cultural traditions. Both held to the Melanesian custom of reciprocal respects between male line and female lines, while Tonga remained closer to the Fijian and New Caledonian standards of patriliny, seniority, and genealogical rank. Quite possibly the very close relations between Tonga and Fiji could have reinforced the Tongan commitment to patrilineal lines, although the Fijian descent group, an exogamous, patrilocal, and patrilineal clan, differs in its categorical standards of membership from the traditional pro-patrilineal lineage of Tonga. Tonga acquired from Fiji its military "technology," and possibly its megalithic tradition.

The megalithic tradition places Tonga within the technical orbit of the more developed eastern Polynesian societies. Tonga's great stone works were monuments for great chiefs; only its stone fortifications could be considered public works. A unique monument, the so-called Trilithon, is a gateway of three slabs of cut stone, each weighing some 30 tons. Most monuments are chiefly tombs, the greatest of which are but low three- to five-tiered mounds of earth faced with dressed stone. Apart from some stelae and petroglyphs, stone was not an artistic medium. As in Samoa, artistry was on the small scale.

Ecologically, the islands are not prepossessing. The archipelago includes some 160 islands, most quite small and only three of great size: Tongatabu (100 sq. miles), Vavau (46 sq. miles), Haapai (20 sq. miles). Only three other islands, Eva, Niuafo'ou, and Niuatoputapu, were regularly inhabited. Among the large islands, only Vavau is volcanic and very fertile. The others are coral outcrops—makatea islands—whose soils are poorer. What these low and flat coral islands lack in soil quality, however, they gain in general arability. The three main islands supported as many as 25,000 people at a moderately high population density of over 150 per square mile. At the time of its discovery, Tongatabu, the center of Tongan culture, was so densely inhabited a message could be sent by voice alone, it has been said, from one end of the island to the other. Like all island dwellers, the Tongans have had experience with famine, but the general impression the islands have given is of economic adequacy, neither of great abundance nor of dire need. The first Europeans were pleasantly impressed at the sight of neatly fenced plantations and well cared for cultivations of yam, taro, and sweet potato, of stands of plantain, breadfruit, and coconut trees, and numbers of pigs and fowl. Makatea islands often lack lagoons. Fishing, nevertheless, was important, if somewhat difficult. The Tongans, in a cruder version of the Hawaiian fish ponds, built stone walls across channel outlets to dam the fish brought in by the tide.

The first European contact was inexplicably hostile. The Dutch explorers Schouten and Lemaire anchored off Niuatoputapu in 1616 and had to beat off a furious attack. Yet when Tasman came a generation later (1616), his reception was friendly. Tasman saw neither weapons nor fortifications, and came away with the impression of "friendly" islands. Wallis stopped for only one day in 1767, so that between Tasman's visit and the Tongan's first real experience with Europeans in the person of Cook and crew, some 130 years had passed. Cook's first visit (1773) was brief. On his return call four years later, the islands were already in great political turmoil. The warrior chiefs of Vavau were on the move, the Tui Tonga was losing his grip, and Cook's own life was, then unknown to him, imperiled. Cook could not fail to sense political turbulence, but there was little open violence and he christened Tonga the "Friendly Islands." However, when the London Missionary Society arrived in 1797 to take up its strenuous labors, the political fever had reached its peak, and for the next half century missionaries, traders, diplomats, and soldiers of fortune did all in their power to help a new nation come to life. In 1845 a chief from an important family was finally crowned King George I.

Like Samoa, Tonga became deeply involved with Europe and yet did not surrender its own traditions. The new monarchy was fashioned on the cut of the old. Chiefs and gentry retained their customary privileges, and commoners remained where they had been. The shift from dominant and honorable land tenure to European standards of private property was relatively simple. As late as 1941 Beaglehole could write:

> Despite years of contact with an invading western European culture, village culture has adapted itself with very considerable success to the strains and tensions that engendered. There has been adaptation but not extinction (1941:4).

Tongan culture is among the better known in Polynesia. An early account going back to 1806 describes the period of greatest political evolution. An anthropological study of 1920 recaptures the traditions and recollections of earlier periods and presents an authentic account of the Tongan social system. These major studies, the first by William Mariner, who spent four years as an adopted son of the chief of Vavau, and the second by Gifford (1929), are supplemented and in all important respects corroborated by subsequent studies.

Genealogical Traditions

The traditions concern mainly the sacred Tui Tonga dynasty, which came to an end in 1845 with the coronation of George Toupou as a Christian monarch. By generation count, the dynasty dates back to A.D. 950, with Tangaroa-descended Ahoeitu. The offspring of the Sky-God and a Tongan woman, Ahoeitu lived in the sky and was sent down with his half-brothers to rule. However, only he held the divine right, and his brothers were reduced to the position of ordinary chiefs. The origin tales state the familiar themes of sibling hostility. Ahoeitu had been killed by his half-brothers while still in the sky. He is sent to earth to rule after his resurrection. As a descendant of the god, Ahoeitu replaces, according to the tale, a previous Tui Tonga who had been descended from worms, an interesting variation on the Samoan viewpoint. Similarly, an origin tale recorded by Mariner, as known only to chiefs, tells a Cain and Abel fable of two sons of Tangaloa who divide the land and live separately. One is industrious, the other indolent and envious of his richer brother, who is also the younger. He kills his industrious brother and his family is punished by being made black-skinned and the family of the murdered brother are made wealthy and fair-skinned (Mariner 1817:I, 122). The references in the traditions to an earlier Tui Tongan dynasty lack details. By omissions, the traditions imply autochthonous origins for the original Tongans. The positive assertion is of original separation of people and rulers. This separatist tradition was later applied to the Tongan court, which had imported its administrative corps from Fiji.

Several Tui Tonga lists have been compiled by various authorities, including the Tongan court. Drawing upon the official registers, and reconciling discrepancies among six of the fullest genealogical records, Gifford has produced the most responsible version of traditional Tongan history. This is what I have drawn upon for the following summary of main events.

Little is recorded about the first ten Tui Tonga other than the nature of royal succession—from father to son—and the observation that the tenth was called also *hau*, the Tongan title for secular ruler. The tenth Tui Tonga may actually have given a new turn to the office, for he is also supposed to have started the practice of uniting the sacred with secular chiefly lines through intermarriage.

With the eleventh, the famous Tui Tonga Tuitatui, the turn is unmistakable. His rule, beginning ca. 1200, coincides with the occupation of Samoa (by Samoan accounts), and with the introduction of monumental stone works. His name, which means "Lord-who-strikes-the-knee," is explained by the traditions as a reference to his striking those who came near him—because he feared assassination. When a ruler must defend his personal boundaries with a stick, the quality of his position has surely changed. Although the first recorded assassination of a Tui Tonga does not take place for another 200 years, it is the concept of encroachment, of breakdown of "distance," that stands out as important at this earlier time. Succession continues to be filial, for when Talama, the twelfth ruler, had no son and heir, he had to create a ritual version of proper inheritance. The rule passed to Talama's brother, but first a wooden image was made to be the "father" who "died," leaving the brother as the filial successor.

With the assassination of the 19th, 22d, and 23d, Tui Tongas, Tongan dynastic history enters a new period of violence and instability. The circumstances of the first assassination are not known, but the second, Havea II, was liquidated by Fijians at the instigation of Tongan chiefs who dared not themselves defy the royal tapus. Thereafter the royal presence inspired no such awe. Takalaua, the twenty-third Tui Tonga, was the victim of fellow Tongans who struck the mortal blows themselves. The saga of their pursuit through all the Tongan

Islands, through Samoa, Uvea and Futuna, points to new political conditions; for the traditions say that during the pursuit through Tonga all its islands were brought under political control, and Futuna was occupied as a Tongan colony. The comment on the conquest of Tongan islands implies a new form of sovereignty, a change from traditional and sacred headship to political overlordship.

The nature of administrative reorganization that occurred in the very next royal generation also suggests a new political orientation. Takalaua's son and successor divided the royal authority, retaining for himself the priestly and sacred side and yielding to his younger brother the temporal powers. This reform—so much in the Polynesian character—comes toward the end of the Tongan occupation of Samoa. In specific pattern it is a close parallel to the Samoan political doctrine of bipolar rule. A new title was created, Tui Haa Takalaua, and a new lineage the Haa Takalaua (not to be confused with the patrilineal lineage of the Tui Tonga Takalaua) was elevated to lower but complementary authority. In Tonga as in Samoa, the lower overcame the higher. The office of Tui Haa Takalaua became the powerful one, and the traditions no longer dwell on the history of the Tui Tongas. They are left behind as voluptuaries, enjoying indolence, good food, and beautiful women. The action shifts to the temporal and more energetic quarters.

Shirley Baker, a missionary on Tonga who has recorded the traditional accounts of the new secular office, writes that the division of authority was intended to safeguard the sacred ruler from future assassination. The Takalaua was made hau and was given a direct and permanent linkage with the Tui Tonga line by agreement of perpetual intermarriage between their two lines. The Tui Tonga line would marry Takalaua women (cited by Gifford 1929:85).

By 1610 the central authority divided again. The then Tui Haa Takalaua named a younger son to be his temporal representative, creating still another title, Tui Kanokupolu, and elevating to prominence the Kanokupolu lineage. Sir Basil Thomson, the first British Prime Minister of Tonga, was told that the Takalaua had wearied of the burdens of his office and passed it on to a younger man. Caillot offers the more interesting and, I believe, more credible explanation for this second repartition: Takalaua, having become more powerful and more like the Tui Tonga, asserts and affirms his new standing by establishing his own secular and complementary counterpart. Ultimately, it was the Kanokupolu line which overcame all and founded the present day Toupou dynasty in Tonga.

Both basically hau-type rulers, the Tui Haa Takalaua and the Tui

Kanokupolu were immediately locked in rivalry for the supreme power, with one another and with other chiefs. The third Kanokupolu, known as "The Hunchback," was at war with his son who had illegitemate designs on the Takalaua title. The fifth Kanokupolu was overthrown by a local chieftain who had already taken command over all of Vavau. In 1777 Cook was witness to the thwarted effort of a woman to wrest the succession for herself from her father, the seventh Kanokupolu. The eighth incumbent was assassinated in a widespread plot promoted by his brother and the subordinate chieftains. Each time the successor was stronger and more ruthless; his power and effective authority exceeded that of Takalaua and, of course, left Tui Tonga in the shade. Gifford sums up the last stages of pre-European Tongan history succinctly:

> The Tui Haa Takalaua had declined in power even more rapidly than the Tui Tonga and so fell an easy prey to the grasping Tui Kanokupolu. The similarity of functions of the two offices made the absorption the easier (1929:29).

The Archeological Record

The most recent archeological survey affirms the close early Melanesian connections of Tonga and provides indirect evidence that its culture is as ancient as the Samoan (Golson 1961). Thus far, archeology has produced neither radiocarbon dates nor stratigraphy that would reveal either the actual time of earliest occupation, and of the original separation from Samoa, or the specific sequences of cultural development. Glottochronology, however, dates the Samoan-Tongan separation at between A.D. 300–530 (Elbert 1953). By the time of the Tongan occupation of Samoa, both had undergone some 900 years of independent development.

For internal development, the archeological source is McKern's pioneer study of surface remains (1929). McKern was able to deduce a developmental sequence from stylistic variation and from information supplied by genealogical traditions, which identify all major tombs and other works with a particular Tui Tonga. If the traditions are correct in dating the *langi,* for example, as late as ca. 1200, then, of course, we are dealing with relatively recent history and the probability of error in assigning dates is reduced.

McKern's survey found no evidence to suggest that Tongan culture was anything but a local development. The Fijian influence was strong but not overpowering; and whatever Tongans imported they reshaped in their own style.

Mounds of various types, shapes and style of construction are the most conspicuous archeological feature on the Tongan landscapes. McKern (1929:70) identified the following five types:

1. *Esi*—raised circular mounds on which chiefs and their families prepared to take their ease. They symbolized, of course, chiefly separation and elevation, and they also gave a view of the sea—as a rule one of the privileges of status in Polynesia—and were high enough to catch a fresh breeze.
2. Pigeon mounds. Chiefs snared pigeons from artificial elevations, while commoners snared them directly on the ground.
3. *Tanuanga*—very small burial mounds, no larger than an ordinary grave site where the common people were buried.
4. *Faitoka*—large earthen mounds shaped like truncated cones, within which ordinary chiefs and their principal retainers were buried. The bodies were placed in stone vaults. The faitoka are quite large. The largest on Haapai has a diameter of 110 feet at the base and 40 feet at the top, and a height of 15 feet. This belonged to the most important family on the island.
5. *Langi.* McKern found 45 royal tombs, a number in excess of the number of known Tui Tonga. But the sacred chiefs sometimes built a tomb in one place and then decided to locate it elsewhere. Thus there are just 37 tombs at Mua, the ancient capital of the Tui Tonga on Tongatabu. Six are on Hoopai and two on Vavau. All langi are immediately recognized as different from faitoka. They are rectangular, as against the circularity of the lesser form. As they follow the succession of Tui Tonga, the langi evolve in monumentality. The earliest are rectangular earthen mounds. They acquire stone facings and monumental character starting in the thirteenth century and reach their climax in the sixteenth with the great five-stepped Telea (29th Tui Tonga) tomb. After the establishment of the Tui Kanokupolu, a rapid decline in quality and size sets in, and the last langi return to the old earthern form.

The Trilithon known to Tongans as "The burden of Maui carried on a carrying stick" (*haamongaamaui*) ushered in the megalithic age. Built by Tuitatui, it was intended, Tongans say, as a reminder of fraternal unity. It was Tuitatui's message to his sons not to quarrel. Two great upright limestone slabs united by a massive cross-piece convey the message.

Among more strictly utilitarian works, Tongans built great stone fortifications resembling the Maori *pa.* The preoccupation was with the symbolic, however. For example, a crude stone wall ran across an isthmus on Vavau, erected, according to tradition, as a memorial to primogeniture. When the first-born was a son, a stone was set in place so that eventually the wall recorded all the senior scions of the district. The comparison with the Tahitian marae, whose stones were also lineage "documents," comes immediately to mind.

Historical Recapitulation

Gifford (1929:349), drawing both upon McKern and the traditions, has postulated four main epochs of Tongan history: *Predynastic* (A.D. 500–950); *Classic* (950–1450); *Decline and Disintegration* (1450–1845); *Renaissance and European Acculturation* (1845–to present). This classification of the historical trajectory can hardly be improved upon, since it is based upon specific and decisive events. With only minor amendment it can be converted to express the course of evolution of the status system.

In the light of Golson's more recent work, the Predynastic should probably extend back to the beginnings of the Christian era, giving it a duration close to a millenium. Mainly on the basis of negative evidence, the Predynastic would appear as an era of small communities without central authority. However, taking New Zealand as a model, we can leap to no conclusions about segmentary organization. Perhaps monuments cannot be built without a central authority; a central authority of the Maori form of waka ariki can, however, exist without monuments.

The Classic, an age of central authority opening with Ahoeitu and closing with the period of assassinations, resembles the Traditional society. Authority is mainly religious, and the social structure is categorically discriminatory, maintaining pro-patrilineal lineages, branched and ranked by seniority. The period divides readily into two distinctive phases: an early phase from 950–1200, when the authority of the Tui Tonga may be presumed to have been more completely religious, and a later phase starting at 1200 with Tuitatui, or perhaps with his predecessor referred to as the hau. During the second phase, which includes such impressive evidences of chiefly prowess as the Samoan occupation, the strengthening of the military establishment by way of new relations with Fiji, and the start of monumental architecture, the central authority has moved out into new and more kinetic demonstrations of power. The megalithic tradition alone reveals new aspects of power in the ability of the Tui Tonga to carry out the works administratively and in the symbolic equation of the "made" monumental with the organic monumental (the inherent stature of the royal line). Architectural monumentality stands for one dimension of growth, the Samoan occupation for another. In its later phase, the

Tongan traditional order gains in power and enters upon a cycle of growth and expansion. Has it changed basically in structure? That is difficult to say, because there is so little specific information. As long as the Tui Tongaship retained its own hold, the traditional lineages and traditional patterns of succession and of patterned kinship relations between male and female lines were in all probability unaltered. The entire social structure was, in fact, "keyed" to the Tui Tongaship.

There is reason to believe that the system of land holdings which found the commoners in a condition of exceptional inferiority had undergone a gradual evolution starting with the Tongan Traditional, or Classic period. All information agrees that the land title was traditionally held by Tui Tonga. He allocated holdings by rank and received honorific tribute in first fruits. When the character of land relations reached the point where commoners could be evicted at will (Thomson 1894:230), we do not know. Interpolating from other Polynesian societies, including Samoa, we can assume that the specific character of tenure depended on the nature of Tui Tonga authority. Religious chiefs held honorable tenure and received honorific tribute. The dividing line between this form of tenure and political tenure with freedom to grant lands and to evict would have come during the late phase of the Classic, since all traditional accounts agree that the system of land tenure first observed by Europeans had already been in force under the strong Tui Tonga. If this is indeed the case, Tonga is an example of direct transformation from Traditional to Stratified resulting from steady accretion in the powers of the Tui Tonga.

Gifford's "Decline and Disintegration" is, of course, the Open society, but at a different level, for it marks the breakdown of an apparent Stratified society and not merely the prelude to stratification. However, the political characteristics of the Tongan "Open" are essentially those of the violent Open societies everywhere in Polynesia: sanctity declines; the gap widens between sacred and secular authority; war rearranges status and power; political turbulence intensifies; control of lands shifts from the royal authority to local chieftains.

The Tongan "Renaissance," coming largely under European influence, restored the central authority and stabilized the Stratified society. George I (Tupou), a descendant of the Kanokupolu line, assumed all three titles to which he had genealogical claim, thus returning—though under a European title—all powers that had once been divided to their single source. The system of land tenure under the new regime was the same as under the strong Tui Tonga. All land belongs to the crown. The nobility have their own estates under "feudal" tenure, and from government estates land grants of at least 8.5 acres are given as tax holdings to each male Tongan as he comes of age (Nayacakalou 1959). Today, as in the past, holdings are individual not collective.

The Status System

As a cognate system, the Tongan is the more powerful version of the Samoan. We have only to compare Tui Tonga with Tui Manu'a, both Tangaroa-descended. The latter declined very rapidly from a religious eminence; the former achieved commanding stature comparable to that of a Hawaiian high chief. Western Samoa shared the Tongan respect for power and contempt for weakness, but did not act upon this doctrine as fiercely as did the Tongans. Both versions of the same system adhered to the bipolar patterns of balances. The Samoan pattern promoted restraints; the Tongan intensified powers. Both were committed to the wide distribution of honor throughout the entire population, but the Tongan system of land tenure undermined in the most serious manner the advantages of formal respects granted by a courtly kinship system. To state the differences epigrammatically: Samoa espoused form foremost, Tonga power. The Tongan system was therefore aggressive and developing.

Primogeniture

The first-born son took the title, the social position, and the leadership in the family. The higher the office and rank, the stronger was the commitment to primogeniture. Lower-ranking chiefs pushing upward through the avenues of power could bypass the genealogical roadblock, but the traditional ranks could not. In the organization of the family, a bastion of traditionalism, and in the structure of the Tui Tonga lineage, the rights of the first-born, the *ulumatua,* were not to be set aside. There is no certainty on the other hand, that primogeniture was as crucial to succession to the two great collateral lines of Tui Tonga. Both titles, Takalaua and Kanokupolu, were fought over from time to time, and in the later times (eighteenth century) the Tui Kanokupolu was appointed—in the Samoan manner—by his fellow chiefs, acting as electors.

Primogeniture is unquestionably a foremost element in rank, but within a pattern that allows—outside the Tui Tonga descent line—for variability. The pattern includes the factor of sex: the sister outranks her brother in formal honor. It offers a choice between direct filial succession to authority and collateral, that is, younger brother. In principle, honor and authority are separable; in practice, honor has a claim and a sister may succeed to command (cf. Gifford 1929:20). When the younger brother succeeds to authority, the first-born son (or paternal nephew) is left "high and dry," or as a contender. The actual preference as revealed by the genealogies is for filial succession.

Seniority of Descent

Tonga combined traditional grading of ranks by relative seniority with a pattern of bilateral ranking based upon the constant superiority of a sister's to a brother's line. The first established the bases for public or general rank; the second modified deferences and respects owed to general rank within the domestic sphere. Public rank is, to be sure, the basic rank, and so Tongan concepts of seniority of descent may be considered to be the same as those of traditional eastern Polynesia. The differences lie in the relationships between closely related families. In eastern Polynesia, families stood to one another as senior-junior, regardless of their public rank but simply by virtue of relative seniority of brothers. In Tonga, relative seniority was joined by the constant hierarchy of the sexes. Eastern Polynesia followed through the implications of seniority consistently; Tonga juxtaposed the seniority principle with one of an entirely different character. Thus the Tongan appearances are traditional; the specific pattern is distinctive.

In eastern Polynesia, to continue with the comparison, gradation by seniority may encompass—Maori is a good example—a substantial part of the ethnic community. In principle, there is no reason why this should not be true of Tonga as well. All chiefs are related to one another and all can claim theoretical descent from the Tui Tonga. Through the titled chiefs, all of Tonga knits theoretically into one vast genealogical net along which the public rank of each person can be precisely charted. In theory, each great lineage is, as in eastern Polynesia, a branch of a larger concept of connection that goes beyond the range of actual kin ties but lends authenticity to the scheme of rank founded upon seniority. Early Tonga of the Classic period may have been organized in this way. Gifford could not, however, discover family genealogies, outside the royal lines, which reached back earlier than 1600. Genealogical discontinuities are easily understood as a consequence of the breakdown of some lineages and the rapid growth of others in a period of social disorder. Conceivably, in earlier periods all were linked by seniority. Those are conjectures. What is actually known is a system of limited application of the seniority principle. Major lineages, Gifford observes, branched into minor and dependent lower-rank segments. Small lineages were less fully differentiated. The most traditional form of segmentation involved finally the related royal lineages of Tui Tonga, Haa Takalaua, and Haa Kanokupolu.

Male Line

The principle has already been stated. Very much as in Samoa, the male line organized power and all utilitarian functions; the female lines controlled the more abstract honors. Tonga, though, was more strongly bilineal than Samoa, which had moved farther along toward more even-handed bilaterality. Thus, while the Samoan aiga united male and female lines within a corporate kinship community, the Tongan equivalent, the *haa,* was what Gifford has called a patrilineal lineage. It was more specifically pro-patrilineal. The haa was the focus of power and the central unit of Tongan social organization. It was not, however, the whole of the social organization.

The patrilineal principle is founded upon the elementary conditions of sexual equivalence which place all nuclear males within the same realm, with potentially interchangeable roles, but regulated and separated by grade (order of birth). Equivalence being a single realm represents, so to speak, a single track. It invites rivalry and competition despite gradation. For this reason alone it is a political realm.

The bilineal principle is founded upon the elaboration of the equally elementary conditions of sexual complementarity of siblings of opposite sex. Brother and sister occupy eternally distinct realms; they move on different tracks. They are, in principle, noncompetitive, and their relationships are patterned to be nonpolitical. They "relate" via respects which assert distance.

Parts of all social structures are built around these two elementary conditions. Tonga has developed them in its own manner. The relationship between brother and sister was known as *fakaapaapa*—"to reverence, to respect, to honor (Gifford 1929:21)." Honoring was through avoidance. Brother and sister lived in different houses after the age of ten. Thereafter they no longer ate together or conversed. Eating is a domestic and familiar action, and its patterning in Tonga, as everywhere in Polynesia, defines status relationships precisely. In Tonga, inferiors never ate in the presence of superiors. Even Tui Tonga respected the elders of his family by not eating in their presence.

Brother-sister avoidance is per se a reciprocal display of respects, an even-handedness. Tonga, however, was wholeheartedly dedicated to status inequality. No two persons held the same rank. The sister was superior to the brother on the single coordinate of respects. Gifford says: "As the sister is superior in rank to the brother, so also are her children, both male and female. Moreover, the sister's children are superior to the brother's children (Gifford 1929:22)."

It is these unequal relationships of honor that create counterparts to the patrilineal organization of the haa. The descent lines of brother and sister may coexist within the same haa (which was not exogamous), or occupy distinct lineages. They form in either case a special ritual kinship community that exchanges respects in a rather intricate manner. As brother and sister avoid each other, their offspring interact powerfully. Cousins intermarry, even though by kinship classification they are "siblings." As children of siblings of opposite sex, they complete the pattern: the separation in one generation is overcome in the next and introduces still another variant of sexual complementarity—that between husband and wife.

Tongan cross-cousin marriage was common enough, but not preferred. The preferred relationship between brother and sister lines was not merger as resulted from intermarriage, but continued distinction. The *fahu* (sister's children) maintained the connections and the ritual separation by their economic rights over their mother's brother and over his line of descendants. The fahu may appropriate property freely. In return they are owed deference and respect. The brother's line is donor under compulsion, a reduction in status; the sister's line has the honor to make demands and to receive deference. "The institution of the *fahu*," says Gifford, "is a one-sided non-reciprocal affair (1929:23)." From the single and limited standpoint of the movement of goods, that is so. From the broader point of view of the brother-sister relationship, fahu carry out their part in a pattern of status balances—reciprocity. The sister, for example, has honor, but not political status. Her offspring, however, have both the honor of deference and the political status of seizing or of demanding property. The fahu are defined as "above the law (Gifford 1929:23)." This gives them a regal equivalence.

The fahu relationship is presently widespread in Tonga. In the past it was a ritual connection restricted to chiefs. One can readily understand the restriction, for fahu complements an authentic political right with a ritual counterpart. The ancient relationship between Tui Tonga and Kanokupolu is illustrative. When Tui Tonga married a Kanokupolu daughter, as became customary, his son and heir—to take only this crucial example—was fahu to the Kanokupolu son and heir. Thus the basic superiority of Tui Tonga and his line over the Kanokupolu line was reinforced, and yet also softened, for there is a difference between an authentic political right and its ritual counterpart. This, of course, is a limited statement of the pattern in "ideal" form. Kanokupolus were, of course, the dominant political authority and Tui Tonga line was in recession. Consequently, ritual political and authentic political rights joined in a new equilibrium.

As people have ritual political rights over mother's brother, they must submit themselves in deference to father's sister, the awesome *mehekitanga.* She is the supreme being in the family and is owed the avoidances of brother to sister. Herself a subject of avoidance, she has jurisdiction over marriages (familiarity). Her very high honor undoubtedly combines the privileges of sisters over brothers and of the older generation over the younger. Fathers and fathers' brothers are also owed respect, but that of generation alone.

In relations between husband and wife and between paternal and maternal families, the patterning is simple. The man is the executive of the family regardless of rank; correspondingly, the paternal side is *eiki,* or chiefly, the maternal, the lower or "commoner."

Genealogical Depth

Only the Tui Tonga lineage going back 39 generations had depth. The Takalaua and Kanokupolu as junior branches are as old. All other chiefly descent lines are recent. Granted a drastic realignment of lineages after 1600 would interrupt descent lines, the utter failure of all lines other than the royal to retain some connection with the past expresses a point of view. Late Tonga certainly had polarized its attitudes, leaving the traditional genealogical doctrines in the care of royalty and basing distinctions among all other lineages upon other considerations.

Linearity

By and large, strict patriliny (linearity) was aristocratic and confined to the major royal lineages. Linearity was a direct function of political strength. The strong retained their patrilineal descent lines and kept their lineages intact. The weak had to seek advantages wherever they could, searching out matrilineal connections, affiliating with expanding lineages, or being absorbed by them.

Sanctity

Tonga, like Samoa, had made sanctity widespread but without—until the last days of the Tui Tongaship—reducing the concept of central focus. The royal family (Tui Tonga) as Tangaloa-descended held the sanctity and the forceful powers that are attributes of divine or semi-divine chiefs. All others held degrees of sanctity, in principle, proportional to their rank. Like the Samoan, the Tongan gradation in sanctity covered the wide spectrum from the incandescence of near-divinity to the moderate patterns of respect for elders in all families. In this respect more traditional than Samoa, Tonga had retained at every level the concept of tapu, never quite reducing sanctity to the lower status of simple decorum. At the same time, all people had mana, which the gods bestowed upon those who lived by right conduct.

If we are to take necessary account of contradictory information, the quality of sanctity enveloping the Tui Tonga can be described in very general terms only. Early missionary sources described the Tui Tonga as "divine," as "high priests," as personifications of a god. They called attention to his being referred to as *atua* ("god"). Gifford's information a century or so later led him to moderate the earlier impressions of royal sanctity. The Tui Tonga, he concluded, was neither priest nor god; as the highest male chief he was the most sacred male in the country (1929:75). Undoubtedly Tongan reflections on the Tui Tonga have been affected both by Christianity (rule by a Christian monarch) and by the apparent decline in the stature of the royal line within relatively recent times. By Mariner's time (1806), a wave of religious skepticism was sweeping the islands and, of course, respect for Tui Tonga had diminished. On the other hand, the character of the Samoan Tui Manu'a would lead to the supposition that missionaries had overstated the case for an anciently divine ruler. A tradition of divine descent does not necessarily endow a line with divinity.

The details of royal tapu, which are reliable though incomplete, indicate, however, that as between the Tui Manu'a, on the one hand, and Tahitian and Hawaiian alii, on the other, the Tui Tonga was somewhere in the middle. Thus the Sky-god Tangaloa is quoted in a Tongan myth as saying: "The funeral of the Tui Tonga shall be as my own funeral (Gifford 1929:289)." Indeed, offerings were placed at the royal tombs (langi). Langi, Tongan for "sky," is also a reference to Tui Tonga (Gifford 1929:289)—at least a hint of his being regarded actively as a sky-being like Tangaloa. First-fruits (*inasi*) were also a religious offering in which Tui Tonga, to cite a phrase from Gifford, "was treated like a god (1929:103)." He was subject, of course, to the usual avoidances, as was Tui Manu'a. But in the Tahitian and Hawaiian tradition human sacrifices—a god-like prerogative—were offered in his behalf. Like the Tahitian high chief, when Tui Tonga entered a house it could no longer be occupied by its owner. Nobody could eat, drink, or sleep in the house in which he did. His separation was carried so far that he alone was not circumcised or tattooed. Violation of the royal tapu need not, however, cause death. In this respect, the awesomeness of the tapu was reduced. But a false oath on the royal kava bowl caused immediate death. The distinction would seem to be in terms of lapse of decorum as against an outright offense. Some acts of obeisance toward Tui Tonga appear as moderate versions of Tahitian and Hawaiian custom—for example, the spread of royal tapu to a house, but not to all ground touched; the carriage of Tui Tonga and his tamaha in a palanquin but not out of fear of tapuing all he touched. The *moe-moe*, the deferential touching of the soles of the royal feet with the back of one's hands, seems a milder form of the Hawaiian prostration. No specific information suggests the Tui Tonga was in any way as "incandescent" as the Hawaiian pio chiefs.

Tui Tonga remained almost to the very end the focus of sanctity. By rank he was closest to divine descent, and junior chiefly families sloped away. Like Hawaiians and Samoans, all other Tongans had a parallel relationship to other, although definitely inferior, deities. While their mana and tapu was thereby inferior, it was, nevertheless, within the sacred order. The Tui Takalaua and Kanokupolu spoken of as "secular" authorities were, of course, only second in relative sanctity to the royal line, enjoying the tapu prerogative—for example, human sacrifice—of great chiefs. Their "secular" character was in reference to administrative function as hau counterparts to Tui Tonga, and as junior and lower-ranking kin with constant obligations of deference.

Like Tui Tonga on a narrower front, each lineage chief held the tapu of association with (but not as priest) tutelary deities and ancestral spirits. The *haa* itself was a spiritual congregation as a body of patrilineal kin. One prominent Tongan even told Gifford (1929:29) that *haa* means "sacred," confusing it with *ha*. The point of view, though, is relevant. All chiefs and gods had some common qualities. In the most specific manner, a chief could eat a turtle, a sacred animal, usually the incarnation of a god, because, as the Tongans believed, they were closer to the gods and therefore less affected by the sanctity of the turtle. (Mariner 1817:II, 133). The general belief was that chiefs and gods had spirits that were essentially alike (Gifford 1929:316).

Deference giving at least the impression of sanctity was owed to all persons in some relationship or other, whether chief or commoner, man or woman. Since commoners, as Mariner was informed, had no "souls," but expired finally at death, it is questionable whether they come within the category of tapu. Information on this question is vague. Yet the obligations of kinship parallel so fully those of royal tapu that regardless of the apparent logic suggesting categorical distinctions between chiefs (spiritually akin to gods) and nonchiefs, each family or household may be regarded as a minor kingdom or small congregation. As such, it offered in its own domestic domain the honors and the appearances of sanctity enjoyed by the chiefs.

Kinship, to anticipate an idea developed in a later chapter, is a domestic status system which finally gives honor to all, at least in principle. Tongan kinship illustrates this central function most decisively because *here* public and domestic status systems were most fully parallel and coextensive. In the Tongan family, women were sacred to their brothers and to their brothers' children. Men had sanctity as fathers, as paternal uncles, as husbands and heads of families, as seniors, and, of course, as first-born. Each position of ritual subordination was offset by an opposing position of ritual superiority, and vice versa. The fahu is someone's mother's brother, and even the great mehekitanga must defer to her husband. Tapu owed to a Tongan father was virtually equivalent to that owed Tui Manu'a. Thus it was tapu to touch the father's head, to play with his belongings, to defile by contact his food or bedding. Even inadvertent violation brought illness, a decisive indication of actual sanctity, rather than mere decorum. The father also had the power to offset the effects of his tapu.

Tohunga

The crafts were not, as in Samoa, organized and autonomous bodies. The title of tufunga was rather an individual honor held in a family and transmitted to the eldest son. The family did not thereby become a tufunga family in the Samoan sense of controlling a craft. It did, however, hold the honor of the title, which from the Tongan status doctrine of constant inequality was limited to a single person at one time. Precisely what the honor of tufunga title meant we do not know. It must have been important enough for families to want to adopt an outsider as the new title-holder if no insider had the proper skills. The family lacked in fact all but the more superficial control over the title. It provided the mechanics of hereditary transmission, and undoubtedly training. The title itself was conferred by the lineage chief and, if important enough, was then confirmed by Tui Tonga or by a delegated representative. The honor of the title then was of public rather than of domestic origin. In the "guild" system it is the membership that autonomously regulates its own hierarchical order. In Tonga the title, being a gift of a chief, was a chiefly prerogative. It was a chiefly benefice sometimes given as a reward, since the recipient of the title was always an inferior in rank. While the title, as Mariner reports, did not confer official rank but a degree of respect (Mariner 1817:II, 93), the ranking of the crafts established a new graded order of subchiefly standing. As a parallel organization of rank—but without religious quality—the Tongan crafts system resembles the Tahitian *arioi.*

As given by Mariner, the three highest-ranking crafts were in order: canoe-builder, whale tooth cutter, and funeral director. A second range included in order: stone masons, net makers, fishermen and large house builders. A third range included tattooers and club carvers; and, finally, making up a bottom and without title; barbers, cooks, and farmers, in that order. The order of ranking differs from the Samoan, but the principles are similar, involving respect for highest skills, for major symbols of status and for religious significance. The relatively low rank of the tattooer and club carver is not explained, nor do we know why of all crafts and occupations only these two were not ordinarily hereditary.

The upper range, restricted to chiefly attendants (*matapule*) and their descendants, were the elite corps. All other of the listed crafts were open to ordinary commoners. Barbers, cooks, and farmers were commoners exclusively. The unfortunately scant information does not permit too specific comparison with Samoa. Yet the Tongan tradition that carpenters were children of Tangaloa connects with the Samoan doctrine in its suggestion of a descent grouping. There is, nevertheless, no hint of the Samoan "guilds" in Tonga. But, for that matter, there is no information on the kind of relationship between artisan and patron, whether based on ritual exchange, as in Samoa, or pecuniary.

Priests

In the Samoan manner, priests were *taula* and not artisans. They had power and influence, but since they were the possessed rather than possessors, their status was not high. No chief, for example, was ever a priest. As Mariner remarked of Tui Tonga and his heir, they were too high in rank to be servants (possessed) of the gods (1817: II, 141). Evidently the same principle applied to chiefs in general: the incompatibility of being in command and being commanded. The position of Tui Tonga was special, for as direct descendant his connection with the god was organic.

Unless actually possessed, the taula had no unusual social standing. When they served at shrines they performed minor duties and conveyed offerings to the gods. In important sacrificial offerings of a human being or of a person's finger joint, they had only an indirect part. When possessed, however, the taula was then a new figure inspiring the reverence of the highest ranks. But then it was the god he stood for; the awe he evoked was for his possessor. Like tufunga, priests had the dignity of hereditary succession within a family (as a rule, from father to son). The will of the gods being subject to caprice, any adult was likely to become an unexpected medium, more often in modern times than anciently (cf. Gifford 1929:317).

It is by comparison with the great societies of eastern Polynesia that Tongan priests seem so unimpressive as a social body. Yet the priests of the great lineages were still remembered long after their death. They were appointed by chiefs, and some by Tui Tonga, and were thus closely associated with the centers of power. The island of Niuatpputapu, for example, was governed for a time by a hereditary priest called Maafu (Williamson 1924:II, 256). The general standing of a priest depended, of course, upon the stature of the lineage and of its gods. While commoners were also taula, their jurisdiction was a low one. When a new taula suddenly declared himself, he had to be confirmed in his status by Tui Tonga or a lower chief, or else his office would lack the stature of belonging to a lineage.

Matapule

The most important specialists were the ceremonial attendants of high chiefs, the matapule. Mariner's description endows them with great importance. They were managers of ceremonial and they were often assigned very specific duties, such as beating a drum, or eating the remains of Tui Tonga's meal, or joining Tui Tonga in death. Others were counsellors and ministers, navigators, the keepers of records, the executive officers and guardians of morals and of public order (Mariner 1817:II, 92).

Most matapule held titles of rank as befitted their close and often intimate associations with chiefs. Some were raised-up commoners selected for unusual ability. Whether matapule were an elite corps of specialists serving only Tui Tonga and lower-ranking chiefs, or whether they were a social rank as Mariner thought they were, is a moot point. In rank, Mariner places matapule just below chiefs. Even though but one person in a family held the actual matapule title and responsibilities, the Tongans thought of his entire family, including his descent line, as matapule. All had distinction as matapule since the title and its regal associations went together, and as landed aristocracy and as distinguished tufunga as well.

Matapule were evidently a developing social class spreading out and gaining distinction over time. The office goes back to Ahoeitu, and may well have been from the very start the Tongan version of the Samoan tulafale. At least the pattern of joining two distinct lines of status, one strictly genealogical and another from another order, is reminiscent of Samoa. Before long, foreigners, men from ranking families of Fiji, Samoa, Rotuma, and the Tokelaus were brought in to join the Tui courts. Representing a genealogical order—by tradition only—of a different realm, they were on different tracks. They could neither compete with local chiefs nor offend their tapu. By intermarrying with Tongan families, they soon enough merged with the local nobility. As matapule, however, they retained their social distinctness. Matapule would seem, therefore, to have had a double or perhaps an ambiguous character. In their distinctness which defined their role best, they represented an extension of tufunga—of tufunga with special relationships to official authority. The three top skills listed by Mariner, to which should be added navigator, were restricted to matapule, that is, to the courts of Tui Tonga and other high chiefs. In their general position as a social class, they fell within a hierarchy that was, as matapule, outside the traditional system of Tongan rank, but as Tongans with good family connections they moved within their appropriate genealogical scale. The matapule to a very high chief was himself chief to a lower-standing matapule. The status of highest ranks is then crisply categorical; that of lower levels, rich in ambiguity and flexibility.

Falefa

In the court of Tui Tonga, which demanded to be set apart from all other high centers of authority, the matapule came under the jurisdiction of four high chiefs of tui stature. These tui and their lineages—known as the "four houses" (*falefa*)—were joined with the Tui Tonga as ritual ministers or ministries. Tui Tonga dealt with them and they dealt with the matapule. Tongan sources have never properly explained the significance of the falefa. The pattern of organization, though, seems clear enough. At the highest level of rank, an upper nobility is interposed between ruler and attendants. As matapule functions spanned a gamut from artisan to ritual attendants, so too did falefa occupy roles that were officially dedicated directly to the enhancement of Tui Tonga's sanctity, and when the occasion arose they moved decisively into political action. Guardians of the royal dignity, they also took part in the selection of the successor. Like the matapule, the falefa, too, were partly of foreign origin.

The first falefa began with Ahoeitu. About their early period we know only this: the "third" house was in charge of stone-hewing and tomb-building for Tui Tonga, the fourth house was constituted as the royal guard. The houses and their functions were reorganized during the reign of the luckless Tui Tonga Takalaua. The charter of the second falefa period has been officially passed down. It declares: "They shall rule relatives, in allotting all my things, my kava ring, and my feasts, and my funeral, and my burial, and of anything of mine that is allotted they will do the allotting (Gifford 1929:66)." These broad and far-reaching responsibilities are what gave to the falefa chiefs their political capability, subject, of course, to the continued powers of Tui Tonga. The charter then specifies the duties of each "house." The four were grouped by pairs. Those of the right hand were the autochthonous Tongan chiefs and were allotted the most formal ritual tasks such as sounding the shell trumpets, singing the funeral dirges, and managing the funeral and its dances at the death of Tui Tonga. Those of the left hand were foreigners and had charge of the more practical tasks of distributing the shares of food and of assigning the many jobs that were part of the royal funeral.

Toa

Tongan traditions, supported by observations of European visitors, suggest that serious warfare was a late, in fact a post-contact development. Early wars were overseas, with Samoans, Fijians, Futunans, Uveans. Cook found the Tongans to be peaceable. Shortly after, however, the Tui Hala Fatai led a war party of some 250–300 canoes on a free-booting raiding mission in the Fijian Islands where they spent two years in fighting and plundering and also taking part in Fijian civil wars (Mariner 1817:I, 77). In the late eighteenth century, domestic civil wars had ignited all the Tongan islands. Fortifications sprang up everywhere, naval fleets were constructed, arms were obtained from Europeans, military alliances were sealed and broken, able warriors were sought out and promised rewards. War had become a deadly interest and the organization of land and naval powers a task of vital urgency. Eyewitness accounts dwell on tactics, on plans of attack and defense, on mid-battle maneuvers, on the morale of troops, and on the skill and daring of commanders. We know nothing of early Tongan styles of fighting. In the period of the civil wars, warfare had gained in professional discipline, certainly in part due to European tutelage, although it never did reach acceptable standards of combat efficiency. Vavau's chief, Finow, had taught his men to press forward and not break ranks without command. Yet when he had the excellent opportunity of catching his enemy in the deadly crossfire of newly acquired cannon, he refrained, explaining to sorely disappointed young Mariner, that such guns should be used only against fortifications (Mariner 1817:I, 195). However, once the fortifications were breached, the slaughter of its defenders was as thorough as could be desired.

Combat units were led by professionals, that is, by men chosen for skill and prowess and not automatically by rank. Details on battle order are contradictory. Gifford, however, thought he could distinguish between a "company," or *matanga,* and a "regiment," or a *kongakau.* The first was led by an ordinary chief, or *eikitau;* the latter, by a district chief. Since war was inevitably in the cause of a great chief, he was naturally in overall command as the architect of the great strategy. The lower commands were the tacticians. Tui Tonga, as incumbent, was too sacred to fight. No such restrictions impeded claimants to the sacred throne.

Commoners could and sometimes did distinguish themselves in battle. The man who brought in ten enemy heads won a title and a land grant. For somewhat less spectacular feats, he won the momentary right to drink from a chief's kava cup. The professional cadres of warriors were matapule and their descendants who lived in the chief's compounds, associating freely with them. Their rewards were minor, for only chiefs benefited substantially from the gains of war.

Wealth

We do not know enough about the pre-European economy to compare it specifically, as we really should, with the Samoan. From incomplete information we recognize at once general similarities; for example, the focus on exchange and on the circulation of goods rather than on display. From Tonga, incidentally, we have a precise example of contrast with eastern Polynesian displays of corpulence in children. Here servants were put to death if they overfed the chief's daughter and caused her figure to lose its shapeliness. The chiefly somatype was, Polynesian style, massive, but acquired naturally and not from forced feedings.

The issue in Tonga, as in Samoa, was sharply focused on the ability to give and the power to demand goods. Samoa—more formal and more complex—had elaborated an intricate series of complementary exchanges of valuables for foods. In Tongan exchanges, the pattern was of equivalence—valuables for valuables, food for food—and thus more readily invidious. Details of Tongan exchanges are not entirely adequate for full comparison with Samoa. On marriage exchanges for which information is comparable, the distinction between complementary and equivalent but invidious is clear. In Tonga the families of bride and of groom were obliged to give each other only equal amounts of objects of value, but to return double the contribution made by their own kinsmen. In other words, the intermarrying families had to declare their absolute equivalence before one another and their exceptional worth before their own kin. Internal or domestic property exchanges were even more markedly symmetrical in the fahu.

The political sphere expressed only inequality. Tui Tonga was donor to falefa and matapule and so was every chief who supported a provincial court of matapule and of fighting men. Giving to the Tui Tonga was, of course, religious and token. Giving to a hau, the more secular authority, was tribute declaring at once the nature of political subordination. The Tongan uses of property seem prodigal and extreme by comparison with Samoa. Hospitality was unrestrained. Early visitors thought the quantity of provisions shared out was "incredible." All who had goods spent lavishly; all who had power demanded fiercely. Tui Tonga as religious being depended upon willing giving. Haus, however, had arbitrary sovereignty, and what they needed they could seize. The right to seize, the privilege of acquiring, and, above all, the capacity to expend actively and conspicuously were the signs of genuine status. For important persons, property was an acute necessity, poverty unimaginably embarrassing. Since wealth was limited and much of it was expended, the economy was inevitably centric—unlike the Samoan. The final burden fell on the "peasants," the commoners. When they were recipients, they were stigmatized as lowly; when they were ritual givers, they were denied direct access to Tui Tonga. Finally, land, the ultimate source, was concentrated and then allocated by rank and by power. The lowly were the working force, not the possessors of wealth. Wealth, if by now this point still has to be made, was in principle distinct from subsistence.

Political Hegemony

Except for mother's brother, an extraordinary example of a contrary pattern, masculine status relationships were clearly defined in terms of power. The common descriptions of power use the adjective "absolute," whether in reference to Tui Tonga, a hau, or to the male head of a household. Rights over life and to property were not in fact absolute, but conditional upon circumstances in most instances. Eyewitness examples of capricious and cruel behavior imply, nevertheless, an impulse to go beyond the limits of common decency. The fabulous Tukuahu, who had the left arms of one dozen cooks amputated only for the personal conceit of distinguishing them from all ordinary cooks, eventually paid for his excess with an insurrection that cost him his life. Even in recent times chiefs horsewhipped subjects who had annoyed them. Power was equated with the awesome and had to be exercised up to the very margins of propriety. The zealots went beyond. The power of the high was matched by the meekness of the lowly if this missionary observation about Tui Tonga is to be believed:

> If he wishes to satisfy his anger or some cruel fancy, he sends a messenger to his victim who, far from fleeing, goes to meet his death. You will see fathers tie the rope around the necks of their children whose death is demanded to prolong the life of the divinity (Williamson 1924:I, 151).

Punishments were naturally severe. Mariner saw his patron, Chief Finow, kill a man and his wife only on suspicion of having withheld the tribute of whale's teeth. Commoners who broke the food taboos were severely thrashed or beaten to death. Adultery was a capital offense.

Power flowed down the lines of hierarchy, and in principle each superior down to head of household had great powers over the life and property of his subordinates. In practice, it was the commoner who was the universal subject of all powers, and it was the upper ranks who had the forcefulness to evade subordination. In a system which had established the crude pattern of master and victim as a relationship akin to that between awesome god and a human being, the commoner was the victim. He was the labor force, the ordinary warrior, the worker on the land, moved about by his chief; his daughters were at the sexual disposal of any chief. He was the proper sacrifice in behalf of a chief.

Power was an attribute of hierarchy; it also sustained hierarchy. Thus when the power balances were upset, as when the Tui Tongaship was divided in order, as it has been said, to preserve it, the effect was the opposite, for reduction implies and therefore foreshadows decline. Rank, of course, being defined as durable and eternal, was unaffected by reductions in power. Without power it commanded only respect, in Tongan terms a feminine and not a masculine prerogative. In the end, therefore, Tongan power passed to a queen, undoubtedly in the new and enlightened European tradition, but still an extraordinary shift in the traditional balances between power and respect for which the way had already been smoothed.

Weakness was inevitably disastrous to position and to personal safety. The weak lineages were immediately attacked and, if defeated, were absorbed. Equals fought to reduce each other. Fighting, in the Polynesian tradition, was fierce, aiming at destruction and reduction. They destroyed crops, and tortured and then killed prisoners.

The older and classic Tongan tradition had an orderly hierarchy and a strongly focused center of power. Tui Tonga ruled over all, held all land title, the power to recruit labor for public works, and to demand human sacrifice. The period of civil war following his decline may be attributed directly to the Tongan commitment to the doctrine of the hierarchy of powers. The confusion of political alliances and antagonisms during this period appear to be nothing more than chaotic clashes of personal ambitions. Yet George Tupou, by unifying all traditional titles, reminds us how durable was the doctrine of orderly hierarchy of powers.

Western Samoa and Tonga had in common the pattern of opposing strong and weak. The Samoan version was crude; the Tongan, through its recognition of gradations, much more refined.

The Structure of Status

Like the Samoan, the Tongan status structure is built around two distinct principles: one, in a sense linear, represents the clear gradations of genealogical rank via patriliny and seniority; the other, complementary, sets off one type of status against another. The structure as a whole can be visualized as in a state of balance, in which case status can be recorded in three dimensions: as up and down the traditional ladder of graded rank; and—as an adjunct to this linear conception of rank—also laterally, as when, to take but one example, Tui Tonga defers to his sister's daughter, the sacred tamaha. A position along one coordinate is, as we have already observed, not identical (it must in fact be different) with a position along the other.

The state of balance is, we need hardly say, as unreal as a single still photograph is as a statement of an energetic process. Status is by definition an energetic condition. While Polynesian status systems are in varying degrees active, the Tongan is among the most active. The structure is stable in that the two coordinates are retained. The points on the coordinates, to carry out the geometric imagery, are unstable. In human terms, persons who are ambitious cannot change the absolute laws of genealogical rank as they have been established in Tonga, nor can they alter the order of complementary statuses, without, that is, destroying the original structure. The structure does, however, allow for shifts in power relationships, offering several leverage points for such shifts.

Shifts in power converted complementary into opposing or antagonistic relationships, allowing the lower to overcome the higher. It was in the course of such antagonisms that the genealogical orders, held to be constant, were, in fact, rearranged. When a lineage was conquered and absorbed, its chiefs were reduced to commoners. By historic (post-European) times, the number of lineages had been substantially reduced. The chiefly grade, therefore, was reductive; the commoner status, expansive. The commoners, "landless" and thus reduced in status, formed the most rapidly growing economic class. Since matapule were attached to the households of chiefs, they, too, were reduced numerically in the general decline of the lineage. From the standpoint of genealogical rank, Tongan society had become polarized between the mighty and the lowly.

Genealogical Rank

Tui Tonga represented in its prime an absolute rank incorporating all virtue and all significant powers. If it was not the true senior line, it was the symbol of seniority. In the associations between Tui Tonga and his falefa and matapule, between Tui Tonga and his junior collateral lines of Haa Takalaua and Kanokupolu, and between Tui Tonga and his sister and her daughter, we see in one tight nexus the essential character of the Tongan status structure. Each of these relationships defines another aspect of what is meant by genealogical rank in Tonga.

Falefa–matapule are not just a ministerial court. Their constitution is part of the larger configuration of what is meant by the pinnacle of rule. Against the absolute, categorical, and truly autochthonous character of Tui Tonga, falefa–matapule stand as dependent, heterogeneous, and utilitarian. Half of the falefa have a quasi-lineal connection with Tui Tonga as representatives of old and important chiefly lines. The other half, being foreigners, represent a genealogical discontinuity. Since this organization was not accidental, but deliberate, its significance must be sought for in terms of the structure of status. The native falefa are smaller versions of Tui Tonga and have a parallel if lower status. The foreigners, who are free of the tapu, are his complements. It is in this sense that the common category of falefa is heterogeneous, more specifically dual. Falefa in relation to matapule are as Tui Tonga is to them in respect to hierarchy and to the contrast between sacred and utilitarian. For whereas falefa are the practical counterpart to Tui Tonga's sanctity, the matapule are the more utilitarian attendants of the falefa. The matapule organization is a reduced version of that of falefa; part foreign, part native, part linear, and part discontinuous.

The relationship between Tui Tonga and the Takalaua and Kanokupolu lines starts from the closest association and then diverges, moving successively from a complementary opposition to open antagonism, and finally to unification. The events leading to this conclusion can be correctly ascribed to the clash of personal ambitions. Their patterned course conforms to Tongan conceptions of structure. The division of authority converts a linear into a complementary relationship, and the subsequent intermarriages which introduce the fahu and its own asymmetrical patterning of status completes once and for all the conversion. This conversion, it will be recalled, was peculiarly unstable. While it reduced the collateral line to the kinship status of a mother's brother in one respect, it had endowed it with great political potential by the grant of powers under duress. The formal concept of structure envisioned, shall we say, a stable pattern; history introduced the impure ingredients. The balance of statuses between a man and his sister and her line divided the prerogatives categorically and noncontroversially, displaying the two sides of genealogical rank. Tui Tonga's eldest sister, the female Tui Tonga and her daughter, the tamaha, acquired highest honor and no more. It is at the obverse side of the genealogical pattern—that of mother's brother, where the honor is also reversed—that the categorical division of prerogatives failed to maintain itself. When the line holding power was also subject to fahu it was, logically enough, not the reductive quality of fahu that prevailed, but the elevating quality of power.

Eiki

On the coordinate of genealogical rank, Tui Tonga and his two close collateral lines form one coherent unit which is recognized by the use of *sinae* instead of the more common *haa* to designate their lineages. The etymology of *sinae* is obscure; it means to some Tongans a transcendant rank (Gifford 1929:33). In the same way, tui is a transcendant title of chiefship, implying sanctity and ultimately eligibility to the Tui Tongaship (Gifford 1929:126).

Eiki, like Samoan ali'i, stands as a broader and therefore lower category of rank on the genealogical scale. Like matapule, the term has its focus in the position (chief) and extends by courtesy to all kin, grading off on the genealogical scale to commoner. Eiki escape the indignity of generality. High-rank chiefs (*eiki motu, eiki taupotu, eiki toho*) are distinguished from petty chiefs (*eikisii*). Eiki unlike tui were free to marry commoners. Their offspring were then derisively known as "half-shells." But the child of a high-ranking mother, while still unfortunately incomplete because of his commoner father, gained somewhat in stature because of the higher respect owed to the woman (Gifford 1929:123).

Even though eiki is qualitatively distinguished from tui in important ways, all chiefs share respects of sanctity and distinguishing prerogatives that set them off from commoners. The life of the chief had to be different and his inherent superiority had to be recognized. For the most part, difference was set off by tapu. Chiefs also employed the bizarre to accomplish the same objective of separation. Gifford tells that King George Tupou had the unique distinction of a tattooed penis (1929:127). By the same token, an act of great distinction, such as extraordinary military valor, entitled a commoner to consideration as a "petty chief." The capricious and often meaningless cruelty of chiefs—such as those who tormented men with elephantiasis of the testicles, or cut off men's arms, or commanded commoners to dive from cliffs into the boiling surf—to fetch bananas—also comes under the heading of the bizarre.

The children of chiefs had no formal position (taupou, manaia) equivalent to those of Samoan ali'i, but they, too, were differentiated from others. The sons were attended by a gathering of young men; the daughters were carefully groomed and oiled to bring out their natural beauty.

All eiki had similar prerogatives of distinction. Only one in a family or lineage held the family name as a formal title of authority. The crucial distinction therefore was between titled and untitled chiefs. In Tonga, title and genealogical rank—in contrast with Samoa—moved along the same coordinate. When lineages subdivided into minor segments, a new title was created and a branch of a family was thereby elevated. All titles decend in chiefly lines (cf. Gifford's Titles of Chiefs, 1929:132–40).

Matapule (As a Rank)

As a gentry, matapule have the special significance of having formed the genealogical ranks by intermarriage. Most are of new lineages, having come to Tonga from abroad in later times; one group came from Samoa in 1600. Their status as gentry comes from possession of the title, which elevates the family name; from their close associations with high chiefs, from whom they acquire a derivative status; and from their welcomed intermarriage with eiki families. The Tongan dictionary defines *matapule* as a "man of honorable rank or status; gentleman, etc." While the etymology is not certain, it is most probably a compound of *mata* in its meanings as: that which is at the front; at the right side; at the head of; the forward prong; the cutting edge of a knife; etc., and of *pule* in its meaning of rule and authority (Churchward 1959). Etymology implies the function correctly as the forward or the efficient end of rule, behind which lies the chiefly source. The matapule have honor as the chief's instruments. As instruments rather than as instigators, they naturally occupy a status lower than that of causative chiefs—although, as previously noted, matapule have genealogical rank independent to a degree of their derivative status. Their positions, however, as Gifford explains, "correlated largely with the power and influence of the chiefs they served (1929:140)."

Mariner spoke of *mua* ("one who leads or goes ahead [Gifford 1929: 109]") as a class or rank below matapule. Gifford does not corroborate this interpretation, pointing out rather that the term designated matapule distinguished by having an eiki parent. In the royal kava circle, the man who is first by virtue of eiki basic rank, of matapule derivative status, and of tufunga skills is known as the *mua* (1929:109).

Gifford is correct in doubting whether *matapule* belongs in the scheme of rank at all, if by rank we mean only order of seniority. But Tongan rank cannot be circumscribed within this single dimension. The example Gifford cites of a man indignant at his relatives being rated as matapule when by blood they were eiki (1929:141) demonstrates the local point of view which saw matapule as a grade. Any eiki, as Gifford points out, outranked the highest matapule (1929:112).

Tua, the commoners, are directly at the bottom of the genealogical scale. They are the end product of junior lines, in itself a stigma; they take in all who have lost worth through loss of efficacy, and they are the residue of indifferent (status-wise) marriages. Although Mariner was told *tua* had no souls (Mariner 1817:II, 105), Gifford found no tendency to regard them as a distinctive breed. On the contrary, the tua, though separated by a major chasm of ritual avoidances from chiefs, was always part of the chief's family. The kinship connection was evidently welcomed as a valued link—or as a long tether—that created still one more contrast (somewhat in the manner of the religious bond between ali'i and kauwa in Hawaii) between high and low status. In the "old days" a chief's commoners were his own low kin who served him (Gifford 1929:114). In this respect, they occupied a position in the status structure parallel to but, of course, lower than that of matapule. Commoners were then the untitled attendants.

Tua, then, are a low, but not a degraded class. The term is a reference equal to our "boor," the country yokel whose manners are not refined. His lowness is, of course, real. He was the one who ate the leavings of others, he was a "pig," an empty "banana stalk," the last to eat in a ritual distribution, and whose portion was often the decayed meat. Crucial to his low status was his dependency on the lands of others. In a society that esteems rootedness in a hereditary estate, the tua was the tenant. Needless to say, he did not suffer material privation. Thomson properly corrects those missionaries and well-meaning friends of the poor who portrayed the tua as miserable "slaves" and "serfs." Their major disability was, of course, honor. But even this they could win to a degree by outstanding performances. Some stigma of "vassalage and serfdom" must have been attached to these people for the royal decree to have set them free in 1862 (Gifford 1929:113).

Finally, slaves and other war prisoners (*popala*) formed an alien category, of no great importance. They were often captive eiki and matapule held for degradation. After suitable torture, most prisoners were put to death.

Status Rivalry

In the classic Polynesian manner, status rivalry began at the top between senior and junior scions of the divine line. First causes are never known and we can only try to imagine why the grandeur of a god-descended chief should be challenged when still pristine. Once it has been challenged, even if only with partial success, pristine and sanctified power has lost its virginity and is fair game. In every other instance in Polynesia the results of dividing an authority into apparently separable components intensified status rivalry by making the goals—of secularized power and authority—more readily attainable. Men cannot fight gods until the latter have been reduced from their incandescent eminence. In Tonga, too, we recognize the same process. The divine authority surrenders an important measure of efficacy and is reduced; secular authorities test one another freely in the arena of sheer power. As victors gain power, they are more approximate to the reduced celestial but humanly based authority. Tui Tonga does not need to be overthrown; he need only be ignored. Mariner's Vavau chief had already risen in his own estimation to ignore the then Tui Tonga. The rise of religious skepticism spoken of earlier reflects, of course, the intrusion of Christianity. But since the skeptics were not themselves Christians, their new-found secularism may be attributed to the greater immediacy of military power. We should not overrate the importance of religious skepticism, however, for did not the victorious Kanokupolu absorb and enrich itself with the prestige of Takalaua and Tui Tonga ancestry? The question really is, what was the traditional Tongan religion concerned with? The answer surely is power. The skeptics were questioning the sources not the basics. Power in Polynesia was meaningful when tangible and capable of meeting worthy challenges. The old Tui Tonga accepted challenge by promoting tangible growth. In the challenge he faltered, the monolithic facade revealed a crack, and the rest is Tongan history. The efforts at mending, such as intermarriage with strong secular lines were inevitably self-defeating since they reduced the pristine authority, despite fahu, and gave to the lower order the requisite gloss that heretofore had been the distinguishing mark of the one exceptional line.

Descent Group Organization

It has been customary to describe Polynesian descent groups from the viewpoint of hypothetical beginnings in small, local communities of kin that enlarge by creating new branches and eventually achieve their maximum size and their complete segmentary order. Peter Buck, in particular, has been drawn to just such a conception of natural, vegetative increase, implying thereby that chiefship is a response to growth. Buck may have been describing correctly general processes of social enlargement, but, of course, from a hypothetical rather than from a genuinely historical perspective. Gifford, also drawn irresistibly to the organic analogy of a tree, nevertheless, reverses the perspective by examining the Tongan haa as a cultural concept. The Tongans see their descent group, in the words of one chief informant, "as the people belonging to a great chief, all related by blood to him (1929:30)." All Gifford's informants agreed on a definition of a haa as a body of kin of graded rank gathered around a nucleus of related chiefs (1929:30). A community may be presumed to have preceded the chiefly organization, but it is the chiefly organization in the Tongan pattern, more generally in the aristocratic pattern, that controls the structure of the community. Thus what Gifford says about the Tongan patrilineal lineage is acutely relevant, as all foregoing evidence has shown, to our understanding of Polynesian descent groups generally. "Everything" he says, "points to the necessity of a line of powerful chiefs for a nucleus about which the lineage groups itself. Without such chiefs it appears to wilt and die and its membership gradually realigns itself with other rising lineages (1929:30)."

Haa is not an organic term like waka, iwi or hapu. It is so abstract a conception of an aggregate of people that a most distinguished informant, a man who had been premier of Tonga, thought, as we have noted, that it was *ha* or "sacred." Consensus of Tongan opinion renders it as tribe, class, family. It refers to persons under a chief and it refers to persons of a locality. Like ngati in eastern Polynesia, haa is always the prefix to the name of the group. In formal address the group's name will not be mentioned without the prefix. In this respect, haa has seemingly the quality of an honorific, accomplishing for a corporate group what the title tui does for a chief. I would guess it is this honorific feature of haa that Gifford's informant had in mind when he spoke of it as sacred. If, as all evidence indicates, the haa is a physical, indeed, a biological manifestation of the efficacy of a chief, then, of course, it is almost literally a sacred attribute, a category of honor comparable to that of the family name. Gifford offers an example to illustrate how haa is, in fact, an extension of a family name. Haa Ata he notes is not the name of a recognized lineage, but designates Ata, presumably a minor chief, and his lower-ranking relatives and followers.

If haa honors the name, the name evidently must be worthy of bearing the title haa. Gifford, for example, describes two kinds of lineage names, one deriving from the family name of a chief, the other from a place. In the first instance the god is the chief, in the latter only locality. In Gifford's examples, locality haa are headed by lower-ranking officers, such as matapule (1929:31). In either case, the continuity of the name, which is no mere formal matter, depends on the circumstances surrounding the source. The continuity of a chief's lineage depends upon the political fortunes of his family. As long as the chiefly line is vigorous, the name and the bonds persevere no matter where the people live. Locality lineages change names with a change in place of residence. Since continuity in aristocratic society is more honorable than discontinuity, the locality lineages would by such standards of judgment alone fall within the lower position. The hundreds of locality names collected by Gifford, each with a haa prefix, poses the intriguing possibility that early Tonga had been divided into two great categories of descent group; one, that of royal and closely related haa, and the other of numerous and quite small locality haa. With the rise to prominence of a chief, a locality haa would convert to a chief's haa. The differences between the two categories go beyond continuity of name or other formal honors. Locality lineages are destined to remain small; chief's lineages have potential for almost limitless growth. Thus, after 1600, a major turning point in

Tongan social history, the entire organized population had fallen into only 13 great lineages, most headed by an important chief.

Tongan haa and Samoan aiga appear immediately as distinctive organizations of kin. The former is strongly patrilineal, the latter bilateral. The haa units in enlarged form are more nearly autonomous and complete as a self-governing body than the aiga, which must constantly confront a deliberative fono and at the same time deal with the formal problems of having to reconcile its masculine and feminine wings. In the usual social classifications, haa is a lineage, aiga a bilateral kindred. If we exaggerate—as is easy to do—these differences, we may well obscure the common origin in common concepts of the two. The closeness of Samoa and Tonga in most other respects cautions us to seek for the cognate.

The haa is, in fact, the tama tane of the Samoan aiga. The fahu defining one set of relations with a mother's line and reverence for father's sister defining extraordinary respects for the female side of the paternal line, gives to each person in a haa a set of female wings comparable to those with which Samoans are endowed. Both systems share bilineal features which differ in specific application but not in fundamentals. Samoa offers the tama fafine jurisdiction over properties administered by the tama tane. In Tonga a man may be perhaps uncomfortably aware of the jurisdiction of his sister's son over his property. The major differences would seem to be political-honorific. Samoa had united the two wings of the family under a common concept and formal title; but had divided the jurisdiction over titles between aiga and fono. Tonga had formally divided the wings, but required them to maintain a ritual linkage. The Samoan is, as we would say today, a system run by committee—for every impulse an available restraint. The Tongan is a more powerful system run by chiefs.

The haa is the prototype of that hybrid social system that does not sit easily in established categories. Its constituency is mainly kin, and its honor depends in large measure upon continuity of descent. But espousing growth as its other component of honor, it welcomes aliens and even dual membership. Descent is patrilineal, but chiefs welcome their maternal kin as permanent residents. When a strong lineage absorbs a weaker, the internal composition becomes more political than consanguineal. The haa lives comfortably with all modifications. It occupies, as a rule, a compact territory; it can also be scattered over several islands. It requires for its honor only that its chiefly lines retain relatively strict adherence to patrilineal descent. Lesser persons flesh out the haa without being organic to its structure. Those of no social consequence, as Gifford reveals, are not members of a haa at all, but are victims of the rise and fall in the political fortunes of haa.

Lineages are ranked precisely in a table of organization recited by orators at formal occasions. However, despite formal commitment to seniority, lineage rank in Tonga is like that of Samoa, political and variable. Chiefs within a haa are ranked by seniority, but command is political. Gifford lists several examples of higher-ranking chiefs being ruled in the haa by lower-ranking but more powerful relatives. We do not specifically know whether all lineages were ranked in some all-encompassing heraldic college or whether the rank order itself was a worthy privilege. The available heraldic texts list only a few major haa in their prologues, an intimation, at least, that the Tongan lineages were not all bound together within even a spiritual community such as the Samoan Great Fono.

Williamson, as well as Radcliffe-Brown, believed that all Tongan chiefs were ultimately related to Tui Tonga (1924:I, 167–68; III 231), admitting, of course, the absence of specific evidence. Conforming as it does with Samoan traditions of Tui Manu'a, the assumption offers a reasonable explanation for the early sovereignty of Tui Tonga, who was evidently not a conquest chief. We have also the alternative analogy with Raiatea and its religious confederation which preceded genealogical links. Tongan "internationalism" adds credence to the Society Islands' analogy. In actual genealogical fact, only the sinae lineages are specifically related to Tui Tonga. All other known lineages are new, and their records do not antedate 1600.

So far as is known, therefore, the royal lineages formed one kinship unit that subdivided into several major branches. In 1920 there were three branches of sinae, sinae eiki, the branch closely related to Tui Tonga, and two other branches, one representative of chiefs related to Tui Tonga in early times, and another of chiefs related to him presently. The heads of several of the 13 lineages now extant are indirectly related to Tui Tonga, but there is no suggestion of any consistent genealogical connections comparable to those of the traditional eastern Polynesian status lineages.

All large lineages form branches or segments directly in accordance with the number of chiefs or chiefly titles they possess. Observing the fourfold subdivision of the great Haa Fale Fisi (the Fijian-derived lineage), Gifford comments: "Apparently the presence or absence of haa subdivisions depends upon the prominence of the chiefs within a haa and the number of their people (1929:39)." When the haa subdivides, one chief remains head of all, the original tutelary deity is retained for all; but each subdivision assumes its own name, that of its chief, and the common title of haa.

Segmentation

Segment I refers to the administration under the Tui Tonga. It began with Ahoeitu as a religious community and then gained enough authority to carry out monumental works. With the appointment of the Tui Haa Takalaua and of Tui Kanokupolu, Segment I had transformed itself from a religious and generalized authority to a more powerful and more immediate central administration with such specific economic jurisdictions as land allocations and the fostering of trade between Tongatabu, the center, and the other islands. Not until more recent times did the central administration find it either possible or necessary to concern itself with the utilitarian economy beyond its immediate reach. At the very peak of his power, Tui Tonga found his effective secular authority limited to his home island. Outlying islands owed him first-fruits and not political tribute. Still, the concept of a secular authority had arisen and its consequences were spreading outward. On Tongatabu, as witnessed by Cook, the Kanokupolu, the new regal authority, presided over food taboos; his deputies inspected farms and issued instructions on what to plant, on how much to consume, and how much to conserve for ritual and for war.

The Tui Tonga's authority faded rapidly after 1784, when the royal succession was forcibly seized by a member of the Tui Kanokupolu lineage. Thereafter Tonga was ruled by a hau who exercised arbitrary authority, it is said, over all properties. But civil war came so hard on the heels of this new political phase that the specific authority of the hau can hardly be evaluated. It could only have reached to the limits of his actual military power.

There are hints in the early reports of the London Missionary Society that Tongatabu had been divided among three "districts," one directly under the Tui Tonga, and thus the capital, the others under related chiefly lines. This information, suggestive of a traditional segmentation as, for example, on Raiatea, is too vague to be designated a Segment II.

It seems rather that Tonga did not have a territorial administrative organization with appointed officials and designated regional jurisdictions. By a more informal and more characteristically "feudal" arrangement, the Tui Tonga delegated large tracts of land (*tofia*) to chiefs of great lineages who sub-enfeudated to lower chiefs. In return, chiefs agreed to military aid and to ritual tributes of foods and *koloa.* When Cook reported "30 districts" on Tongatabu, he must have been referring to these principal land tracts held by the major lineages.

Those major lineages are Segment II. They are the more intimate land-holding agencies, and their chiefs were in virtually all respects sovereign in their own jurisdiction. Each major lineage was a replica of the entire administration.

Segment III was the subdivision, and for its part a replica in most respects of the major branch, dependent on the major as the major was on the Tui Tonga or his representatives. The nature of dependency must be seen always in the dynamic context of shifting power relationships that could suddenly turn the tables, the minor branch becoming commander of the entire lineage. Moreover, in the endless late period civil wars, new dependencies were suddenly formed as first one lineage and then another gained control over an island and established itself on others. Dependency of alien lineages, however, was only a matter of offering tribute and not, as in Hawaii, submission to another administration.

Segment IV was the patrilocal household, for which there is no generic term. In sharp contrast to Samoa, Tonga had no villages, only centers of power and of authority dominated by chiefs' households. Major households formed themselves into a compound that incorporated patrilineal and matrilineal kin along with others who were attendants, warriors, and servants. So very little is known about the life of commoners in ancient Tonga, but that they were dispersed among landholders as tenants or as kin tenants seems reasonably certain. There is no reason to doubt they maintained bilateral kinship links and enjoyed some if not most of the honors of domestic status. But lacking the village, the common agency of local autonomy and democracy, the Tongan commoner, by contrast with his more fortunate Samoan compeer, was fully dependent and subordinate.

A hierarchy of successive dependencies was the ancient Tongan scheme. Samoa had interposed at all strategic points clusters of deliberating agencies which held off and muted potential internal authorities. In Tonga there were few blocks. Dependency was in direct proportion to personal power.

13

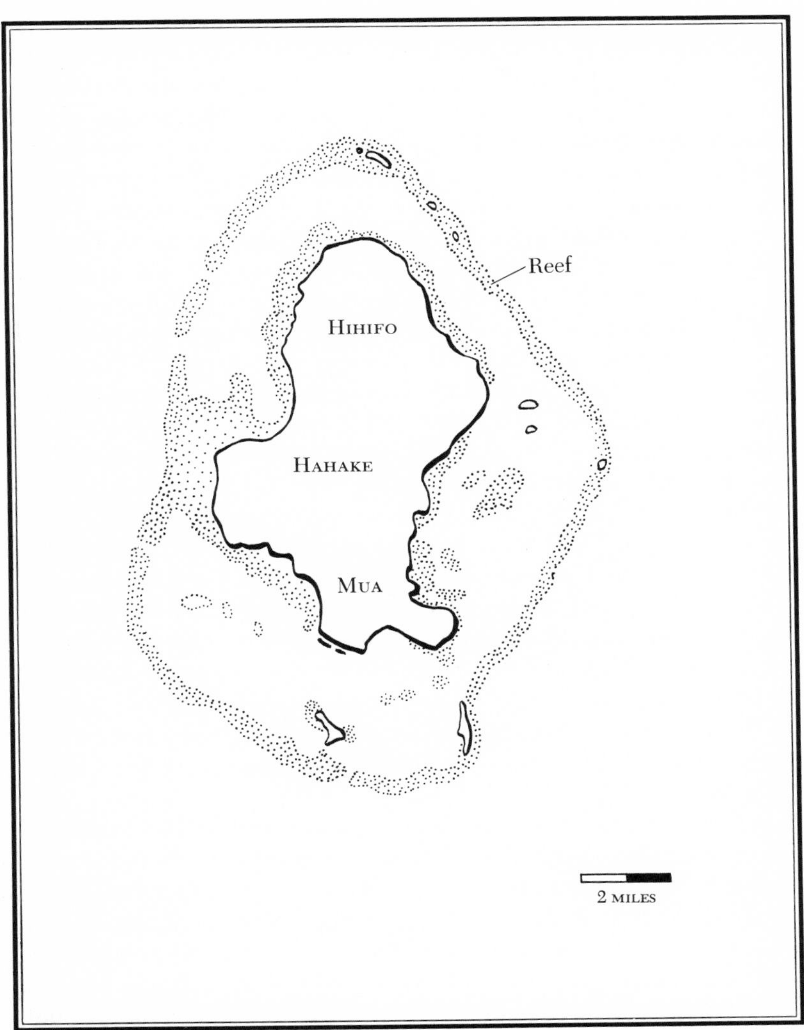

Uvea

UVEAN CULTURE, AS BURROWS WAS THE FIRST TO OBSERVE, IS ESSENTIALLY Tongan. The languages are very close, and the traditions of both speak of specific and continuous connections. Ignoring in this instance the economic connotations of colonialism, we may describe Uvea as having been a Tongan colony for several centuries beginning perhaps in the twelfth. When local rule was reestablished, it simply continued the older tradition. The pattern of relationship during the "colonial" period is unfortunately obscure; but there is no reason to suspect a material interest. One gathers that Tonga loomed as a moral authority over the Uveans, and that Tongan prestige was at stake in the security of its reputation there. The Tongan investment was to place representatives of its royal lines there and to defend their honor. When visiting royalty had her tapa robe accidentally splashed by an Uvean child, the Tongans had to invade to remedy the affront. When the Tongan dynasties had been overthrown, the home country made serious though ineffectual attempts to restore the loss.

There is some difference of opinion between Tonga and Uvea on how they got together in the first place. The Tongans claim conquest and the Uveans say they had sent to Tonga to ask for a chief. I would assume that for Uvea there was an advantage in having authentic links with a source as august as Tui Tonga. The Tongan rulers integrated with but did not merge with the local lines, never relinquishing their genealogical discreteness. It is unlikely—although the distance is not very great—that Uvea would have become embroiled in the shattering events that reverberated through Tonga in its later period. It was at best a very remote province, sheltered from the immediate political concerns of the center and thus more representative of an earlier Tonga.

As a small volcanic island of some 23 square miles, Uvea could well be, ecologically, a part of the Tongan archipelago. Though formed around volcanic craters, it resembles Haapai more than it does Vavau. Erosion has created the low silhouette and openness of terrain of an atoll. It even has a large lagoon. The combination of volcanic and atoll features has given the Uveans the multiple advantages of fertile and level crop lands, ease of movement, secure fishing, and generally speaking, economic diversity. The island is unusually well-watered. The windward side, catching the moist winds, is excellent for wetland taro. The craters are great lakes of fresh water, and even the dry central zone produced some crops. Yam, taro, and breadfruit were the main crops. Fish, pig, and domesticated fowl balanced the diet. Even in the late European period the population was well in excess of

4,000, indicative of a favorable habitat. If there were economic problems, they would have resulted not from general conditions, but from the distribution of soils. Some villages monopolized good wetland soils; others had to rely upon shifting horticulture of arid uplands. Such inequities would have been of more consequence for settlement patterns than for nutrition. There was an abundance, for example, of other foods, the coconut in particular. But wetland cultivators had to organize for irrigating and draining fields that were, however, nearby; dryland farmers were obliged to scatter and move about. There is no specific evidence of fighting for land.

The scale of public construction was small, as befitted a remote province whose rulers were well below the rank of Tui Tonga. The tradition was Tongan. The royal tombs, small versions of the homeland models, were earthen mounds faced with lava slabs. The great tomb, also called Tongatapu, measured 30 feet by 15 and was only three feet high. The backrests of chiefs on the marae were crude boulders. Both scale and quality imply an unassertive central authority. Irrigation was a local village enterprise.

European discovery and occupation was late, and so the task of undoing the native culture lagged a bit behind other Polynesian islands. Wallis, whose name the island bears, was the discoverer in 1767. He sent a scouting party for a quick look and left. The first crisis came in 1825 when the adventurous George Manini, arriving as a passenger on a European schooner, settled among the Uveans and, because he had the credentials of being half Hawaiian, thought he should be their king. They took his claim seriously enough to kill him. Several years later they were obliged to treat the crew of a British bark in the same way, although for lesser provocations. But in 1838 they accepted a French Catholic mission and helped them fight off a Protestant "invasion" from Tonga. Then King Lavelua sealed this new victory over the Tongans by converting to Catholicism. The island became a French protectorate in 1888. When Burrows arrived in 1932 for a three-month survey, the traditional religion and political system was all but forgotten. What remained was the language and what may be called the domestic or household culture and, fortunately, mission records dating back almost a century which offer at least some hints as to aboriginal conditions.

Genealogical Traditions

Father Henquel, who served on Uvea between 1889 and 1919, compiled most of the traditional history. His reports are at best fragmentary and particularly vexing because they do not consistently distinguish between minor local and high chiefs. They are most useful as accounts of conditions that just preceded the European epoch.

The traditions do not deal with the actual first settlement. They start rather with two brothers who had arrived from New Zealand, having paused on the way in Tonga. They live under a local chief. When he dies, it is they who send to Tonga for a replacement. They have the stature of founders because they initiate a major epoch by shifting the chiefly pedigrees from small and perhaps undistinguished lines to that of the majestic Tui Tonga. This era may be dated as early as 1150 or as late as 1450. The latter date would fit the Tongan traditions of the Uvean "conquest" more closely. The first such Uvean ruler is said to have been named by Tui Tonga himself. His successor came from the next lower line of Tui Haa Takalaua; and, finally, a new dynasty was formed from even lower-ranking chiefs who had been sent over from Tonga as bodyguards. The most notorious of the latter was Havea the Arrogant, who earned his soubriquet as a mean despot who had brought about his own downfall by going too far. The last straw was his insufferable habit of convening his council of chiefs night after night. Finally, two young men who could no longer bear to see their elderly father submitted to such abuse deposed Havea and divided the rule between themselves. They, too, were Tongans by genealogical connection, but evidently undistinguished. They prove to be the last rung of the Tongan ladder and the last link with its authority. In the time of Havea, disputants over a land title had come before Tui Tonga saying: "We came to see you because we are having a dispute over your island, Uvea (Burrows 1937:22)." Shortly, the island was to be for Uveans only. The brothers could not preserve the peace. They became embroiled with a strictly local Uvean chief over a dog fight, accused of having "rigged" the decision, and were defeated in a war that quickly became political. The victor, having vindicated the honor of his dog, had also inadvertently put an end to the Tongan dynasties. The era of Uvean independence dates from 1600 and is represented by the truly autochthonous Takumasiva dynasty. The Takumasivas were said to be cruel despots. They were attacked and briefly replaced by Tongans, and they were the target of one revolt after another, but they were able to come back and to hold on. The breakaway comes during the period of decay of Tongan authority at home and is thus an extension of Tongan history. The break seems to have caused nothing more than a genealogical discontinuity in the Uvean system of government. The system remained in the old mold and simply changed, partly in response to Tongan characteristics, but in the main from inherent internal rivalries and discontents.

The Status System

The principal features are Tongan, though revised and diluted. An impression of vagueness may have been conveyed by the incompleteness of information and lack of specific detail. Nevertheless, there is no putting aside certain positive indications that traditions of genealogical honor, sanctity, and chiefly power, to name the key constellation, had indeed been modified. Revision of these features may be taken for granted, considering that the Uvean status system lacking the Tui Tonga is but a partial version of the original. Without a pinnacle of divine majesty, all aspects of status are simplified and reduced. Relative distances between the ranks were perhaps unchanged. If the summit had been lowered, so had the base. Tonga, it will be recalled had elaborated a familial code of honor that was comparable in design if not in scale with royalty and thus compensated for the distance between Tui Tonga and commoner. Uvea had either lost or perhaps never had a comparable system. Fahu is a specific example: it had been general in Tonga, but was restricted to royalty in Uvea. Conceivably, Uvean royalty being of Tongan descent and tradition had brought their own institutions, preserving them for themselves. Who then were the true Uveans? Probably, early Tongans. A system representing Tonga at the peak of its traditional powers was imposed, one may speculate, upon a more generalized Tongan base. Since what was imposed was partial, the net effect had to be dilution, away from the Tongan intensification of its central source.

Primogeniture

All first-born, male or female, were honored with property exchanges at birth, the male alone, however, qualifying as a leader. There are no references to their sanctity. The Uveans had departed from primogenitural exclusiveness, reinterpreting the concept as a principle of sequence of birth order. Succession to command moved down the fraternal line until finally even the youngest son had absolute eminence in his generation as the sole bearer of the honor. The Uvean system is a handsome compromise between exclusive and distributive ideas of status.

Seniority of Descent

The compromise with primogeniture has its repercussions in the organization of lines of descent. Uvea did not neglect seniority; it insisted only that the first-born of first-born cannot take up his command until all his father's brothers had had their turn. *Sub specie aeternitatis*, the principle is sustained, allowing for interruptions. In the short span, where the realities of power lie, it is the interruptions that matter most. Traditional Polynesian seniority is focusing and isolative; the Uvean compromise dilutes and blends. Like all other compromise systems, it too has to improvise new criteria of discrimination. Among the three royal Uvean lineages, the seniority principle had been so compromised that successions were in fact decided by appointment or by force of arms. It had become as Burrows put it, "elastic (1937:71)."

Male Line

The Tongan viewpoint was preeminent in giving political preference to males, to patrilineal descent and to patrilocal residence without sacrificing flexibility. When there was no male heir, a woman succeeded, but to preserve, of course, the interests of the lineage. By Burrows' count, as many as one-third of all marriages accepted residence with the wife's side for the sake of specific advantages. These figures are to be judged, however, in the light of contemporary interests, presumably more utilitarian. The principal divergence from Tongan standards was in the degree to which Uvea had narrowed the gap between brother and sister and their respective descent lines, particularly among ordinary families. While insisting upon avoidances, Uvea did not elevate sisters above their brothers, except among royalty. Thus the daughter of the high chief's sister, and her descendants, stood before him and his own line as a sacred lineage, known (in close correspondence with the Tongan) as the *Tamahaa.* As sacred counterparts to the royal male lineage, the latter held power of fahu over the chiefs, but limited to ritual property. The fixation of fahu within a lineage undoubtedly follows—though in reverse—the Tongan pattern of relationship between Tui Tonga and his Tui Kanokupolu lineage, the source of his own fahu privileges. In the etiquettes of precedence, those of the Tamahaa outranked the chief, just as in Tonga the tamaha of Tui Tonga had the highest rank in the land. A Tonga-Uvean comparison on fahu suggests opposing trends in further development of a traditional respect relationship. In Tonga there were indications that fahu had begun as a royal privilege and then spread outward, in a wave of democratization, to the common man. In Uvea, if we accept Burrows' judgment, the process was reversed (1937:170).

Sanctity

Information on religion is most incomplete. Sketchy details imply, nevertheless, a chiefly sanctity, comparable in principle to that of the Tongan, as well as an extension of some sanctity to all mature males. All objects set aside for high chiefs were tapu, but not his person. Distance was maintained rigorously, of course, although there were apparently no specific injunctions against touching his body or avoiding contact with what he had touched. The missionary Bataillon has described traditional deferences (cited in Burrows 1937:73). When the people saw their high chief, even from a distance, they sat down and remained silent. They would not utter his name, or look at him straight on, or address him in the vernacular. Only sacred chiefs could eat turtle. It is not known how chiefs defended their sanctity against either accidental or deliberate abuse. Since they did have the power of putting to death, they may have taken a personal hand in severe breaches. What is known is that when they had imposed a conservation tapu on crops, violations were automatically punished by a god.

The degree of sanctity in the domestic sphere may be judged by eating habits, on which there is some information. It was tapu for children to eat with their fathers and wives with their husbands. Such separation is surely an aspect of sacred status, but must be distinguished from royal sanctity, which was an aspect of religious power. The former merges imperceptibly with etiquette (as in Samoa); the latter stands forth clearly as divine or god-like. In either realm the Uvean focus was on the acquired, the secured position, never upon potential alone. At least there is no evidence that even the royal firstborn were regarded as sacred. Power was given by the gods to those who had shown some merit or had taken their fancy. Both chiefs and priests shared powers as spokesmen, as mere representatives of the gods. Holding hereditary title (in principle), chiefs may be designated as scheduled representatives, while the priests were made oracular at random. Judging by the text of prayers, neither had any but a modest role in the affairs of power. The congregation is embarassed that the mischievous god has mistreated them before their chief. They urge him to give up his wrath and turn loving. The power of the representatives was in dealings with the people, and not with the gods.

Tohunga

Priest and craftsmen were distinct categories. The former stood to craftsmen as they did to chiefs. Chosen at random, they laid down no line of descent. Their honor was ephemeral. Tufunga were the master craftsmen of the three esteemed skills, canoe making, house building, and dye (turmeric) preparation. The titles of honor were inherited, probably as in neighboring Futuna within selected lineages. Healers formed a lower category of inherited skill. There is no information on the organization of the crafts, and no references to the warrior as specialist.

Wealth

All families regardless of rank were democratically involved in ritual feasting and property exchanges; all were obliged to put on the best possible show. Royalty had a few additional obligations, but the distinction was not categorical. In general, standards of display and rank differences were not conspicuous. The first missionaries were surprised to find they could hardly tell which house belonged to a chief and which to a common man. Burrows sums it up: "Respectful behavior is much more in evidence than material insignia (1937:75)." There are no clear indications, either, of a central role for chiefs in the economy, ritual or material. The circulation was between families and lineages, not, as far as we know, islandwide.

Political Hegemony

It is the haughty and capricious power of the chief that is remembered. Nothing is said of his administrative accomplishments. Presumably he was a traditional ariki, exponent of divine power and conserver of crops. Administration was in the lower jurisdictions of lineage and household heads. We should not assume that the examples of arrogant powers are necessarily typical. They may have been recorded as strikingly bizarre and thus would throw the picture out of balance because there is so little else to stabilize it. One example is of special interest because it matches the Tongan style. A human body is said to have been used as a torch to illuminate a royal birth feast. If the story is perhaps apocryphal, it does illustrate the symbolic gulf that awesome power creates between the high and the low. Somewhat less flamboyant is the apparent custom of burying subjects alive with their chief (Burrows 1937:69). The early missionaries were convinced that chiefs held the lives of their subjects too cheaply. So were the Uveans, whose traditions speak of the assassination of despots who indulged in excess.

The Structure of Status

The principal commitment was to traditional rank—established, however, upon criteria that have not been fully elucidated, but unquestionably predicated upon an etiquette of precedence as codified in the kava circle. Polarization was a key feature: in the old days, in terms of upper-rank Tongan and lower rank native; in the later period, of indigenous rule, of those within and those without the kava circle. The dichotomy was relatively stable and governed etiquette more than it did "life style."

Genealogical Rank

The paramount chief over all Uvea was of *aliki* rank, but in a realm of his own as bearer of the unique title of Lavelua, presumably an old family name. Aliki retained its distinction as aristocratic, and was the title of chiefs of notable or royal lineages. Occasionally it was granted to notable leaders of lesser families. It was a title of office only, but had some of the attributes of a rank, since all formed the special council (*kau aliki*) of the Lavelua.

Heads of lesser or junior lineages were known mundanely as elders (*matua*), who, like aliki were also ranked. Matapule were matua who had been chosen to enter the kava circle as a bridge between the two realms of royal-common or, in a replica of the Tongan court, between foreigner and autochthone (in reverse). Commoners, or *taua,* are described in Uvea as those who sit outside the kava circle.

Descent Group Organization

Burrows' description of Uvean social organization must be evaluated in the light of the European authority, which favored a central native administration over officially created districts. Our interest, however, is with the older and more traditional order, even though only its shadow organization can now be discerned. In the older system, to sum up, Segment I was the ritual organization that covered the island under Lavelua. Segment II were the constituent lineages, not necessarily linked up with each other. The royal lineages were part of a larger ramified organization; the commoner lines may have been. The royal lineages differed from the commoner in their tendency to hold together, and thus to grow larger. Commoner lineages split more readily. The former were referred to as *faahinga;* the latter simply as *kainga.* Faahinga designates an honorable rank or class, and in this sense lifts up the lineage; kainga, on the other hand, has a utilitarian connotation. Its usage, to quote Burrows, "shows that the economic factor has always been fundamental (1937:66)."

Each lineage had a name and a territory within which its members had assured rights to crop land. Primary allegiance was to the paternal lineage and courtesy rights to land were available in that of the mother. The kainga point of view probably fell somewhere between utility and religious obligation. Members could choose economic residence freely, but the norms of kinship held them to their elders, who presided over the ceremonies of birth, marriage, and death and thus enabled them to transmute the efforts of their labor to a higher level.

Segment III was the *api,* a common residence group that shared a single cookhouse even when it occupied several dwellings. The *api* was also headed by a matua or a *taokete,* an eldest son, and had sufficient autonomy as a producing group to declare itself a full-fledged kainga when it had enough substance to hold its own in ceremonial exchange.

One point emerges with some clarity from this too general account, and that is the dependence of a ramified lineage organization upon some ritual connection, which in turn is predicated upon genealogical rank. One is left with the feeling that the Tongan occupation which tended to create a monopoly of rank and ritual pushed the commoner kainga into a freer and less structured terrain.

14

Futuna

FUTUNA, A UVEAN NEIGHBOR, HAD MOVED IN ITS OWN DIRECTION, more directly toward the Open society. Also of the Tongan family, the Futunan language is closest to Tikopian and Uvean, and only more distantly related to Tongan and Samoan. If one is obliged to select some particular cultural leaning, it is probably toward Samoa, the reputed source of a major founding dynasty. The Tongan cultural reflections, are, as Burrows had observed, subdued despite military contacts, and despite very close relations with Tongaized Uveans who had lived among the Futunans for a long time. Having beaten back several Tongan invasion attempts, the Futunans had also turned their backs upon political innovation from that direction. Thus the Open society which had made its appearance upon part of Futunan territory was an internal development upon a presumably ancient and general western Polynesian foundation.

The intensity of political antagonism in Futuna owes much to features of terrain, to the uneven distribution of arable lands, and to periodic famine. There are two islands, Futuna proper and smaller Alofi. Both are volcanic, but otherwise ecologically distinct. The main island is arable mainly along its moist coastal lowlands, while on Alofi, all lands, including the central plateau, could be planted. Futunans confined to the rim of their much larger island were, in fact, locked-in; Alofians could spread out. Estimates of population density thus misrepresent, in this instance, the true economic situation. Futuna with some 2000 people on 25 square miles seems falsely underpopulated by comparison with Alofi, whose 1800 were dispersed over only 11 square miles. The local traditions leave no doubt, however, that it was the Alofians who were the constant victims of Futunan land hunger.

Both cultivated the usual high island crops—taro and yam as staples, coconut, breadfruit, arrowroot, banana, and sweet potato as supplements. Both raised livestock (pig, dog, and fowl), snared pigeons and other birds, and fished. Neither island had a lagoon, so that fishing was reduced to a minor industry. The diet may have been varied, but evidently not bountiful. The Futunans, especially, worked hard. They put to use even the most distant and small plots of fertile soil, and they drained and irrigated the coastal swamps. Famine was not uncommon. After a brutal storm they were driven, it has been said, to the excesses of cannibalism, infanticide, and pillage. One can hardly disagree with Burrows judgment that land shortage was "a factor in war (1936:130)."

Futunan technical skills were, like the Uvean, unimpressive. They used stone freely to line irrigation ditches, and to face house platforms, burial mounds, and dams, but uncut and untrimmed. Ceremonial structures were rudimentary. The village *malaes* were clearings surrounded by rough-hewn coral slab backrests. The royal tombs were low mounds. Only wood was carved to represent ancestral images.

In their encounters with Europeans, Futunans displayed some of the intransigence that had earlier repulsed the adventurous Tongans, but with somewhat less success. They startled their amiable discoverers, Schouten and LeMaire (1616), by plundering their vessel when they had been invited simply to trade. After a costly skirmish, the Futunans understood what was desired of them and invited the Dutch to stay, to no avail. They were not disturbed again for almost two centuries, until the London Missionary Society's *Royal Admiral* hove to. This reception, too, lacked cordiality, impressing even the determined evangelists with the inopportuneness of their visit. They left after three days. But Futunan insularity had been breached. Shortly thereafter, in 1841, Father Peter Chanel attempted the first Catholic mission on Futuna. He was executed by a high chief who saw the perils of Christianity to his authority. His son and successor recognized rather the opportunities, and converted—unleashing thereby a zeal for reform that amazed, even terrified their teachers, who could barely restrain the exuberant enthusiasm of such ardent pupils. The islands then quickly became French protectorates, and in 1923 were formally annexed.

When Burrows came in 1932, traditional religion and government had, of course, disappeared. What remained was the "daily routine," presumably in aboriginal form. The French mission, however, had left good records of its own inquiries. It is from these, in the main, that the Futunan past must be reconstructed. Futuna is somewhat better known than Uvea; important details are missing, but the general outlines that permit us to place Futunan society within its western Polynesian social milieu are discernible.

Genealogical Traditions

The traditions describe three periods: of first settlement, of the early chiefly dynasties, and of recent political history that starts in the nineteenth century with the final conquest by Futunans of Alofi. They have little to say about origins, and leave open the question whether the islands had been settled by a single line or by several. Burrows thought the latter was more probable, citing the independence of the Alofi traditions from those of Futuna proper. On the larger island, the lineages of chiefs of Tua, one of two great districts into which Futuna had become divided, claimed descent from Samoan royalty; those of rival Singave from an independent royal line that bore the divine title of *fakavelikele*. Alofi, having been virtually depeopled by the avid Futunans, understandably has nothing to say about its own origins.

Singave implies an early religious sovereignty of its fakavelikele over all, without disputing the common legend of an early period of local group autonomy. Eventually, the traditions record, some, such as Tua, Singave, Asoa on Futuna, and Alofitai on Alofi, became dominant centers, conquering and otherwise absorbing the others. Alofi, for example, was brought under Asoa, which was in turn incorporated under Tua. Then Tua and Singave faced each other as irreconcilable rivals, disputing boundaries, and above all the great prize of Alofi, but not it would seem, the question of actual political hegemony. Like the West Samoans they were concerned with the broader concept of mastery and not with the specifics of rule; with who was for the moment the *malo* (victor) and who the *lava* (weak).

We have been left with only the dimmest view of this early period. Because the lists of chiefs are incomplete, they cannot date its duration. Futuna is presumably at least as old as Uvea. As for social systems, the records suggest that Tua from earliest days was under the jurisdiction of a single royal dynasty. At one time the rule was divided peaceably when an heir to the ritual authority chose instead the new title of Tui Saakafu, which carried the special prerogative of distributing food at public feasts.

The history of early Singave suggests a more turbulent evolution. The earliest chiefs had divine powers, then women are said to have ruled, and finally a military triumvirate replaced the traditional chiefs and divided the district into three related territories. Warriors loom over all the histories. In Tua they dethrone royalty, but not until the nineteenth century; and in once independent Asoa an arrogant toa defied the traditional chief by setting his backrest at a higher level and by having kava served to him in the royal manner. This example of insubordination, and a Tuan account of open rebellion against the traditional chief, along with the record of conquest and consolidation illuminates, if barely, the general direction. If the early authority had been religious, it had also turned aggressive and expansionist.

From this perspective, Burrows' demarcation of the reign of the great Veliteki over Tua as the beginning of a new era is entirely apt. A traditional chief, Veliteki completed the subjugation of Alofi with savage thoroughness. There are several versions of this final solution of the Alofi problem. According to one, the ruler was saddened by the hard lot of his own people. He urged them to play more, work less, and feed instead upon the flesh of the enemy. The version Burrows found the more credible is that Veliteki had sent his people against Alofi because they were near starvation after a severe hurricane. They ate everyone there except for three men. Servant, who had first collected this account, adds his own rational comment. Had the people gathered the coconuts and other vegetables which the storm had spared, they would have been adequately nourished at home. If not the custom, then the fashion for cannibalism dates from this period. According to Chevron, hungry Futunans did not always go abroad for flesh. They sought victims even among their own kin. Mothers, he insists, had been known to eat their own children (cited by Burrows 1936:36).

The later period, beginning after 1800 with the consolidation of the two great Futunan powers, moves rapidly into new stages before the European outlook has time to take over. Veliteki is succeeded by a warrior chief from a new line. In one more war in 1841 with Singave—after the mission had been established—Tua is victor and now declares a single authority, but only briefly, for with the sudden death of the new monarch the new dream of unity, so devoutly desired by Europeans, fades. Futuna was only to taste greatness, not to enjoy it!

The Status System

Characterization is difficult for several reasons, which are now self-evident. Principally, the record is incomplete. But the society itself, subject to diverse influences, may have evolved a generalized pattern. By contrast with the great and strongly delineated status systems of Samoa and Tonga, the Futunan appears all the more undefined. As Samoan in derivation, to which has been added the Tongan and, in some unspecified manner the Tikopian, its generalization is a likely development. Whatever the reason, no feature commands attention. The focus is blurred. Nevertheless, the Tua and Singave distinctions and their history of transformation help place the main orientation. The style is mobile and flexible, with outlets for the enjoyment of power and for the refinements of graded etiquette. If we consider Singave at the time of its military triumvirate, still another significant feature suggests itself: an implacable rivalry between diverging systems, one more fully open than the other.

Primogeniture

The first-born son (not the daughter) was greeted at birth by a series of feasts and exchanges of food between his father's and his mother's families. The display of economic efficacy became part of his prestige record. It did not sanctify him and it did not set him apart.

The concept would seem to have been limited to the immediate religious statement of linkage between the economic and the birth cycle and not with the promulgation of a major being or of a superior line. In qualifications for office, being first-born was a factor, not the standard criterion (Burrows 1936:88).

Seniority of Descent

The evidence is partly negative. If so remarkable a social feature as seniority is not mentioned by a professional observer, it probably did not exist. On the positive side, the absence conforms, as we would expect, with the Samoan plan of grading family and person by general criteria of family and accomplishment. The genealogical records of the high chiefs reveal no pattern of succession consistent with so orderly a procedure as seniority. Of a total of 26 successions (combining Tua and Singave), only eight involved kinsmen of a known degree.

Male Line

In this respect, Futuna is closer to Tikopia than to either Samoa or Tonga. Patriliny, while not absolute, was customary, in family law more than in politics, in succession to property and title more than to the office of high chief. There is no reference in Burrows' work to Samoan-Tongan bilinearity. On the contrary, his account of the local version of *vasu* indicates a break with the policies of the homeland. Here it had ceased to be an exclusive privilege of a man's sister's son, and had become the right of all male relatives of the high chief to foods brought for distribution before him. At the decisive point of a traditional relationship, the formal division between the line of a man and of his sister had been set aside. What remains of the bilineal complex is a mild avoidance between brother and sister. The maternal line has the same role here as in eastern Polynesia; it is supplementary, making up in what is desired for status, but missing in orthodox patriliny.

Sanctity

In the Samoan manner, sanctity was an attribute of the office and not of the person. Chiefs represented ancestral gods, who accepted them as oracular spokesmen after they had taken office. Chiefs could intercede to divert their ancestral deities from malevolent intent and thereby score a popular success. The great positive actions came directly from the gods and were not benefices of chiefly power. Unless our information is seriously defective, we may believe that Futunans had reduced personal sanctity to a very low magnitude. In many respects the Marquesan common man was more of a sacred being than a Futunan chief. The chiefs moved among the emblems of sanctity which were tapu; they in their own person were not. Certain birds and fish and, of course, the turtle were tapu and reserved for chiefs. The turtle, a traditionally sacred creature as an agent of the gods, was specially set aside food for malo chiefs. The slab backrests on the malae were tapu to all but the designated chief, and whoever touched the ornamented house beam in the house of the high chief of Tua would be stricken dead by divine agency. Sanctity emanated directly from the gods, not from the person. The chief was their spokesman, indeed their lineal descendant, but in no way even metaphorically their rival. Futunans had thus rejected the elevation of a living being beyond a moderate degree. They expected their chiefs to move freely among them and to work as they did. The basic concept is Samoan (Manu'a), but the scale is much reduced. Tui Manu'a was a most exalted eminence and from him the grades of sanctity diminished, but to a point where all had some touch of it. In Futuna the touch of sanctity was the province of chiefs and titled persons only; all others were free of it, and the difference between the most exalted and the common was narrowed.

The Futunan concept of graded sanctity is in fact analogous to traditional ranking by seniority, and may be either a parallel form or simply a revision of the latter. As apotheosized ancestors, the gods have taken their own rank from the lineages, introducing into an otherwise mobile society an absolute order. The structure having been made rigid, the person remains free, within the range of his own kindred. The places are fixed; he is not ordained from birth to fill them. In its own greatly abbreviated form, this Futunan conceptualization of the interplay between form and freedom is surely Samoan.

Tohunga

Tufunga in Futunan designates merely the possession of a skill and is not a title of honor. The master craftsmen were the outstanding carpenters, the canoe and house builders, who then bore the graphic title "adze handles" (*kau toki*). Whether they may have had special privileges, we do not know. It would be extraordinary if they did not, for the titles were the property of chiefly lineages only; they could be bestowed as an added honor upon a chief. In Tua only two lineages held it, and in Singave only one. A lower title was *lautsilo,* for supervisors of turmeric dyes. Evidently in the same class was the hereditary *tui*—the most exalted of the western Polynesian titles—who was privileged to hold the front of the great net upon occasions of ritual fishing.

Fragmentary information on priests describes them as oracles (*vaka atua*) of the gods, an hereditary office. If the chiefs represented major ancestral deities, the priests probably spoke for the host of "inferior spirits" who were mainly bearers of misfortune (cf. Williamson 1937: 97), and would therefore be at a lower level.

In the narrow sense, the warrior is an occupational specialist. That he is everywhere called toa states for us the Polynesian view that he is a person apart, not tohunga but in another order of skills. In Futuna the toa was always a potential chief, and actually within the realm of chiefs even when not an office-holder. The title was the privilege of only the most distinguished fighters, those who had won prominence. Since being malo was after all the true test of chiefly competence, the great warrior was a natural though not the inevitable candidate. All toa rated a backrest. The warrior who set his own above that of the chief and arrogated to himself a royal role in the ritual of the kava service exceeded his actual rights without, however, outraging the established order.

Wealth

The obligation to share goods and foods so that one never consumed or used only that which was his own was felt by all families regardless of status. The rationale, as the Reverend Gunn learned, was religious. To eat only one's own food was to die (1914:208). Thus all families engaged in countless exchanges, item for item, with other communities, seizing the opportunity offered by any special occasion. Economic insularity is metaphoric death in all of Polynesia, where the low is that which is heavy, inert, and does not move outward. Everywhere chiefs assumed the major obligation to energize by circulating widely and actively the produce of their jurisdiction. In Futuna, too, the chiefs had the privilege of the larger role. They presided over the annual harvest festival, and over feasts to propitiate the gods in times of famine; and as polygynists they multiplied their marital exchanges. The distinction is largely quantitative, and not too great at that. Gunn (1914), who has described harvest festival exchanges, does not mention chiefs, leaving one to assume they were in the name of the individual households. There are no hints of rivalry in the economy; the leading concepts are generosity and reciprocity.

Political Hegemony

The nature of political authority is only hinted at, leaving us with but a vague intimation of the nature of relationships between dominant and subordinate. If we grasp at all the slender straws of evidence left by the traditions, we shall remain afloat long enough to perceive a pattern that is more brute than political. The reported liquidation of Alofians is a case in point. Admittedly, since there is no information to the contrary, one is drawn to interpreting each "clue" from the standpoint of a Western Samoan model. If there is no evidence of economic integration or of political hierarchy among related communities to oppose such an idea, a Samoan-type seems a plausible interpretation. Bearing on this is the image of a chief as a priestly figure, and of the village and its fono as the authority that organized collective labor and promoted economic interchange. As a high priest, the chief had extraordinary powers of a metaphoric nature—that is, the imposing or lifting of tapu. If he had authority over the lives of his subjects, the examples that have come down are of intervening to save a life. He was evidently an instigator and organizer of war, drawing upon his divine connections to improve prospects for plunder and destruction (cf. Burrows 1936:85).

As in Samoa, chief and fono were in complementary balance, the former dealing with the great elevated events, the council with details. In the event of a "grave crime," it was the council that judged and punished. In an example Burrows gives, the culprit is compelled to slaughter his pigs and to take up his crops and provide a feast (1936:98). The idea, one may imagine, is to restore an asocial malefactor by forcing him to be an extravagant giver. In Singave, the balance of power had seemingly shifted more decidedly to the fono, until presumably the military triumvirate had restored centralized authority. In one instance, a ruler took the hint from popular neglect and renounced his office.

I think we may distinguish two concepts of power, one internal, postulated upon balance, gradation, and equilibrium, and the other external, demanding a powerful demonstration of strength. The enemy had to be reduced. His property was seized, his crops were destroyed.

The Structure of Status

The system is of titles, not of class, or of genealogical rank in any organized way. The principal titles are traditional, the high chief as *aliki sau*, the subchiefs as *aliki*. Only one person at a time held one of these titles, the others, even the close relatives were *seka*, the non-titled, the common people. Distinctions are inevitable, nevertheless, so that the family of the sau had at least one royal prerogative, the vasu. Among lower aliki even this was lacking. The vasu, in any case, like the turtle for the malo chief, was a prerogative of form.

The Futunan equivalent of genealogical rank is the kava circle, a meticulously graded society of luminaries. The kava circle resembles the Samoan fono stripped of executive function. With the usual exceptions, membership favored the holders of hereditary titles. The exceptions were the toa, that is, if they were otherwise untitled. In Tua, the kava circle recognized three grades; the aliki sau and his aides, such as food distributor, and messenger, along with the most eminent of the aliki; the aliki of all inhabited villages; and finally a grade of reserve chiefs who were temporarily without a constituency. In Singave, where political life was more austere, this last category was ignored. In Futuna, as in Samoa, political and ritual gradation coincide and resemble rank by seniority. But here the system has been reconstituted on different principles. We know what these are in Samoa. Perhaps they are the same in Futuna.

The term *seka* is undefined, but if it was an appropriate designation for the relatives of chiefs, it must have at worst a neutral connotation. Only defeat was degrading. The untitled commoner was a free man, owing his chiefs respect but not servility. Such economic burdens as there were fell upon the chiefs, leading the missionaries to lament: "Chieftainship leads to poverty (Burrows 1936:89)."

Descent Group Organization

Our knowledge of the Futunan organization is too fragmentary for full discussion, and I shall confine myself to setting forth some tentative implications from such information as is available. To start with the broad historical pattern, the traditional record has suggested to Burrows a radical evolution from once politically significant lineages who had occupied their own extensive territory to a system of political districts such as Tua and Singave (1936:71). In the new system the surviving lineages were very much reduced in size; those who shared a common territory were neither related to one another nor necessarily to their chiefs. The traditions refer to older districts such as Asoa as *kutunga*, the term for lineage, and then describe how they were conquered, absorbed, or dispersed. In the later history only the royal lineages retained an interest in pedigree; all others stopped reckoning beyond five or six generations, thus conceding a shallow and fragmentary structure. In short, the hypothesis of transformation is credible. What is most unclear is the nature of early connections among lineages, if any. The belief of some Futunans that Fakavelikele was once the national god suggests a ritual unity similar, perhaps, to that of Manu'a under Tui Manu'a. The character of the transformation would then have been somewhat different.

On segmentation, only broad features can be discerned. The antagonism between the politically independent districts of Tua and Singave is clear. But there may be cause to suspect a ritual relationship (rituals of antagonism) that implies a partnership. The alternation of malo and lava, symbolized by the right to the sacred turtle, demonstrates at least a common religious understanding. Perhaps this is too fragile an association. In that case, Segment I is each of the two island divisions. While the chief was a religious figure, he had the power to wage war—a political authority for a religious end—but no utilitarian economic functions. His fono, which was not fully representative of subordinate groups and villages, did not represent the material interests of the villages either.

Segment II refers to constituent villages, each governed by a lower-order chief and a fono of household representatives. A village could comprise a single lineage, but most brought together unrelated kin and gave to their constituency a distinct and complementary organization. Dropping below the status of the higher order, the villages assume more utilitarian functions. They deal with crime, and they organize one of the systems of agriculture and fishing. Their chief is a lesser priest who might be represented in the district fono.

Segment III is the abbreviated kutunga, a pro-patrilineal lineage, generally localized, and headed by its senior male, who was known either as its *pule*, leader, or *taokete*, eldest son. Each kutunga bore a name either from a founder, the totemic animal associated with its god, or most simply from its place of residence. The type of name may once have described its quality or grade. Each possesses traditional land holdings, which are kainga, and thus distinct from the collective taro gardens, which come under the jurisdiction of the village. Kainga lands are a birthright, inalienably associated with the lineage, so much so that even when they are abandoned permanently others are reluctant to claim them. At the same time, they are available to a woman's children, who are not in fact authentic members of the lineage. But this is evidently a matter of courtesy and respect. The pule is the administrator of the lands, responsible for allocating to each household its share.

Village lands have been collectively improved and lie compactly in the vicinity. The kainga is a strip like a Hawaiian ili that runs from the central plateau to the beach. This arrangement can be said to give each lineage a true sample of the island's terrain, an equity transcending economic value, since on Futuna the basic crop lands are those of the irrigated flat lands.

For reasons that are now obscure, some lineages control the important titles, including that of *sau,* and others do not even claim an hereditary craft, or important priest. Thus they differ in prestige and significance even though as lineages they are not formally ranked. If formal rank had been an earlier characteristic, vestiges are observable among the royal lineages (cf. Burrows 1936:72).

Finally, each constituent household was a fraternal extended family held together by the preference for patrilocal residence. It was often referred to as kainga, perhaps because it was the true and ultimate economic unit that tilled its own lineage segment and negotiated through its membership in the *fono* its rights within the village.

15

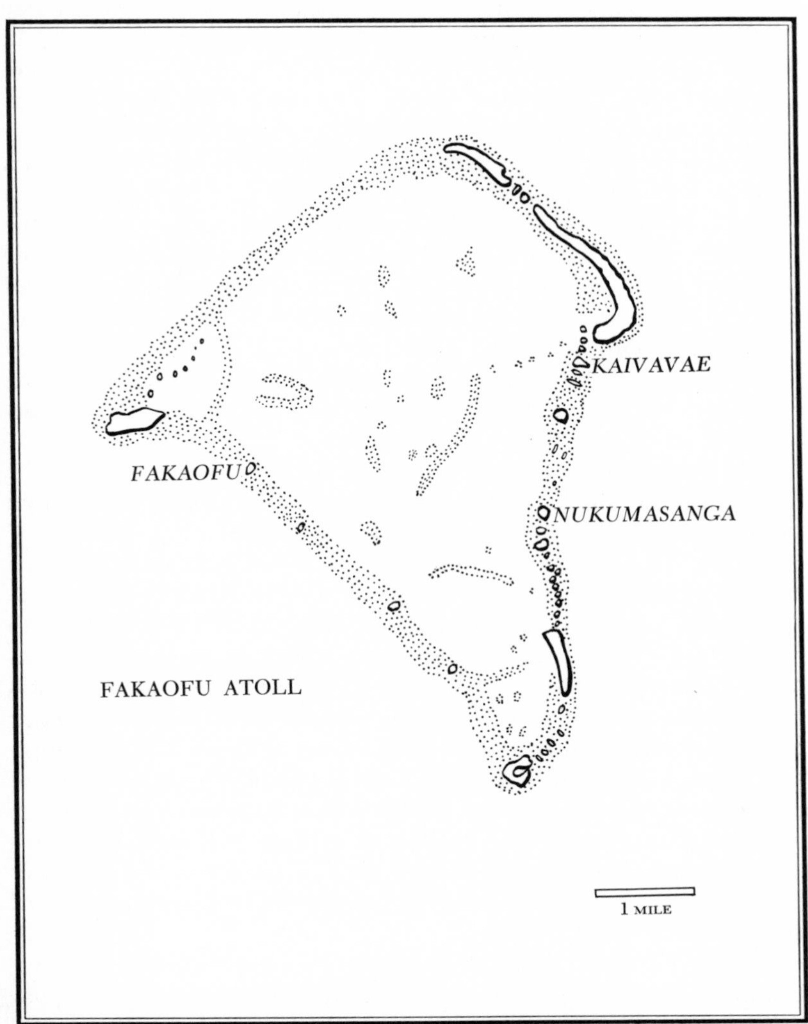

The Tokelaus

COMPRISING FOUR WIDELY SEPARATED ATOLLS OF SOME FOUR square miles of combined land areas, the Tokelaus are among the poorer habitats of Polynesia. Yet in aboriginal times they had held a population estimated as high as 1200 and had created, according to their traditions, what may be described as a miniature "conquest state." Tokelauan culture is fundamentally Manu'an, with some important modifications. Where Manu'a had replaced seniority with more flexible criteria for office, the Tokelaus had established a balance between seniority and age. As politics had encroached upon seniority in Manu'a, age had superseded the claims of seniority in the Tokelaus. Thus, while Manu'a had become an Open society, the Tokelaus after an early fling at political expansionism had settled down to the more stable traditionalism of its elder citizens, a pattern shared only with Pukapuka and Ontong Java. Insofar as one may think of "gerontocracy" as a more primordial political pattern, the Tokelauan version of Manu'an culture may be considered as an example of social recidivism.

The history of these small islands is one of great complexity. If Samoa was the core of Tokelauan culture, several other societies from both eastern and western Polynesia had undoubtedly helped shape its edges. The Tokelaus traditions—which are consistent with the actual distribution of "traits"—specify additional connections with Tongareva, with Manihiki-Rakahanga, with the Ellice Islands, with Tonga, and with Pukapuka. MacGregor, struck by the seemingly archaic character of the social system, conjectured that the atolls still retained the early Polynesian traits brought there by first migrants from Micronesia. To consider the Tokelaus as "early" Polynesian in that sense would require us to assume the unlikelihood of long and continuous occupation of tiny islands with a known record of savage and devastating storms. It is simpler to attribute the unusual features of Tokelauan society to its complex and, in more recent years, very painful history of culture shock brought about by foreign intrusions and by drastic depopulation.

Of the four atolls, only Olosenga had ever cultivated taro in pre-European times. The others depended upon fish, coconut, and pandanus fruits, a diet of stark simplicity. The cultural and political center was Fakaofu, which at 500 people per square mile was also the most densely populated. Such density is all the more extraordinary when we consider that this atoll is simply a collection of 60 islets each rising barely 10 feet out of the sea, and only one of these large enough to sustain a solitary village. By the middle of the nineteenth century, and after white contact, two of the atolls, Olosenga and Atafu, had already been totally abandoned. The real subsistence problem was not food, but fresh water and, of course, the implacable threat of sudden disaster.

First discovered by Quiros in 1606, the Tokelaus were not visited again by Europeans until 1765, when a British vessel touched briefly on Atafu. More active relations began after 1841, when French and American explorers arrived in short succession. The United States Exploring Expedition of that period produced the first anthropological report on Tokelauan life, including some evidence that the atolls had been visited by European-born Hawaiians some years before—still another strand in a complex history (Hale 1838–42).

Hurricanes battered Fakaofu in 1846 and again in 1852. After the first of these, many left the island. But the second brought help from Samoan-based missionaries, who then made a permanent place for themselves on the atolls. The most severe blow to the continuity of Tokelauan culture was struck by Peruvian slavers, whose raids between 1852 and 1870 drained the islands of their human population. Some 240 were reportedly removed from Fakaofu in 1863 alone. Finally, in 1877 the Tokelaus came under the more stable authority of Great Britain, and more recently under the New Zealand mandate of Western Samoa, which granted local autonomy.

The persistence in the Tokelaus of a recognizable Polynesian culture in the face of such damaging rents in its social fabric says much for the durability of the basic pattern. In 1932 MacGregor could still record the nature of domestic life. The traditional religion and chiefly organization had faded almost to the point of extinction, to be sure, but enough survived to provide, even if dimly, a glimpse into the capabilities of the Polynesian tradition under circumstances that fostered reduction and regression.

Genealogical Traditions

The traditions reflect rather accurately the historical diversity of the Tokelaus. They reveal themes which are eastern Polynesian, and a concept of man as emerging from maggots, in the true Samoan tradition. Some claim Samoa as the origin point, others claim Rarotonga. They also refer to the conquest of an indigenous population by later migrants. All chiefly lines are, however, traced back to a Kava, who was known as The Definer of Boundaries. The genealogical lists are understandably incomplete. One of 19 generations collected by MacGregor carries back to the eighteenth century; a list of 11 chiefs compiled by Hale in 1841 would also place this Kava after the time of Quiros. An earlier date, nevertheless, is almost certainly the more likely, since Quiros had already observed a chief being carried about on a shoulder-borne litter by bearers who were shading him with palm leaves. The atolls were then quite prosperous. Quiros also saw large double canoes that could carry upwards of 50 persons, and great quantities of fine mats—in Tonga the hallmark of royalty.

Two decisive events are assigned to the early founding period. The first is the royal repartition of Fakaofu lands among family heads; the second, the conquest of the other and alien atolls by Fakaofuans. The formal division of lands on so small a territory would seem to be in the eastern Polynesian tradition of granting to the paramount chief the titular honors over the economy. As definer of boundaries, the chief stands as the literal founder of the social order. Within this same tradition, the next generation embarks upon territorial expansion. Kava has two sons, one who succeeds him as ariki; the other, as chief warrior, undertakes the conquest of the adjacent atolls. Nukunono, already in political turmoil, is the first to fall. Fakaofu sends a resident overlord to collect a coconut tribute. Atafu is conquered in retaliation for a raid. Olosenga becomes a tributary dependency. This micro-state was short-lived. It was an untenable political extravaganza, and the Tokelaus—in one of the rare reversals of this kind in human history—went from conquest state back to the more traditional forms of genealogical dependency. Famine had compelled the Nukunonans to abandon their mother atoll; Atafuans simply fled from their Fakaofuan aggressors. On Olosenga they had all starved to death. Fakaofu then colonized the atolls with its own people and retained their traditional loyalties; according to the traditions, nothing unusual happened until after the European encounter.

The Status System

In its understatement of seniority, in its recognition of the duality of male and female descent lines, in the quality of sanctity of chiefs, in the honoring of crafts, and, most strikingly, in the counterpointing of chief and council, the Tokelauan status system is Samoan, but on a much smaller scale. Scale is a factor, however, that governs the behavior of a pattern. The grandeur and the range of honors inherent within the Samoan system were attributes of its magnitude, with its broad prospects for mobility within the social hierarchy. The Samoan system was tropically florescent; the Tokelauan barely unfolded its buds. The Samoan system expanded in the warmth of aggressive ambition; the Tokelauan settled finally for the quiescence of gerontocratic conservatism.

The precise character of Tokelauan gerontocracy does not emerge too clearly from earlier writings. Williamson, who saw clearly the balance between respect for age and concessions to descent, believed, however, that the Tokelaus once had "pure gerontocracy (1924:I, 377)." Discussing only the present system, MacGregor notes a subtle but important distinction between succession to the high chiefship (Tui Tokelau) and membership in the village council. In the former, succession was traditionally by primogeniture; in the latter, succession was by age. Ruler and councillors were all, however, apt to be old men, since the successor to the chiefship would not be invested in office until he was well along in years. Age was a dominant consideration, yet the distinction is not to be ignored, for it suggests as between Tokelauan ariki and council a parallel to the distinctive ways in which Samoans chose their ariki and their matais.

Primogeniture

The first-born was the *tama sa,* the "sacred child," the center of honor in each family. If male, he was drawn into a very close relationship with his *matua sa* ("sacred mother"), who held a parallel position of honor as the eldest sister of his father. Adopted by the senior representative of paternal aunts, he had the distinction of being removed from his parental household, in effect a sororal household because of matrilocal residence, and allowed to reside at the very center of his patrilineal line. The honors of primogeniture were thus divided across the generations into masculine and feminine domains. Primogeniture was therefore more prominent in the Tokelaus than in Manu'a, although restrained and compromised by reverence for age. The first-born male should head the kindred, and is groomed for such leadership from birth. He does not, however, take command until his father's brothers have ruled in order of their seniority. It must be said, then, that if primogeniture opened the way to authority, only the maturity of age secured it.

Seniority of Descent

Considering the ambiguity about primogeniture, seniority understandably faded. Whatever the earlier customs had been, it had finally become the practice to select the high chief, the ariki, from among the four principal families who had the distinction of descent from the first dynasty. According to Newell (1895), they simply elected their oldest male, ignoring seniority of descent. The royal lines had the honor of notable descent, but were not ranked.

Male Line

The basic pattern was dual. The Tokelauan version of the western Polynesian tradition was tilted, but only slightly, in the direction of favoring the female line because of the preference for matrilocal residence, which gave economic ascendancy to the household of the mother and her sisters. The residential patterns, however, varying as a rule with status, restored traditional Samoa-Tonga balances. A first-born son, as we have observed left his mother's household to reside with his paternal aunt and eventually set up his household on his father's land (MacGregor 1937:43), thus sustaining the continuity of the male line. The male line held the important authorities of ariki and kindred head, as well as the special respects and supernatural powers vested in its senior female representative, the father's sister. In view of matrilocality, the balance seems to divide along the utilitarian-honorable axis, a traditional division.

Genealogical Depth

The chiefly families traced descent back to first beginnings. No pedigrees have been collected from nonchiefly lines.

Sanctity

Sanctity, as a minor quality, was the birthright of all first-born, male or female, of priests, and of craftsmen. As a major quality, it pertained only to the ariki and to the high priest and was then essentially an attribute of office. The concept was in this sense basically Manu'an, although on a somewhat reduced scale. We do not have enough information, however, to compare Manu'an and Tokelauan concepts in detail.

Missionary reports hint at gradual reduction in the sanctity of the high chief over time. Originally the ariki may have been the high priest of Tui Tokelau, the tribal god, and may then have been known by that sacrosanct title (Turner 1884:8). In that event, his sacred status might have been analagous to that of Tui Manu'a and Tui Tonga. He is said to have been able through intercession with the gods to regulate the weather and the food supply. We do not know whether he was then innately sacred. Subsequently, some sources say, the authority was divided, the title of Tui Tokelau lapsed, the son became ariki, and the sister's son became the priest of Tui Tokelau, the god (MacGregor 1937:50).

The foregoing information is unfortunately vague. The sacred character of the ariki has been described in somewhat more detail. We recognize in him attributes of traditional sanctity. The power to curse to death those who opposed him puts him in the realm of chiefs with awesome powers, but with the important modification that a curse is neither an automatic punishment nor a summary execution, its effect depending, after all, upon the state of morale of the victim. From a western Polynesian standpoint, the power of the curse would seem to have established an analogy between ariki and a matua sa, equating the power of both not with politics but with the supernatural. The person of the ariki was tapu. He avoided association with all lower ranks, received special foods, ate from a special dish, and at his funeral was honored as though he were the god of fire. The locus of supernatural power, though, was definitely with the gods rather than with persons (cf. Lister 1892).

Tohunga

Less formally organized than Samoan craftsmen, the Tokelauan tufunga were, nevertheless, a group of highly honored men. While distinct from priests, who were taula, they performed priestly rites in the course of their work carried out under the sponsorship of gods. Skill gave them wealth, authority, and sanctity, and was, accordingly, the sole competitive avenue to status. The master craftsmen were titled, an unusual distinction in a society that had gone so far in abolishing formal statuses. Canoe building was the supreme technical profession. The master canoe builder was the esteemed *matemai,* the priest of his craft, master designer, and supervisor of the work of apprentices and journeymen. Other honored crafts were those of house builder, fisherman, tattooer, and circumcisor. We are not told how craftsmen were recruited nor how they rose to distinction in their profession. Presumably, skills tended to remain within a family, for MacGregor had observed carpenters instructing their sons and their nephews.

The evident importance of the crafts must modify the impression of gerontocracy, for as MacGregor has said, "When a man had established a household of his own and had become skilled in man's crafts, he assumed an authoritative position within his kindred (1937:43)."

Wealth

Wealth was not as dynamic a factor in status as in Samoa, if only because there was so little to aspire toward. Possessions served more to conserve than to advance. They sustained the reputation of a family but gave it no permanent advantages over others. Wealth, valued for its contribution to physical well-being, must surely have enhanced the prestige and influence of a family, but—in contrast to Samoa—influence was not readily translated into formal position. The advantages of wealth, while surely not unimportant, were general. The smallness of the economy and the unremitting obligation of kindred heads to support the general welfare impeded accumulation. Seniors who inherited larger shares of family lands reallocated periodically in accordance with need. In any case, the poor seem to have had the good sense to marry into wealthier families.

Wealth apparently fell into two distinctive categories: land, essentially a subsistence commodity, and mats, a prestige commodity. The trend to equalization affected the subsistence economy most strongly, leaving the kindred heads free to accumulate substantial quantities of mats which they distributed and exchanged in behalf of family etiquette and ritual.

Political Hegemony

From rather incomplete information we have only hints as to the nature of the political authority in the Tokelaus. After the collapse of the central authority on Fakaofu, each island was ruled by its own ariki and council of elders. The former paramount chief is described simply as a "patriarchal head" who "had full authority over all the people and established their laws, which he enforced by his power to curse anyone to death (MacGregor 1937:50). The local chief on each island presided over a village council and ratified the election of its members. The council dealt with land disputes and with serious infractions of the law, and directed community enterprises connected with the ceremonial life. As in Samoa, the relation of the ariki to the council was more ceremonial than practical, the actual administrative role being held by his executive officer, his "talking chief," referred to by some Tokelauans as *faipule* and by others as *puseve*. MacGregor speaks of the rights of the ariki to the property of his subjects. His examples suggest that this may not have extended over lands, which were solidly under control of the kindreds, but only over special items such as unusual foods and objects. In short, the suggestion is that here, as on Manu'a, the focal authority was of a ritual nature, while the diffuse authority dealt with the more secular affairs. The ariki is thought of by Tokelauans as a center of power more in deference, it would seem, to his dignity than to actual rights.

Rank

Rank was generalized rather than graded. The four founding families on Fakaofu represented a royal lineage, but—insofar as we know—without title, for only the incumbent chief was aliki, or *tupu*, or Tui Tokelau. Lacking title, these families seem also to have lacked all the formal distinctions of class or rank. If they were separated from the population at large, it was by virtue of the exceptional privilege of supplying the ariki, and not by style of life. We must assume that if observers of the experience in Polynesia of the London Mission Society did not speak of an ariki class, it probably did not exist, at least in their time. If the Tokelaus were not in Polynesia, we would hardly think of its social system in such grand terms as class or rank. It is in their particular historical context that we recognize the four families as "royal," as analagous to a chiefly rank, and as an extreme attenuation of western Polynesian aristocracy.

All kindreds (kainga) named elders who served as their heads (matais) and who were advised by the body of elders. In the village council the elders were arranged by a hierarchy of age, on the model of genealogical rank in the fully aristocratic societies. Age hierarchy is analagous to genealogical rank insofar as it stands for an organic sequence, a given of nature. The distinction between the two modes of hierarchy is nevertheless a critical one. Genealogical rank has the honor of absolute organic continuity. It is an unbroken chain of being that links the lowest to the highest. The essential quality of age hierarchy is precisely its organic discontinuity. The genealogical grading focuses upon discriminating segments of a descent line; that of age focuses upon persons and generalizes the branches of the line. The generalizing of kin is, from the point of view of status, reductive. Thus age hierarchy may be visualized as a reduced version of genealogical rank in a Polynesian context. In a more general historical perspective, the reverse may be stated, namely, that genealogical rank is an elevated version of age hierarchy.

In another respect age hierarchy comes to resemble an achieved status, drawing upon the accomplishments of durability and experience. It is an achieved status without stress, only barely differentiating the given from the made. Craftsmen and priests represented a more specialized grade of achieved status, but, again, with a minimum of rivalry. Craftsmen were chosen, it would seem, by their kinsmen; the high priest inherited his office, and all other priests were chosen by the gods. In more ancient times, there were warriors who might have represented the fully assertive side of status. Like Samoa, then, the Tokelaus offered a wide range of honors. No one had an unworthy status.

Descent Group Organization

Only the four chief families retained a well-defined organization of branches that were represented on all the islands of the group. Among these, it was presumably the right to elect an ariki that held the branches together. Among other kindreds, the prime consideration of group unity was the ownership of land. MacGregor seems specific on the point that when land was divided the descent group itself divided, with no other links to bind them. To the extent that land rights united families, land shortage would separate them. To acknowledge a kinsman was equivalent to opening a request for land. The short pedigree was more prudent, more conservationist. The example of a specimen kindred MacGregor offers extends for only five generations, a short genealogy even by Tokelauan standards.

The concept behind the original division of lands by the high chief of Fakaofu was undoubtedly within an older tradition of segmentation; that is to say, the land titles would move down lines of descent that branched from a common source. Inasmuch as the tradition is still recalled, we must assume that consciousness of common unity was, if no longer an economic factor, still alive. The regulation of landholdings was most definitely, as in Samoa, the province of the local community, yet the sentiment of economic unity cannot be ignored. In Traditional societies, of course, the same pattern of organization prevailed: sentiment of economic unity with the Segment I chief, and practical economics at the lower levels. Where the Tokelauan system differs is in the apparent discontinuity between local descent lines and those of chiefs. Connections might have lapsed from successive depopulations, yet one cannot escape the suspicion that the structure of the system itself, which had become so fully dependent upon economic utility, tended toward dissolution of a ramified order. After all, even on the much richer island of Manu'a economic utility accomplished this, being offset there by the hierarchy of fonos, the repositories of titles and honors.

In recapitulation, the Tokelaus suggest very much, as in Manu'a, the dissolution, or the fading away of a traditional segmentary kin group organization. The process was, to say the least, spasmodic. When Fakaofu ruled the atolls, Segment I had the primordial structure of a state. When that ended, the four atolls reflecting descent lines from Fakaofu assumed, perhaps only approximately, the structure of a segmentary lineage organization. Thereafter the magnitude of the structure was reduced. At most a sentiment of Tokelauan unity prevailed, but the individual atoll became the new Segment I. This entity had the elementary Samoan structure that combined a ritual figure as the islandwide authority and a more fully secular council that represented the local families. The kindreds may very well have been related. Their formal relationship to one another, however, was not through kinship but through the political agency of a council. The jurisdiction of the council defines the character of this Segment I. It is most aptly described as quasi-ritualistic, since ritual was the main concern of collective interests.

Segment II was the kindred, or *'ainga,* a kin group reckoning descent and inheriting property from a common ancestor bilaterally. The details about 'ainga organization are not as clear as might be desired. Still, the basic Manu'an structure does show itself. Some notion of male line stands as the core of leadership and, indeed, as the focus of landholding. The matai, as representative of the patrilineal core, directs the use of land and provides for continuity of its transmission along a male line. The system provides, however, for a distinction—as in Manu'a—between transmission and administration, both highly honorific prerogatives, and direct utilization. The most direct utilization, a lower-status interest, is represented by matrilocal residence. In this respect the Tokelaus have reversed the Manu'an plan, dispersing the male line and converting the female line into the direct working group—in effect, a reduction.

The concept of a male line preserves the traditional Polynesian point of view as to structure. The reality of the structure, that is, the formation of working groups, represents still another Polynesian concern, and that is economic flexibility. The patterns of landholding observed by MacGregor are extraordinarily diverse. He says, for example, "Many landholders have left the complete control of the land to the eldest daughter of the family, and the sons have only a share in the products. In some families the children all inherit alike; in others the eldest son and daughter receive larger shares than the younger children (1937:58)." So broad a range of possibilities of landholding must, of course, diversify considerably the actual structure of the kindreds. In the final analysis, even the concept of kindred leadership seems to have been ambiguous. While the concept of fraternal and then of filial succession to the mataiship is still consistent with a patrilineal core, the provision that the senior male should succeed opens the gate quite widely to other more flexible arrangements.

Segment III is the household, matrilocal as a rule, but subject to every other convenient arrangement. Here again, the male line, represented by father's sister and her brother's son as codirectors, is the core. In this respect the household recapitulates the structure of the 'ainga.

16

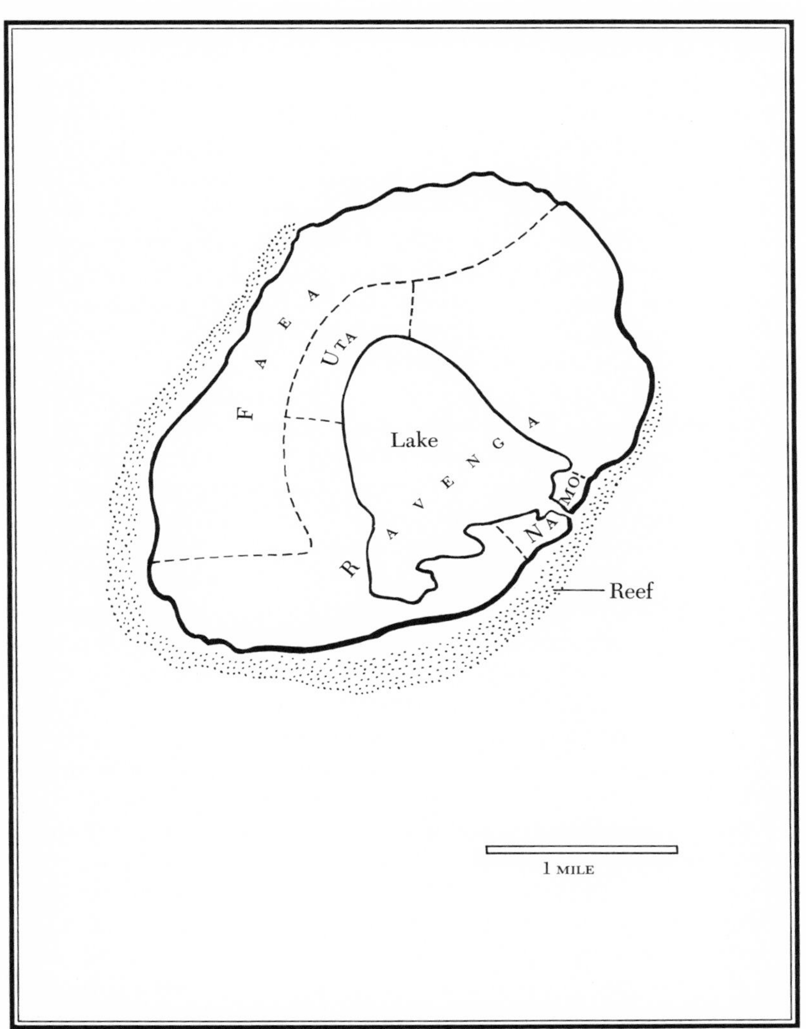

Tikopia

TIKOPIA IS A DISTANT BRANCH OF SAMOAN CULTURE SETTLED DEEP IN Melanesian territory and much closer physically to Santa Cruz, the New Hebrides, and the Solomons than it is to its original home base in western Polynesia. Its alien location and the remarkable diversity of its intercultural connections should have given to Tikopian society an atypical character, but despite a history of migrations between it and such distinctive centers as Samoa, Tonga, Rotuma, Uvea, Pukapuka, Ontong Java, Banks, and Santa Cruz, Tikopia is very typically, in fact, intensely Polynesian. Rather than having bred some new and strange cultural concoction, hybridization has had a generalizing effect. Tikopia fits as readily into the eastern as it does into the western Polynesian picture. Specific affiliations with each of its ancestral components can be identified, yet it is surprisingly different from any one of them.

The Samoan ancestry is attested by such archeological evidence as the presence of early Samoan-type adzes (Firth: 1961), and more definitely by language. Samoan and Tikopian are as close to each other as is, for example, Tahitian to Hawaiian, indicating by Elbert's calculations (1953) that they had separated sometime after A.D. 930, or, in terms of historical events, shortly before the end of the Samoan Traditional. In that case, Tikopia, on the Maori–Society Islands analogy, may have retained earlier traditional features that in Samoa had undergone progressive transformation. Tikopia stands even more strongly as an apparent example of Tonga in its Traditional phase. It has the primogeniture, the seniority, the patriliny, and the segmentary lineage, lacking mainly the centralization of authority and the economic stratification of later Tongan society. Basic patterns of kinship structure, among the best diagnostic features of common descent in Polynesia, also leave no doubt as to the basically Samoan–Tongan provenience of Tikopia. While Tikopia may therefore be taken conveniently as one of the historical variants of an underlying Samoan–Tongan social pattern, its position is obviously more complex. Apart from Melanesian influences which could have emphasized the categorical preferences for patriliny along with the differentiation of female lines, there are the contacts with Pukapuka, one of the bridges between eastern and western Polynesia. But if Tikopia absorbed eastern traits through Pukapuka, their effects are not readily identifiable. The most specific and thus the most positive link with Pukapuka is actually through the unusual and distinctively "non-eastern" absence of terminology for senior and junior siblings. This "negative" trait is shared in Polynesia only among Tikopia, Pukapuka, and Ontong Java.

In Tikopia alone it has no functional counterpart in the kinship system, and must be regarded therefore as intrusive.

Among the Samoan–Tongan satellite societies, the closest Tikopian associations are with Futuna and Uvea. By Elbert's calculations (1953), these three are linguistically more cognate than Tikopian is to Samoan. In view of this association, Tikopian society may be considered as a close variant of the Uvean-Futunan type. Of the three, Tikopia is most fully representative of the Traditional society.

Tikopia is not a poor island, but with a density of some 400 per square mile it is heavily populated—on the verge of over-population—for a high island. Even with most of its three square miles under intensive cultivation, and with good growing weather, there are no reserves and no surplus for foreign trade. At best, Tikopians must control their appetites for two lean months each year. In not infrequent bad times they starve—or commit hunger suicide. Understandably, therefore, Tikopians have become expert in population planning.

Taro is the main crop. Open cultivations cover up to one-fifth of the land area, reaching almost to the mountain summit. Everywhere else where there is a spare patch of land, in a coconut or breadfruit orchard, or in a banana grove, they fill in with extra plantings. Taro grows well, yielding at least two crops a year, but it demands an annual rotation that leaves half the acreage lying fallow. By the eighteenth century Tikopia could no longer afford the luxury of pig and fowl.

Technically, Tikopia falls among the more backward Polynesians. Its outrigger canoe, its most complex construction, is among the simplest of Polynesian vessels. Houses are crude pole and thatch structures that rest directly on the earth. Apart from low walls of selected boulders, there is no work in stone. The arts are rudimentary, confined to simple geometric designs on canoe hulls, and in tattooing. Barkcloth is simply stained with turmeric.

Tikopia is among the best described of the Polynesian societies, having been intensively studied by an eminent anthropologist. When Raymond Firth first came to Tikopia in 1929, half the population was still pagan, while even the Christians were at least socially conservative. The aboriginal culture was essentially intact. The culture was still aboriginal in 1952 when Firth returned with a professional associate (James Spillius) for a restudy. The restudy verified earlier impressions and charted some important trends in culture change. Fortuitously, Firth and Spillius came upon Tikopia this time in its moment of crisis, just after the island had been swept clean by a hurricane. Their detailed account of how the people managed during a famine—reconstruction was relatively simple—brings to light, as no other observed events can, the Tikopian scale of values.

Tikopian experience with Europeans came late. Quiros sighted the island in 1606; Peter Dillon in 1798 was the first to disembark and to start the Tikopians on their fortunately amiable associations with European civilization. Dillon made four visits in all, his last in 1827. He was followed a year later by Dumont D'Urville. Both explorers published extensively, giving us a reasonably coherent and reliable historical record of over a century. These records, it is pertinent to note, verify fully the Tikopian traditions for the same period. The effects of contact with Europeans were mild: they were more economic than political. Tikopians acquired metal tools—axes, adzes, knives—but, having little to offer in trade, shipped out as hands on whalers or to European plantations in Fiji. They brought back goods, remaining true, nevertheless, to their own ways. A Christian mission was not established until 1911. The island had become a British protectorate in 1896 under the rule, however, of the local chiefs.

Genealogical Traditions

The traditions, ignoring actual historical connections, insist as a point of honor upon autochthonous origins from gods who are distinctively Tikopian. When a lineage wishes to undermine a rival, it slyly imputes a foreign—for example, a Pukapukan—origin to it. Each lineage speaking for itself, and as a matter of common doctrine, claims rootedness in its own land. Primordial beginnings go back to general founders, to male and female deities unconnected with present history. Specific origins of the lineages and their heads start with a group of brothers, the "Brethren," to use Firth's translation. In conventional Polynesian fashion, the Brethren lock all lines into a single hierarchical source. The Brethren are celestial beings drawn to be human and to establish themselves terrestrially. From the start they reveal the central issues and lay down the broad plan of organization of the future society. In one version of this origin tale, the first-born—ordinarily the one who should lead the way for all the others—blocks the descent by remaining partly in the womb, whereupon the second in line delivers himself outside the normal order of descent by springing from his mother's head. As a result of this incident of the lower overcoming the higher, he is awarded two great prizes, breadfruit, the constructive gift, and thunder, storm, and other powers of destruction. Then a wrestling match among the four great founders results in the further dividing of the four major crops (breadfruit, coconut, taro, yam). The division of the food crops bears some resemblance theoretically to the early land divisions of other Polynesian societies. The Tikopian version, however, is more in the totemic spirit, in that this division is at once categorical—as land boundaries are not —and binding, insofar as each is individually incomplete. The legend, it should be said, sharpens distinctions that in life are far less categorical. Up until very recent times each of the major divisional chiefs held some special ritual control over one crop; the paramount ritual chief then transcends this division by his general responsibility for the whole (cf. Firth 1961).

Tikopians think of their history as falling into three definite but unlabeled stages. The first, as just considered, deals with general beginnings, with the first efforts of sky beings to establish themselves on earth and then to cut off passage between earth and sky. The second recapitulates the first, but in more specific form. Particular and known branches of men form themselves on earth and the heretofore free movement between territorial and celestial realms is finally ended. The final stage, with a duration of no more than 10 generations, is contemporary, and describes the antagonisms, the displacements of people, conquests, and the final consolidation of the contemporary rank order. All three stages are set in an energetic atmosphere of turmoil and antagonism, as befits circumstances of social creation. The point of view is physical: Antagonism is the source of energy for the transformation of gods into men and of men back into gods.

The second stage brings forward *Atua i Kafika* whose forms symbolize the social cosmos. As *Atua* he is a god, the "high" god of Tikopia; as ariki Kafika he is the high sacred chief; and as *Kafika* he is the name of one of the four major descent groups and of its leading lineage, and of its temples. *Kafika* is god, chief, organic assemblage of people, and sacred place. He is the center of religion, of rule, of social and economic life. All else is dependent and peripheral—but not subsumed under Kafika.

The origins of Kafika are involved in processes of celestial–terrestrial transfers. Most commonly in Polynesian cosmogenesis the gods establish themselves, or their descendants, as earth-beings. The initial movement is simply downward, from sky to earth. Tikopia, by contrast, postulates movement in both directions. Atua i Kafika is an example of a god who had already acquired a terrestrial and human character and then only later reestablished himself in celestial and spiritual form.

Kafika originates in the Pu Ma, "The Respected Ones," twin gods arrived on earth to be the permanent celestial links with Tikopia. They are immediately locked in conflict with those sky gods known as the Brethren and with preexisting persons for full possession of the island. They succeed in establishing a Kafika dynasty which is simultaneously Pu Ma-descended, but in action reminiscent of Samoa, installed by a kinetic effort. Subsequently, the son of a Kafika chief is caught up in a land dispute and is killed. He is at once installed in the sky as the Atua i Kafika. The Christian parallel is obvious, although we may have here nothing more than a convergence of general ideas. The Kafika as human covered the gamut of necessary powers. As "culture hero" he founded the social order; as a total power he had the capacity to destroy. Since he was a transformer, he was, of course, contentious, fighting against immigrants but also trespassing upon neighboring territory. He met his death appropriately (in the Samoan style) at the hands of a man who had the low standing of a younger son, but who had thus the honor of converting a chief into a god. When contentious Kafika had been turned into a god by an act of violence, his clan carried further the dialectic of transformation by declaring itself to be "above the strife." Had Kafika done the killing, his descendants now reason, he would have remained human.

Kafika withdrew from contentions, but it could hardly remain a center of social significance without being a center of contention itself. In the Tikopian cosmology nothing comes of calm. Firth was understandably astonished to learn that Tikopians inconsistently accepted the primacy of Kafika and then attacked its credentials. Others of the four great clans challenged the Kafika claim to priority in descent, and even clansmen—but not of the direct lineage—implied, in the lowest slur of all, that Kafika were not autochthonous but had come from Pukapuka. Disparagement of a supreme religious authority expresses perhaps little more than ordinary resentments. In the Tikopian historical context, disparagement is, in fact, a form of contention and is, therefore, energizing and vitalizing.

In the third stage of Tikopian history, contention is finally and fully human. The history reads as though each successive era recapitulates its own past in a more specific and narrower compass—like an inward-turning spiral. This last phase has Mangaian overtones, but not a Mangaian conclusion. The descendants of Pu Ma had branched into three royal divisions, the Nga Ariki (Kafika, Tafua, Taumako), who occupied one-half the island and accepted tribute and contributions from two subordinate divisions of late-arrived foreigners, Ravenga and Faea. The origins of Ravenga are not known. Faea claim to have come from Ontong Java. This kind of hierarchical order was common enough in Polynesia, and so, for that matter, was its abrupt disruption. Ravenga insolently suspended its tribute and was immediately attacked. It was reduced to a sole survivor who was then allowed to found a new descent group, the Fangarere. Its antecedents having been reduced to virtually nothing, Fangarere rose to equivalent standing as one of the four major divisions of Tikopia with an ariki at its head. One generation later, Faea was invaded and all but a few stragglers were driven out to sea and never heard from again. Faea never rose again; its survivors founded only small and low-ranking lineages.

These wars, which cleared the land of most of its low-ranking foreigners, came during the eighteenth century just before Dillon's visits. It is altogether reasonable to attribute Nga Ariki expansionism directly to population pressure, as Firth does. This was the time when Tikopia had begun to feel the strain of husbanding pigs and fowl. The Tikopian explanation follows considerations of status: the insolent refusal to acknowledge the ritual supremacy of Nga Ariki. When the Nga Faea were expelled, land shortage was hardly a compelling reason, because the full occupation of their territory was very slow.

Firth describes Tikopian society at this time as "somewhat unstable." Chiefs, he elaborates, fought one another for power and prestige; toa were troublesome. Among the Nga Ariki, no one challenged Kafika's ritual status. Tafua tried to undermine Kafika's social ascendancy. Taumako, having taken the lead in the Ravenga war, seized most of the new territory and enriched and strengthened itself. The invasion of Faea was mainly a Tafua enterprise, an indication of the urge of rivals to catch up with one another. Tafua and Taumako were open rivals for social superiority. So were Ravenga and Faea in their better days (1961:122ff.).

Tikopian status rivalry of this period resembles the Mangaian pattern in its initial phases. But whereas the Mangaian gained impetus and finally reached a culmination in a new political management, the Tikopian rivalry simmered down and then cooled. The royalists won all the battles. Blood flowed, but the system remained untouched. It survived external and internal threats and crises. Twice members of the Raropukan sublineage of Kafika resorted to regicide. Assassination however, gained them nothing, but cost them their own social standing.

The Status System

As an apparent composite, the Tikopian status system incorporates Tongan patriliny and primogeniture, but little of its idealization of sheer powers. On the other hand, the marginal role of senior descent lines as sources of rank, and the blurring of social separations are in the Samoan mode. The pattern of kinship respects is general western Polynesian. The system, nevertheless, assumes its own clear character as Traditional almost in the classic eastern Polynesian manner. The focus of status is in religion. Political and economic powers are sufficiently subordinate to ritual supremacy to allow the system to retain a unitary character.

Primogeniture

The superiority of the first-born is virtually unassailable. The *urumatua,* the senior son, is singled out for ritual honors at birth. He will carry the family name, its leadership, its heirlooms, and most of its land. The respects owed the father as *potestas* belong to the urumatua as well, inasmuch as both, at the proper time, share the authority. Father and eldest son are in the domestically unenviable situation of being co-rulers. Antagonism is almost inevitable.

Tikopian traditional history must remind each generation anew that antagonism is the price of social priority. Contention begins at home when father and son occupy the same track. The father is preeminent until his senior son reaches social maturity and assumes his right to be at the center. The authority is then divided, and the antagonism, which may be said to call attention to the social potency of each, builds up. The filial threat is fittingly strongest in the households of senior lineages, where all honor is at stake. In these households the senior son must remain behind after his marriage as the heir and executor of his father. Among the poorer commoner families, there is little to stay at home for.

The urumatua and the younger children are contrasted in a polar pattern of respectful awe for the former and kindly indulgence for the latter. Thus with respect to this pattern, the relationship between elder and younger siblings is parallel to that between the awesome father's sister and the indulgent mother's brother. That is to say, the first-born son has a position which is intensely patrilineal—as it must be since he carries on the name. The younger would seem to be analogous to the mother's side. This interpretation of the organization of a sibling group appears less extreme when it is considered that the junior males may be expected to be celibate and so have no part in carrying on the patrilineal line.

Seniority of Descent

The founding traditions are not unequivocal on this point, but there are accounts that derive the core of the population, its major descent lines, from a single sibling group. They raise questions about seniority of descent, and they allow for the principle of ranking all descent lines by seniority. They do not, however, specifically and categorically document the rank order of the four great "clans" (*kainanga*) by seniority. The issue may have been deliberately left open and vague so as to satisfy an evident requirement of argument about pedigree. One tradition cited by Firth does derive the major rank order of the four kainanga from order of birth (1961:30–32). But is this the authentic record? Tikopians disagree. For the contemporary period, Firth learned, there is no direct correspondence between the traditional rank order of the four kainanga and the order of seniority of their ariki. In this respect the pattern differs from the traditional eastern Polynesian, where the lineage takes its rank from that of its ariki. Tikopia recognizes, rather, two separable orders of rank, one fixed, the other variable. Tradition has locked in the rank order of the kainanga. The seniority of their chiefs depends upon the outcome of all their intermarriages and thus upon their personal pedigrees. But the actual rank of a chief, as in a modern aristocracy, depends upon the rank of his constituency. His islandwide seniority is only hypothetical.

The apparent disjunction between the rank of chiefs on an extended genealogical network and the rank of their "clans" can be readily seen as entirely consistent with the preoccupation for safeguarding the notion of clan equivalence. Clear-cut seniority must compel a corresponding subordination.

On the other hand, seniority of descent poses no such problems of safeguarding equivalence and autonomy among the lineages of each kainanga. Although rank in prestige and ritual precedence does not correlate exactly with genealogical seniority, the relationship is close enough to have allowed Firth to conclude: "a lineage sprung from a senior ancestor exercised wider and more inclusive rights than a lineage sprung from a junior ancestor (1959:223)." Leadership could deviate, but tended to return to the senior line. The senior male of the senior lineage then acquired genealogical eligibility for the arikiship; that is, for chief of "clan."

Male Line

Tikopia may be exceptional in the strength of its commitment to patrilineal succession and filiation, but it is still within the Polynesian family. Firth found no exceptions to the rule of patriliny "in the overt legal sphere (1936:346)." No one could ever belong to his mother's lineage for any reason. No rule can, of course, be absolute. Immigrants who married the daughters of Tikopian chiefs could assimilate through the wife to the prestigious lineage of the chief. In the beginning, at least, the line would have matrilineal descent. The example, to be sure, does not violate the rule. It is relevant, though, as a contrast to Mangaia, which guarded itself against precisely this type of upgrading. Mangaia sought segregation; a more liberal Tikopia opened a gap.

At the far pole from Samoan descent and filiation doctrine, Tikopia is not too deviant from the Tongan on this specific issue. The differences widen as we take account of the broader kinship pattern and its delineation of male and female line. In this area we recognize western Polynesian standards, but characteristically more general, and less elaborated. Tikopia acknowledges the special status of father's sister and of mother's brother without the extraordinary emphasis given to these antipodal relatives by Tonga. Tikopia lacks the explicit fahu relationship, for example. On the other hand, the practice of giving daughters a substantial share of household lands—equal to that given the eldest son—(Firth 1936:182) carries economic bilaterality much farther along than does the Samoan aiga. Tikopia cherishes sheer patriliny only where it means most, namely, in the spheres of ritual and honor and specifically in asserting rootedness in a line of descent. But women are also from the line and must carry away some share in its honors. Thus, land patrimony is divided with sister; the father's sister is given some equivalence in avoidance respects with father; and the sister's child is accorded the respects owed to a descendant of the line even if it is resident in and member of another *paito*. Thus the western Polynesian delicacy in openly calling attention to these extensions of a descent line is in broad pattern certainly fully matched by Tikopia.

Genealogical Depth

The issue of roots, or, to use the Tikopian term, *tafito* ("origin, source, cause, beginning, base"), is central in genealogical disputes. The honor of a line depends upon (a) priority (b) "sprung from the land." The disputants seek to downgrade each other by challenging on either or both points. The new and short lines of immigrants are low —but, one must add, "all other things being equal." The commoner kainanga is "old," but was overcome in battle and then allowed to rise. Immigrant lineages compensate for their newness by connecting with the adoptive chiefly lines. Contemporary Tikopian genealogies are generally shallow, the longest going back only 18 generations.

Sanctity

Like Samoa, Tikopia understates sanctity, and grades respects for all persons almost imperceptibly from high tapu to ordinary courtesy. Tapu is an attribute pertaining to descent from the gods, and differentiates the four ariki, the great Kafika in particular, from all others. The distinctions, to repeat, are quantitative, for as Firth points out, personal sanctity is largely a function of the kinship system (1936: 183). Any man's head, for example, is tapu to his children, but they are permitted to delouse him upon his request. A chief, however, would never ask his children to violate the intimacy of his body or of his possessions. The distinction between religious avoidances as they involve the person of an ariki within his household and in the carrying out of his ritual roles, and the "ordinary" respects as they are shown to kinsmen, is, of course, subtle though undeniably well-defined. The subtlety is in the underlying religious conception that almost all Tikopian families are god-descended and have their own and direct access to familial deities. Respect avoidances, focused as they are on key progenitive points, are honoring the sanctity of descent, or, in more specifically religious terms, the lines of connections with gods. Chiefs, as we have seen in other western Polynesian societies, are more directly linked to the gods, and so their sanctity is more immediate and stronger.

As representative of the god, the Kafika, for example, is directly responsible for the prosperity of the land, for its growth. His sanctity is in this respect specifically religious and the deference shown him is symbolically relevant to his god-like status. Thus, when the chief loses a tooth, the wail of mourning is raised in his house and his sons gash their foreheads. Firth calls this "a conventional tribute of affection to the aging man for the food that he will now be unable to consume (1936:185)." But it is really dismay at failing powers. In the same vein, coconut cream is the food of chiefs (1961:104); coconut cream—as Firth explains in an entirely different connection—is the source of semen (1936:482); food and sex are the two principal media of growth and prosperity, and the chiefs, as elsewhere, are honored in each. Precedence in eating and the receipt of first-fruits (*muakai*) are the sacred respects, the counterpart to the chief's religious position as the terrestrial agent for god-bestowed food, and hence as "owner" of all resources.

Despite the chief's vital progenitive and nutritive role in the spiritual sense, the "distance" between him and the community is unremarkable, and the sentiment he inspires is not awesome.

Tohunga

As in Samoa, the honor paid the craftsman (*tufunga*) and the utilitarian requirements for specialized products are not commensurate.

Tufunga as a title expresses another dimension of status and an unusually active arena of status rivalry. The major statuses of rank are genealogically fixed, more or less, and since they enter into spheres of religion, they impose restraints upon open rivalry. In the crafts such restraints are somewhat diminished. Tufunga are free to boast of their own skills and to belittle the work of their competitors—but only in general and not by name. Sensitivity on this account is acute; and a man who senses himself as belittled will stop work at once and sulk. Rivalry, as Firth observes, functionally stimulates group effort and is unquestionably a positive social value. From the more limited perspective of the Tikopian, skill is surely a measure of efficacy in a realm not dominated by chiefs. The distinction of being a skilled craftsman with its gratifying rewards of prestige and, more concretely, wealth is open to all men.

Tikopian tufunga are part-time specialists. Whether they are tatooers, sennit plaiters, net makers, bowl makers, canoe makers, or fishermen, they are only somewhat more proficient than the amateurs, who are also substantially self-sufficient. Why then are they employed? The answer must be that important undertakings can only be elevated above the ordinary by drawing them into the spheres of ritual and social and economic exchange. In Tikopia, the tufunga does not control the rituals, but his labor is part of a ritual undertaking when goods are exchanged and persons of honor exchange services and goods. A craftsman may have personal standing only. As a rule, however, he represents a branch of a lineage that has already won a reputation for skill. Thus while Tikopia does not quite have the formally organized Samoan "guilds," the parallel between craft paito and lineage-like "guilds" is self-evident. The parallel is even more striking in view of the ritualization of crafts which in Tikopia gives the paito headman the special position as priest of the craft. The Tikopian organization, we gather from Firth, is more informal than the Samoan. No paito has a crafts monopoly, nor, for that matter, is the paito organized directly around the craft. The title itself is informal, to be won by reputation and not as in Samoa and Tonga bestowed by a chief or other official. The skills are not ranked.

In Samoa–Tonga style, tufunga does not apply to priests or to ritual leaders. The realm of artisan, though involved with ritual, is distinct from that of intermediary with gods. Chiefs and ritual elders called *pare* are responsible for ritual, holding, as a result, a higher office and status. Tufunga, then, is ordinarily subordinate to his pare. The pattern is, of course, Tongan, where the functional unit also divides between ritual director and subordinate executor.

Wealth

Differences in material standards between ariki and commoner are minor, even on the rather small Polynesian scale. The house of a chief has more things in it, but is, in Firth's words, "no more sumptuous than that of a commoner (1939:34)." Chiefs may even have less land and thus be basically poorer than commoners. The issue is neither abundance as such, nor conspicuous display; it is the ability to control a ritual circulation of goods. The chief must have wealth. It must be freely available to him—if not from his own family holdings, then from his community. Ready availability is in deference to the ariki as a religious figure and defines his place in the grand circulation of goods, to be understood as material manifestations of natural abundance. Tikopia is, in fact, as close to the traditional ideal as a Polynesian society can be in its conceptions of wealth. The ariki is a giver of basic prosperity. Next to the god, he is the initiator of the grand cycle and is responsible for keeping in motion the distribution and redistribution of foods. All who give to him are honored by being literally drawn into the lines of connection that run between chiefs and gods. Circulation is certainly the most conspicuous and pressing economic obligation of ariki. He is the giver of feasts on his own account and the sponsor of all kainanga-wide and islandwide rituals, which also involve energetic consumption. Only secondarily must he use wealth to establish his god-like separation. But since the separation of chiefs is not in Tikopia conspicuous, the "aura of abundance" that must envelop them need not be very conspicuous either. Some part of chiefly abundance is specifically display, as when chiefs are prodigal in economic exchanges with one another. For the most part, though, the chief's bounty is directly in the interests of his community, for ritual, as mentioned, and for public works, such as an aqueduct, for example.

The chiefs are the regulators of accumulation. Because their priestly role demands of them a full sense of public responsibility, chiefs, as Firth has put it, "are the proper persons to control large quantities of food, to have a number of valued objects stored away in their houses (1939:243)." Others, including commoners, can be wealthy in lands, in orchards—that is, in basic resources—or in goods (mats, barkcloth, bowls) but they dare not project their wealth beyond their station. In the past the ariki would have punished unwarranted ostentation by seizing the property or by having the offender killed. Wealth as an attribute of status had not in Tikopia escaped from its embeddedness in religion. It could not help being a factor in status, simply because it was an undeniable demonstration of efficacy in production, and in social relations, which had almost as much to do with family prosperity as the direct tillage of the soil or the cultivation of trees.

When we visualize the Tikopian ariki as imposing limits upon display and accumulation, we are correctly perceiving a broad-gauge regulator. Pressure does, nevertheless, build up. All persons have ritual and social obligations; heads of groups feel the pressure most because they must be donors. To fall short while others are efficaciously active can only be depressing. "Wealth becomes a subject of comment and envy" (Firth 1939:53). People are provoked into quarrels over lands and boundaries, sometimes into battle. The invasions of Ravenga and Faea are extreme examples of aggression; the impulse of chiefs to push cultivations aggressively into all uncultivated patches anywhere expresses the same tendency more moderately.

In the final analysis, it is the concept of land tenure that most accurately describes the central economic motives. By religious title the ariki of the kainanga is "owner" only in the sense of being spiritual custodian and endower of land with honor and mana. All households share equivalent title on a hierarchical basis. Each has continuity of residence, the right to transmit down the descent line, to subdivide among contemporary kin, and, of course, to acquire new extensions. Each subdivision of a kin grouping has significance as a spiritual entity precisely insofar as its relationship to land and crop is equivalent to that of ariki. Tikopia is not a quantitatively egalitarian society. As a Traditional society it approaches a consubstantial egalitarianism. The notion of a spiritual community is to be taken quite concretely as specific connection with ancestral deities. The crop that gives the land its meaning is, as Firth (1939) explains, an aspect of the god, either as his head or his body. The tiller thus is reproducing divinity. The four major crops are each associated with one kainanga in the narrow totemic sense of subdivision of responsibility for a spiritual aspect of life on the island. In short, all Tikopians are within the same religious community as equivalent though unequal portions of the whole.

Political Hegemony

Having declared himself "above the strife," the ariki Kafika adjusted the chiefship to conform to the traditional pattern of high rank and low power—in the secular orbit. The traditions do not declare that he renounced the possession of power. He retained his divine potential but with self-imposed restraints. By traditional evidence, then, Tikopia took a retrograde political step, reducing power instead of increasing it. The parallel with Maori suggests itself at once and reminds us again that in political evolution retreat is as possible as advance.

In the new order we observe how Kafika in some spirit of self-reduction gave away lands from his specific descent line to help the needy. On the other hand, it was the second-ranking Tafua ariki who carried out aggression against Ravenga and forced distant kinsmen off lands to favor his own sons. Similarly, it was the branches of the kainanga that proved to be contentious, asserting their forcefulness against their higher authority. Forcefulness, self-assertion, even aggression do not erect harsh dominance–subordination relationships in Tikopia. These fitful winds of rivalry and contentiousness only roil the waters. When they subside, all is smooth again. Ravenga and Faea were not brought under the yoke. They were cleanly eliminated, and so the egalitarian ideal was undisturbed. Fangarere, the commoner clan composed of the few survivors, was reduced, to be sure, as an accretion to Nga Ariki, but then it was given an ariki and thus an equivalent status in the quadrumvirate of chiefs. The nature of this quadrumvirate asserts most significantly the Tikopian concept of hierarchical political order. Not only is Kafika highest and most restrained, but each ariki is given a portion of the whole without which the entire system is incomplete. Other Polynesian societies compelled or resolved to divide the authority followed other alternatives. They divided along religious-secular lines or they divided geographically. Either course created an incompleteness that led to new conflicts for reconciliation or recombination. A single community having been broken apart will make the effort to reconstitute itself. The four Tikopian ariki remained within the same religious community, each in charge of a major crop—an embodiment of an ancestral deity—and thus inextricably interdependent. This Tikopian subdivision is as the totemic tradition of central Australia, where each religious body has responsibility for its segment of natural reproduction.

Tikopia offers only few glimpses into the more common Polynesian vista of awe-inspiring powers, of gods and men who create and recreate, who elevate and reduce, who inspire both exaltation and terror. The more power-minded societies had offenders against chiefly dignity killed; Tikopian ariki asked them to commit suicide. The Tikopian conception is more along vegetative lines, of slow growth and of continuity. Subordinates occupy a lesser branch, but they are on the same tree.

The Structure of Status

The theme of the status structure is gradation of honor and prerogative. All status differences once labeled and defined in terms of principles of differentiation can be represented as polarized. In Tikopia we can also put forth a series of status oppositions of ariki and commoner, autochthonous and late comer, rich and poor, sacrosanct leader (ritual head) and member of congregation, and the like. But to be true to Firth's own meticulous rendition of the Tikopian ethos, we must heed his admonition not to overstate the distinctions. Polarization of status is here on a small scale. The system is unitary, bound by genealogy and tradition, with some allowance for minor divergences through military distinction (toa) in the past or for accretions of wealth, as in the present.

Genealogical Rank

Rank has its origins in the four great chiefly lines, each of which is represented in the kainanga by its own paito. The chiefly, or *paito ariki,* bears the name of the chiefly line, which is also that of the kainanga. Only the head, and that would generally be the senior male of the senior line, is actually chief with all the ritual and secular privileges of the office. His patrilineal kin have distinction as members of the honored paito ariki, but one does not gather from Firth that they are addressed as ariki. His sons and brothers, who are his executive officers, are known rather as *maru,* also a title of office.

Ariki appears thus not as a generic title of rank but, in combination with the great ancestral name, as a specific title held by only one person at one time. In Samoan fashion, the title carrying the honor of the line is considered as bestowed. The chief is almost necessarily the scion of the senior line, but that is only one of the two required lines for office. His designation by leading men from kainanga other than his own by people whom he does not rule (Firth 1960:172) endows the title with the double quality of the organic and the made, that which has descended directly from the deity and that which has been contributed by the congregation.

The arikiship is so closely identified with traditional and religious origins that the title is fixed and confined to four incumbents—quite the opposite of the Samoan condition. The concept of ariki is focal; he is central and his prerogatives are precisely defined. As we have already observed, he is the source of all rank. What is not clear is the point at which a chiefly paito ends and a commoner paito begins. The privileges of association with paito ariki are not extraordinary, but they do include deference, in itself a sufficient attraction to hold persons to the chiefly "house." Needless to say, the paito ariki are the largest. Eventually the junior branches fall off as they do in New Zealand. Presumably there is some hypothetical point of status "maximization" where the attraction of autonomy and the prestige of being a ritual elder outweighs the honors of being a junior and anonymous member of a ranking paito. Since the public judges relationship to the ariki by genealogical grade, the falling-off point may be vague, but it is undoubtedly detectable.

The aristocracy of chief's relatives is expansive as Firth's figures for lineage growth between 1929 and 1952 show (1959:235). By lineage count, of course, there are never more than four ariki paito. But as these expand more rapidly than commoner lineages—between 1929 and 1952 they had gone from 19 percent to 23 per cent of the total population—their proportion among lineages will also increase. In Tonga, the powerful lineages absorbed the weaker without increasing the aristocratic segment of the population. In Traditional Tikopia, the relative increase is accounted for partially by absorption but mainly by failure to segment and thus establish a new lineage. In the past, when all the ariki paito formed an exclusive intermarrying caste, their rate of expansion would have been slower than that observed by Firth and Spillius in 1952 when the barriers to intermarriage with commoners had all but collapsed.

The persons closest in grade to the ariki are the men of his immediate household. They are the maru, described by Firth as "executive official[s] responsible for law and order (1936:289)." As the ariki has the ultimate authority in his control of ritual and in his privilege of enunciating general policy (such as the undesirability of thievery or the merits of population control), the maru carry out his intent as secular representatives. They enforce the food tapus in anticipation of ceremonial festivity, oversee public works, and look after the general well-being of the people. *Maru,* meaning "shade" or "shelter" (Firth 1936:289), expresses fully the benevolent side of the ariki household. A dirge for a departed maru recalls: "He lived as a maru of this land; this land used to obey him. He was a true *maru,* his mind was good; he was not angry, he fed the commoners (Firth 1936: 289)." When offended, the maru could show the sterner qualities of ariki by commanding a suicide at sea.

The common folk fall into two divisions: an upper, represented by paito headed by a ritual elder (*pure, matapure*); and a lower, whose lineages had only an ordinary and secular headship. Upper-division commoners have thus the distinction of a status analagous to that of ariki paito. The pure or matapure are not in the generic category of ariki, but they come close to the broad concept of ritual chief in all respects but genealogical grade. They have direct connection to ancestral deities; they are, in principle, the senior males of the senior line with honor of descent, and—perhaps of decisive importance—they are nominated and ratified as ritual heads by the kainanga ariki. Ratification may be seen as still another strand in the multiplicity of connections the chief has with his dependent lineages. From the standpoint of status, however, the pure and his paito are thereby drawn into the realm of the chief. The patterns of succession and of investiture are analogous and, of course, deliberately nonidentical. The pure and their lineages seem at first glance to be like the eastern Polynesian rangatira in their middle status between true aristocracy and commoner. Their genealogical foundations, however, are different, for the pure are not simply junior branches of the chiefly lines. Rather, they are, according to Firth, fresh aggregates of families, some indigenous to Tikopia and some descended from immigrants (1939:187). They are lineages with some claim to autonomous first origins. Firth implies, therefore, that it is the lower and nonritual paito who are the low scale, and products of the ariki lines. These low-status paito evidently lack rank order, in contrast to the upper-division groups, who share in the ritual precedence of their pure.

There is a curious and perhaps significant reversal in the pattern of status classification between Samoa–Tonga and Tikopia. In the former it is the upper ranks who are finely categorized. In Tikopia, categorization is generally crude, but given this crudity it is the generic category of commoner that is refined rather than that of ariki. The term for commoner, *fakaarofa* is not, of course, derogatory. *Arofa*, the stem, refers to warmth and sympathy. *Faka* is the causative prefix, so that the reference is to a status calling forth benevolence. When we recall the distinction in attitude toward eldest son and younger children, we recognize a parallel in public status. To be indulged and looked after is by no means equivalent to being despised. Dependency is, nevertheless, demeaning. The unrestrained Tikopian scorn is for the "bats," the poor families who have nothing of their own and because of poverty are dependent upon others. Fakaarofa have dignity in their economic standing. The pure fakaarofa controlling their own ritual life enter still a different category.

From Firth we learn for the first time what is the actual distribution of a Polynesian population by status category. In 1929 Tikopians fell into three almost equal grades of ariki paito, pure paito, and plain fakaarofa. This count expresses formal distinction only. The actual classification of persons by more general criteria of having distinction would, as Firth frequently points out, be more complex. Wealth, a source of considerable honor, does not correlate precisely with formal rank and neither does occupational distinction.

To summarize: By economic criteria, Tikopia is a classless society.

Gradations and their categories draw upon a variety of criteria, among them seniority, traditional history, ritual roles, wealth, and skills. The genealogical criteria are, however, foremost, endowing the system with a fundamental stability.

Status Rivalry

Tikopian traditional history, probably because it speaks more eloquently for the internal viewpoint of the islanders, has impressed even so dedicated a functionalist as Firth with its turbulence:

> Tikopia men of rank seem to have been almost obsessed by a thirst for prestige and power, and a hunger for land, and ready to resort to violence to secure their ends. This was a time . . . when there were many *toa* and they were trying, by force or stratagem, to kill one another off so that each might rule simply, and the land own obedience to him alone . . . (1961:124).
>
> As it was said, "In the land of olden time each man objected to the land obeying another. Each said that the land should stand under him (1961:122)."

The résumé, suggestive of the Open society, contrasts a turbulent past with a gentle present. Of immediate interest is the clear indication of social resilience. Elsewhere in Polynesia obsessions with power and prestige shook societies to their foundations and sent their most cherished traditions of authority crashing into the dust. In Tikopia, when the dust had settled and the bruised and battered had come to their senses and were able to assess their gains and their losses, they must have been delighted to discover that all was as before. The smaller pieces had moved on the board; the major pieces stood more or less where they belonged.

We can always propose "structural" explanations for Tikopian durability. In wars, however, the outcome is more important than internal structure. If Ravenga had won, the outcome could have readily led to a Mangaian system—or if subordinate lineages had actually overcome their chiefly superiors! Still, there is something to be said after all for the stabilizing effects of Tikopian patterns of equivalence which evidently reduced rivalry among the Nga Ariki and then among all four kainanga even after the commoner Fangarere were admitted to the ritual confederacy. Since Kafika was in fact ritually superior, equivalence was not absolute. Religious transcendence, however, is less likely to draw fire than temporal dominance. In the temporal domain, consensus was the rule, while the weight of religious prestige was offset by the Kafika traditions of being "above the strife."

The threat to social stability was more likely from below, where economic issues prevailed: Land shortage was chronic and land was crucial for status. The war against Ravenga was at least in part a response to land shortage. Since this war was officially sanctioned, its economic aims were realized in an orderly fashion. No individual warriors gained sudden or unusual powers. Ritual supremacy held firm.

Land shortage was, nevertheless, a constant threat to the amity of the paito and, for that matter, to the household. On this truly critical issue, the Tikopian solution—celibacy of the younger brother—was unique. Offhand, such a "solution" appears perilous, because by Polynesian standards celibacy reduces status. But as it reduces his status, it simultaneously strips the victim of the means for effective revolt. He has no natural following. The fact that the celibacy of junior brothers also limits population and relieves the economy can have only a secondary and much delayed bearing upon the pressures of status rivalry. Status rivalry and the economy are, of course, interdependent—but only after rivalry has already been generated. Short of revolution, rivalry represents only the natural antagonisms of those who are recognized as worthy.

The restudy of Tikopia after one generation brings to light more subtle but unquestionably far-reaching changes in the Tikopian status system. Those changes, accurately recorded by Firth and Spillius, have affected relations between commoners and chiefs and are therefore also to be considered as aspects of status rivalry. They are not as dramatic as the turbulent events of the pre-European period, but they are surely more decisive, for they are in keeping with the irresistible and global trend toward reduction in social differences based on pedigree and the creation of new differences based upon individual abilities.

The traditional status system had not changed drastically between 1929 and 1952. It was gradually eroding. Rank endogamy, for example, was accepted in traditional Tikopia as a valid if not rigid principle. By 1929, marriages between chiefs and commoners had already become frequent. By 1952, the expectation of endogamy had virtually disappeared and two-thirds of all chiefly marriages had taken place with commoners (Firth 1959:207). Respect for aristocracy had not vanished. Intermarriage occurred rather as a form of hypergamy, lifting the commoners onto higher ground, where they merged with the aristocracy. The influence of Christianity upon the standing of the chiefs was not as drastic in Tikopia as it had been elsewhere in Polynesia. The church contributed, nevertheless, to the erosion of chiefly status by undercutting the ritual significance of the kainanga ariki. The four great chiefs had to depend more upon traditional respects for their hereditary position and upon consideration of their economic capabilities than upon religious efficacy. Under these circumstances, among others, the first-ranking Kafika had lost ground—as measured by rate of increase in numbers of households—to the third-ranking Taumako and to the commoner-descended Fangarere. While the chiefly lineages of each of the four kainanga had grown faster than their commoner paito, their rates of increase were almost in inverse proportion to their traditional ranking. Taumako had more than doubled in size and Fangarere paito had increased by 80 percent (in round numbers). Kafika had only increased by about one-quarter, and Tafua by some 30 percent (that is, at the average rate of increase for the population as a whole).

Rate of increase in size is a fair measure of efficacy of leadership and is thus at least indirectly a gauge of actual social standing. By these objective standards, Taumako—followed closely by Fangarere—had begun to emerge as the new dynamic centers. The Ariki Taumako had become the foremost holder of cultivatable land (Firth 1959:165) and "fear of Taumako expansion (Firth 1959:201)" was openly expressed. Expansion was simply the desired outcome of aggressively pursuing land-holdings through all legitimate means (by marriages and by moving into all uncultivated and thus available land parcels). Expansion occurred in a new economic atmosphere of greater household autonomy, which may explain why it provoked fears. Firth learned of a number of instances where elders brothers, the traditional custodians of the land, had gone beyond ordinary privileges of stewardship to deprive younger brothers of their rights (1959:165). Even ariki had become "land grabbers" as their interests turned from ritual to land. Such a portentous shift in interest is revealed, to quote Firth, "in the actions of the pagan Ariki Taumako in using land control directly as an instrument of religious and political policy (i.e., as a threat) (1959:171)."

The magnitude of these shifts in value should not, as Firth cautions, be overestimated. Even under stress, traditional concepts of honor had not changed much, and the image of chiefs as spiritual centers of the community, had only barely blurred. If it is really true that disaster shakes a society down to the very bedrock of its values, the great hurricanes of 1952 and 1953 and their aftermath of severe famine should reveal once and for all the solid foundations of Tikopian cultural life. That two anthropologists—one with a background of intimate knowledge of the island—should have been on the scene as expert reporters is one of those scientifically gratifying fortuitous events that are all too rare in our discipline.

With food very scarce, theft was common. The people stole from each other as well as from the chiefs. Only the chiefs, their close kinsmen, and the maru resisted the impulse to steal. The chiefs took effective control, rationed the food supply, tried to stamp out theft, collected and redistributed shares in the earnings of overseas Tikopians. In return, they were cherished. In principle, at least, the general public was prepared to starve so as to preserve the chiefs at all costs. Loyalty to the chiefs persisted despite the haunting memory of the Ravenga and Faea wars. The commoners feared that once again the chiefs would expel them to preserve themselves.

The shortages of food curtailed ritual to the point where people felt that life was going out. In some manner, nevertheless, the major ritual obligations (mortuary in particular) were met. Those who could afford an offering appeared; the others stayed away. The usual hospitality toward casual guests and more distant relatives was abandoned. But for an honored guest, the sacrifice of personal convenience was made—and the last stores of food brought out.

Descent Group Organization

The small Tikopian population is historically diverse, in fact insistently so, but linked together through intermarriages into a single kindred. The community can therefore enjoy the deeper satisfactions of separation, autonomy, and particularity without any sacrifice of the practical benefits of bilaterality. The principles of organization are familiar: Honor is lineal, utility lateral; honor seeks separateness, utilitarian kinship promotes connections.

Impressed by Tikopian particularism which endows each of the four kainanga with substantial autonomy, Firth reasoned functionally that their ritual relations are an effort to overcome excessive autonomy. From the standpoint of aristocratic values, however, the emphasis is in reverse. The ritual community guards the small population against the anonymity of general and bilateral kinship. The character of the ritual community is such that each kainanga comes under a particular jurisdiction, preserves its own traditions, and—by the totemistic analogy—asserts its organic individuality. The organic concept of Kafika ritual supremacy is set off against this counterpoint of separation. When we consider Tikopian society as a structural entity, the issue in any case ceases to be that of autonomy versus unity in the utilitarian sense of whether the island community holds together or breaks up. One counterposes the other in a pattern that demands both. Tikopian thought, as the traditions reveal it, moves easily between these two poles.

In the classic traditional manner, Segment I represents an essentially ritual unity among discrete and economically self-sufficient groups. Through their ariki and their ritual elders, they take part in the islandwide productivity rites known as "The Work of the Gods," an annual and prolonged series of observances to promote crop fertility and success in fishing. Having been initiated by the *atua i Kafika* who is worshiped by all four kainanga (cf. Firth 1940a), the ritual cycle acknowledges simultaneously the ascendant position of Ariki Kafika and the distinctiveness of the three others, each of whom has his special privileges. Ariki Kafika is also a physical center in ritual. He signals the start of the cycle and his home base of Uta is the ceremonial center of the island. In earlier days the theme of one and many was carried out by placing Kafika temples in each of the kainanga territories as well. Kafika ascendance, then, is by no means a vague concept. The symbolism of a pinnacle is entirely concrete. However, it is deliberately nonpolitical and disassociated from power.

Segment II is the kainanga described by Firth as a corporate entity whose ariki combine ritual and economic powers. It is worth mentioning that Firth's initial impression of the ariki was of a religious figure. Upon restudy and rethinking, he has concluded that he had understated his temporal role (1959:256). The ariki, he shows, are responsible for "law and order": They address the fono (in Tikopia a solemn assembly like a joint session of Congress) on grave issues such as overpopulation or the prevalence of theft; they receive a portion of the wages of Tikopians who have worked abroad and redistribute it among kainanga men; they receive first-fruits and gifts; they proclaim the food tapus and the maru enforce them; as the crisis of the hurricane showed, they have the ready writ of leadership. Finally, the land title (i.e., the cachet of honor) is vested in them and they settle land disputes. The jurisdiction of an ariki is specifically confined, but since the kainanga is no longer a compact residential body, those who live near an ariki fall under his general temporal jurisdiction; the ritual authority, however, stays at the home base. The ritual jurisdiction of the kainanga retains its primacy.

From the standpoint of its core, the ariki descent line, the kainanga, has a lineage structure. The ariki lines are patrilineal and pure, but the commoner lines are not. The immigrant lines, having been adopted by the chiefs and attached to their lines, hold thereby a jural legitimacy as lineage members. But they lack the authentic honor of descent; they have rather the lower status of a graft. It is from this lower perspective that the kainanga loses distinctness as a lineage, and it is presumably for this reason that Firth prefers to label it a "clan," a useful label because it is very general.

The dispersal of kainanga membership all over the island may be said to reflect first the condition of smallness. Wherever people live on a three-mile-square island, they are in close touch. Second, the focus being general ritual and not economic, the disadvantages of dispersal vanish altogether. The kainanga arouses strong feelings of pride and of superiority in precisely its growth and outward expansion.

Segment III, the paito, a categorically patrilineal lineage, is a branch, either organic or grafted, of the kainanga, and in principle holding rank by seniority. Higher-category paito, being headed by a pure, are lower-rank replicas of kainanga, but even those without a ritual elder are religious bodies possessing their own tutelary deities and a personal representation before them. The lack of a ritual elder deprives a paito of full status in more general ritual observances but not of religious representation before its own god.

If the kainanga are traditionally the stable descent groups, embedded in beginnings and in fundamental divisions, the paito are the growing areas, the locations of subdivision. Yet segmentation, a "natural" lineage process, is considered by Tikopia as unfortunate, if not calamitous. The aim, evidently, is to retain parallelism with the kainanga and thus support the sense of subgroup autonomy. The expectation of junior-brother celibacy, as Firth observes, would act to restrain subdivision (1959:223). The drastic subordination implied by celibacy is not in fact always realized. On the contrary, it is the rejection of junior subordination precipitated in a quarrel that splits the paito and begins a course of gradual estrangement between the original "house" and its new branch. Estrangement demands symbolic differentiation, but not the rupture of genealogical connections. When a paito divides, no one need move. The lands are divided, and ritual procedures are altered in a move Tikopians call "to turn aside (Firth 1959:239)." When the ritual differences are publicly recognized, autonomy has been established. Firth's penetrating analysis of Tikopian segmentation compels us to reexamine Buck's overly generalized vegetative picture of New Zealand branching. The process may be far more an aspect of internal structure than is represented by the bucolic image of people filling up an ecological zone and then moving on. In Tikopia, the issue is autonomy, and autonomy is a primary condition for honorable status.

The reference to paito as a "house" implies coherence and intimacy. From the point of view of size, these expectations of closeness should be easily met: the population of a paito averages out to about 40. In general, the paito is in fact a more compact, a more intricate, and a more pragmatic version of the kainanga, especially with respect to land-holding. Its household constituents are nonetheless scattered, and their compulsions toward coherence are still, in the main, those of ritual and of honor. Religion is generally centripetal. Honor is more specific, and that is one reason why chiefly lineages are the more cohesive and faster growing. In the contemporary period, however, wealth of a head-man has begun to compensate for rank.

The ultimate and the utilitarian segment is the household, a fraternal joint family whose head by tradition is the senior brother. He is the day-by-day custodian of the land and the director of labor. He is the secular and pragmatic authority. Patrilocality gives the household the patrilineal cast of kainanga and paito. Economic ties, however, are bilateral. Daughters have rights to household lands during their lifetime. Thus, a married man may expect to cultivate plots to which he has rights of patrilineal descent, along with those which belong to his wife, who may be of a different kainanga and paito. Cultivation, of course, is not necessarily a matter of title (honor), but of utility.

The District Organization

Present-day Tikopia is divided regionally into an eastern (Ravenga) and a western division (Faea). The earlier division was tripartite, but since it then pitted the Nga Ariki in their own district against Ravenga and Faea, the point of view was still that of moiety. The district division expressed then the actual locations of the kainanga, distinguishing between chiefs and autochthones, on the one hand, and commoners and immigrants, on the other. After the Ravenga and Faea expulsions, the chiefly kainanga, it will be recalled, began to disperse, maintaining, however, foci of concentration. The present moiety is still rivalrous, but on a somewhat different basis. Their rivalry, entirely a matter of sentiment, pits, in effect, their representative kainanga against each other—all but Kafika, which is the only one of the four to be evenly disseminated in all four, just as in the past it had maintained its temples in all kainanga centers. Thus eastern Tafua sees itself as pitted—but symbolically—against Taumako, while Kafika is still above the strife. The sentiment of regional rivalry surely sustains the traditional commitments to kainanga autonomy and particularism in the face of new pressures for utilitarian self-effacement of groups.

The scattering of households—in large measure also a result of war—(but not of power centers) affects the character of the villages. In its composition, a village (*potu* or *kainga*) is a compact version of the district. It reassembles residentially all who are divided by descent line—of kainanga, paito, and household. It combines the disparate lines into a common fono and submits them to the authority of a chief, the highest-ranking resident. The village does not override any other affiliations. On the contrary, its inner order in turn recreates the linear classifications. The overall village order seemingly transforms—through concentrations—what is only a sense or sentiment of unity of a district into a more pragmatic unity of common action: Villagers fish together and help each other in harvesting. Unlike the Samoan village, the Tikopian does not own land. However, there are two kinds of village: one of the composite structure as just described, and another that is a compact paito and resembles, therefore, the Maori kainga. If we seek to describe the political character of the potu, we must look toward the social standing of its chief and toward the linear qualities of its members. In short, neither the district nor the village in Tikopia has crystallized politically.

17

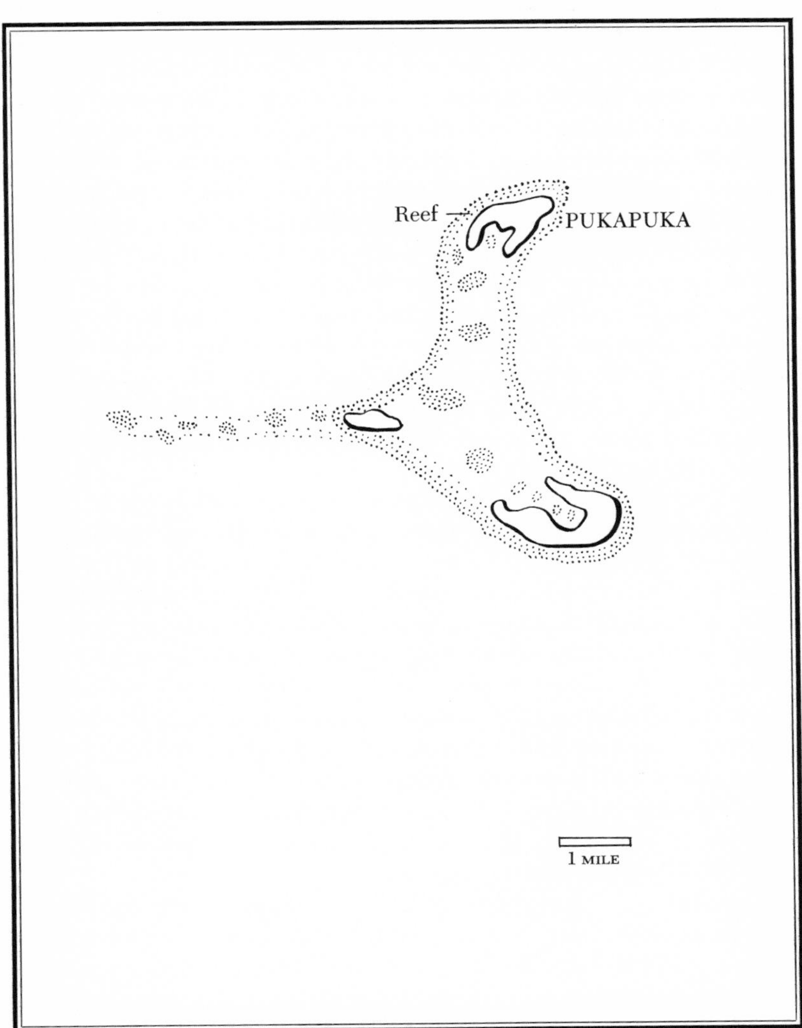

Pukapuka

MIDWAY BETWEEN THE SAMOAN AND COOK ISLANDS, PUKAPUKA presents understandably a picture of historical ambiguity. Until its linguistic identification has been verified, we cannot say confidently whether Pukapuka society was originally eastern and had come under Samoan influence or an old western that had been modified by its contacts with the Cook Islands. The leading authorities (Beaglehole and Beaglehole 1938) suggest still another possibility, namely: a truly archaic Polynesian culture severely simplified by an atoll environment and, of course, affected by later history of diverse Melanesian and Polynesian connections. One would only question the assumption of antiquity. Local traditions postulate a settlement date not much earlier than A.D. 1200 (parallel with that for Manihiki), and thus within the range of atoll occupation dates generally. Among atolls Pukapuka is peculiarly subject to devastating storms that alone would make very long continuous occupation an improbability. A settlement date of 1200 places Pukapuka with the prestratified phases of eastern and western Polynesia, a situation in accord with local history.

The nature of the balance between "eastern" and "western" characteristics yields no decisive clues as to place of origin either. The patterning of relationship terms is unmistakably eastern. The structure of kin groups, on the other hand, is western, suggesting an elaboration of Samoan concepts of male line–female line duality. In a similar manner, status terminology is eastern, and the status system is western. The culture is conceivably a composite of both areas. I have included it among the western Polynesians because it resembles Samoa far more in overall character than it does Manihiki. As a status system, the parallels are also strongest with the west. The traditions of the Pukapukans, it must be said, finally, refer to connections with Manihiki, Tonga, Niue, the Tokelaus, and Samoa, but do not positively identify the original homeland.

In evolutionary perspective, therefore, Pukapuka does not take its place as a specific branch of an established tree (for the time being), but as a cultural "hybrid." As a contrast to Manihiki it demonstrates the social diversity possible even under the very rigorous conditions of atoll life. In its apparent fusion of a "Hawaiian" type of kinship system with a "dual" organization, it demonstrates how loose the "fit" between kinship pattern and kin group can be. As a status system it illustrates the diversity but also the durability of "traditional" patterns.

The atoll of Pukapuka consists of three islets with a combined land area of 1,250 acres (2 sq. mi.). In recent times only one of the islets has been inhabited, the population residing in three villages on the lagoon shore. The remaining islands serve as reserve lands and are visited only occasionally. The basic food supply for the population of 630 comes, therefore, from a land area of only .5 square miles, giving a normal population density of 1,260, by far the highest in Polynesia. Such density is made possible by a reliable supply of fish and coconuts. Taro, cultivated in carefully prepared pits filled with plant material and fertilized with leaves and ferns twice a year, barely meets subsistence needs. In times of drought or storm, the crop is lost altogether. The Beagleholes observed what they believed to be a typical cycle of six months when food is abundant and the remainder of the year, between July and October, when all food is scarce. Famine has been chronic, and a major concern of village authorities, who are responsible for the communal taro beds, is to guard them against theft, always a serious problem. Pulaka, bananas, and pandanus complete the vegetable diet. Of these, only the pandanus, hardly an esteemed food, is abundant.

Technical skills were adapted, of course, to the material limitations of atoll environment. Tridacna shell was used for adzes, and conglomerate coral took the place of traditional stone in the construction of religious enclosures and of small-scale agricultural works, such as taro beds. Uncarved and crudely shaped coral slabs sufficed as god-images. The Pukapukas were uninterested in ornamentation and decoration generally. In short, material culture was essentially though not altogether utilitarian.

The atoll fell within the European orbit rather late, but effectively. Commodore Byron was the discoverer in 1765. A century later the London Missionary Society had established itself and had converted almost all the inhabitants. In 1863 the native culture suffered still another blow when the assiduous labor collectors from Peru carried off some 100 men and women. But the aliki did manage to return. In the same decade, Pukapukans volunteered for labor in the Philippines. They found the work unrewarding and returned home bringing back recollections of still another cultural experience. In 1892 Great Britain annexed the atoll to its Pacific possessions, and for most of its recent history it has been administered by New Zealand represented by a resident agent. As exporters of copra, the Pukapukans are now enmeshed, if moderately, in the cash economy of the world market.

Thus when Ernest and Pearl Beaglehole arrived in 1934 for Bishop Museum, much of the traditional culture was gone and largely forgotten. Even the language was disappearing, being replaced officially by Rarotongan. New political forms combining English and local concepts had already pushed aside traditional chiefship, and the older ideas of kinship and family were losing their hold on the young. Nevertheless, in the course of over seven months the Beagleholes salvaged a great deal and succeeded in relating a current state of affairs with a more traditional past. The greatest loss was in information on religion. Presumably much ambiguity about the cultural and historical position of Pukapuka may be laid simply to incompleteness of information. At the same time it is also clear that Pukapuka could not have failed to develop anomalous cultural features because (like the Tokelaus) of an extraordinarily turbulent and disruptive history. On small atolls, even moderate disturbances are easily magnified.

Genealogical Traditions

After they have established the concept of initial settlement, the traditions focus on disorder. The founder is said to have been Mataliki, who is also known as an ancestral deity. He is thought to have come from Tonga and to have established a line of aliki that endured for 22 generations, or some 500 years. Although the traditions refer to immigrants from several sources in and outside of Polynesia, they also claim that the aliki lines, at least, were founded in utmost purity—reminiscent of Hawaii and Tonga—from the offspring of a brother–sister marriage. The event of highest interest for the Pukapukans as they recollect their history is a natural catastrophe, a great seismic wave that swept over the atoll some 300 years ago. This event divides Pukapukan history into two major periods which may be designated as pre- and post-catastrophic.

The early, or pre-catastrophic, seems to have been one of restlessness, leading finally to a state of chaotic disorder. The traditions of this period tell of arrivals, but note as well a series of departures to distant parts (named as Tonga, Niue, the Tokelaus, the Gilberts and Manihiki). Then, just before the seismic wave, the atoll was convulsed by strange disorders, seemingly provoked by the discontent of Wauguna, an extraordinary woman who is described as both sorceress and as sexually wanton. She led a large company of followers on an orgy of debauchery. Under her influence they violated all tapus, tore down gravestones, and leveled the religious maraes. When finally abandoned by her lovers, she called down the ire of the gods. The seismic wave was their answer. Fittingly, Wauguna was one of the few whose lives were spared.

The natural cataclysm seems only to have added a new dimension to Pukapukan disorders. With the population terribly reduced in numbers, and with food and crops all but totally destroyed, the atoll was driven by new torments. The new chief, the notable Maina, undertook to conserve the remaining food supply and to control looting by resettling all the scattered families into a single village. He assumed personal control over the entire economy. He took upon himself the management of the taro beds and of fishing expeditions. He set up taro reserves and posted guards who were authorized to kill thieves. These measures were effective during his reign only. His son and successor could not sustain the central authority because he could not safeguard the taro beds against increasingly more powerful raids by presumably guerrilla bands that defied both the authority of the chiefs as well as the power of the gods in whose name the reserves were guarded.

The utter collapse of traditional standards of decorum is documented again in the record of the reign of Alatakapa, the twelfth aliki, who is portrayed as a cruel and violent ruler. During his tyrannical administration, an extraordinary antagonism developed between the elders—the secular power—and the young men. Traditionally, the younger men brought foods to the elders, who arranged for a proper distribution. But with food scarce, the elders kept all for themselves. The young men retaliated angrily by entering the forbidden reserves, thus defying at once all sources of authority. A full-scale insurrection followed. Before it was settled, the paramount chief and his entire lineage had lost their lives. The new chief had to face an attack from a new, but more traditional quarter—from a priestly party—which he succeeded, however, in resisting. The passions of political antagonism finally subsided and by the middle of the nineteenth century, a generation before the calming influence of Christianity could be felt, the inherent rivalries had settled into a more placid pattern. Thus when four eligible lineages put forth their own candidates for the paramount alikiship, the new solution was not to fight but to accept a quadrumvirate—a solution resembling the Tikopian style.

Were it not for the Wauguna episode which is attributed to the pre-catastrophic, one would have at once a handy economic explanation for Pukapukan political disorder: poverty rends the social fabric; prosperity mends it. The Wauguna disorders suggest rather deeper layers of discontent, perhaps with the social system itself Pukapukan violence does not follow the common norms of Polynesian status rivalry. The dissidents seem unduly iconoclastic. They aim not merely for the vein in the throat of the aliki; they go for the social foundations. They apparently reject the rationality of economic necessity, as well as the absolutes of the religious order. The traditions, of course, are incomplete, and probably omit the crucial political events that might portray Pukapukan rivalries as closer to familiar Polynesian standards. As in Mangaia, poverty may in fact have been an unsettling condition. If the food supply failed, it was reasonable, within the Pukapukan traditions, to blame the paramount chief and his lineage gods.

The Status System

In terms of traditional norms, the Pukapukan status system may be visualized either as underdeveloped or as deteriorated. The latter seems the more likely, simply by historical evidence—late date of settlement and connections with Cook Islands, on the one hand, and Samoa–Tonga, on the other. Structure also suggests deterioration. Examined in detail, Pukapuka exhibits all the traditional principles of status, although in modified and, more concretely, in attenuated form. We detect at once pale yet recognizable reflections of primogeniture, of seniority of descent, of male line, of genealogical rank, of chiefly sanctity, and of all traditional interests in political power. As a western Polynesian society, Pukapuka has carried sex-line dualism past the Samoan standards. On the other hand, it has not gone as far as the Tokelaus in a "gerontocratic" direction, but has rather adapted age and genealogical seniority to the complementary or dual pattern.

Primogeniture

Primogeniture holds for peripheral areas and not for the more traditional office of aliki. In more recent times, at least, the aliki could name any of his sons as successor. On the other hand, primogeniture was the normal basis for the selection of the *mayakitanga* (an apparent composite of Samoan *taupou* and Tongan *mehekitanga*), or "sacred maid," who as first-born daughter of the aliki symbolized his sanctity and prestige. Beauty was a prerequisite and could supersede the qualification of order of birth. But since beauty in the sacred virgin was the equivalent of efficacy in a chief, the principle remains the same. We recognize, too, the traditional respects for order of birth in feasts given in honor of first-born children.

In kinship classifications, Pukapuka did not use the conventional distinctions between senior and junior siblings that are characteristic of almost all Polynesian and Malayo-Polynesian systems. Since its "system" is in all other respects so typically eastern Polynesian, an assumption of lapse is reasonable, and so, for that matter, is the probability that the principle of primogeniture, generally, was in decline.

Seniority of Descent

On the related question of seniority, the evidence is unclear. There are no definite indications of genealogical ranking of descent lines. If primogeniture did not regulate chiefly succession, a traditional order of senior lines could hardly have developed. Nevertheless, only some patrilineal lineages held the aliki titles. The Beagleholes also say that sometimes "junior lines" usurped the rightful succession (1938:239). The implied presence of a concept of junior lines reinforces an assumption of decline in the significance of both primogeniture and of seniority of descent.

Male Line

The honoring of the male line occurs within a social setting of sex-line duality that in Pukapuka emerges more decisively than in Tonga or in Samoa. The Samoan distinction between tama tane and tama fafine has its counterpart here in two distinct sets of lineages, one matrilineal the other patrilineal. The former were more nearly—though not exclusively—domestic and secular; the latter, more political and religious. Thus the chiefship (aliki) went from father to son only in particular patrilineal lineages. If there was no direct male heir, the title lay open until an acceptable male of the lineage, often a brother, claimed it. Women never assumed the title, and if a male of the maternal lineage laid claim, he had to be adopted first, so that he was in effect an authentic title holder. The paternal lineages were called *po*—a reference to their special connections with the dead. In Pukapukan, po is the underworld and the cemetery. Each po (lineage) was represented by its own ancestral deities, priests, and burial grounds. On the economic side, the po controlled the very important coconut groves, certain lands, and the houses. Its economic character is emphasized in the synonym *kainga*. Like the Tikopian kainga, the po were categorically patrilineal.

The matrilineal lineages (not to be confused, as the Beagleholes remind us, with the Samoan tama fafine) represent a true matrilineal line. They are called *wua,* a reference to the female generative organs, and had in 1934 as perhaps in the past more limited and more secular functions. In the recent past they organized group fishing and supplied teams for athletic contests. They held specific ritual roles at marriages and births, when they assumed responsibility for food distributions. Like the Samoan tama fafine, each wua guarded the public behavior of its members, punishing them for misdeeds. The wua did not, however, have the religious right to curse either its male line or its counterpart patrilineal lineages. With a general decline in formal organization, the wua had lost even more of their earlier role, but they still retained the truly secular responsibility for the private taro beds.

The Pukapukans had only a vague recollection of the aboriginal wua. Their traditions suggest a more extensive and more coherent organization in the past. They refer to a division between seaside and inland wua (moiety organization), each divided again into two major lineages or *keinanga*. By analogy with eastern Polynesia (Mangaia, for example), the inland–sea division suggests a religious moiety. The tradition itself is vaguely totemic in deriving one division from land animals and the other from sea creatures. Conceivably, maternal and paternal lineages were once more evenly balanced.

Given the ambiguity of available information, the Beagleholes have prudently resisted the temptation to explain wua and po either historically or sociologically, yet one cannot overlook the general relationships with familiar western Polynesian sex dualism. The Pukapukan system appears to be a variant of the Samoan by virtue of general categories of sex-line privileges, and of the Tikopian by standards of categorical descent. In all these systems it is the male line that focalizes and the female lines that diffuse. Thus po and wua fall within general western Polynesian patterns of dualism. Here, the designations po and wua help define the metaphoric character of sex-line dualism rather clearly. The wua speak for the more general and, really, for the more diffuse quality of birth; the po, for the more specific and indeed focal continuity of a line as it joins its ancestry, and as it occupies an immovable site in a cemetery. Po and wua are metaphorically complementary and structurally equivalent.

In the mayakitanga, the metaphoric association is reminiscent of Tonga, but the structural implications are distinct. In Tonga the mehekitanga was an honored female who headed an honored line. The Pukapukan sacred maid is a virgin and thus a terminal person. Through her, only the chief is honored and not his female side. It is the wua that conveys the honors for the female lines.

Genealogical Depth

Since it is evidently only the aliki lines that go back to the founding settlers, the traditional principle is upheld.

Sanctity

Because of the premature collapse of local religion, our knowledge of concepts of sanctity are inevitably vague, in particular of the Pukapukan ideas of mana. Since the Beagleholes do not discuss mana, we must assume that in their day at least it had ceased to have meaning. Still, the available information, though fragmentary, is not too puzzling, portraying as it does a familiar western Polynesian doctrine of chiefly (aliki) sanctity derived from the gods and assumed only as a prerogative of office. Insofar as the aliki office is concerned the quality of sanctity appears to be a lesser version of that associated with Tui Manu'a.

Pukapukans were no longer sure about the exact circumstances of the sanctity of the aliki, but there was no doubt that his sanctity was associated only with the office and not with the person as heir apparent. The question was whether he was treated as sacred after his investiture or only when he officiated at the marae in his capacity as aliki and priest. Majority opinion leaned to the latter and more traditional view, regarding the aliki as god-descended. He acquired unusual powers after public ratification. Then the god acknowledged the candidate by sending a rainbow; the incumbent, for his part, revealed his seizure either extravagantly by falling into a trance or moderately by developing goose flesh. The manner of instruction declared him to be a high priest as well. As chief-priest he prayed for prosperity and long life. He was thereafter above criticism and outside the realm of practical economic affairs. His curse was feared, but for bringing illness, not death. The gods, however, sent a lightning bolt to blast anyone who touched the sacred garment worn by both priests and aliki. As sacred, he was removed from the general public. The sleeping quarters he shared with his wife were inviolate; he entered the house through a private doorway. He had his own bench, his own resting places, and his own portion of beach. People moved away as he walked among them. His intimate possessions became tapu from contact with his body and were thrown into the sea when discarded. He was the religious guardian of prosperity, and thus immediately vulnerable when the economy failed.

The sacred maid was the religious complement of the chief and in no respect his rival. She, too, was a source of religious powers that brought prosperity. Her induction resembles that of chiefs elsewhere in Polynesia. Taken on a circuit of the island, she was greeted with explanations of: "You are making a circuit of the island—to bring us prosperity (Beagleholes 1938:238)." Her person and surroundings were tapu. The lineage god severely punished sacrilege against her, bringing illness or death. In the Pukapukan version of sacred origin, the concept may be: the cutting off of a human descent line for the sake of economic continuity. In those Pukapukan concepts of royal responsibility we may venture to see an explanation for disorders provoked by economic deprivation.

There is no mention of food offerings to the chief from the island as a whole, an implication, if the chief really did not receive first-fruits or other formal offerings, that his lineage acted purely as donors and not as redistributors. The centers of redistribution were the villages and not the island chief. Since the chief was removed from economic activities, we may infer that the economy was at best a secondary and perhaps a minor element in status. We might then attribute displays of affluence to sheer exuberance of feeling. By the same line of reasoning, the meanness of the old men, stealing from reserves, and watchfulness against being cheated at formal food distributions could be accounted for by the absence of a clear chiefly standard for the estimation of wealth.

Tohunga

Craftsmanship was not strongly developed in Pukapuka, and while skill was admired and in some crafts well honored, there was little scope for the expert. The term *tohunga* (or cognates) does not occur. There were only three kinds of expert: the canoe builders, known as *tangata tau waiva* or *tangata mawatu;* the healers, known as *tangata yila, tangata wotu,* or *tangata vivayiva,* depending on their specialty; and priests called *wata* or *tangata wai atua.* The difference between terms such as *tohunga* and *tangata* is that the former is a special title of honor, the latter means simply "person." Tangata would seem to be a term of understatement of the status of the craftsman, but we cannot safely make that judgment on linguistic grounds alone.

Canoe building was an honored craft held by particular families only as an unofficial monopoly. The chief craftsman was assisted by his own relatives, whom he taught. The work of canoe building was carried out with a degree of ceremoniousness that mainly honored the chief carpenter and his assistants. They were well fed with the best foods while working, and received at the end a variety of gifts such as sennit, fish hooks, and the like. The building terminated in a great feast. Since the principal material rewards were in food for direct consumption, craftsmanship was an avenue to prestige and influence but not to wealth. The same was true of priests and of curers or medicine men. Speaking of the latter, the Beagleholes say:

> For his services the medicine man was paid whatever the patient thought fit. A small food gift was usually sufficient. He received ample recompense for his trouble in the social prestige that accrued to him as a prominent individual of the community (1938:335).

The practice of medicine was open to all who were granted the gift through a dream given him or her by the god of the lineage. Like the chief, a warrior, or seer, the medicine man had manamana.

The priesthood was also a rather unrestricted calling. It was open to old men who had the right dreams and the ability to experience trance. Priests were associated with the god of their paternal lineage and served for only two years unless they had special gifts, in which case they might continue to serve for a lifetime. The position was one of great honor, and even after retirement the priest either became a medicine man or joined the governing council of the old men, where his priestly qualifications gave him a more effective voice in village or island affairs. The priests were maintained by generous offerings of food brought them by close relatives and by the paternal lineage. They received a portion of all feast products, and special gifts of food whenever their intercession with the god was successful.

Toa ("warriors") are mentioned in the Pukapukan traditions in a way to suggest they were not merely warriors but specialists in fighting. The Beagleholes report that each toa was escorted by one or more young men who carried his weapons. In one tradition, the chief is said to have assigned several of his toa to assist the elders in a battle. The toa also possessed mana. We have no further information, but the scraps of information we do have suggest an honored specialist category. The toa were of the lineage of the chief and acted also as his general executive.

Wealth

Despite poverty, Pukapukans insisted upon an active cycle of feasts and gift-giving. Reciprocity was a norm, but was not mandatory. The poor were not expected to return food gifts, and guests were often given gifts freely and unilaterally. Even in formal exchanges there was no expectation of equivalency of return. A token was acceptable. Nevertheless, honor was not altogether irrelevant. Returns were evaluated, even if informally, and the temptation to return more than one had received "to shame" the original donor was not unknown (Beagleholes 1938:91).

The account of economic exchanges we are given by the Beagleholes is remarkably comprehensive, although we cannot be certain how fully it reflects the past when traditional chiefship had given its focus to the status system. The Beagleholes see the Pukapukan economy functionally and demonstrate the role of feasts and exchanges in binding families and villages. They leave us less clear on the direct motives underlying the formal distributions. Every event of importance—and there were very many—was memorialized with an expensive feast. There were numerous occasions when gifts were exchanged. I count at least a dozen types of feasts, each distinctively named. They feasted the chief, the village guards, canoe and house builders, participants in contests and sports, marriages, births, deaths, the special affairs of lineages, religious rites, phases of the moon, and changes of season. I assume that each feast was a statement of economic efficacy that declared the state of prosperity of the donors. The quantities of food given away were often prodigious and excessive. Large quantities of food could not be consumed and were allowed to rot (Beagleholes 1938:92).

The invidious element was present, though definitely not conspicuous (in accordance with the pattern of understated status rivalry generally). In the past, the aliki set standards of generosity, drawing upon the reserves of his own paternal lineage rather than upon public contributions for feasts given in his name. He was then pure donor rather than redistributor. An extraordinary contrast is presented—extravagant generosity, on the one hand, and meanness, on the other. The successful were the prideful donors. What, then, were the circumstances of thieving from the food reserves? Did people steal so as to be publicly generous or were there two distinct standards—one of giving and another of taking? The aliki were unquestionably the reliable givers.

Political Hegemony

Earlier concepts of chiefly power must be deduced from fragments of traditional history. Reference to oppressive chiefs and to rivalry between chief and priest bring to mind at once the familiar Polynesian themes of power as the capacity for violence, of violence as a potential prerogative of high position, and of a divine connection manifesting itself through some aspect of terror. The knavery of elders who withhold food from the community they are pledged to serve is recognized as unethical, yet even as the traditions single out such events they portray at the same time a real connection between authority and the arbitrary imposition of self-interest. Pukapuka does not fall within the class of powerful chiefships in Polynesia, at least insofar as we know from fragmentary evidence. If it had once resembled more closely a Tongan or a Cook Island model, its evolution would be in the contrary direction: from power to conciliation; from centrality to collectivism; from paramount chief to divided and carefully counterbalanced authority between sacred aliki, who exercise the broad and spiritual dominion, and the council of elders who share as a body—in the spirit of compromise and conciliation—the secular powers that regulate the economy and practical affairs. The pattern, as the Beagleholes reconstruct it, is more Samoan than Tongan in the period that first precedes the European occupation. By then, ritual forms of antagonism, such as wrestling matches to settle boundary disputes and competing games between maternal lineages, had begun to loom more conspicuously over the Pukapukan social landscape than wars and feuds.

The Structure of Status

Viewing the qualification of age as a distinctive coordinate of status —as we did in the Tokelaus—expressive of a genealogical discontinuity and of achievement in terms of durability and the accretion of experience, the status system appears as dual. Aliki and langatila, who are the subordinate chiefs, occupy the genealogical coordinate; the elders (*tupele*), who form an administrative council to the paramount chief, are on the coordinate of achieved status. Their senior citizen is their leader and is simultaneously spokesman of the chief and of the people. He was called *wola,* and it is not difficult to see him, especially since he had priestly powers as well, as a counterpart to the Samoan talking chief. The tupele is complement to the genealogical ranks; it is the official body that grants high status to priests, medicine men, craftsmen, and warriors who have reached the top of their professions. It is the crafts union, so to speak, of those who have made it on their own.

As in Tikopia, the highest chiefly rank held no secular authority, but the lower-ranking chiefs who headed sublineages were secular leaders over their own small patrilineal kin groups. The highest genealogical rank was sacred, but while highest sanctity was definitely a prerogative of high genealogical rank, it was not (as we have seen) limited to rank. The distinction between rank and achieved status was in scope of jurisdiction. The high chief was related to the lineage god who was the dominant or islandwide god. The jurisdiction of the commoner priests was either subordinate to that of the aliki, or of a local nature. All sacred persons (including toa) possessed mana, but only the aliki was entitled to all the special tapus of separation, and only he was believed to be actually descended from the gods, a fundamental distinction.

The holders of genealogical rank formed a very small group. They included only the actual heads of patrilineal lineages and sublineages. We might include the mayakitanga among them. There is no statement in the Beagleholes' work to tell us whether the kin of the aliki were also considered as aliki. Evidently they were not, although there was clearly some distinction in status between the four patrilineal lineages entitled to name an aliki and those that were exclusively commoner. Most of the population were commoners, or, as the Beagleholes put it, without rank. They were referred to as *te kau,* the people, or as *te tama,* the children. There were no derogatory statuses other than epithets designating undesirable personal qualities.

Descent Group Organization

Segment I stands for the entire atoll, which carries a tribal name *ulu-u-te-wahi* and is conceived of as having common descent and was thus a kindred. A paramount aliki was its sacred and priestly ruler and a grand council of elders representing the villages acted until recently as a royal council with authority to administer intervillage and islandwide affairs. What these affairs actually were, the people no longer remember distinctly. Presumably, as the Beagleholes believe, they dealt with land boundaries and with the periodic distribution of reserve lands. Such tangible economic matters were discussed by the tupele in the presence of the public. The aliki and his executives advised, but the final decisions were with the elders, who were, in fact, the more durable agency of administration than the aliki. If the tupele duties were as the Beagleholes believe them to have been, Segment I has stature as a strongly administrative body. The nature of the genealogical authority falls within traditional western Polynesian patterns: The representative of genealogical rank divides the authority with the villages, whose representatives are not ranked but—in a more radical departure from the Samoan system—are the elders. The economic power seems to have been with the villages.

The question of Segment II is seemingly complex, but perhaps only because of fragmentary information. Again there is an apparent balance between a matrilineal division of the atoll into "land people" and "sea people," and a patrilineal organization representing the village. The characteristics of the matrilineal moieties are very poorly remembered. Since there is no evidence that they were actually territorial, they were conceivably metaphoric entities cognate, perhaps, with the

Mangaian priestly organization that divided the powers between land and sea. Since games and contests now pit the individual maternal lineages against each other, it is likely, as the Beagleholes believe, that in the past the moieties also opposed each other in such matters. If this were so, the moiety would stand as a ritual organization and thus as clearly complementary to the village, a major political and economic entity. The matrilineal society represented its dependent lineages and sublineages presumably in a metaphoric manner, organizing them in an implied opposition that took account of the totality of creation (cf. creation myth, Beagleholes 1938:222–23). It did not organize them, to the best of anyone's knowledge, substantively.

The village has always been, as it could hardly have failed to be, the truly substantive organization. This very small atoll contains three villages, each representing various paternal lineages. The structure is Samoan insofar as the territorial emphasis outweighs the genealogical. While lineages constitute the village, it is the village as an organization that claims primary loyalty. It is the village community that discusses the eligibility of membership. To be unaffiliated with a village is, as the Beagleholes say, to be "lost and outcast (1938:221)." The village is known as *matoyinga;* it controls its own lands and has its own governance. In earlier times, before the seismic wave, each of the three villages was autonomous. Later, one village, the residence of the dominant aliki, became the administrative center for the atoll, maintaining itself as the head of a territorial organization that consisted of a tripartite grouping, each part of which, in any case, had a recognized and exclusive jurisdiction over its own economic affairs. At no time, it would seem, was there ever an island control of land, reefs, or other resources. The central administration realigned boundary lines according to population growth. But since the paramount aliki and his council employed ritual wrestling matches to resolve discontent, his jurisdiction is recognizably cognate with the ritual authority of Segments II in other Traditional societies.

Pukapuka, however, had divided its lands into several jurisdictions. The village controlled only those lands designated as communal village lands; the two sets of lineages controlled the rest. As a co-owner of lands, the village had an equivalent status to that of the lineage, and thus a powerful claim upon the loyalty of the residents. If the village seems to have held an edge in the claims, it is not because it had more to offer, but because what it offered was bestowed as an "extra," available to an outsider. As a lineage member, one's land rights were by contrast a "given," and subject to intrafamilial decision.

However, as the focus of maritime activities and of bonito fishing, in particular, the village had definite economic ascendancy. The village council selected the crew, distributed the bulk of the catch, and was at the center of fishing ritual.

The po and wua lineages are Segment III. Each of the four wua was headed by its oldest member, male or female, who was its official gift-giver at feasts honoring all its first-born children, and its official representative at meetings where wua feasts, games, and competition were planned. We do not know for certain if the wua were ranked. They are described as though they were in fact of equal standing. The patrilineal po, on the other hand, were ranked as noble or commoner. Four of the seven could nominate an aliki from their lists; the remainder are commoner by status. Thus the po are the custodians of traditional honors that differentiate the population by grade. The wua are custodians of another order of honor that grants its membership complementary rather than hierarchical statuses. As co-land–holders, po and wua stand to each other as equivalent counterparts to the village economy. Each, however, has its own mode of internal organization within which the po combine the affairs of lands, rank, and religion, while the wua are altogether less comprehensive. The po, headed by aliki, represent the traditional order; the wua, headed by elders, seem to constitute themselves as the structural counterparts of the tupele. Or, to put this more directly: po are to wua as aliki are to tupele. That both lineage systems are genuinely coordinated within a common moral order as well is suggested by the power of the gods of the po to punish certain offenses committed within the wua.

Po and wua have branched out into sublineages which may be considered as Segment IV. The sublineages of the wua are known as keinanga. Thirteen are recorded, so they are rather small. The keinanga are inexplicably exogamous, and have tended to take upon themselves the actual economic authority over the taro beds. Thus the wua have receded to a more formal and perhaps more ritual position. Since the keinanga are not actually identical with the Pukapuka concept of consanguinity within which marriages are forbidden, their rule of exogamy has an independent moral force. But why should exogamy be confined to a subdivision of the wua? The Beagleholes venture an historical hypothesis: The wua at one time resembled the conventional matrilineal clan. When they subdivided, they transferred their exogamy along with their functions to the smaller constituencies. Well, perhaps it was so. Considering the relative smallness of the keinanga within the social structure as a whole, its exogamy may perhaps be understood as a metaphor for consanguinity. That is to say, if the ultimate functional entity is the patrilocal and exogamic household, then in conformity with the consistency of balanced dualism, the maternal unit would acquire structural equivalence by taking on exogamy.

The subdivisions of the po are known as *wakavae* (21 are listed). These stand for a section of the cemetery, but like their parental po may have had in the past a wider range of functions, that has since been forgotten. According to uncertain information, the heads of the wakavae were langatila, an intimation that in its po Pukapuka came close to sustaining the traditional order of segmentation.

18

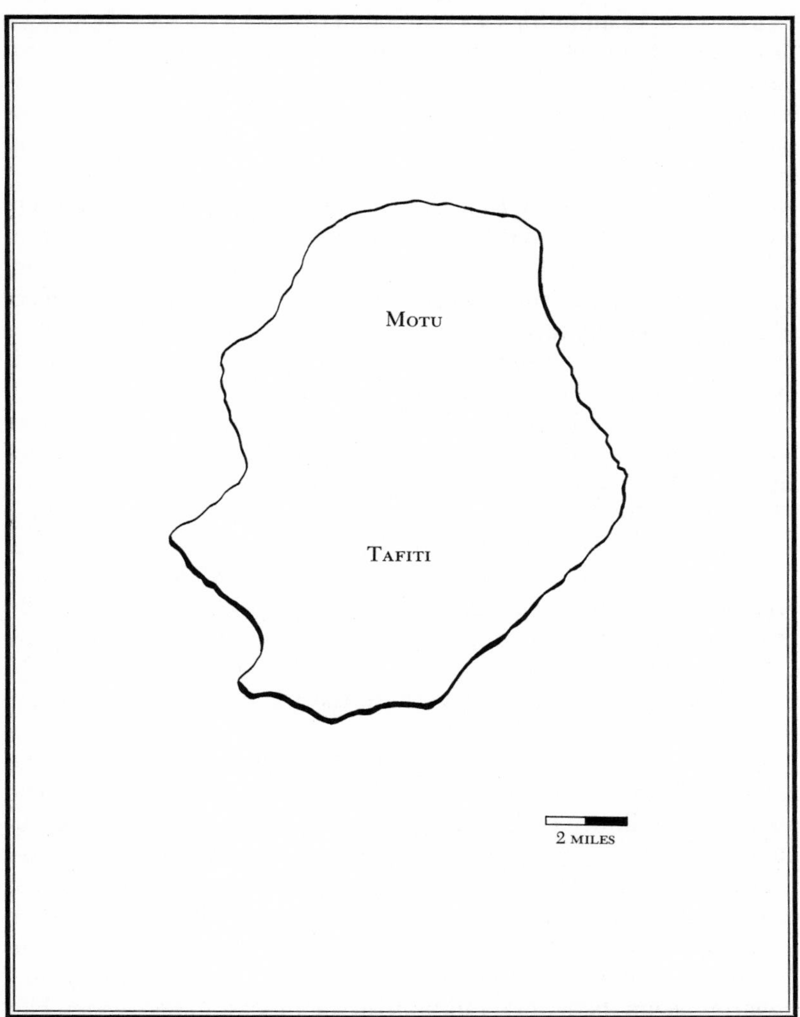

Niue

NIUE, LIKE PUKAPUKA, COMBINES CULTURAL FEATURES OF EASTERN and western Polynesia. The language is evidently Tongan; the kinship system is generalized and thus eastern; the pattern of social relationships is reminiscent of the Marquesas. If linguistic dating is to be relied upon, Tongan and Niuean separated at about A.D. 500 (Elbert 1953). On the strength of this indication of antiquity, we might justifiably consider Niue as an example of an early Polynesian type which had not developed the specialized features of kinship and status that finally distinguish eastern and western Polynesia. The Niuean cultural configuration is consistent with this possibility. On the other hand, the traditional history of Niue and, of course, its geographic position insist upon a strong Tongan connection. The first paramount chief was supposedly Tongan, but since the actual reflections of Tongan culture are faint, at best, we must assume either a thin overlay despite propinquity, or else a rapid erasure. Either possibility, archaism or later simplification is reasonable.

Although it is a large island of some 100 square miles, Niue does not offer an easy living. It is an elevated atoll that has lost its inner lagoon and has gained only the fertility of decomposed coral rock. The fertile soils lie in scattered pockets, mainly along the coastline. Cultivation is in the end rewarding, but difficult and time-consuming. Water is scarce and droughts are frequent. Thus while crops of taro, breadfruit, yam, coconut, sugar cane, and arrowroot can be ample, the threat of famine is real. In the past they raised fowl; more recently only the wild rat and fish have been the main source of protein. Fishing is important but difficult because the island has a very narrow ringing reef.

The terrain of coral rock is rugged but undulating and presents no natural divisions that might have contained the warring tribes. The population, following the distribution of the most fertile soils, occupied mainly the coastal regions, leaving the great interior and elevated plateau as a relative desert; and as a neutral zone where a ritual capital that seems to have represented the entire island was located.

The discovery and foreign occupation of Niue was late but swift in its effects. Cook was the discoverer in 1774. In 1830 Protestant missionaries began their work and by 1849 the process of conversion had been hastened by a Samoan zealot. In 1861 Peruvians carried off several hundred Niueans, and in the same period a great many other islanders went voluntarily to work in Samoa. British rule was established in 1900, carrying forward the transformation. Thus when Loeb (1926) arrived in 1923, there was little left to observe. He spent seven months recording native recollections, in Niuean, so that what information he does present has some special claim to authenticity.

Genealogical Traditions

The traditional history is vague and hardly to be trusted. Chronological inferences are totally unreliable, since the Niueans had no interest in chiefly genealogies. They do record three immigrations and perhaps only the last of these, as Loeb believes, may be accepted as historically credible, on the grounds that it is recited in some detail. This refers to the coming of Mutelau from Tonga very late in the eleventh century and the establishment for the first time of a central authority over the entire island. Mutelau, who is credited with a Niuean mother, forcefully overcame the traditional division between the north and south and established himself as *patuiki*—supreme chief. A list of nine paramount chiefs follows Mutelau within the space of a single century. None could hold office for long and all are described as fearful of the responsibility. Even Galiega, whose reign is described as prosperous, was killed by a subject for some trifling cause. His successor was then killed in battle, and the chief who came after him died in a famine and was eaten by rats. The last of the early patuiki was Pakieto, who died after only one year at the helm. Thereafter and until the people became Christian, the island was ruled by a council of local chiefs. But even collective authority could not keep the peace. After conversion, a new line of Christian chiefs was founded but with no greater success. This short-lived dynasty ended in 1917.

What the traditions evidently intend to document is the ineffectualness and, in effect, the ultimate insignificance of central authority. No chief ever founded a true dynasty. All were chosen for military prowess and none could consolidate his power. The patuiki is presented as a paradoxical figure. He emerges only as a war leader, and then is expected to display the qualities of a priest whose religious powers would promote islandwide prosperity. On Easter Island a similar concept was more reasonably set within an annual cycle. But on Niue the patuiki had no natural exit when nature did not cooperate. The local priests were not his natural allies.

The Status System

Niue had no genealogical rank and no developed system of hereditary chiefship. All major positions were won by force, or, as in the case of nationally prominent priests, by a sudden display of divine possession. Only among families (that is, in the domestic sphere) did leadership move along the more traditional lines of primogeniture. In all cases ability outweighed traditional rights. Percy Smith has compared Niue with Mangaia. The comparison is apt insofar as it touches on the doctrine of military authority. The Mangaian status system was dual, however; that of Niue was more like the Marquesan with its single standard of status.

Primogeniture

The special position of the first-born was fully recognized. The male inherited the largest share of land and, if he demonstrated ability, headed the family. He then became custodian of its properties, received produce and other goods from his juniors, arranged his sister's marriage, and was entitled to take up the family mana at the death of his father. He was the keeper of family genealogies, and acted as the family priest. If he was a forceful person, he imposed his authority over his more distant siblings as well.

Male Line

Loeb shares, at least in part, the opinion of Thomson his amateurish predecessor, that Niue is in transition between "matriarchy and patriarchy." The reference as usual is to the role given to a female side, to indications of what we have described as sex-line duality. The characteristic western Polynesian dualism is, however, rather undeveloped in Niue, which in this respect is closer to Tikopia than it is to Tonga. The focus in powers, in respects, and in genealogical concepts is, in fact, strongly masculine and patrilinear. When Loeb speaks of women as having a "high position" in society, and as being listened to in family councils, he is describing values that verge on the informal rather than a structural feature. There are no indications of a female line or of any sororal or maternal social realm. The "matriarchal" feature can only refer to the rather minor honoring by the brother of the sister with the exalted title of *mahakitaga,* and thus putting her within the western Polynesian category of distinguished females. For Niueans, *mahaki* (which seems to mean "very great, excessive") elevates, but only in the nominal sense, the sister above the brother, who is addressed by the more conventional honorific, *tugane* (cf. chap. 21 on kinship.).

Genealogical Depth

Few genealogies go back more than five generations, but those of warriors go back nine, suggesting some tendency toward a formal structure.

Sanctity

Loeb recognized in Niuean concepts of *mana* the traditional Polynesian traits (1926:184). It was the source of potency, of success, an attribute of persons and of objects. The well-employed spear had mana, as did its capable thruster. The Niueans, however, saw mana as a freely available power accessible to all. They were less interested in how mana was acquired than in its display, in the test. Thus they did not speak of their gods as having the disposition of mana at their command. They evaluated, rather, the potency of the god's mana by the success of his human protégé. The focus seems to have shifted from supernatural force as the primary agency of effectiveness to efficacy itself as a proper vehicle for the supernatural force. At the moment of defeat on the battlefield, the warrior designated the new holder of his mana. Had the quality failed him or had he indeed failed it? If the answer is the latter, then Niue does indeed represent the fully open society. Mana was, in fact, transmitted by consent, from father to son as a rule, but nevertheless as an act of human agency and not as an independent genealogical process. When a child's feet were placed on its father's head, the father's mana flowed into the child. Men who withheld their mana were derided as "stingy." The transmission of mana had become an act of investiture. Fathers decided when the son —preferably the first-born—was ready by being worthy of the ceremony of passing on the skill.

The relationship between mana and sanctity does not emerge clearly in Niue. One would assume a connection, because successful people (high mana) were family heads and thus priests authorized to set restrictive tapus on crops and property. Loeb likens the tapu to a curse. Yet in the examples of tapu violation, the supernatural punishments are patently unreliable. The violation was interpreted as a personal affront and had to be punished openly. When a warrior learned that children had desecrated his tree tapu, he killed them and provoked a feud. This narrative bears out the idea of the primacy of personal efficacy.

In its treatment of the "sacred" chief (patuiki) the Niueans accepted the traditional forms but not their spirit. The patuiki was sacred simply by virtue of his high office as natural rainmaker, as priest of plant fertility. He had no hereditary sanctity, of course, but the rites of installation, his ritual separation from the common people, and his special privileges are those that designated sanctity elsewhere in Polynesia and are definitely akin to those associated with Tui Tonga. His subjects prostrated themselves before him, gave him first-fruits, and addressed him in chiefly language. Withal, he had no active powers. He strikes us as an artificial figure of sacred power rather than as a true presence. He is no more than the facsimile of a Tui Tonga. Since he is judged only by efficacy, he is pathetically vulnerable. When crops fail his powers are gone and he may be put to death. He has been elected because of his military prowess, over which he had control, and is put into a situation—by a logic that identifies military prowess with supernatural efficacy that should work for crops—over which he has none. Many patuiki, the traditions tell us, saw the pathos of their plight and accepted the high post reluctantly. One has bared his feelings in this forlorn refrain (Loeb 1926:54):

> I wish that a foreign ship would come
> That I could give up my kingship
> I like to be a king
> But no one else likes me to be king.

Tohunga

Any skilled person in any endeavor was called tufuga and credited with mana. Since the title was so freely applied, it does not imply a specialist category. In any case, Niuean crafts are among the most indifferent in Polynesia. Percy Smith thought the Niuean house was about the most poorly constructed in all the Polynesian islands. The ancient canoes were very small, wood carving was crude, and stone was worked only into adzes.

There was no organized priesthood either. Loeb regards the *taula-atua* as "shamans" rather (1926:165), because they were "possessed" by the gods and thus had temporary though extraordinary powers to cure and to aid the success of special enterprises. The ordinary religious rites, such as offerings to family gods, were the province of each household head who was, in effect, the family priest.

Wealth

All families joined in rivalrous feasts and food exchanges. In the fakalofa, families tested one another. The aim was to set down a donor by returning more. The donor was obliged, however, to honor the economic potency of his recipient by making a great effort. One gathers that warriors were most sensitive to the challenges of what was in effect an economic mode of interfamily warfare.

The obligation to fare well in economic rivalry may have been an important motive for going to war. The strong seized lands from the weak and acquired an affluent following who financed the fakalofa.

No one else had wealth. The patuiki, no longer an imposing warrior, was often poor. Wealth, it would seem from the few details we have, was used contentiously and not luxuriantly.

Political Hegemony

In Niue more than in any other Polynesian society status had become fully polarized between strong and weak, power being defined almost exclusively in terms of raw physical mastery. The Niueans had come to respect only the visible, the manifest properties of power. If we could accept the historical hypothesis of their Tongan and Samoan ancestry, then we may conceive of the Niueans as stripping themselves of metaphor to reach the bedrock of Polynesian values. The patuiki is the true symbol of their implacable doctrine. Once removed, even if in name elevated, from the actual arena, he can only fade. The battlefield was the Niuean marae, the source of glory, of strength, and quite literally the focus of sanctity.

The accounts of Niuean life, whether from the pen of Smith (1902, 1903) or of Loeb always return to the themes of war and of antagonism. Any challenge, any slight, provokes a violent rage or a terrifying depression. Injured or insulted Niueans either attack or commit suicide. We rarely imagine them at rest, rather restless, planning an assault or ablaze with rage on the battlefield. Having stripped away the etiquettes of aggression along with much of the formal gradations of social arrangements, the Niueans had reduced themselves to sheer dependence upon circumstance. Yesterday's friend could be the immediate foe. The traditions document treachery so appalling that Loeb feels compelled to interpret this theme as moral revulsion: They speak of treachery so much because they despise it. I accept his interpretation insofar as it supports my own views on Niuean reductionism, on their submission, perhaps reluctantly, to an ultimate state of antagonism.

The major conflict was between the endogamous divisions of Motu and Tafiti; the motives are not well known. The record of a 50-year war between them may imply no more than the indecisiveness of sheer antagonism rather than a definite political aim at conquest. Yet Mutelau had created a conquest state. When the central power was soon eroded, a weakly ineffectual but nonetheless traditional concept of ritual unity replaced it. The political ideal was diluted and denatured; it became regressive. The antagonism remained. The judgment of history would declare the Niuean chiefs to be more aggressive than political. The long-range aim is no more than the assertion of strength. Political aims are for their part more complex and technocratic. Thus the great struggles between the two divisions that had insisted from the start upon their separateness did not supplant in the least any of the interior antagonisms. Neither side was capable of visualizing, let alone carrying out, the policies of accomodation among potential or, better still, proper allies. Easily provoked, they fought constantly, evidently on all fronts—Motu against Tafiti and neighbor against neighbor. Short of extermination, they had no means for bringing an end to feuds. Many families had given up a settled life for the precarious safety of caves and the hardships of the wild brush because they could not escape embroilment. They quarreled bitterly over property rights, understandably; but also over honor (even more understandable). A group of villagers, mortified at their constant defeat in a sporting contest, set upon their tormentors, boarded them up in their huts, and burned them alive. Warriors of different villages arrogantly taunted each other until they provoked a fight which turned at once into a general combat between the villages.

The narrative of Niuean wars portrays unmistakably the conflict between the social ambition to conquer, to reduce, to annihilate an enemy, and the individual toa who must portray his own style of arrogant virtue on the battlefield. The traditions are against the flamboyant act, as exemplified by the warrior who had his thighs bound up with rope. He proved his point and his side was defeated. They applaud the sole survivor who patiently plans and plots a treacherous revenge which brings about the total annihilation of the enemy.

If domination is so total, hegemony can barely be political. There seem not to have been enough survivors to form a subordinate class.

The Structure of Status

The structure is binary—it is not actually graded—and is thus rudimentary, stripped down to the brute distinction between strong and weak. The patuiki, who is surely the traditional ariki, illustrates through his instability, the absoluteness of status polarization. He does not head a graded order. He may be either a great warrior or a nonentity. As the former, he stands for the strong; as the latter, he has become a virtual outsider.

Niue recognized three kinds of people: warriors, servants of warriors, and the weak. In a formal sense one may see a reflection here of a graded status structure. The servants themselves are arranged upon a scale of honor and their higher grades are allowed merit. There is no doubt, however, about the central concept. It is unequivocally that of subordination. The Niuean traditions speak of the toa as "the strong generation that jumped into the forts and killed the people inside (Loeb 1926:57)." The brave warriors were the leaders. When they held command they were then *iki*—in the Marquesan manner. The iki were the pick of the warriors. They were not—as were their Marquesan counterparts—politically skilled, but they did have the priestly prerogatives.

The servants of the toa were known as *fekafekau*, a term that means "dependent." There were three grades, one reserved for captives of distinction—an enemy chief—was, according to Loeb's information, honorable. The common dependent was one who attached himself to a warrior in exchange for a parcel of land and protection. The lowest grade were called "crabs" because they were dependents who were entitled to no special rights.

The lowest order were the *lalo tagata*, described as the "faint-hearted." They were wanderers who had no settled domicile and no connections with a paternal line. They sought refuge with their mother's kin, a concession of weakness. Apart from these broad categories of status, Niue recognized holders of special titles, almost all of which referred to some military office or duty.

Descent Group Organization

It is regrettable that so little concrete information is available on the organization of descent groups. For Niue could be a most important test case of relationship between status and descent. Specifically, the absence of genealogical rank might be expected to rule out the possibility of a segmentary lineage organization. What information we do have indicates that the expectation is in fact correct. But the evidence is incomplete and hence inconclusive.

Communities and villages were representative of bilateral kindreds referred to as *tama* ("child") which means here literally "descendant of." Village names bore *tama* as a prefix indicative of organization around a founding ancestor. Since residence was patrilocal, in the main, the tendency would be for paternal lines to form a focus; all others, as in the Samoan system, would be more widely dispersed. Presumably, for this point is not too clear, related extended families (*fagai*) occupied the same village. The term *fagai*, meaning "those who eat together," seems cognate with *kainga*, which has a similar meaning. On the composition of this common eating and land-holding kin group, Loeb is ambiguous, but he does define it as a shallow kindred going back only three or four generations in all collateral lines (1926:66).

Thus far the social system represents the bilateral underpinnings of all Polynesian descent groups. What is lacking is the slightest hint of a traditional pro-patrilineal lineage structure. According to what we know about the chiefship, the system would be fundamentally Marquesan. Strong chiefs collected more dependents about them, some who were not kinsmen. But in any case the kinship composition was bilateral, while the chiefly descent line, drawing upon ability rather than heredity, could hardly have remained patrilineal. It is fair to assume that if Niue had no extant genealogies by the end of the nineteenth century (cf. Smith, P. 1902, 1903) it was because the genealogical concern had long been insubstantial. Smith, for example, thought they were unusual in this respect. In short, the absence of genealogies is not inevitable (as in the Marquesas), but is consistent with a fully flexible grouping of related people around a chosen chief. Flexibility of affiliation serves the political interest of chiefs, but disturbs the more parochial interests of families in retaining firm control of productive land by restricting claims. The traditions hint at drastic efforts in the past to correct the dispersal of kinship claims to land. Important and powerful families, it is said, fostered incestuous sibling marriages to confine the lines. The reasoning is logical, for it was the larger families that were most fully bilateral. Whether the observation itself is historically correct, we do not know.

The Niuean analogue to the segmentary lineage structure can be represented only vaguely. Taken as an isolated example of social structure, the forms are barely discernible. The comparative approach sensitizes our vision, however, by providing frame, scale, and a reflecting background.

In the time of Mutelau, Segment I was temporarily the "conquest state," uniting under a single political authority two antagonistic and supposedly endogamic divisions. We have few details on the character of the central authority. It was represented by a capital which gave a religious and political focus. We deduce some administrative functions from the presence of a council representing the major chiefs, and the appointment of an officer to represent the patuiki and his council in each village fono. A note in the traditional record that Mutelau had appointed a conquered chief as chief roadbuilder indicates substantial secular interests. At one point the political system had begun to resemble those of the Stratified societies.

The central authority declines swiftly. First the patuiki converts—more likely reverts—to a ritual figure and then is abandoned altogether, leaving the central administration in the hands of the council of chiefs who then were charged with preserving the peace. The means seem formidable, even though ultimately ineffectual. Each chief was represented by a stick. All the sticks were tied into a bundle which bound them all to a common cause. Whoever then broke the peace was considered guilty of sacrilege. A well-conceived institution had been created, but nothing could contain the contentious temper of a people who accepted the judgment of wives as to whether a husband was aggressive and worthy or timid and contemptible.

Segment II includes each of the great moieties of Motu and Tafiti. We know less of the administrations of each principality than we do of the central administration. Each, the traditions say, was governed by a war chief who had seized the power by internal conquest or had risen to command a military alliance. Since the grandfather of Mutelau was the chief of Motu, hereditary succession was another possibility. At one time a woman was military commander of Motu in a war against Tafiti.

Segment III comprised the essentially autonomous family groups headed by warrior chiefs. These expanded or contracted and changed their internal composition in accordance with military fortune. Since there were eight major iki with jurisdiction over eleven villages, each of these unnamed kindreds was rather large. These groups were definitely political and subject to strong authority. The chiefs received first-fruit tribute, and had some authority over lands and produce, but not the ultimate jurisdiction over its distribution. The relationship between the warrior chiefs and the villages is not altogether clear. Apparently the heads of fagai constituted the village fono and the leading warrior was their head. The relationship would then be one of balance of military effectiveness—quite different from the Manu'an system.

Segment IV were the fagai, extended families cohering about related males and their families. The senior male, if forceful, acted as head. He was priest, land administrator, fono representative, and ritual director—the focus of its economic capability.

The fagai is a nearly autonomous productive unit. It is limited to the village as a constituent of a higher chief and not, insofar as one knows, as an organic branch of a general kindred. On this point, the data are inadequate. In any case, there is no hint of ranking fagai.

19

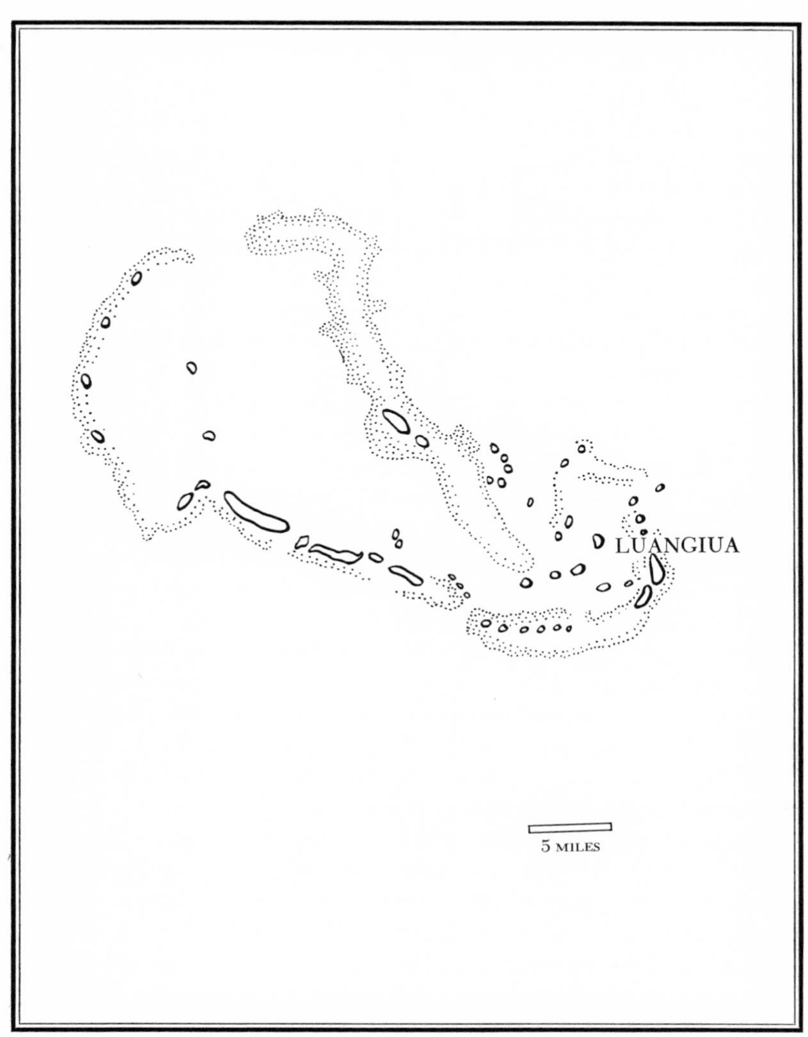

Ontong Java

ONTONG JAVA, A CORAL ATOLL DEEP IN MELANESIAN TERRITORY, is the fourth example of a simplified form of "traditional" society. Like the Tokelaus, Pukapuka, and Niue, Ontong Java had neither a developed system of genealogical rank, nor of segmented lineages. In each instance the question arises whether apparent simplification is to be explained by the preservation on those atolls of early or archaic Polynesian traits or by later modification. If the latter, was simplification then a response to physical environment or to historical causes? In each case the answer is different. As for Ontong Java, the suggestions from glottochronology are that the language is of western Polynesian provenience, related more closely to Samoan than to Tongan, and separated from the mother stock as early as A.D. 300. Since the break with Samoa and Tonga was evidently sustained, a presumption of archaism is not unreasonable. The historical situation, however, is quite complex, indicating, as in the case of Pukapuka, the presence of a composite culture. At least the physical types suggest diverse ancestry, as if the island had received castaways from neighboring islands. Shapiro (1933), who found evidence of a Micronesian physical strain, questioned whether the population was indeed Polynesian. The Ontong Javanese have no traditions to account for their origins. We must consider the culture, therefore, as an example of the differentiation of an ancient western Polynesian type under complex historical conditions.

To my knowledge, the land area of the atoll has not been recorded. The entire atoll complex consists of a great many islets distributed along a lengthy reef, each of very small size. If estimates of the earlier population as 5,000 are correct, this would be by far the most heavily populated, if not in all probability, the most densely settled of the Polynesian atolls. It is evidently a good atoll habitat.

When the island was first studied by Hogbin in 1928, the population had declined to 700. The older and traditional chiefly authority had already disappeared, but in other respects the culture was still largely traditional. Actually, European influence did not make itself felt until well into the nineteenth century. Germany annexed the atoll in 1893 and then handed it over to the British in 1900, who administer it under the Solomon Islands' protectorate.

Genealogical Traditions

Hogbin evidently made no great effort to collect native traditions. Undoubtedly there were no extensive genealogies to collect, but we have very little information on native traditions generally. The one historical episode Hogbin did record seems quite important. This is the account of the setting up of a paramount chiefship over each of the two tribes, an event dated by Hogbin at approximately 1800. Prior to 1800, each tribe had at its head a priest-chief known as *maakua* who was responsible for economic prosperity. In time of calamity he was expected to commit suicide or else his tribesmen had him drowned. In 1800 the son of one of the maakua of one of the tribes set himself up as a despot. He was opposed, but the example took hold and each of the two tribes was then ruled by a powerful chief. The peak of high chiefly power was reached in 1875 after European contact and declined after 1915, when the new chiefs were chosen by the British representative. Apparently at no time did one ruler govern the entire island. Hogbin supplies the further information that once the paramount chiefship (he uses the term "king") was set up the position was hotly contended for among a variety of claimants. The new paramount chiefs were titled *heku'u,* a term that does not occur elsewhere in Polynesia.

The Status System

Primogeniture

The first-born male assumed leadership of the joint family only if he was also the eldest male, regardless of generation, in the family. The principle therefore was age seniority not primogeniture.

Seniority of Descent

Seniority of descent was not acknowledged. Leadership and title went entirely by age seniority.

Male Line

The joint family, actually a short lineage going back no more than six generations, claimed descent through males for a common male ancestor. It was headed by a religious leader, the maakua, and was the principal land-holding group. In other words, the male line was predominant in status. The maternal line held domestic prominence, since residence was matrilocal and a group of sisters owned and transmitted to their female descendants the taro gardens. The coconut groves belonged to the male line, which also composed the fishing party. The female group owning the taro gardens was the direct equivalent of the fishing party of males. Each was headed by its oldest or senior member. The lack of equivalence was in the male holding the religious and political offices and the real titles of status. When men were well-to-do, they brought their wives to live with them, thus starting a new female taro garden–owning group. When both families were wealthy, residence was ambilocal, and when both were poor it remained matrilocal. Wealth then added some patrilocal bias. The key issue in sex line, though, was symbolized by the balance between fish and taro, on the one hand, the main items in what I would call the purely domestic diet, and the coconut, on the other hand, the largely ritual crop, used in payments and in ceremonial exchanges. The coconut was the status foodstuff and so was the exclusive prerogative of the male line. The balance between male and female line was carried out further by brother-sister avoidance taboos, a mode of mutual respects and honoring, an expression of equalization of merit. The role of the mother's brother as a generous donor of gifts is perhaps to be understood as a balance against the more forbidding religious and secular authority of the paternal line headman. But the donor role, honorable as it is, lacks the distinctively honorific status of the paternal line, leaving the balance on that side.

Genealogical Depth

There were evidently no distinctions in genealogical depth between joint families headed by maakua and others. No genealogies exceeded six generations and there was no interest in connecting joint families with one another.

Sanctity

Sanctity was contained in the ceremonial regalia of the priest-chief, specifically in his necklet, his fan, his mat, and his staff. He bore the priestly title of maakua, but his person had no sanctity until he assumed the regalia, which was known as his *alii*, a term the Ontong Javanese translate as "sacred." It was then that bearers went before him to warn people away. The local concept of sanctity is unique in having materialized a title so strongly. It is nonetheless typical of the western Polynesian idea of the sacred as an attribute of office rather than of person. In the broadest sense, the local concept is but an extreme restatement of the general doctrine that alii endows a being with divine qualities. The Ontong Javanese concept in its particularity clarifies the general Polynesian point of view.

The maakua as a priestly head appears here as a highly generalized facsimile of ariki. He was held responsible for the general prosperity and well-being of the atoll. If the people suffered, the maakua would have to die by suicide or public execution. His normal death became the occasion for renewal rites which promoted crop fertility. His illness, if it interfered with his duties, required him to step down and hasten his demise. Such a degree of intimacy in association between a maakua and what were in fact divine events implies a special attribute of person comparable to that of an ariki. There is no reason to doubt the local concept of alii as the source of sanctity, even as we detect a fusion of the broader with more specialized doctrine. All local or village maakua shared the same attributes of sanctity as the high priest.

Tohunga

There are no titles of skill and no professional standards or traditions of specialized ability other than tattooing. The tattooer alone is a professional and is paid in coconuts. Canoes, houses, mats, tools, and other artifacts are made by the older men, for whom a particular skill is but one trait of their general capability. The heads of families are the capable men. They are also the maakua and the sorcerers.

Wealth

The capacity to make substantial distributions of coconuts, mats, and other property upon the major ritual occasions, and to pay liberally for all services was the ultimate source of status. Poverty, if not actually demeaning, is reductive. The poor were lowered in esteem and reduced in social significance. They were dispersed, and had no totems and no religious center around which to cohere. They did not name a maakua, an acknowledgement of their generalized inferiority and loss of efficacy. The principles regulating the cycle of wealth, social unity, religious and political effectiveness are common and entirely self-evident. Because of inherent simplicity, the operation of the cycle is seemingly predictable. In aggressive systems the poor (the weak) are quickly converted to dependency and thus incorporated within the wealth-status cycle of dominant leaders. Probably because the intensity of status rivalry in Ontong Java was evidently well below, let us say, Niuean levels, the rate of assimiliation of the weakened poor was slow. Hogbin's figures show that at least three-quarters of the families on the atoll owned coconut lands on several islets and so were wealthy. Open competition for land was evidently subdued and land title was held to be inalienable. If people were poor it was because of poor management or bad luck and not because of political deprivation. Moreover, while the pressure to acquire goods (coconuts) was real enough, it was restrained by strong feelings against overdoing and by collectivization of the ritual obligations. The limits of proper display were narrow. If 16,000 coconuts was the most magnificent distribution a family could make at a betrothal, 17,000 was derided as meaningless ostentation. The head of the family was distributor, but as the representative of all who shared in the obligation. Returns were precisely equaled; escalation was prevented. Wealth, to be sure, is dynamic; its dynamism is sometimes controlled. As on Pukapuka and on Niue the taro beds had to be heavily guarded against theft, a serious vice and an index of subterranean antagonism.

Political Hegemony

Headmen (maakua) represent kinsmen and, of course, rule in their interests. If they overstep propriety, they are likely to be deposed. Their power speaks for the collective will. Abuses were common enough so that we are not likely to forget that even this distant Polynesian outpost acknowledged traditional beliefs in the exaltation of power. If there is no clear evidence of an exultant ambition to expand the family and to enlarge the sovereignty, there is adequate documentation, even in an ethnographic work as unremittingly functionalist as Hogbin's, for the opportunities successful and capably directed families had for expansion. The sudden appearance of a "king," an extraordinary event for this seemingly peaceable atoll, testifies to undercurrents of ambitions and of social antagonisms which the ethnographer had not fully explored. We are obliged to turn away from Hogbin's bland functionalism to discover for ourselves the local concepts of power as revealed by local history. The information is scant but suggestive.

There is the evidence, to begin with, of serious conflict between a maakua and his kinsmen. If he is to be deposed, it is another claimant, another senior figure who accepts the challenge and engages the tyrant in single and hand-to-hand combat. Evidently he must win the duel if he is to prevail. What happens when the challenger is defeated? We do not know. There are records, however, of widespread conflict, of armed battles between factions. If the unpopular maakua can be deposed by force alone, then power as a worthy end in itself has established its own traditional place alongside of responsibility for family welfare. An example of a maakua withholding coconuts for the private use of his immediate family identifies again the conflicting claims of personal and social status. Personal status may indeed be inauthentic in the Ontong Java code of honor. It registers, nonetheless. Some degree of hardness is expected of a headman if he is to be able to exercise the great sanction—banishment. The family title to land is inviolable. The individual is subject to a higher authority. If banished (for what cause?), he joins the socially deprived. He is disposed therefore to accept the traditional authority. Power is undeniably responsible, provided it can assert itself and meet challenges.

Thus the sudden rise to power of a heku'u, a paramount chief over a tribe, is not altogether inexplicable. In general we see this event as a transposition of the domestic battle to a "national" plane. Hogbin's account is tantalizingly brief. The traditions say only that Ke Hangamea formed an army some eight generations ago (eighteenth century) and assumed forcible command of the Luanguia, one of the two tribes. He ruled his tribe by terror until he met his own violent death. For many years thereafter others fought bitterly for the prize so suddenly vacated. When finally stabilized within a lineage, the royal power was no longer as despotic, though it remained strong and capable of overriding the local authorities. When one of the new line of paramount rulers had put down a revolt, his authority and that of his successors was fixed, and thereafter, as Hogbin says, "The will of the king seems never to have been disputed (1934a:227)." The authority of heku'u was confined and restrained, however, by the definition of the office as magisterial. He was to be judge and not potentate, and powerful as he was, his jurisdiction did not transcend his own tribe. Here we seem to have a political counterpart to the morality of economic constraint. Ontong Java is unusual in having two distinct tribes living in close proximity and united in ritual without having developed traditional antagonisms. It is a cause of either incomplete historical information, or of the presence of an unidentified inhibitor of conflict.

The Structure of Status

The system is still another variant, in simplified form of the Traditional society. In the heku'u, the system has turned toward the Open society, but in a limited and formal sense only, for he did not open up the avenues to power—insofar as is known—to his followers. Maakua, on the other hand, held traditional priestly headships, even without genealogical rank. Their offices are traditionally rooted in the origins of the people. While each of the major maakua does not have a specific link with all of his predecessors, he is part of a generalized traditional history. While each is a potential political leader, in the Marquesan style, little mobility has in fact been generated. The position of the priestly headman is in the end more constrained by religious obligation than it is energized by its economic and political potentialities. As in any status system without genealogical rank, the outlook is for flexibility. The system is not "open," because we have no evidence either that a genealogical order had been overcome, or that rivalry for power and position had been elevated to a serious concern.

The system is not Traditional either. We simply detect a general kinship with the concept of priestly chief and of the hierarchy of statuses. The hierarchy is confined to maakua, who are recognized but not titularly distinguished as major and minor depending upon the size and importance of the family groups they headed. There seems to have been no term that can be rendered as commoner and no designation of unworthy status. Ontong Java is the classless society, although it recognizes grades and social differences. It is unpolarized even as it recognizes weakness and strength and wealth and poverty. It has distinguished families that customarily are headed by major maakua, but not an aristocracy. In Ontong Java we recognize the intimations of more traditional Polynesian organizations, but we do not see their characteristic developments.

Descent Group Organization

The traditions assume a common origin of all Ontong Java from the local gods, Ke Pa and Ke Papa, so that the entire atoll can be conceived of as a single kindred but only from the most general point of view. The notion of common descent has no bearing on actual relationships. The atoll has two tribes that are identical in organization and custom, but are totally separate, linked neither as ritual complements nor as political antagonists. They see themselves rather as duplicates. When one had set up a kingship, the other followed suit.

Segment I, therefore, is not the atoll but the tribe, which is presumably a kindred, although there is no specific information on this matter. The concept of tribal leadership, as we have seen, has been unstable. In the traditional form that preceded 1800, a senior maakua was the head, essentially as a religious leader presiding over rites at tribal *malae* and having as its center a village. The Ke Hangamea rebellion introduced—on a small scale—a military dictatorship; and finally, a less despotic and more traditional dynasty of heku'u evolved on the basis of magisterial authority. Thus the evolution of tribal authority parallels the political transformations of the great Polynesian societies that had developed a state. One would not dignify the Ontong Javanese regime by so formidable a rubric as "state." The requirement of multi-tribalism, for example, was not met. The heku'u is interesting precisely for its parallelism with conquest chiefs, revealing on a miniscule scale some processes of state development, and reminding us again how susceptible even an archaic or undeveloped Polynesian system really is to political centralism.

The tribe comprises a number of small patrilineal lineages known as *manava kanaka* ("male belly") whose relations with each other have not been clearly defined. While they are undoubtedly interrelated through bilateral kinship, they are not linked together by any formal genealogical plan. These lineages, which Hogbin prefers to describe as "joint families," are exogamous (Mangaian style) and strictly patrilineal (as in Tikopia). The large lineages are totemic and have a religious center presided over by a maakua; the small ones, lacking totemism and a religious leader, are incomplete and thus of low status. The lineages are basic economic groups, owners of common coconut lands and groves—usually an islet.

The economy, as we have observed, is in fact divided. The male line controls the major prestige crop and has the special distinction of owning an islet, the distinguishing trait of being wealthy. A female line (unnamed) based upon the residential unity of sisters controls the taro lands which run in strips surrounding the domiciles. A fishing group of males crosses lineage lines to base itself upon an informal constituency. Only the coconut crop came under the formal jurisdiction of a maakua. The pattern is familiar as western Polynesian with new variations. The male line is focal ritually but is dispersed residentially; the female line has a residential focus and no ritual center. Through the religious chiefs, moreover, the manava kanaka are linked directly to the religious center of the tribe, which may therefore be regarded as a congregation of patrilineal lineages. The residential groups of sisters and their families are, by contrast, discrete entities. Thus the pattern may be variant, but the underlying principles of unity and dispersal are constant. Segment II is, strictly speaking, the patrilineal sector only. The matrilocal side, which is its economic counterpart, is the residential unit, the household, and is Segment III. Structurally, the joint sororal household is not in fact a segment of the lineage in the sense of being a lower order of it. It is an arm of it, giving to the sisters a unity that counterpoints that held by brothers in the manava kanaka. The structure, in other words, is dualistic in the western Polynesian traditions. As many as six families live under one roof, but they have no formal head, and thus no central jurisdiction either over the house itself or the taro plots. The absence of a head person asserts in still another way the fractional character of this female side.

20

The Status Lineage

ARISTOCRACY, ROOTED IN PEDIGREE, CONSIDERS DESCENT A MATTER of honor. In traditional Polynesia, where honor was, more specifically, a matter of mana, the line of descent was the measure of religious worth. The Maori spoke of their descent lines as their "mana," and described specific descent from a line of senior males as the "erect penis" in order to assert the phallic quality of the pattern: mana, honor, and descent. Honor came from many sources, and descent had ceased to follow the straight and narrow paths originally desired of it. Nevertheless, no matter how important achievement itself had become, and no matter how seriously descent lines were rearranged and disarranged, descent remained the one constant and authentic source of honor. Honor, could, of course, be associated with accomplishment, but since accomplishment was the product of mana, and mana was always a transmitted and transmissible quality, the accomplishment, too, had to be transmissible to be authentic. Authentic in the Polynesian sense of the term means just that: the association of honor with mana. Mana as a variable quality gains or loses potency in the course of transmission. Deep genealogies, straight genealogies, and genealogies richly staffed with illustrious persons transmit the full charge of mana. Mana moves most powerfully down the senior lines, causing them to grow and proliferate. The junior lines, receiving only the weaker impulses, lose religious efficacy, become at best dependents, and so fall low in honor, and sluggish in growth. Descent, in brief, is the pivot of the status system. Whatever happens in status of any consequence is immediately registered in rules of descent, and in the organization of descent groups. When we draw together now the Polynesian principles of descent and the course of their variations, we are, at the same time, recapitulating a portion of the history of Polynesian status systems.

To say merely that descent authenticates honor and that therefore status and descent are interdependent is to assert only what is common knowledge. Nevertheless, an important question is implied in the statement, and that is whether the genealogical organization of Polynesian society can be understood precisely except as a product of the status system. What do we mean by "understood precisely"? Any approach to Polynesia—or to any other social tradition for that matter—yields some understanding. Polynesian society can be understood generally as a social system that effectively nurtures itself, maintains its morale, defend itself against dangers, and provides for its continuity over the generations. From this general point of view of society as an effective adapting organism, descent may be described as a system of classifying persons into units of kin that will efficiently carry out necessary tasks. Descent can be understood thus as rules of affiliation, or as rules of subdivision of kin groups. Since membership in a kin group conveys a variety of rights and corresponding responsibilities, descent may be considered, more specifically, as the valid, the truly authentic way of participating in such rights and responsibilities. Whether seen as the means of forming kin groups, as a method of affiliation to kin groups, or as the vehicle for transmitting rights and exacting responsibilities, descent appears in general social theory as a technical rule, as a device for establishing effective order among kin. This functional view of society and of the role of descent in perpetuating good order is altogether reasonable. It describes as well as modern general social theory can, the "physiology" of a society. It has the merit of being applicable to any society, Eskimo or Hawaiian. It has, however, little value for history. To be sure, descent in Polynesia, whether pro-patrilineal, pro-seniority, or bilateral does indeed define kin groupings, and it does authenticate affiliation and rights. The historical question, however, is always: What are the characteristics of variability? Questions about change are of necessity specific, and can only be answered in specifics. The specifics of history that delineate change are patterns, and the central characteristic of pattern is organization of components. In Polynesia, descent falls within a pattern of which the focal concept is honor, and to which all other components are subordinate. It has been easy to demonstrate the focal role of honor in descent. We have seen in every Polynesian society how the rules of descent, the organization of descent groups, the varieties of affiliation, and the varieties of rights, have been directly dependent upon fluctuations in the concepts of honor.

Only history can define the character of institutions. The modes of social change and, above all, the conditions to which institutions are most sensitive reveal their specific functions. Descent, to repeat, is most sensitive to status. The rather precise mutual dependency between status and descent is not that of ends and means. Descent is not really a *means* to status, it is at the *heart* of status. It is one of the concrete measures of a social concept that is either intensely concrete or has no social meaning at all. The statement, then, that descent is most sensitive to status means specifically that one measure of status is sensitive to all other measures of status. The concept of descent is itself composed of several very concrete measures—measures of the antiquity of pedigree, of its masculinity, of its seniority, of its chiefly accomplishments, of its directness, and of its relations to other pedigrees. The genealogical measures of status are essentially quantitative and are calibrated to a scale of some precision. The scale must be reasonably precise because at some point or other it must draw the line between chiefs and non-chiefs and between authentic chiefs and raised-up chiefs. Whatever alters the pattern of such vital discriminations in rules of honor must necessarily register its effects upon rules of descent.

Rules of descent establish two different but related orders. One is by tradition basically religious, the other is preeminently social. The religious order is represented by a particular descent line, as a matter of course the descent line of a chief. The social order is represented by the actual association of kinsmen to the religious line. While the religious order of the descent line concerns itself with the past, with founding ancestors, with their chain of mana, and with the catalog of ancestral honor, the social order is concerned with the present, with common action, and with present honors and their rewards. The two orders are totally interdependent, because a descent line without its active kin group is like a religion without a congregation. The descent line is the vital center of the kin group, and the kin group gives concrete substance to the promise of the descent line.

All descent groups have this same basic structure: a central descent core representing some vital principle and a congregation of kinsmen. Descent groups differ, though, in how they define this central core, its rules of descent, and its rules of affiliation and of common action. Clans and lineages have in common the concept of honorable ancestry which they transmit down either a male line or down a female line—or, in some instances, down both lines. Because Polynesian descent follows more complex rules of transmission and of affiliation, it has been necessary to distinguish it from clans and lineages and to enter it into a class of its own, which I have called the "status lineage." Polynesian descent groups have, in fact, long been recognized as distinctive enough to warrant special classification. Gifford (1929), impressed by their characteristics of branching, or of ramifying, first called them "ramages." This term has gained popularity. It has been adopted by Firth, by Sahlins (1968) and in modified form by Murdock (1960). Others, including Goodenough (1955), have simply called them "nonunilineal" descent groups, and Davenport (1959) has suggested the still more descriptive "multilinear." Ember (1959) finally, has proposed the very general term, "sept." Each of these terms arises from a close and perceptive study of the Polynesian groups, and each is suitable. But none is precise in that none deals with the actual content of descent. "Ramage" simply ignores descent and selects a feature that is, in fact, common to all extensive lineages. If branching is the issue, then all lineages are ramages (as well).

"Nonunilinear," as Murdock observed, has the serious disadvantage of being negative. A negative term implies disorder, a departure from what should be, and is, in the case of Polynesian descent, clearly irrelevant. "Multilinear" is indeed precise, but it does not identify what the choices are about. Status lineage is a precise term, and identifies the true principles of linearity. Status lineages, as I have demonstrated, are characteristic of all Polynesia, and probably of other parts of the world as well. Strictly speaking, the designation "status lineage" applies to all lines of descent that convey honor, whether through a single line or several. There is no real difference between the preferential patriliny of Maori and the absolute patriliny of Tikopia. The difference is only that of degree. Maori, as a prototype of eastern Polynesian descent groups, acknowledges some diversity in genealogical sources of honor and so offers alternative descent lines. Tikopia also acknowledges diversity, but combines the Polynesian ideals of patriliny and seniority. Common to both is the concept of status descent. If Tikopia were observed as a social isolate, outside the context of Polynesian history, it would be reasonable to classify its paito, as Firth finally did, as a "clan." Similarly, the Mangaian kopu, which ideally is both fully patrilineal and exogamous, classifies readily as a patrilineal lineage. There is every reason to believe that all Polynesian descent groups belong to one common system. If we are to deal realistically with evolving systems, taking account of their variability, then classification must establish first the underlying and common principles of organization of all Polynesian descent groups. That this organization depends upon principles of status has been demonstrated in every instance.

The status lineage has been presented as a special form of lineage, a type of descent group common to very many societies, in one form or another. True lineages are organizations founded on selective descent from known ancestors. They commonly rely upon a single rule of selective descent through sex line.

Fortes (1953) has noted that lineages are central to the organization of "middle range" societies, societies that stand midway between the very simple tribal peoples and civilizations. It is easy to see why this should be so, for lineage is an aristocratic concept in one important respect: in the reverence for pedigree. Where the specific genealogical reverence is lacking, other types of descent groups are formed. Clans, for example, differ fundamentally from lineages insofar as they ignore specific genealogical descent lines and accept instead a generalized and often mythological ancestry. Lineages are specific in tracing descent back to founding ancestors. It is aristocracies, as a rule, that have this specific point of view about ancestry. It is the primitive aristocracies, moreover, that constitute the middle range of social systems.

All large lineages assume "corporate" functions that give them continuity of control over political, economic, and ritual affairs. They all grow by a process of branching, which, as we have seen, achieves for each branch and segment a high degree of administrative autonomy without loss of the genealogical connection. In Polynesia, and in all other lineage systems, for that matter, the traditional and common undertakings of lineages are subject to the authority of a chief, who is, as a rule, its principal genealogical link to the main descent line. The genealogical position of the chief authenticates his administrative role and determines the corporate functions of his subdivision. In other words, how members of a lineage subdivision act together depends upon their concept of ancestry. Their concept of ancestry also controls the growth of lineages by imposing a powerful feeling for genealogical unity. The sense of genealogical unity is strong in most tribal societies. When clans and lineages represent themselves as genealogically distinct, they still enter into wider coalitions. They form phratries or confederations, align themselves as moieties, intermarry, and join in bonds of ritual and economic exchanges. For each line that divides them, they develop linkages that reunite them. The idea behind the lineage is a concept of permanent linkage to a founding ancestor. As against the improvised links one kin group establishes with another discrete kin group, the branches and subdivisions of a lineage are held to be bound to each other organically. The stronger the veneration for the original descent, the stronger the internal links. Aristocracy, by endowing a chiefly descent line with the highest honor, has the capacity for developing the most branches and for retaining their loyalty and unity most stubbornly. We have seen lineage branches break away and oppose the center, the main stem. But when antagonistic cleavage develops, the tradition of the lineage is already nearing the point of dissolution.

The status lineage in Polynesia differs from the broader class of "conventional" lineages in the lack of exogamy and in its lack of full commitment to either male or female descent lines. Or, to state the difference positively, the conventional lineages hold to categorical rules of exclusion and of affiliation; the Polynesian status lineages, to flexible rules. Polynesian flexibility, as we have seen, is primarily political, and it is for political reasons that the status lineage is so highly variable an organization. How vital are exogamy and categorical unilineal descent to the concept of lineage? Are Polynesian descent groups a subclass of lineages despite these deficiences? The answer to both questions can only be that the decisive trait of a lineage is the concept of a known line of descent from a founding ancestor. Sex-line descent is only one of several linear principles of relationship to a founding ancestor, and exogamy is one of several ways by which one linear group can be set off from another. Seen from the perspective of categorical sex-line descent, the status lineage seems to be somewhere between unilateral and bilateral. To evaluate the proper significance of this intermediate position, we must remind ourselves again that all descent is finally bilateral. All unilateral systems may be readily visualized as modifications of basic and inescapable biliterality.

In some sense one is always a member of the enlarged community to which both parents belong. Thus when we speak of unilineal descent and of unilineal descent groups, we have in mind the lines along which special rights and privileges and special kinds of membership are passed along. These special rights and privileges may indeed be the most important, but they are never the only ones that are relevant. The uses of lands and properties, participation in ritual, and membership in the religious community, the use of names, claims upon ritual aid, marriage rights, the organization of respects, the uses of kinship titles, and the patterns of kinship relations are all examples of specific rights which are allocated along sex lines. Societies differ in their systems of allocating such special privileges. They may enforce high exclusiveness on names, on the use of kinship titles, on the organization of respects and on marriage rights, and be more permissive on residence and property rights. They may distinguish between rights to use property and rights to transmit property, between avoidance respects and the respects of license, between authentic residence and courtesy residence. Rights that move along a line of descent may be balanced in terms of equivalence, as in bilineal descent; they are more often complementary, transmitting secular privileges down one line and ritual prerogatives down the other. Finally, they may be strongly asymmetrical, one line having the bulk of authentic privileges and the other entitled to minimal courtesy rights. No lineages, no matter how categorical, exclude members of outside categories altogether. Each type establishes its own categorization of authentic and courtesy rights, and each type allocates specific authentic privileges along both parental lines. Thus Polynesian status lineages differ from categorical lineages only in degree or in the specific patterning of allocation of rights. Linearity is not a generalized characteristic of descent groups: it always refers to specific privileges. Linearity in

Polynesia follows very specific criteria, as has been shown: male line, seniority, general genealogical distinction. The status lineage does have this special feature: Criteria of descent differ in accordance with genealogical rank or status distinction. The appearance of descent differs for chiefs and for commoners. In Traditional Maori, for example, high chiefs are members of essentially "unilineal" descent lines which authenticate their rank and authority. Commoners, whose concern with status authentication is general rather than specific, are in this respect bilateral, and it is only their concern with more utilitarian considerations of economy that confines them to a single line. In the Stratified societies, only the upper ranks can be said to belong to a lineage organization at all. Commoners are part of both a political organization and part of small kindreds.

In drawing necessary distinctions between the Polynesian status lineage and the conventional sex-line lineages, we should not leave the impression that Polynesian descent is exclusively concerned with honor and that conventional matrilineal and patrilineal lineages follow principles of descent that are solely utilitarian. On the contrary, the concept of descent, of a descent line, of ancestry is always a matter of honor. As the evidence on matrilineal descent has demonstrated, a line of pedigree through a female line does not correlate with any known material conditions of life such as means of subsistence, patterns of residence, or the social and political position of women (Schneider and Gough 1961:655 ff.) The notion of descent is essentially symbolic. Since it symbolizes an important aspect of a social identity, it asserts the worthiness of a group. Unilinear descent, with its categorical notions of inclusiveness and exclusiveness, represents different standards of honor from bilateral descent, which is, in theory, all-inclusive. I am speaking now only about the concept of descent and not about the organization of descent groups. While descent may be a concept of honor, descent groups are organized for a variety of purposes. Thus, from the point of view of the symbolic meaning of descent as a concept, Polynesian multilinearity does not differ materially from the unilinearity of matrilineal and patrilineal lineages. Strictly speaking, all lineages are "status lineages," but for the sake of clarity it is necessary to distinguish between a fixed concept of status as in matriliny or patriliny, which can then ignore all other concepts of status, and a more fluid concept of status that is responsive to other conditions of status. The differences become truly marked in their effects upon the organization of descent groups.

Polynesian multilinearity should also be distinguished from nonunilinearity. The first term more accurately refers to the number of specific genealogical options that can be claimed for identification with a particular pedigree, as well as for affiliation with a descent group. The latter refers broadly to affiliation alone. Since affiliation may be for temporary political or economic reasons, it need not involve continuity of descent or linkage to a pedigree. In this form of truncated descent, the point of view is not linear at all.

By and large, it is high-rank descent in Polynesia that is multilineal and low-rank descent that is nonunilineal. How then does nonunilineal differ from bilateral? Bilaterality I take to be a view as to the equivalence of maternal and paternal kin and their descent lines. It is a positive doctrine that honors both lines equally. The traditional theory of descent in Polynesia is multilinear in that it incorporates several criteria of honor. Insofar as these concepts of honor stand for the ideal—as in combining male line, seniority, and an unbroken line from important chiefs—they may indeed be considered as "unilineal." The combination of ideal principles represents in Polynesian thought a single and a unilineal principle of descent. Most descent lines, however, are in fact compromises in which each principle is then separately evaluated. The compromises are properly regarded as postulating multilineal descent. We must recognize at once therefore that Polynesian descent lines are always complex. In the Traditional societies the highest ranks are, by status criteria, unilineal; the next higher ranks are multilineal; and the lowest ranks are simply nonunilineal. This kind of complexity by heterogeneity can hardly be expected to foster stability. Thus in the Open and Stratified societies, particularly, a general shift has occurred in which the component of sex line has been reduced in significance, so that by Traditional society standards all upper-rank descent has become multilinear. By categorizations based on sex-line descent alone, descent in Polynesia eventually becomes "bilateral." The term bilaterality does not fully describe these new conditions. The concept of bilaterality is, nevertheless, relevant and indeed important, for it describes a new status for women and for the female line in general.

Clearly, then, there is no single viewpoint from which to describe Polynesian concepts of descent or descent group organizations. As for the Polynesians, their affiliations to pedigree and to group depend upon their status, on the one hand, and upon their interests and ambitions, on the other. Chiefs have two considerations. One, is to establish their own affiliation honorably to an honorable descent line so as to authenticate their mana and hence their authority. The other is to affiliate to themselves people who will contribute to their power (Aginsky and Hiroa 1940). In this way they unite authority and power. Commoners may have some realistic interest in affiliating honorably to an honorable line, but really not much. Their interests are best served by affiliating "politically" to rising chiefs, and to chiefs who will offer them the best living conditions. I have presented only the extremes of differences. Polynesian history, and the theory of Polynesian descent group organization, points to even greater diversity in mode and interest of descent group affiliation. Such diversity can lead only to marked descent group variability. Chiefs, in particular, must weigh carefully the short-range and long-range implications of choice among multiple possibilities. All choices are potentially dangerous because all are made in the context of status rivalry. The more acute the rivalry, the more dangerous the choice. At the same time, nevertheless, status rivalry as we have seen, increases the options for all.

Are status lineages more unstable than categorical sex-line lineages? It would seem so. When large lineages follow rules of seniority, they form a hierarchical organization based on high-ranking senior lines and lower-ranking junior lines. The Polynesian status lineage is, in this respect, closely related to a broad class of ranked lineages. Ranked lineages—and there is strong historical evidence to show this—tend to evolve politically. Their senior lines become ruling lines, and in the course of branching, senior lineages become dominant and ruling lineages. All types of ranked lineage, including the "status lineage," evolve politically because their hierarchical organization serves as an effective model for political centralization. The Polynesian status lineage would seem to be the more unstable form of ranked lineages. It should be said, of course, that finally political pressures render all categorical social systems unstable. In Polynesia the pressure is particularly acute because kinship bilaterality sanctions variability in alliance. In categorical sex-descent lineages, where kinship classifications clearly separate out maternal from paternal lines, shifting from the lineage of one parent to that of another is possible but unorthodox. In Polynesia such shifts are, on the whole, not only possible but proper. The multilinear quality of the status lineage results, then, from a particular combination of elements from the status system—superiority of the male line, seniority, genealogical depth, mana, etc.—and from bilaterality, an element of the kinship system.

The variable nature of Polynesian kinship classifications and their interaction with principles of descent is discussed in the next chapter. The present chapter deals specifically with principles of descent as they affect the formation of descent groups. In this context, bilaterality is seen as the organizing principle for the total kinship community. The status lineages draw upon the total and undifferentiated bilateral kinship community and organize it around chiefly lines. The status lineages become the specific agencies of common action and of economic and ritual rights and, traditionally at least, encompass all. Still, the bilaterality of kinship classifications gives all persons "brothers" and "sisters" in many, and hypothetically in all the constituent lineages. The sibling relationship, which extends avoidances or marriage restrictions to "third cousin," but includes recognition of relationship almost indefinitely, is no light formality. It does not, however, guarantee authentic rights in one another's lineage; it makes authentic rights possible. Thus, persons can, in fact, move freely from one status lineage to another. When Polynesian status lineages become "mixed," it is often through the addition of distant kin. Distant siblings are distinguished from near siblings. But this distinction is rather ambiguous as compared to the distinction between sibling and cross-cousin in communities composed of categorical sex-line lineages. This ambiguity of distinction between near and distant relatives introduces a strong element of competition for members among the various status lineages. It would seem, here, that the reality of a bilateral kindred must facilitate the ultimate dissolution of the status lineage. The kindred is always present as a refuge.

The ambiguity of affiliation to the status lineage has raised the question whether it can be properly considered a descent group. Fortes, it will be recalled, citing the common definition of descent group as having membership based on continuity of descent either from one parent, or from both parents under conditions of endogamy, noted that the Maori hapu lacked either qualification. He recommended that Polynesian kin groupings of the Maori type be considered as "kindred groups." He defined "kindred groups" as "corporate political associations whose members are linked by common kinship ties." A "kindred group" is, of course, not a lineage. Even though the Maori hapu is, in fact, largely endogamous insofar as its commoners are concerned and so, in this respect, can be designated a bilateral lineage, Fortes' general objection is well taken. Except for Tikopia, the membership of all Polynesian status lineages includes persons who have affiliated bilaterally rather than through a single line of descent. On the other hand, the leadership of a status lineage does represent a specific descent line which gives continuity of succession to the group. Status lineages are, as a rule, named after their founder; and his notable descendants represent the lines of descent which are the backbone of the lineage and its branches. In Traditional

Polynesia, leadership is linear. The question, then, is from which point of view are we to look at Polynesian kin groups? From the point of view of their leadership they are descent groups. From the point of their general membership they often are, as Fortes calls them, "corporate political associations." Since the kin groups are formed around leadership and expand or contract and branch according to the qualities of their leadership, it is from the perspective of leadership that they have historical significance.

In contrast to the direct continuity of succession of categorical sex-line lineages, the status lineage has a composite or complex history of succession. Complexity involves opposing interests of honor, which is lineal, and of utility, which is nonlineal or bilateral. The shifting nature of these interests is an important condition of social evolution generally in Polynesia and regulates rather precisely the patterns of variability of the status lineage. Pro-patriliny is the ideal of honor when combined with seniority. The more fully the ideal is realized, the more fully does the status lineage approximate a conventional descent group.

The status lineage is the total structure that is segmented in a characteristic way. In conventional lineages, which also segment into various levels (maximal, major and minor lineages), the structure of each level is a replica of all the others. The levels differ structurally only in degree of inclusiveness. The Polynesian traditional segments differ as well in structure, that is, in characteristics of descent of their chiefly lines. Considering Maori as the eastern Polynesian model, we observed a gradation of highest degree of patriliny among waka chiefs to lowest degree of patriliny among hapu heads. On the other hand, the waka, as the most comprehensive body of kin, was most fully bilateral in its general composition, while the hapu, with preferential residence at the paternal side, was likely to have a more patrilineal composition. The most patrician hapu were the most fully patrilineal; the more plebeian hapu, the most fully bilateral. The preference of high ranks for exogamy and of low ranks for endogamy fostered this important distinction in descent. This characteristic structure of the status lineage is a product of the basic principles of status by which the senior male line has highest rank and highest authority.

In organization by function, the status lineage resembles conventional categorical sex-line lineages that have not developed central political authority. In the traditional forms of the status lineage, upper-level segments have essentially ritual functions and the lower-level segments carry the political and economic functions. Social theory that is concerned only with the practical life of groups is apt, therefore, to ignore the upper levels as relatively unimportant. Presumably this is why Fortes and Firth have considered the Maori hapu as though it were an isolated grouping. The tendency, as we have repeatedly observed in Polynesia, of upper-level segments to gain political and economic power, demonstrates rather conclusively the unity of the entire segmentary structure. Moreover, the functional character of segments is a product of the differential quality of order of descent. In the Traditional eastern Polynesian societies, in particular, the highest-ranking chiefs are the most sacred. Their authority is largely religious, and being religious it transcends local and utilitarian interests and so establishes a sense of social unity without recourse to political power. Political and economic interests are always narrower and sectional, and in the Traditional order they belong more appropriately to lower-order segments. High chiefly interests are cosmopolitan. Low-rank interests are parochial. In the course of Polynesian social evolution, the chiefly point of view is not lowered to the parochial level. Rather, the formerly parochial interests in economy and specific administration are elevated and, of course, reorganized. Transformation of the functions of segments is then another aspect of status lineage variability linked with changes in the position of chiefs. All variability in structure and function of the status lineage, we may say further, is linked with changes in the status system, specifically with changes in degree of adherence to rules of seniority, to male-line descent, to sanctity and to their economic, political, and religious prerogatives.

When reverence for descent is itself an integral part of lineage loyalty, lineage growth is necessarily by branching. The formation of a branch reconciles divergent interests—the collective interest in retaining the link to the source, and the more personal interest in achieving recognition as a founder. Founding a lineage is always a primary source of honor. Lineage honor, however, depends on qualifications of age (lineage depth) and of seniority, so that branching is not quite free. Under fully traditional conditions, a new branch from a junior line has no standing. In the political atmosphere of status rivalry, however, a new branch may grow quickly and achieve standing by virtue of numbers and military force. Branching under these circumstances is not only an irregular but also an antagonistic process. Normally, the branch should not turn against the trunk. In the Open societies it does. Traditional branching responds to two conditions: to vegetative increase that fills up a valley or other compact productive zone, and to dissension. In the former colonists start a new branch, retaining connections with their kin. Since the senior line has strongest authentic rights, it is up to a junior line to move out. In the latter, an ambitious junior line moves out to gain status as a founder. The first form of branching is orderly and slow, but the second can be speeded enormously, depending upon the political temperature. In whatever way new branches are formed, antagonism among them is common, even though ranking by seniority imposes upon them an order of respects. Despite the antagonisms of political rivalry, the branches do not willingly break from the main stem. Lineage unity is maintained, because with very few exceptions there are always two keys to status, that of genealogy and that of power. Neither by itself can open the door. Thus we observe that even after the status lineage has been replaced by a territorial organization in the Stratified societies, it is the commoners whose lineage links have been broken. Royalty continues to regard lineage descent as honorable and as the key to legitimacy.

The status lineage, then, has its own characteristics of branching. In every instance, the specifics of lineage growth and of formation of branches and of segmental levels depend almost precisely upon the organization of the status system. The specific interdependence which I have brought out in each preceding chapter explains how in this basic respect, as well, the status lineage, has not only high variability but direction. It moves under the peculiar conditions of Polynesian life toward its own downfall, as the branches fight one another, dominate one another, and finally absorb and destroy the weaker.

Residence and Economy

One side of the status lineage is genealogical honor; the other side is power. The focus of power is territory. As a result, the status lineage is compelled to seek a territorial unity. The chiefly lines representing the mana and honor of the status lineage are dispersed, but retain their unity because of powerful genealogical interdependence. The genealogical bonds being weaker for commoners, their source of unity is common residence on the land. Commoners gain honor from their resident chiefly line; chiefs gain power from their resident commoners. In the Traditional societies, these interests draw together chiefs and their kinsmen, regardless of rank. The patrilineal preference together with patrilocal residence for highest ranks stabilizes the ruling descent lines, giving them a traditional territory even when some of their genealogical luster derives from ancestral lines located in other territories. Chiefly mana guarantees territorial integrity and so safeguards the economic interests of all residents. Among the Maori of New Zealand, it will be recalled, the iwi chief metaphorically associated territories with parts of his own body, identifying them closely, in other words, with his personal honor, establishing thereby a continuity of interest in a specific territory.

I have reviewed these familiar facts to emphasize the actual continuity of land and descent in a system that authorized their discontinuity by virtue of the rule of bilaterality. Polynesian bilaterality does, of course, allow persons to take up authentic residence on maternal as well as on paternal lands. But honorable residence favors, in fact, continuity of residence, normally on patrimonial lands. Eggan, for example, in commenting on the advantage of flexibility in bilateral kinship, has noted, however, the difficulty such systems have in "providing social continuity and in transmitting property and position (1955:494)." The status lineage overcomes this difficulty but only as long as it retains its traditional status system and fixes the honor on the male line. Goodenough (1955), dealing with the same problem, sees the central issue as one of providing continuity for the inheritance of lands. Residence and descent, he argues, are adaptations to the problems of equitably distributing land-holdings. Where land is abundant, fully unilineal systems are most feasible, but where land is scarce, as on small islands, more flexible systems of residence and descent develop. If land were indeed the issue, then New Zealand and Manihiki, for example, would have very different descent systems, which, of course, they do not. And if equitable distribution were the issue, we would have found Polynesian political life inexplicable. Land rights, residence, and descent are interdependent, to be sure. The nature of their interdependence is to be explained, however, as a complex balancing of the dual interests of economy, on the one hand, and of status and power, on the other. In the Traditional societies, these dual interests are complementary. Economy, now used in the subsistence meaning, remains the concern of local and low-level segments. Among the Maori, the hapu, the true land-working groups, were headed by rangatira and not by ariki. In Manihiki-Rakahanga Segment III, matakeinanga headed by *whakamaru* were the centers of economic administration, and in Tongareva the economic centers were the households. Western Polynesia presents generally a more complicated picture because of the greater variety of descent group systems. The basic principle of complementary division is, nevertheless, the same. The economy remains in local hands, and the local interests are essentially autonomous. Economic autonomy is part of the flexibility of residence and descent of the local and lower-level segments, whose members could shift residence according to personal advantage. Flexibility was in residence and use of lands, but not in transmission. Transmission is still another concept, and is associated with the integrity of the status lineage and its lands. Land cultivations were under the principal jurisdiction of a ranking headman, generally a senior male whose office came under the rules of preferential patriliny and patrilocality. Thus even at the lower segmental levels it was still the status system that unified economy, descent, and residence. Since, as a rule, those who shifted residence for economic or status advantage were the lowly, their flexibility did not affect the fundamentals of land tenure. In this differentiation of a status line with continuity of jurisdiction over lands, and a genealogically variable populace with discontinuous use of lands, the traditional status lineage was a model for the still further differentiation between status line and populace that developed in the Open and Stratified societies.

Adoption

If marital residence, which gave rights to land in either maternal or paternal lineages, carried out the implications of bilaterality for the utilitarian interests in economy, the adoption of children carried out those implications still further, but in a more complex manner. In all of Polynesia adoption was a common practice among close relatives. Adoptions were so frequent that Rivers was moved to speak of a "communism" in children. Adoption generally involved absolute transfer. In Manu'a, children moved freely from parental to collateral households, now living here and now living there. In the face of such freedom, adoption seemed superfluous. This ease of transfer, of residential mobility, seems to have been part of a rather general Polynesian conviction most forcefully expressed by Tikopians who told Firth: "It is bad for a child to adhere only to his parents; it belongs to the larger group, the *kaino a paito,* and must stand in an equal relation to all therein (1936:205)." This is the principle that lineage transcends household, that the linear interests of a higher-level segment are superior to those of a lower level.

An adoption had a personal as well as a social side. The personal is familiar. Childless couples, families that had lost a child, families that were too small and could feed more, desired additions. And the desire for addition is easily explained as part of the strong affection of Polynesians for children. The desire of a family for a source of support, or the interest of a family in placing a child in safe and prosperous custody, represents the straightforward utilitarian interests in adoption. The social side of adoption was concerned with more abstract principles of defining the relations between two families, of adjusting inequities in lineages, or of strengthening a lineage. The idea just mentioned of the child as belonging to the lineage and not gripped by the narrow parochial interests of personal family is part of the social doctrine of adoption.

Firth, in reviewing conditions of adoption in Polynesia, concluded that "adoption often acts as a mechanism of compensation or equilibrium when there is institutional maladjustment (1936:595)." Among the examples he offered were the Maori use of adoption to revive a land interest in a maternal lineage that would otherwise lapse for nonoccupancy and the Mangaian transfers of children to a maternal line to offset the disaster of military defeat. Firth does not imply, however, that compensation is the sole function of adoption, for each society, he noted, improvised on the possibilities of adoption for its own specific purposes. Unfortunately, information on adoption is not detailed enough to allow for a systematic comparison of these specific purposes. What information we do have suggests a distinction between western Polynesian uses of adoption as one of the several ways in which descent lines of a brother and of a sister may carry out exchanges and mutual honoring, and eastern Polynesian uses strictly in the interests of lineage that involve no special relationship between the families of the donor and the recipients of the child. This distinction—a tentative one at best—may be related to the general pattern of male line–female line duality in western Polynesia and the more unitary pattern of male line–female line equivalence in eastern Polynesia. These general characteristics are described in the following chapter on kinship.

Everywhere in Polynesia, adoption was more often a demand than an offer. The Beagleholes, whose account of adoption in Pukapuka is most comprehensive and illuminating, ask: What are the advantages for the giver? In Hawaii the issue was not advantage but of an incurred obligation being met by giving up a child on demand. To refuse was to risk the danger of reprisal by sorcery. In Mangaia, giving up a child for adoption was often the only way to spare it from the human sacrifices conquering tribes demanded of the conquered. Mangaia had also developed an orderly procedure of alternately allocating children between the paternal and maternal sides. The paternal side kept the first-born son so that its lineage interests were defended. But the alternation of offspring—which was not automatic but subject to negotiation—must have had the opposite effect of stressing bilaterality in the face of the unilineal lineage principle of exogamic patriliny. The Maori similarly used adoption to stress bilaterality of lands against the unilinear principle that united patrilocal residence to patrilineal descent.

These examples of adoption imply, however, submission to general principles of social organization with no clear evidence of specific personal benefits other than those of necessity. In Pukapuka, as the Beagleholes have brought out, adoptions brought two families into mutual relations of honoring. To be asked for a child was to be honored, and only the esteemed kinsmen were asked. Commonly, adoptions were by cross-uncle and cross-aunt—a special western Polynesian respect relationship—and by their descendants, who were cross-cousins to one another. These lines exchanged children and used these exchanges as the basis for appropriate property exchanges. The rationale of the ritual exchanges of goods as a validation, in effect, for child exchange is self-evident. Absolute adoptions known as *kokoti,* "to cut," were negotiated to repair a "break" in a lineage. Since the lineage is a status organization, the repair, we must assume, must convey honor. The giver, it would appear, is honored by being considered worthy of "repairing" a descent line. The ethnographies do not, to my knowledge, mention the consideration of mana. Yet, if mana is an aspect of descent, it would be reasonable to assume that in adoptions families exchanged mana. If this were really the case, it would mean a concept of dual transmission of mana—a unilinear and a bilateral transmission. In view of Polynesian commitment to both systems of descent, this speculation is by no means unreasonable. In Pukapuka, equalization of lineages was definitely an important motive in adoptions. The Beagleholes give the example of a man who, having been adopted originally out of his father's lineage, subsequently adopted his sister's son, whom he presented to his father's lineage. In this society, with its dual lineages, there seems to have been the greatest concern with maintaining the balances. The families who agreed to do this thereby added to their own honor. Pukapuka had also partial adoptions, evidently of a utilitarian nature. These, known as *wangaia,* "to feed," involved only change in residence, not in descent. The adopters undertook to feed the child, and received the child's food allotments from its parental village. This form of partial adoption, whose purpose is to bind villages in material respects, seems part of the more general pattern called by the Beagleholes "sponsored affiliation," by which persons "affiliate" to another village, becoming partial members of the "corporation" but without taking up residence there.

The Pukapukan pattern of respect relations was repeated in slightly different form in Western Samoa, where the adoption of a child put in motion a set of ritual exchanges equivalent to those of marriage between two families. Here, as in Tonga, the common adoption was by the cross-uncle or aunt of a nephew. But while the Samoan adoption merely linked two families without implying succession to chiefly title, those of more politically oriented Tonga did introduce the child into the line of succession.

The notion of adoption as linkage was most fully developed in the Marquesas, where adoption, according to Handy (1923:82), was, like marriage, the source of political advantage. Between chiefly families, adoption established a political alliance. The rites of adoption were, accordingly, commensurate with the importance of the event, which —going far beyond simple family linkage—united the genealogies of the lines as marriage would have done. As in marriage, a series of symmetrical gift exchanges validated the transactions. In the western Polynesian manner (not surprisingly, since the Marquesas retained the western patterns of kinship), the father's sister and the mother's brother, the cross-aunt and uncle, carried out the rites of adoption, rather than the actual and the adopting parents.

In the case of nonchiefly families, it was the personal interest that was more important, an interest in adding to the size of the family for the material advantages of work and service and for the religious purpose of having descendants who could make proper death offerings.

Marquesan adoption practices would appear to represent the entire Polynesian pattern of satisfying personal interests, of linking families, of enriching genealogies, of promoting political advantage, and of actual honoring of families. In this fully bilateral society, adoptions were still another device, but only at the political level of chiefs, for carrying out fully the possibilities of bilaterality. "The object of bringing about a union of families was the acquisition of wealth, social prestige, and power," as Handy so succinctly puts it (1923:82).

In the Marquesas, particularly, we see adoption not only as a universal and personal custom allowing families to remedy their excesses and insufficiencies in children, but as a singularly appropriate means of adding still more flexibility of linkage to an already highly flexible status lineage organization.

Patterns of Variability

All social systems are variable, so that strictly speaking we cannot classify them as "stable–unstable" except perhaps on some hypothetical gradient. On such a hypothetical gradient, the status lineage would place at the "unstable" end among tribal society descent groups. What, however, do we mean by "unstable"? Can we really say that a system has an ideal structure—let us say, the Traditional—

and that departure from the ideal is a sign of instability? Stability, in this sense, has a needless moral connotation. It may suit functionalist theory, which regards "equilibrium" as the summum bonum of social life, but hardly historical theory, which sees change, development, growth, conflict, and opposition as the most characteristic social processes. Thus we may consider variability not as "instability," in the sense of inadequacy and structural defect, but as inherent flexibility. If a status system resembles a game (not play) in its rules, in its goals, and in its provision for choices in how to apply the rules, it will, like a game, produce variable patterns. However, unlike a true game, which can always start from the beginning again, each new combination changes the rules to a degree. Chiefs do not make their own rules in Polynesia any more than they do elsewhere. As chiefs, they have the privilege of varying the rules. In Polynesia they vary the rules of status and they vary the rules of descent—one of the keys of status. The system represents the traditional rules. "It" does not change itself. "It" is changed by chiefs and by their ambitions. Variability, therefore, is not to be explained solely in terms of chiefs or solely in terms of the abstraction we call a "system."

In the preceding discussions of Polynesian societies and their characteristics of status and descent group organization, I have tried to show the interplay between the personal factors, presented through the histories of chiefly lines, and the social factors, presented through an analysis of systems. In this chapter, intended as a summary and as a pulling together of findings, I am concerned only with variability as an expression of the interaction of systems. It should be understood, however, that the energy for variability is not in the system as such, but in the responses of persons—chiefs and all other ambitious men and women—to the systems.

The variability of the Polynesian status lineage seems to have been influenced by two different sets of conditions, one perhaps external, the other internal. The external conditions are those of geography and are observed in the distinction between the social systems of western and eastern Polynesia. The internal conditions are those of response to status rivalry and are observed in the distinctions among Traditional, Open, and Stratified societies. Variability is, therefore, complex. Status rivalry may be a constant factor, but its effects differ in detail in western and in eastern Polynesian societies. Yet, since Polynesia is after all a relatively homogeneous culture area, we must also ask whether the original differences themselves are not also related to internal processes of development. In the next chapter I present the hypothesis that western Polynesian kinship systems have been in process of change and have finally evolved eastern Polynesian forms. In this chapter I present a parallel hypothesis for the descent group organization.

Ignoring for the moment the range of differences, we can say that in western Polynesia descent groups have two characteristics that distinguish them generally from those of eastern Polynesia; these are a concept of kinship duality, and a concept of locality which is also, as I shall explain, part of a concept of duality. Kinship duality is a concept that recognizes patrilineal descent lines, on the one hand, and a maternal side, on the other. Locality, very strongly expressed in the Samoan tradition in particular, sets off common residence against common descent as sources of common interest. Kinship duality sets off common interests in status and authority as vested in patriliny against other common interests vested in a female and her line. As Firth once said, Polynesia has only patriliny and not matriliny. Kinship duality does not oppose in symmetrical fashion a patrilineal against a matrilineal line. It opposes a patrilineal lineage principle that is generally and, in the case of Tikopia, exclusively through males to a variety of descent principles that identify a line as descended from or linked to a woman—a sister, or a father's sister, or a mother's brother. This line itself may then go through males. The oppositions in kinship duality are in relative balance. Opposition between lineage and locality, on the other hand, is not. As Mead has demonstrated for Manu'a, the local group whose fono governs status has reduced the significance of the descent groups. In eastern Polynesia, again speaking generally, kinship with respect to sex line is unitary and so are—in the Traditional societies—lineage and residence.

Are these differences to be considered as matters of separate streams of diffusion into Polynesia, or can they be related to evolutionary direction? The answer, I think, is self-evident from the evidence that has been presented. The status lineage is the product of the status system and is most directly influenced by evolutionary changes in that system. This implies that whatever may have been the aboriginal Polynesian descent group organization, its development and its ebb and flow has followed the history of chiefly lines and of chiefly prerogatives.

There is good reason to assume, as Goodenough has suggested (1955) that the earliest Polynesian descent groups may have been small and localized and concerned primarily with land. Thus kainga (or "cognates") is the one term for a kin group that is common to all but three Polynesian societies (Niue, Mangaia, Marquesas), and we cannot be certain that these three did not ever use this term for a kin group. The variety of meanings of the term reveal its general realm of application. It stands for the bilaterally extended family in Samoa, Tokelau, Uvea, Futuna, and Tonga. In Ontong Java it refers to a related idea, as the collective term for consanguinal and official kin of one's generation. The Tikopian kaina, "place where fires are burning," is sometimes the term for village, and in Pukapuka, kainga is a synonym for the paternal lineage. In eastern Polynesia it means relatives generally, or a territory, either the village or food plantations, or a more general strip of land. The most generalized references are in Tahiti and in Hawaii, where it means one's heritage and the homeland, respectively. Either as kindred or as land-holdings, the reference is bilateral and for the most part local.

Only in four societies, all of western Polynesia (Samoa, Uvea, Futuna, Tokelau), is kainga the common term for a descent group. The Tokelaus, as a Samoan colony, carried the kainga with them. But Uvea and Futuna as Tongan satellites have kainga as a descent group, while in Tonga the reference is only broadly to bilateral kinship. Quite possibly the lineage concept of haa replaced kainga in Tonga. If kainga, as seems likely, was an early Polynesian bilateral descent group, then, of course, we must assume it had been replaced almost everywhere in Polynesia. Tikopia and Maori support such a suggestion, for in these societies kainga refers to the village, whereas the common residential groups, such as the paito and hapu derive from a specifically lineage terminology.

To carry forward this frankly speculative reconstruction of Polynesian descent groups, we proceed to the hypothesis that the organization of Polynesian kin groups evolved from two different sources, from the small and utility-minded land-holding group of bilaterally related persons, the kainga, and from the comprehensive genealogical networks organized around chiefly lines. Both systems meshed, and since they were not fully incompatible, the kainga could retain for long its own character and its relative autonomy. We can thus visualize the growth of Polynesian societies proceeding through certain general stages: (I) when the society was small, the kainga was proportionally large and the chief was its head; (II) when the chiefship began to expand, the status lineage ramified and the kainga remained relatively constant in size; (III) when the status lineage underwent, in concert with drastic changes in chiefship, a major reorganization, the kainga was then either drastically modified or brought close to dissolution. The stages just depicted are, of course, hypothetical and schematic. In each society the relationship between local group and ramified status lineage was played out according to the vicissitudes of local history. In Samoa, for example, the village organization fused aiga, the representative of the kainga form, with the fono, the expansive organization of chiefly titles. In the Samoan context, the concept of locality had grown, but it was the hierarchically ranged fono organization that encompassed the political system.

This basic division between bilateral land-holding units and propatrilineal status-granting units underlies all Polynesian social systems, except for the special cases of the Stratified societies. Whatever the merits of the historical hypothesis, the dependence of the ramified lineage organization upon chiefs and upon basic principles of status is, from the available evidence, incontrovertible. If the status lineage depends upon chiefs, we cannot postulate a direct evolution, except in the broadest and most schematic terms. Polynesian genealogical traditions demonstrate how chiefships have waxed and waned. Manu'a seems to have experienced a decline in chiefly authority, as have Futuna and Uvea. The arikiship must surely have been an old institution, judging by its universality in historic times. Accordingly, the ramified status lineage must also have been old, but probably not as old as the kainga.

Our specific interest, however, is not in historical reconstruction, but in factors of variability in status lineage organization. We turn now to the dependency between status system and status lineage.

The broad evolutionary developments from Traditional to Open to Stratified societies define the very general transformations of the status lineage from a kinship to a political organization and its eventual replacement by a district or territorial organization. These developments are summarized in the final chapter, status and evolution. At this point our concern is with the more specific patterns of variation that underlay the more general developments.

Variations in degree of adherence to the principle of seniority of descent are of particular significance, and are most fully illustrated from western Polynesia. Samoa, Pukapuka, Ontong Java, and Niue all ignored descent seniority. Their descent groups reveal the following features: The Samoan aiga was not fully segmentary. While the hierarchical organization of the fono depended ultimately upon titles held by families, it was the regional system, the fono itself, that administered and transmitted titles. Since honor came from the fono, the aiga had no obligation to foster exclusiveness. And, as Holmes (1957) has remarked, the number of people tracing descent from the founders of a title could be enormous and widespread. A person already had wide choice of affiliation. If he were ambitious, he would choose the aiga that had the best and most titles to bestow. Thus affiliation was not simply bilateral, but by status. But because of the indirectness of transmission of titles, the Samoan aiga was a diffuse and broad-based status lineage.

Pukapuka, a variant on the Samoan theme of sex-line duality, was able to sustain a segmentary lineage structure by developing distinctive maternal and paternal lineages. The patrilineal lineages were the sources of wealth and of rank, but in the absence of seniority, the lineages were not ranked. Categorical affiliation through sex line gave definition to the lines, clearly singling out chiefly from nonchiefly lines and separating very decidedly the "royal" from the commoner patrilineal lineages. While each lineage formed its own subdivision, the major lineages were not interrelated, but simply formed separate descent groups. Ontong Java may be described as a Pukapukan system on a much smaller scale. In the absence of seniority, lineages retained their linearity through exclusive male-line descent; they were neither ranked, branched, nor interconnected.

Niue, still another Samoan variant, with no recognition of senior lines and with no strong commitment to patriliny, had the most flexible kin group organization. Local kindreds did not ramify, but were drawn together by the rule of powerful warrior chiefs. In the absence, further, of any genealogical rank, attachment to the fagai was for economic or political reasons.

Seniority of descent lines, like any other principle of kin group organization, cannot be considered apart from other principles of affiliation and descent. How descent groups will be organized in the absence of seniority depends upon other conditions, such as the organization of sex lines, general genealogical distinction, and the attractions of power. The absence of seniority, nevertheless, can be detected in special characteristics of branching and segmentation. Without seniority, the pressure of bilaterality and the requirements of land-holding can only create genealogically discrete groupings.

We can see the specific role of seniority in descent group structure even more advantageously among those western Polynesian societies where the royal lines followed traditional principles of seniority and where commoner lines did not. This was the situation in Uvea and Futuna, and in the Tokelaus. We noted that in Uvea the royal linages which were ramified in the traditional manner were, in fact, known as faahinga, a term cognate with the Tongan haa and carrying the significance of an honorific descent from a distinguished founder. The commoners belonged to nonramified and economic kaingas. In Futuna the katunga were ramified when they were royal and were essentially unconnected with one another when they were commoner. On both islands the royal lineages grew more rapidly than did the commoner lineages. The Tokelaus, with their special interest in combining principles of seniority and reverence for age, created a nonramified kindred organization that regulated the basic economy, along with four descent lines of aliki that retained a lineage organization through pro-patriliny and partial seniority.

The examples of Uvea, Futuna, and the Tokelaus pose the question: Why did not the senior, pro-patrilineal descent lines of the hereditary chiefs encompass wider sections of the community? The answer, I think, lies in political history. In the eastern Polynesian Traditional societies, ariki founded lines that grew progressively by seniority-ranked branches. But political conquest is a nongenealogical method of growth. The royal lines and subject lines remain distinct. Uvea, Futuna, and the Tokelaus are examples of conquest states that had eventually achieved political stability, but the split in descent group organization remained. In eastern Polynesia, the departures from the pattern of pro-patrilineal and seniority-ranked branches could all be attributed to the effects of conquest and to the growth in political power. The fate of the Tongan haa, a counterpart to the status lineages of eastern Polynesia, illustrates for western Polynesia the same political processes. In the case of Manu'a the process of variation was nonviolent, evidently the end result of a more quiet form of status rivalry.

The Village Organization

Thus far we have considered the complementary duality between status lineages formed from chiefly descent lines, and local and economically oriented kin groups comprehended by the concept of kainga. Chiefly lines and local economic groups form opposite ends of a common social system, certainly in Traditional societies. Even when the chiefship has assumed substantial powers, the local group represented by the village can retain its independent organization. The village is not simply a condition of residence; it is, rather, a collective organization, a most important expression of "home rule." In Manu'a, the village organization, having evidently replaced the family lines as the manipulator of status, was able to infuse the status system with the vitality of fresh opportunities for advancement. It did so by granting local headmen the vote of approval or denial of titles and privileges. Apart from this example of direct involvement in the politics of status, villages worked lands together, reallocated land-holdings according to need, granted permission for outsiders to take up residence on village lands, arranged for the cultivation and guardianship of public lands, received distinguished visitors properly, and organized local public works and local ritual. In New Zealand, the hapu, a descent group segment, and the kainga, a residential unit, were sometimes one and the same. By and large, however, the village was specifically a compact territorial unit that brought local descent groups into some collective management and gave representation to each household. It is the village with its strong autonomy that is the powerful complement to chiefly majesty and authority. Thus we must consider the loss of the village or, in any case, its absence, as a matter of profound difference in social organization. The difference is that of chiefs dealing either with autonomous corporate bodies or with dependent households.

Among the group of eighteen Polynesian societies, seven had no village organization at the time of European contact; These are Easter, Mangaia, Marquesas, Tonga, Mangareva, Society, and Hawaii. In other words, three of the Open and all of the Stratified societies had apparently abandoned the village organization. What assurance have we that these societies had, in fact, once possessed a village organization? The evidence is circumstantial, but reasonably compelling. The majority of Polynesian societies had villages; the village organization spanned eastern and western Polynesia; Maori, a probable branch of the Society Islands, and Futuna and Uvea, outposts of Tonga, had villages. If the offshoots had villages and the parental stock did not, the explanation could be that they had developed villages later. This seems to me the less likely explanation since all the societies without a village organization are of the same political type. The Stratified societies, in particular, and those Open societies that had evolved feudatory land relations were antagonistic to the autonomous village organization. When powerful chiefs organized populations around their own land holdings, there was no longer place for the village organization. The older and more traditional village organization depended, as we have seen, on two conditions; the autonomous tenure of its own lands, and autonomy in social life. In the traditional view of social relations, chief and commoner had a balanced relationship of, let us say, ritual to economy. When the chiefs seized the economy, the new relationship became strongly antagonistic. The balanced relationship was parallel to the male line–female line duality of each in its own realm. The relationship became antagonistic when chief and commoner entered the same realm.

At this point of antagonism, the status lineage literally cracked. In the traditional form the status lineage had tendencies to evolve in two directions, in the direction of indefinite expansion by branching, so as to incorporate the entire genealogical community, and in the direction of actual subdivision. The evolution of the status system along the lines of political power combined, it would seem, these two tendencies, elaborating the chiefly lineages through the traditional modes of branching and subdividing in the sense of dropping the commoners from the branches.

It cannot be said that the status lineage went through an "inevitable" evolution, but it is clear that the quality of flexibility of the status lineage—which offered to contenders for genealogical rank such a variety of options—was well suited for rapid evolutionary development.

21

Principles of Kinship

ANY SOCIAL STRUCTURE CAN BE REPRESENTED AS A COMPLEX INTERweaving of several systems of classification that combine and separate people by different standards and therefore in numerous ways. As a result, all persons have multiple social identities or statuses; what they may lack in honor or consequence in one category, they may gain in another. If all systems of categorization were equivalent, the sum of lacks and gains in status would eventually balance. In social systems as strongly rank-conscious as those of Polynesia, the varieties of classification offer compensations, but no true balancing out of pluses and minuses in status. In the final analysis, the status system dominates the total system of social categorization. We have had good reason to consider the status system as the broadest and most general scheme of social classification, for rank encompasses not only the total ethnic community of interacting tribes, but has an all-Polynesia significance as well. The status system embraces the organization of descent groups by virtue of its control of principles of leadership. Descent groups, as we have seen, respond almost directly to changes in the status system. We now wish to consider whether the kinship system—that is, categorization by relationship terms—is also under the influence of the status system, and if so, to what degree and in what manner.

Status system, descent group organization, and kinship system are the three principal ways in which the Polynesian genealogical network is subdivided. The status system, the most far-reaching, the most cosmopolitan, and the most public mode of classification, is concerned primarily with leadership and authority. The descent group organization, being segmentary, is a more local, more parochial, and more intimate classification. The segments are concerned with common action in ritual and economy. Yet the status system opposes the utilitarian interest in unity with its own persistent requirements for the separation of high and low ranks. In the end, each society works out its own form of reconciliation between these opposing interests. The kinship system, being anchored in the most intimate and sheltered realm of households and local groups, is more immune from these conflicts of unity and separation. In the Traditional societies, kinship is fully coextensive with status system and descent group organization, providing the rules for very broad and general patterns of respects. In all forms of Polynesian society, however, kinship has its exclusive place in the domestic realm, where it draws up its own and exclusive categories of honor and worth. It is within the kinship system primarily that what is lacking in honor and consequence in other areas of genealogical classification is compensated for. The status system readily ignores internal differentiations among persons of commoner status. The kinship system gives these differentiations prominence. All first-born, for example, have domestic honor within kinship that entitles them to deference and respect. If one is not senior to a sibling, he at least has ascendancy of generation as parent. In many other ways the kinship system guarantees to each some measure of honor. Kinship honor, however, does not balance out the honors. The senior male of a commoner family is only a big man in a small pond. And we have also seen how the reduction in economic and ritual significance of commoner families has, in effect, reduced the role and hence the status of the family senior in the course of Polynesian status evolution. Nevertheless, as long as the family organization itself remains intact, all, even pariahs, are spared the indignity of total lack of honor.

We can say at once, then, that the kinship system is also dependent upon the status system. The dependency is, however, loose, in the way perhaps in which the life of a remote peasant community is both ultimately affected by national policy and yet generally remote. In crisis, the remote and loosely related dependencies are suddenly made to respond to national policy. Even so, their smallness and parochialness give them some immunity. The same may be true of kinship systems in response to crises of the status system. At some point they surely must respond, but the narrowness of their interests is a safeguard. If we were to rank the three systems of genealogical classification by the criterion of sensitivity to disturbance, we would place the status system first, the descent group organization second, and the kinship system last.

That kinship is, nevertheless, a "sensitive" system can be judged from the rather wide variations between the patterns of classification of eastern and western Polynesia, and within each cultural zone. We may consider these basic variations as having been brought about by internal differentiation, since all Polynesian kinship systems share a common vocabulary (see Appendix 2) as well as common underlying principles. We know, of course, that no kinship system is encompassed by its standard vocabulary. The terms, their meanings, their patterned formations, are themselves an abstraction of all that is actually involved in kinship relations. Nor need a kinship system be confined to a single vocabulary. In Polynesia, for example, standard terms define certain broad categories that relate kinship to social status. Other and more specific terms establish, whenever necessary, the immediate connections between relatives for more utilitarian purposes. A kinship system, therefore, has several vocabularies. The Polynesian standard vocabulary includes only terms of reference by which the speaker simultaneously identifies himself and his referent. Outside the standard vocabulary, the speaker has great freedom. He may refer to clusters of kin from an impersonal standpoint, identifying them as "siblings" or "cousins" or first-born. Again, from the personal point of view he may describe a kinsman precisely and uniquely. Only the standard vocabulary of reference is fully generalizing. If kinship reference is general, reciprocal, and formal, kinship address is by name and is, by contrast, personal, intimate, and nonreciprocal.

Polynesian standard kinship terms have their own meanings which are current. These meanings are expressed through currently understandable metaphor. The kinship systems are most readily understood, therefore, as organizations of paired or reciprocal relationships, each of which is defined by some metaphor that conveys ideas of honor and worth. Insofar as these paired metaphors which are contained within the kinship terms have some conceptual unity, we may speak of a kinship "system." The "system" in this sense is more a product of a literary or mythological imagination than of social logistics. Since Polynesia is spared the categorical imperatives of exogamic groupings and of precisely channeled marriages, it is also free of the obligations for sharply categorizing kinsmen, and for maintaining set channels for the interchange of spouses between set groups. The kinship systems, in short, have logistical freedom, and thus are free to develop categories around what are conceived to be the central interests of the culture, namely, honor. Honor enters into the warp and woof of the social fabric, giving it design and content. Each paired kinship relationship contributes its distinctive pattern to the whole design. I use the image of a woven design with its connotation of stability advisedly, even though the Polynesian kinship systems are, in fact, highly variable. But the variability is not that of a dynamic system adjusting itself to the material problems of economy and marriage, but that of a conceptual system preoccupied more with the etiquettes of respects. Kinship systems cannot and do not ignore the material conditions of life. They need not, however, delegate all their categories to attend to the same issues. Households, local groups, and kindreds deal with the utilitarian aspects of life. The specialized categories deal with the ideals of status.

There is the choice of approaching Polynesian kinship systems from their periphery, so to speak, or from their center. The periphery is literally the maximum ascending and descending generations, the center, the generation of Ego. From the Polynesian point of view, as their metaphors disclose, the grandparent and grandchild generations represent a linear dimension of a beginning and a continuation that encompasses the kindred and gives it general coherence. The center, which represents a lateral dimension, conveys quite a different concept: that of separations and of differentiations. Stated most abstractly, the periphery encompasses the whole; the center segments it.

Grandparents and Grandchildren

Polynesia readily generalizes the category of founders, ancestors, and grandparents, to obscure distinctions of sex, line, and ascendance. The most common term is *tupuna* from *tupu*, "to arise," "to increase," "to cause to grow," and *puna*, "prolific as a female" (Tregear 1891). The grandparents are thus the initial progenitive forces and are analogous within the kinship system to the organic concept of a Segment I to the descent group organization. Only three societies—Tonga, Manu'a, and Uvea—have different terms. Tonga and Uvea "reduce" the grandparents to *kui*, which has the opposite connotation of age and weariness. Manu'a extends the meanings of *tama* to establish a single idea of line encompassing grandparents and grandchildren and parents and children. Manu'a thus carries out the theme of a kinship periphery in the most general form possible. If Tonga and Uvea reduce grandparents to kui, they still remain with the general Polynesian tradition in terms for grandchildren. They retain tupuna, converting it into a more general category of "ancestor."

Grandparents are not specifically honored. Like grandparents everywhere, they are more warm than distant and respected. The viewpoint is, therefore, complex. The imagery of organic growth, of a source of growth, is, of course, elevating. Generality, on the other hand, is not. High honor demands specificity. As sources, the grandparents transcend the specific Polynesian interests in social status. Moreover, the generation gap confronts grandparents with the very young who are not quite in the orbit of specific honors.

Grandchildren are generally *mokopuna*, which Tregear (1891) derives from *moo*, "a path, a line of direction" and from prolific *puna:* The grandparents are source and the grandchildren continuity. The generations define each other as linked processes in the formation of a kinship community. They create the general framework of kinship, giving it a biological and metaphysical character. As reciprocals, tupuna and mokopuna are precisely balanced in degree of generality and in specific content. With minor exceptions, they state a common doctrine for all Polynesia.

Parents and Children

The generations of parents and children gain specificity and, accordingly, intensity of concern with honor, when we consider Polynesia as a whole. Whereas the grandparent–grandchild concepts are relatively constant, surely because of their abstractness, the parent–child concepts, because of their greater specificity, are subject to much greater variability. Generally speaking, eastern Polynesian systems are the least discriminating and western Polynesian the most. The range of variability extends from the Hawaiian, which is capable of reducing the parent–child generation to the same level of abstractness as grandparent–grandchild, to societies of western Polynesia which distinguish by sex, and by linearity, and between cross and parallel relationships. Hawaii may be unusual in its freedom to express such general ideas as "parent" as well as "child." All other eastern Polynesian systems acknowledge gender and most distinguish lineal from collateral at the generation of children. The Marquesas, although central to eastern Polynesia, are exceptional in that they retain many of the western Polynesian concepts of classification and behavior.

In eastern Polynesia the common parental term is *matua,* whose meanings bear on ideas of maturing, of growing, of quickening (as a foetus in its womb), of largeness, and of abundance. In Hawaiian, *makua* means "full," "thickset" (cf. Tregear 1891). From these organic connotations, meanings of makua extend into ideas of honoring. It is also the noun for "benefactor" and "provider," and for "master" and "owner." Thus, as tupuna stands for the beginning of the organic line of growth, so matua stands for the maturing phase and for a more concrete quality of a kin line. Concreteness is in the gender distinctions. Tupuna may stand for a single generative line; matua, with gender, represents two evenly bilateral lines. The general concepts of parenthood are variable even in eastern Polynesia. The Marquesas and their Mangarevan offshoot associate the mother (kui) with ancestors in their less exalted form (cf. meanings of *kui* or *kuikui* as "blind," "weary," "aged" [Tregear 1891]), but retain the paternal image as the one who gives body. The parental concepts in these societies tend toward the dual, since two evidently complementary ideas are being expressed, maturing and ageing. In the Tokelaus, on the other hand, it is the mother who is honored as *matua* while the father receives the more neutral term *tamana.* The reversal here may be due to the special circumstance of matrilocal residence and the association of the mother with agricultural growth.

Eastern Polynesia generally draws no lineal-collateral distinctions at this generation level. Nevertheless, there are two exceptions, Tongareva and the Marquesas. In Tongareva father and mother take on intimate-meaning terms, and uncles (*taueka*) and aunts (*matua-*

wahine) emerge with metaphors of honoring. The intent would seem to be not bifurcation of line, but the more general differentiation between close–distant, affection–honor. Bifurcation, however, is clearly the Marquesan intent. The Marquesan distinction is, broadly speaking, in the western Polynesian tradition, for it lifts up the cross-uncle and aunt with special terms. These terms, *tunane* (mother's brother) and *tuehine* (father's sister), are only minor variants of *tunana* (a woman's brother) and *tuehina* (a man's sister). What they presumably imply is that a mother's brother is as a woman's brother, and a father's sister is as a man's sister. That this is truly what the Marquesans had in mind is made quite clear by terms for parallel uncle and aunt. Handy does not supply all the kinship terms, but the terms he does cite for mother's older sister (*tua'ana kui*) and for father's younger brother (*teina motua*) are modeled upon the Marquesan terms for older and younger sibling of same sex, respectively, *tua'ana* and *teina*. In other words, uncle and aunt terminology derives from principles that define distinctions between siblings. What these principles are I discuss under the "Sibling Generation," below. But in anticipation of that discussion, we may note here that the principles of sibling differentiation are the same for all Polynesian societies. This doctrine that siblings of opposite sex are functionally and structurally a different pair than siblings of same sex has in western Polynesia become the basis for a major elaboration of cross relationships. By distinguishing between a man's relationships through his sister, and a woman's relationship through her brother, the cross-relationships emphasize the duality of the sexes. While eastern Polynesia also recognizes the same doctrine, it has not developed it, except in the Marquesas. We can hardly overlook the historical significance of the Marquesan example, which appropriately bridges both traditions. Fully dualistic, western Polynesia places mother's brother and father's sister as conceptual opposites. But in the more bilateral and evenhanded tradition of eastern Polynesia, the Marquesas equate these cross-relatives. Their standard kin terms have equal value (see discussion under "Sibling Generation"), and they are also referred to as the *pahu pahu,* meaning "to burst forth" (Tregear 1891). The term connotes organic growth and so falls within the conceptual frame of terms such as *tupuna* and *matua.* Offhand, it seems rather strange that a relationship modeled on that of brother–sister should convey a generative sense. Yet this must be the Marquesan meaning of preferential cross-cousin marriage. If the children of mother's brother marry the children of father's sister, the cross-uncle and aunt are indeed the procreative kinsmen of the parental generation. They are procreative, moreover, in a special and exalted sense, because their children are in fact "brother" and "sister" to each other. Their marriage is therefore an equivalent of the sacred Hawaiian brother-and-sister marriages.

Except, then, for the Marquesas, the earliest representative of western Polynesian society in the area, eastern Polynesia understates the cross-relationships. Western Polynesia emphasizes them by placing them at the first ascending and descending generations. What is essentially only a nominal distinction in eastern Polynesia assumes major importance in western Polynesia, which singles out mothers' brothers and fathers' sisters and, correspondingly, cross-nephews and nieces. But the distinctions persons draw between the children of their siblings of opposite sex and those of their siblings of same sex are not, in fact, recognized by their own children. In other words, the cross-relationships are essentially cross-generational. Polynesia can safely ignore the apparent inconsistency of referring to the parents of some siblings as "uncle" or "aunt" and of others, also referred to as sibling, as "parent," because—lacking exogamy—it has no categorical descent lines to identify.

In western Polynesia, mother's brother and father's sister are commonly polar. The maternal uncle is *tu'asina,* a term based on the *tu'a* stem which means "common" (Churchward 1959). The designation is "low," within the kinship pattern as a whole: The man is in a subordinate status to his sister and to her children. The pattern, it should be noted, is variable, in itself a characteristic feature of western Polynesian kinship.

The key features of the generalized pattern are seen most clearly in Tonga, which may be the prototype for western Polynesia as a whole. In Tonga, of course, the sister outweighs her brother in formal honors, and he outweighs her in formal powers. Their relationship is thus brought into complex balance. What he holds in actual power over his sister he surrenders in ritual power to her children. Since the maternal nephew is of the "child" generation, his ritual ascendance reduces the uncle by still another step, so that he is as much reduced to his sister's child on this scale as he is to his sister.

Reasoning from a more general point of view about this form of avunculate, Levi-Strauss (in Hymes 1964:46) has devised the following formula: "The relation between maternal uncle and nephew is to the relation between brother and sister, as the relation between father and son is to the relation between husband and wife." Thus, as he explains further, if the relations between uncle and nephew and between brother and sister are both friendly or "positive," the relations between father and son and between husband and wife will be antagonistic or "negative." Or the reversal of "positive" and "negative" can occur; or, if in the first pair one is negative and the other relationship positive, a parallel situation will occur in the second pair. If relations between husband and wife are "positive," that between brother and sister will be "negative"; and, if the relationship between father and son is strained or "negative," that between maternal uncle and nephew is familiar or "positive." Tonga, as Levi-Strauss defines "negative" and "positive," fits the formula precisely. Husband and wife have a friendly relationship, brother and sister are tapu to each other and the tapu between father and son is counterpointed by the familiarities the nephew is allowed with his maternal uncle.

No social formula can be expected to operate precisely, but the central idea that kinship patterns are constructed around parallels and opposition can be demonstrated to apply to the organization of honoring relationships among kinsmen. Since honor in Polynesia can be more precisely defined in terms of ritualized behavior than in the more general terms of casual behavior (such as Levi-Strauss' citation from Gifford [Hymes 1964:47] that the Tongan wife "does not harbour the least thought of rebellion against him [the husband] on all domestic matters, she yields willingly to his authority"). The patterns formulated around honor can also be more precisely described. It is necessary to demonstrate, of course, that these kinship patterns are, in fact, organized around honor rather than around the more general sentiments of freedom and restraint. That honor is the central issue at least in the cross-uncle–aunt and cross-nephew relationships is readily shown.

From the standpoint of honors, the central constellation for Tonga involves: (a) the brother–sister, (b) husband–wife, (c) father–child, (d) mother–child. Mother's brother and father's sister are reflections of the special character of these four relations. The brother–sister avoidances are not manifestations of strain, but rather the opposite: they pay honor to each other through the respectful demeanor of avoidance. Their relationship is dual and balanced in the manner already described. The status relationship of husband and wife, on the other hand, is unbalanced, since the man, regardless of his or his wife's rank, has both the domestic authority and the honor of being recognized as the "chiefly side." Between father and son, the status relationship represents the power of the ascendant generation. The father has the authority and is entitled to avoidance respects. Between mother and son, the respects are more equal, except in the case of the first-born, who assumes the authority of potential office. Finally, the father is quite permissive toward his daughters in a counterpoint to his more formal relations with his sons. Another equation of respects may thus be stated: father is to daughter as mother's brother is to sister's son; father is to son as father's sister is to brother's child.

Within this pattern the father's sister appears as the opposing figure to the mother's brother. The term for father's sister, *mehekitanga,* derives its significance from the element *mehe,* which means "precious," and "envied." The etymology of *kitanga* is obscure. It may be related to *tanga,* "to be assembled," but this is far from certain. In any case, mother's brother is the "commoner" to the envied and respected father's sister. Tongans also describe the mother's brother as the "male mother" (Gifford 1928:24), an obvious further reference to his lowered status. Correspondingly, a man's maternal nephew (or niece) has the extraordinary designation of *ilamutu,* while a woman's brother's children have only the kinship status of the term *tama,* or "child." In the total design, *ilamutu* looms large as the *fahu.* The etymology of the term suggests the quality of the relationship; it is composed of a nominal stem *ira* with the designation of a "birth mark" and a verbal suffix, "to cut short," "to mutilate." In Hawaii the *iramaku* is the official executioner; and the term generally means "a destroyer." From etymology we deduce that what is destroyed is like a birthmark, namely, an inherent quality. The Tongan ilamutu, who is "above the law," is symbolically the destroyer of his maternal uncle. His powers over his uncle's property and his extraordinary right to seize his uncle's sacrificial offerings give him a divine ascendancy. The implication of ascendancy is enormous, because it represents a reversal of the normal hierarchy of the power of generations. The younger generation in this instance overcomes the higher, a recurrent theme in western Polynesian concepts of status.

Following now upon Levi-Strauss' formulation, the overall pattern of equivalences and oppositions involving the so-called parental and child generations appears as follows: through his sister, a man loses ritual or symbolic power and suffers a reversal. Through her brother, a woman gains an ascendancy equivalent to what a man has over his children. Through his mother, a child gains an ascendancy over a male of his parental generation. Through his father, a male submits to an awesome respect relationship before a female of his mother's generation. The key element is the concept of sex opposition as the switch-over point for status. Within consanguinity, the brother–sister pattern is the key. In marriage, an affinal and "made" relationship, a male immediately overcomes genealogical inferiority via his wife. The woman surrenders her genealogical position through the agency of her husband. Sexual complementarity, in short, balances out the kinship honors.

From the perspective of strongly unilinear systems, the quality of the cross-uncle and cross-aunt pattern would seem to balance out the stress of a line of descent. In patrilineal societies, the mother's brother, as Radcliffe-Brown sees it, represents freedom, as against the restraints of the male line. In matrilineal societies, it is likely to be the reverse. Pro-patrilineal Tonga would seem to fall in with this logical pattern rather neatly. But as Levi-Strauss has already remarked, descent is but one of the several factors that defines the avuncular relationship—to which we must add the observation that descent itself is not always a single factor. Tonga is "patrilineal" for some purposes and dual for others.

What these multiple factors forming the cross-uncle, cross-aunt relationships are (the so-called avunculate is obviously not a complete or isolable relationship), only the close study of patterns of variation will reveal. The Samoan pattern is, of course, cognate with the Tongan, but key elements are different. Tonga counterbalances mother's brother against father's sister; Manu'a shifts the emphasis to the father's sister, who stands apart as the ilamutu, just about blocking out the mother's brother from special consideration. He has, however, high status as *tamā* and as a member of the general category of parental generation males. Some Manu'ans, Mead reports, say that the mother's brother, who does after all have ritual obligations, is also an ilamutu (1930:138), an indication it would seem, that the term is held to be some kind of an honorific title. The most convincing evidence that Manu'a thinks of ilamutu as a title of honor is, of course, in its application to the father's sister rather than to the maternal nephew. The applicability of the term to the paternal aunt is evidently in recognition of her special role as one who can cut off the brother's line by her curse of barrenness. Her brother's child stands in the lowered class of victims. Her own child, who may be the *tama sa,* or "sacred child," or only the *tama fafine,* has, of course, derivative powers and status. The general pattern remains cognate with the Tongan, but its emphases have been shifted.

In Manu'a the concept of an ilamutu, with its privileges of taking property, has moved up one and two generations. In the two-generation shift, only the term is involved, for the father's sister is still equivalent in function to what she was in Tonga. In the one-generation shift, ilamutu appears as the title of the eldest sister of a titled man in a family of rank. Her rights to a fine mat from the dowry brought into a family must then be regarded as equivalent to the fahu rights of the Tongan ilamutu. In this instance we see the political aspect of the ilamutu relationship shifted from nephew to sister. The terminological patterns outline this shift. The Tongan reciprocals of mother's brother-sister's son is *tu'asina-ilamutu;* that is, in broad conceptual terms, dependent–master. In Manu'a the same reciprocals are: either *tama-tama fafine,* a "normal" generational distinction; or, *ilamutu-tama fafine,* with its even more emphatic stress upon the status of the ascendant generation. Information from Holmes (1957) that Manu'a also referred to the maternal nephew as *tama sa* underscores what is really the essential point, the great versatility of the cross relationships. Rivers and Mead, and more recently Gilson (1963) and Holmes (1957), derive these cross-relationships from the patterned connection between brother and sister. Their reasoning is unassailable. The sister is a special link with the ancestral gods and she and her line are entitled to the honors of sanctity. This honored line goes up to the generation of great grandfather and down to the generation of her own children. Ego's patrilateral cross-cousins are, accordingly, distinguished in their quality, even if not by terminology.

If the cross-relationship patterns depend upon the quality of the tie between brother and sister, we can readily understand the differences in the Tongan and Manu'an configurations. Tonga, as observed, declares a striking contrast between the power of the brother and the honor of the sister. Manu'a moderates this pattern by understating the brother's powers. Perhaps, then, it is the power gradient between brother and sister that is central. Differences between Manu'a and Western Samoa point in this direction. In Manu'a, the powers of the maternal nephew are reduced because, by the analogy of the Tongan formula, there is no need to counterbalance an overweighty brother. That is, the man and his sister's children are already in a proportionate relationship. In Western Samoa, where the political power of the male is very strong, the nephew is elevated above his maternal uncle in ritual powers. Here the sister's children are *tama sa* ("sacred child") and inherit their mother's power to curse. They are elevated more than in Manu'a, but since the maternal uncle is not, in fact, reduced, less so than in Tonga.

Brother–sister respects are the constants in western Polynesia; the variables are in the bearing these respects have upon the relations between nephews and maternal uncle. Two features define this special relationship: the terms, which are, after all, titular and connotative and not merely semiotic, and the appropriate behavior. Wherever nephews are designated as ilamutu or *tama sa,* they have high honor.

Wherever mother's brothers are designated either by *tu'a* (the stem) or *fae,* they are reduced. Father's sister as *masikatanga,* as ilamutu, or as *matua sa* is elevated. With respect to behavior, the maternal uncles are reduced still further when their maternal nephews have power over them through fahu. Even within western Polynesia, patterns of reduction and elevation in this constellation are variable with respect both to terminology and behavior. Mother's brother is reduced titularly in Tikopia, Tokelaus, Tonga, Uvea, and Futuna. He is elevated in Samoa, Ontong Java, Pukapuka and Niue. From the same titular point of view, the maternal nephew is elevated (he is nowhere reduced) in Tikopia, Tokelaus, Ontong Java, Uvea, Tonga, Samoa. He is not elevated in Pukapuka, Futuna, and Niue. The father's sister is elevated in Tonga, Samoa, Tikopia, Futuna, Uvea, Tokelau, but not in Ontong Java, Pukapuka, and Niue. Appendix 7 shows the patterns at a glance, revealing their complexity. What is clear at once, however, is the antiphonal nature of mother's brother to father's sister, with the dominant position given to the aunt. When she is elevated, her counterpart in mother's brother is almost inevitably reduced. But when he is elevated, she is never reduced. Terminologically, they are never represented as honor equals. A similar antiphonal relationship holds for mother's brother and his maternal nephew. Again, the nephew may not, in fact, be elevated; he is, however, never reduced.

The complexity of the pattern appears in the lack of correspondence between terminology and behavior, a not surprising lack since Polynesia has always known how to separate form from function. The most constant figure is that of father's sister, whose title is almost inevitably the counterpart of respects due her. The nephew figure is slightly less constant in this respect. The mother's brother, however, exhibits the most discrepancy between behavior and title. This variability may reflect two pressures within a kinship system: one, to preserve the dignity of the higher generation—thus upgrading the maternal uncle—and the other to allow the lower to overcome the higher ritually through the mother and thus counterbalance the reduction through the father. Appendix 9 also shows that the position of the maternal uncle cannot be related meaningfully to a concept of descent. The question is whether the variable patterns of honor and deference in western Polynesia can be laid to any single factor. This question, however, is best left to the end of the discussion.

The extraordinary variability of the fahu designation and privileges is a good example of the improvisory character of the male–female balances in western Polynesian kinship patterns. As a rule, the maternal nephew, known also as the fahu, has specific powers over his uncle. Within Polynesia, this kinship "trait" may have spread from Tonga to Western Samoa, and to Futuna and Uvea. Its absence in Manu'a may have resulted, of course, simply from lack of direct contact. Yet since Manu'a and Western Samoa were not, in fact, isolated, we are obliged to consider as well the possibility of rejection because of incompatibility. By virtue of its command over an ascendant generation, the fahu goes against the grain, resembling in this ritual respect political power which is also innovative and "made." Fahu power differs markedly therefore from father's sister power, which has the natural authority of the generation behind it. The essentially political character of fahu in western Polynesia is brought out in its tendency to jump from a domestic to a strictly political orbit.

In Western Samoa, to be sure, the *tama sa* ("sister's child") has fahu prerogatives and powers by having acquired the powers which, in Manu'a, belong only to the father's sister. But in Tonga, Futuna, and Uvea, fahu had served as an instrument of the power of one lineage over another. In Tonga the Tui Tonga descendants exercised rights over their related Tui Kanokupolu line through the fahu. In Uvea, a late Tongan branch, the political pattern was reversed, but the basic concept was the same. Here, the descendants of the father's sister's daughter had ritual rights over the paramount chief, who represented to them a mother's brother's line. According to Burrows, the Uvean specialization of fahu took place in relatively recent times (1937:170).

Futuna introduced still another variant. The ruler's sister's son had the central *vasu* (fahu) privilege. He had rights to all foods brought as ritual offerings to the paramount chief, but then had to share with all who claimed kinship with him. Thus the role of ritual redistribution went from the male line, in whose name it was collected, to the female line, in whose name it was redistributed. The ready transference of fahu from a domestic to a political orbit defines the interior significance of this relationship for Polynesia. It speaks for the doctrine of the lower overcoming the higher and is thus a particularly appropriate way of balancing out political authority.

As for parallel relations (fathers' brothers and mothers' sisters), these are recognized as equivalents and so are taxonomically merged with parents in western Polynesia. Insofar as patrilocal residence is preferred, the entire paternal side looms up—father, father's brother, and father's sister are the dominant figures. The mother's brother, who by residence rules is distant, is brought close, but at the disability of being reduced. Residence is therefore still another factor in the balance of kinship statuses. In accordance with Tongan doctrine, the wife entering a foreign household accepts reduction regardless of her inherent rank and so, of course, does her brother in respect to her new household. But in accord with principles of balance, what she surrenders in status to her husband she gains in relation to her brother, that is, to the household she has left. Residence has been seen to play a constant role in status. For example, the rule is consistent that matrilocal residence is lowering and patrilocal residence elevating. But this rule may be stated in still another way, namely, that a residence pattern is reductive when it is at variance with the line of status descent. Thus, since marriage must always lower a woman axiomatically, she should in all equity receive a compensation. In western Polynesia the compensations are very formal; in eastern Polynesia they are more improvisory. But the sense of an equity which status always demands is ever present. The western Polynesian principle of balances of status in reference to residence shows itself with particular forcefulness in the Tokelaus, where status moves patrilineally and residence is matrilocal. Here a woman brings into her own household her brother's first-born son. In this way he acquires, as MacGregor explains, a patrimonial link. He is spared, at the same time, the status disability of living within the undistinguished household of mother's sisters.

This consideration of the residence factor is germane, needless to say, to the proper characterization of the parental generation, since the cross-relatives are inevitably the outgroup, whereas father's brothers are the most common insiders and share in the great respects owed a father. In the kinship pattern as a whole, mother's sisters are grouped with mothers in an undistinguished category.

The rather general nature of this category is reflected in terminology for children. A woman's children appear simply as *tama* everywhere in Polynesia. But a man's children acquire the distinctive and honorable designations of *foha, tamaroa,* or *atalii.* The term *foha* refers to a bulb or tuber and connotes organic growth; *tamaroa* and *atalii* have chiefly connotations. Distinctions between a man's and a woman's child occur only in those western Polynesian societies that acknowledge the male–female dualism. In these instances, it would seem, a child who has taken a reduction through his father's sister picks up a gain directly through his father. The calculus of gains and losses operates relentlessly.

Sibling Generation

In its classification of siblings, Polynesia, speaking generally, asserts two main distinctions: relative seniority and sexual opposition.

The patterning of these distinctions is particularly precise in eastern Polynesia. Siblings of the same sex face each other as senior–juniors and ignore their gender; but siblings of opposite sex face each other by gender and ignore their relative rank. In other words, either gender is declared equivalent, or rank is; siblings are either on a scale of rank, or in two domains of gender. They may see themselves as hierarchical and close, or as divergent and distant. The terminology makes these distinctions quite clear. The terms for senior and junior establish metaphysical contrasts; those for siblings of opposite sex place both on the same plane.

All of Polynesia acknowledges the same key principles of classification, but where eastern Polynesia has finally fixed upon one unequivocal pattern, western Polynesia has experimented with various combinations of these two distinctions.

Eastern and western Polynesia are, of course, within the same kinship universe, as can be seen from the table of shared terms (see appendix 6). Thus their divergence on terms for senior sibling, even in instances when the principle of classification is the same, can only mean that on this issue the two subareas had reached a critical point of separation. There are other reasons for believing seniority to be the principle upon which a major divergence had occurred, and I shall discuss these shortly.

In eastern Polynesia the senior sibling is *tuakana* a term constructed upon *tua* cognate with *atua* or deity (cf. Tregear 1891). The reciprocal of *tuakana* is *teina,* which Elbert (1957) has defined from the Hawaiian as a "weak person," "trying to walk," "moving slowly." The reciprocals thus oppose god-like power to human weakness. The siblings of opposite sex, on the other hand, are both designated by semantically equivalent terms (*tuangane* and *tuahine*), both formed around the *tua* stem. These terms occur almost everywhere in Polynesia, and thus throughout all of the area this one concept of the god-like quality of brother and sister to each other stands as a formidable constant. In view of the high degree of variability of other kinship principles, we may safely assume that this exalted relationship of brother and sister to each other is a core trait of early Polynesian kinship. Of course, to speak of the brother–sister pattern as relatively invariant is to refer only to taxonomy. The implications of the principle for secondary terminologies—as in cross-relations—and for behavior are, needless to say, remarkably variable. Even so, the related concept, that of seniority is even more variable. On this issue, even terminology has been subjected to pressures for change.

In western Polynesia the contrast between senior and junior evokes a different image. The senior is often *ta'okete,* a term compounded of *ta'o,* meaning "under pressure," "under restraint," "weighing down," "keeping a secret," and of *kete,* or "abdomen." The term suggests the Melanesian idea (cf. Malinowski 1929) of magic stored in the abdomen, referring as it does to a force held weightily in check within the body. The reciprocal term for junior remains the same. The contrast is thus again between a strong force and that which is weak. The eastern Polynesian opposition, however, suggests two realms: one celestial, the other human; the western postulates a single physiological reference with a contained force at one extreme and weakness at the other. If we were to regard western Polynesia as the older, then we might speak of eastern Polynesia as having intensified the seniority distinctions. Quite obviously, eastern Polynesia is firmly committed to the senior–junior opposition; western Polynesia is uncertain. Altogether six of the nine western Polynesian societies have no general or standard terms of reference for senior sibling. These include such an old society as Manu'a, along with Tikopia, Futuna, Tokelaus, Pukapuka, and Ontong Java. Since Manu'a (with Futuna and Tikopia) has the *teina* term meaning "junior," it is reasonable to assume that the "senior" term present in cognate Tonga had been abandoned.

Whatever the history of seniority usages, these western Polynesian societies have set up different sets of distinctions between siblings of same and of opposite sex. In Tikopia, for example, siblings of same sex are *taina* to each other and those of opposite sex are *kave,* regardless of seniority. Taina has, here the connotation of endearment and of closeness. Kave, on the other hand, meaning "to send away," connotes estrangement. Thus the Tikopian sibling distinctions fall within the usual Polynesian concepts of placing the brother–sister pair into a separate category. But a new point of view has arisen. Both kinds of sibling pair are reduced; the same sex pair to low status and the opposite pair to nonstatus. Since the terms lack gender as well, the stripping process has been thorough. Pukapukan sibling terms are different, but in principle their meanings are in this radical Tikopian tradition.

Manu'a, the older culture, is closer to what must have been the earlier tradition. In the term *tei* for junior siblings, it retains the older usage. And while it has no standard terms for senior, it can describe, for example, older sister of a woman and of a man as *uso matua* and *tuafafine matua,* respectively (Mead 1930:126). Moreover, when issues of status become exigent, as in families of rank, the eldest sister joins the category of father's sister as ilamutu. Manu'a, in brief, is conversant with seniority. Still, indicative of western Polynesian pressures to subdue seniority, the standard term for siblings of same sex is *uso,* which in its meanings of "umbilical cord" and "heart of a tree" (Pratt 1960) emphasizes closeness rather than hierarchy. At the same time, *tausoga* for siblings of opposite sex lacks the exaltation of the *tua* terms. Western Samoa shows a different emphasis by elevating siblings of same sex as *tua'a,* the common Polynesian seniority term. In Manu'a, *tua'a* had become a title of special honor applied to the parents of a chief.

Futuna represents still another variant. Siblings of same sex are all reduced to *taina. Ta'okete* is then reserved for the exclusive use of the first-born brother or for the senior male of the senior line of the kin group. *Ta'okete* assumes then both a political and an absolute quality. Siblings of opposite sex are elevated to *tuanga'ane.* Reductions are balanced by elevations, but gender is lost.

The Tokelaus illustrate a variant of the Futunan type. Absolute seniority-juniority is expressed through *kimua-kimuli,* but same sex siblings are reduced to *taina;* and opposite sex siblings are in the standard tradition, *tuangane* and *tuafafine.*

Finally, among this group of societies that has rejected relative seniority, the most deviant is Ontong Java, which does not distinguish at all between the same sex and opposite sex sibling pair. The "brother" is simply *kainga,* or "kinsman," and the "sister" is *ave,* the "one sent away." This example caps the demonstration that the quality of the sibling terminology may depend upon the presence or absence of the relative seniority concept.

Among the three remaining western Polynesian societies which do acknowledge relative seniority, the sibling terminology does in fact follow the standard patterns. Only Niue varies the pattern by designating the sister as the *mahakitaga.* But the variation is, after all, minor, since as the equivalent of a father's sister in Tonga, she is raised up to a parallel exaltation with her brother.

Cousin Terms

A pattern of classification can define only one of the multiple interests of kinsmen in each other. A kinship classification by its very nature is exclusive and focal. Thus Polynesian ego generation classifications draw attention to generation, to seniority, and to the distinctions between complementary and equivalent siblings. By permitting the exclusion of distinctions between lineal and collateral descendants, they may create the impression that all are "siblings." In fact, the total kinship vocabulary is far more extensive than the standard terms indicate. What Mead has said about Manu'an kinship must surely be true of all Polynesian systems, namely, that all fine discriminations can be, and are, made. The question for Polynesian systems is not therefore whether they lack cousin (or uncle–aunt) terms or classifications, but rather the nature of these. The Futunan reference to "cousins" as *mataitama* ("headman's children"), or the Samoan *tasimai* ("first issue"), points out their honorable character, or the more neutral suffix *keke* defines a line as distinct from one's own.

Tending to ignore the cross-relationships altogether, and to minimize the importance of complementary respects between brother and sister, eastern Polynesia is prepared to distinguish only generally between lineal and collateral descent lines, that is, between own siblings and cousins. The distinction, however, is not grossly taxonomic. Cousins and siblings are not placed in truly separate categories, but are differentiated within the standard sibling category by means of seniority terms. For example, while siblings of same sex are *tuakana-teina* by virtue of their own order of birth, cousins or collateral siblings are senior–junior to one another by reason of seniority of their parents or of their ancestors. Thus a Maori will acknowledge and so honor a younger "cousin" as *tuakana,* but never a younger lineal sibling of same sex. In the important respect of seniority, then, eastern Polynesia fully recognizes the opposition, specifically the ascendant–deference opposition, between lineal and collateral lines. It seems clear, however, that the distinction is intended to demonstrate the transcendant importance of a senior line of descent and not the rather minor and/or general consideration that the offspring of one set of parents are really different from those of another. What is remarkable about this kind of eastern Polynesian distinction is its extraordinary flexibility and ambiguity.

Western Polynesia is, of course, far more complex in allowing for both the cross- and the lineal-collateral distinctions. The emphasis is here predictably upon patterns of cross-relations rather than upon seniority, with the result that distinctions are categorical and unambiguous. Again, where eastern Polynesia pays its respects to the senior or tuakana line, western Polynesia pays its respects primarily to the descendants of a sister's line. The respects as they affect cross-cousins need not be taxonomic, which is only one form of notation. In fact, despite the strong western Polynesian interest in the cross-relations, only Ontong Java and the Tokelaus specifically and consistently identify the cross-cousins terminologically. Elsewhere, and including the Marquesas, they are recognized behaviorally or by descriptive terms that characterize rather than classify.

Behavioral recognition ranges between the conceptual poles of avoidance and preferred marriage. At either extreme the theme is special honor. The Marquesas and Tonga, two related and ancient centers, favor cross-cousin marriage; all others who recognize the category enjoin avoidances. In accordance with their own specializations of status, in Tonga the fully aristocratic society brings together in marriage only the cross-cousins of high rank; the more democratic Marquesas encourage such marriages in all families. Marquesan cross-cousin marriage is unquestionably the behavioral response to the special ceremonial bond between a child and his father's sister (*tuehine*) and his mother's brother (*tunane*), the pahu pahu pair. A marriage with the child of the pahu pahu pair would thus presumably be fruitful and energetic, although Handy, it should be remarked, sees it more pragmatically as a means of bringing two families together. But all marriages bring families together. In this instance, cross-cousin marriage brings together two especially potent and thus significant lines.

Tongan cross-cousin marriage is more restricted, but in the same conceptual dimension. Among families of rank for whom the fahu is most consequential, the otherwise divergent lines of a brother and sister are brought together. The fahu relationship necessarily favors the matrilateral form of cross-cousin marriage, the nephew being in the position of demanding his maternal uncle's daughter. His superiority as the fahu is then fully in accord with the conventional Tongan doctrine that the husband is superior to his wife and to her brothers. As fahu, he adds superiority over his father-in-law. In chiefly families, this marriage overcomes the distance that might otherwise exist between political rights of a fahu and the insularity of separate lines. Taxonomy is surely not irrelevant in kinship. And the fact that in the Marquesas and in Tonga the cross-cousin marriage is seen as a "sibling" union emphasizes all the more the point that the cross-relationships are so extraordinary they can be used to overcome one form of the incest taboo. In this respect, these cross-cousin marriages are, as I have already observed, the conceptual equivalents of the Hawaiian brother–sister marriage. In the Hawaiian case, understandably, it is the potency of seniority and general genealogical quality that is recognized as overcoming the power of the brother–sister tapu.

The point about the relationship between kinship taxonomy and behavior is not that single patterns are formed, but that variability results. Pukapuka and Tikopia do not recognize categorical distinctions between siblings and cross-cousins and do not allow them to marry. Both established rather special respects that succeed in differentiating behaviorally and descriptively siblings from parallel cousins and cross-cousins. Pukapuka, elaborating on the theme of the cross-sex versus same-sex division, recognizes first the special relationship between cousins of opposite sex, who are said to be *kainga wakama* to each other. By contrast, cousins of same sex are *teina* to each other, mutual juniors. Such cousins have equivalence, but on the grade of low status. Wakama relatives are higher. The children of opposite sex of kainga wakama gain in stature. They enter into avoidance respects, become sacred to each other and become known as *wale atua,* that is, god-like. The children of same sex of the kainga wakama continue as taina. In Pukapuka, it will be recalled, there are neither brother–sister avoidances nor cross-uncle–aunt relationships. The base line for the respect patterns has moved down the generations. Cousins of opposite sex become the equivalent of cross-uncle and aunt, and the wale atua become the precise mirror image—as the avoidance pair—to the marrying cross-cousins of Tonga and the Marquesas.

Tikopia is back with the conventional balance of generations with its recognition of the cross-uncle–aunt pattern of complementary respects and indulgences. Brother and sister are joined in mutual respects. The major distinction, then, is between parallel cousins, who stand toward each other as *fakalaui,* that is "without restraint," and cross-cousins who are by contrast *fakapariki,* or under "avoidance respect." Obviously, as Firth observes, the cross-cousins carry out the roles of their parents. The father's sister's children claim the ascendancy of their mother's sanctity and are superior in honor to the matrilateral cross-cousins. In Tikopia the fahu is transformed from power to honor alone or, to state the principle more abstractly, from action to form.

Whether the distinctions are taxonomic or behavioral, the cross-cousin pattern asserts duality of line as a corollary of the more basic principle of the necessary separation by complement of brother and sister. But since duality is, after all, a very general concept, it can enter into a variety of patterns even in a region so closely knit as western Polynesia.

Thus, the Tokelaus, a very small demographic version of the Samoan social system, represent still another pattern of duality. Here, cousin terminology has been elaborated to the fullest degree. Tokelauan taxonomy makes all the distinctions: patrilateral and matrilateral cross-cousin; parallel cousin of opposite sex on father's side, and parallel cousin of opposite sex on mother's side. At the same time, it can combine into one common category (*uso,* in the Manu'an manner) all same-sex siblings and cousins, uncles and aunts who are collaterally close, and into another (*tausoga*) all siblings of opposite sex along with all distant relatives of opposite sex regardless of generation. The contrast between *uso* and *tausoga* illustrates the point of view: same sex is close; opposite sex is more distant. In its general tenor, this Tokelauan formulation of duality is standard for western Polynesia. What is unique is its taxonomic rendition. The merging of generations refers to still another principle of classification to which I shall turn directly. The cross-cousin terms, *ilamutu* and *tuatina* both merge generations. Ego's *ilamutu* are the entire line of descent from his father's sister, who may or may not be his sacred mother (*matua sa*). His *tuatina,* on the other hand, are the entire line that includes his mother's brother and descendants. The weighting of honor through semantics and degree of specificity is clearly on the father's side. The terminology looks like "Omaha." Yet it hardly clarifies anything to use this label, since Tokelauan kinship structure has little in common with the common Omaha system with its exogamous patrilineal clans and its cross-cousin marriage. In any case, one must explain a variant from the point of view of its own genetic stock and not from a general model.

We may say then that Tokelauan cousin terminology reflects western Polynesian principles of kinship which elsewhere in the area appear in behavioral rather than in taxonomic form. Specifically, the merging of generations states taxonomically the behavioral principle of the linear relationships proceeding from mother's brother and father's sister. In the fahu specifically, and in the Samoan, Tikopian, and Pukapukan systems generally, a parallel relationship is set up between the line of a father's sister vis-à-vis the line of mother's brother. It seems thus redundant to mention that the matrilateral–patrilateral distinction clearly delineates these lines.

This is not to say that in the Tokelaus taxonomy and behavior have finally been harmonized. For example, it is the father's eldest sister only who is matua sa, or "sacred mother," and it is her descendants alone who have the ilamutu prerogatives, even though *all* father's sisters' children carry the honorific designation. Similarly, it is only the mother's elder brother who has ritual privileges. But since tuatina is generally the subordinate status, it is hardly relevant that his prerogatives be restricted to the senior line. The extreme dualism expressed in cross-cousin terms is fully in harmony, on the other hand, with the marked structural dualism that separates residence and the domestic economy from leadership descent, and ritual relations. The combination of patrilineal preferences with matrilocal and sororal households inevitably separates siblings from cousins, and matrilateral and patrilateral cousins from each other. This factor of separation probably accounts for distinctions descriptively drawn between parallel cousins of mother's and of father's side. However, the examples of dualistic Pukapuka and of matrilocal Ontong Java, both with nondifferentiating cousin terminology, reminds us again that kinship taxonomy is not bound by any single formula.

Variations

Seen from the perspective of western Polynesia, the kinship configurations just reviewed must appear bewilderingly variable. No two western Polynesian kinship systems are identical even when they are as historically cognate as Western and Eastern Samoa. By contrast, the kinship patterns of eastern Polynesia seem exceptionally stable, although, as we see at once, even these fall into several types. In itself, social variability is not a remarkable phenomenon. Islands experiencing only sporadic contacts with one another will inevitably diverge. Our interest at this point, however, is not with general variability, but with characteristic and systematic direction. Variability in this instance is not random. We recognize at once a major axis of kinship variability along which eastern Polynesia becomes differentiated from western Polynesia, and two minor axes along which each has become internally differentiated. Insofar as both the major and the minor axes represent variant forms of the same basic principles of classification, we may assume their interdependence. If we can explain internal variability in western Polynesia, we should, using similar premises, be able to explain the major differentiation of the kinship systems of the two great regions of Polynesia. Both forms of differentiation can be described in terms of (a) principles of dualism, and (b) principles of seniority. We have already touched on the suggestion that dualism and seniority may be moving in opposition to each other. This suggestion, to repeat, arises from sibling terminology which states the principle that sex equivalence goes with seniority, sexual complementarity does not. The principle does not, of course, specify incompatibility, but judging from the patterns of variability it opens up, so to speak, a choice between emphasis upon one or the other. Seen in broad perspective, western Polynesia seems to have been abandoning seniority in favor of dualism, while eastern Polynesia has been following the reverse course in abandoning dualism in terminology in favor of seniority. At the same time, Tonga a primary center for the west, and the Marquesas a primary center for the east, have evidently retained both dualism and seniority.

The nature of the choice is not difficult to understand from a Polynesian point of view. Either preference yields a hierarchical pattern—a Polynesian necessity. The patterns, however, are different. Dualism is qualitative and categorical, while seniority is in practice quantitative and relative. From this observation we may go further and say: Dualism plus seniority allows for the most formal and rigid organization of kinship statuses; dualism without seniority focuses attention on more narrowly familial or domestic status; seniority without dualism offers the freest and most expansive statement of kinship statuses. These propositions suggest some of the broader implications of choice, but do not account for the choices, for which much more specific historical information is needed.

Evidence for high variability of the dualism–seniority pattern, particularly in Western Polynesia, points unmistakably to acts of choice. Each element in the pattern is variable, whether we deal with taxonomy or with behavior. Among the nine western Polynesian societies, only Tonga, Uvea, and Niue use regular terms for senior sibling of same sex. Samoa preserves the junior term (tei) of the pairing. Six elevate the father's sister; four elevate the mother's brother. Six, as we would expect, elevate the sister's children, but only four do so formally through the fahu. All, however, have institutionalized avoidance respects between brother and sister, while three (Samoa, Tonga, Tokelaus) carry out complete avoidances. With respect to terms, we observe a parallel instability. Ilamatu (or cognates) is the most variable, referring most commonly to sister's son, but also to mother's brother (Ontong Java), father's sister (Manu'a), and descendants of father's sister (Tokelaus). Differentiating terms for mother's brother and father's sister are only somewhat more stable.

The constancy of avoidance respects between brother and sister is consistent, of course, with the view that this, rather than a concept of descent, is the nuclear relationship in western Polynesian dualism. The central importance of the brother–sister as defining the cross-relationships has been recognized by Williamson, who saw in the relationship a matrilineal vestige, but more incisively by Mead, who brought out its structural significance. What she says about Manu'a applies with equal force to all of western Polynesia: "The *ilamatu* and *tama fafine* relationships are really the outcome of a brother and sister relationship, rather than of special attitudes towards father's sister or mother's brother (1930:138)."

In short, the relationship between the type of brother–sister relationship and the organization of a wider kinship configuration is unquestionably complex. But it is not random. What specific conditions, we may now ask, act upon the relationship and thus upon the configuration? This question cannot be answered satisfactorily in the light of present knowledge. Some kind of answer is suggested, however, by what we know of the fahu. The fahu, an expression of the power and authority of the father's sister, develops, as we have seen, as a political prerogative. When it does so, we observe first that it begins to overshadow the relationship between a man and his sister—an observation Mead has made about the fahu equivalent in Western Samoa, and which is clearly observable in Futuna and Uvea. In Tonga, Futuna, and Uvea, we observe again how the pattern of respects as it affects brother and sister and the cross-relatives is drawn away from the domestic sphere, where it had originally formed, and is converted to political utility by chiefs and the highest-ranking families. In short, there is some reason to suppose that the pattern is responsive to political interests. We know, for example, specifically, in the case of Tonga, that the political forms of fahu, of tamaha, and of the Tui Tonga fefine were relatively recent developments. When the fahu became a political prerogative, it had ceased in Tonga, as in Futuna and Uvea, to be an ordinary kinship usage.

Insofar as respects conform to a calculus of balances, the cross-relationships tend as a whole to form themselves into coherent patterns of mutual dependency. From the standpoint of structural theory alone, we might expect that all other cross-relationships would depend upon the brother–sister pattern, simply because this is a central pattern in almost all Polynesian kinship systems: the concept of brother and sister as a divergent pair underlies the cross-relationships in general. Is there also empirical support? As Appendix 7 shows, eastern and western Polynesia are moving in opposite directions on this point. Eastern Polynesia has no brother–sister respects and no elaboration of cross-relationships. In western Polynesia, respects and the cross-relationships coincide. The Marquesas, the one eastern Polynesian society to acknowledge cross-relationships, have no formal brother–sister respects. But preferential cross-cousin marriage may be taken to be a form of respect. The Marquesan example indicates, however, how complex and variable the patterning of the cross-relations can be. In western Polynesia, for example, the patterning of respects ranges from extreme avoidances to general expressions of deference. Six societies impose various forms of avoidance, among them Pukapuka, which ignores true brothers and sisters and places the greatest restrictions upon the distant wale atua. We might expect to find that the strongest respect patterns (i.e., avoidance) would be associated with the fullest elaboration of cross-relations. Such an association is likely, but certainly not absolute. The balances, after all, can move in several directions. There is, in fact, no precise rule that relates degree of respects with degree of cross-relationship development. From a more general point of view, however, it does appear that a gradation of respects, starting with the strong avoidances of Samoa and Tonga and proceeding through the more general and weaker respects of Uvea, Tipokia, and Niue, leads finally to near extinction of brother–sister respects in all of eastern Polynesia, except at its archaic Marquesan center.

Reduction in function could conceivably lead to reduction in terminology as well. Function, however, does not demand terminology; it is terminology that demands a function. Reduction, in other words, is a downhill process; once begun, it should meet few impediments. Building up is, by contrast, a more energetic and more difficult process.

The question of reduction versus building up comes immediately to the fore when eastern and western Polynesian taxonomies are compared. Murdock (1949) has reasoned on long-range logical grounds that the simple form of the Hawaiian system was the historical basis for the more discriminatory taxonomies of Malayo-Polynesia. Burrows, on the other hand, interprets contemporary (short-range) distributions to mean reduction. He notes, for example,

> . . . part of the western Polynesian kinship complex emphasizing certain close collateral relatives was abandoned in central Polynesia [eastern Polynesia] in favor of a simple kinship system of the type known as "Hawaiian." This type even lacks specific terms distinguishing father from mother. The distribution of such terms supports the suggestion that this simple Polynesian terminology is not old, but was brought about by the abandonment of some old terms (1938:125).

More recently, Lane (1961) has presented evidence of reduction from "Crow," a dual system based on matrilineal affiliation and descent in Banks and New Hebrides, attributing simplification to great population reduction. If the Hawaiian system is a reduced version of, let us say, Tokelauan, the demographic factor cited by Lane cannot in this particular case be a valid explanation.

Undoubtedly a variety of powerful circumstances affect taxonomy, but in the final analysis it is the logic of the classification itself that must be the ruling factor. Since all Polynesian kinship categorizations denote honors, respects, and worths, they must be most sensitive to changes in concepts of status. The examples of two lately formed societies in western Polynesia, namely, Pukapuka and the Tokelaus, leaves no doubt that both reduction and elaboration have been going on simultaneously. The question of a long-range trend, however, is not that easily put aside. The historical facts are that eastern Polynesia has simpler classifications and is also the more recent area. Such old Polynesian centers as Tonga, Samoa, and the Marquesas have dualistic terminology, an indication, though not conclusive proof, of retention of older forms.

Reduction is but a general term for a process that demands a more specific description. Specifically, reduction has been shown to be a transformation from dualism to bilaterality. Dualism postulates two essentially nonrivalrous, but hierarchically organized tracks of social status. Bilaterality concedes a single and thus a fully rivalrous track. Dualism, as I have said before, is a qualitative categorization, whereas bilaterality, when it is differentiated by relative seniority, is quantitive. Thus dualism tends toward the formal, bilaterality toward the pragmatic and, in a broad sense, the political. The shift from dualism to bilaterality may be considered, therefore, as one aspect of a broader political process.

The political process, referring specifically to the pragmatic interests of chiefs in power, can affect kinship classifications and behavior from two sides: kinship usages are drawn directly into political service, as in the examples of fahu; and they are withdrawn from common circulation. The political is, of course, status in the public domain, just as kinship per se is status in the domestic domain.

In "kinship society," both domains are extensions of a common status system. We may think of that extension associated with office, rank, and power as the *public status system,* and the categories of terms and behaviors of kinship in their strictly familial aspect as the *domestic status system.* The public status system uses kinship as a means of entry into still higher categories of honor and power. Domestic status is smaller. It may, in parallel fashion, extend into family offices; ultimately it stands as an end in itself, as the final and irreducible measure of personal honor. In the domestic status system, all persons are at least hypothetically superior at one point or another to someone else. All kinship statuses are fully relative. In aristocracy, on the other hand, public statuses become fixed. Thus, if a person has a fixed status in one order, he is assured of a relative status in the other. The two orders are not in balance in terms of magnitude, but they are in a qualitative equilibrium. The domestic status system stands in the way of extinction of status.

From this point of view, the simplification of taxonomy implies a reduction in the significance of the domestic status system. In eastern Polynesia, the etiquette of kinship behavior is also reduced. There are no brother–sister respects and no significant etiquettes in the cross-relationships. Seniority offers a single quantitative distinction in place of the variety of qualitative kinship polarities. The qualitative distinctions function dyadically, in principle. Quantitative distinctions of seniority allow for every range of discrimination, from that between one senior and one junior to that between one senior and a community of juniors. In the latter case, statuses can become fixed in the public status system. In this special sense, public and domestic status seem to evolve in concert. In eastern Polynesia, the quantitative principle has taken over in public and in domestic status. The gap of honor and honoring between the highest and lowest ranks is actually widened. A qualitative difference has constancy, but quantitative differences can be diminished almost to the point of extinction.

The case for reduction in kinship categorization as a byproduct of broader shifts in basic concepts of status is handily argued in general terms; a strong case should be more detailed. We can, in fact, see the process of reduction more minutely. We can see it in what is clearly a step-by-step extinction of those categories expressing duality. In western Polynesia, for example, duality is asserted at three generation levels, parent, ego, child. The Tokelaus are the only example of such a three-generation assertion, however. The common taxonomic dualities are at parent and child generations. In eastern Polynesia outside of the Marquesas, the cross-uncle and aunt duality has been eliminated, and iramatu has been extended to all nephews and nieces—a variant form of attenuation by generality. In the Society and Hawaiian Islands the iramutu kin term has disappeared, and extinction of duality is complete. We may assume extinction as an historical probability because Maori, having broken away earlier, still retains iramatu. Conceivably, the Hawaiian herald and executioner, the royal iramaku, is the last vestige of what was formerly a kinship term.

Kinship is surely sufficiently independent of politics, of line of descent, of residence, and of any other single factor so that changes in categorizations of terms and patterns of behavior will not ever follow a fully consistent course with respect to any single variable. The categorizations define reciprocal honors; the terms act very much like titles; and variability in western Polynesia, in particular, is considerable precisely for those classifications which entail the most specific honors. But "sensitivity" to status does not correlate rigorously with particular changes in status system. Nevertheless, one broad and very general observation may be valid: The growth of the pragmatic interest runs counter to the domestic status system; political expediency runs counter to form.

Evidence for the association between political pragmatism and kinship reduction is definitely not conclusive. Neither, it must be said, is it inconsequential. Taking into account both taxonomic and behavioral distinctions, we list four societies as having fully reduced kinship systems—Niue, Mangaia, Society, Hawaii. Niue, the most politically "open" of the western Polynesian societies, has evidently been seriously reduced from its previous and probable Samoan–Tongan type. Mangaia is a late derivative of Society, having been separated off well after the Maori had left. Thus a possible date for Society kinship reduction could be the short period between A.D. 1350 and 1500. Easter Island terminology is so close to the fully reduced pattern that we may include it as an example without fear of forcing the argument. These five societies had eventually achieved the most dispersed kinship communities. Marquesan society was not deficient in the pragmatic interest. It had not, however, abandoned its commitment to the principles of kinship unity; and though peoples were indeed dispersed, they attached themselves to chiefs as kinsmen. Kin dispersal had not, to be sure, gone too far in Mangaia. But then Mangaia was probably already in the late Society tradition. Mangareva, with its iramutu terms for all nephews and nieces, seems at first glance to defy this apparent rule. When we take note, however, of its history as a probable branch of the Marquesas that had established itself after A.D. 1100, its degree of reduction from its parent culture is, in fact, quite substantial.

Reduction proceeds in all areas of categorization. In western Polynesia, seniority and dualism offered alternatives and it was seniority that retreated. In eastern Polynesia, more remote from the Melanesian sources, it was dualism that gave way. Under the pressures of restless status systems, neither concept has a claim to permanence. In the east, even seniority had given way as a classifier to more complex and more expedient criteria. Perhaps it is only a matter of time before the concept of more expedient criteria would have invaded the domestic status system as well. Kinship systems always stand for the superiority of the organic, the categorical, and the formal. In the end, they are no more immune to the advantages of the "made," the expedient, and the flexible than any other system of social order.

22

The Economics of Status

CIVILIZATIONS RARELY DEVELOP UPON AS RUDIMENTARY AN ECOnomic basis as that of Polynesia. The ancient Polynesians were, of course, well-nourished; and their chiefs were often super-nourished. But their diet of palm fruits, of root crops, and fish, occasionally lifted up with the flavor of pork, fowl, juicy dog, or human, was crude, more appropriate for "simple" tropical forest farmers than for ambitious states. To meet the costs of military conquest, of religious monuments, and of public works, states need ready reserves of negotiable merchandise and of high-energy foods that store well. Except for starchy (though vitamin-rich) poi, Polynesia had no ready food reserves to compare with the cereals of Europe and the Near East, or the maize and beans of the American Indian. The Polynesian reserves were on the trees, in the ground, or in the sea. What was harvested was almost without exception destined for immediate consumption. If other civilizations have grown upon economic doctrines of conservationism, the Polynesian has fulfilled itself more upon the opposite doctrine of giving away and of eating well. Mariner's patron, Chief Finow, divined at once the distinction between the European and the Tongan economy. Having pondered a description of money, he explained to his more civilized protégé that Europeans are unfortunate in that they would be drawn to hoarding (Mariner 1827:I, 263). The Polynesian economies preferring generosity to accumulation illustrate both the limitations and possibilities of the absence of capital.

Only a few societies—and these like Tahiti, Hawaii, and the Marquesas were among the more monumental—had such rudimentary capital as livestock. And only in the Hawaiian Islands were pigs numerous enough to be classed as a capital reserve available for exchange. In the main, pig and fowl were barnyard creatures, minor elements in the economy, and nowhere (as in Melanesia and New Guinea) outstanding symbols of wealth and status. Like crops, they were consumption goods, and so there was little of the compulsion toward excess of production that elsewhere starts primitive economies on the road to modernization. Durable goods were for the most part products of honorable production and destined for honorable use. Whether made by tohunga or by wives of chiefs, they were scarce commodities circulating among elites and symbolizing elite exchanges: Items such as ornaments, feather capes and helmets, or girdles, or finely woven mats and tapa cloth serving specific symbolic purposes can be considered as "capital" only in the narrowest sense but as capital, nevertheless, since they were also traded and converted into other goods, on a small scale. Utilitarian objects were household goods and moved slowly. Polynesia did not ignore commerce; it subordinated commerce—utilitarian exchange—to a greater interest in ritual circulation of goods.

If we choose to think of Polynesian economies in terms of so modern a concept as "gross national product," we may reckon services as its third major category of "income." It is in this realm of productivity that Polynesian economies begin to approach the diversification of complex societies. The guilds of Samoa and the professionalization of skills in Open and Stratified societies still reflect ritual concerns more than they do utilitarian growth of the economy. Yet insofar as role diversity enlarges the scope of "payments" (gifts of reciprocal exchanges), thus intensifying the movement of goods and spurring patrons to increase production and hasten collection so as to come within the sphere of elite services, the effect upon the economy is stimulating. Role diversity, while it stimulates patrons to energize, so to speak, the economy, creates at the same time a new and energetic elite of artisans, priests, poets, genealogists, custodians, and administrators, who are themselves patrons. The economic effect is doubled, but the impact is more upon velocity of circulation than upon increment of commodities. In material commodities, Polynesia remained forever primitive.

The economic primitivism of Polynesia appears in strongest relief against the picture of economic specialization in the much smaller societies of Micronesia, Melanesia, and New Guinea. By contrast with these "simpler" societies, the Polynesian economic processes were rudimentary. Aboriginal Polynesia had no entrepeneurship in goods, no systems of finance, no concepts of interest, no currency, no creditor–debtor relationships, no systematized trade, and none but the most elementary systems of temporary accumulation. The quality of an economy then is no direct reflection of political integration. The economy expresses more directly the character of the status system. In Polynesia, the simplicity of the economy is an accurate image of the rather single-minded and elementary conceptions of goods held by the chiefs.

As distinct from general economic activities, an economic system has always a distinctive character that accords with the social system of which it is an integral part. The Polynesian economy takes its character from the forms of aristocracy in the area. Granted, Polynesian aristocracies moved through a range of variations that included serious challenges to the aristocratic tradition, that tradition was never overcome. All Polynesian economies may be considered, therefore, as aristocratic economies. Precisely because market features were so conspicuously absent, there is reason to regard the Polynesian economies as elementary forms of the aristocratic type. What distinguishes the aristocratic economy from other types is its insistence that all respected economic activity conform to the standards of genealogical rank. First and foremost, the economy in all its phases—production, circulation, and consumption—serves to measure, to allocate, and to validate honor. All economic systems must conform in some degree to utilitarian or maximizing principles if they are to deal with scarce means, and the ancient Polynesian system was no exception. For that matter, no economic system, including the contemporary market economies, ever does, nor can it, yield fully to sheer utilitarianism as a dominant principle. All economies work out some relationship between the utilitarian and the honorific. It would be simplifying to say merely that aristocracies emphasize the honorific as against the utilitarian. The point is rather that aristocracies favor a particular patterning of honorific–utilitarian. This pattern, moreover, is not rigid but variable and evolutionary in that it changes with changes in the status system. What can be said of a general nature, though, is that the major concern of the ariki is with the honorific aspect in the main, and that lower ranks are concerned more with the utilitarian aspects of the economy. It is this particular relationship that gives rise to variability.

The apparent relationship between rank and a focus either on honor or utility suggests, offhand, that when the traditional authority of the ariki is high, the economy will be slanted toward the honorific, and that when lower ranks become dominant, the bias will shift towards the utilitarian. This suggestion is generally supported by the information. The relationship, however, is more complex, because efficacy, a utilitarian measure, is also one of the tests of ariki status. Honor, then, tends to dominate economic circulation and consumption everywhere in Polynesia, while production tends to represent a balance between the role of the sacred, an aspect of honor, and the technical. But this is a statement of the economy from the point of view of the chiefs. Seen from the point of view of the commoners, the economy is in all respects basically utilitarian. The preoccupation of the commoners in almost all Polynesian societies was with subsistence pure and simple. In most societies the commoner had neither the obligations nor privileges of a full ritual life. Thus, if the commoners were poorer than the chiefs, the economic pressures upon them were correspondingly lesser. Economic pressure rested most heavily on the ariki, and because the pressure on them for maintaining a high rate of circulation of goods in validation of their status was so great, they were inevitably the driving force of the economy as a whole.

The distinction I have drawn between honor and utility as economic motives is but a rephrasing of the older and still useful distinction between prestige and subsistence economies. These two economies, as they have been described, differ in the ends they serve and in their manner of operation. Subsistence economies are essentially rational, conforming closely to economic standards of maximizing scarcity in all three phases of production, exchange, and consumption. The prestige economy has always an atmosphere of sheer extravagance, which is, in fact, its distinctive feature. The center of attention, though, is not on wastefulness, but on form, on the correct manner of doing things. The subsistence economy is narrow; the prestige economy, broad.

The terms "prestige" and "subsistence" economies may give the unfortunate impression that a society has two economies, one devoted to prestige and the other to nutrition. The terms are meant rather to call attention to economic duality, to a polarization of attitudes. Having posed the issue of duality, we need to understand its true nature. That these opposite economic attitudes may conflict is clear enough from the example of Mangareva, where the economic demands of status were at the expense of the subsistence of the weak. The Mangarevan example points to circumstances, essentially those of poverty, when these attitudes are in inherent conflict and suggests, therefore, that conflict between them is always latent. Mangareva, however, was exceptional, and all other Polynesian societies sustained these two attitudes in a complementary relationship.

I do not think it is stretching the meaning of sanctity too far to say that the prestige economy was in ancient Polynesia the sacred economy, for it is concerned either with ritual associated with the gods or with chiefly power, which was basically a sacred power. In that case, the subsistence economy is the secular economy. The relationship of prestige to subsistence aspects of the economy is in effect parallel to and an extension, in fact, of the sacred–secular complementarity. The two attitudes oppose one another in the same way that the sacred–secular oppose each other, by encroachment. Under conditions of economic stress, and particularly when lower ranks achieve social importance, the status part of the economy tends to convert to more utilitarian purposes. The sacred part of the economy, in other words, becomes progressively desanctified. The reverse is also true. The subsistance and utilitarian interests of the economy are drawn into the sacred and honorific realm, as when craft guilds with their religious and honorific prerogatives are formed. These shifts in boundary between the two economic attitudes are no mere changes in abstract realms, but reflections of active status rivalry and of intense social conflict. They are, hence, of the greatest social interest.

The oppositions and instabilities of relationships between these complementary attitudes disturb the economy as a whole. There is, in fact, only one economy, one set of material resources, and one source of manpower to service both aspects. In one respect, therefore, an expansion of one aspect is at the expense of the other. The central concept of modern economic theory, the rational management of scarce means, applies then to the Polynesian economy as it does to our own, for with a dual and contradictory set of pressures, the economy faces scarcity no matter how rich the material resources. The subsistence factor in the economy is inevitably the more stable, for it fluctuates only with the relatively small changes in population (over the short run). The status factor on the other hand, is, by definition, expansive. Expansiveness, extravagance, exuberance, conspicuous display, prodigality—these are the requirements of economic utilization for the chiefly ranks. These honorific criteria have significance only against the constant of scarcity. The status economy, in short, is always an economy of scarcity. Status itself is by definition a scarce commodity. And so long as wealth remains both a criterion and a prerogative of status, its significance, like that of currency, depends upon its scarcity. Much of the character of a society depends upon how the economic problem of scarcity in its status aspect is managed. The possible solutions are few. Productivity can be increased; the food supply (subsistence aspect) can be squeezed tighter; enemy tribes can be raided, subdued, or conquered, bringing in their resources; tightening of the subsistence aspect can be general or selective, that is, imposed on the commoners; chiefs can contend with one another for scarce supplies; and, finally, the scale of status spending can be reduced. All of these solutions are actually found in Polynesia. In every instance the solution chosen had a profound effect upon the social system as a whole. In every instance, too, the solution followed an economic rationale. Economic rationality, in short, is no less a feature of the status side of the economy than it is of the subsistence side. The difference between the two sides is not one of economic rationality but of standards of utility.

I have suggested that the honorific side of the economy is associated with chiefs and the subsistence side with commoners. This distinction can be carried a step further by suggesting that the honorific side is associated with the public economy, that is, with the broad circulation of goods, and that the subsistence side is associated with the domestic or household economy, that is, with the narrow and internal circulation of goods. The distinction between a public and a domestic economy is related to the parallel distinction I have already drawn between public and domestic status systems. The chiefs, representing the public status system, utilize the economy in its interests. The domestic economy refers to the organization of production and the circulation of goods within the narrower orbits of familial kinship. The standards of utility differ in these two economic spheres even in chiefly houses.

This distinction between public and domestic economic spheres is a necessary one if we are to understand the economic role of the chiefs. Functionalist theory (cf. Hogbin 1934, Sahlins 1958) attributes to the chief the role of economic redistributor with the utilitarian function of rationally allocating foodstuffs and other materials. While he does so in a ritual manner, the theory maintains, the effect is to produce a necessary reallocation of goods. The chief satisfies his honor and the economic needs of his community at the same time. The theory is appealing because it follows the satisfying logic of dealing with the end product. The chief's sense of honor, the whole organization of status, are but means to the one end of organizing the economy so that all subsistence needs are met. Even extravagant and conspicuous consumption, Malinowski has argued, serves to promote morale, to enhance the standing of the chief and so enable him to be even more effective in his economic role. Sahlins has carried this general theory one step further, insisting that the power of the chief, therefore, is proportional to the richness of the resources he must manage. Power enables the chief to carry out his economic role. The larger that role, the more power he must have. As Sahlins sees it, stratification in Polynesia is essentially a measure of chiefly economic efficacy. The special merit of Sahlins' version of functionalist economic theory is that unlike the older Malinowskian statement, essentially a philosophical reflection, his can be verified or not. As Sahlins argued his case, the degree of chiefly power and of social stratification should be greatest in materially rich societies and least in the poor societies. Mangaia and Mangareva, however, are outstanding examples of poor societies with strong chiefs and marked stratification. On the other hand, Maori and Manu'a are far richer and have weaker chiefships and systems of graded rank rather than social stratification. The correlation sought by Sahlins does not hold because the role of the chief in the economy is more complex than his analysis has made it out to be.

The point is that the chief's role in the economy is directed by dual interests, that of his honor and that of the well-being of his community. These interests are not necessarily incompatible or antagonistic; ideally they are in harmony. But since this ideal is rarely realized, the chief must juggle the two components, following, however, two fundamental rules: he must meet all obligations of honor, and he must win and hold support. We saw a similar problem in kinship in the balancing of the ideal of high-quality descent lines against the more pragmatic necessity of attracting followers. Within the broad guidelines of Polynesian principles of status, the manner of juggling, and the outcome, are necessarily a matter of chance, of unpredictable circumstances. Strong chiefships, which are always associated with social stratification, represent, as we have seen, the outcome of severe status rivalry. This outcome is indeed predictable. What is not predictable is the nature of the engagement in status rivalry and how it will draw upon the economy. We can, however, describe some of the characteristic ways in which Polynesian chiefs have utilized the economy for its dual purposes. In a general fashion I have described some of these ways in the specific accounts of social structure. The present chapter focuses more directly upon the economic roles of the chiefs.

The Economic Roles of Chiefs: Production

Karl Polanyi succeeded admirably in defining fundamental economic types through their systems of exchange. There is no doubt that in Polynesia, too, the systems of exchange or, preferably, the circulation of goods can differentiate economic variability quite sharply. Even so, the organization of production, the technical facts of scarcity and abundance, and cultural attitudes toward produce, foods, and commodities, as well as the value placed upon productivity as an end itself, are also important economic variables. They are not mere reflections of the systems of exchange but are combined with exchange systems in varying ways.

Logically, the first question asked about production is quantitative. Are the societies rich or poor, are their habitats fertile or infertile? Rich societies with fertile lands advance in one direction; poor societies with more barren lands stand still and make do. We already know that the quantitative factor does not work quite so directly in Polynesia. But the fact that a condition does not produce a uniform result does not minimize its significance. Quantity of production is indeed a crucial economic condition, with profound social and cultural consequences. In Polynesia productivity was a general measure of chiefly efficacy. Poverty was demeaning. Abundance brought out the cultural patterns in their full splendor. Scarcity reduced them to their most meager forms. Abundance supported rich and costly rituals. Scarcity stripped ritual life to the bone. Productivity affected the forms power took, but not its forcefulness. In this connection we need to bear in mind that to Polynesian aristocracies form was foremost and sheer power itself a pragmatic necessity.

When we consider productivity from the point of view of the chief —the most significant perspective—we must take account of the two-sided nature of his role. One side is his religious role, based on the general theory that his sanctity and his mana are in the final analysis responsible for the well-being of his community. The other side is his technical role, based on his authority to direct labor and his knowledge of techniques of agriculture and of fishing. The relationship between these two sides is variable, while each stood as a measure of specific qualities of efficacy, religious and technical. The logic of the Polynesian theory of chiefly mana would lead us to expect a single measure of efficacy. In practice this was not the case. Polynesians more often than not distinguished between the religious and the technical role of chiefs, between religious and technical efficacy. It is to these distinctions and their forms of variability that we turn first.

In the Traditional societies, the religious side of production was either the province of the highest level ariki, of ariki in concert with priests, or of priests alone. The technicalities of production were the exclusive prerogatives of low-level chiefs. Among the Maori, for example, only village chiefs of rangatira rank organized the work. The ariki, as chiefs, had no role in production at all except insofar as they were priests (tohunga), in which case they officiated at agricultural rituals, but only at the level of the hapu (Segment III). On the other hand, the higher-level (Segment II) chiefs of ariki rank, the heads of iwi, took a commanding role in exchange or circulation. Since the hapu was the productive unit, we cannot say that production was a household activity; it was rather a low-level public activity. Chiefly mana may have affected the well-being of the iwi generally, but in the specifics of agriculture the public generally contributed its own mana to the growing crops; the chiefs did not monopolize the religious side of the production.

Maori illustrates two principles which hold firm in the Traditional societies: the religious management of production is more honorable than its technical management; and management of circulation is more honorific than the management of production generally. Underlying these principles is the valid enough assumption of an appropriate division of the economy in such a way that the commoners bring food into being and freely honor their chiefs with offerings. The chiefs put their honorable mark, so to speak, on the produce, send it into circulation as honorably marked produce, and the populace—having started the cycle with food as raw material—receives it back in a new and honorific form. This economic cycle belongs to the status aspect of the economy. Food, of course, nourishes no matter how ingested and this cycle is not to be described as non-nutritive. But that is not the point. Nutrition is in the Traditional societies more or less a domestic issue. Nor is this status cycle an ordinary religious affair within which food, as Mauss has reasoned, conveyed to its consumers some mystical quality or supernatural powers. Polynesians valued food enormously without, however, devising a specific theory as to its spiritual nature. The Maori considered their kumara crop to possess the vital spirit, called *mauri*, but did not consider this mauri as transferable to people. What the cycle transmitted was honor, merit, worth. These status attributes were not contained in the food but in the action that conveyed the food. Mauss, who had so brilliantly demonstrated the spiritual significance of economic exchange in the primitive world, argued needlessly, it seems to me, that value lay in the commodity, when in fact it lay in the action. The commodity, to be sure, must be worthy of the action, but it is the action that validates the value.

How do we really know value lies in the action of circulation rather than in the commodity? There are several lines of evidence. One is negative. As Firth (1940) has pointed out in his rebuttal of Mauss, there is very little evidence from Polynesia that exchanged objects do contain, as Mauss believed, a spirit of mystical quality that is transmitted to the receiver. On the other hand, an irregularity in the form of exchange or distribution was invariably regarded as an affront to honor.

The focus on circulation is not constant. When chiefs begin to feel the economic pressures, they are obliged to attend to productivity as a technical and as a religious process. Status rivalry makes its demands upon the economy, upon primary sources of wealth, upon land and upon crop. Hence, the paramount chiefs in Stratified societies, having secured their position by conquest of the economy, found themselves in control of production. Those who had risen from the lower ranks of authority were already experienced as directors of agriculture and as administrators of lands, and brought new standards of efficacy to the top levels.

Even so, the technical management of lands and crops was delegated to subordinate or to lower ranks, so as not to obscure the primacy of the religious link between the gods, crops, and the community. The religious concept demands an allocation of roles and a permanent pattern of economic circulation. The ariki stands to the people as a god. As the deity is the primary source of food and must therefore receive back a portion of it—a divine economic circulation—so the chief, the divine exemplar, must occupy a parallel place as a center of circulation. Others must be the producers from whom he is to receive. If the ariki were both primary producer and circulator, he would be literally outside the religious community. He would be like a god without people, a solipsistic absurdity. That he does, nevertheless, involve himself in production may be taken as a compromise before the exigencies of power. The compromise, such as it is, never violates the basic religious conception of the ariki's place in the economy. Insofar as he is top ariki, his economic role remains primarily religious. The authority of the chief to impose controls upon consumption (rahui) represents the other side of his interests in production. From either side he is compelled to regulate the dimension of the disposable crop, that part of production which must circulate ritually, that is to say, within the chief's religious orbit. As the chief's interest grows in the productive side, the rahui simultaneously becomes a direct expression of his sovereignty and power. I take this development as evidence of pressure to sustain the enlargement of the circulatory network. From ordinary and acceptable conservationism, the rahui becomes a direct test of the chief's power to preempt the circulation of foods.

The centralization of authority in public works is another important development. The question it poses is whether we are to attribute centralization to the requirements of a public works program, as proposed, for example, by Wittfogel (1957), or to credit a central authority with developing a public works program as one of the measures for its own stability. The so-called irrigation thesis as put forth by Wittfogel and others has relied only upon the facts of association between major irrigation projects and strong central authority. The thesis offers an abstract explanation of the association and takes for granted the materialist assumption that, in general, it is a subsistence necessity that brings into being the appropriate social institutions to cope with it. The scientific weakness of the thesis lies in its failure to examine historical evidence, on the one hand, and to evaluate difficult cases, on the other.

Strong central authority does, in fact, coincide with extensive irrigation projects in Tahiti and in Hawaii. But evidence from genealogical traditions demonstrates that growth in political centralism was a product of war. In the contest for power, economic capability added enormously to the strength of a chief. The chiefs who could promote production through terrace irrigation were the most successful, as the Hawaiian traditions tell us. We know, in fact, from the example of the Ifugao in the Philippines, that massive terrace irrigation can be organized without the aid of any central authority at all. On the other hand, we have the examples in Mangareva and Tonga of a strong central authority evolving without benefit of a public works program.

We need not, however, consider the Polynesian examples as directly contradicting the irrigation thesis, since ability to organize irrigation projects was indeed a key factor in political evolution. We do need to consider the entire process of political and economic development less mechanically and more fully in the light of interactive processes. In Polynesia the process of status rivalry sets political evolution in motion and this, in turn, draws heavily upon economic resources and means for its continued development.

Information on western Polynesia presents a somewhat different picture, because here no public works were associated with production. Neither Samoa nor Tonga, the heavily populated areas, utilized terrace irrigation, even though all conditions for its successful employment were present. On one point the correspondence with eastern Polynesia is precise, and that is the higher rank of the authorities vested with the religious concerns of insuring crop fertility and the privilege of imposing the rahui or its equivalent. On this matter, Tongan traditions are particularly interesting, because they recount the division of the central economic authority into a religious sphere held by the Tui Tonga and a secular side held successively by the Tui Ha Takalaua and Tui Kanokupolu. The technical authority won ascendancy. However, the ascendancy of the technical economic authority was, according to all available information a political event.

The absence of rahui in Niue, Ontong Java, and Pukapuka may be attributed to the utilitarianism of poverty combined with a general weakness of religious authority. In Ontong Java and Pukapuka, the taro reserves were guarded by a constabulary against theft.

Economic Scarcity and Abundance

It is naïve to consider the level of economic productivity as an independent factor creating economic and social institutions. A question such as, How does scarcity and abundance affect a society? is too general to be meaningful. The real question, rather, is, How does a Polynesian system, with its particular economic expectations, fare under poverty or riches? Since Polynesian societies can be similar in basic culture whether they occupy atolls or high islands, relatively rich habitats or barren islands, they cannot be regarded as having been molded by their different material environments. The same basic status system existed on all Polynesian islands, posing everywhere the same basic economic demands. Scarcity everywhere posed problems of adaptation, and abundance provided opportunities. Neither adaptations to scarcity nor the exploitation of abundance followed a mechanical course. In every instance there are options, the play of chance and of human intentions. Scarcity, however, always offers fewest options, and we should expect to find, therefore, that the poorer Polynesian societies have more in common than the richer.

Scarcity Conditions

When we speak of scarcity in Polynesia, we must introduce two qualifications: one, that all Polynesian societies are subject to famine resulting from drought or storm; and two, that all Polynesian societies, no matter how poor, are able to carry out some of the economic obligations of ritual and status. What then do we mean by scarcity economies, since the term is inevitably elastic? Lacking figures on production, we can distinguish only generally and imprecisely between scarcity and abundance. By Polynesian standards a scarcity economy would be one that can barely, if at all, carry out the obligations of status, an abundant economy one that can carry out these obligations richly. There are no readily measured difference between rich and poor Polynesian economies by standards of subsistence alone.

There are two kinds of scarcity settings in Polynesia, those on atolls, and those on high islands with special ecological shortcomings. All students of Polynesia have noted the relative simplicity of atoll-based cultures. We have seen, for example, that no Open or Stratified societies were formed on the atolls, an indication that ecologically undifferentiated islands do not support notable social and cultural changes. Granted that atoll ecologies are culturally limiting, in general, can we specify just what kinds of social and cultural limits they impose and what the precise limiting factors are?

The political histories of Manihiki and Tongareva show contrasting solutions to apparently similar economic circumstances. The former organized the peaceable use of resources, the latter was driven to battle for coconuts and land. Scarcity may have been a more significant factor in promoting war, however, than this comparison reveals. Figures on population density—crude as these are—show Manihiki as at least 20 percent below Tongareva, which, at 333 persons per square mile, may have felt the pinch more strongly. All the other atolls in the present study were as crowded an Tongareva and almost as combative. Of the densely occupied atolls, two had evolved temporary "conquest states" and two continued to fight indecisively. But then the outcome of war is even more subject to chance.

Among high islands, the Marquesas, Easter, Niue, and Mangareva qualify as difficult habitats, although for different reasons. Only Mangareva was chronically unproductive. Easter, while a poor island, was evidently underpopulated. Niue and the Marquesas had rich soils but experienced prolonged and severe droughts. All four had to contend seriously with the stress of scarcity. In the Marquesas, for example, approximately one-quarter of the breadfruit crop went into a famine reserve and so was withheld from the normal channels of supply. Niueans, on a large island, endured the burden of living along the coasts near their fishing grounds and traveling great distances to cultivate their interior taro plantations. Mangarevans came to rely more on fish than on breadfruit for food. These were, so to speak, the utilitarian responses to shortage: underpopulation, food reserves, extra effort, and shift in emphasis from scarce crops to more abundant fish.

The cultural responses bear out our observations on the atolls to the effect that economic stress undermined the traditional order of genealogical rank and generated chronic political instability. Three of the four scarcity examples are Open societies and Mangareva was the most unstable of the Stratified. All four were wracked by predatory warfare and in all four the control of wealth became major sources of power and status.

The Mangarevan case merits close study, for it reveals how central authority and social stratification can evolve in the midst of, or even through poverty, contrary to theories that emphasize economic "surplus." As we know from the examples of Tonga, Tahiti, and Hawaii, abundance is indeed an important economic factor in the evolution of chiefly authority. But then so is scarcity. Neither economic condition has a creative role in political evolution, but each enters the picture and influences the outcome. Active warfare, always a potential generator of strong political authorities, does not, for example, spring from objective scarcity. The Hawaiian Islands, an outstandingly favorable physical environment, were as much the scene of battle and wars of conquest as poverty-pinched Mangareva. The drive for power through conquest has its own impetus and its own interpretations of economic scarcity. Mangarevan warfare, though, was more desperate, more utilitarian, more directly concerned with conquest of food lands. Even so, Mangarevans like fellow Tongarevans, could not resist the destruction of enemy breadfruit trees—the symbol of victory—at the extraordinarily high cost of long-range impoverishment of the entire island. But if they cut down the trees, they also restored the ecological balance by exterminating the enemy or by compelling those in hiding to forage for recent corpses. In this respect, at least, warfare had become ruthlessly utilitarian.

It is to the acute Mangarevan sense of the scarcity of land that we may attribute this politically immature policy of eviction rather than of reorganization of conquered populations. Yet some of the adaptations to eviction from productive lands were instrumental in social and economic diversification. At some point in the course of Mangarevan warfare, the commoners, really the weak, had been evicted from the land and been converted to professional fishermen, a lowly status. At the same time, more ambitious landless took up skilled crafts and acquired high status in this way. If scarcity was a factor in diversifying the Mangarevan economy, it also narrowed it in other ways; for apart from the Marquesan famine alleviation, when chiefs drew from reserves to feed a needy community, Mangareva was alone in Polynesia in having converted chiefly food distributions into a welfare activity. Finally, the abortive rise to power of a commoner line is an example of the triumph of utilitarianism over aristocratic privilege that may be attributed to scarcity.

Conditions of Abundance

If poverty sharpened the appetite for land, wealth did not necessarily dull it. The rich Polynesian societies could choose freely between the courses of peaceable or of predatory expansion. They chose both. Tikopia and Manu'a, for example, expanded peaceably, while Tonga, Tahiti, and Hawaii chose conquest. The Maori, curiously, were most covetous and expansive when they had just arrived in New Zealand and had before them almost limitless frontiers, and were most peaceable after they had fully occupied the land. The covetousness of scarcity and the predatory expansiveness of the wealthy differed, however, in basic aim. For the poor chiefs, ambition was of necessity more narrowly economic. They coveted the lands, often regarding their enemy occupants as impediments to be removed. Their ambitions were fierce but small. The point of view of the rich, on the other hand, was primarily political. They could of course use more wealth, but their interest was in controlling people. It was not territory alone they set out to seize but jurisdiction. This was how the arii Taimai explained the Tahitian political economy to Henry Adams. Wealth mattered less than power, and while the royal rahui was a source of supply, its imposition was a test of strength, a challenge to subordinate chiefs.

In distinguishing between the economic emphasis in the predatory expansion of poor societies and the political emphasis in the predatory expansion of the rich, we must avoid too excessive a categorization. All Polynesian status systems include both the economic and the political elements, and in all the political and the economic are intertwined. If the distinction is the subtle one of emphasis, it is, nevertheless, a demonstrable distinction. The logic of the distinction can be explained as follows: Because high productivity was a dual measure of efficacy, of religious and of technical accomplishment, we are justified in considering wealth or abundance as the normal condition of Polynesian status systems. The abnormality of poverty is demonstrated by the curtailment of ritual and the decline in the stature of the ariki. The toa came to command, reducing the ariki either to insignificance, or confining them to the role of priests, within which they had only minor obligations of hospitality and of distribution. The decline of the ariki is not to be laid to poverty alone, any more than his durability is assured by wealth. The turning point was challenge and he need not be challenged. But if a determined challenge did come, poverty was more likely to mean defeat and wealth victory. When wealthy ariki sustained the challenge of lower-ranking warriors by their ability to draw them into their own service, they emerged from the conflict in full chiefly majesty, their dual religious and secular prerogatives enlarged.

For eastern Polynesia, New Zealand, and the Hawaiian Islands exemplify the two political patterns made possible by favorable physical environments. Population density in Hawaii was far greater than in New Zealand, but at under 50 per square mile still well below the average for Polynesian high islands. Both societies drew upon their natural resources to the full, the Maori expending their surpluses on great rivalrous feasts, the Hawaiians on supporting a great administrative establishment. The Maori focus was almost exclusively on ritual and display; the Hawaiian, on a balanced combination of display and utility. The Maori economy received its strong impetus for growth—apart, that is, from the demographic factor—from intertribal rivalry; the Hawaiian, from political antagonisms. The pressure upon the Hawaiian economy was by far the greater, for any economic weakness was politically dangerous. Thus the Hawaiian Islands show evidence of the most intensive cultivation. Some valleys were terraced and irrigated to the crown of their mountain peaks. In New Zealand, by contrast, land was underused. Abundance in the service of display alone allows high chiefs to withdraw from active concern with production. But when abundance is drawn into the service of politics, the necessity of tight control draws even the highest ariki into the actual administration of production. Thus it is neither wealth nor scarcity that determines the role of the chief in production, but the uses of wealth.

Manu'a and Tonga represent parallel examples from western Polynesia. Both shared richly endowed lands. One stabilized a social system emphasizing the decorum of status; the other, caught in political wars, reduced the high chief, the Tui Tonga, to his religious role only, splitting the rule between religious and political authority. In this respect, Tonga differed from Hawaii, where the alii held firmly to both functions. However, it was not until very late in Tongan traditional history that the split occurred. Evidence on this point is far from conclusive, yet there is reason to suppose the greater relative poverty of Tonga played its part in undermining the full authority of the sacred ruler. As in Hawaii, warfare and political rivalries were economic strains that the poorer economy could bear less easily. In the end, the Tongans felt they could no longer afford the annual tribute to their paramount.

Economic Specialization

The significance of specialization lies in its role of diversifying the economy, giving it more interactive agents and more complexity with respect both to the organization of production and the system of exchange. General economic theory holds specialization to be a by-product of high productivity, on the one hand, and of the diversification of social needs, on the other. The assumption is logical enough that an economy will not have specialists until it can afford them and wants them, but since the theory does not claim that specialization *must* arise with an economic "surplus," it is uninformative on the very question of greatest interest, namely: how does specialization arise? With its wide range of forms of specialization, Polynesia can illuminate some of the factors in their evolution. In the history of specialization, Polynesia is not at the lowest level. All share in the common respect for the expert, the tohunga. Respect for skill is surely a basic human trait. But the Polynesian concept of tohunga is more than general respect. By conferring the title, the Polynesians have converted a general human concept into a specific system of status, drawing the expert into the orbit of aristocracy. Thus, viewing the forms of variation and the historical elaboration of specialization from the perspective of Polynesia, we see in the honoring of the expert the source of the whole development. The concept of expertness does have its roots in the actual nature of skills, as in the exceptional skill required to fashion a seaworthy canoe. It is the elaboration of the system of skills, the formation of professions, of guilds, and the incorporation of the tohunga into the order of statuses—in short, the growth of specialization—that we must attribute to the basic concept of honoring the expert. This, however, remains to be proven.

Can we really distinguish between expertness that grows around the nature of the skill and expertness as a status that learns to monopolize a skill? It is easy to show the close interdependence of these related but differently focused processes, but can we sort out which is the leading idea? To a degree we can.

A broad survey of Polynesia brings to light two relevant considerations: One is the close association between the elaboration of titles generally, and the elaboration of the crafts and specialties in particular; the other is that except for stone work, the level of skill required in Polynesian manufactures remains relatively constant. For all its remarkable political development, sophistication of religious doctrine, and virtuosity in the verbal arts, Polynesia has always been a technologically unremarkable area.

Economic specialization was least developed on all five of the atolls, as well as on Niue. All six societies are distinguished by relative poverty. Yet the elaboration of the crafts on Mangareva leads us to doubt that productivity was the decisive factor, although it was evidently a significant one. Specialization was in fact costly not because the specialist ceased to be a food producer—food production was not that tightly organized—but because work undertaken by specialists was honorific and had to be ceremonialized by feasts and gifts. It is this honorific aspect of specialization, the fact that titles of specialization were extensions of the status system, that compels us to see it not as a technical development but as part of a complex social institution. It can hardly be expected to correlate with single factors. The more general relationship between the least differentiated status systems and the least elaborated forms of craft specialization does seem to hold true, however.

We are speaking, of course, of titled specialists, since only titled specialists in Polynesia formed the cadre of diversified roles that affected the economy. The six societies did not lack for skilled men to carry out specialized tasks. To cite but a few examples: the Ontong Javanese who depended upon high skills for adze making, canoe making, weaving, housebuilding, and fishing, called upon the older men, a corps of untitled specialists. Apart from priests, only the tattooer occupied a titled craft. On the remaining atolls, only the canoe makers were titled craftsmen. On Niue, with its remarkably loose status system, tufuga was a designation for people with skills of any sort but not a title. All other specialties were carried out by untitled, and hence by economically undifferentiated, craftsmen.

A crude but useful measure of degree of elaboration of specialization is given by the number of titles of occupational specialists in use within each Polynesian society. Interestingly enough, the number of titles corresponds generally to the level of politicalization of the status system. It follows, in other words, the main course of social evolution in Polynesia, from Ontong Java with one title (tattooing specialist), to Hawaii with over 40. Representing crafts, professions, administrative offices, and religious specialties, the growing list calls attention indeed to increasing complexity, on the one hand, and to honorific multiplication, on the other. The Hawaiian list includes, for example, technical officials along with such courtly offices as steward in charge of king's food, masseur and steward of the royal chamber pot, and the king's pipe lighter (cf. Malo 1951). The Hawaiian royal household accounted for most of the titles, in keeping with the general principle that statuses breed at the top. Administrative and religious office diversified most rapidly and the crafts most slowly, judging by the outcome in Hawaii.

Each of the major societies seems to have developed its own special area of elaboration of titles. The Hawaiians were outstanding in administrative and household posts. Tahiti lacked the administrative organization of Hawaii and built up its religious offices. It had more military titles and a greater degree of craft specialization. Mangareva, in keeping with its small size, lacked administrative offices, but had richly developed religious specialization, including a category of scholars. Finally, among the complex Stratified societies, Tonga had the most fully diversified ranks of craft specialists. These specialties included such titled occupations as the supervision of gathering shellfish and crabs, canoe building, navigation, cutters of whales' teeth, funeral directors, stone masons, net makers, fishermen, large house builders, tattooers, barbers, cooks, poets, prostitutes, and circumcisors. In addition, the Tongan administrative corps was second only to that of Hawaii. Among Open societies the Marquesas had well-developed craft specialization but were richest in servant terms. They had 15 terms for domestic help. There were notables for administrative positions. Small Easter Island with its meager resources had a good list of craft titles, many servant titles, but no executive offices. In the two well-to-do Traditional societies, Maori and Manu'a, the main titles were in the crafts.

The three main areas of specialization refer to expansion of chiefly roles, of priestly roles, and of tohunga roles, the three main functional statuses of Polynesia. The number of titles seems to provide a fair index of area of development and defines for us somewhat more precisely the character of leadership. By this index, Hawaii was the most fully matured status system, while Tahiti and Mangareva fell behind in lacking a diversified administrative corps. Tonga, with its organization of matapule, was closest to the Hawaiian system.

From the standpoint of political development, the lowest level is marked by the expansion of the crafts alone. By expanding administrative and religious offices, a society evolves a corps of officials who are linked to the main chiefly and priestly ranks, if not as extensions of these ranks, then as dependencies. Thus the entire central corps of officials is enriched. The craft specialists, on the other hand, were an independent status and developed along with, or as a parallel social group. Tonga and Hawaii illustrate the emergence of strong and independent statuses of craftsmen. The Tongan hereditary crafts gave their members a parallel status to that of the administrative gentry, and the Hawaiian crafts, with their smaller measure of corporate identity, were relatively lower in the scale.

We may turn now to a more concrete concern with the conditions promoting craft specialization. From our general knowledge of Polynesian status systems, we would predict that given tohunga as a basic title of honor, its holders would be caught up in the same passions of status rivalry that moved chiefs and priests, and would use skill, their special attribute, to advance themselves. The evidence we have just surveyed indicated indeed that all three divisions of status advanced together. Since status rivalry is a complex process, the evolution of all three cannot be even. The one evidently definite rule is that the chiefly sphere, the most powerful and energetic, evoles most rapidly, and inevitably influences the development of the priestly and the occupational specialties. All three spheres are, in fact, closely interrelated. In the traditional theory of status, the ariki commanded all three. He was the master of administration, the master of religion, and the master of the main skills. The expansion of public interest in honor broke the ariki monopoly on virtue and led to the division of what were once unified prerogatives. In this division, the occupational skills—being devoid of the attributes of political power—naturally came to occupy the lowest rung on the scale of honor. The occupations were not only lower, but, even more important for their status, they were beyond the fray. Being uninvolved in the combats for power, they began to form an independent center in society.

Mangaia and Mangareva illustrate this independent status of the crafts in a context of violence. The Mangaian craftsmen, even if of enemy tribes, were offered safety and position. In Mangareva, craft skills rescued the landless from the lowest status. Crafts were the alternative to land-holding as a source of honorable status. Because of the violence of status rivalry, the crafts offered defensive positions. In the Marquesas, where status rivalry centered more on wealth than on sheer power, the crafts offered opportunities for active engagement, and hence for a greater share in the rewards of status. Tonga seems to have been in a different situation. Here the main conflict was between lower-ranking chiefs, the exponents of sheer political power, and the sacred Tui Tonga, a conflict in which the crafts were not involved. Like their counterpart guilds in Western Samoa, the Tongan craft organization had the character of a traditional estate in an overall status system that had systematically elaborated all the ranks.

To return now to our original question. What spurred the development of the crafts? Was it economic necessity or status? Since status rested on realities, economic necessity can hardly be ruled out, but we can say conclusively that the crafts—having been established as honorific from earliest times in Polynesia—developed always under the aegis of the status system.

Perhaps this point can be most clearly illustrated by changes in the status of fishermen. Fishermen were a highly specialized craft, with an independent status in all the Stratified societies. Except for Niue, specialization was not quite so strongly developed in all the Open societies. On the atolls, all men fished and all were qualified. In the remaining Traditional societies, Manu'a, Maori, and Tikopia, all men fished, but fishing skills were more clearly defined and experts were recognized. The conclusions to be drawn are clear enough. No specialization develops when dependence on the skill is as absolute as it is on atolls. Specialization tends to develop, rather, in secondary economic areas. Finally, when fishing specialization does develop, it becomes established as a lower status activity. Tikopians, for example, referred to canoes as "the orchards of the commoners (Firth 1939: 117)." Why did fishermen become a lower status in a maritime civilization so dependent on the food of the sea? The answer would seem to be that status had become identified with power based on land-holdings, and on crops which were central to all honorific exchanges.

Systems of Exchange

The giver is *magister*, the receiver *minister*, Mauss wrote and so defined the central principle of honorific exchange. In the most elementary form of this kind of exchange, the giver acquires honor for goods, the receiver goods for honor. If the exchanges move in one direction only, this sheer inequality of goods versus honor would stand as a true social equation. Such an equation, however, is the mark of powerful discrepancy between rich and poor and strong and weak. It represents charity and charity is a product of civilization, not of the primitive world. In the primitive world, including Polynesia, the equation is modified to allow honor and goods to move in both directions, either equally or unequally. In simple reciprocity, *magister* and *minister* alternate roles; each is in turn debtor–creditor insofar as honor goes. Since it is only temporary, the debtor position is not dishonorable, but it holds the potential of being dishonorable. This potential is the force that compels an appropriate return. As long as *magister–minister* alternate in regular fashion, the cycle itself is honorific. Each enhances the other, somewhat in the way in which two men on one saw work together. While the receiver is surely dishonored when he cannot meet his obligations, the giver too is dishonored to a degree, because the cycle has been disturbed, and he has involved himself with an unworthy partner. In simple reciprocity, then, the partners begin with an assumption of their status equivalence and they combine to enhance one another. In more complex systems of reciprocity, status equivalence is either denied or remains to be established. In these systems the equations vary. If equivalence is denied, inequality is "programmed" into the system, so to speak. If equivalence is to be established, then the system serves as a test, as for example in the case of the Maori hakari or openly rivalrous potlatches generally. Given the presence of these three status conditions within a system of exchange, we should expect to find a range of variability within Polynesia. Systems of honorific exchange are in no case more stable than the status systems they represent.

Perhaps no other set of conditions defines the state of affairs within a status system quite so precisely as the conditions of honorific exchange. Exchanges are the code through which status information is communicated. A code is expected to be precise and is taken with utmost seriousness. When the Maori chief who received slightly less in an offering than his status traditionally entitled him to, sought a violent revenge, it was because a precisely measured affront to his worth had been announced. Exchanges are not the only codes of status, but they are the only quantitative form of coding and, hence, the most explicit and most precise. Dress, ornamentation, housing, and special privileges of one sort or another are other important sources of coded information about status. These are general symbols, though, and even when more fully defined still lack the precision of a set of exchanges.

In an aristocracy, participation in a cycle of economic exchanges is not the source of status, nor is it normally a test of status. It is, rather, the prerogative and documentation of status. But if it is documentation, why is documentation necessary, since (as in Polynesia) knowledge of genealogy itself reveals the basic information? The explanation would seem to be that status in Polynesia is not normally a passive position but a position promising efficacious actions. The economy is the supreme symbol of efficacy, standing equally as symbol of efficacy for the gods, for chiefs, and for commoners. Honorific economic exchanges are to be considered, therefore, as coded statements of efficacy. In aristocratic societies, these statements follow a strict protocol, conforming to genealogical precedence and avoiding aggressive ostentation, for ostentation is challenge. Protocol exchanges are not actual demonstrations of efficacy, insofar as what is exchanged is often a token; they are statements about efficacy. Do not people actually exchange information about efficacy in the ordinary events of their lives, especially in very small communities where nothing is secret? Undoubtedly they do. Honorific exchanges, however, are not ordinary events. They are ritual, and as ritual they translate the commonplace into a higher sphere of worth. From this point of view, the honorific exchanges are a language of ritual which all communicants use to honor and to elevate to a higher moral plane their concepts of personal worth.

Polynesian exchanges are most usefully considered from the point of view of chiefs and from the point of view of family heads. Chiefly exchanges, as Polanyi has generally described them, have the special quality of centricity. The chief is a center of distribution and of redistribution. As distributor, he is a center of hospitality and generosity, as well as a fomentor of the exchange system in general. As redistributor, he has the more specific prerogative of circulating goods among those from whom he has collected. Household heads are also centers of distribution and of redistribution, but in a different sense. Whereas chiefs redistribute ritually, the redistribution of household heads is utilitarian, serving subsistence only. Household heads' honorific exchanges are with other household heads.

Exchange, then, in Polynesia serves dual interests: the interests of honor, in which case the precise forms of circulation and of reciprocity act as a ritual language, a mode of honorific discourse; and the interests of subsistence or the utilitarian interests. As in the organization of production, dual interests are in unstable balance. As both interests state their claims to the same sources of supply, they conflict. The conflict between honorific and utilitarian interests is more turbulent in the sphere of circulation than in production, since circulation is the true domain of highest-ranking chiefs and the very center of honor in the economy. Our analysis, therefore, should focus on this area of conflict rather than upon the formal description of systems of exchange. In keeping with this focus, I should like to start with a consideration of the most stable forms of economic coding and conclude with the most actively changing ones.

Display of Productivity

The direct and passive display of productive capacity was confined to eastern Polynesia, where it took so moderate a form as compared, for example, with the Trobriand yam structures, that we can only assume it was relatively unimportant. The ornately carved *pataka*—food storehouse—of the Maori chief is the closest parallel to the Trobriand yam display, but is unique in Polynesia. The commonest form of conspicuous display was the custom of fattening. Corpulence implied wealth and chiefly qualities of solidity and strength. Fattening was confined to Manihiki-Rakahanga, Mangaia, Mangareva, Easter, and Tahiti. It was absent in Maori, Tongareva, Marquesas, and Hawaii. In Tahiti, only grown women fattened themselves to enhance their attractiveness. But in Mangaia, Easter and Mangareva children were fattened and then displayed to the admiring public. Mangarevans who could afford to fatten up only the first-born children of rank took this honorific task seriously, stuffing the miserable children with poi and cudgeling them if they refused to eat.

Tongareva had no forms of passive display. Marquesans ornamented food pounders, an act, however, of honoring food, not of displaying it. Hawaiian display was highly sophisticated. I have brought out the relative unimportance of passive display in Polynesia to add emphasis to the Polynesian preoccupations with exchange, an interactive and hence dynamic mode of display. In status as in mechanics, the measure of force is the energy of motion. Mass must be moved. It must be assembled and circulated, and moved outward into wider orbits. That which is inert is low in vitality and hence in standing. So, whoever is vital and efficacious is the mover of food—the natural image of life-giving properties.

The Feast

We should define the feast broadly to include within our scope what the Polynesians do: eating together in one place as well as the eating together at separate places, but from the common stock and in honor of the same event. Thus we would include under "feast" the distributions of foods to absent guests and the carrying away of foods by present guests. Food as the primary expression of life-giving force must inescapably take its place as the symbol of social unity. Those who exchange fundamental properties of life through food must stand in some parallel relation to that conferred by the sexual bond. The connection between sex and food can hardly fail to be understood by societies as organically minded as the Polynesians.

It has often been said that exchange of food creates a bond (cf. Bell 1931). The bond, of course, is already present, so that what is created is but another ligament of it. Exchange of goods does not, for example, create a marriage tie; it adds its own validation, which is to say that it links concepts of productivity to concepts of genitality. Productivity, at the same time, defines the qualities of the agents as matching their social standing. What the feast creates then is another dimension, or another strand of relationship that is always multidimensional and that is bound by more than a single ligament. Our present concern is a limited one, not to explore all the ties that bind, only those that define the status of the bodies bound, the donor and the receiver.

The giver of a feast is, of course, in the most important sense a *magister,* a momentary exponent of efficacy, of productive potency. The giver authenticates the event and establishes its honor by relating it to another domain or to another cycle. An event in isolation is inconsequential and, hence, illegitimate. It lacks significance unless annexed to events and processes whose credentials have already been established. Feasts in Polynesia, as elsewhere, occur at the events of transformation. They mark beginnings, conclusions, and passages in the lives of persons and families, and in the affairs of the broader community. They honor the life cycle—births, baptisms, maturations, betrothals, marriages, and deaths—and the beginnings and terminations of economic and political actions. In the most general sense, the feast brings productivity, itself a phase of movement, into relationship with all social and personal phases of movement. The life processes, for example, are meshed with the cycle of productivity. The donor has the signal honor of acting as initiator. He acts as a mover of goods, as an enlarger of the area within which foods and other produce circulate. As the donor of a feast, he has the chief-like prerogative of assembling an enlarged congregation. As he moves food from the narrow confines of the immediate circle outward into others, or conversely, as he draws food from the outer zones to his own center for redistribution, he is displaying a genuine power to circulate productivity, a power that is, in the Polynesian conception, that of the gods. The event in whose name the motions have been engendered is then transported out of the ordinary. The feast, or exchange, generally expresses productivity in quantitative terms and so becomes a true measure of efficacy. Like the productive cycle, exchance must also have its own closed and interactive cycle. There is room for "leakage" out of the system, but the recipient, if he is worthy, must himself turn donor. If the recipient is *minister,* in the equation of hierarchy he is not automatically inferior. No exchange is calculated upon such elementary dyadic terms; the relationship between donor and recipient is defined, rather, by the broader pattern, which includes other elements besides those of donor and recipient. In general terms, the patterns of feasting will be found to bear a relationship to more fundamental concepts of status, to the organization of ranks, of classes, and of chiefly powers. Space does not permit an exhaustive study of feasting in all of Polynesia. The following survey is confined to high islands whose agricultural production is diversified and which represent among themselves all the basic forms of status system.

To begin with the Traditional Maori, reciprocal feast-giving was the prerogative of all families regardless of rank, whether aristocrat or commoner, for the intimate family occasions of baptism, marriage and death. The ordinary householder moved foods modestly and moderately within the narrow inner circle of close kin. Rank extended the circle outward and more prodigally to more distant groups, and in honor of more general political and economic affairs. Chiefs dealt with construction, with crops, with the change of season, and with relations with outsiders. The internal circulation is friendly, for donor and recipient are in the same community, or else are extended the courtesy of being regarded as members.

The outermost feast, the great *hakari,* was a major confrontation between iwi or between hapu; it asserted militant superiority and was indeed a metaphoric declaration of war in which the display of productive efficacy was the weapon. The hakari may be said to have been a temporary substitute for war, since it was given by one group unilaterally as a way of resolving a dispute. The atmosphere of the great hakari was deliberately made tense and fearful. The guests took the food to be potentially dangerous to them and the hosts feared the crop-damaging magic of their guests. In this antagonism we read at once the message of the hakari: the donor threatens his possible enemy with his productive force. The enemy tries to overcome it. The display of food upon enormous pyramidal stages, some over 100 feet tall, is in itself an effort to overwhelm by setting forth in one concentrated image all the productive effort (a year's labor) of the community. The scale of display is perilously extravagant, as if to say: In opposition to the outside we make a supreme effort. If the hakari brought the donors to the point of utter depletion, that was the message: In the logic of war, to risk all to gain all. The opposing side was not obliged to return an excess. The antagonism here was between production and antiproduction.

Like a war party, the great hakari is collective; it represents the hapu or iwi as corporate bodies and serves to define their worth. Ritual combat is in the collective name or in the name of an honored person and not necessarily in that of the chief. The chief is organizer and master of ceremonies and not the central protagonist. His honor is involved in the assembly of the foodstuffs; the manner of distribution leaves no doubt that family heads are in fact also donors. They search out recipients, usually kinsmen, to bestow a parcel of food upon them. It seems that individual distributions are, in fact, friendly. They are given by name and by rank in the spirit of honoring. It is the collective effort, the pooling of all resources, the awesome display of the forcefulness of hapu or iwi, that conveys, as it should, the atmosphere of menace.

Antagonism need not separate. The hakari draw the hapu and iwi into new and wider relationships, compelling each to consider the other as involved in the productive process. As judge, in effect, each compels the other to transcend utility, to leave its parochial zone and to accept the risk of crossing the perilous boundary that separates autonomous divisions. Thus to think of great intertribal food distributions as utilitarian is to invert the traditional Polynesian concept. The aim of the hakari is not to nourish, but to exalt. Traditional Maori exalted the community equally with its chief.

Mangareva had three kinds of feasts: *takurua* were given either by powerful families or by tribes to celebrate the important events of life cycle, completions, installations, and political discussions; *kai pure,* strictly religious affairs held on the marae; and *maninitori,* marriage exchanges that affirmed the status superiority of the male side. In the takurua, the chief assembled food from all families, and the Ruler of Food, a priest, or else a spokesman of the chief, allotted portions to names and titles in order of rank. Rank received a particularized allotment; commoners received their food on a common spread. Thus, a quantum of food (productivity unit) was matched with a quantum of rank or potency. One quantum of title was made equivalent to the mass of commoners as a single entity. In the religious kai pure, the status of the population was defined in a slightly different manner. The notables ate on the marae as inner members of the sacred congregation; the common people ate their food outside. In the maninitori, the food exchanges defined very clearly the metaphoric inferiority of the bride's family. The female side allowed itself to be used as a human carpet of the groom and then accepted corresponding inferiority by receiving a larger offering of food from the groom than it had originally given.

The Marquesas present a similar organization, with variations apparently in accord with the greater autonomy of local chiefs. The same basic occasions were used by families and tribes to display the utmost limits of their productivity. The chief or headman was the center; he was collector, organizer, and distributor. All contributed to share in the distribution, and all received individual allotments in recognition of their name and status. Where Mangareva emphasized the strict hierarchical order, the Marquesas made an issue of the spatial separation of statuses. At the large intertribal feasts, a special platform was allocated to each tribe and to each social status, chiefs, master craftsmen, warriors, chiefs' sons, daughters, women, children, old men, etc. There does not seem to have been the Mangian effort to reduce by generalizing status. The concept of feasts (*koina*) was, as Handy has said, religious. The aim was not to reapportion the bounty of a harvest, but to honor productivity by giving focus and climax to consumption. As everywhere, in fact, the people lived meagerly for as long as a year so as to eat to excess in one great exuberant display of appetite and bounty. The modest ration stands for utility, excess for honor. In the light of this formula, all Marquesans participate in the pooling that creates honor. In the Marquesas, the excess that is postulated by a great feast can overcome the excess that is represented by war. The very great feasts accepted contributions from the enemy and so transcended hostilities.

Perhaps the subordination of fighting to feasting does indicate, as I have suggested earlier, an equation between two modes of efficacy. In the rivalrous feasts (*koika hakahiti*) between antagonistic chiefs, this equation (as in the Kwakiutl potlatch, which is referred to as "fighting with property") is literally stated. The parallel to the Maori hakari is self-evident. In the Marquesas, the emphasis seems to have shifted, however, from the group to the figure of the chief.

Marriage, considered a political alliance, demanded, appropriately, a very substantial feast that only the very wealthy could support. That is to say, the overcoming of a real or potential antagonism needs a correspondence in productive force. With respect to food, both sides gave an equal number of feasts and, in contrast to Mangaia, the bride as well as the groom walked over the deferentially prostrate bodies of the other side in a dramatic portrayal of political equivalence. Nevertheless, the male side asserted its inherent formal superiority by giving double the quantity of durables as gifts. In the betrothal feasts, the guests play an unusual role. They are free to snatch and carry off anything they can lay their hands on, as though they were plunderers. Seizure, it may be assumed, substitutes for the subordinate role of *minister*. In a fundamental sense, the military theme equalizes all parties. The hosts have dropped their antagonism to form an enlarged party and now allow their guests to act as the honored antagonists.

In Mangareva, poverty alone would have divided the population into donors and receivers. The poor were the constant recipients, but only upon circumscribed occasions. Reciprocal feasting in honor of great events, or lavish displays of hospitality, had become the fully exclusive privilege of nobles and wealthy. The concept of a closed circle of honorific circulation accords with the fact that the landless had become inert entities by Mangarevan standards. Thus, chiefs who had the specific obligation to include their entire dominion in the annual breadfruit distribution tried to exclude the poor. Public resentment of such ungraciousness testifies to the emergence of a utilitarian conception of benefice. The chief's evasion, on the other hand, speaks for the conservatism of the older tradition that the circle of distribution includes only the worthy. The obligation to give food to the poor is for Polynesia a revolutionary idea made inescapable by the breakdown of local economic autonomy. The Mangarevans responded conservatively to the revolutionary obligation. The chief included his entire constituency in a mandatory distribution. All, even children in the womb, received an allotment. Landowners or lessees having contributed in the first place, remained honorably within the traditional circle of reciprocity. The poor were the categorical *ministers,* the permanent outsiders.

When honorable guests who were outsiders by virtue of distance arrived for the first time they were, in the opposite manner, treated with utmost deference. Food and durables were thrown toward them from a distance. Having paid deference with property, the hosts performed war dances, evidently a counter-statement that illustrates, at the same time, the analogy between property display and military power. Similarly, Mangarevan war leaders gave food to the enemy during a lull in the fighting, or taunted him with an insolent offer.

The modes of giving can add precision to the modalities of antagonism and friendship.

Marriage, in contrast to the related Marquesan pattern and to Polynesia generally, called for a clearly one-sided distribution of food and goods by the male side. "The male side," the text declares, "provided the clothing, the food, and the goods (Buck 1938a:131)." The pattern is distinctive only as an intensification of a general stress upon the special honor of the male side.

To compare feasting in Tahiti and Hawaii with much smaller Mangareva, we must turn to the district organizations, the comparable units of reciprocal exchange. On the national level, foodstuffs and other goods moved upwards as tribute to be subsequently redistributed in a variety of forms. I shall consider the political circulation of goods separately. Our immediate concern is with the feast as a ritualized set of events. In Tahiti, the local arii had a role in food distribution comparable to that of the high chief in the Marquesas, Mangaia, and Mangareva. They were the focus for the religious rituals that demanded the assemblage and reapportionment of a crop among the established order of ranks. The position set aside for commoners was generalized, and the public was obliged to scramble for a share, "to bring them luck," Tahitians said. The meaning is not obscure when we recognize that the crop dedicated to the gods, the priests, and the holders of divine powers had been sanctified. Aristocrat and commoner are brought into communion even as their respective places in the allocations of sanctity are carefully defined and set in opposition to one another. In the Tahitian formula: the high-born are in the fixed order, a good fortune; the masses are contestants for it, an honorable, because an energetic role, yet reduced because to a degree generalized. The source of good fortune is, of course, the arii who sets the course.

Since feasts were given only in the name of chiefs to commemorate their own events of passage and completion, the reciprocity of food exchanges was contained within a restricted network from which commoners were excluded. The commoner, the source of productivity in the economic sense, was not a ritual entity in the circulation of goods. His produce entered the system anonymously and assumed ritual significance only in the name of a chief. As an anonymous giver he was, perforce, a nonentity as receiver.

Marital exchanges, inherently rivalrous and antagonistic because they must define the opposition and therefore the potential antagonism between two families compelled to surrender their alienness, required each to demonstrate economic capacity, but not to overcome.

The intent seems rather to proclaim a balance. If the bride were socially inferior, her side gave more. To compensate for social inferiority by the privilege of giving is to go against the antagonistic spirit that one expects of marital exchanges.

Fragmentary knowledge of Hawaii on feasts points, nevertheless, to further elaborations of the exchange pattern in conformity with a new social and political order. The Hawaiian concern evidently was to accommodate the traditional principle of separation of rank within a political conception of national unity. The *makahiki,* the great four-month long national harvest festival, illustrates how this was accomplished. The ali'i nui, the religious and administrative center of the festival, established the ritual sequence, the order of feasts, and set in motion the monumental circulation of the harvest within the domain. Wherever he officially presided over the collection, the subsequent redistribution went in order of ranks and overlooked the common people (Malo 1951:141). The commoner was outside the major cycle of which the great ali'i was the visible center; but the commoner was included within all of the internal distributions over which the paramount chief was the presiding spirit. He was also included, however, as both donor and recipient in the small local feasts when the island chief came to dedicate a *heiau.* But we have no information on the manner of distribution.

When we turn to western Polynesian feasts, we encounter a new principle, or possibly an old principle, for we had observed it in the Marquesas, that of complementary exchange. Eastern Polynesia, generally, seeks a quantitative measure of efficacy. In western Polynesian societies, quantity is but one additional measure in a system of qualitative distinctions between two kinds of goods that generally are set to move across one another on distinct tracks. If one side to an exchange gives one kind of property, the other repays with another. To simplify the description of this exchange, for the moment, for the sake of formulating an exchange "model" we may speak of one as high-honor durables (*toga*) based on fine mats and ornamental objects, and the other as food. The Polynesian categorization is more complex. In Samoa, for example, food is included in the category of *oloa* along with houses, weapons, tools, and ornaments. Even here, the basic exchanges are in terms of mats, which are the product of a specially honored labor of women, and foods, taro, pigs, fowl etc., the generalized productivity of patrilocal households. *Toga* and *oloa* (to use the Samoan terms) are unquestionably complements and have, as shall soon become clear, a parallel significance to male line–female line duality, but they are evidently not equal. Mats, the gifts of chiefs, are the higher value as the product given by chiefs to lower-ranking talking chiefs.

Exchange of durables for food gives the feast the appearance of barter. When a Samoan village receives a visiting chief with a feast, he and his party reciprocate by distributing fine mats and tapa then and there. Host and guest maintain a level—more or less—equilibrium of status. None is either *magister* or *minister,* and the guest is allowed the courtesy of a nominal superiority. The sociology of this transaction is equalization; its religious concept is along similar lines, namely, the declaration of parity between two modes of productive efficacy. In still another manner, the food cycle is brought into relation with that of manufacture. Perhaps, it is permissible to think of the toga–oloa exchange as a further permutation of what seems to be the more conventional exchange that occurs when artisans (tohunga) are feasted for bringing a complex artifact into being. Even closer to the western Polynesian form of toga–oloa is the pattern of exchanges set in motion by Maori ariki when they visit other communities. His hosts feast him and he provokes exchanges of precious durables. The toga–oloa pattern may be said to have crystallized into a relationship that ordinarily exists in a more fluid state.

We therefore approach variability in the western Polynesian feasting pattern from a basic conception of complementary balances as distinct from that of hierarchical alternation in eastern Polynesia. I believe that the fundamental variants with status can be described most economically through three societies on which information is also satisfactory, Tikopia which illustrates the Traditional pattern; Samoa (Manu'a), the Open; and Tonga, the Stratified.

In Tikopia we see the basic complementary pattern enmeshed in so complex a series of exchanges of foods and durables that it is almost obscured. Nevertheless, if we take as our guide Firth's splendid chart on marriage exchanges (1939:323), we see at once that the kinship group of the husband gives "valuables" (*koroa*) to the chief of the wife's clan, bowls and sennit to the parents of the bride and to her kinship group generally, and beads and sennit to the women of the bride's family. Her side gives pandanus mats and barkcloth. As for foods, the female side (bride) gives raw food and receives in return cooked food. Male and female sides are set on different exchange tracks, to be sure, but not in categories of value. They have divided the durables and they have divided the foods so that one side does not loom over the other as markedly as, say, in Samoa. The giving of valuables to the chief of the wife's clan is probably a factor of balance with patriliny. On the other hand, the evident understatement of exchange duality seems to be in accord with its minor place in the structure of kinship groupings.

The pattern of complementary exchanges, it should be noted, involves only equals; it holds between families in their domestic interests and is not associated with chiefs in their political aspect. The major chiefs deal with food. They may receive durables as presents along with the *muakai* ("foremost foods"), a first-fruits offering; their position establishes them in the eastern Polynesian mode as centers of the food cycle. By giving food to the chief, Firth remarks, the commoner maintains his ancestral connections, which may be translated as: The chief meshes productivity with the genealogical cycle. Since the Tikopian chief cannot command an offering, and will only grumble when it is not made, we must assume it is less his honor than that of the donor's that is involved. For his part, the kainanga ariki gives feasts in honor of his own life cycle, starting with his election to office.

Returning to Samoa and its strong complementary patterns: here economic duality of male and female branches characterizes the status of chiefs as well. Toga is the donation of the male line in marriage and of the chief in his formal relations with his talking chief. Male line and chiefly line are brought into correspondence through the ritual of the feasting exchange, as indeed they are in the genealogical organization. We would misrepresent the Samoan pattern, however, if we left at this point an impression of preponderance. If toga has a higher value, it is not excessive. As the movement of food has highest honor in Tikopia, it has incontestable honor in Samoa. The difference between toga and oloa is between a product that is consumed, and so must be actively and perpetually renewed, and one that endures. One is regenerative, the other is additive; one stands for bounty, the other for scarcity. By intermarriage, exchanges are balanced between families and, in principle, equalized. It is the chief for whom the balance is postulated as difficult. Within his community, he is the constant donor of toga, the source of the scarce and essential adornment which has, it may be permissible to say, the power to elicit foodstuffs for feasting from the lower order of rank. Within his community, the chief would be in a state of economic entropy. His outside connections, however, restore him. He feeds his honored guests and they present him with toga. In short, he sustains economic equilibrium by fulfilling the chiefly obligation to move outward.

Tonga exhibits a weak form of the Samoan pattern. Koloa (mats, tapa) and foods are still on different "tracks," but only as representing the most formal expression of the idea and without a clear-cut delineation of lines. At the marriage feast, for example, each side assembled both sets of produce from among its kin membership. Women gave koloa, and men food and kava. First the groom's side set its produce before the bride's house in two parallel rows, an inner of koloa and an outer of food and kava. Then the exchange was reversed at the groom's house. Thus only sex and not sex line is recognized. Each side receives the same kinds of goods and in equal quantity. When the gifts were subsequently distributed among the kinsmen of bride and groom, respectively, each original contributor received double the amounts, even at the cost of utter depletion of the households of bride's and groom's parents. The Tongan point of view in these exchanges is therefore quantitative far more than it is qualitative. While the marriage exchange is represented as a powerful display of productivity, the partners are not directly invidious. The return of double is not potlatch since it is internal and therefore not antagonistic.

The issue may well be to achieve depletion at the center for the sake of filling the surroundings, so to speak. What impressed Mariner so strongly about Tonga was the constant commitment to feast or starve. Whether domestic, provincial, or national, the feast had to represent excess in the name of the chief who was the assembler and donor. In distribution, the shares went down by name, and order of rank among notables. In national feasts, the gods were first and the commoners last. As the lowest, they received the offering to the gods after it had rotted. They are made to appear as the post-recipients, as receptacle for a product that had already completed a major itinerary in the cycle.

To recapitulate briefly, feasting exchanges, whether between equivalents or among the ranks, are obligated, it would seem to delineate the principles of status rather closely. Western Polynesia, in the three examples cited, suggests that economic duality dependent upon a system of intricate balances becomes a highly specialized form inconsistent with either strong patriliny or a vigorous concept of power. Power, in particular, is a function of quantity.

The Utilitarian Interest in the Economy

If we consider the traditional ariki as the very embodiment of the honor principle in the economy, and the lower-level chiefs as the exponents of the utilitarian principle, then, of course, we formulate a social equation in which the relationship of these two economic principles to each other would vary as the relationships between ariki and lower-level chiefs. This rather abstract equation is, in fact, historically correct for Polynesia. The reason it holds so well is that each side of the equation is bound by firm limits. The economic side is bound by the inexorable law of scarcity of goods, and the political side is bound by the social rules of status, which by definition impose a scarcity of honor. Whether we start with politics to explain the economy or with economics to explain the polity, we are involved in the same equation.

We have been dealing with this equation all along. At this point, however, I wish to document the interaction and its historical resolution as it is revealed in two fundamental economic institutions, those of tribute and of land-holding. Both involve chiefship and both are transformed, losing in the course of transformation their connotations of honor, and gaining at the same time a new focus of utility.

Tribute

Chiefs received goods in a number of ways, through reciprocal exchanges and through a formal system of collection. Our concern is with the latter, since tribute is a constant in Polynesia and we have no doubt at all that it is one common institution that is undergoing systematic variation. Williamson has already called attention to the transformation of "first-fruits" offerings into a compulsory system of tribute. What had been a freely given religious offering became a tax. We need to examine more closely the process of transformation.

Tribute and land-holding were consistently interdependent in Polynesia. The right of the chief to tribute was associated with his rights to the land; the nature of the tribute he could command depended on the quality of his land rights. Weak rights went with weak collections, strong rights with strong collections. To take Maori as our first example. The ariki received two kinds of offerings, one was from subject, that is, defeated tribes who brought occasional presents of food and were then assured of aid in case of enemy attack. The other was a first-fruits offering from the iwi. In the first case, the offerings were a token of conquest. In the second, they acknowledged the sanctity of the ariki. According to Maori belief, the first fruits offerings to ariki began as religious offerings to their ancestral gods. We thus have an external offering respectful of the power aspect of chiefly status, and an internal offering respectful of its sacred aspect. One was compulsory, the other traditional. Both involved reciprocity. Tribute to power was reciprocated by a utilitarian service, to which, however, a token gift was added. Tribute to sanctity was reciprocated by honor in the form of equivalency, for the chief reciprocated all offerings with a gift of equal or greater value. Under the circumstances of reciprocity, undergiving to an ariki was offensive. The ariki also had rights to sea mammals, flotsam and jetsam washed ashore, and all the plunder of war. In other words, he was entitled from within his tribe to the exceptional and not to the ordinary. Since the external tribute was occasional, it too had the quality of the exceptional.

As Maori ariki sought to emphasize that their role in the economy was honorific and nonutilitarian, so did the Mangaian. But with their supremacy lost, their place in the economy was small compared with that of the Temporal Lord, who redistributed conquered lands for tribute and services. The Mangaian ariki, it may be said, conducted the honorific economy, collecting for feasts, though not through the formality of first-fruits; the Temporal Lord and the district chiefs managed the utilitarian economy. The concept of economic honor was not confined to the ariki. All giving, Buck has brought out, was a mark of respect. The utilitarian outlook did not suppress the concept of economic honor; it simply grew up large beside it.

The utilitarian outlook was strongest in the Marquesas and in Mangareva, where high chiefs redistributed seized lands for tribute and services, and organized collections upon a fixed tax system. But the Mangarevans recognized first-fruits as well. The Marquesans frankly used land as a resource for building centers of personal power, attracting followers, and exchanging subsistence for the means of power. Out of four breadfruit crops, the tribal chief received as his due the entire first crop, which contributed substantially to his reserves. He also received the customary tributes of special or exceptional items, but this was very small compared with his substantial interest in the ordinary food crops. The Mangarevan high chiefs took as their right two of the three breadfruit crops, according to the French missionary observer, Laval. They distinguished between rent *kai 'akareva* and first-fruits, *matikao mua,* thereby dividing collection into a small honorific sector and a very large utilitarian sector. The presence of first-fruits in Mangareva and its absence in the Marquesas may be attributed to the presence of the traditional ariki in the one and not in the other, since first-fruits were essentially a tribute to the sacred chief. It would appear, then, that an honorific tribute is not necessarily dislodged with the growth of chiefly power. A new form of utilitarian tribute grows up alongside, coinciding with the change in land tenure from the traditional kinship form to that based on the power of chiefs.

The nature of first-fruits in Tahiti and Hawaii further illustrates this general principle. In Tahiti, the matahiti was the honorary first-fruits offering to the high chief and was divided formally for redistribution into three parts: one for royal household, one for priests, and one for the people. The matahiti was not the mainstay of the chiefly establishment. For his pressing and steady needs, the high chief depended upon the resources of the raatira, the landed gentry whose bonds with him were political. Similarly in Hawaii. Here the makahiki was a harvest festival but was also the occasion for great tributes to the supreme chief, or moi, of foods, articles and ornaments. This tribute was also divided into three parts: one to the moi, one to his court, and one to the priests. The return to the people was in the honorific form of rain, prosperity, and happiness, as Handy has explained it. The heart of the economy was under technical administration. The makahiki itself has been regarded by scholars as a tax, on the grounds that its collection was supervised and the contribution mandatory. In addition, the high chief's konohiki, or land and labor supervisors, levied demands upon all landholders under his jurisdiction as his needs dictated. In both Tahiti and Hawaii, high chiefs had the power of seizure.

Handy has described the Hawaiian makahiki as a first-fruits tribute converted to a tax. In this respect, Hawaii had carried an honorific economic institution to its utilitarian culmination under royal auspices. That the makahiki collection was still richly embedded in concepts of honor and in a framework of ritual demonstrates the relativism of the utilitarian interest. No matter how much Polynesian economies elaborated their utilitarian interests, they still remained bound to traditions and doctrines of aristocracy. As aristocratic power grows and changes its characteristics, it transforms in its wake the royal institutions, giving them continuity with the past. In Tonga we saw how first-fruits tribute coexisted with a highly technical administration of the economy under the secular chiefs. When the Tui Tonga was finally overthrown by the lower-level technical chiefs, the first-fruits collections were also abandoned.

Land-Holding

In the system of tributes, the transformation was from voluntary giving within a pattern of mutual honoring to compulsory giving within a pattern of unequal reciprocity. This pattern expressed to a considerable degree the mutual advantages that could be claimed from unequal status and power. As long as status inequalities were based on genealogical rank alone, the inequality of reciprocity was essentially symbolic, a matter of etiquette more than of substance. They became matters of substance when unequal status and power were registered in terms of land. There is hardly any doubt that the concept of land-holding was pivotal to the Polynesian economy as a whole.

Can one describe a growth of utilitarian interest in land, considering that land to farmers is the very being of utility? We can, insofar as we refer to the interest of chiefs in land. In the Traditional societies, for example, the ariki gave the stamp of honor to tribal lands. This is all that is meant by "titular ownership." The high-level ariki had no "stewardship" over tribal land, since all caretaking was the responsibility of lower-level segments, the real holders of the land. The Maori tribal chief could rally the entire iwi to fight off an aggressor because an attack on the land was an attack on his honor. He had no direct or immediate interests in the land to defend. In a number of Traditional societies, the high ariki endowed the land with his mana, making it fruitful. This, too, as we have seen, was a relationship of honor to the land.

The record shows that the honor relations between high chiefs and land was actually unvarying in Polynesia, being essentially a key high chiefly interest in Traditional, Open, and Stratified societies. The variations were in terms of accretion of other interests—of utilitarian interests, in administering productivity, and in securing political services and powers. The utilitarian interest was always present, but in the Traditional societies as a prerogative of household heads or of smaller lineage chiefs. Our evidence has shown that one way, and perhaps the principal way, in which actual administrative authority became a high chiefly prerogative was by the advancement of the technical chiefs. As they advanced, they enlarged their traditional authority, changing it to the extent that the new authority extended over those who were not near kinsmen and were, therefore, in a new and utilitarian relationship to them. The mutuality of interests of near kinsmen in Polynesia was accepted as an end in itself, but when others were brought into the household, mutuality was in terms of reciprocal benefits. This household pattern prevalent in all of Polynesia was evidently the root pattern for the newly elevated chiefs to follow in dealing with outsiders brought within their jurisdiction.

It is indeed true that a household head or local chief maintained a utilitarian mutuality of reciprocal benefits with all persons in his jurisdiction, near or distant kin. He was compelled, nevertheless, to distinguish between kinsmen and dependents if he was not to undermine the sentiments of kinship. Dependents were stamped with distinctive inferiority. Among the Maori, they were the menials. As menials they were in a different category of inferiority from that of kinsmen, who were graded by seniority. Their relationship to the household head had less kinship sentiment and was closer, therefore, to sheer utility.

The utilitarian relationship may be also described as a function of the gap in status. The Traditional societies maintained gradations in rank; the Open and Stratified created clear divisions. These divisions were expressed and communicated through the language of economic exchange, or of economic relationships generally.

The relationship to land expressed this division in the most decisive manner because land was the material focus of status. The material counterpart of genealogical rank was formulated precisely in terms of rights to the Mangarevan "rat," the commoner who had no rights as terms such as title and ownership by distinguishing among kinds of rights to land. Every kind of right conveyed an equivalent measure of honorific status, ranging from the high ariki and his strictly honorary rights to the Mangarevan "rat," the commoner who had no rights at all. The rights of commoners to land in Traditional societies were made honorable by the nature of the kinship claim, which was inherent rather than contractual and, hence, utilitarian. Contractual relationships were also honorable, in the feudal manner, in proportion to the rank and status of the lessor. The least of the honorable claims was that of pure livelihood, the most utilitarian. This was the claim of the Hawaiian commoner, whose tenure on the soil was rarely challenged. The Hawaiian outcasts, the kauwa, had no honor at all, and their lands, accordingly, were distinct and beyond the pale, not part of the regular hierarchy of administration.

Status and specific land rights were linked, but in the traditional systems only in a one-way relationship. Land rights followed upon rank. The transformations in land tenure of the Open societies were to make land tenure and status mutually interdependent to a high degree, but not fully, since there was no substitute for genealogical rank. The impetus for profound changes in land rights came, as we learn from the histories, from an interest in power, an attribute of genealogical rank, and was propelled by the technical chiefs, who opened up new ranges of status.

Power in this setting was defined as the ability to move up the ladder of land rights contracts and to stay there. Power was the ability to break a contract and to negotiate a better one. Power, thus, was the ability to compel others to serve one's own interests in status. Compulsion rested on the reliable formula of stick and carrot, the carrot in Polynesia being a specific land right. In the sense, therefore, that land rights were transferable in the interests of chief's status, land had become a commodity. It never became a marketable commodity under native conditions, but it did become a utility, safeguarded by a modified aristocratic code that restricted land holdings to those who accepted contractual relationships of personal subordination.

If the lower-level chiefs were quick to see the possibilities for status advancement in land contracts, the ariki, with their more austere concepts of genealogical rank, held, if they could, to the older traditions. Their traditionalism favored the sacred and "higher" form of honor, and made it easy for them to leave the lower-ranking privileges of administering lands to the lower-level chiefs; to preserve, in short, the traditional pattern. Mangaia and Tonga offer the clearest examples of this traditional division between priestly roles and land-administrator roles. To be sure, the ariki had to yield authority under pressure. The division that followed, nevertheless, was for Polynesia a natural one. How "natural" it was we can see from the example of Hawaii, where even with supreme authority the high chiefs still delegated administrative authority to lower-ranking technical officers. Hawaii, however, is to be considered the outstanding example of expansion of the ariki's economic role. The supreme authority, the moi, may have delegated technical authority, but it was he who now regulated all land contracts. What has been called the "spoils system" in Hawaiian land distributions was the ultimate expression of the utilitarian interest in land for aboriginal Polynesia. Hawaii had gone so far in regarding land as commodity that its chiefs had no difficulty in understanding capitalist land-holding traditions. Shortly after the establishment of Christianity and Europeanized rule, the institution of fee simple created a true class of landowners in the Hawaiian Islands. In New Zealand, as a significant contrast, the chiefs bitterly fought the British to preserve the traditional system of land rights of kin groups.

23

The Rituals of Status

WE MAY DEFINE RITUAL AS ACTION THAT TRANSPOSES AN EVENT from the literal to the metaphoric. While the literal, being inevitable, must be acceptable, it is, nevertheless, objectionable on the grounds of being inconsequential, of being literally no more than it is. The literal is asocial because it differentiates by person rather than by category; it is transient because it does not enter into binding concepts; it remains within its given sphere and has the social disability of utmost parochialness. Finally, it is a raw event and therefore incomplete. The metaphoric, literally a transfer from one sphere to another, endows the event with the added significance of merger and of compression; it, too, is a transposition, a move into a precisely defined state that establishes the social viewpoint once and for all. Metaphor, the "language" of ritual, imposes its own categories and its own meanings which can be rejected only at the risk of defying the concept of community.

The rituals of rank authenticate position by defining it as sacred and so divesting it of connotations of literalness. The chief may have the literal power to subjugate, to intimidate, and to put to death, but it would not serve him unless he had demonstrated the metaphoric qualities of power, that is, its extension into other spheres. In the preceding chapter we considered the transposition of rank and its powers into spheres of economic productivity. In this chapter, an extension of the preceding, we are to consider other modes of metaphoric elaboration. The subject is complex, and a full treatment of the ritualization of status is beyond the scope of the present work. I have therefore chosen to illustrate only some of the metaphoric demonstrations, emphasizing those of dominance and of separation. Dominance ritual refers directly to power. Separation ritual establishes the quality of power as coming from outside, on the analogy of god:man. Dominance and separation are thus interdependent according to the axiom of Polynesian aristocracy (but not unique) that power separates, and separation authenticates power. There is here an implication of proportion. In principle, separation and power should increase in concert with the evolution from Traditional to Stratified societies.

Transposition as a metaphoric leap has merit in itself, regardless of the specific character of the sphere into which it has landed. As a demonstration of efficacious energy, it stands in contrast to the inert and passive. Content, nonetheless, is uppermost. Ritual can be said, as Durkheim has noted, to sanctify, to transpose to a divine state, and the Polynesian concept of tapu has indeed an abstract and generalized merit. The preoccupation with exact form, the essential quality of a rite, indicates the concern with specific content. In one respect, form is a code to be accurately deciphered; in another, it stands for the new locus which is to correspond in its preciseness to the point of departure. It is the nature of aristocracy to define itself by precise gradations. Generality destroys it. Thus, the exigency of ritual form.

As a system of motions, ritual must act upon consistent principles of mechanics, even if metaphoric. Consistency is as pertinent, if not mandatory, to metaphoric as it is to mechanical systems. In either case, a break in the system is interpreted as dangerous. Breaks must be repaired and changes warded off. The metaphoric system in aristocracies is logically the province of ariki and of high priests. As the operators, they are honored; as honored by one set of qualities, they are qualified to be its operators. Perhaps it is not really necessary to reassert the aristocratic principle that the elevation and separation of chiefs to give them dominance is in the interests of the religious order, which is postulated upon gradation and diminution from pinnacle to bottom.

The absolute association between ritual, beginnings, terminations, and, in particular, with rites of passage exemplifies, it would seem, a specific law of metaphoric mechanics, namely, that motion on one plane makes possible motion on another—as if, for inertia to be overcome, one transposition must help the other. I have chosen to illustrate the principle of interactive transpositions, to coin a cumbersome phrase, from rites of passage, which are unquestionably the central concern. I shall begin, however, with a primary concept, the metaphoric assertion of dominance. The expression of dominance can take a dyadic form in which one is ascendant, the other deferential in corresponding measure. The more extreme the demonstration of ascendance, the more abject the counter-show of deference. Ultimately, deference is reduced to servility, and status separation reaches its widest. The gradient of progressive polarization can be observed through Maori, Mangaia, Mangareva, Tahiti, and Hawaii in eastern Polynesia, and Tikopia, Samoa, Niue, and Tonga in western Polynesia.

Among the Maori, where the chiefs mingled freely with the people, working side by side with them in the fields, there were no signs of servility. On Mangaia, the priestly ariki were approached even by the Temporal Lord on all fours, but only when they were holding services in the sacred precincts of the marae. On Mangareva, however, the situation was far more complex. Although the akariki had great political power and sanctity (tapu), there is no evidence of ritual servility. The principle holds well, however, for Tahiti and Hawaii. On Tahiti, servility was shown by baring the breast, and on Tonga and Hawaii by the more extreme form of prostrating oneself before the ruler.

This distribution suggests that servility deference was the product of a fully developed Stratified society. The Mangaian form of servility was confined to religious services, while Mangareva appears to have been exceptional because it was the most "open" of the Stratified societies. Since in the Open societies chiefs enforced servility upon the weak, we must evidently distinguish between ritual and utilitarian servility. The Stratified societies, having successfully combined sacred and secular authority, also combined ritual servility with the utilitarian forms. The occurrence of the identical patterns in western Polynesia confirms the hypothesis. In Tonga, for example, a commoner bowed in the presence of a chief and all persons of lower rank touched the soles of a chief's feet either with the back of the hands, stooping low to do this, or—in a more pronounced gesture of respect—by placing the chief's feet upon his head. Only Tonga in western Polynesia had servility deference before chiefs.

Servility deference differs in two main respects from other forms of expressing subordination. Being confined to a simple sequence of gestures, it is an individual act. The response is not confined to a special ritual occasion, but is the obligatory obeisance to rank. Ritual servility is not to be confused with true servility, since it was demanded of persons of rank who were in no sense servile. In Tonga the Tui Tonga himself offered the gesture of extreme obeisance to the tamaha, his father's oldest sister. In Tahiti and Hawaii, ranking chiefs prostrated themselves before the supreme moi. If not true servility, neither is it insignificant, for what it denotes is the potential power of the highest rank. Hawaiian chiefs avoided contacts that would submit them to prostration obeisance.

Servility deference was an extreme form of deference, and hence relatively rare in Polynesia. All societies including the Traditional had socialized forms of deference, which were social acts of the community and were confined to special occasions. Deference by a community gives to the act a civic character, and deference upon an established occasion further shifts obeisance from person to institution. In such a setting, we have deference without servility.

When a high chief visited a Maori village, for example, the community tore down its defensive stockade to create a special entrance for him. In this act of ritual deference with its connotations of submission, the context was of mutual honoring. The chief's visit was an honor, and the deference response was in proportion. To take an opposite example, when the Hawaiian high chief visited each district or subdistrict at the conclusion of the makahiki, he was met with a ritual display of hostility. Spears were hurled at him as he stepped from his canoe and with the aid of his retinue he warded them off. In this instance the chief came in the aspect of conqueror to collect the tribute due him. The display of actual ascendance was reciprocated by actual submission (paying the tribute) and by ritual hostility. Gluckman has argued from African data that similar "rituals of rebellion" have the useful function of discharging hostile feelings in a harmless way (1955). Judging by the frequency of insurrection in Hawaii, this particular "ritual of rebellion" was irrelevant to the actual state of political affairs. The relevance of this type of ritual is not that it is an effective device for dealing with tensions and conflicts —life would be remarkably simple if this were so—but that it is a sensitive barometer of the social climate. To weather watchers, barometers are of the greatest importance.

All Polynesian chiefs were "weather watchers," sensitive to the slightest changes in public appraisal of their mana. If they did not react instantly to a slight, the signs of change were read by the public as well. The Hawaiian ritual of reception would seem to have been an acutely sensitive device, measuring the intent of the subjects and the defensive agility of the chief. Everywhere in Polynesia lese majesty was the official and acknowledged form of challenge to chiefly authority. This is true of aristocracies everywhere. Rituals of ascendance–deference more specifically are the coded communications by which the members of a community test the tonus of the status system. Ascendance ritual asserts the quality of status and deference ritual acknowledges it. Thus it has been reported of the Maori chief: "He was quick to resent any act that he deemed a *takahi mana*, a disregarding or belittling of his prestige! . . . A breach of etiquette was quite sufficient to lead to serious trouble (Best 1924:I, 389)." An example of serious trouble is given by Firth, who tells of the man who gave a chief less than a full calabash of food as a gift, an offense known as whakahawea ("to despise the recipient"). For this slight he was killed and then, in the Maori tradition of reciprocity, his kin were treated to a feast by the offended chief.

Personal Sanctity

Personal sanctity was the most characteristic form of Polynesian ascendance display. Respect for sanctity was the complement of deference. Sanctity of the chiefly person and, by extension, of his possessions and surroundings was respected in all Polynesian societies, including those often described as "democratic." The Maori, who resented imputations of servility, were as respectful of the personal tapu of chiefs as were the Hawaiians. So, for that matter, were the very politically-minded Marquesans. The differences among the Polynesian status systems were not in the granting of deference to personal sanctity, but in the style of tapu and in the response to lack of proper deference. The style of tapu display was a matter of extension and of rigor. Or, we might say more generally, it was a matter of how profoundly the concept of tapu separated chiefs from commoners. Polynesian societies differed in degree of separation of chiefs from commoners as measured by how they applied the concept of personal tapu. In the Marquesas, for example, Nuku Hivans accepted very rigorously the sanctity of the chief's head; the less aristocratic southern islands of the Marquesas did not. In a general and undoubtedly impressionistic manner, we can trace a gradient of style of tapu in terms of rigor and extension of application across all of Polynesia.

Deference to personal tapu is the religious form of avoidance respects, and does not necessarily have connotations of servility. Avoidance respects in kinship have their foundation in incest taboos, in avoidances of in-laws, and are the common property of mankind. Aristocratic societies like the Polynesian have evidently constructed their public status systems upon these elementary foundations. Respects that are so deeply rooted in kinship can hardly denote servility.

Among the Maori, sanctity was proportional to rank, in keeping with the system of finely graded status. All men had some degree of sanctity. But while women were generally noa, those of highest rank, the tapairu, the first-born daughters of a chief were also tapu. In the case of chiefs, the avoidances were more severe. They ate apart and no commoner dared touch the person of a chief or his belongings. The head was especially tapu. Conquered lands were made sacred by symbolic association with a part of the chief's body. This association involved only the prestige of the chief with the land. It did not as in Tahiti, for example, restrict its normal uses. The high priests, who were also sacred, were fed by their sisters, who put the food directly into their mouths. Violation of tapu was supernaturally punished, generally by insanity.

In Mangaia, the Temporal Lord, having come to power by force, was not sacred. Only the high priests had personal sanctity, which was confined to their bodies, and only insofar as they were concerned with religious duties. Sanctity was in respect of the religious office, and infringement was punished automatically by the gods. Sometimes, however, the priests took action.

The Marquesas illustrate still another kind of Open society pattern, but again in accord with the organization of status. All males had some sanctity centering about the head. Tapu increased with rank, adding houses and possessions to the realm of the sacred. Avoidances were not very severe, as a rule, but on Ua Pou and Nuku Hiva commoners could not enter the chief's house. Disrespecters of chiefly tapu were killed by witchcraft or by open violence.

In the Stratified societies, personal sanctity was restricted to the rulers and their immediate family. In Mangareva, this extended to the royal person, his personal property, his own residence, and the residences associated with his heirs, which included the house of the pregnant queen, the huts where she lived with the royal child, and the houses where the royal child was brought up in seclusion. The high chief himself speared to death those who ignored the royal tapu. Personal sanctity included the royal consort in Tahiti, and was generally more far-reaching than in Mangareva, covering everything in the least degree connected with the royal couple, including the sounds in the name of the paramount arii. All words in the language that contained these sounds had to be changed. Neglect of the royal tapus was punished by death.

Hawaii brought the concept of chiefly sanctity to its peak in Polynesia. Not even the shadow of a person was to fall on the person or possession of a high chief. Any action that might give the appearance of challenging the honor of the chief was lese majesty. All such violations were punished by a brutal death. To quote Malo: "The punishment inflicted on those who violated the tapu of the chiefs was to be burned with fire until their bodies were reduced to ashes, or to be strangled or stoned to death. Thus it was that the tabus of the chiefs oppressed the whole people (1951:84)."

Western Polynesia reveals a somewhat similar gradient of heightened and broader-ranging sanctity of chiefs, along with increasingly drastic punishment of offenders as we move from Traditional to Stratified societies. Firth has noted: "The system of personal *tapu* is not highly developed in Tikopia (1936:183)." A man's children respected the sanctity of his head, his person, and belongings. In the case of a chief, these restrictions applied more widely and were more strictly regarded. Violations were punished in some way by the anger of the gods. Personal sanctity was of minor importance in Manu'a as well, because, as Mead has observed; "The Samoan conception of rank as a question of title rather than of birth was highly unfavorable to the maintenance of *tapus* of rank (1930:122)." Tapu was associated not with the person, but with the title, except in the case of the truly hereditary office of Tui Manu'a. In the case of other chiefs, most of the tapus of respect for person and his intimate possessions had become forms of etiquette and not respect for sanctity. Tapu of the Tui Manu'a was comparable to that of Maori and Tikopian ariki, with an added touch of the Tahitian restriction on use of sounds in the royal name. In the Manu'an case, this was restricted to the use of the word *moa* (poultry), the family name of the Tui Manu'a. Mead has stressed, nevertheless, that the concern in Manu'a was not so much with a transgression against the sanctity of the high chief as with protecting the inadvertent transgressor who might otherwise be afflicted with boils.

The sanctity of the Tui Tonga was certainly more awesome than that of the Tui Manu'a, and his powers were correspondingly greater. Nevertheless, while the sanctity of his person, possessions, and intimate associations was fully respected, tapus were of the same kind that prevailed among the population at large. They were part of the general system that made fathers tapu to their children, sisters to their brothers, paternal aunts to their nephews, and persons of higher genealogical rank to their inferiors. The difference was only that violation of the supreme chief's tapu was punishable by execution, whereas among the populace only general afflictions were imposed by the gods.

Rites of Passage

Van Gennep demonstrated the common elements in passage rites, and contemporary theory (cf. Cohen 1964), in the spirit of the times, has interpreted passage as "crisis" and ritual as its therapy. Ritual promotes catharsis and safely discharges anxieties. Pregnancy and parturition rites, for example, relieve natural anxieties about child birth, puberty rites cope with oedipal disturbances, funeral rites master grief and social derangements, and so on. The magnitude of ritual should be in proportion to the gravity of the "crisis." If applied to Polynesia, the therapy theory of ritual compels the extraordinary conclusion that the life of the aristocracy was anxious and disturbed, that of the commoner serene. The Polynesians seemingly thought otherwise. Having associated ritual with genealogical grade, they varied it in accordance with power and other qualities of status.

Maori. It is logical to start with the ritual of childbirth, the beginning of the life cycle. Birth, according to Firth, was most ceremonious among the aristocracy and the most important ceremonies were for the first-born males. Buck concurs: The children of commoners were born with "little trouble or fuss (1949:950)."

The Maori had no rites to mark the transition from youth to maturity. This is a striking omission, since elsewhere in Polynesia male superincision had the significance of a transition. Perhaps since the induction to rank with its consolidation of mana came in infancy, any further gain of prerogatives of rank was superfluous at adolescence. The Maori were drawn more to formal education that taught esoteric and exoteric lore in schools conducted by priests. Ritual avoidances demarcated the special status of the honored mother and, at the same time, that of the infant, who represented at that very moment the appearance of a distinctive line that must emerge as separate or die out. If the jurisdiction of the birth was violated, the infant would be aborted. It was considered as being transposed to the realm of its appropriate deity; to Io, if of highest rank. When the infant was to receive a name from the genealogy, it was then metaphorically transposed to the jurisdictions of war, of power, and of knowledge. A weapon pressed against the hand symbolized war, the sacrifice of a slave its power to command life or death, and a bird pressed against an ear opened the mind to awareness. These three attributes "fixed" the mana to the infant.

Ritual grief is inevitably a deferential act, if not directly in behalf of the deceased, then before his mighty patron, the specter of death. The Maori, who were not overly deferential to the living, did not hesitate to submit before the dead. Mourners gashed themselves and women, the most violent, tore their breasts. If the deceased was of high rank, a slave was killed in his behalf and his widow took her own life. Both would then accompany the departing soul. Self-inflicted violence would seem to be the deference counterpart of an act of extreme ascendance. The mourners are putting themselves down; the widow virtually joins the category of the slave.

Mourning has generally two phases. Self-abasement acknowledging the supremacy of death is followed by a reversal in which the erstwhile mourners assert their own supremacy. Maori concluded mourning with the distribution of extraordinarily valuable gifts, jade and whalebone clubs, and with monumental feasts in proportion to rank. Those from among whom the genealogical vacancy will be filled are privileged to move up. The extravagant praise of a chief at death, compared with the more modest acclaim he received in life, indicates that he, too, had been elevated. He was then "the horn of the crescent moon" that had broken off, "the lofty mountain" that had been leveled to the ground.

Mangaia. Birth ritual was confined to families of rank. A feast in her honor aided the mother in her labor: One productive cycle abets another. If the child was first-born or otherwise distinguished, he was dedicated to the tribal god and made into a person who could be both sympathetic and contemptuous (Buck 1934:350). In its principal lines, Mangaian birth ritual resembled that of Maori, with one important difference: In Mangaia, the human sacrifice seems to have been omitted. In its place was a more moderate display of ascendance. The infant in an important family was raised on the shoulders of kinsmen, an act of symbolic fealty. Human sacrifice in Mangaia attains importance at the investiture of the Temporal Lord, where it attests to the power of mature status.

The investiture of the Temporal Lord was the major ritual. The victors in triumphant procession marched seven times around the island. The first march around was violent, and they killed all who crossed their path. The remainder were peaceable and were directed toward each of the major maraes which had now come under the central jurisdiction. At the central marae, a captive was sacrificed and his ears were cut off and placed on the altar. These represented the division of the island into its right and left parts. Then the ears were cut into small portions, one for each local jurisdiction, and deposited at each local marae. Among the Maori, a comparable act of investiture was to attach the land to the conqueror by merely naming it after a part of his body.

In mourning rites, Mangaians displayed more violent feelings than the Maori. The bereaved gashed themselves and submitted themselves to the reduction of cutting their hair, blackening the face, and wearing garments that smelled of decay. Then, in a contrary spirit, they fought violent sham battles with neighboring communities. Gill, the first to describe these intermural combats, which the Mangaians called the "younger brother of war," thought of them as a thrashing of the ghosts in each district. Buck, reasoning along similar lines, saw them rather as a way of disposing of the life principle of the deceased. Either interpretation is feasible; it is the choice of form that is significant. The mourning combats resemble the investiture of the Temporal Lord. The theme of antagonism is verified in the funeral dirges. In one, Tane is reviled in a bitter verse that says: "You are not weary for you have eaten / may you be plastered with filth / and even defecated upon / Man is (as good as) a god (Buck 1934:195)." Other funeral dirges, known also as war dirges, ask for a warlike spirit.

Marquesas. Birth ritual was open to all children, bearing out the impression of the Marquesas as the most "democratic" of the Open societies. Just as consistently, the first-born were greeted with more elaborate ritual and the first-born of chiefs with the most. The maximum ritual is the most interesting. A conch shell trumpet announced the birth and thereafter the infant was honored by the erection of a decorated shrine in his behalf, by the planting of trees, by the construction of a new house, and by the preparation of cloth, ornaments, a canoe, a sacred adze. Shortly after his birth, the child was betrothed with elaborate rites, and sometimes during his childhood he participated in a great memorial festival to honor his ancestors. The erection of the shrine was to strengthen the child's spirit, a rite clearly analogous to the Maori rites for consolidating mana. Handy has made the point altogether clear that all the rites of birth and early childhood were to honor the child, to elevate him to his proper status.

With their belief in opportunities for all, the Marquesans did more to honor children than any other Polynesian society. Even the first public appearance of the first-born child of rank was celebrated with a major festival. Because of the continuity of honorings and elevations in status, rites at adolescence do not stand out as particularly important. Nevertheless, circumcision at puberty was followed by costly tattooing. Ornamentation of the body was an outstanding public event celebrated with a major feast. Just before marriage the boy was introduced once more to society at a festival during which songs composed in his honor were sung. These rites that moved the child and youth up the stages of honor added increments of status to him and, of course, enhanced the prestige of his family.

The details of the rites bring out some of the specific concepts of honor. For example, the first-born children of chiefs did not enter a dwelling through the doorway but were passed through a specially made opening in the thatch above the door, until the house specially constructed for them had been completed. Among the Maori it was a point of honor for high chiefs never to enter the house of another through the regular doorway. These customs must surely be cognate. If they mean the same in the Marquesas, they define the infant immediately as of chiefly stature. All evidence points to the fact that the honoring of high-status infants was not really in the interests of the status of the family but was intended for the child. Handy specifically states this to have been the case in the festival that first introduced the infant to the public and recited his genealogy. He says:

> The feast that followed being in honor of the child the mother and father could not participate—a tapu apparently based first on the respect due from parents to their sacred first-born, and secondly on the practical idea of preventing parents from taking personal advantage of what belonged to or was in honor of their child (1923:93).

Marquesas shared with Maori the practice of a human sacrificial offering as part of the deference to children. But whereas Maori associated this with birth ritual, the Marquesans associated it with the piercing of the ears between the ages of six and ten and with tattooing. For boys, ear piercing accompanied circumcision so that the sacrificial deference clearly marked a stage in physical maturity, a more realistic association in the Marquesas than in New Zealand. All other human sacrifices were offered at the very great events in the lives of actual chiefs or in the affairs of the community.

Mourning rites for chiefs and important priests were distinctive in their demand for human sacrifices and in their imposition of tapu restrictions on the entire tribe. For one month no fire could be lighted or any work be done. As soon as a chief's death was announced, warriors went out to seek human victims. According to Dordillon, up to ten victims were killed and laid at the foot of the bier. Children were sometimes buried alive with the body of an inspirational priest. The expression of mourning has been described by observers as rather violent. The American missionary Alexander wrote in 1833:

> The funeral rites beggared description for obscenity, noise, cruelty, and beastly exposure. They lasted several days, and were the darkest days I ever saw. Companies came from all parts filling the air with loud wailings, dancing in a state of perfect nudity around the corpse like so many furies, cutting their flesh with shells and sharp stones til the blood trickled down to their feet, the women tearing out their hair, both men and women knocking out their teeth, indulging in the most revolting licentiousness, and feasting to excess, while muskets were fired and seashells were kept a-blowing with a long deep sepulchral sound during the whole night." (cited by Handy 1923: 106–8).

Whatever more specifically religious significance the funeral rites undoubtedly had, the graphic but too brief description just quoted does bring out the themes of extreme deference in the self-humiliation of the mourners. Human sacrifices, the Marquesans believed, would bring blessings of fertility from the gods. Extreme deference, was the price for fertility in analogous fashion to the political convention that deference was the price for succorance. The honoring of the very powerful *tau'a* (inspirational priests) was the most deferential, a sacrificial victim being offered for every part of his body. In this way the dead priest was deified or elevated in power.

Mangareva. Birth ritual between royalty and commoners differed largely in degree as well as in the fact that the royal heir had to be born on the royal marae if he were to claim the office of supreme chief. Chiefly children, generally, were born on a marae, while commoner children were not. Chiefly families also observed special pregnancy ceremonies. When conception was recognized, the woman discarded her previous garments and went to live in a specially constructed new house that was either on a hilltop—a common chiefly location—or else was surrounded by eight fences where she was removed from the rest of the community and guarded closely by priestesses. Even a high chief could be put to death for violating the tapu of his pregnant daughter. In advance of parturition, still another house was constructed for the residence of the infant, and the stages in its construction were celebrated with food distributions. The pregnant princess was carried around the island from marae to marae where a lock of her hair was cut.

Pregnancy ritual in the case of the royal heir seems to have had two themes: one was the elevation to the highest honor of the child-bearing mother, and the other was a prenatal investiture of the heir-to-be. The visits to the maraes were surely investiture, while a great many ceremonies systematically added honor to the woman. When the eaves for the infant's new house were cut, the woman was presented with the ritual of a brief but bloody sham battle. Later she was taken to the sea to sit in the water upon a fattened person of chiefly rank. Back on the shore she then sat on a seat of wealth—of barkcloth heaps and fine mats. She witnessed processions of fattened youths and pleasant games. Each event was accompanied by chants sung by the rogorogo and, of course, by food distributions in the name of the supreme chief. Immediately after birth, the royal infant was invested with sanctity on the marae and then it and its mother were secluded in a series of four special huts, spending some 10 days in each. At the conclusion of this period of some 40 days, the child was conveyed to the royal nursery on the mountain summit where it and the royal attendants were enveloped in strict tapu, and remained in isolation for 12 or 14 years. During this time, they were heavily fed to take on the corpulence of a chief.

Fattening was definitely a passage rite, with its stages of seclusion, its transitional acquiring of body mass—a form of being grown—and the public appearance. The house of seclusion was a sacred precinct and the coming down from the mountain was a festival occasion that in the case of the heir lasted up to three days. The privilege of fattening was open to all families, but only the wealthy could afford it and so—for the most part, in any case—it was the first-born who were so honored. Such children were called "cherished children"; those not first-born simply "fattened children." Mangarevan fattening was not just a matter of putting on weight. It had the qualities of ritual exaggeration. Laval who witnessed the rites wrote as quoted by Buck (1938a:118):

> "They made their public appearance, decorated with *toga* (cloth) and flowers and supported by their relatives, because —even fatter than carnival bulls—they could not walk without stumbling or collapsing under their own weight. . . . As they appeared before the crowd anxious to see them, the people shouted with sheer admiration and the one who aroused the most admiration was considered the champion."

Supercision was a minor rite performed only on the sons of chiefs toward the end of their stay at the house of isolation. Commoner youths substituted for the operation a simple tying of the prepuce with a ligature. Tattooing also began at puberty and was associated strictly with rank. High ranks tattooed family crests and could afford complete and elaborate tattooing. Successful warriors were the most extensively tattooed (Buck 1938a:177).

We have no accounts of rites of investiture of the akariki, although the religious initiation of priests has been described in detail. Since an observer of the caliber of Laval is not likely to have overlooked important rites, there is cause to suppose this was not for Mangarevans a major ritual event. Quite possibly the birth rites for the royal heir took the place of formal investiture ritual.

The great ritual emphasis was on death. The elaborateness of mourning was proportional to rank and wealth, and mourning was accordingly the major occasion for the ritual display of the standing of the deceased and of his kin. Insofar as death is considered, as it was in Mangareva, a felling at the hands of the gods and thus a humiliation, funeral rites have the obligation to restore some balance to human self-esteem by a marshaling of all the signs of human greatness. If a commoner has been felled, it is a small event, but if a chief, the counter-action must be of monumental importance. This was the way it was in Mangareva and in all of the Stratified societies. In Mangareva, where even a commoner could be king, the rites for those of low birth followed a simplified version of the royal pattern. In the other three Stratified societies this was not so. Royal funerals created, in addition, as Buck has remarked, a political problem of the succession and held the threat of open violence.

The akariki's death was announced in wailing as an attack by a shark. The people were gathered to the main village where they mourned in the traditional fashion of beating their heads, biting their hands, and cutting their skin. "Some committed acts of violence on others to adequately express their grief (Buck 1938a:481)." They feared unfriendly gods in the after-world, and each family therefore appealed to its own ancestral gods for aid, and offered them presents. The mourning of close kin was more restrained and more concerned with lamentations of loss. In the course of ceremonies the expressions of grief were gradually replaced by more joyous themes. Songs were introduced for the pleasure of the audience and a new refrain marked the change. For example (Buck 1938a:487):

> Behold, the dawn appears
> The light increases,
> Rosy rays are spreading

Thereafter the treatment of the corpse was one of honoring accented by the song: "Give the chief a sacred headdress/ A headdress adorned with red plumes/ with a whole ivory ornament." In the course of this new mood, flattering speeches extolled the deceased, recited his distinguished genealogy, and mentioned the distinctions of all important persons present. These were political speeches testing the popularity of the succession. If the succession was not approved, this was the time to proclaim opposition.

Funeral feasts went on for a lunar month, during which time the royal corpse (wrapped in at least 20 wrappings of barkcloth) was presented at each of the different districts and islands. When it was finally interred in a cave, great quantities of precious barkcloth were laid with the corpse.

Other events of importance honoring the royal corpse included a fish dance that displayed the gracefulness of noble women, an honorary duel to display the skill of warriors, the killing of sacrificial victims, some of whom were commoners and others who were of chiefly descent, and finally a period of tapu on the sea, a restriction that penalized the landless fishermen.

Tahiti. Birth ritual in Tahiti was rather more important than in Mangareva, because in the Society Islands the chiefly heir assumed the title and the deference due to it from the moment of birth. Some form of ritual attended the birth of all first-born, including those of commoner families. In the royal family all children were honored to a lesser degree, but the first-born was honored with human sacrifices. Tahitian birth ritual resembled the Mangarevan in basic outline. There was the proclamation of a six-day tapu on all normal activities on sea and shore, but not at the deep mountain areas, where no one ordinarily lived. The public retired to this region, fearing only the manslayer who was sent among them to fetch human sacrifices. The confinement took place in a newly constructed and consecrated house behind a fence and on the sacred grounds of the ancestral marae. The royal child was taken to the royal marae, where sacredness was imparted to it, and it was taken on a tour of all the district maraes within its jurisdiction. There were two basic differences: In Tahiti the ritual was dedicated to the honoring of the child and not to elevating the mother, and all important events in the ritual were accented with human sacrifices. The rationale of these differences is not difficult to comprehend. Since the infant acquired rank and title at birth, there was no need to precede with an elevation of the mother. Thus in Tahiti, it was the child who was taken to each marae and not its pregnant mother. The human sacrifices associated in Tahiti with all major chiefly events belong, therefore, with the infant.

The first human scrifice came at the ceremony on the marae attaching sacredness to the infant. This was an occasion for homage of servility deference to the child and its royal parents. The father was the first to pay homage to the child. The next human sacrifice followed the ceremony on the marae. Messengers were sent to the districts to announce the birth and to set a red pennant on each district marae. When the messengers left, a victim was sacrificed. This part of the ritual was strictly political, for each district then had the option of either accepting the flag and administration or tearing it down and declaring open insurrection. When the heir apparent after a 14-month ritual seclusion with his mother was taken on a round of visits to each district marae, he was received with a human sacrifice in each. The victim was placed beneath his canoe as a roller. For other than royal children, there were rites on local maraes but no human sacrifices and no ritual seclusion. The ordinary first-born were honored only with feasts and property distributions.

In Tahiti, by contrast with Mangareva, the "initiation" rite was circumcision and not fattening (which was a secular interest). When the heir apparent was circumcised on the family marae, several victims were offered up, suspended by sennit strings through the ears, like caught fish. In the case of ordinary circumcisions, the parents pierced their skin so they too would bleed. A religious rite, circumcision took place on the family marae when the boy was 15 or 16 years old. It does not seem to have been an important ceremony. There are not sufficient details by which to judge whether circumcision was in fact a transition rite.

The royal inauguration might be considered a ritual continuation of the pre-inaugural rites that began with the early childhood of the heir apparent. The official inauguration dealt in the symbols of sacredness; the only recognition given to the political theme was the moment when the ruler standing in the sea awaited the arrival of two deified sharks. If he was indeed the legitimate ruler, the sharks nuzzled him. If he were a usurper, they would avoid him. Human victims were sacrificed to emphasize sanctity and specifically to honor the gods. A great display was made not of the ruler's power, but of the sanctity of his vestments, all of which were carefully displayed to the public audience.

This formality, which made much of the insignia of rank and the flourishes of speech, song, and gesture, was carried over into the rites of mourning, which added the specifics of wailing, self-laceration, and ritualized violence. The Tahitian form of violence, called *heva,* was more intense still than in Mangareva. If the deceased had been royal a band of young men of the collateral lines and from among the retainers formed themselves into a troupe of the "bewildered" and sallied out periodically among the people beating, seriously wounding, and killing any they met on their path. As in Mangareva, this was the time to assault one's enemies. This "reign of terror," as Henry describes it lasted indefinitely, at least over a month, and had to be put down by chiefs of other districts. In that case, whole districts might become involved in hand-to-hand combat. The priests could end the heva readily by changing their form of dress and declaring the mourning finished.

It seems rather strange at first thought that Tahitians, who had carried human sacrifices to a frenzied peak by Polynesian standards, should not make a human offering at the death of a ruler. There were so many occasions for human sacrifice that its omission in the case of mourning must have its own special meaning. They offered human sacrifices for the foundation stone laying of a central marae; for washing the first-born; for planting the royal pennant on local maraes; for introducing the royal child to the public; for the circumcision of the heir-apparent; for the coming of age of the royal first-born; for inauguration of the ruler; for perforating tapa cloth to make a royal feather girdle; for the first piercing of the cloth by the needle; for completing the ruler's loin cloth; as a roller over which the royal canoe passed in its visits to new lands; for awakening the tutelary god to preside over battle; for invoking the sovereign to be victorious in battle; for opening hostilities; for support to the ruler in defeat; for closing hostilities and pledging peace; for erecting a house of sacred treasures of the marae. This, the complete list, brings out the theme of auspicious beginnings. We must assume therefore that the death of the sovereign was to the Tahitians a momentous anticlimax. Presumably this was so because the royal death brought no interregnum; the heir-apparent had already been designated at birth. If human sacrifices are interpreted as examples of extreme servility deference, the heva must be considered a second-rate form of servility deference. Does the designation of the grotesque and violent band as "bewildered" also carry out the connotation of a lower form of servility deference? I think it does, inasmuch as the directed is always more consequential than the random.

Hawaii. Malo tells us "The women of the poor and humble classes gave birth to their children without paying scrupulous attention to matters of ceremony and etiquette (1951:182–84)." The most scrupulous attention was paid, though, to royal births. Mangareva began its attentions at the time of recognized conception. Hawaiian royalty, profoundly interested in genealogical purity, began its ritual concern prior to the first mating—but only in behalf of the highest-ranking first-born. For the offspring to acquire the highest degree of sacredness and mana, this first mating was made a public religious ceremony. First the royal pair were separated and guarded by priestly keepers. They were kept apart until the girl had completed a menstrual period and had been ritually purified by a bath. She was then escorted to a tent of tapa cloth set up in public where she waited for her consort. He arrived bearing a staff with an image of the deity which he planted outside the tent before he entered. The priests prayed for a fruitful union and the multitude waited until evening when the ritual of mating was completed.

A new round of ceremonies began when conception was announced. *Meles* were composed to eulogize the genealogy of the chief-to-be and were sung and danced to by the royal hula company. They sang and danced continually until the child was born. When conception was announced, the couple refrained from further coitus until after the birth and the subsequent purification of the mother.

Parturition itself was relatively unceremonious. The midwives, however, were women of high rank. If the child was the hoped-for boy, he was taken to the royal heiau, where the navel cord was cut in a simple ceremony marked by the sacrifice of a single pig and a prayer for his long life and reign. Hawaii is noteworthy for not having imposed any public restrictions in connection with the royal birth and for not associating the royal birth with any form of servility deference. Royal sanctity was not asserted through human sacrifices. Far more than in Tahiti and Mangareva, Hawaii relied upon the formality of prayer and incantation and display of insignia to present the image of sanctity. The public could view the setting of the royal mating but it was not asked to participate in the sequence of marriage ritual. The public reaction was not an issue in royal ritual, and in this respect royalty and the public were more separated than they were in other eastern Polynesian societies. The closest association was between royalty and the high priesthood.

Among ordinary families, pregnancy rites concerned themselves with the more mundane interests in the child's physical welfare and moral qualities, and these concerns dictated the foods the pregnant woman was encouraged or forbidden to eat. Similar practical interests governed the treatment of the umbilicus. If the cord was not safeguarded from rats, the child would develop a thievish nature (Handy and Pukui 1958:78). For first-born only, a domestic sacrament was held that required the consumption of a pig (parallel to the royal sacrifice of a pig), or a fish substitute, and other special foods which when eaten would safeguard the child from malicious influences and give it a good character. Then the child was presented to the family and friends at a feast when gifts were brought for it. The higher the rank, the more extensive the feast and the greater the quantity of gifts received.

The difference between the highest-rank and low-rank pregnancy and birth rites was therefore more than a matter of elaborateness. The difference was also in kind. For royalty, the rites asserted or endowed with sanctity; for the commoner, the rites gave only secular qualities. The distinction thus was between honor and the utilitarian interests, the traditional distinction between noble and commoner.

Hawaiians practised subincision without rituals of passage. The purpose of subincision was simply to facilitate coitus and to enhance the pleasure in it. Handy and Pukui insist there were no puberty rites in Hawaii of any sort, and attribute their absence to the sexual freedom of adolescents. Boys, having been fully weaned at the age of four or five, were initiated into the men's house through rather simple rites. By leaving the company of women, who were noa, and entering the company of men, the child gained in status. He was dedicated to the god Lono the Provider. This initiation was in part a general fertility rite and in part a specific rite to promote the growth of the child. The parallel ritual for royalty was the initiation of the youth into the temple service. Both forms of the ritual were transition rites in that they marked a passage from female food to men's food, symbolized mainly by pork. Since the Hawaiians regarded food—as distinct from mother's milk—as sacred, the passage was from secular to sacred. In the case of royalty, the transition was to highest sanctity; in the case of commoners, to the more common form of sanctity by which men were differentiated from women.

The great political ritual was the building of a heiau. The construction and consecration of this great temple was undertaken specifically to ask the gods for military victory or to make the crops flourish. It signalized at the same time the consolidation and sanctification of royal power. The ceremonies were most awesome in time of war, since war was both threat to royal power and the means of its extension. It was then that human sacrifices were offered. In contrast to Tahiti, where the central authority was not nearly as strong, Hawaii made rather little use of human sacrifice, reserving these offerings for wartime. But even for a war heiau, the consecration rites called for few human sacrifices and the victims were chosen from among criminals. The victim was dedicated to Ku, the god of war, from whom an omen was asked. Until the omen was granted—the appearance of deep sea seaweed—a general tapu on sexual intercourse was in force over the land. This tapu, according to Malo, might last only ten days or months or even years. Those who broke the tapu were put to death. As in the parallel Tahitian inaugural ceremonies, it was the gods who commanded attention and the ruler served as a high priest. It was the god who commanded deference. When the image of the god specially carved for the occasion was carried to the sea by the priests in a mad and headlong rush, they killed anyone who got in their way. And when priests carrying the image in a procession on the temple grounds made an error, they were put to death for an act of sacrilege to the god. Violence, nevertheless, was not the central theme, but as in all other major ritual, worship. The great offerings were of food especially pigs. As Malo observed, the power of the Hawaiian ruler was conceived to be religious, depending upon the favor in which the gods held him.

Thus royal funeral rites were rites of deification. These rites did not call for the violence that marked mourning in other Polynesian societies. For a high chief—but not the supreme ruler—the mourners followed Polynesian tradition in knocking out front teeth or gashing the head and body (Handy and Pukui 1958:156), but they did not seek to kill innocent victims. Instead they indulged in an orgy of sexual passion.

Manu'a. We may deal more concisely with the western Polynesian variations in status ritual by confining the comparisons to Manu'a and Tonga, both very closely related societies, one representing a transitional phase between Traditional and Open; the other Stratified. A comparison between Manu'a and Tonga is particularly interesting, because while both were very sensitive to the proper etiquette of status, one had understated political power and the other had evolved quite a formidable political authority. The comparison considered in relation to what we have learned from eastern Polynesia should reveal somewhat more clearly the influence of political power upon the development of status ritual. Tonga, it will be recalled was warlike, Manu'a was not.

We have no information on birth rites in the family of the Tui Manu'a, the highest rank, so that we cannot say if there was actually a qualitative distinction between this sacred rank and all others. The birth of a first-born was considered much more important than that of all others, but no ritual distinction was made for sex. In the case of a first-born, the mother if she had been a *taupou* (that is, the first-born of a chief), would return to her own village to give birth in the setting of highest rank. The major difference evidently between high and low rank was in the size of the gift exchanges, which in the case of a first-born was substantial. In the case of later-born children of ordinary households, only a small feast with only small property exchanges was held. The birth feast, Mead has explained, was in behalf of the mother rather than for the child, and for that reason the sex of the child was of no great consequence. Some minor restrictions on the expectant mother were for the benefit of the child's health, in the main. There is no hint of deference ritual; the complementary gift exchanges while honoring mother and child expressed the balance of status between the two sides of the family.

Circumcision was merely an operation and not a ritual; first menstruation was ignored. Slightly more ceremonious was the introduction of the boy to the council of young men, the *aumaga,* an event that gave adult status. When a youth, boy or girl, assumed the title of manaia or taupou, the occasion was ceremonialized with gifts of toga to the talking chiefs, who responded with eloquent flattery. This, as Mead has brought out, was the standard ritual for the assumption of a title or privilege.

Even the installation of the Tui Manu'a, a solemn act of sanctification, followed the same basic pattern, devoid of servility deference or of any other sign denoting physical powers. There was a procession to the altar led by the talking chiefs, food offerings of distinguished foods, fish, pigs, chickens, and cooked bananas. Then the ruler's sanctity was made official by anointment with coconut oil. Finally the Tui Manu'a reciprocated the honors by distributing toga to the high-ranking talking chiefs.

By eastern Polynesian standards, the reaction to the death of the Tui Manu'a was also muted. Although his rank was acknowledged over all Manu'a, the tapus banning work and the lighting of fires was confined to his own village. Elsewhere people paid their respects by not wearing anything on the head until the period of mourning had closed. In western Samoa, where war was common and chiefly power was especially formidable, mourning followed the violent customs of eastern Polynesia. Mourners rent their clothes and hair. They gashed their scalps and singed their flesh. They did not attack others.

Tonga We have no detailed information on birth rites on Tonga generally, and none specifically for the family of the Tui Tonga or other chiefly ranks. A ceremony at age two honored the parents.

Tonga differed from Manu'a in holding some minor rites for first menstruation and for circumcision of adolescent boys. Both rites were celebrated with feasts and distribution of gifts. In the case of the Tui Tonga's daughter, the entire countryside took part, men bringing kava and food, women durables. The rites were accompanied by brief seclusion and minor tapus. The Tui Tonga was too sacred to be circumcised. For the same reason he was not tattooed.

There is not enough information on the installation of a Tui Tonga to allow a comparison with Samoa. However, the death of the Tui Tonga and of other major chiefs has been described in some detail. Rites of mourning expressed antagonism and devastation. In the words of Mariner (1817:I, 111) the extravagant feasts alone "threaten to leave the place desolated." In the Western Samoan style they arranged for acts of ritual violence. Women simply appeared forlorn. Men (except for warriors for whom only outward violence was appropriate) attacked themselves. They gashed their bodies, pierced their cheeks, and clubbed their heads. They exclaimed, "with your death, destruction and war will come." Then they engaged in ceremonial combat and killed anyone they encountered on the road. When his daughter had died, Mariner's patron, Chief Finow, ordered general combat between parties of women and parties of men, each representing the north and the south regions of his domain. At the death of the chief himself, a principal wife was strangled to accompany him into the afterlife. But even as the mourners were encouraged to express their feelings in controlled violence, they were urged by the heir to the chiefship to control true excess. "Life is already too short," he reminded them. "The land is depopulated. The principal chiefs and warriors are fallen, and we must be contented with the society of the lower classes (Mariner 1817:I, 411)."

Rituals of Separation

Unlike rituals of servility deference, the rituals of separation are quite general. Having only to indicate that their subject is in a distinctive and honorable category, they can be freely improvised. Maori, for example, are distinctive, I believe, in separating the mode of chiefly entrance to a house from the ordinary entrance. The full elaboration of a distinctive chiefly language in Tonga and Samoa, whereas in Tahiti and Hawaii only the vocables of a high chief's name could not be used, are examples of improvisation subject to no known rule of chiefly authority other than the general recognition that separation itself is clear-cut.

All separation rituals of ariki have in common the theme of personal intimacy that arises from the concept of personal sanctity. For them, separation is very much a matter of avoiding contact, touch, contamination. Equal in importance is the theme of uniqueness, of being first, of being the only one entitled to first-fruits, to certain fish, to certain ornaments and insignia, to have a house on a hill, on the highest mound. The tapu and uniqueness of high-born is part of a complementary pattern that imposes the opposite on low-born. If high-born receive individual and deferentially offered allotments of food at a feast, the low-born eat en masse and scramble for their food. If the relation of high-born to land is honor, that of a low-born is utility. If highborn are cosmopolitan, low-born are parochial. What is lese majesty but a break in the pattern of polarity?

Technical or nonariki statuses have their own modes of separation from those beneath them. Craft organizations and their ritual separate tohunga from ordinary men and separate one set of skills from another. As middle statuses, they lack the special rituals of personal tapu and the special requirements of uniqueness. As a class, these middle ranks are eligible for the more pragmatic prerogatives of status such as wealth in commodities and in lands and a share in power. Middle ranks therefore are not a shadow aristocracy but rather an elevated commoner class. Unfortunately we know too little about the status systems of the middle ranks to carry the comparison with the ariki statuses very far. The system divides the prerogatives, giving ritual plus pragmatic prerogatives to the ariki status and pragmatic prerogatives with markedly reduced ritual to the lower statuses. What is not clear is the nature of the interaction set up by this division. Is there a pull upward toward ritualization of the lower ranks, giving them an opportunity for ritual separation, or a pull downward toward breaking down the ritual isolation of the ariki?

Historical evidence on this point is far from complete. What there is suggests that the expansion of the Polynesian middle class or technical statuses in the Stratified societies was accompanied by increasing of ritual separation of the high chiefs. This increased separation can be judged from the intensified exercise of personal tapu between the traditional stages and the stages of stratification. A reasonable interpretation of this association of events is that ritual separation is a constant in aristocratic societies and it responds to a challenge by asserting itself all the more strongly. That this phenomenon of increasing ritual separation is distinct from the accompanying phenomenon of increased personal power that is expressed in tapus involving servility deference can be seen from changing patterns in other forms of ritual separation. In the changing patterns, for example, in rituals involving food and sex.

Food and sex were conceptually related in Polynesia. Raw food was a masculine concern, cooked food a female concern. At the same time, and as a second element in the status equation, food and sex were conceptually related to rank. Among Maori, for example, chiefs promoted the growth of raw food in their own domains and their presence was antagonistic to the growth of food of other tribes. As for sex, there was the familiar division between the sacred or most honored male and the common and least honored female. The varying combinations of these basic concepts gave to each society its distinctive version of food and sex separations.

To start with Maori as the best example of a Traditional eastern Polynesian society, the distribution of food and eating were most emphatically distinguished in ritual significance. Distribution was most honorific and was at the same time a link with the people. Eating was for ranking chiefs a more complex ritual act, because cooked food was antithetical to tapu. Only low-ranked women or slaves cooked, and on ceremonial occasions chiefs ate apart. It was always bad form for Maori hosts to be present when their guests were eating. Food could not be brought into the Maori meeting house or it would pollute its sanctity and that of its occupants. Eating, or the preparation of food for eating, was no form of communion among the Maori but rather one of the rituals of separation between ariki and the populace. There was, however, no domestic separation in eating among the Maori. The family, including the women, ate together and food was prepared in the common residence. Hawaii, by contrast, had carried separation of eating to an extreme, separating husband and wife and requiring separate cook houses for men's food and women's food.

The principles of separation are reasonably clear. With respect to food, polarity takes several forms: abundance and poverty, giving and receiving, circulating and producing, raw and cooked, of which the first component is usually the higher honor, the second the lower. Raw food enters into the honor of association with abundance, giving, and circulation. Cooked food is the end product, the terminus of a cycle. How does one honor a terminal offering? The prototype for a terminal offering is the offering to a god. The ariki receiving food as a god does so in his quality of distinctness. The ultimate transmitter of the food is either a commoner woman or a male menial. In either case, someone at the opposite end of the social scale. In this way the distance between food giver and ariki is made to appear equivalent to the distance between ariki and the god.

24

Status and Evolution

WE TURN FINALLY TO A MORE GENERAL VIEW OF POLYNESIAN evolution, taking as our vantage point the major processes of enlargement and diversification. The growth of the political community represents the fulfillment of chiefly ambitions and of Polynesian status ideals. In this respect it is a progressive structural modification and a focal point of cultural development. Enlargement refers both to community and to power, each an aspect of the other. Whether or not the appearance of a more powerful central authority represents a general evolutionary advantage for Polynesia is a matter for moral philosophy to decide. Since enlargement was bitterly resisted by many who had their own clear opinions about social progress, we are justified only in recognizing it as an objective advantage for chiefs. Perhaps, what is good for the chief is also good for the community at large. Diversification refers to community and to status. Local groups take on new structural and functional characteristics and at the same time new statuses and new privileges are created. By the terms of Polynesian interests and ideals, diversification, too, is progressive as fulfillment and as compensation for losses sustained in the course of political evolution.

Enlargement and diversification are counterpart processes in constant response with each other. What is enlarged diversifies, and what diversifies tends to enlarge. Both processes are products of antagonism, specifically of status rivalry, and each may be viewed as an adjustment to the other within a social context of strong oppositions. It is doubtful that either enlargement or diversification could develop in an atmosphere of social passivity. Purists rule sentiment out of social structure. Yet it is precisely the sentiments of rivalry that convert formal rules into action and transpose abstractions into the real events of history. From a structural point of view that considers history as a dimension and not as an obstacle, antagonism appears as neither accidental nor pathological. It is the ultimate testing ground of efficacy in Polynesia. It is the measure of the authenticity of status. It is, in a manner of speaking, the source of energy for transformation. Status rivalry has been a vital factor, specifically, in the transformation of the segmentary organization, the main area of enlargement and diversification.

Variations in Segmentation

By all available evidence, the modes of segmentation of Polynesian social groupings depend upon the character of the status system. The orderly branching of descent groups in New Zealand, in Manihiki-Rakahanga, in Tongareva, and in Tikopia is unquestionably a derivative of the eastern Polynesian Traditional status system with its strong adherence to genealogical rank based on seniority of descent. The Tikopian example is particularly telling because of its very close similarity to Maori, despite a western Polynesian cultural environment and kinship system. Tikopian stress on the male line is more categorical than Maori, but apart from this minor difference both societies share a common status system. Since their segmental nomenclature is different, it is more reasonable to attribute Tikopian segmentation to independent forces than to diffusion from eastern Polynesia, particularly since the more powerful cultural influences upon Tikopia have been from Samoa, where status system and mode of segmentation are quite different.

The coincidence between type of status system and mode of segmentation has, of course, been brought out in every society I have described. But the fact that such coincidence can be demonstrated for a western Polynesian society that belongs to a different social tradition adds particular weight to the probability that the association is significant. The Tongan haa supplies evidence from another side. In theory, the haa segmented itself, or ramified, in the Maori manner, but only so long as genealogical seniority remained intact as a principle of rank. When the status system changed, the pattern of segmentation and the internal organization of the segments was correspondingly altered.

I shall return to the Tongan example in another context when I discuss the effects of status rivalry upon segmentation. Status rivalry, as we have repeatedly observed, alters first the status system; and the alteration of the status system transforms both the general pattern of segmentation and the internal structure of the segments, giving to the social structure an appearance of atypicality. In some instances atypicality may be due not to the transformation of a Traditional status system but rather to its underdevelopment. Ontong Java is the clearest such case. Lacking genealogical rank, its descent group organization never ramified. Gerontocratic Pukapuka formed a dual organization of maternal and paternal lineages which subdivided but not in hierarchical order of the Maori type. Similarly, in the Tokelaus, where age was more significant than seniority, only the chiefly lines ramified, while the commoners formed unranked kindreds. The Tokelaus, however, are distinctive in this respect in having been at one time a "conquest state" ruled by a powerful chief, the Tui Tokelau, who established a traditional Polynesian descent line.

The deviation of descent group structures from the common norms of genealogical segmentation can be attributed to two opposite conditions: one, the fact that a society had not developed descent seniority; and two, the disruption of senior descent lines by force. For Polynesia as a whole, most examples of atypicality, however, come from societies with histories of strong status rivalry and can be explained, therefore, from the special circumstances produced by imposition of strong central authority. Strong central authority disturbs the segmentary order by imposing a territorial (district) organization that at first coexists with the segmented ordering of kindred, but then reduces the kindred organization to a smaller scale. Speaking more generally, we may describe political power as disruptive of kinship unity. Since I have already brought out the details of such disruption, it is appropriate at this point to consider the process in more general terms.

From the most general point of view, an interesting evolutionary change seems to occur in the imagery of kinship unity. In eastern Polynesia the traditional imagery of segmental unity is biological, as expressed in the Maori terms *ivi* ("bone") *hapu* ("pregnancy") and *whanau* ("giving birth"). This imagery gives way in "Open" Mangaia to a district organization that has no consistent nomenclature but visualizes the entire island biologically as a fish. In the Hawaiian Islands the district nomenclature is more abstract; it is spatial, or territorial, as in *aka puaa* and *ili* referring, respectively, to boundary markers and to a thin strip. Whether Hawaii ever had Maori terminology is purely a matter of conjecture, but Mangaia evidently did, for the traditional terms are still extant even though no longer applied. I offer the example of apparent change in imagery not because this was itself the most characteristic transformation, but as a more vivid way of underscoring the more typical shift from an organic to a dictated order of subdivision. The biological image expresses segmentation as inherent development; territorial terms lack such connotation. The distinction is parallel to that between the ariki and haka-iki (Marquesas); that is, between hereditary and sacred authority, and achieved or "made" chief.

In Western Polynesia, however, segmental terminology is not organic. Terms refer instead to the common interests of a people in food lands (kainga) or in common residence (paito, whare, or "house"). The distinction in imagery between this pattern of nomenclature and that of the Hawaiian is not quite as antithetical as the Maori–Hawaiian, but is nonetheless striking.

The major change, of course, has been in actual social arrangements. The substitution of a territorial system of subdivision for one of kinship branching has long been regarded as a major divide in human history. Apart from introducing new structural arrangements of great importance, this change has introduced a parallel change in outlook—apart from the specific imagery implied by terminology—from that of a natural to a political order. Kin groups bud, branch, and unfold. Territorial groups are created by chiefs. They express human agency. In this expression, they assert a radically new social idea.

The orderly patterns of social variability in Polynesia uncover for us the details of transition from which we derive more general principles. I have selected the following as particularly important.

1. The segmentary organization is the model for the territorial organization. Superficial similarities alone, such as the frequent occurrence in territorial divisions of a four-level order, as in kinship segmentation, suggest at once a common pattern. Just as the genealogical network was subdivided into major and minor segments, so was the total political community subdivided into major and minor subdivisions headed by a hierarchy of chiefs. Put in general terms, we may say: one kind of hierarchical organization generates only a parallel hierarchical organization; the territorial organization is the political expression of the segmentary organization in its more developed form.

Polynesian genealogical traditions describing the formation of territorial divisions confirm this general observation. The traditions describe two ways by which territorial divisions were formed. In one, representing only a minor modification of the traditional segmentary pattern of kinship, chiefs allocated specific territories to their sons. In the older or more traditional form, we will recall, a younger son simply moved into unoccupied territory where his household could grow into a lineage. The traditional focus was on the natural growth of the kin group. Following the allocation of specific lands, however, the focus became territorial. A chief could not allocate lands, however, unless his authority had grown well beyond that of the traditional ariki, who was a ritual rather than a political figure. That the social climate of such an allocation was strongly authoritarian is borne out by the inevitable conflicts that broke out among these newly formed divisions.

The second type of territorial formation was historically an outgrowth of the first, and resulted from wars over lands. Victorious chiefs arbitrarily divided an island into divisions, placing over them loyal and friendly chiefs or warriors regardless of kinship affiliations. If the first step of allocating lands to sons revealed a new and more political point of view, still within the framework of kinship, the second step went farther still in acknowledging the pragmatic necessities of military victory or defeat which put utility above traditional kinship obligations. Nevertheless, it was only in the Hawaiian Islands where the new territorial organization had broken completely with the old segmentary order. Elsewhere, a composite system was established under which the major subdivisions were territorial, while their branches, headed by local chiefs, continued to follow the traditional pattern of segmentation. In this composite organization, the territorial divisions replaced, as a rule, segments I and II, leaving more or less intact III and IV.

2. *Upper level segments are shadow organizations for the formation of the proto-state.* This is corollary to the first principle, and states more specifically how territorial divisions emerge from segmentary organizations. As a rule, the traditional Segment I, is a ritual or honorific organization with little or no corporate character. A proto-state, which is the highest level of political centralism in Polynesia, has very strong corporate character at its territorial equivalent of Segment I. The principle states that the political Segment I is a converted form of kinship Segment I. It implies more generally that a ritual organization, by laying down the basic traditions and sentiments that unify a people, provides the framework for a fuller political unity to follow. Ritual ties precede the political ties, and the shadow falls before the substance comes into view in a developing system.

The operation of this principle is fully exemplified in Polynesia and demonstrates that war, not economic utility, is the crucial factor in strengthening Segment I. Warfare is often the only substantial ground for political unity. On the principle already so fully elucidated by Evans-Pritchard (1940), segments of politically noncentralized societies assert themselves as units when seriously confronting segments like themselves. Thus in war the Maori waka unite against other waka, and iwi unite against other iwi. When the wars subside, unity dissolves and the actual authority of Segment I chief becomes potential. Persistent warfare always strengthens some authority, but whether strengthening will be at segments I, II, or III depends on the military scale. When a Maori hapu attacked another, neither the iwi nor the waka were necessarily drawn into the fighting. These higher segments responded when the honor of their respective ariki became involved. On large islands, therefore, localized wars could rage without activating the potential political power of a Segment I. On small islands, on the other hand, vital interests and threats to chiefly honor were more easily aroused. Thus central authority brought about by the political build-up of a traditional Segment I was in fact achieved more readily on small islands where there was warfare. The examples I have described in the text are Tongareva, where a supreme ariki held a temporary political grip over the entire atoll, Mangareva, where a proto-state had been formed; Futuna, whenever a major district became dominant; the Tokelaus, which had been a conquest state, and Mangaia, where a secular paramount chiefship had emerged in the course of wars. A vigorous Segment I does not in itself create a proto-state. It may only institute despotism. A proto-state, at the very least, organizes the economy. Despotism, which is the power of intervention and interference harshly exercised, is seemingly a preparatory condition for the state. Small islands favor the emergence of despotism. Even so small a Polynesian society as on Ontong Java had its despotic ariki. Among the small islands and atolls, only Manihiki-Rakahanga with its strong sentiment of membership in a single descent line avoided both wars and chiefly despotism. On large islands, in the Societies, in the Hawaiian and Tongan archipelagoes, the growth of central authority through an invigorated Segment I demanded extraordinary effort. There the choice was either a proto-state or sheer decentralization. Mangareva, a transitional proto-state on a very small island, demonstrates again the point about ecology as offering opportunities and imposing obstacles but not as creating.

Again, it is the Segment I ariki who uses his traditional office and prerogatives to transform the system. In every example of Open and Stratified society it was the traditional head of a traditional kinship Segment I or a close kinsman who instituted the transformation.

3. *The territorial organization may develop alongside the traditional segmentary organization.* Just as aristocratic status systems transform themselves by establishing a parallel scheme of achieved statuses, so apparently does the traditional segmentary system give way by coexisting with a parallel and evidently rival territorial organization. The dual status system has a dual social structure as its counterpart. Structural dualism is a natural outcome of the fundamental social dualism of aristocracies, which assert the tradition of genealogical rank for themselves but not for commoners. Thus, as the Polynesian record so clearly shows, whenever ariki established a district organization they retained, if they could, the traditional kinship segmentation for the royal lines. This was reasonable, since the Polynesian segmentary order depended more or less precisely upon the vigor of genealogical rank. Mangaia, Marquesas, Society, and Tonga are the best examples of such dual social structure.

4. *The territorial organization carries out the destruction of traditional segmentation.* This principle is a corollary to no. 3, and is based

upon the observation that wherever political districts have been established the island-wide segmentation has apparently lost its orderly character of branching. It could not be otherwise, since kinship and politics are in the long run inherently incompatible. Although principles of kinship and politics can be and, in fact, are adjusted in some compromise, they pull in opposite directions, so that in the end ruling lines are reduced to formal and politically inconsequential positions, as in Mangaia, or devise a fully pragmatic solution, as in Hawaii. The Polynesian segmentary order is undermined when appointed chiefs replace genealogically qualified chiefs. The segmentary order is, therefore, hit hardest in its middle range, which, as the evidence shows, is evidently the first to disappear. Segment I can remain intact because it represents the line of ariki. It holds to its traditional ritual and religious prerogatives and its head is as always the traditional ariki scion of the senior line, by "hook or crook." Segment IV, representing the domestic level, remains intact, since it is already pragmatic and based on economic utility. Segments II and III are most vulnerable, because they produce the basic leadership for political and economic organization.

5. *The territorial organization is a product of chiefly power.* I have already presented evidence demonstrating that while the segmentary order was visualized as organic, the territorial organization conveyed the sense of human agency. Why was the territorial organization imposed? From the perspective of Hawaii, where political organization was most fully carried out, it would seem reasonable to argue the conventional doctrine of economic utility, calling attention to the size of population and its territory and the ecological diversity encompassed by territorial strips reaching from shore to mountain top. The argument would be that a territorial organization is a more effective one than the traditional ramified order. Yet a traditional ramified order was very effective in New Zealand, and a variant of this order worked well in the Samoan Islands. It is Mangareva, an atoll-sized island, that raises the most serious question about economic utility. Here the Temporal Lord had divided the island into six pie-shaped divisions, naming a military governor over each. Each major division was further subdivided into nine subdistricts, creating a total of 54 divisions for a population of only 2,000. Mangarevan history is uncompromisingly clear in depicting this fine subdivision as the political expedient of carrying out warfare. The same political expediency underlay the Hawaiian "spoils" system. From the chiefly subdivision of lands among sons, to the Hawaiian territorial division ran a direct line of political evolution entirely in the interests of chiefly power.

6. *Dual divisions are antagonistic.* Particularly on smaller islands, Polynesian societies tended to form dual geographic divisions, such as a north–south; shoreside–lagoonside; west–east. These divisions were formed out of various antagonisms. Separation did not reduce antagonisms, but—rather—inflamed them. Thus, territorial divisions are distinct from moieties, which start from the assumption of a basic unity, and then carry out some form of ritual opposition. Dual territorial divisions rejected outright the possibility of unity and waged ceaseless war. Easter Island pitted the royal tribes of the west against the commoner tribes of the east, just as Mangaian Ngariki were pitted against commoner Tongaiti. In the Marquesas, descendants of a senior line formed a western coalition against an eastern coalition organized around descendants of a junior line. Mangareva was divided into eastern and western coalitions before a clear-cut victory unified the island. On Futuna, traditionalist Tua battled more open Singave for the ascendancy. If the genealogical traditions are correct on this point, then, in some instances, at least, the dual division preceded the formation of hierarchical territorial divisions. That is to say, basic antagonisms provoked wars and the new territorial organization attempted pacification by substituting a new hierarchical order for territorial dualism. In all instances cited, the divisional antagonisms were on issues of status, of royalty against commoner, of senior against junior line. We cannot say these antagonisms were inevitable. But they were logical by Polynesian standards that found only hierarchy natural. When hierarchy was disrupted or was incomplete, it was logical to try to restore it. Since segmental hierarchy depended both on kinship sentiment and upon the structural facts of genealogy, a reconstructed territorial hierarchy was the only effective way of restoring an already disrupted order.

7. *The proto-state creates a new synthesis of traditional and territorial organizations.* While the Stratified societies had all established territorial organizations, the central authority had, nevertheless, to assert traditional genealogical distinction to validate its rule. This necessary validation bears out the inference that the territorial hierarchical organization was viewed as a legitimate reconstruction of the old order, just as a Segment I ariki had legitimized the entire traditional segmental organization under him. Thus, the new territorial organization had far-reaching effects upon the entire structure of kinship and power—but it was not in itself a revolutionary innovation. The Stratified societies were, in all respects, stronger aristocracies.

Variations in Status

Insofar as status defines leadership, the organization of status defines the organization of groups. As the segmentary order coincides with graded genealogical rank, variations in the traditional order of status coincide with variations in segmentation. The precise nature of the interaction eludes us, although all available evidence points directly to the status system as an important generator of social change. The processes of integration differentiated descent- and residence-based groups. Simultaneously, the same processes differentiated statuses and status-based groups. The status differentiations, we have observed, include specialization of ariki functions, specializations of priestly functions, specializations in administrative organization and in the conduct of war, the expansion of titles and of honorable positions generally, the enhanced political position of women, and the emergence of a "middle class." This process of differentiation was accompanied by a powerful tendency toward status polarity, as expressed in sharp distinctions between strong and weak, between conquerors and conquered, between royal and common, and between landed and landless, concluding, finally, with class endogamy and the appearance in Hawaii of pariah outcasts. In following the transformations of segmentation, we noted some dependency between polarity and hierarchical subdivision. Hierarchy, having set the stage in the first place for antagonistic dualism, succeeded in bridging emergent dualism and so managed to subdue antagonisms. A similar, but by no means identical, relationship could be traced between status differentiation, which closed gaps, so to speak, and status dualism, which polarized differences. Some aspects of status differentiation can be explained as means of bridging the gaps. The immunity from abuse of enemy craftsmen in Mangaia is one example of a bridge between victor and defeated. The formation of pakaora in Mangareva may be described as a bridge between noble and commoner. Since traditional status systems were graded, and only moderately dualistic, there is reason to interpret status differentiation as reconstructive, as restoring patterns of gradation, although in a new form that had been disturbed by status rivalry. In this respect, then, status differentiation was to traditional graded rank what territorial divisions were to traditional segmentation: Both were reconstitution processes. The repeated appearance of processes of reconstitution implies that hierarchy is a most durable social pattern. When it is overcome in one way, it reconstitutes itself in another. Judging by the course of human history, there is every reason to regard hierarchy as the durable principle and status polarization as a transient phase. In Polynesia, however, polarization was still a highly vigorous principle. While the Stratified societies had overcome, as it would seem, the crude polarities of strong and weak, they replaced these with the more solidly established distinctions between landed and landless. As I have explained previously, land tenure in aristocratic societies is primarily a matter of honor. Thus, while the "landless" toilers on the land were, as a rule, adequately nourished, the nature of their relationship to the land was profoundly different from that of titled tenure. The landless were not "degraded," for Polynesians restricted degradation to a small minority. But the landless were a low class more sharply separated from royalty than were commoner Maori from ariki. At the same time, bearing out the hypothesis of gap closing, the Hawaiian commoners had political avenues open to them allowing them to rise to very high administrative office.

The principles of status differentiations and polarizations may be expressed as follows:

1. *The differentiation of chiefly role was a response to status challenge.* The traditional differentiation was organic and related to segmentary level that assigned a ritual role to Segment I chiefs, and a utilitarian role to Segment II. Under pressure from contending lines, the division occurred at Segment I, differentiating ariki by adding priestly and economic titles and offices.

2. *Economic chiefly roles eclipsed the purely religious roles.* We attribute this development to the character of status rivalry, with its increasing emphasis upon political power via economic advantage, such as feudatory land relations.

3. *Rank and power entered into varied and shifting combinations.* Power, measured by criteria of control over lands and agricultural production, was always the prerogative of rank, which is to say that status rivalry notwithstanding, aristocracy, finally, had the upper hand in Polynesia. Economy was not an aristocratic concern when it was primarily a domestic concern, as in most traditional societies. Economy became an aristocratic concern when it became an instrument of political power, for the traditional Polynesian reason that power was the legitimate concern of aristocracy. The genealogical traditions of Mangaia, Mangareva, and Tonga, for example, suggest, however, that religious power could be regarded as superior to the economic power. Polynesian history demonstrates, nevertheless, that when the highest ranks took the religious powers and the secondary ranks the economic power, the latter inevitably became ascendant. The ability of lower ranks to acquire lands, and so build their own centers of political power, as in the Marquesas, is part of the general picture of shifting combinations of rank and power. The rise to power of lower ranks was, in general, the "price" paid by the higher ranks for

their own ascendancy. The variety of rank and power combinations in Hawaii, particularly, illustrates the general process of status diversification in which the economic powers themselves have become increasingly specialized.

4. *Priestly diversification corresponded to general patterns of status differentiation.* In Traditional societies, priestly titles and offices were aligned with graded rank. In the Open societies, the priesthood reflected the state of status rivalry. The traditional rule that status demanded a counterpart in sanctity was faithfully followed and was most fully exemplified in the Hawaiian Islands, where every craft and every status had its own cult and its own priests. In Maori, the traditional rule revealed a patterned relationship between the abstract and the esoteric religious doctrines and the highest ranks, and between the more concrete and utilitarian religious doctrines—such as fertility rites—and the lower ranks. This orderly pattern was the actual doctrine of the *whare wananga*, the schools of knowledge. It is presumably this basic and traditional distinction between upper-rank and lower-rank religion, with its counterpart in the status of priests, that was the general guiding principle in priestly diversification. Priestly diversification was both horizontal—as in the Mangaian distinction between Island-High Priest and Shore-High Priest—and vertical—as in the distinction between high-status hereditary and cult-associated priests and groups of free enterprise prophets and seers in Open and Stratified societies.

5. *Craft diversification corresponded to general patterns of status diversification.* This principle has already been discussed in Chapter 22, on the economics of status. I would repeat, however, the general observation that diversification of status through craft skills evidently counteracted the more general loss of status when systems of land tenure changed. Polarization of land tenure was offset by the provision of new honorific statuses available to commoners. But in the strong hierarchical organization of crafts, we see the persistence of traditional patterns of genealogical rank, sanctity, and separation. The crafts, like the Tahitian arioi, model themselves upon traditionalism.

6. *Administrative diversification corresponded to general patterns of status differentiation.* Administrative complexity can no more be separated from the pragmatic factor of complexity of problem than can crafts specialization from sophistication of technique. This is to emphasize again that cultural elaboration is never simply an elaboration of form. Nevertheless, the manner of administrative growth, as well as the basic impetus for growth, comes from the status system.

That administrative offices and titles developed in proportion to centralization of authority can be explained generally as a response to political complexity. Specifically, however, we see emergent administration as another example of a series of "made" positions, in contrast to the organic allocation of administrative positions in the Traditional societies. In Tonga, the matapule and in Hawaii the kalaimoku and the konohiki were agents of the central authority. As agents, they formed a new relationship that was distinct from the traditional relationships of status and the more newly-formed relationships of contract, exchanging services for land. Agents exchanged services for what may be called bureaucratic statuses. Bureaucratic status was a very special form, so specialized, in fact, that in Tonga matapule were foreigners and in Hawaii the kalaimoku and many konohiki were commoners.

Administrative agents were part of the growing chiefly establishment, and their special status must be seen as part of that particular segment of tribal or national organization that included servants, warriors, and advisors. We may state therefore a corollary principle:

7. *The chiefly establishment or royal court formed a specialized sector of the total status system.* An establishment that binds persons specifically to a paramount chief tends to specialize statuses, because the nature of the relationship draws upon contradictory principles. Traditionally, high status (that is, genealogical rank) depended upon actually heading a segment or being eligible to do so. In Open and Stratified societies, status depended upon heading a territorial division. Membership in the chiefly establishment, insofar as it was not associated with segment or district rule, was accordingly in this respect alone a low status. But low basic status was balanced by privileges and powers that assumed consequence in a social setting where power had become consequential. In the Stratified societies, servants or retainers had the privilege as agents—extensions of the paramount chief—of exercising arbitrary powers in his name. This power put them in a different category from ordinary servants. Being an agent was a specialized form of achieved status, since it was often outside the realm of genealogical rank.

8. *Diversification of warrior status corresponded to general patterns of status differentiation.* The elaboration of warrior statuses paralleled elaborations of the crafts of priests and of administrators, and must be considered, therefore, in the broader context of status elaboration, rather then simply and directly as responses to the technical requirements of war. In the Traditional societies, military commanders were holders of genealogical rank. But evidently the menace

war held for genealogical rank imposed a more pragmatic outlook that drew upon military prowess regardless of rank. Thus toa as a title of honor came to include ranks and achieved statuses—traditionalist warriors who fought only in the cause of their own lineage, dependent warriors who formed part of the chiefly court, and free-lance warriors who were called upon almost as mercenaries for a specifically contracted price. In some Stratified societies, moreover, the level of military organization had gone so far as to establish an officer cadre or a military table of organization.

9. *The political position of women advanced with status differentiation generally.* Between Maori with its view of women as noa (common) and the Stratified societies that gave women the opportunity for the highest political office there seems to have been a wide gulf in social outlook to be bridged. That the gulf was bridged may be laid, on the one hand, to some loopholes in traditional doctrine and, on the other, to the general widening of avenues to political office in Open and Stratified societies. One loophole in doctrine was in the balancing of genealogical factors. Where primogeniture, seniority of descent, or general genealogical distinction overwhelmed the doctrine of male-line superiority, women became eligible for honor. Even among Maori, in exceptional cases, women rose to influence. As I demonstrated in chapter 21 on principles of kinship, the emergence of bilaterality as against the traditional focus on patriliny was a weakening of the aristocratic principle of categorical exclusiveness of descent lines. The second loophole was in the western Polynesian theory of status complementarity which gave power to the male line and honor to the female line. Judging by the honoring of the tapairu in New Zealand, both eastern and western Polynesia had, in fact, some common understanding of a principle that was given fullest expression in the western area. For women to rise to political prominence, therefore, it was necessary in eastern Polynesia for the balance to shift in the direction of primogeniture, seniority, and general genealogical distinction. It was necessary in western Polynesia for honor to be transposed to power. Since honor in western Polynesia also had teeth, as in the cursing power of the father's sister, the transition was not difficult. Nevertheless, the proper political atmosphere was necessary, for in Tonga the female paramount Queen Charlotte came from the Takalaua, a lower-ranking line that had finally overshadowed the more traditional and sacred Tui Tonga. In eastern Polynesia it was the Marquesan system of emphasizing primogeniture that brought women to chiefly office. The same basic genealogical principle in the context of acute status rivalry brought women to the highest chiefly

office in Tahiti and in the Hawaiian Islands. The eligibility of women for the chiefship is still another example of the general status differentiation of Polynesian populations.

The Formation of Economic Classes

Economic stratification in Polynesia was one of the consequences of diversification of concepts of land tenure. Using these terms rather loosely, we have spoken of the formation of a "landless class." There is some justification for speaking of "landed" proprietors and "landless" commoners in a society where land rights were personal rather than legal, where title was a function of status rather than of impersonal contract, where land could be seized or given but could not be bought or sold in a market. The justification, as I have explained before, is that within the framework of aristocratic land concepts, the very important distinction between the right to dispose of lands and the disability of being subject to someone's disposition is parallel to, although not identical with, concepts of ownership and tenancy in a market economy. The disability of being transferred from land or even evicted for improper performance is parallel to, although not the same as, loss of tenancy for failure to pay the legally contracted rent. The most appropriate analogy is with feudalism and its graded conception of superior and inferior land rights. Between the superior land rights of the disposer and the inferior land rights of the disposed lies a social and economic gulf as wide as that between landed and landless in a market economy.

The sources of economic stratification are readily detected in the Traditional societies, where the ariki holds "title" to the lands of his segment. Title, however, is an assertion of honor; it is the link between the land and its productivity and the mana of the chiefly line. Chiefly title enhances the land in the formal sense of endowing it with honor and in the more practical sense of adding to its productivity. In the gradation of chiefly function generally characteristic of the Traditional societies, the more immediate and practical management of land rests with heads of lower-ranking segments, even with heads of households. Thus, if we consider the distinction between superior and inferior rights in Traditional societies, we find that where the social gap is greatest, the superior rights are least pragmatic. The superior rights are most pragmatic in that they include privileges of actual management when the social gap is most narrow. In other words, the pragmatic forms of land rights are most democratic.

In the Traditional societies, moreover, rights of honor are so much more important than rights of management that there is no strong chiefly interest in fostering social separation on such practical details as management of labor on the land. The democratic land tenure of Traditional societies may be explained, therefore, by the concept of honor that does not involve high chiefs in the practical affairs of agriculture. Their honor is met when they receive first-fruits as token tribute and when the lands prosper generally.

Changing forms of land tenure must correspond, therefore, to changing forms of chiefship. And since the chiefship responds to status rivalry, new forms of land tenure emerge in the course of status rivalry. Thus, each of the principal manifestations of status rivalry seems to have had some counterpart effect in diversifying relations to land. The appearance of a land administrator (*tuha whenua*) in Tongareva and in other Traditional societies, for example, moves the segmental level of land administration up a grade or more, and so narrows the social gap in that respect. While traditional land administrators simply reallocate lands democratically according to need, the point of importance is that allocation has become a higher-level function. Once the function has been made legitimate, the manner of its exercise will depend upon specific political conditions.

Scarcity, when it is an objective condition, must, in the final analysis, prompt a pragmatic solution. Thus, the scarcity conditions on atolls seems to have favored the introduction of administrative controls—in periodic reallocation already mentioned in the posting of guards to protect public taro beds. Some wars were also stirred by food shortage. War made lands and produce instruments and rewards of power.

As we have seen in all the examples brought to light, warfare is a complex series of events whose consequences may be unpredictable in specifics but whose general effects can be charted. War polarized social relationships in Polynesia, with its implication of victory as the sign of high mana and of defeat as the stigma of low mana. In traditional status, where groups were highly unified by kinship, social polarization was between traditionally opposing groups and not within the producing community. The relationship to land, or to put it another way, the quality of land rights, was invariably one of the specific measures of status. Thus, even in the Traditional societies the defeated "outsiders" were required to demonstrate subordinate land tenure to the victors, offering tribute as the sign of inferiority. Tribute is quite distinct from offerings of first-fruits. First-fruits, as I have explained, move within patterns of honorable exchanges and this movement defines the organic community of honor. Tribute, on the other hand, is a strongly polarized economic relationship.

If warfare polarized the economic relationships between victor and vanquished as communities, it also diversified the victor communities insofar as they took captives. Captives in Traditional societies held subordinate tenure until such time as they could be incorporated either by marriage or by adoption. Insofar as warfare dislocated internal populations, driving the weak to seek shelter with stronger kinsmen, the community acquired still another form of land tenure, that of dependent relatives or "servants," as in New Zealand.

In the Traditional societies, to be sure, kinship set its own general pattern upon land tenure, equalizing, more or less, both the economic benefits and the benefits of honor. Nevertheless, many of the varied forms of land tenure that emerged fully and vigorously in the Open societies were foreshadowed, so to speak, in those Traditional societies that were warlike.

The major economic innovation of the Open societies was the feudal concept of land as reward for service. Whereas the Traditional societies, committed as they were to the unity of land, status, and kinship, were content with tribute as the sign of subordination, the Open societies, more pragmatic and flexible, seized the lands of the vanquished and redistributed them internally in accordance with political merit. Thus they at once widened the gap between dominant and subordinate tenure as between communities, and diversified still more the varieties of internal land tenure by adding that of master–client, or "lord" and "vassal." As in European forms of feudalism, the lord–vassal relationship, or the equivalent in Polynesia, was itself highly variable. Insofar as vassalage was the reward for valor, it was honorable and, under some circumstances, the lord had only nominal claims of subordination. A new principle of land tenure was, nevertheless, introduced: The management of land in terms of distribution and in terms of production was a prerogative of high-level chiefs. This principle was expressed in a variety of forms, in successive subleases and in clientage where the patron accepted upon his land those who had voluntarily declared their weakness and subordination. Thus, as the gap between the dominant and subordinate forms of land tenure widened, it was simultaneously filled by a variety of intermediate forms.

Polynesian traditions curiously do not account specifically for the quality of land tenure of the internal commoners, even though they detail minutely the appearance of vassalage and clientage and the facts of land expropriation of conquered enemies. Yet it is reasonable enough for central authority self-consciously concerned with reconstituting the community upon new foundations to pass over suggestions of commoners as an expropriated class. Be that as it may, we do not know how the Tahitian menahune or the Tongan commoners descended, so to speak, in the scale of honorable tenure. In all probability the commoners were not expropriated as were the foreign conquered. That is to say, they were probably not rooted out and then resettled; their lands were not seized. In the Marquesas, it has been reported, chiefs moved suddenly from roles as guardians of kin group lands to despots. This must have happened in the Stratified societies as well. Powerful chiefs now involved in pragmatic issues of land, wealth, and power increased their jurisdiction. The gap widened not by the "fall" of the commoners, but by the ascent of the chiefs. But chiefly ascendance was clearly no isolated phenomenon. It occurred within a disturbed social atmosphere of polarization and of such social differentiation that kin groups were no longer intact. The basic unity of land, status, and kinship was broken as part of the historic process that changed the nature of the Polynesian chiefship. The subordinate tenure of commoners in the Stratified societies set the seal upon this process as a whole.

Transformation of Ethos

A number of rather specific indicators point to significant changes in public mood and values in the course of social transformation in Polynesia. We have seen evidence of increasing antagonism, of greater violence and cruelty, of growing despotic power and of a powerful antithesis between the strong and the weak as characteristic of the Open and Stratified societies. The genealogical traditions attribute this "new" atmosphere to the fever of status rivalry, to the ambition of chiefs, and to the raging wars and insurrections they provoked. Since status rivalry is, after all, an attack upon a traditional order, even when it is within the "rules of the game," it must necessarily generate antagonism and then benefit by an atmosphere of violence. Much of the social transformation of Polynesian social life cannot be accounted for in terms of social structure per se. The most fundamental changes in kinship, in the organization of descent groups, in the qualifications for and the authority of chiefs, in land tenure, in basic status relationships could hardly have occurred except in the appropriate atmosphere of violence and of antagonism.

An *ethos* may be defined as the symbolic elaboration of social atmosphere or public mood. In wars, in insurrections, in fratricidal conflict, violence and antagonism may be fleeting states even though socially consequential. War, like a temper, blows over, and social life is restored to its previous state. Violence, antagonism, menace, suspicion become fixed in the public consciousness when they are incorporated in a substantial doctrine, when represented in art and ritual, when given a symbolic and therefore a lasting significance. Ruth Benedict spoke of an ethos—by which she meant precisely the symbolization of sentiment—as a "precipitate of history." Since violence seems to have been so decisive a factor in Polynesian social evolution, the atmosphere of antagonism inevitably called forth a supporting ethos. In Polynesia, ethos of antagonism is reflected most acutely in religion, in the character of the gods, in the nature of the after-life, in the prominence given to omens and to sorcery, in human sacrifice and in the ritual treatment of enemies. The common religious groundwork of Polynesian religions allows us to trace methodically, although, needless to say, not precisely, those variations in practices and beliefs that reflect changing ethos.

Character of the Gods

The Traditional societies saw the spiritual cosmos as dual, as divided between good and bad spirits. Maori dualism was antiphonal, pitting Tane, the god of knowledge, against Whiro, the god of evil, in fierce combats. Whiro, finally defeated, descended into the underworld, or Po, where in league with other spirits he continued to assail the world, bringing sickness and death. The significant point, however, is that Tane was victorious and hence basically dominant. All the Traditional societies for which adequate information is available had mischievous spirits, but always subordinated to the dominant and benevolent gods and spirits. In Manihiki-Rakahanga, the gods were under control of the ariki, as they were in Tongareva, and so could be relied upon as beneficient. Ontong Java had a "god of evil," who existed, however, within a pantheon of ancestral spirits, or kipua, who were the dominant powers. Benevolent ancestral spirits were also dominant in Tikopia. In the Tokelaus, the Tui Tokelau was a deified paramount chief who, with other ancestral deities, could be relied upon to look after the community. Dualism here was expressed between a benevolent band of inland spirits who fought for control with the mischievous sea spirits. When these "outsiders" were victorious, the Tokelauans were in trouble. Still another group of mischievous spirits, the Ngaveve, who ran off with men's souls making them temporarily mad, were regarded more lightly as pranksters. Samoans feared aitu demons and ghosts of the dead who brought illness and often lured people to their death. Tangaloa, the major deity, and ancestral gods who could punish, nevertheless, for neglect were the major spiritual forces. These were subject to control.

The spiritual threat becomes more specialized in the Open societies. In Mangaia, for example the principal deity was Rongo, god of war (cf. Rongo as god of agriculture in New Zealand), who demanded human sacrifices. The tribal gods demanded unswerving obedience, according to Buck, a suggestion of a somewhat more awesome character than family gods had in Traditional societies. Tane, on the other hand, was in one song reviled for having allowed a man's son to die, with the imprecation: "May you be plastered with filth/ and even defecated upon/ Man is as good as a god."

The Marquesans came under the helpful protection of tribal gods, who were deified chiefs or priests, and of a great many creation and departmental gods, tutelary spirits who were divinized local chiefs and priests, and all the occupational deities. Evil spirits were highly specialized. They were all female, attacking pregnant women and children in particular. Cannibal ogresses, *vehine hae,* assumed the form of beautiful women and lured men into caves, where they devoured them.

The evidence for specialized antagonism between men and gods on Easter Island is not very strong. Makemake, the god of the birdman cult, seems to have overshadowed the once dominant Tangaroa cult. As god of warriors under whose auspices the reigning incarnation of the god could pillage and inspire fear, he may be regarded as antagonistic.

Niue finally had a great many gods, very many of whom were troublesome, devouring the food and bringing famine, killing children, and causing people to steal. There is no evidence, however, that the antagonistic spirits were dominant. Perhaps it is the Niuean form of dualism that states the issue best. They believed in a good and younger Maui and in an evil and older Maui who were in more or less balanced opposition. The younger tried to be helpful and the elder tried to thwart him.

The Stratified societies shared with the Open societies a pattern of spiritual specialization. This tendency reached its high point in Hawaii, where a god existed as a counterpart for every form of social specialization. The common people in Hawaii had their own gods who represented, as a rule, the more narrow interests of craft and locality. The alii worshipped the major and more general gods. In the Stratified societies, a concept of deistic hierarchy corresponding quite closely to political hierarchy seems to have replaced the dualism of the Traditional and Open societies. The emphasis was on the power of the major deities and upon the theme of specialization. Malevolent spirits, while prominent, were simply a class among many. If human sacrifice is a measure of the awesome power of a god, then the major gods of Tonga, Tahiti, and Hawaii came within this category.

Nature of the After-Life

Polynesians imagined the after-life as reflecting more or less the present state of social affairs. Thus, while the Traditional societies anticipated some punishment for wrongdoers in the after-life, they did not sort out personal fates by rank or social class. All Maori, regardless of rank, for example, had the same options awaiting them in the po, or underworld. Pukapukans thought of adulterers as being thrown into a hot fire, but set up no close distinctions in the po, which was a genial place where the entering souls entertained the gods with stories, songs, and dances. Tokelauans thought of an unpleasant purgatory only for the uncircumcised. All others lived in a paradise, Tualiku, where they danced and ate all day. According to Turner, however, there was some danger from demons, who seized and enslaved unwary spirits.

Among the Open societies, the Marquesas, Mangaia, and Niue distinguished the after-life by social status. The Marquesas imagined three levels of lower regions, the lowest a paradise for chiefs, an average middle for middle ranks, and a miserable upper level for the weak and defeated. For the Mangaians, only warriors lived in a pleasant upper world to defecate upon all others who wandered disconsolately in a miserable lower world. Warriors were swallowed by Rongo, through whom they passed into the upper world. All others were swallowed by Miru, an ugly old cannibal woman, and then passed forever into a burning oven. Niue also had two heavens, one occupied by wonderfully accomplished women, but not by the spirits of the dead, the other a less pleasant place where rats gnawed the heads of men who had not died on the battlefield. Finally, among Open societies, Easter Island had no dual conception of the after-life. All went to a happy after-life if they had obeyed all the tapus.

Strong differentiation of the after-life was characteristic of all the Stratified societies. Tongan chiefs went to Bulotu, a paradise; according to Mariner, the souls of commoners perished at death. Mangarevans visualized five after-worlds, each subdivided into several districts according to social class. In the sky was hapai, the best afterworld, which admitted only good spirits. The bottom-most realm was the Te Piaoi, a hungry realm for the souls of those who had died of starvation and of commoners who had died without proper burial. Tahitian spirits of the dead traveled a road until they came to a forking where they were met by a god who directed them, as he chose, to the right or to the left. Those who went to the right entered a voluptuous paradise; those to the left flew into a crater to the domain of Taaroa, where rank was not respected and all, including paramount chiefs, did menial work for the gods. Eventually these were converted into three classes of spirit: good spirits who were always helpful to their kin; spirits who were helpful as long as they were well treated; and very dangerous spirits who could be easily turned to strangling or devouring their own kin. In Hawaii, the lower world for those of poor mana was seen as a desolate and ghostly place, bare of grass, flowers, and trees, where the famished shades of men strove vainly to appease their hunger by feeding on butterflies, moths, and lizards (Handy 1927). The high ranks reveled in a heavenly paradise.

Omens

Preoccupation with omens signifies quite naturally a high degree of uncertainty and insecurity. Dangerous undertakings, such as war, almost inevitably called upon the divinatory skills of priests. If the signs were wrong, the war party turned back. The reading of omens cannot be considered unusual in war. Omens become truly significant as indicators of ethos when they enter areas less clearly dangerous than war. When they precede all or most undertakings, they point to a generalized state of insecurity. Without exception, the Stratified societies were the most deeply concerned with reading the auguries of success or failure. The Samoans, for example, had never developed the interpretation of dreams and paid little attention to omens. Divination among Tongans, however, was a highly developed art. No important action was undertaken without appropriate oracular consultations. Sneezing, the appearance of birds, of lizards, of shadows, of lights, of lightning and of thunder presaged some disaster. The same was true of Mangareva and Tahiti. The Tahitians had many omens, according to Henry, of impending disaster, war, conspiracy, contention, death and sickness. They expected a miraculous sign, such as the approach of sharks, to accompany the inauguration of a paramount chief. Of all Polynesians, the Hawaiians were the most concerned with omens, carrying the search for auguries into more areas and developing the skills of divination to the highest degree in Polynesia. Of special importance was the preoccupation with signs in connection with housebuliding. Hawaiians systematically taught dream interpretation to children as though it were a catechism (Beckwith 1932).

Self-Indulgence

There are some indications that the symbolic statements of violence, antagonism, menace, and insecurity were accompanied by expressions of self-indulgence to form a coherent pattern. This pattern viewed from the perspective of the Traditional societies is best described in developmental terms as the casting off of restraints and the upsetting of traditional balances. Unfortunately, we have only incomplete information on this subject. Information is full enough to pose the problem but not full enough to establish a definitive tendency. Infanticide, for example, would seem to be a good measure of self-indulgence because it involves decisions on sexual restraints and on child-rearing. Among Traditional societies, infanticide was generally uncommon and, if practiced at all, was for stern necessity. Tikopian infanticide was mainly for population control, when crops were poor. Maori put infants to death in the privation of military sieges. On the other hand, in Futuna at the "open" end of the Traditional scale, infants were killed for such trivial reasons as not lying quietly on their backs and so interfering with the desired head-flattening. Among Open societies, there is no mention of infanticide for Easter Island or for Mangaia, but female infanticide was very prominent in the Marquesas, judging by the extraordinarily unbalanced sex ratio. Niueans felt compelled to get rid of infants who cried in wartime by throwing them into a ravine. Among the Stratified societies, it was Tahiti and Hawaii that had established status infanticide as a common practice. Our information, however, is mainly from the Rev. Ellis, who may have had some interest in overstating the miseries of paganism, but it is confirmed by other sources. The arioi society of Tahiti as a crop fertility cult was barred from producing children at the same time that it set an example of sexual indulgence. In the main, however, infanticide served to sharpen social class differences. Offspring of socially unequal liaisons were systematically put to death. According to Ellis' estimate, as many as two-thirds of births were put to death. By his own account, though, this figure is surely excessive, since, as he reported, infanticide was mainly a high-rank practice and was less common among farmers and raatira. Some parents, he claims, confessed to having killed as many as ten of their children at birth. The number of infanticides by a couple, one of whom was of inferior rank, determined the degree to which the inferior party would be elevated in rank. In any case, Ellis has said Tahitians regarded the rearing of more than three or four children as burdensome.

In Tahiti, male infanticide was apparently most common, but the Hawaiians followed the Marquesan tradition in doing away with girls. Ellis estimated the Hawaiian rate also as two-thirds of all births, attributing it to the same causes as in Tahiti, that is, to the desire for keeping descent lines pure.

It should be evident from its apparent absence in Tonga and in

Mangareva that infanticide is no absolute by-product of stratification in general, but rather a self-indulgent adaptation to developing caste consciousness that concerned itself with genealogical questions but did not interfere with marriage or with sexual relations outside of marriage. Neither Tonga nor Mangareva valued genealogical purity to the same degree as Tahiti and Hawaii. Marquesan infanticide has been explained by Linton as the reluctance of women to endure the difficulties of child-rearing and not—as to be expected from an Open society—for genealogical reasons (1939).

Self-indulgence is most readily expressed in sexual license, a personal choice generally free of economic and political imperatives. In Polynesia, where pre-marital sexual freedom was everywhere established custom, sexual self-indulgence took the particular form of excess, of elaboration of sexual play and, apparently, if incomplete information can be trusted, of greater freedom for adultery. Traditional Polynesia counterpointed sexual freedom with symbolic demonstrations of total restraint. The sacred maid chosen from among young women of high rank exemplified the high honor associated with self-denial. As a rule, female chastity was a privilege of rank, so that men did not necessarily expect to marry virgins. Thus, the preference in Niue for a wife who had been chaste suggests an expansion of the honor concept in an Open society which made available to many what was the privilege of the very few in the more traditional societies. The counterpoint between chastity and freedom took many forms. Thus, in Manihiki-Rakahanga, all high-ranking young women were expected to be virgins before marriage, while no sexual restraints were imposed on lower ranks. If chastity was a traditional feminine virtue, indulgence was a traditional masculine merit. Men of high rank were free to exercise fully their special influence over women. Thus, polygamy was honorable and monogamy the lot of the ordinary man in several Polynesian societies.

The evolution of Polynesian sexual behavior must probably be considered against a rather complex pattern of traditional beliefs: premarital sex as innocent play; adultery as a highly disruptive social vice; selective chastity as a special source of female honor; sexual attractiveness among the young as a mark of personal honor; the female genitalia as a "seat of misfortune" (Maori); sexual aggressiveness as a symbol of masculine honor and status; and, finally, decorum as the appropriate manner of sexual courtship.

Variations of the pattern seem to correspond with departures from traditional norms of social status. Pukapuka traditions, for example, speak of a severe period of social disturbance accompanied by sexual license and debauchery instigated interestingly by a female chief (a major departure from tradition). In this period, the sexual taboos were broken and women provoked one another by deliberately seducing husbands and then violating decorum by exposing the affair. Eventually the traditional balances and restraints were restored.

Futuna and Uvea departed from tradition by introducing prostitution. In fully "open" Niue, adultery, even though punished severely, had become common. Women befriended women so as to seduce their husbands, and men killed the husbands of the women they coveted. Traditional masculine superiority was defied as women, according to Loeb, preferred to marry dependent males from dependent families so they could rule them. Loeb has recorded cases of women killing their husbands in anger. Finally, the powerful families defied the incest rules. Yet these examples of anti-traditionalism must be considered against the opposite example of preference of upper-rank men for marriage with virgins.

Mangaia, too, while upholding the tradition of pre-marital sexual freedom generally, expected chastity of all daughters of high-ranking families. In contrast to Niue, Mangaia presents a more orderly picture of sexual behavior.

The Marquesas, because they presumably had no ariki tradition to follow, had no interest in chastity at all. At least the unofficial status of a girl suffered if she did not have an active sex life. Polyandry was a further departure from tradition, insofar as it asserted masculine subordination in marriage to the highest degree. Since a man accepted subordinate status in a polyandrous household, partly at least because the wife was very attractive, he was a victim as well of the highly cultivated erotic lure of the talented Marquesan women. Much as the Marquesans honored the erotic, they reacted to adultery violently. Men killed adulterous wives and jealous wives committed suicide from grief and shame. Perhaps the very strong emphasis on sexual desirability and on erotic technique intensified the shame of adultery, for even in the freedom of pre-marital sex a rebuff could lead to suicide.

Tongans promoted the double standard, restraining the sexual freedom of high-born girls and giving the greatest license to men of rank, who had "the run" of all women of low rank. A chief, accordingly, had sexual rights to all women of his district, including married women. Thus, since adultery was an issue only when status equals were involved, it was understandably rare. Low-ranking men would not dare sexual involvement with high-ranking women.

Post-marital sexual license received fuller rein in the Society and

Hawaiian Islands. In the Society Islands, however, sexual license was in the interests of religion and was socially regulated insofar as the arioi, a specialized group in a sense isolated from the ordinary community, were the traditional libertines. Ritual license in Tahiti brings out the cultural theme of opposition to the traditional restraints in family life. And while this contrast between traditional restraint and religious sexual license is in itself indicative of changing ethos, of departure from the more moderate contrasts of the Traditional societies, it is in its well-regulated form still within the traditional pattern.

If missionary accounts are to be fully believed, the true break from the traditional order seems to have begun in Hawaii, where sexual self-indulgence was becoming established as a regular feature of married life. Malo, who had begun to judge Hawaiian life by Christian standards, was deeply troubled by the decline of traditional Polynesian morality among upper-rank Hawaiians and among the associates of the royal court. Upper-class married women assumed the normally masculine privilege, as in Tonga, of sexual license with lower-class men. Men of the royal court added sodomy to the register of acceptable sexual behavior and among these, in a sense, urbanized circles, sexual games spiced the social life of families. In one popular game, men rolled little balls toward the outspread legs of women seated before them. If the pellet struck its target, the couple retired for sexual intercourse. The real point of interest in this and similar games is that the players were married persons. No other Polynesian society sanctioned adultery quite so openly. Hawaii was also unique in Polynesia for having developed intoxicating beverages which, as Ellis reports, then spread to Tahiti.

Changing attitudes toward athletic sports also chart the transformation of ethos. Again Hawaii stands out as a region of growing professionalism. The most popular sports were boxing and wrestling. Great public bouts that pitted professional fighters againset one another drew crowds of excited partisans who wagered heavily on their favorites. Professionalization of sports may be understood, of course, as part of the general process of increasingly narrower specialization in the Stratified societies. Hawaiian society had drawn the lower ranks quite generally into the technical services of administration. Through professional sports, they drew even the very low strata into the areas of entertainment. The popularity of boxing and wrestling, the bloody violence of the bouts together with the sexual social games, points curiously to the emergence of the urbanized taste for refined sensationalism in a society that had never developed a true urban center. From Malo we gather that the Hawaiian court had begun to create positions of honor without serious functions. The organization of Hawaiian life generally had become bureaucratic, freeing gentry from their traditional obligations of administration and from their traditional roles as exemplars of conduct. The loosening of these often austere bonds freed the gentry for a life of greater self-indulgence, while games and sports supplied the excitement to make up for the drop in tension from loss of social responsibility.

Evolutionary Direction

All the evidence leads to the conclusion that direction was introduced into Polynesian social and cultural variations by the action of the status system. The status system exercised a powerful control over all major social relations by acting as the medium of organization and as the guide for social morality. In a more general vein, it can be said that the principles of aristocracy were the constant measure of all social relations that deeply concerned the Polynesians. As the application and organization of these principles varied, so did Polynesian cultures vary as a whole. Thus the tendency of Polynesian aristocracy to evolve from Traditional to Open to Stratified forms seems to have given to Polynesian evolution its general direction.

If we are to attribute direction in Polynesian evolution to the status system, we must take care not to endow status systems with the qualities of prime movers or first causes or even of engines of history. There seems little advantage to reducing the overwhelming complexity of historical development to a single set of "causes," even for the sake of manageableness. What the evidence has revealed is not status system as "cause," but status system as constantly involved in change as well as in conservation. A status system is, however, no independent apparatus that changes itself and in so doing changes its society. Incorporating rules of conduct that define and measure honor and worth, status systems respond to all material conditions of life. They respond to wars, to quarrels, to rivalries, to foreign contacts, to physical dislocation, to economic abundance and scarcity, to the personal character of chiefs, and to historical traditions. It is difficult to imagine to what of significance status systems are not responsive. What seems to give constancy at all to the interaction between status and society is the characteristic function of a status system to assert and preserve fixed rules of conduct insofar as those affect honor and worth.

In Polynesia, principles of status are never abandoned as a whole. Some particular principle—seniority of descent, for example—may be abandoned. For the most part, status principles are bent, stretched, evaded, and so the traditional status systems gain flexibility and new characteristics. I have found no instance of total modification of a status system. All variants form part of a connected series.

This series does have direction, a direction that expresses an increasing degree of political power and authority, on the one hand, and an increased measure of social distinctions and oppositions, on the other. There is substantial evidence that status rivalry has been the constant factor in setting these directions. While it is proper to describe status rivalry as an inherent characteristic of Polynesian—if not of all—status systems, we recognize the range of rivalries as broad and the types of status conflict as diverse. No two Polynesian societies exhibit quite the same patterns of rivalry. Nor, for that matter, are any two Polynesian status systems identical. The evolutionary directions are *general,* but nevertheless real and significant.

How far can we go in defining the direction of evolution of Polynesian status systems? Can it be said that every Open society had been Traditional and that every Stratified society had been Traditional and then Open? I have dealt with this question from both a morphological and an historical point of view. Morphological study, taking account of a continuous series of variations, demonstrates the logic of a developmental series from Traditional to Open to Stratified. Historical reconstruction, even when supplemented by archeology and documentary words, is inherently uncertain, as almost all Polynesian scholars have conceded. Historical reconstructions assume credibility, however, if all sources of interpretation tend to coincide. In Polynesia, morphological interpretations, the evidence from historical or genealogical traditions, and—in two important instances (Marquesas, Easter Islands)—evidence from archeology either support or in no case contradict the hypothesis that the general direction of Polynesian social evolution was from Traditional to Open to Stratified. The hypothesis gains in credibility from the parallelism of such development in both eastern and western Polynesia, regions that had diverged in other cultural respects.

The case for direction of evolution is by no means complete. The hypothesis seems most complete in its application to eastern Polynesia and for a short series such as Maori, Manihiki-Rakahanga, Tongareva, Mangaia, Mangareva, Tahiti, and Hawaii. We do not know the Marquesas Traditional and our information on Easter Island is sketchy at best. Western Polynesia presents an even more problematic picture because of the diversity of what I have felt compelled to group together as Traditional societies. The case for direction in Western Polynesia rests quite satisfactorily, however, upon a coherent (i.e., continuous) series including Tikopia, Manu'a, Western Samoa, Futuna, Uvea, Niue, and Tonga. Even if we exclude Niue for reasons of insufficiency of data, or as problematic in any case, this sequence is a very close parallel to that of eastern Polynesia.

Evolution generally is considered an irreversible process. But the assumption of irreversibility drawn from organic evolution has yet to be verified in the case of social evolution. The Polynesian case as an example of short-range and local evolution does not clarify the question. From a morphological point of view alone, there is no reason why status systems cannot revert to older or to less politicalized forms. The western Polynesian outlying islands may be examples of general lapse without benefit of status rivalry from a more formal system of traditional status. Western Samoa seems to have been able to oscillate between Traditional and Open forms. We know, too, that Stratified societies shifted back and forth between centralized and decentralized phases. But since we have no definite information on conditions of land tenure, we cannot say whether these shifts were from Stratified to Open.

On the grand scale, evolution brings to light major processes of technical accumulation and of adaptation. To some degree, the narrow compass of small area variations also reveals technical additions in such forms as stone work, terracing, and irrigation. But technical developments and technical economic adaptations are rather minor aspects of Polynesian evolution. The smaller Polynesian scale brings out rather more subtle processes of differentiation of a common core, such as the intensification of traditional features or the readaptation of traditional features to new uses.

Intensification refers to the process by which cultural features assume greater prominence within the overall pattern of organization. Functionally weak patterns are strengthened, optional relationships become categorical, and the nominal becomes actual. The strengthening of political authority under the stress of status rivalry is the leading example of intensification and is seemingly its source, for all examples of intensification are essentially aspects or by-products of political power. When Segment I takes on corporate character as the locus of chiefly authority, it has responded to political intensification. Segment I in Stratified societies may be regarded as an intensification of the "shadow" form of Segment I in Traditional societies. Caste is an intensification of rank, making of optional avoidances categorical separations. The low-status dependent tenure of commoners in Stratified societies is an intensification in parallel fashion of the honorific titles to land held by traditional ariki. In Traditional societies, the distinction between chiefly and commoner tenure was essentially ritualistic. In the Stratified the distinction had become essentially pragmatic and was, accordingly, intensified. In the Marquesas, we had an indicated example of sudden shift from honorific to pragmatic title, from the assertion of honor over land to an assertion of control. Since honor implies control, this shift is to be regarded as an example of intensification. In the evolution from Traditional to Stratified, all status relationships involving separation are, as I have demonstrated in Chapter 23 on rituals of status, intensified. Finally, the apparent transformation of ethos from balance to antagonism and from moderation to violence illustrates intensification on a broad scale.

Insofar as intensification produces an alteration in traditional patterns, it demands readaptation to new functions. Intensification and readaptation, therefore, are linked processes. Again, all examples of readaptation are most readily explained as adjustments to the strengthening of political authority and power. And in this broad respect readaptation is a by-product of intensification. The entire political apparatus, which includes the territorial organization, the hierarchy of officialdom, and the administration of the economy, is really a readaptation of the old segmentary organization to the new requirements for stabilizing the intensified authority of the ariki.

This discussion of social evolution in terms of processes described as "intensification" and "adaptation" emphasizes the extraordinary continuity of the traditional Polynesian social pattern. In place of continuity we may speak of adaptability. The pattern is as adaptable to small coral atolls with populations in the hundreds as it is to high island archipelagoes with populations numbered in the hundreds of thousands. Of greater interest, to my mind, is the resilience of the aristocratic pattern in the face of severe internal disturbance and intense status rivalry. Status rivalry implies mobility. Polynesian aristocracy has evidently been able to preserve itself against the powerful claims of lower ranks for a place in the scheme of honor by accommodating itself to utility and, at the same time, strengthening its claim to exclusive representation of cultural ideals. Thus, while Polynesians repeatedly rejected despotism, they never rejected the principles of aristocracy. Malo's account of decadence at the royal Hawaiian court suggests a potential weakness in the system. Corruption enters when status has become nominal and has lost responsible functions. Yet we should not exaggerate the signs of "decline" in Hawaii. By all evidence, Polynesian aristocracy at the time of European occupation was, in fact, entering upon a new stage of growth.

Appendixes

I

Settlement Dates

	TRADITIONS	ARCHEOLOGY	LINGUISTICS
Maori	A.D. 950	A.D. 1000	A.D. 1000[a]
Manihiki-Rakahanga	A.D. 1300	. . .	A.D. 500[a]
Tongareva	A.D. 1400	. . .	A.D. 500[a]
Mangaia	A.D. 1100	. . .	A.D. 500[a]
Easter Island	A.D. 400	A.D. 386 ± 100[h]	A.D. 500[a]
Marquesas	300 B.C.	124 B.C. ± 150[b]	100 B.C.[a]
Mangareva	A.D. 1200	A.D. 1100	A.D. 1000[a]
Society Islands	A.D. 900	A.D. 1022 ± 90[c]	700 B.C.[a]
Hawaiian Islands	600 B.C.	A.D. 124[d]	A.D. 500[a]
Samoan Islands	A.D. 750	220 B.C. ± 90[e]	1500 B.C.[a]
Tonga	A.D. 950	. . .	1500 B.C. (?)[a]
Uvea	A.D. 1150	. . .	A.D. 530–930[f]
Futuna	A.D. 1400	. . .	A.D. 530–930[f]
Tokelaus	A.D. 1650	. . .	. . .
Tikopia	A.D. 1450[g]	. . .	A.D. 530–930[f]
Pukapuka	A.D. 1200	. . .	. . .
Niue	A.D. 750	. . .	A.D. 300–530[f]
Ontong Java	. . .	. . .	A.D. 300–530(?)[f]

a. Emory 1963b
b. Suggs 1961
c. Sinoto 1963
d. Shutler 1961
e. Davidson, Green, Buist, and Peters 1967
f. Elbert 1953
g. Firth 1961:165
h. Heyerdahl 1961:394

2

Historical Relationships from Linguistics

	Cognate percent		Cognate percent
Maori		*Samoa*	
Rarotonga	83	Tikopia	76
Tahiti	73	Futuna	74
Hawaii	71	Uvea	70
Tikopia	71	Tonga	66
Easter		Rarotonga	67
Tikopia	67	*Tonga*	
Hawaii	64	Uvea	86
Marquesas	64	Futuna	74
Marquesas		Tikopia	70
Rarotonga	75	*Uvea*	
Mangareva	73	Tonga	86
Tikopia	67	Tikopia	78
Mangareva		*Futuna*	
Rarotonga	73	Tikopia	83
Marquesas	73	Uvea	83
Tahiti		Tonga	74
Rarotonga	85	*Niue*	
Hawaii	76	Tikopia	68
Maori	73	Tonga	64
Marquesas	68	Samoa	63
Hawaii		*Ontong Java*	
Rarotonga	79	Futuna	62
Maori	71	Tikopia	62
Marquesas	69		

From data of Elbert 1953

3

Standard Terms of High Honor

Maori	ariki	rangatira	. . .	. . .	. . .	tohunga	. . .	toa
Manihiki	ariki	rangatira	. . .	. . .	. . .	. . .	taula	. . .
Tongareva	ariki	. . .	. . .	. . .	. . .	. . .	. . .	. . .
Mangaia	ariki	rangatira	. . .	. . .	. . .	ta'unga	. . .	toa
Easter	ariki	. . .	. . .	. . .	. . .	tohunga	. . .	mata-toa
Marquesas	haka-iki	anatia	. . .	. . .	. . .	tuhuna	. . .	toa
Mangareva	atariki	ragatira	. . .	. . .	. . .	tu'uga	taura	toa
Society	arii	raatira	. . .	. . .	. . .	tahu'a	tauha	toa
Hawaii	ali'i	. . .	. . .	. . .	. . .	kahuna	kaula	koa
Samoa	ali'i	. . .	tui	. . .	. . .	tufuga	taula	. . .
Tonga	eiki	. . .	tui	matapule	hau	tufunga	taula	toa
Uvea	aliki	. . .	tui	matapule	fau	tufunga	taula	. . .
Futuna	aliki	. . .	tui	matapule	sau	tufunga	. . .	toa
Tokelaus	aliki	. . .	tui	. . .	fau	tofunga	taulaitu	toa
Tikopia	ariki	. . .	. . .	. . .	. . .	tufunga	. . .	toa
Pukapuka	aliki	langatila	. . .	pule	. . .	. . .	tauila	toa
Niue	iki	. . .	. . .	pule	. . .	tufuga	taula	toa
Ontong Java	alii	. . .	. . .	. . .	. . .	. . .	. . .	. . .

4

Standard Terms of Low Honor

Maori	tutua, ware, taurekareka, pononga
Mangaia	'ao, ivi panga
Easter	kio, harumanu
Marquesas	vai-noa, kikino meau, tupenoa, tautua
Mangareva	'urumanu, u'iga, kio, kiore
Society	manahune, taata ino
Hawaii	kauwa, mahelele
Samoa	itua
Tonga	tua, polata
Uvea	taua
Futuna	seka
Tikopia	fakaarufa
Niue	fekafekau, tupa, lalo tagata

There are no terms for Manihiki, Tongareva, Tokelaus, Pukapuka, and Ontong Java.

5

Standard Terms of Consanguinity

	Manu'a	Tonga	Uvea	Futuna	Tokelaus	Tikopia	Pukapuka	Niue	Ontong Java
GF	tamā	kui	kui	tupuna	tupuna	tupuna	tupuna	tupuna tane	kipunga
GM	olamatua	kui	kui	tupuna	tupuna	tupuna	tupuna	tupuna fifine	kipunga
GCiL	tamā	mokopuna	mokopuna	makopuna	makupuna	makopuna	makopuna	mokopuna	mopunga
F	tamā	tamai	tamai	tamana	tamana	tamana	matua tane	matua tane	kamanga
FB	tama	tamai	tamai	tamana	tamana	tamana	matua tane	matua tane	kamanga
FSi	ilamutu	mehekitanga	mahiki-tanga	masakitanga	matua sa	masikatanga	matua wawine	matua fifine	kinga
M	tinā	fae	fae	tsinana	matua	nana	matua wawine	matua fifine	kinga
MB	tamā	tuasina	tuasina	tu'a tsinana	tuatina	tuatina	matua tane	matua tane	lamoku
MSi	tinā	fae	fae	tsinana	matua	nana	matua wawine	matua·fifine	kinga
(W)B[1]	tuagane	tuongaane	tuangaane	tuanga'ane	tuangane	kave	tua tane	tugane	{ hangau kainga
(M)Si[2]	tuafafine	tuofefine	tuafafine	tuanga'ane	tuafafine	kave	tua wawine	mahakitaga	'ave
oLB	. . .	ta'okete	ta'okete	taina	kimua	taina	taina	{ matakainaga ta'okete	{ hangau kainga
YB	tei	tehina	tehina	taina	kimuli	taina	taina	tehina	{ hangau kainga
oLSi	. . .	ta'okete	ta'okete	taina	kimua	taina	taina	ta'okete	'ave
YSi	tei	tehina	tehina	taina	kimuli	taina	taina	tehina	'ave
(M)S	atali'i	foha	foha	tama (vosa)	ataliki	tama	tamatane	tamatane	kama
(W)S	tamatane	tama	tama	tama (vosa)	tama	tama	tamatane	tamatane	kama
(M)D	afafine	ofefine	ofafine	ta'ine	afafine	tamafine	tamawawine	tamafifine	kama
(W)D	tamafafine	tama	taahine	ta'ine	tamafafine	tamafine	tamawawine	tamafifine	kama
(M)SiS	tamafafine	ilamutu	ilamutu	ilamutu	ilamutu	{ tama tapu iramutu	tamatane	tamatane	lamoku
(W)SiS	tamafafine	tama	tama	tama (vosa)	tama	tama	tamatane	tamatane	kama
(M)SiD	tamafafine	ilamutu	ilamutu	ilamutu	ilamutu	iramutu	tamawawine	tamafifine	lamoku
(W)SiD	tamafafine	tama	taahine	ta'ine	tamafafine	tamafine	tamawawine	tamafifine	kama
(M)BS	atali'i	foha	foha	tama (vosa)	tama	tama	tamatane	tamatane	kama
(W)BS	tama	fakafotu	fakafotu	fakafotu	tama sa	tama	tamatane	tamatane	kama
(M)BD	tamafafine	ofefine	ofafine	ta'ine	tamafafine	tama	tamawawine	tamafifine	kama
(W)BD	tamafafine	fakafotu	fakafotu	fakafotu	tamafafine	tama	tamawawine	tamafifine	kama

Source: Manu'a (Mead 1930), Tonga (Gifford 1929), Uvea (Burrows 1937), Futuna (Burrows 1936), Tokelaus (MacGregor 1937), Tikopia (Firth 1936), Pukapuka (Beaglehole and Beaglehole 1938), Niue (Loeb 1926), Ontong Java (Hogbin 1931b, 1934), Maori (Buck 1949), Tongareva (Buck 1932a), Manihiki-Rakahanga (Buck 1932b), Mangaia (Buck 1934),

Maori	Tongareva	Manihiki-Rakahanga	Mangaia	Marquesas	Easter	Man-gareva	Society	Hawaii
tipuna tane	tupuna	tupuna	tupuna	tupuna	tupuna	tupuna	hui tupuna	kupuna kane
tipuna wawine	tupuna	tupuna	tupuna	tupuna	tupuna	tupuna	hanahana	kupuna wahine
mokopuna	mokopuna	mokopuna	mokopuna	moupuna	makupuna	makupuna	mootua	mo'opuna
matua	tira	metua-tane	metua	motua	matua tamaaroa	motua	metua	makua kane
matuakeke	taueka	metua-tane	metua	teina motua	matua tamaaroa	motua-iti	metua	makua kane
matuakeke	matua-wahine	metua-wahine	metua	tuehine	matua tamahahine	kui-iti	metua	makua hine
matua wahine	papa	metua-wahine	metua	kui	matua tamahahine	kui	metua	makua hine
matua keke	taueka	metua-tane	metua	tunane	matua tamaaroa	motua-iti	metua	makua kane
matua wawine	matua-wahine	metua-wahine	metua	tua'ana kui	matua tamahahine	kui-iti	metua	makua hine
tungane	tuangane	tuangane	tungane	tunana	tuakana	tugane	tu'ane	kaikunane
tuahine	tuahine	tuahine	tua'ine	tuehina	tuahine	tue'ine	tuehine	kaikuahine
tuakana	tuakana	tuakana	tuakana	tuaana	tuakana	tuakana	tua'ana	kaikua'ana
taina	taina	teina	teina	teina	taina	teina	teina	kaikaina
tuakana	tuakana	tuakana	tuakana	tuaana	tuakana	tuakana	tua'ana	kaikua'ana
taina	taina	teina	teina	teina	taina	teina	teina	kaikaina
tamaroa	tama	tama	tamaroa	tama	poki-tamaaroa	tamaroa	tamaiti	keiki
tamaroa	tama	tama	tamaroa	tama	poki-tamaaroa	tamaroa	tamaiti	keiki
hine	tamahine	tamahine	tamaine	mo'i	poki-tamahahine	mo'ine	tamahine	kaikamahine
hine	tamahine	tamahine	tamaine	mo'i	poki-tamahahine	mo'ine	tamahine	kaikamahine
iramutu	toate	iramutu	tamaiti	i'amutu tama	tama-iti	iramutu	tamaiti	keiki
iramutu	toate	iramutu	tamaiti	tama	tama-iti	iramutu	tamaiti	keiki
iramutu	taukohera	iramutu	tamaiti	i'amutu	vovo	iramutu	tamahine	kaikamahine
iramutu	taukohera	iramutu	tamaiti	mo'i	vovo	iramutu	tamahine	kaikamahine
iramutu	toate	iramutu	tamaiti	tama	tama-iti	iramutu	tamaiti	keiki
iramutu	toate	iramutu	tamaiti	tama	tama-iti	iramutu	tamaiti	keiki
iramutu	taukohera	iramutu	tamaiti	mo'i	vovo	iramutu	tamahine	kaikamahine
iramutu	taukohera	iramutu	tamaiti	mo'i	vovo	iramutu	tamahine	kaikamahine

Marquesas (Handy 1923), Easter (Metraux 1940), Mangareva (Buck 1938a), Society (Handy 1930a), Hawaii (Handy and Pukui 1958).

NOTE: For Manu'a only, (M)SS = atalii

1. (W)—woman speaking
2. (M)—man speaking

6

Distributions of Standard Kinship Terms

	Tupuna	Mokopuna	Tamai	Tamana	Mehekitanga	Fae	Foha	Tuasina	Matua	Ilamutu	Tuagane	Tuafafine	Tuakana	Teina	Ta'okete	Tama	Afafine	Kui
Manu'a			×						×	×	×	×		×		×	×	
Tonga		×	×		×	×	×	×		×	×	×		×	×	×	×	×
Uvea		×	×		×	×	×	×		×	×	×		×	×	×	×	×
Futuna	×	×		×	×		×			×	×			×		×		
Tokelaus	×	×		×				×	×	×	×	×		×		×	×	
Tikopia	×	×		×	×			×		×				×		×		
Pukapuka	×	×							×			×		×		×		
Niue	×	×			×				×		×			×	×	×		
Ontong Java	×	×		×						×						×		
Maori	×	×							×	×	×	×	×	×		×		
Tongareva	×	×							×		×	×	×	×		×		
Manihiki	×	×							×	×	×	×	×	×		×		
Mangaia	×	×							×		×	×	×	×	×	×		
Marquesas	×	×							×	×	×	×	×	×	×	×		×
Easter	×	×							×			×	×	×	×	×		
Mangareva	×	×							×	×	×	×	×	×	×	×		×
Society	×	×							×		×	×	×	×		×		
Hawaii	×	×							×		×	×	×	×		×		

7

The Cross-Relationships: Honoring

	MB(T)	MB(B)	FSi(T)	FSi(B)	SiS(T)	Fahu	B-Si Respects
Samoa	o	+	+	+	+	o	A
Tonga	—	—	+	+	+	+	A
Futuna	—	o	+	o	o	+	A
Uvea	—	o	+	o	+	+	R
Tokelaus	—	+	+	+	+	o	A
Tikopia	—	+	+	+	+	o	R
Pukapuka	+	o	o	o	o	o	A[1]
Niue	+	o	o	o	o	o	R
Ontong Java	+	o	o	o	+	o	A
Maori	o	o	o	o	o	o	o
Tongareva	o	o	o	o	o	o	o
Manihiki	o	o	o	o	o	o	o
Mangaia	o	o	o	o	o	o	o
Marquesas	+	+	+	+	+	o	R[2]
Easter	o	o	o	o	o	o	o
Mangareva	—	o	—	o	o	o	o
Society	o	o	o	o	o	o	o
Hawaii	o	o	o	o	o	o	o

Note: (T)—terminology; (B)—behavior; o = normal; + = elevated; — = reduced; A—physical avoidance; R—respect behavior

1. cross-cousins only 2. cross-cousin marriage

8

Ecological Character

	Type	Area (sq. miles)	Estimated Population	Density (per sq. mile)	Irrigation
Traditional					
New Zealand	high	102,000	100,000	1	
Manihiki	atoll	4	900	225	
Tongareva	atoll	6	2,000	333	
Uvea	high	23	4,000	174	×
Futuna	high	25	2,000	80	×
Tokelaus	atoll	4	1,200	300	
Tikopia	high	3	1,300	433	
Pukapuka	atoll	2	630	315	
Ontong Java	atoll	. . .	5,000	. . .	
Open					
Mangaia	high	27	3,000	111	×
Easter	high	55	4,000	73	
Marquesas	high	408	100,000	50	
Samoa	high	1,210	60,000	50	
Niue	atoll	100	4,500	45	
Stratified					
Mangareva	near-atoll	6	2,500	416	×
Society	high	593	200,000	334	×
Hawaii	high	6,445	300,000	45	×
Tonga	atoll and high	250	25,000	100	×

Sources: New Zealand (Burrows 1939b), Manihiki (Buck 1932b), Tongareva (Buck 1932a), Uvea (Burrows 1939b), Futuna (Burrows 1939b), Tokelaus (Burrows 1939b), Tikopia (Firth 1939), Pukapuka (Beaglehole and Beaglehole 1938), Ontong Java (Hogbin 1934), Mangaia (Buck 1934), Easter (Metraux 1940), Marquesas (Handy 1923), Samoa (Mead 1937), Niue (Smith 1902), Mangareva (Buck 1938), Hawaii (Jarves 1843), Tonga (Gifford 1929).

9

Basic Kinship Patterns: Western Polynesia

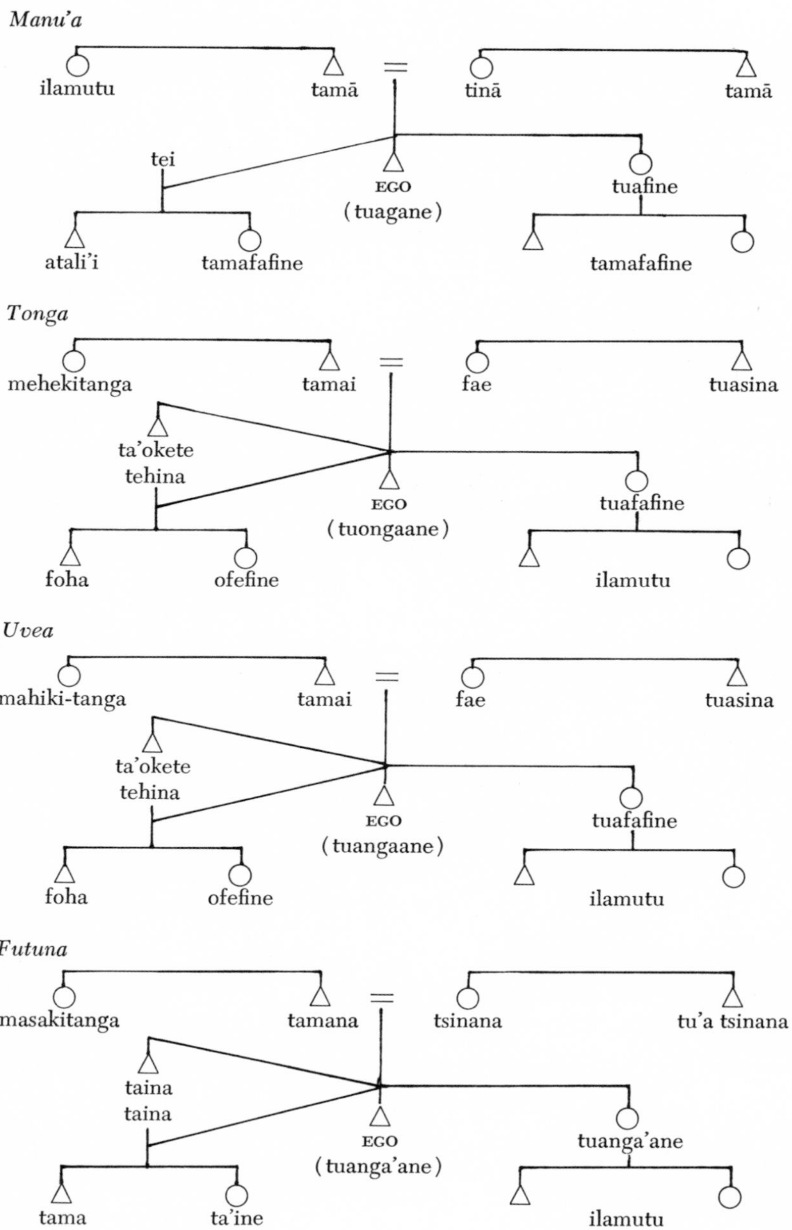

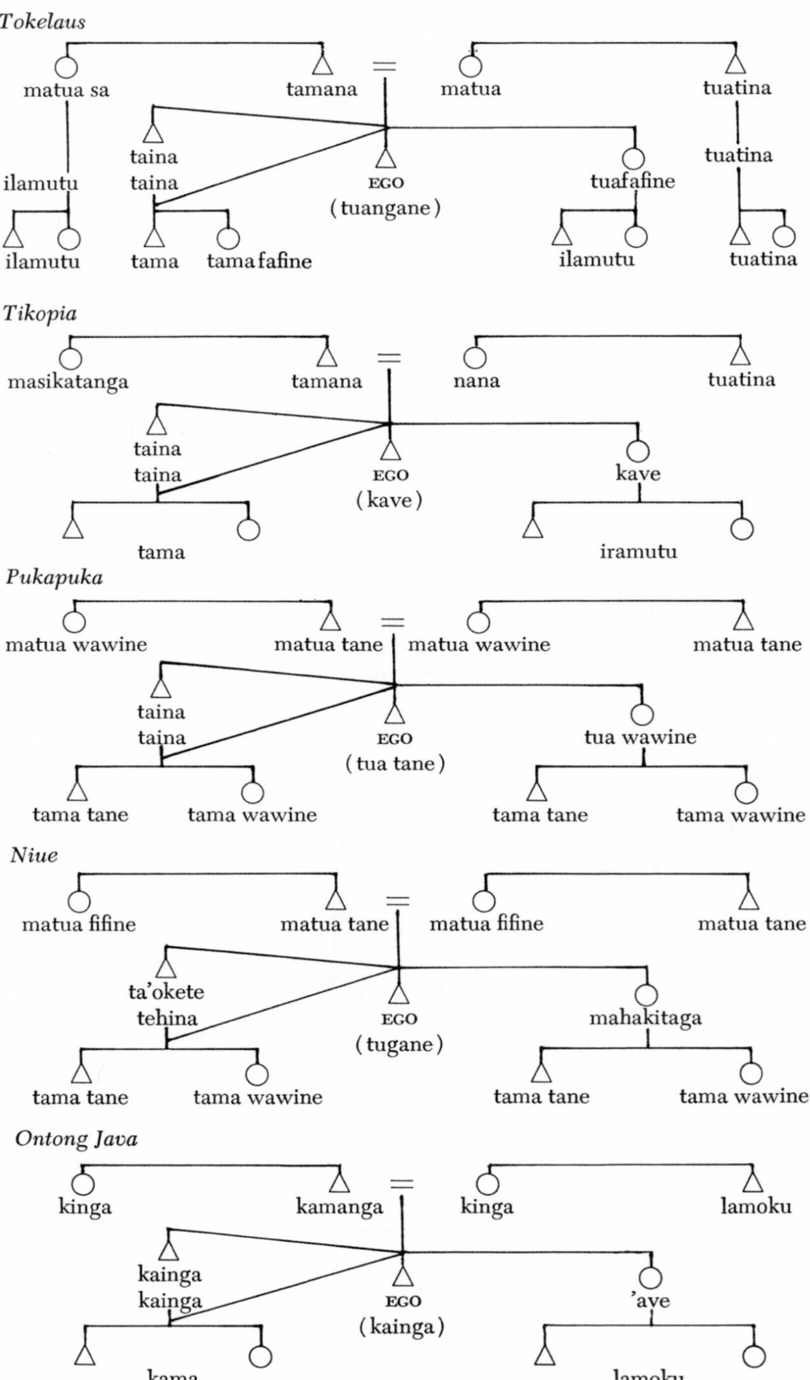
Tokelaus
matua sa
tamana
matua
tuatina
taina
taina
tuatina
ilamutu
EGO
(tuangane)
tuafafine
ilamutu
tama
tamafafine
ilamutu
tuatina
Tikopia
masikatanga
tamana
nana
tuatina
taina
taina
EGO
(kave)
kave
tama
iramutu
Pukapuka
matua wawine
matua tane
matua wawine
matua tane
taina
taina
EGO
(tua tane)
tua wawine
tama tane
tama wawine
tama tane
tama wawine
Niue
matua fifine
matua tane
matua fifine
matua tane
ta'okete
tehina
EGO
(tugane)
mahakitaga
tama tane
tama wawine
tama tane
tama wawine
Ontong Java
kinga
kamanga
kinga
lamoku
kainga
kainga
EGO
(kainga)
'ave
kama
lamoku

10

Basic Kinship Patterns: Eastern Polynesia

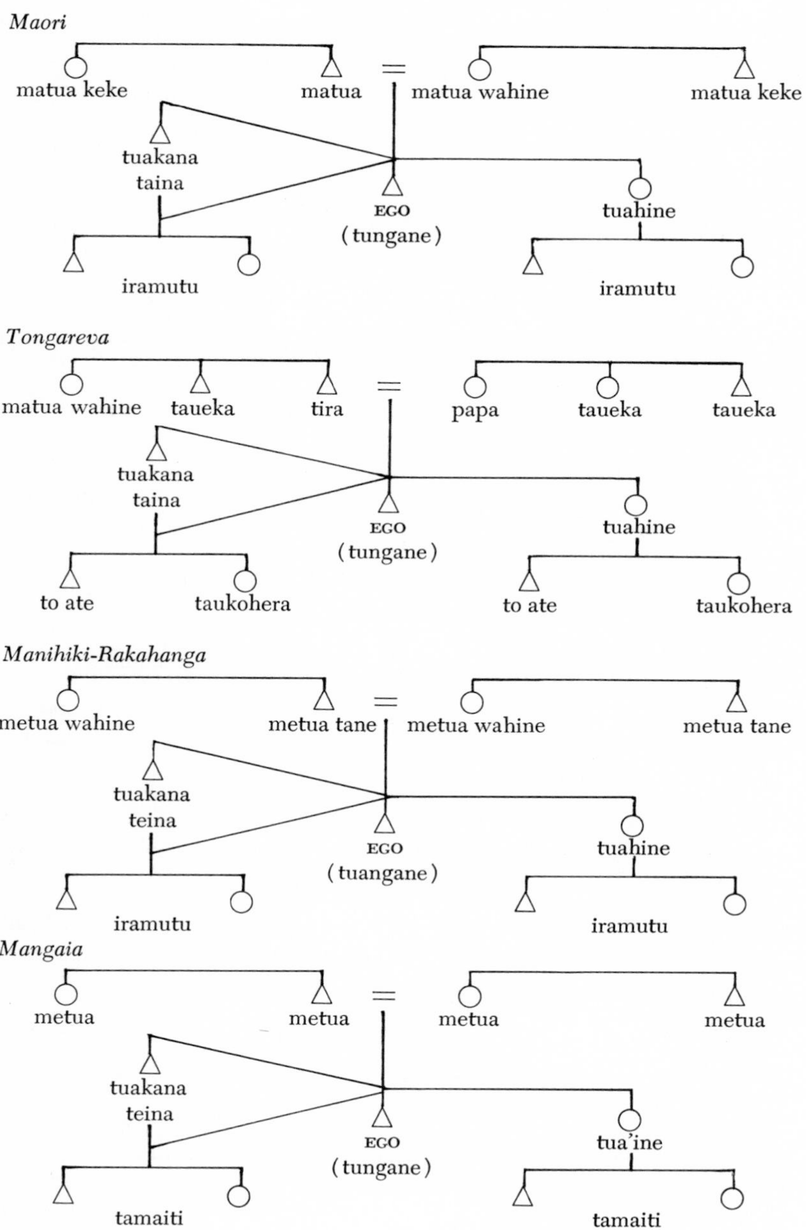

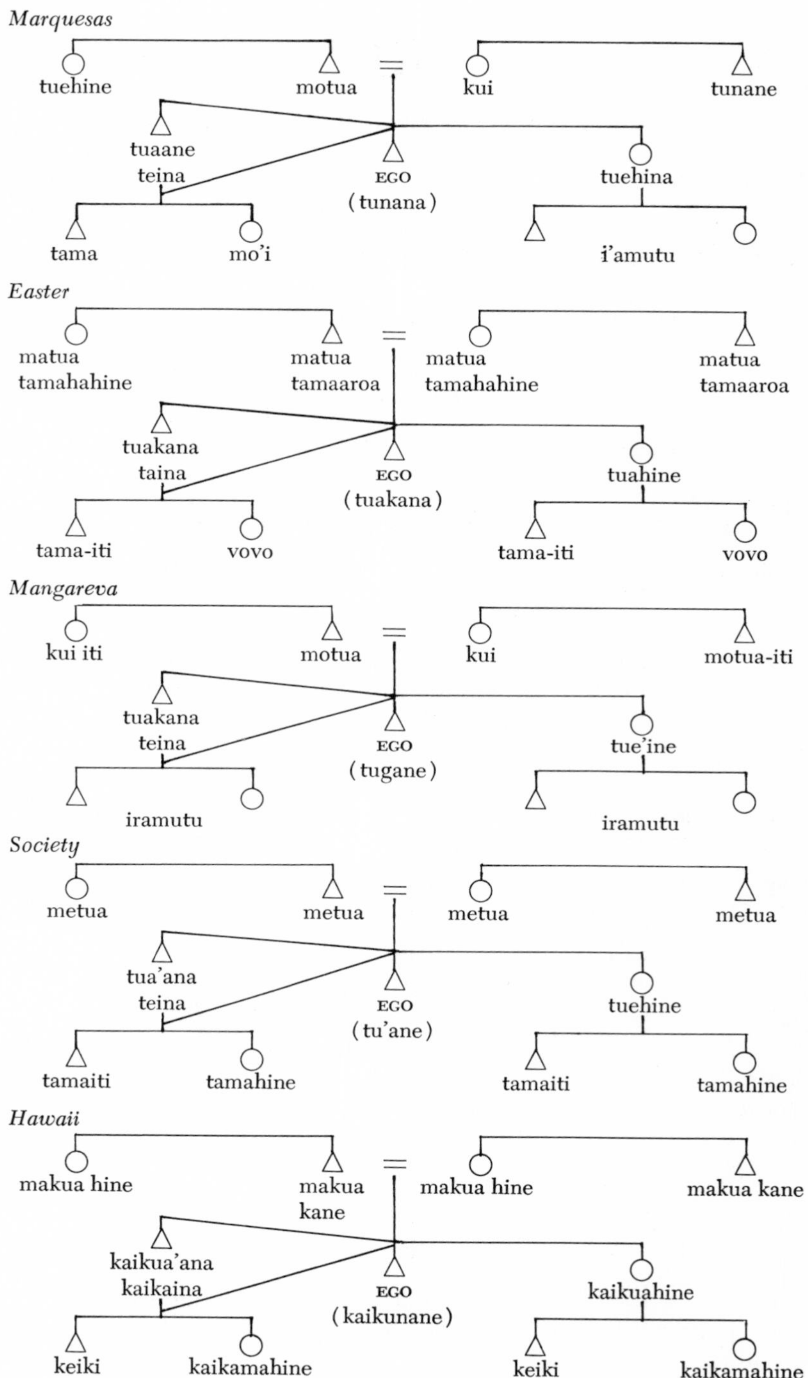
Marquesas
tuehine
motua
kui
tunane
tuaane
teina
EGO
(tunana)
tuehina
tama
mo'i
i'amutu
Easter
matua
tamahahine
matua
tamaaroa
matua
tamahahine
matua
tamaaroa
tuakana
taina
EGO
(tuakana)
tuahine
tama-iti
vovo
tama-iti
vovo
Mangareva
kui iti
motua
kui
motua-iti
tuakana
teina
EGO
(tugane)
tue'ine
iramutu
iramutu
Society
metua
metua
metua
metua
tua'ana
teina
EGO
(tu'ane)
tuehine
tamaiti
tamahine
tamaiti
tamahine
Hawaii
makua hine
makua
kane
makua hine
makua kane
kaikua'ana
kaikaina
EGO
(kaikunane)
kaikuahine
keiki
kaikamahine
keiki
kaikamahine

Bibliography

Adams, Henry

1947 *Memoirs of Arii Taimai e Marama of Timeo Tooarai Terrinui of Tahiti, Tauraatua Iamo*. New York: Scholars Facsimiles and Reprints.

Agee, H. P.

1927 Hawaiian Agriculture Prior to 1860. *Hawaiian Planters Record* 31:154–63.

Aginsky, B. W., and Te Rangi Hiroa (Sir Peter Buck)

1940 Interacting Forces in the Maori Family. *American Anthropologist* 42:195–210.

Aitken, Robert

1930 *Ethnology of Tubuai*. Honolulu: Bernice P. Bishop Museum Bulletin 70.

Alexander, W. D.

1890 A Brief History of Land Titles in the Hawaiian Kingdom. *Hawaiian Annual for 1891*, pp. 105–24.

1891 *A Brief History of the Hawaiian People*. New York: American Book Company.

1917 Overthrow of the Ancient Tabu System in the Hawaiian Islands. In *Hawaiian Historical Society, 25th Annual Report*, pp. 37–45.

Andrews, Edmund, and Andrews, Irene P.

1944 *A Comparative Dictionary of the Tahitian Language*. Chicago: Chicago Academy of Science.

Archey, G.

1949 *South Sea Folk*. Wellington, N.Z.: Auckland Museum. *Handbook for Oceanic Ethnologist*, 2d ed.

Barnett, H. G.

1949 *Palauan Society*. Eugene: University of Oregon.

Barrau, Jacques

1956 *Polynesian and Micronesian Subsistence Agriculture*. Mimeographed. Nouméa, New Caledonia: South Pacific Commission.

1963 (ed.) *Plants and the Migration of Pacific Peoples: A Symposium*. Honolulu: Bernice P. Bishop Museum Press.

Barrow, T. T.

1956 Human Figures in Wood and Ivory from Western Polynesia. *Man* 56:192.

Barthel, Thomas S.

1958 *Grundlagen zur Entzifferung der Osterinselschrift*. Universität Hamburg. Abhandlungen aus dem Gebiet der Auslandskunde. vol. 64.

1961 Zu einigen gesellschaftlichen Termini der Polynesier. *Zeitschrift für Ethnologie* 86:256–75.

Beaglehole, Ernest
1937 Cultural Peaks in Polynesia. *Man* 176:138–40.
1957 *Social Change in the South Pacific: Rarotonga and Aitutaki.* London: Allen and Unwin.

Beaglehole, Ernest, and Beaglehole, Pearl
1938 *Ethnology of Pukapuka.* Honolulu: Bernice P. Bishop Museum Bulletin 150.
1940 The Polynesian Maori. *Journal of the Polynesian Society* 49: 39–68.
1941 *Pangai, A Village in Tonga.* Wellington, N. Z.: Polynesian Society Memoirs vol. 18.
1948 *Some Modern Maoris.* Wellington, N. Z.: New Zealand Council for Educational Research.

Beckwith, Martha W.
1932 *Kepelino's Traditions of Hawaii.* Honolulu: Bernice P. Bishop Museum Bulletin 95.
1940 *Hawaiian Mythology.* New Haven: Yale University Press.
1951 *The Kumulipo: A Hawaiian Creation Chant.* Chicago: University of Chicago Press.

Beechey, Frederick William
1831 *Narrative of a Voyage to the Pacific and Beering's Strait . . . in The Years 1825, 1826, 1828.* London: Colburn.

Bell, F. L. S.
1931 The Place of Food in the Social Life of Central Polynesia. *Oceania* 2:117–25.
1932–33 Functional Interpretation of Succession and Inheritance in Polynesia. *Oceania* 3:167–206.

Benedict, P. K.
1942 Thai, Kadai and Indonesian. *American Anthropologist* 44:576–601.

Benedict, Ruth F.
1934 *Patterns of Culture.* Boston: Houghton Mifflin.

Bennett, Wendell Clark
1931 *The Archaeology of Kauai.* Honolulu: Bernice P. Bishop Museum Bulletin 80.

Best, Elsdon
1903–05 Notes on the Art of War. *Journal of the Polynesian Society* 13:11–13.
1924a *The Maori.* Wellington, N. Z.: Polynesian Society Memoir no. 5, vols. 1 and 2.
1924b *Tuhoe, Children of the Mist.* 2 vols. New Plymouth, N. Z.: Polynesian Society.
1925 *Maori Agriculture.* Wellington, N. Z.: Dominion Museum no. 9.
1927 The Discovery and Settlement of Rarotonga by Polynesians. *Journal of Polynesian Society* 36:122–234.

Beyer, H. Otley

1948 *Philippine and East Asian Archeology*. Manila: *National Research Council of Philippines* Bulletin no. 29.

Biggs, Bruce

1957 The Story of Kupe: Himiona Kaaira. *Journal of Polynesian Society* 66:216–48.

1960 *Maori Marriage: An Essay in Reconstruction*. Wellington, N. Z.: The Polynesian Society.

Bijlmer, H. J. T.

1928 Results of Anthropological Researches on Different Indonesian Tribes. In *Third Pan-Pacific Science Congress* (1926) *Proceedings*, pp. 2405–7. Tokyo.

Birket-Smith, Kaj

1956 *An Ethnological Sketch of Rennell Island: A Polynesian Outlier in Melanesia*. Det Kongelige Danske Videnskabernes Selskab. Historisk-filologiske Meddelelser. vol. 35, no. 3. Copenhagen: Ejnar Munksgaard.

Bishop, Marcia Brown

1940 *Hawaiian Life of The Pre-European Period*. Salem, Mass.: Peabody Museum.

Bligh, W.

1792 *An Account of The Mutinous Seizure of The Bounty*. London: Nicol.

1937 *The Log of the Bounty*. London: Golden Cockerel Press.

Boas, Franz

1896 The Limitations of the Comparative Method in Anthropology. In *Race, Language and Culture*, pp. 270–80. New York: MacMillan.

Bonk, Wm. J.

1961 Prehistoric Man in Hawaii. *Archeology* 14:88–94.

Bougainville, Lewis de

1772 *A Voyage Round the World . . . in the Years 1766, 1767, 1768, 1769*. Translated by J. R. Forster. London: Nourse and Davies.

Bovis, E. de

1855 État de la Société Tahitienne, à l'arrivee des Europeéns. *Revue Colonial* 14:368–408, 510–39.

Boyd, William C.

1950 *Genetics And The Races of Man*. Boston: Little, Brown.

Brigham, W. T.

1900 *An Index To The Islands of The Pacific Ocean*. Honolulu: Bernice P. Bishop Museum, Memoir vol. 1.

Browne, Arthur H.

1897 An Account of Some Early Ancestors of Rarotonga. *Journal of the Polynesian Society* 6:1–10.

Bryan, Edwin H. Jr.

1938 *Ancient Hawaiian Life*. Honolulu: Advertiser Publishing Co.

Buck, Sir Peter H. (Te Rangi Hiroa)
1930 *Samoan Material Culture.* Honolulu: Bernice P. Bishop Museum Bulletin 75.
1932a *Ethnology of Tongareva.* Honolulu: Bernice P. Bishop Museum Bulletin 92.
1932b *Ethnology of Manihiki and Rakahanga.* Honolulu: Bernice P. Bishop Museum Bulletin 99.
1934 *Mangaian Society.* Honolulu: Bernice P. Bishop Museum Bulletin 122.
1936 *Regional Diversity in The Elaboration of Sorcery in Polynesia.* New Haven: Yale University Publications in Anthropology, no. 2.
1938a *Ethnology of Mangareva.* Honolulu: Bernice P. Bishop Museum Bulletin 157.
1938b *Vikings of the Sunrise.* New York: Stokes Press.
1939 *Anthropology and Religion.* New Haven: Yale University Press.
1944 *Arts and Crafts of the Cook Islands.* Honolulu: Bernice P. Bishop Museum Bulletin 179.
1945 *An Introduction to Polynesian Anthropology.* Honolulu: Bernice P. Bishop Museum Bulletin 187.
1949 *The Coming of the Maori.* Wellington, N. Z.: Whitcomb and Tombs.
1951 *Report of the Director for 1950.* Honolulu: Bernice P. Bishop Museum Bulletin 205.
Burney, J. A.
1803 *A Chronological History of the Discoverie in the South Seas or Pacific Ocean.* 5 vols. London: L. Hansard.
Burrows, E .G.
1936 *The Ethnology of Futuna.* Honolulu: Bernice P. Bishop Museum Bulletin 138.
1937 *The Ethnology of Uvea.* Honolulu: Bernice P. Bishop Museum Bulletin 145.
1939a *Western Polynesia.* Gothenburg: Ethnographical Studies, Gothenburg Museum, vol. 7.
1939b Breed and Border in Polynesia. *American Anthropologist* 41: 1–21.
1940 Culture Areas in Polynesia. *Journal of the Polynesian Society* 49: 349–63.
Burrows, Edwin G., and Spiro, Melford W.
1957 *An Atoll Culture, Ethnology of Ifaluk in the Central Carolines.* New Haven: Human Relations Area Files.
Buschan, G.
1923 *Die Polynesische Kultur in Australien und Ozeanien Asien.* Stuttgart: Strecker und Schroeder.
Caillot, Eugene A. C.
1910 *Histoire de la Polynesia Orientale.* Paris: E. Leroux.
1914 *Mythes, Legendes et Traditions des Polynesiens.* Paris: E. Leroux.

Callenfels, P. V. Van Stein

1936 *The Melanesoid Civilizations of Eastern Asia*. Bulletin of the Raffles Museum, Singapore Straits Settlement, series B, 1:41–60.

Capell, Arthur

1962 Oceanic Linguistic Today. *Current Anthropology* 3:371–431.

Capell, A. and Lester, R. H.

1945–46 Kinship in Fiji. *Oceania* 15:171–200 and 16:109–43.

Carter, George F.

1950 Plant Evidence for Early Contacts With America. *Southwestern Journal of Anthropology* 6:161–82.

Chang, Kwang-Chih

1956 A Brief Survey of the Archeology of Formosa. *Southwestern Journal of Anthropology* 12:371–86.

1957 On the "Polynesian" Complexes in Formosa. *Bulletin of the Institute of Ethnology Academia Sinica* no. 3.

Chang, Kwang-Chih, Grace, George W., and Solheim, William, III

1964 Movement of the Malayo-Polynesians. *Current Anthropology* 5: 359–406.

Childe, V. Gordon

1946 *What Happened in History*. New York: Penguin Books.

Christian, F. W.

1910 *Eastern Pacific Islands*. London: R. Scott.

Chubb, Lawrence John

1930 *Geology of the Marquesas*. Honolulu: Bernice P. Bishop Museum Bulletin 68.

Churchill, W.

1911 *The Polynesian Wanderings*. Washington, D. C.: Carnegie Institution of Washington Publication 134.

1912 *Easter Island. The Rapanui Speech and the Peopling of Southeast Asia*. Washington: Carnegie Institution of Washington.

Churchward, C. Maxwell

1959 *Tongan Dictionary*. London: Oxford.

Codrington, R. H.

1891 *The Melanesians: Studies in Their Anthropology and Their Folklore*. Oxford: The Clarendon Press.

Cohen, Yehudi

1964 *The Transition from Childhood to Adolescence*. Chicago: Aldine Publishing Company.

Cole, F. C. C.

1913 The Wild Tribes of Davao District. In *Field Museum of Natural History, Anthropology Series*. Vol. 7, 2:49–203.

1922 The Tinguian Social, Religious and Economic Life. In *Field Museum of Natural History, Anthropology Series*. Vol. 4, 2:231–493.

1936 Family, Clan and Phratry in Central Sumatra. In *Essays in Anthropology Presented to A. L. Kroeber*. Berkeley: University of California Press.

Collocott, E. E. V.
1921 The Supernatural in Tonga. *American Anthropologist* 23:415–44.
1921 Notes on Tongan Religion. *Journal of the Polynesian Society* 30: 152–63; 227–40.
1924 An Experiment in Tongan History. *Journal of the Polynesian Society* 33:166–85.
Colum, P.
1937 *Legends of Hawaii*. New Haven: Yale University Press.
Cook, Captain James
1784 *A Voyage to the Pacific Ocean*. 3 vols. London: W. and A. Strahan.
1955 *The Journals of Captain James Cook: The Voyage of the Endeavor 1768–1771*. Vol. I. Edited by J. C. Beaglehole. Cambridge: Hakluyt Society.
1961 *The Journals of Captain James Cook: The Voyage of the Resolution and Adventure*. Vol. 2. Edited by J. C. Beaglehole. Cambridge: Hakluyt Society.
1967 *The Journals of Captain James Cook: The Voyage of the Resolution and Discovery, 1776–1780*. Vols. 1, 2. Edited by J. C. Beaglehole and Cambridge University Press: Hakluyt Society.
Coon, Carleton S.
1962 *The Origin of Races*. New York: Alfred A. Knopf.
Corney, Bolton G.
1913–19 *The Quest and Occupation of Tahiti By Emissaries of Spain in 1772–76*. London: Hakluyt Society Works, 2d series, nos. 32, 36, 43.
Coulter, John Wesley
1931 *Distribution of Population and Utilization of Land and Sea in Hawaii*. Honolulu: Bernice P. Bishop Museum Bulletin 88.
1933 *Land Utilization in the Hawaiian Islands*. Honolulu: Printshop Coy.
1941 *Land Utilization in American Samoa*. Honolulu: Bernice P. Bishop Museum Bulletin 170.
Crocombe, R. G.
1964 *Land Tenure in the Cook Islands*. London: Oxford University.
Cumberland, K. B.
1949 Aotearoa Maori: New Zealand About 1780. *Geographical Review* 39:401–24.
Davenport, W.
1959 Non-Unilinear Descent and Descent Groups. *American Anthropologist* 61:557–72.
Davidson, J. M., Green, R. C., Buist, A. G., and Peters, K. M.
1967 Additional Radiocarbon Dates for Western Polynesia. *Journal of the Polynesian Society* 76:223–30.
Davies, John
1851 *A Tahitian and English Dictionary*. London: London Missionary Society.

De Young, John E.

1953 An Analysis of the Hawaiian Cranium in the Light of Racial Affinities and Relationship to Migration Routes of the Original Proto-Polynesians. In *Proceedings of 8th Pacific Science Congress.* Quezon City, Philippines.

Dibble, Sheldon

1909 *A History of the Sandwich Islands.* Honolulu: T. G. Thrum.

Dillon, Peter

1829 *Narrative and Successful Result of a Voyage in the South Seas.* 2 vols. London: Hurst Chace.

Dole, Sanford B.

1893 Evolution of Hawaiian Land Tenures. In *Hawaiian Historical Society Reports,* nos. 1–18. Honolulu.

Dordillon, Msgr. I. R.

1904 *Grammaire et Dictionnaire de la Langue des Iles Marquises.* Paris: Belin-Chadenat.

Duff, Roger

1950 *The Moa-Hunter Period of Maori Culture.* Wellington, N. Z.: Canterbury Museum Bulletin 1.

Durkheim, Emile

1947 *Elementary Forms of the Religious Life.* Glencoe, Ill.: Free Press.

Dyen, Isidore

1965 *A Lexicostatistical Classification of the Austronesian Languages.* Indiana University Publications in Anthropology and Linguistics, Memoir 9.

Eggan, Fred

1954 Social Anthropology and the Method of Controlled Comparison. *American Anthropologist* 56:743–63.

1954 Some Social Institutions in the Mountain Province and their Significance for Historical and Comparative Studies. *Journal of East Asiatic Studies* 3:229–335.

1955 *Social Anthropology of North American Indian Tribes.* Chicago: University of Chicago Press.

Elbert, S. H.

1953 Internal Relationships of Polynesian Language and Dialects. *Southwestern Journal of Anthropology* 9:147–73.

1957 (with Mary Pukui)
Hawaiian-English Dictionary. Honolulu: University of Hawaii.

Ella, Rev. S.

1892 Samoa. In *Proceedings of Australasian Association for the Advancement of Science 4th Meeting,* pp. 620–45.

1895 The Ancient Samoan Government. In *Australasian Association for the Advancement of Science Report* I (no. 6):396–603.

Ellis, Wm.

1825 *A Journal of a Tour Around Hawaii.* Boston: Crocker and Brewster.

1853 *Polynesian Researches During a Residence of Nearly Eight Years in the Society and Sandwich Islands.* 4 vols. London: H. G. Bohn.

Ember, Melvin

1959 The Nonunilinear Descent Groups in Samoa. *American Anthropologist* 61:573–77.

1962 Political Authority and the Structure of Kinship in Aboriginal Samoa. *American Anthropologist* 64:964–71.

Emerson, Nathaniel

1909 *Unwritten Literature of Hawaii.* Washington, D. C.: Bureau of American Ethnology Bulletin 38.

Emory, Kenneth P.

1924 *Island of Lanai.* Honolulu: Bernice P. Bishop Museum Bulletin 12.

1928 *Archaeology of Nihoa and Necker Islands.* Honolulu: Bernice P. Bishop Museum Bulletin 53.

1933 *Stone Remains in the Society Islands.* Honolulu: Bernice P. Bishop Museum Bulletin 116.

1934 *Tuamotuan Stone Structures.* Honolulu: Bernice P. Bishop Museum Bulletin 118.

1939 *Archaeology of Mangareva and Neighboring Atolls.* Honolulu: Bernice P. Bishop Museum Bulletin 163.

1943 Polynesian Stone Remains. *Studies in the Anthropology of Oceania and Asia.* Papers of the Peabody Museum of American Archaeology and Ethnology, vol. 20. Cambridge.

1962 Report on Bishop Museum Archaeological Expeditions to the Society Islands in 1960 and 1961. *Journal of the Polynesian Society* 71:117–20.

1963a Review of Heyerdahl, Archaeology of Easter Island. *American Antiquity* 28:5605.

1963b East Polynesian Relationships. *Journal of the Polynesian Society* 72:78–100.

1965 *Kapingamarangi. Social and Religious Life of a Polynesian Atoll.* Honolulu: Bernice P. Bishop Museum Bulletin 228.

Emory, Kenneth P., Bonk, W. J., Sinoto, Y. H., and Yoshiki, H.

1959 *Hawaiian Archaeology. Fish Hooks.* Honolulu: Bernice P. Bishop Museum Special Publication 47.

Emory, Kenneth P. and Sinoto, Yosihiko H.

1964 Eastern Polynesian Burials at Maupiti. *Journal of the Polynesian Society* 73:143–60.

Englert, P. Sebastian

1948 *La Tierra de Hotu Matu'a: Historia, etnologia y lengua de la isla de Pascua.* Chile: Padre Las Casas.

Epling, Philip J. and Eudley, Ardith A.

1963 Some Observations on the Samoan Aigapototo. *Journal of the Polynesian Society* 72:378–83.

Farmer, Sarah Stock

1855 *Tonga and the Friendly Isles With a Sketch of Their Mission History.* London: Hamilton Adams.

Ferdon, E. N., Jr.
1957 Notes on the Present-Day Easter Islanders. *Southwestern Journal of Anthropology* 13:223–38.

Firth, Raymond
1929 *Primitive Economics of the New Zealand Maori.* London: G. Routledge.
1930–31 Totemism in Polynesia. *Oceania* 1:291–321, 377–98.
1936 *We, The Tikopia.* New York: American Book Company.
1939 *Primitive Polynesian Economy.* London: G. Routledge.
1940 *The Work of the Gods in Tikopia.* London School of Economics and Political Science, Monographs on Social Anthropology, 1 and 2.
1940 The Analysis of Mana. *Journal of the Polynesian Society* 49:483–510.
1951 Privilege Ceremonials in Tikopia. *Oceania,* vol. 21, no. 3, pp. 1–177.
1955a Privilege Ceremonials in Tikopia: A Further Note. *Oceania* 26.1:1–13.
1955b The Theory of Cargo Cults: A Note on Tikopia. *Man* 55: art. 142.
1956 Ceremonies for Children and Social Frequency in Tikopia. *Oceania,* vol. 27, no. 1, pp. 12–50.
1957 A Note on Descent Groups in Polynesia. *Man* 57:art 2.
1959 *Social Change in Tikopia.* London: Allen and Unwin.
1960a Succession to Chieftainship in Tikopia. *Oceania* 30:161–80.
1960b Woodworking Ornaments. *Man* 60:art 27.
1961 *History and Traditions of Tikopia.* Wellington, N. Z.: The Polynesian Society.
1967 *Tikopia Ritual and Belief.* Boston: Beacon Press.

Fletcher, H. J.
1930 The Use of Genealogies for the Purpose of Dating Polynesian History, *Journal of the Polynesian Society* 39:189–94.

Fornander, Abraham
1878–85 *An Account of the Polynesian Race.* 3 vols. London: Kegan Paul.
1916–20 *Fornander Collection of Hawaiian Antiquities and Folklore.* ed. by Thos. Thrum. Honolulu: Bernice P. Bishop Museum Memoirs nos. 4, 5, 6.

Forster, John
1960 The Hawaiian Family System of Hana, Maui. *Journal of the Polynesian Society* 69:92–103.

Forster, J. R.
1778 *Observations Made During A Voyage Round the World.* London: G. Robinson.

Fortes, M., and Evans-Pritchard, E. E.
1940 *African Political Systems.* London: Oxford.

Fortes, Meyer

1953 The Structure of Unilinear Descent Groups. *American Anthropologist* 55:17–41.

1959 Descent, Filiation and Affinity: A Rejoinder to Dr. Leach. *Man*, November, p. 309, December, p. 331.

Frake, Charles O.

1956 Malayo-Polynesian Land Tenure. *American Anthropologist* 58: 170–72.

Freeman, Derek

1964 Some Observations on Kinship and Political Authority in Samoa. *American Anthropologist* 66:553–68.

Freeman, J. D., and Geddes, W. R.

1959 *Anthropology of the South Seas. Essays Presented to H. D. Skinner*. New Plymouth, N. Z.: Thomas Avery & Sons.

Freeman, Otis W.

1951 *Geography of the Pacific*. New York: Wiley.

Fried, Morton H.

1957 The Classification of Corporate Unilineal Descent Groups. *Journal of the Royal Anthropological Institute of Great Britain and Ireland*, vol. 27, no. 1, pp. 1–29.

Garanger, Jose

1964 Recherches Archéologiques dans le District de Tautira. *Journal de la Société des Americanistes* 20:5–18.

Gifford, Edward Winslow

1924 *Tongan Myths and Tales*. Honolulu: Bernice P. Bishop Museum Bulletin 8.

1929 *Tongan Society*. Honolulu: Bernice P. Bishop Museum Bulletin 8.

1949 Excavations in Viti Levu, *Journal of the Polynesian Society* 58:83.

1951 *Archaeological Excavations in Fiji*. Anthropological Records, University of California, vol. 13, no. 3.

Gifford, E. W. and Gifford, D. S.

1959 *Archaeological Excavations in Yap*. Anthropological Records, vol. 18, no. 2.

Gill, William

1856 *Gems from the Coral Islands. . . . Savage and Christian Life in the South Sea Islands*. 2 vols., London: Ward.

Gill, William Wyatt

1880 *Historical Sketches of Savage Life in Polynesia*. Wellington, N. Z.: Government Printer.

1885 *Jottings from the Pacific*. London: The Religious Tract Society.

1890 The Genealogies of the Kings of Rarotonga and Mangaia. *Australian Association for the Advancement of Science Report* 2: 627–37.

1894 *From Darkness to Light in Polynesia*. New York. Religious Tract Society.

Gilson, Richard P.
1963 Samoan Descent Groups: A Structural Outline. *Journal of the Polynesian Society* 72:372–77.

Gluckman, Max
1955 *Custom and Conflict in Africa.* Glencoe, Ill.: The Free Press.

Goffman, Erving
1956 The Nature of Deference and Demeanor. *American Anthropologist* 58:473–502.

Goldman, Irving
1955 Status Rivalry and Cultural Evolution in Polynesia. *American Anthropologist* 57:680–97.
1957 Cultural Evolution in Polynesia, A Reply to Criticism. *Journal of the Polynesian Society* 66:156–64.
1958 Variations in Polynesian Social Organization. *Journal of the Polynesian Society* 66:374–90.
1960a The Evolution of Status Systems in Polynesia. In *Selected Papers of the Fifth International Congress of Anthropological and Ethnological Sciences.* Philadelphia: The University of Pennsylvania Press.
1960b The Evolution of Polynesian Societies. In *Culture in History,* edited by S. Diamond. New York: Columbia University Press.

Golson, Jack
1959 Culture Change in Prehistoric New Zealand. In *Anthropology of the South Seas,* edited by Freeman and Geddes. New Plymouth, N. Z.: Avery Press.
1961a Report on New Zealand, Western Polynesia and Fiji. *Asian Perspectives* 5:166–80.
1961b Review of Suggs—Ancient Civilizations of Polynesia. *Journal of the Polynesian Society* 70:498–508.

Goodenough, Ward
1955 A Problem in Malayo-Polynesian Social Organization. *American Anthropologist* 57:71–83.
1957 Oceania and the Problem of Controls in the Study of Cultural and Human Evolution. *Journal of the Polynesian Society* 66:146–55.

Grace, George W.
1959 The Position of the Polynesian Languages Within the Austronesian Family. Bernice P. Bishop Museum Special Publication 46, *Supplement to International Journal of American Linguistics,* vol. 25, no. 3.
1964 Movement of the Malayo-Polynesians: The Linguistic Evidence. *Current Anthropology* 5:361–68.

Gracia, P. Mathias
1843 *Lettres sur les Iles Marquises.* Paris: Gaume Freres.

Grattan, F. J. H.
1948 *An Introduction to Samoan Custom.* Apia, Western Samoa: Samoan Printing and Publishing Co.

Green, Roger
1961 Moorean Archaeology: A Preliminary Report. *Man* 61:169–73.
1966 Linguistic Subgrouping Within Polynesia: The Implications for Prehistoric Settlement. *Journal of the Polynesian Society* 75: 6–38.

Greiner, Ruth H.
1923 *Polynesian Decorative Designs.* Honolulu: Bernice P. Bishop Museum Bulletin 7.

Gudgeon, C. M. G.
1907 The Tohunga Maori. *Journal of the Polynesian Society* 16:63–91.

Guiart, Jean
1963 *The Arts of the South Pacific.* New York: Golden Press.
1963 *Structure de la chefferie en Melanesie du Sud.* Paris: Institut d' ethnologie, Travaux et Memoires 66.

Gullick, J. M.
1958 *Indigenous Political Systems of Western Malaya.* University of London, London School of Economics, Monographs on Social Anthropology.

Gunn, Wm.
1914 *The Gospel in Futuna, with chapters on . . . the New Hebrides, the People, Customs, Religious Beliefs, etc.* London: Hodder and Stoughton.

Haddon, A. C. and Hornell, J.
1936–38 *Cances of Oceania.* Honolulu: Bernice P. Bishop Museum Special Publication 27–29.

Hale, Horatio
1846 *United States Exploring Expedition, 1838–1842 under Command of Charles Wilkes . . . Ethnography and Philology.* Philadelphia: Lee and Blanchard.

Handy, E. S. Craighill
1920 Some Conclusions and Suggestions Regarding the Polynesian Problem. *American Anthropologist* 22:226–36.
1923 *The Native Cultures in the Marquesas.* Honolulu: Bernice P. Bishop Museum Bulletin 9.
1927 *Polynesian Religion.* Honolulu: Bernice P. Bishop Museum Bulletin 34.
1928 Probable Sources of Polynesian Culture. In *Third Pan-Pacific Science Congress* (1926) *Proceedings* 2:2459–68. Tokyo.
1930a *Marquesan Legends.* Honolulu: Bernice P. Bishop Museum Bulletin 69.
1930b The Problem of Polynesian Origins. *Bernice P. Bishop Museum Occasional Papers,* vol. 9, no. 8, pp. 1–27.
1930c *History and Culture in the Society Islands.* Honolulu: Bernice P. Bishop Museum Bulletin 79.
1931 *Cultural Revolution in Hawaii.* New York: American Council, Institute of Pacific Relations.

1940 *The Hawaiian Planter.* 2 vols. (vol. 1). Honolulu: Bernice P. Bishop Museum Bulletin 161.

1951–52 The Hawaiian Family System. *Journal of the Polynesian Society,* vols. 60–61.

Handy, E. S. C., and Handy, Willowdean Chatterson

1924 *Samoan Housebuilding, Cooking and Tattooing.* Honolulu: Bernice P. Bishop Museum Bulletin 15.

Handy, E. S. C., and others

1933 *Ancient Hawaiian Civilization.* Honolulu: Kamehameha Schools.

Handy, E. S. C., and Pukui, Mary K.

1935 *Ohana, The Dispersed Community of Ohaka.* Honolulu: Institute of Pacific Relations.

1958 *The Polynesian Family System in Ka'u, Hawaii.* Wellington, N. Z.: The Polynesian Society.

Harding, J. R.

1957 A Carved Pumice Head from New Zealand: A Preliminary Report. *Man* 57:art. 119.

Hargreaves, R. P.

1963 Changing Maori Agriculture in Pre-Waitangi; New Zealand. *Journal of the Polynesian Society* 72:101–15.

Hawkes, Jacquetta, and Woolley, Leonard

1963 *Prehistory and the Beginnings of Civilization.* New York: Harper and Row.

Hawthorne, H. B., and Belshaw, C. S.

1957 Cultural Evolution or Cultural Change: The Case of Polynesia. *Journal of the Polynesian Society* 66:18–35.

Heine-Geldern, Robert

1928 Die Megalithen Sudostasiens u ihre Bedeutung für Die Klarung der Megalithenfrage in Europa u Polynesien. *Anthropos* 23:276–315.

1932 Urheimat und Früheste Wanderungen der Austronesier. *Anthropos* 27:543–619.

1942 Conceptions of State and Kingship in South East Asia. *Far Eastern Quarterly* 11:15–32.

1945 Prehistoric Research in Netherlands Indies. In *Science and Scientists in Netherlands Indies,* pp. 129–167. New York: Southeast Asia Institute.

1952 Some Problems of Migration in the Pacific. *Wiener Beitrager zur Kulturgeschichte und Linguistik* 9:313–62.

Henry, Teuira

1928 *Ancient Tahiti.* Honolulu: Bernice P. Bishop Museum Bulletin 48.

Heyerdahl, Thor

1952 Problems in Polynesian Anthropology. In *International Congress of Americanists,* vol. 30, Cambridge.

1952 *American Indians in the Pacific*. Stockholm, London: Allen and Unwin.

1961 (ed.) *The Norwegian Archaeological Expedition to Easter Island and the East Pacific*. Vol. 1: *Archaeology of Easter Island*. Monographs of the School of American Research and the Museum of New Mexico, no. 24 pt. I.

Himiona, Kaamira

1957 The Story of Kupe. *Journal of the Polynesian Society*, 66:216–48. Translated by Bruce Biggs.

Hobbs, C.

1946 *Southeast Asia 1935–45*. Washington, D. C.: Library of Congress.

Hobbs, Jean

1931 The Land Title in Hawaii. *Hawaiian Historical Society 40th Annual Report for 1931*.

1935 *Hawaii: A Pageant of the Soil*. Stanford, California: Stanford University Press.

Hobhouse, L. T.

1937 Aristocracy. In *Encyclopedia of Social Sciences*. New York: Macmillan.

Hocart, A. M.

1915 Chieftainship and the Sister's Son in the Pacific. *American Anthropologist* 17:631–36.

1927 *Kingship*. London: Oxford University Press.

1929 *Lau Islands, Fiji*. Honolulu: Bernice P. Bishop Museum Bulletin 62.

1950 *Caste*. London: Methuen.

Hogbin, H. Ian

1930 Transition Rites at Ontong Java. *Journal of the Polynesian Society* 39:94–112, 201–20.

1931a The Sexual Life of the Natives of Ontong Java. *Journal of the Polynesian Society* 40:23–34.

1931b The Social Organization of Ontong Java. *Oceania* 1:399–425.

1932 Polynesian Ceremonial Gift Exchanges. *Oceania* 3:13–39.

1934a *Law and Order in Polynesia*. New York: Harcourt, Brace.

1934b Mana. *Oceania* 6:241–74.

Holmes, Lowell D.

1957 Ta'u: Stability and Change in a Samoan Village. *Journal of the Polynesian Society* 66:301–38.

1958 An Appraisal of the Kon-Tiki Theory. *Oceania* 29:127–31.

Hornell, James

1946 *Water Transport, Origins and Early Evolution*. Cambridge: Cambridge Press.

Huizinga, Johan

1955 *Homo Ludens: A Study of the Play Element in Culture*. Boston: The Beacon Press.

Ii, John Papa
1959 *Fragments of Hawaiian History.* Honolulu: Bishop Museum.

Janse, Olov R. T.
1947 *Archaeological Research in Indo-China.* 2 vols. Harvard Yenching Institute Monograph Series, vols. 7, 10. Cambridge.

Jarves, James Jackson
1843 *History of the Hawaiian or Sandwich Islands.* Boston: Tappan and Dennet.

Josselin De Jong, P. E. de
1952 *Minangkabau and Negri Sembilan.* The Hague: Nijhoff.
1952 *Levi-Strauss's Theory on Kinship and Marriage.* Leiden: Rijksmuseum voor Volkenkunde, Mededelingen no. 10.

Kamakau, Samuel Manaia-Kalani
1964 *The People of Old.* Honolulu: Bernice P. Bishop Museum Special Publication 51.

Keesing, Felix M.
1950 Some Notes on Early Migrations in the Southwest Pacific Area. *Southwestern Journal of Anthropology* 6:101–19.
1953 *Social Anthropology in Polynesia.* New York: Oxford University.

Kelly, Leslie C.
1949 *Tainui.* Wellington, N. Z.: Polynesian Society Memoir No. 25.

Kennedy, D. G.
1931 *Field Notes on the Culture of Vaitupu, Ellice Islands.* Wellington, N. Z.: Polynesian Society Memoir 9.

Kennedy, Raymond
1942 Contours of Culture in Indonesia. *Far Eastern Quarterly* 2:5–15.
1945 *The Islands and Peoples of the South Seas and Their Cultures.* Philadelphia: American Philosophical Society.

Kernan, K. T, and Coult, A. D.
1965 The Cross-Generation Relative Age Criterion of Kinship Terminology. *Southwestern Journal of Anthropology* 21:148–53.

Kirchoff, Paul
1959 The Principles of Clanship in Human Society. *Readings in Anthropology,* In Morton H. Fried, ed. New York: Crowell.

Koch, Gerd
1955 *Südsee, Gestern und Heute.* Braunschweig: A. Limbach.

Koenigswald, G. H. R. von
1951 Über Sumatranische Schiffstucher und ihre Beziehungen zur Kunst Ozeaniens. *Südseestudien,* pp. 27–50. Basel.

Koskinnen, Arne A.
1960 *Ariki the First Born: An Analysis of a Polynesian Chief-Title.* Helsinki: Suomalainen Tiedeakatemia Academia Scientarium Fennica. FF Communications Vol. 74, No. 181.

Krämer, Augustin
1902 *Die Samoa-Inseln.* 2 vols. Stuttgart: E. Nägele.
1906 *Hawaii, Ostmikronesien und Samoa.* Stuttgart: Strecker and Schröder.

Krieger, Herbert
1942 *Peoples of the Philippines.* Washington, D. C.: Smithsonian Institution, War Background Studies, no. 4.

Kroeber, A. L.
1919 Kinship in the Philippines, *Anthropological Papers American Museum of Natural History* 19:73–84.

Kuykendall, R. S.
1938 *The Hawaiian Kingdom.* Honolulu: University of Hawaii.

Lamont, E. H.
1867 *Wild Life Among the Pacific Islanders.* London: Hurst and Blackett.

Landtmann, Gunnar
1938 *The Origin of the Inequality of the Social Classes.* Chicago: The University of Chicago Press.

Lane, Robert B.
1961 A Reconsideration of Malayo-Polynesian Social Organization. *American Anthropologist* 63:711–20.

Lavachery, Henri
1935 *Ile de Pâques.* Paris.

Laval, Honoré
1938 *Mangaréva. L'histoire Ancienne d'un Peuple Polynesien.* Braine Le-Comte, Belgium: Maison des Pères des Sacres-Couers.

Leach, E. R.
1951 The Structural Implications of Matrilateral Cross-Cousin Marriage. *Journal Royal Anthropological Institute* 81:23–55.

LeBar, Frank; Hickey, Gerald C.; and Musgrave, John K.
1964 *Ethnic Groups of Mainland Southeast Asia.* New Haven: Human Relations Area Files.

Leenhardt, Maurice
1947 *Arts de L'Océanie.* Paris: Les Editions du Chène.

Lehmann, Fredrich R.
1922 *Mana, der Begriff des "Ausserordentlich Wirkungsvollen" bei Südseevolkern.* Leipzig: O. Spamer.

Levi-Strauss, Claude
1963 *Structural Anthropology.* New York: Basic Books.
1964 Structural Analysis in Linguistics and in Anthropology. In *Language in Culture and Society,* edited by D. Hymes. New York: Harper and Row.

Ling, Shun-Sheng
1957 Kava Drinking in China and East Asia. *Bulletin, Institute of Ethnology, Academia Sinica,* no. 5.

Linton, Ralph
1923 *The Material Culture of the Marquesas Islands.* Honolulu: Bernice P. Bishop Museum Memiors, vol. 8, no. 5.
1925 *Archaeology of the Marquesas Islands.* Honolulu: Bernice P. Bishop Museum Bulletin 23.

1926 *Ethnology of Polynesia and Micronesia.* Department of Anthropology Guide, pt. 6. Chicago: Field Museum of Natural History.
1936 *The Study of Man.* New York: Appleton-Century.
1939 The Marquesas. In *The Individual and His Society,* edited by Abraham Kardiner. New York: Columbia University Press.

Lister, J. S.
1892 Notes on the Natives of Fakaofu. *Journal of the Royal Anthropological Institute* 21:43–63.

Loeb, Edwin M.
1926 *History and Traditions of Niue.* Honolulu: Bernice P. Bishop Museum Bulletin 32.
1933 Die Sozial Organization Indonesiens u Ozeaniens. *Anthropos* 28: 649–62.
1934 Patrilineal and Matrilineal Organization in Sumatra: The Minangabau. *American Anthropologist* 36:1–25.
1949 Social Organization of Oceania and the American Northwest. In *South Pacific Science Congress Proceedings* 4:135–39. Berkeley and Los Angeles: University of California Press.

Luschan, Felix Von
1924 Polynesians Origins. *Journal of the Polynesian Society* 33:78–79.

Mabuchi, Toichi
1953 The Omaha Type of Kinship Terminology Among the Bunun, Central Formosa. In *Eighth Pacific Science Conference.* Quezon City, Philippines.
1951 The Social Organization of Central Tribes of Formosa. *Journal of East Asiatic Studies* 1:43–69.

McAllister, J. Gilbert
1933 *Archaeology of Oahu.* Honolulu: Bernice P. Bishop Museum Bulletin 104.
1934 *Archaeology of Kahoolawe.* Honolulu: Bernice P. Bishop Museum Bulletin 115.

MacGregor, Gordon
1935 Notes on the Ethnology of Pukapuka. *Bernice P. Bishop Museum. Occasional Papers,* vol. 11, no. 6.
1937 *Ethnology of Tokelau.* Honolulu: Bernice P. Bishop Museum Bulletin 146.

McKern, W. C.
1929 *Archaeology of Tonga.* Honolulu: Bernice P. Bishop Museum Bulletin 60.

Malinowski, Bronislaw
1922 *Argonauts of the Western Pacific.* London: Routledge and Kegan, Paul.

Malo, David
1951 *Hawaiian Antiquities.* Honolulu: Bernice P. Bishop Special Publication 2, 2nd ed.

Mangeret, R. P.
1932 *La Croix dans les Isles du Pacifique*. Paris: Missions d' Océanie.

Mariner, W.
1817 *An Account of the Natives of the Tonga Islands . . . with a Grammar and Vocabulary of Their Language Compiled from the Communications of W. Mariner by John Martin*. 2 vols. London: J. Martin.

Markham, Sir Clements
1904 *The Voyage of Pedro Fernandez de Quiros, 1595–1606*. London: Hakluyt Society.

Marshall, D. S., and Snow, C. E.
1956 An Evaluation of Polynesian Craniology. *American Journal of Physical Anthropology* 14:405–27.

Marshall, P.
1927 *Geology of Mangaia*. Honolulu: Bernice P. Bishop Museum Bulletin 36.

Martin, E. J.
1960 Incidence of Bifidity and Related R. B. Abnormalities in Samoans. *American Journal of Physical Anthropology* 179–87.

Maude, H. E.
1959 The Tahitian Pork Trade, *Journal de la Société des Océanistes* 15:55–95.

Mauss, Marcel
1954 *The Gift*. London: Cohen and West.

Mead, Margaret
1928a *Coming of Age in Samoa*. New York: Morrow.
1928b *Inquiry into Cultural Stability in Polynesia*. New York: Columbia University Press.
1928c The Role of the Individual in Samoan Society. *Journal Royal Anthropological Institute* 58:481–95.
1930 *Social Organization of Manu'a*. Honolulu: Bernice P. Bishop Museum Bulletin 76.
1934 Kinship in the Admiralty Islands. *Anthropological Papers American Museum of Natural History* 34:181–358.
1937 *Cooperation and Competition Among Primitive Peoples*. New York: McGraw-Hill.
1939 *From the South Seas*. New York: Morrow.
1957 Introduction to Polynesia as a Laboratory for the Development of Models in the Study of Cultural Evolution. *Journal of the Polynesian Society* 66:145.

Melville, Herman
1846 *Typee*. New York: Wiley and Putnam.
1847 *Omoo, A Narrative of Adventure in the South Seas*. New York: Harper.

Merrill, Elmer D.

1954 The Botany of Cook's Voyages and its Unexpected Significance in Relation to Anthropology, Bio-Geography and History. *Chronica Botanica* 14:161–384.

Metge, A. J.

1957 Marriage in Modern Maori Society. *Man* 57:art 212.

Metraux, Alfred

1937 Easter Island Sanctuaries. *Ethnological Studies* 5:104–53.

1937 The Kings of Easter Island. *Journal of the Polynesian Society* 46: 41–62.

1937 Une Feodalite Cannibale en Polynesie Francaise. *Revue de Paris*, vol. 44, no. 19, pp. 637–61.

1940 *Ethnology of Easter Island.* Honolulu: Bernice P. Bishop Museum Bulletin 160.

1957 *Easter Island.* New York: Oxford.

Miller, C. D.

1927 *Food Values of Poi, Taro and Limu.* Honolulu: Bernice P. Bishop Museum Bulletin 37.

1929 *Food Values of Breadfruit, Taro Leaves, Coconut, Sugar Cane.* Honolulu: Bernice P. Bishop Museum Bulletin 64.

Miller, Gerrit, S.

1924 *The Characters and Probable History of the Hawaiian Rat.* Honolulu: Bernice P. Bishop Museum Bulletin 14.

Milner, G.B.

1961 The Samoan Vocabulary of Respect. *Journal of the Royal Anthropological Institute.* 91:296–317.

Moerenhout, J. A.

1837 *Voyages aux iles du Grand Océan.* 2 vols. Paris: Bertrand.

Morrison, James

1935 *The Journal of James Morrison, Boatswain's Mate of the Bounty.* Tahiti: Golden Cockerel Press.

Moubray, G. A.

1931 *Matriarchy in the Malay Peninsula and Neighboring Countries.* London: G. Routledge and Sons.

Mühlmann, Wilhelm E.

1933 Staatsbildung in Polynesien. *Zeitschrift für Ethnologie* 65:380–89.

1934 Die Begriffe "Atiu Mataeinaa" Ein Beitrag zur Politischen Entwicklung u Besiedlungsgeschichte Polynesiens. *Anthropos* 29: 739–56.

1936 Über den Anschluss der Polynesier an die Südasiatischen Hochkulturen. *Baessler Archiv. Friederici Festschrift* 19:82–91.

1938 *Staatsbildung und Amphiktyonien in Polynesien.* Stuttgart: Strecker und Schröder.

1955 *Arioi und Manaia: Eine Ethnologische Religionssoziologische und Historische studie über Polynesische Kultbunde*. Wiesbaden: Franz Steiner Verlag.

Murdock, George P.

1948 Anthropology in Micronesia. *New York Academy of Sciences Transactions*, series 2, 11:9–16.

1949 *Social Structure*. New York: MacMillan.

1960 (ed.) *Social Structure in Southeast Asia*. New York: Viking Fund Publications in Anthropology, no. 29.

1964 Genetic Classification of The Austronesian Languages: A Key to Oceanic Culture History. *Ethnology* 3:117–26.

Nadel, S. F.

1953 *The Foundations of Social Anthropology*. Glencoe, Illinois: Free Press.

Nayacakalou, R. R.

1955 The Fijian System of Kinship and Marriage. *Journal of the Polynesian Society* 64:44–55.

1959 Land Tenure and Social Organization in Tonga. *Journal of the Polynesian Society* 68:93–114.

1960 Land Tenure and Social Organization in Western Samoa. *Journal of the Polynesian Society* 69:104–22.

Newell, J. E.

1893 Chiefs' Language in Samoa. *Ninth International Congress of Orientalists Transactions* 2:784–801.

Newhall, W. H.

1947 The Kava Ceremony in Tonga. *Journal of the Polynesian Society* 56:364–417.

Oliver, Douglas L.

1955 *A Solomon Islands Society*. Cambridge: Harvard University Press.

1961 *The Pacific Islands*. New York: Natural History Library.

Osborne, Douglas

1956 Archaeological Backgrounds of Pacific Culture. *Davidson Journal of Anthropology* 2:31–42.

Panoff, Michel

1964 L'Ancienne Organization Ceremonielle et Politique des Samoa Occidentale, *L'Homme* 4:63–83.

Parkinson, Cyril Northcote

1957 *Parkinson's Law and Other Studies in Administration*. Boston: Houghton Mifflin.

Pehrson, Robert N.

1954 Bilateral Kin Groupings as a Structural Type. *Journal of East Asiatic Studies* 3:199–202.

Pérouse, J. F. G. La

1799 *A Voyage Around the World, in the Years 1785, 1786, 1787, 1788*. 3 vols, 2d ed. London.

Phelps, Southwick

1940 Puberty Observances in Polynesia and Micronesia. *Sixth Pacific Science Congress Proceedings* 4:145–52.

Phillips, W. J.
1950 Mahua's Account of the Digging Up of the Atua Whenga. *Oceania* 21:152–53.

Piddington, Ralph
1957 Synchronic and Diachronic Dimensions in the Study of Polynesian Culture. *Journal of the Polynesian Society* 60:108–21.

Polanyi, Karl
1957 *The Great Transformation*. Boston: Beacon Press.

Polanyi, Karl., Arensberg, Conrad M., and Pearson, Harry W.
1957 *Trade and Market in the Early Empires*. Glencoe, Illinois: Free Press.

Pollenz, Philippa
1950 Changes in the Form and Function of Hawaiian Hulas. *American Anthropologist* 52:225–34.

Ponsonby, Arthur
1912 *The Decline of Aristocracy*. London.

Porter, David
1815 *Journal of a Cruise Made to the Pacific Ocean . . . in the Years 1812, 1813 and 1814*. 2 vols. Philadelphia: Bradford and Inskeep.

Pratt, Rev. George
1890 The Genealogy of the Kings and Princes of Samoa. In *Australasian Association for the Advancement of Science*, Report no. 2, pp. 655–63. Melbourne, Australia.

Radcliffe-Brown, A. R.
1935 Patrilineal and Matrilineal Succession. *Iowa Law Review* 20: 286–303.
1940 On Social Structure. *Journal of the Royal Anthropological Institute* 70:1–12.

Radcliffe-Brown, A. R. and Forde, Darell
1950 *African Systems of Kinship and Marriage*. London: Oxford University Press.

Raven-Hart, Major R.
1955 Musical Acculturation in Tonga. *Oceania* 26:110–17.

Remy, Jules
1868 *Contributions of a Venerable Savage to the Ancient History of the Hawaiian Islands*. transl. by W. T. Brigham. Boston. Privately printed.

Riesenfeld, Alphonse
1950 Racial Characteristics of the Early Polynesians in Melanesia, *Man* 50:art. 30.
1956 Shovel-shaped Incisors and a Few Other Dental Features among the Native Peoples in the Pacific. *American Journal of Physical Anthropology* 14:505–21.

Rivers, W. H. R.
1914 *The History of Melanesian Society*. Cambridge University Press.
1926 *Psychology and Ethnology*. London: K. Paul, Trench, Trubner and Company.
Rivet, Paul
1932 *Les Oceanians*. Edited by W. R. Dawson. *The Frazer Lectures*. London: MacMillan.
Roberton, J. B. W.
1957 The Role of Tribal Traditions in New Zealand Pre-History. *Journal of the Polynesian Society* 66:249–63.
1958 The Significance of New Zealand Tradition. *Journal of the Polynesian Society* 67:39–57.
Robertson, George
1948 *The Discovery of Tahiti, A Journal of the Second Voyage of HMS Dolphin . . . in the Years 1766, 1767, 1768*. Hugh Carrington, ed. London: Hakluyt Society.
Routledge, Catherine
1919 *The Mystery of Easter Island*. London: Sifton Praed and Co. Ltd.
Russell, M.
1843 *Polynesia or a Historical Account of the Principal South Sea Islands*. Edinburgh: Oliver and Boyd.
Sahlins, Marshall
1955 Esoteric Efflorescence in Easter Island. *American Anthropologist* 57:1045–52.
1957 Differentiation by Adaptation in Polynesian Societies. *Journal of the Polynesian Society* 66:291–300.
1958 *Social Stratification in Polynesia*. Seattle: University of Washington Press.
1961 The Segmentary Lineage: An Organization of Predatory Expansion. *American Anthropologist* 63:322–45.
St. John, Harold
1957 Origin of the Sustenance Plants of Polynesia and Linguistic Evidence for the Migration Route of the Polynesians into the Pacific. Bangkok *Ninth Pacific Science-congress,* Abstracts. p. 19.
Sauer, Carl O.
1952 *Agricultural Origins and Dispersals*. New York: The American Geographical Society.
Schneider, David M.
1962 Double Descent on Yap. *Journal of the Polynesian Society* 71: 1–24.
Schneider, David M., and Gough, Kathleen
1961 *Matrilineal Kinship*. Berkeley and Los Angeles: University of California Press.
Schofield, Graeme
1959 Metric and Morphological Features of the Femur of New Zea-

land Maori. *Journal of the Royal Anthropological Institute* 89: 89–105.

Scholefield, G. H.
1923 Economic Revolution in Polynesia. *Austronesian Association for the Advancement of Science Reports* 16:499–602.

Schrieke, B.
1928 The Evolution of Culture in the Pacific. In *Third Pan-Pacific Science Congress* (1926) *Proceedings*, pp. 2423–2441. Tokyo.

Schultz, Erich
1911 The Most Important Principles of Samoan Family Law and the Laws of Inheritance. *Journal of the Polynesian Society* 20:43–53.

Schwartz, Theodore
1963 Systems of Areal Integration: Some Considerations Based on the Admiralty Islands of Northern Melanesia. *Anthropological Forum* I:56–97.

Selling, O. H.
1948 *Studies in Hawaiian Pollen Statistics.* Honolulu: Bernice P. Bishop Special Publication 39.
1962 Settlement of Oceania; Symposium on Sharp's Thesis. *Journal of the Polynesian Society*, vol. 71, no. 3.

Shapiro, Harry L.
1933 Are the Ontong Javanese Polynesian? *Oceania* 3:367–76.
1940 Distribution of Blood Groups in Polynesia. *American Journal of Physical Anthropology* 26:409–16.
1940 Physical Anthropology of the Maori-Moriori, *Journal of the Polynesian Society* 49:1–15.
1943 Physical Differentiation in Polynesia. In *Studies in the Anthropology of Oceania and Asia.* Cambridge: Peabody Museum Publication, vol. 20.

Shapiro, H. L. and Suggs, R. C.
1959 New Dates for Polynesian Prehistory. *Man* 59:art. 3.

Sharp, Andrew
1956 *Ancient Voyagers in the Pacific.* Wellington, N. Z.: Polynesian Society Memoir 32.
1960 *Discovery of the Pacific Islands.* Oxford.

Shortland, Edward
1882 *Maori Religion and Mythology.* London: Longmans, Green and Company.

Shutler, Richard Jr.
1961 Peopling of the Pacific in the Light of Radio-Carbon Dating. *Asian Perspectives.* 5:207–12.

Simmons, R. T.
1962 Blood Group Genes in Polynesians and Comparisons With Other Pacific Peoples. *Oceania*, vol. 32, no. 3, pp. 198–210.

Simmons, R. T., and Graydon, J. J.
1957 A Blood Group Genetical Survey of Eastern and Central Polynesia. *American Journal of Physical Anthropology* N. S. 15: 357–66.
Simmons, R. T., Graydon, J. J., Semolia, M. M., and Fry, E. I.
1955 A Blood Group Survey of Cook Islands, Polynesia and Comparisons with American Indians. *American Journal of Physical Anthropology* 13:667–90.
Sinoto, Y. H.
1963 Polynesia. *Asian Perspectives,* 7:57–64.
Skinner, H. D.
1923 *The Morioris of Chatham Islands.* Honolulu: Bernice P. Bishop Museum Memoir 9, no. I.
Skinner, H. D., and Bauke, W.
1928 *The Morioris.* Honolulu: Bernice P. Bishop Museum Memoir 9, no. 5.
Skottsberg, Carl (ed.)
1920 *The Natural History of Juan Fernandes and Easter Island.* 2 vols. Uppsala: Alinquist & Wiksell.
Smith, M. G.
1956 On Segmentary Lineage Systems. *Journal Royal Anthropological Institute* 86:38–80.
Smith S. Percy
1889 Tongareva or Penrhyn Island and its People. *New Zealand Institute Transactions* 22:85–103.
1898–99 Hawaiiki: The Whence of the Maori. *Journal of the Polynesian Society,* vols. 7–8.
1902–03 Niue Island and its Peoples. *Journal of the Polynesian Society,* vols. 11 and 12.
1913–15 *Lore of the Whare Wananga.* 2 vols. Wellington, N. Z.: Polynesian Society.
1918–24 History and Traditions of Rarotonga. *Journal of the Polynesian Society,* vols. 27–30.
Solheim, Wilhelm G., II
1963 Eastern Asia and Oceania. *Asian Perspectives* 6:1–7.
Spier, Robert F. G.
1951 Some Notes on the Origin of Taro. *Southwestern Journal of Anthropology* 7:69–76.
Spoehr, Alexander
1949 Majuro, A Village in the Marshall Islands. *Fieldiana, Anthropology, Chicago Natural History Museum,* vol. 39.
1950 Observations on the Study of Kinship. *American Anthropologist* 52:1–15.
1952 Time Perspective in Micronesia and Polynesia. *Southwestern Journal of Anthropology* 8:457–65.
1957 Marianas Prehistory: Archaeological Survey and Excavations on

Saipan, Tinian and Rota. *Fieldiana-Anthropology*, Chicago Natural History Museum, vol. 48.

1960 Port Town and Hinterland in the Pacific Islands. *American Anthropologist* 62:586–92.

Stair, Rev. John B.

1897 *Old Samoa, or Flotsam and Jetsam From the Pacific Ocean*. London: The Religious Tract Society.

St. John, Harold

1957 *Origin of the Sustenance Plants of Polynesia and Linguistic Evidence for the Migration Route of the Polynesians into the Pacific.* Indonesian Sociological Studies. Institute of Pacific Relations.

Steinen, Karl von den

1925–28 *Die Marquesaner und ihre Kunst*. 3 vols. Berlin: Reimer.

Stevenson, Robert Louis

1892 *A Footnote to History, Eight Years of Trouble in Samoa*. London: Cassells.

Stokes, John F. G.

1932 The Hawaiian King. *Hawaiian Historical Papers* 19:1–28.

1933 New Bases for Hawaiian Chronology. *Hawaiian Historical Society 41st Annual Report*, pp. 23–65.

Suggs, Robert C.

1960 *Island Civilizations of Polynesia*. New York: Mentor Books.

1961 *Archeology of Nuku Hiva*. American Museum of Natural History, vol. 49, Anthropological Papers. New York.

1962 Polynesia. *Asian Perspectives* 5:88–94.

Suzuki, Makato, and Sakai, Takuro

1964 Shovel-Shaped Incisors Among the Living Polynesians. *American Journal of Physical Anthropology* 65–72.

Taylor, C. R. H.

1951 *A Pacific Bibliography*. Wellington, N. Z.: Polynesian Society Memoirs, vol. 24.

1965 *A Pacific Bibliography*. 2d. Ed. London: Oxford University Press.

Te Ariki-Tara-Are

1899 History and Traditions of Rarotonga. *Journal of the Polynesian Society* 8:61–88; 171–78.

Thompson, Andrew

1927 Earth Mounds in Samoa. *Journal of the Polynesian Society* 36: 118–21.

Thompson, Laura

1940 *Southern Lau: An Ethnography*. Honolulu: Bernice P. Bishop Museum Bulletin 162.

Thomson, Sir Basil

1894 *The Diversions of a Prime Minister*. London: Blackwood and Sons.

Thomson, William J.
1891 *Te Pito Henua or Easter Island.* Washington, D. C.: U.S. National Museum Report.
Thrum, Thos. G.
1906 Heiaus and Heiau Sites Throughout the Hawaiian Islands. In *Hawaiian Almanac for 1907.* Honolulu.
Tischner, H.
1934 *Die Verbreitung der Hausformen in Ozeanien.* Leipzig: Studien Zür Volkerkunde.
Tocqueville, Alexis De
1955 *The Old Regime and the French Revolution.* New York: Doubleday.
Tregear, Edward
1891 *Maori–Polynesian Comparative Dictionary.* Wellington, N. Z.: Lyon and Blair.
1899 *A Dictionary of Mangareva.* Wellington, N. Z.
1904 *The Maori Race.* Wanganui.
Tregear, Edward, and Smith, Percy S.
1907 *A Vocabulary and Grammar of the Niue Dialect of the Polynesian Language.* Wellington, N. Z.: Govt. Printer.
Turner, Rev. G. A.
1884 *Samoa a Hundred Years Ago and Long Before.* London: MacMillan.
Vancouver, George
1798 *A Voyage of Discovery to the North Pacific Ocean.* 3 vols. London: Robinson.
Vayda, Andrew P.
1956 Maori Conquests in Relation to the New Zealand Environment. *Journal of the Polynesian Society* 65:204–11.
1958 The Pukapukans on Nassau Island. *Journal of the Polynesian Society* 67:256–65.
1960 *Maori Warfare.* Wellington, N. Z.: The Polynesian Society.
1961 Love in the Polynesian Atolls. *Man* 61:art. 242.
Vesson, George
1810 *An Authentic Narrative of Four Years Residence at Tongataboo.* London: Longman.
Vidal, Gormaz, Francisco
1880 *Jeografia Nautica de la Republica de Chile.* Santiago De Chile.
Vlekke, Bernard, H. M.
1943 *Nusantara, A History of the East Indian Archipelago.* Cambridge: Harvard University Press.
Webb, M. C.
1965 The Abolition of the Taboo System in Hawaii. *Journal of the Polynesian Society* 74:21–39.
Webster, Hutton
1943 *Taboo.* Stanford, California: Stanford University Press.

Weckler, J. E.
1943 *Polynesians: Explorers of the Pacific.* Smithsonian War Background Studies 6. Washington, D. C.: Smithsonian Institution.

Wiens, Herold J.
1962 *Atoll Environment and Ecology.* New Haven: Yale University Press.

Wilder, Gerrit Parmile
1928 *The Breadfruit of Tahiti.* Honolulu: Bernice P. Bishop Museum Bulletin 50.

Wilkes, Owen
1964 New Zealand. *Asian Perspectives* 8:98–101.

Willett, F.
1955 A Maori Store-Chamber Slab in the Manchester Museum. *Man* 55:art. 197.

Williams, Howell
1933 *Geology of Tahiti, Moorea and Maiao.* Honolulu: Bernice P. Bishop Museum Bulletin 105.

Williams, John
1837 *A Narrative of Missionary Enterprises in the South Sea Islands.* New York: D. Appleton.

Williamson, Robert Wood
1924 *The Social and Political Systems of Central Polynesia.* 3 vols. Cambridge University Press.
1933 *The Religious and Cosmic Beliefs of Central Polynesia.* 2 vols. Cambridge University Press.
1937 *Religion and Social Organization in Central Polynesia,* edited by Ralph Piddington. Cambridge University Press.
1939 *Essays in Polynesian Ethnology,* edited by Ralph Piddington. Cambridge University Press.

Wilson, Wm.
1799 *A Missionary Voyage to the Southern Pacific Ocean.* London: London Missionary Society.

Winiata, Maharaia
1956 Leadership in Pre-European Maori Society. *Journal of the Polynesian Society,* 65:212–31.

Wittfogel, Karl A.
1957 *Oriental Despotism: A Comparative Study of Total Power.* New Haven: Yale University Press.

Wolf, Werner
1948 *Island of Death: A New Key to Easter Island's Culture through an Ethno-Psychological Study.* New York: J. J. Augustin.

Yanaihara, Tadao
1946 *Pacific Islands under Japanese Mandate.* New York: Oxford Press.

Yuncker, T. G.
1945 *Plants of the Manua Islands.* Honolulu: Bernice P. Bishop Museum Bulletin 184.

Index